Childhood Developmental Language Disorders:

Role of Inclusion, Families, and Professionals

Dimitra Katsarou
University of the Aegean, Greece

A volume in the Advances in Psychology, Mental Health, and Behavioral Studies (APMHBS) Book Series

IGI Global
PUBLISHER of TIMELY KNOWLEDGE

Published in the United States of America by
IGI Global
Information Science Reference (an imprint of IGI Global)
701 E. Chocolate Avenue
Hershey PA, USA 17033
Tel: 717-533-8845
Fax: 717-533-8661
E-mail: cust@igi-global.com
Web site: http://www.igi-global.com

Library of Congress Cataloging-in-Publication Data

Names: Katsarou, Dimitra, 1983- editor.
Title: Childhood developmental language disorders : role of inclusion, families, and professionals / edited by Dimitra Katsarou.
Description: Hershey, PA : Information Science Reference, [2024] | Includes bibliographical references and index. | Summary: "This edited book brings together a collection of chapters that delve deep into the intricacies of language development in individuals with developmental disorders, drawing upon linguistic approaches, therapeutic methods, and inclusive pedagogical perspectives"-- Provided by publisher.
Identifiers: LCCN 2023047107 (print) | LCCN 2023047108 (ebook) | ISBN 9798369319826 (hardcover) | ISBN 9798369319833 (ebook)
Subjects: LCSH: Language disorders in children. | Language disorders in children--Treatment. | Developmentally disabled children--Education. | Developmentally disabled children--Services for.
Classification: LCC RJ496.L35 C475 2023 (print) | LCC RJ496.L35 (ebook) | DDC 618.92/855--dc23/eng/20231103
LC record available at https://lccn.loc.gov/2023047107
LC ebook record available at https://lccn.loc.gov/2023047108

This book is published in the IGI Global book series Advances in Psychology, Mental Health, and Behavioral Studies (APMHBS) (ISSN: 2475-6660; eISSN: 2475-6679)

British Cataloguing in Publication Data
A Cataloguing in Publication record for this book is available from the British Library.

Advances in Psychology, Mental Health, and Behavioral Studies (APMHBS) Book Series

Harish C. Chandan
Argosy University, USA
Bryan Christiansen
Southern New Hampshire University, USA

ISSN:2475-6660
EISSN:2475-6679

Mission

The complexity of the human mind has puzzled researchers and physicians for centuries. While widely studied, the brain still remains largely misunderstood.

The **Advances in Psychology, Mental Health, and Behavioral Studies (APMHBS)** book series presents comprehensive research publications focusing on topics relating to the human psyche, cognition, psychiatric care, mental and developmental disorders, as well as human behavior and interaction. Featuring diverse and innovative research, publications within APMHBS are ideally designed for use by mental health professionals, academicians, researchers, and upper-level students..

Coverage

- Emotional Health
- Neurological Disorders
- Trauma & Stress
- Addiction
- Human Behavior
- Psychiatry
- Cognition
- Anxiety
- Mental Health & Disorders
- Personality Disorders

IGI Global is currently accepting manuscripts for publication within this series. To submit a proposal for a volume in this series, please contact our Acquisition Editors at Acquisitions@igi-global.com or visit: http://www.igi-global.com/publish/.

The Advances in Psychology, Mental Health, and Behavioral Studies (APMHBS) Book Series (ISSN 2475-6660) is published by IGI Global, 701 E. Chocolate Avenue, Hershey, PA 17033-1240, USA, www.igi-global.com. This series is composed of titles available for purchase individually; each title is edited to be contextually exclusive from any other title within the series. For pricing and ordering information please visit http://www.igi-global.com/book-series/advances-psychology-mental-health-behavioral/110200. Postmaster: Send all address changes to above address.

Titles in this Series

For a list of additional titles in this series, please visit: www.igi-global.com/book-series

Handbook of Research on Child and Adolescent Psychology Practices and Interventions
Sanjeev Kumar Gupta (All India Institute of Speech and Hearing, ndia)
Medical Information Science Reference • © 2024 • 632pp • H/C (ISBN: 9781668499832) • US $395.00

African Womanhood and the Feminist Agenda
Maxwell Constantine Chando Musingafi (National University of Lesotho, Lesotho) and Chipo Hungwe (Midlands State University, Zimabwe)
Information Science Reference • © 2024 • 360pp • H/C (ISBN: 9798369319994) • US $230.00

Stabilization Approaches That Empower Clients Through Mental Health Crises
Isabel Logan (Southern Connecticut State University, USA) and Cheryl A. Green (Yale New Haven Health-Bridgeport Hospital, USA & Abilene Christian University, USA)
Medical Information Science Reference • © 2023 • 202pp • H/C (ISBN: 9781799882282) • US $360.00

Modern Perspectives and Current Trends in Asian Education, Psychology, and Sociology
Pannee Suanpang (Suan Dusit University, Thailand)
Information Science Reference • © 2023 • 295pp • H/C (ISBN: 9781668473757) • US $240.00

Developmental Language Disorders in Childhood and Adolescence
Dimitra V. Katsarou (University of the Aegean, Greece)
Information Science Reference • © 2023 • 436pp • H/C (ISBN: 9798369306444) • US $230.00

Changing the Stigma of Mental Health Among African Americans Moving From Denial to Acceptance
LaVelle Hendricks (Texas A&M University, Commerce, USA) and Dimitra Smith (Texas A&M University, Commerce, USA)
Information Science Reference • © 2023 • 367pp • H/C (ISBN: 9781668489185) • US $240.00

Facilitating Social Justice, Service Delivery, and Advocacy Through Multicultural Counseling Competencies
Keith B. Wilson (University of Kentucky, USA) and Si-Yi Chao (University of Kentucky, USA)
Information Science Reference • © 2023 • 369pp • H/C (ISBN: 9781668461556) • US $215.00

Combining Exercise and Psychotherapy to Treat Mental Health
Lara Carneiro (United Arab Emirates University, UAE) and Felipe Schuch (Universidade Federal de Santa Maria, Brazil)
Medical Information Science Reference • © 2024 • 300pp • H/C (ISBN: 9781668460405) • US $325.00

IGI Global
PUBLISHER of TIMELY KNOWLEDGE

701 East Chocolate Avenue, Hershey, PA 17033, USA
Tel: 717-533-8845 x100 • Fax: 717-533-8661
E-Mail: cust@igi-global.com • www.igi-global.com

This book is dedicated to
To my family
My colleagues
and my advisor, Professor Georgia Andreou

Editorial Advisory Board

Table of Contents

Detailed Table of Contents

In this chapter the authors present the educational framework that they believe the lower secondary school teacher of an inclusion class in Greece should know in order to help his/her students integrate into the physics class. This chapter will describe the legislative framework concerning the operation of the inclusion classes, the principles of differentiated pedagogy that can be exploited when teaching students with learning difficulties, the current and pilot physics curriculum, and present differentiated teaching practices in physics.

The worldwide prevalence of students diagnosed with specific learning difficulties (SLD) has increased over the past few decades. Education systems strive to include students with SLD in general classrooms through the implementation of various educational methods and adjustments to the teaching process, although often with limited learning outcomes. This chapter focuses on developmental dyslexia (DD) and explores its primary characteristics while delving into the attitudes, misconceptions, and lack of training among teachers, as their approach significantly impacts the education of students with DD. By describing the key attributes of DD and identifying the resulting learning challenges for students, the chapter puts forth suggested teaching methods and practices based on the current literature. These approaches encompass differentiated instruction, implicit learning, the use of Information and Communication Technologies, multisensory teaching, and student-centered group work.

This book chapter forcefully delves into the paramount topic of inclusive education for children with language disorders, unearthing the undeniable efficacy and significance that lie in furnishing an equitable and buttressed learning environment. The imperative of early intervention and vigilant surveillance takes center stage, spotlighting the fundamental responsibility of pinpointing and redressing individual requisites within multifaceted classrooms. The call within the chapter is collaboration among teachers, speech-language therapists, parents, and invested stakeholders. Through a sweeping scrutiny of empirical investigations and research conclusions, the chapter exposes the resplendent influence of inclusive education on scholastic accomplishments, linguistic outcomes, and socio-emotional maturation in children beset by language disorders. It probes the formidable obstacles encountered, including paucity of resources

Attention Deficit Hyperactivity Disorder (ADHD) affects people diagnosed with it and their families in many ways. Parents of children with ADHD are likely to face challenges in various aspects of parenting their children. This chapter describes a case study of a family of a child diagnosed with ADHD living permanently in Kos. The purpose of this study was to explore through in-depth structured interviews how parents perceive and manage the functioning and organisation of their family, the impact of the child's ADHD behaviour on their daily life, the sources of support they receive and their quality of life. The dominant themes identified were that parents perceive the disorder to affect family functioning and quality of life and seek support in order to cope with the difficulties of daily life. Understanding parents' own experiences is of paramount importance to clinical practice because the way a family functions and the sources of support available to them can have a significant impact on the child and the whole family system.

Parental involvement especially in the early years of education significantly influences the academic and socioemotional development of children with disabilities. Nevertheless, findings suggest migrant parents with a lower socioeconomic positioning typically exhibit limited engagement with their children's schools. In Greece, research exploring parental involvement has largely focused on the dominant middle-class parent group within the general education context. Using an intersectional lens, this chapter shifts focus and explores the social interlocking barriers and facilitators of school involvement among low-income migrant mothers of ASD children with language deficits. Findings shed light to how these mothers' experiences are constructed at the intersections of their multiple marginalized identities within the highly-centralized Greek education system and the narrative of individual responsibilitization and have implications for educational policies and practices that will foster active engagement of mothers who lack cultural and economic privilege.

Caregivers are individuals who provide comprehensive care to those facing challenges and who are unable to manage daily demands independently. Due to the practical and emotional demands they face on a daily basis, it is crucial for them to prioritize self-care to effectively fulfill their caregiving role. Counseling plays a pivotal role in helping caregivers navigate the psychological impact of developmental disorders while also discovering purpose in their caregiving role. This chapter aims to explore the significance and benefits of counseling for parents caring for children with developmental language disorders. Counseling plays a pivotal role in supporting parent caregivers of children and adolescents with language developmental language disorders.

Language development has a significant impact on healthy emotional functioning throughout the lifespan. There is increasing evidence highlighting the existence of specific language deficits on distinct developmental diagnoses, which posits difficulties in various aspects of language, such as language processing deficits, vocabulary and verbal fluency, and pragmatic language impairment. In particular, separate lines of research have unveiled that language problems may exist in conduct disorder, oppositional defiant disorder, and also in populations posing elevated callous unemotional traits. The scope of the present chapter is to summarize key evidence in this area of inquiry, by focusing on the underlying neurocognitive mechanisms involved in language problems. Conducting such analysis will aid in a better understanding of the key behaviours, cognitive mechanisms, and biological signatures of such difficulties that may assist future research in this area of research and designation of more tailored educational and therapeutic interventions.

The present study aims to implement an intervention program on a 2.5-year-old boy with a rare metabolic syndrome, Leukoencephalopathy with brainstem and spinal cord involvement and lactate elevation (LBSL). Although the recorded cases of the syndrome are unknown, there are aproximately100 patients worldwide that undergo treatment. This specific syndrome refers to a genetic biological disorder in expression. An attempt was made to investigate the outcome of an intervention program involving projects based on play therapy for the development of deficit communication skills. The ESCS was used as an

The major purpose of this research study was to detect the significant differences in human figure drawing between the students with learning difficulties and the students without learning difficulties. Moreover, this scientific research aimed to detect the differences between students of different genders with and without learning difficulties. The sample of this study consisted of 80 students who attended elementary school. The 40 were students with learning disabilities and the other 40 were students without learning disabilities. The main research tool used was the Goodenough-Harris drawing test (GH), which was assessed in 20 points. The results showed that the children without learning disabilities outperform children with learning disabilities. The drawing of students without learning difficulties is more detailed and they display more often in their drawing both proportions and symmetries in comparison with students with learning difficulties. Similar results are also observed in the drawings between the two sexes, as girls outperform boys of the same chronological age.

This chapter presents a collection of hypothetical and novel mathematical models and formulas for language development and disorders. The author explores the potential and limitations of using mathematics to understand, measure, predict, and intervene in various aspects of language development and disorders, such as genetic, environmental, cognitive, linguistic, and social factors. The chapter consists of several parts. One part introduces the language development index (SLDI), a formula that measures the level of language development in children with or without developmental language disorders (DLD). Anotehr describes the hypothesis of language disorder inheritance, a formula that predicts the inheritance pattern based on genetic and environmental factors. The third section explains the linguistic complexity index for developmental language disorders and so on. The chapter concludes with a discussion of the advantages and disadvantages of using mathematical models and formulas in language development research and practice, as well as some suggestions for future directions.

Preface

Welcome to *Childhood Developmental Language Disorders: Role of Inclusion, Families, and Professionals*. As editors of this comprehensive reference book, we are delighted to introduce you to a vital exploration of a field that impacts the lives of countless children and their families around the world.

In the journey of childhood development, language acquisition holds a central place. It is a powerful tool that shapes not only communication but also cognition and social interaction. However, for a significant number of children, this journey is not without its challenges. These challenges, often rooted in factors like reduced cognitive function, intellectual disability, autism, genetic syndromes, and other disabilities, can lead to what we term "developmental language disorders."

The world of developmental language disorders is vast and diverse, affecting children of different linguistic backgrounds, with varying etiologies, intensities, and durations. In recent years, there has been a surge in global research dedicated to understanding these disorders and finding effective ways to support affected individuals. This edited book brings together a collection of chapters that delve deep into the intricacies of language development in individuals with developmental disorders, drawing upon linguistic approaches, therapeutic methods, and inclusive pedagogical perspectives.

While there are existing books in the field of language disorders, they often focus on specific disorders or groups of disorders, leaving a gap in the holistic understanding of treatment and special education. Our aim with this volume is to illuminate the multi-prismatic nature of developmental language disorders, shifting the focus from a medical and marginalizing perspective to one that is inclusive and pedagogical.

This book serves as a valuable resource for a wide range of readers. It is intended as academic reading for students of pedagogy, psychology, special education, and speech therapy. Moreover, educators at all levels, from primary to tertiary, can find insights and practical strategies to better support children with developmental language disorders. Clinicians, therapists, librarians, parents, and members of language clubs and associations will also find this book to be a valuable addition to their reference collection.

The chapters in this book span a diverse spectrum of topics, including psycholinguistics, neurolinguistics, etiology and differential diagnosis, genetic syndromes, dyslexia, autism, aphasias, stuttering, psychological problems and language, developmental psychopathology and language, cognitive and linguistic profiles, special education, therapy, inclusion, and the crucial role of schools, families, and caregivers.

We hope that the insights and knowledge contained within these pages will not only deepen your understanding of developmental language disorders but also inspire meaningful actions to support children and individuals facing these challenges. By fostering an inclusive and supportive environment, we can empower these individuals to thrive and reach their full potential.

Thank you for joining us on this enlightening journey into the world of childhood developmental language disorders.

CHAPTER OVERVIEW

Chapter 1: The Social Dimension of Inclusive Education for Students with Cognitive and Developmental Difficulties

This chapter critically examines the social dimension of inclusive education, with a focus on students facing developmental and cognitive difficulties. It clarifies key terms and concepts related to social inclusion and explores the variables affecting the social dimension of inclusive education. The chapter delves into observational studies, sociometric studies, and self-reports from students to understand their social interactions and relationships. It also discusses school intervention programs designed to enhance the social dimension of inclusion and assesses their impact on the daily lives of students with developmental and cognitive difficulties.

Chapter 2: Empowering Language: Fostering Inclusion and Growth through Assistive Intelligence for Students with Language Disorders

This chapter delves into the complex realm of language disorders and their impact on students' educational experiences. It explores various types of language disorders, including expressive, receptive, and mixed receptive-expressive language disorders, and their implications for academic achievement and social interactions. The chapter also investigates the potential of assistive intelligence technologies to empower inclusive education for students with language disorders, emphasizing ethical considerations and a commitment to equity.

Chapter 3: Differentiated Teaching Practices of Physics in Inclusion Classes for Students with Learning Disabilities

This chapter provides insights into the educational framework necessary for lower secondary school teachers in Greece to effectively integrate students with learning difficulties into physics classes. It covers legislative aspects related to inclusion classes, principles of differentiated pedagogy for students with learning difficulties, and the current physics curriculum. The chapter also presents differentiated teaching practices specific to the field of physics, offering valuable guidance to educators.

Chapter 4: Educational Challenges and Perspectives in Developmental Dyslexia

Focusing on developmental dyslexia, this chapter addresses the increasing prevalence of specific learning difficulties among students. It explores the characteristics of developmental dyslexia and highlights the attitudes, misconceptions, and lack of training among teachers that impact the education of these students. The chapter proposes teaching methods and practices based on current literature, including

Differentiated Instruction, implicit learning, Information and Communication Technologies, multisensory teaching, and student-centered group work.

Chapter 5: Fostering Inclusive Education: Collaborative Strategies, Emerging Technologies, and Parental Engagement for Children with LDs

This chapter underscores the significance of inclusive education for children with language disorders and emphasizes the importance of early intervention and collaboration among various stakeholders, including teachers, speech-language therapists, parents, and others. It discusses the positive impact of inclusive education on scholastic achievements, linguistic outcomes, and socio-emotional development in children with language disorders. The chapter also addresses the challenges faced in terms of resource limitations and the demand for specialized services.

Chapter 6: Language, Socio-emotional Skills, School Performance of Children and Adolescents with Developmental Language Disorder According to Parents' Perception

This chapter investigates parents' perceptions of children and adolescents with Developmental Language Disorder (DLD). It explores the developmental history, language skills, socio-emotional characteristics, and school performance of children with DLD based on parental perspectives. The chapter highlights the challenges faced by these individuals, including difficulties in oral lessons, spelling, writing, and reading, and identifies significant relationships between oral language skills and various aspects of school performance.

Chapter 7: Family Dynamics and Socio-demographic Characteristics of Children with Spelling Difficulties

This chapter delves into the correlation between students' performance on a family dynamics test and specific socio-demographic characteristics. It examines the impact of family dynamics on children's spelling difficulties and explores factors such as parental satisfaction with school performance and leisure time utilization. The chapter sheds light on how family dynamics can influence the academic experiences of children with spelling difficulties.

Chapter 8: A Family's Experiences of Raising a Child Diagnosed with ADHD

This chapter presents a case study of a family with a child diagnosed with Attention Deficit Hyperactivity Disorder (ADHD). It explores how ADHD affects the child and the family, emphasizing the challenges faced by parents in various aspects of parenting. The chapter discusses the impact of ADHD on family functioning, organization, and quality of life. It highlights the importance of understanding parents' experiences and their coping strategies within the context of raising a child with ADHD.

Chapter 9: Migrant Mothers of ASD Children with Language Deficits in Greek Kindergarten Classrooms: Barriers and Facilitators of School Involvement Through an Intersectional Lens

This chapter examines the involvement of low-income migrant mothers in the education of their children with Autism Spectrum Disorder (ASD) and language deficits. It employs an intersectional lens to explore the social barriers and facilitators that impact these mothers' engagement with the Greek education system. The chapter emphasizes the need for cultural sensitivity and inclusive educational policies to foster active involvement of mothers who lack cultural and economic privilege.

Chapter 10: The Role of Support Networks for Children and Adolescents with Language Developmental Problems

This chapter explores the critical role of support networks, including family, school, community, and digital networks, in assisting children and adolescents with language developmental problems. It categorizes the assets provided by these networks into external and internal factors, highlighting their significance in helping individuals overcome language developmental challenges and integrate into society.

Chapter 11: Understanding the Developmental Needs of Children with Developmental Language Disorder According to Professionals

This chapter investigates professionals' understanding of the developmental needs of children with Developmental Language Disorder (DLD). It examines how professionals define DLD, the diagnostic criteria they apply, and the challenges they encounter when working with children with DLD. The chapter also explores differences in perceptions among educational psychologists, speech and language therapists, and special education needs teachers, shedding light on training and practice implications.

Chapter 12: Counseling for Caregivers for Children and Adolescents with Developmental Language Disorders

This chapter underscores the significance of counseling for parents caring for children with developmental language disorders. It explores the psychological impact of developmental disorders on caregivers and emphasizes the importance of self-care. The chapter highlights the role of counseling in helping caregivers navigate the challenges they face and discover purpose in their caregiving role.

Chapter 13: Associations Between Language Impairments and Behavioral Problems in Childhood: Neurocognitive Mechanisms and Future Implications

This chapter examines the relationship between language impairments and behavioral problems in childhood, focusing on the underlying neurocognitive mechanisms. It explores specific language deficits in conditions like conduct disorder, oppositional defiant disorder, and elevated callous unemotional traits. The chapter aims to deepen our understanding of the cognitive mechanisms behind language problems, providing insights for future research and tailored interventions.

Chapter 14: Case Study, Communication Abilities of a Child with Leukoencephalopathy (LBSL)

This chapter presents a case study of a child with a rare metabolic syndrome, Leukoencephalopathy with brainstem and spinal cord involvement and lactate elevation (LBSL). It investigates the outcomes of an intervention program based on play therapy to develop communication skills in the child. The chapter highlights the effectiveness of the intervention in improving the child's early communication skills.

Chapter 15: Using the Language Environment Analysis (LENA) System to Investigate Language Input in Greek-Speaking Children

This chapter discusses the use of the Language Environment Analysis (LENA) system to analyze language input in Greek-speaking children. It explores how wearable audio recording and voice analysis can reveal patterns of child-directed speech in typically developing children. The chapter identifies key parameters, such as conversational turn count and adult word count, and their correlation with child vocalizations and electronic device engagement.

Chapter 16: The Human Side of Dyslexia: An Exploration of Children's Self-esteem and Potential Interventions

This chapter delves into the relationship between dyslexia and self-esteem in children. It examines the impact of dyslexia on academic self-esteem and global self-esteem, considering factors such as placement and diagnosis. The chapter also explores interventions to improve self-esteem in children with dyslexia, emphasizing the role of supportive family, teachers, and peers.

Chapter 17: Learning Difficulties and Children's Drawing

This chapter investigates significant differences in human figure drawing between students with and without learning difficulties. It uses the Goodenough-Harris Drawing test to assess the drawing skills of students and compare the results. The chapter highlights differences in the quality and detail of drawings between the two groups and explores the influence of gender on drawing skills.

Chapter 18: Mathematical Models and Formulas for Language Development and Disorders

This chapter presents a collection of hypothetical and novel mathematical models and formulas for understanding language development and disorders. It introduces formulas like the Language Development Index and the Hypothesis of Language Disorder Inheritance, which predict language development patterns and inheritance based on various factors. The chapter discusses the advantages and limitations of using mathematical models in language development research.

Chapter 19: Beyond Words and Numbers: Exploring the Interplay Between Language Challenges and Mathematical Problem-Solving Abilities

This chapter critically analyzes the complex relationship between Developmental Language Disorders (DLD) and mathematical problem-solving abilities in children and adolescents. It explores how linguistic and non-linguistic factors influence problem-solving skills and challenges prevailing assumptions. The chapter emphasizes the need for a comprehensive analysis of this relationship and its implications for inclusive education.

Chapter 20: Navigating Dysphagia in Child Developmental Communication Disorders Using Telepractice Methods

This chapter examines the use of telepractice methods in addressing dysphagia in children with developmental communication disorders. It highlights the advantages of telepractice, such as accessibility and reduced travel, while addressing technical obstacles and privacy concerns. The chapter underscores the importance of modern diagnostic and intervention methods in the era of telepractice, ensuring accurate diagnosis and individualized rehabilitation programs.

IN SUMMARY

In concluding this comprehensive edited reference book, we reflect on the vast and intricate landscape we have traversed in the realm of developmental communication disorders. Our journey has taken us through the multifaceted dimensions of language difficulties, learning disabilities, and the invaluable contributions of professionals, caregivers, and educators. As the editors of this volume, we have witnessed the dedication and passion of countless individuals striving to support children and adolescents facing these challenges.

The chapters in this book have provided a panoramic view of the diverse experiences, insights, and methodologies that converge within the field of developmental communication disorders. From understanding the nuances of language disorders to exploring the intersections of socio-demographic factors and family dynamics, we have endeavored to create a rich tapestry of knowledge for researchers, educators, clinicians, and caregivers alike.

It is our fervent hope that this book will serve as a vital resource, shedding light on the complexities of developmental communication disorders and offering guidance to those who seek to make a meaningful impact on the lives of affected individuals. The research findings, case studies, and innovative interventions shared within these pages underscore the importance of collaboration, inclusivity, and tailored support in addressing these challenges.

As we look to the future, we recognize that the journey to enhance the lives of children and adolescents with developmental communication disorders is ongoing. New technologies, evolving research, and shifting societal perspectives will continue to shape our understanding and approach to these issues. It is our aspiration that this book will inspire further inquiry, innovative solutions, and a steadfast commitment to fostering inclusive educational environments and supportive communities.

In closing, we extend our gratitude to the dedicated authors who have contributed their expertise and insights to this volume. We also express our appreciation to the readers, educators, and professionals who will carry forward the mission of advancing the well-being and potential of children and adolescents with developmental communication disorders. Together, we can continue to build a more inclusive and supportive world for all.

Warmest regards,

Dimitra Katsarou
University of the Aegean, Greece

Chapter 1
The Social Dimension of Inclusive Education for Students With Cognitive and Developmental Difficulties

Ilias Vasileiadis
Aristotle University of Thessaloniki, Greece

Ioanna Dimitriadou
University of Macedonia, Greece

Spyros Koutras
Queen Margaret University, UK

ABSTRACT

The purpose of this chapter is to present firstly - with a critical approach - a clarification of the terms and concepts describing the social dimension of inclusion, with regard to students with developmental and cognitive difficulties, in order to identify differences or convergences. These specific variables are usually examined within observational studies of the social interaction among peers, sociometric studies of acceptance, and studies that require self-reports from the students regarding themselves and their social relationships. Furthermore, the variables related to the social dimension of inclusive education for these students, and their development in each age period, are presented. Finally, the chapter focuses on school intervention programmes concentrating on the social dimension of inclusion, and evaluates the impact of such programmes on the daily school life of students with developmental and cognitive difficulties.

STUDENTS WITH COGNITIVE AND DEVELOPMENTAL DIFFICULTIES

Support for students with cognitive and developmental difficulties has been a subject of scientific study for several decades. Researchers from various disciplines, such as special education teachers, psycholo-

DOI: 10.4018/979-8-3693-1982-6.ch001

gists, speech therapists and others, have defined these specific difficulties, investigated their causality and determined appropriate educational frameworks. However, one of the most significant challenges that arise from studying the international literature on students with cognitive and developmental difficulties is the lack of a universally accepted definition (Genova, 2015). The confusion surrounding the identification of these difficulties is evident from the various terms that have been used over time to describe them, such as generalised learning difficulties, learning disorders, learning difficulties, etc. (Alkahtani, 2016). Nonetheless, most researchers agree that students' cognitive and developmental difficulties are accompanied by deficiencies in adaptive behaviour (social skills, self-guidance, development of learning strategies, functional academic skills, communication, etc.) and manifest during the developmental period (Messiou, 2017).

The term cognitive difficulties implies that these students present slower rates of development and learning compared to their peers and that these specific students are able to manage their cognitive difficulties with adequate support. Thus, with the term cognitive and developmental difficulties, it becomes clear that these students do not perform at the same developmental and cognitive level as their peers and that this deviation may have organic underpinnings and/or be connected to environmental factors (Schalock & Luckasson, 2021). Therefore, according to this approach, in most cases, students with cognitive and developmental difficulties are intellectually lagging compared to their peers and their development is slow and deficient (Richards et al., 2014).

Furthermore, when identifying specific difficulties, attention is devoted to the students' capabilities, the environment in which they are being educated and their broader functionality within the school and social context. Emphasis is placed on social factors (the students' socio-cultural background, dominant school culture, quality of provided support and education) that influence their school integration and performance (De Bruin, 2019). Thus, a student's cognitive and developmental difficulties are not determined as fixed characteristics of said student, but as a result of the student's interaction with the family, school and broader social context (Schalock et al., 2021).

This specific approach contributes to the more effective inclusion and acceptance of students with cognitive and developmental difficulties, as it does not attribute the difficulties solely to the students themselves, but also to their environment and particularly the social context in which they live and interact (Vlachou & Papananou, 2018). More specifically, it is observed that students with more severe cognitive and developmental difficulties are distributed across all socioeconomic strata. On the other hand, the majority of students with mild cognitive and developmental difficulties are found in populations belonging to lower socioeconomic strata; this is because greater challenges are associated with the design of learning programmes for these students, thus leading to more direct impact on the quality of the provided education. Therefore, the prognosis of students with mild cognitive and developmental difficulties can be improved by the fostering of adequate inclusive interventions (Vlachou & Fyssa, 2016). In conclusion, it is noted that the school and broader social exclusion experienced by students with cognitive and developmental difficulties is not directly linked to the difficulties themselves, but rather to the school environment. The type and quality of inclusive policies implemented can either facilitate or hinder students' cognitive and emotional development, as well as their access to social activities in the school daily life (Berghs et al., 2019).

Traditional approaches focus on the cognitive development and the challenges experienced by students with cognitive and developmental difficulties. Specifically, in regard to their cognitive development, these students seem to have difficulty in spontaneously activating and implementing certain cognitive functions. In some cases, the cognitive processes they adopt are insufficient for effective problem-solving and handling, which hinders their communication and social integration. They often struggle to organise incoming information and process it autonomously, which causes their difficulty in acquiring new knowledge and skills (Nteropoulou-Nterou et al., 2017).

However, these observations have been heavily criticised for presenting cognitive and developmental difficulties in a one-dimensional and individual-centric manner. The most significant criticism is that, when particular emphasis is placed on individualised academic skill programmes, the emotional and social development of students with intellectual and developmental difficulties is not facilitated (Lindner et al., 2023). In other words, it is thought that the historical, social and emotional factors that shape and define the image of students with cognitive and developmental difficulties are not taken into account; instead, focus is placed on their cognitive deficits without considering the social factors associated with inclusive practices (Ainscow, 2020).

Several decades ago, Vygotsky (2012) challenged the dominant biological approach of his time, which viewed every cognitive impairment as a result of an organic disorder. Instead, he proposed that developmental and cognitive difficulties in children should be seen as social problems rather than issues of restrictively physical causes. A significant aspect of his work was the differentiation of a primary and a secondary dimension in regard to developmental difficulties. The primary dimension is associated with the cognitive impairments themselves, whilst the secondary dimension is connected to the social aspects that arise from society's attitudes and practices in dealing with cognitive impairments (Ainscow, 2020). Usually, the prevalent tactic is for people to equate these two dimensions unknowingly. This lack of awareness regarding the differentiation of the two dimensions is systematic in nature; as such, it leads to principally social issues being viewed as personal matters that are supposedly associated with a student's organic disorders. Additionally, Vygotsky (2012) greatly emphasised the social consequences of developmental and cognitive difficulties. He acknowledged that, whilst these specific difficulties have inherent consequences, their main effects are of social and cultural character. According to his approach, developmental inadequacy, on the one hand, poses objective challenges, but on the other hand, it also provides incentives for development. Even though a child's developmental trajectory may be complicated due to a developmental impairment of some sort, their emotional and social development could acquire a creative quality, due to the reorganisation of all their mental functions (Akhmetova et al., 2017).

The social position of students with developmental and cognitive difficulties at the school and within the broader social context is usually low and the roles they assume in social activities are mainly passive. Many researchers state that the daily lives of these students are characterised by loneliness and engagement in solitary, often monotonously repetitive activities, either within the school environment or at home (Nilholm, 2021). In reality, students with developmental difficulties remain isolated, without social interactions with their peers, but rather form co-dependent relationships with the adults responsible for their education. The lack of differentiation concerning their degree of socialisation and social position in different educational settings is attributed to the fact that, in most cases, organised activities aimed at enhancing their social inclusion are not provided (Garrote et al., 2017).

As a result, students with developmental and cognitive difficulties interact less with their peers and are mainly guided by adults, which reinforces the co-dependent factor of their relationships. At the same time, the relationships they develop with their peers often lead to conflicts and they themselves might exhibit aggressive and negative verbal and non-verbal behaviour, become divisive or withdrawn (Vetoniemi & Kärnä, 2021). These behaviours often result in the active rejection of these students by their peers. When the co-dependent relationships with the educators become even stronger, the focus is again shifted on the students' difficulties; thus, the exploration of ways to manage the social, educational, or familial factors that make schools dysfunctional and ineffective, not only for students with developmental difficulties but also for all students, is neglected (Broomhead, 2019). A typical example of this is the case of students who do not exhibit any organic disorder, but are partially or entirely excluded from social processes in education, because the inadequacies of the educational system hinder their social integration and adaptation. These students can be described as slow learners, or 'weak' students in educational systems with one-dimensional educational demands and rigid curricula (Graham, 2020).

Thus, students with developmental and cognitive difficulties begin to face social and emotional development challenges mainly because the structure and organisation of the school are more suitable for students without developmental difficulties (Florian et al., 2017): this means that the school's inability to manage the deficiencies and the obstacles to the socialisation of students with cognitive and developmental difficulties is overlooked. For the student population, however, the school functions as an example of how the world is organised and how its protagonists are categorised. From an inclusive perspective, all the aforementioned difficulties are part of an ongoing process of defining and managing daily life in school (Meuser et al., 2023). As a school culture, inclusion shapes and impacts the relationships of all those involved in educational processes in a dynamic and innovative manner. The advantages of inclusion are listed below (Graham, 2020).

APPROACHES TO INCLUSIVE EDUCATION

Over time, various definitions of inclusive education have been formulated. Most valid definitions originate from the United Nations organisation and various conventions, such as the Convention on the Rights of Persons with Difficulties and the Incheon Declaration. According to the Committee on the Rights of Persons with Difficulties, inclusive education is a fundamental right, a principle that values the well-being, dignity, autonomy and contribution of students to society and a continuous process to eliminate barriers in education and to promote cultural reform (Ainscow et al., 2019). Inclusive education means that students facing learning difficulties are being taught with their peers in the same classroom for most periods of the school day (Cobley, 2018).

Inclusive education begins with acknowledging that all children have the right to be in the same educational space (Schuelk, 2018). It is presented as a philosophy that guides educational practices to respect the right of all students to equal education. Inclusive education focuses on increasing the participation of all children, creating systems that equally value all individuals and promoting equality, empathy and respect for human rights (Florian & Spratt, 2013). Other essential aspects include increased placement of students with various difficulties in mainstream schools, equal opportunities for academic and social achievements, the implementation of inclusive pedagogical methods and the creation of inclusive school communities (Messiou & Ainscow, 2020).

Furthermore, inclusive education mainly refers to the type and quality of the relationship that develops between educators and students with and without learning difficulties. It is defined as an integration process that is not limited to a psycho-educational method or a practical design. Instead, it is closely linked to a broader philosophy, according to which every student is accepted regardless of the degree and nature of their difficulties (Ainscow, 2020).

When examining the concept of inclusion, obstacles arise immediately by definition. It is a concept that entails multidimensional and conflicting expressions, which allow multiple interpretations; therefore, at the international level, the tendency is to refer to a broader definition. The primary objective seems to be enhancing human diversity and actions against discrimination and exclusion (Dell'Anna, Pellegrini & Ianes, 2019). Inclusive education's significance is evident from its positive results for all students, both typical and atypical in their development. Successful inclusive education requires school transformation and systemic shifts. However, a significant part of this reform focuses on the design, without considering the resources needed (Florian et al., 2017).

The key factors for implementing inclusive education include the school and classroom levels. School reforms, training and support for all educators in implementing practices for inclusive education, as well as support from school leadership for vision-driven and inclusive education, are required (Schuelk, 2018). The most significant elements that lead to the success of inclusive education are: an official, detailed curriculum and an assessment approach that address all students; the support of the entire educational community towards inclusion policies; an organised and reliable system for monitoring students who may be at risk of developing special educational needs; the guidance of all services involved with students with atypical development by the same principles and goals. Additionally, all educational faculty should encourage the participation of every student in all aspects of school and community life (Cobley, 2018).

The fundamental principles that need to be satisfied for successful inclusion are threefold (Kefalinou, Symeonidou & Meijer, 2020):

- Educational principle: inclusion benefits all students, as it focuses on meeting the diverse needs of learners.
- Social principle: inclusion can promote a more equitable society.
- Economic principle: inclusive schools are likely to be less costly compared to separate schools.

To understand what inclusive education is and how it can benefit all students, one can take a look at the research conducted over the past ten years. Most studies (Nilholm, 2021) have found that students with developmental and cognitive difficulties exist in general education schools. Research reviews provide different insights into the topic, depending on three main variables:

i. the involved parties and their perspectives (students with typical and atypical development, educators, parents, stakeholders, etc.);
ii. the aspects of inclusion being examined (e.g., students' attitudes, perspectives, self-perception, academic performance, etc.);
iii. the school level at which inclusive education programmes are implemented (preschool, primary, secondary, or tertiary education).

In review studies, it appears that students generally have a neutral attitude towards their peers with developmental and cognitive difficulties, but differences were observed in relation to specific individual variables. Girls tended to have more positive attitudes compared to boys, attitudes were more positive towards students with physical difficulties than towards peers with intellectual or behavioural difficulties, whilst students with prior knowledge about diversity showed a more positive attitude towards inclusion (Dell'Anna, Pellegrini & Ianes, 2019). In another study, it was evident that educators generally had a positive attitude towards students with developmental difficulties and recognised the benefits of inclusion for these students and their typically developing peers. Knowledge and understanding of developmental difficulties were identified as crucial factors in the success of inclusion programmes. However, it was also acknowledged that significant obstacles still exist in achieving full inclusion (Göransson & Nilholm, 2014).

Research review categorises the studies into positive, negative, or non-significant, based on their findings. The effects of inclusion on social-emotional skills and students' academic performance with and without difficulties are recorded. Most included studies reported significantly positive outcomes, whilst some found adverse effects or mixed findings (Dell'Anna et al., 2019). Students with developmental and cognitive difficulties benefit in various ways from inclusion programmes. Initially, research shows that they exhibit reduced rates of inappropriate behaviour associated with increased rates of individual learning goals. This aims at their integration into future environments without exclusion and social initiatives. Additionally, they demonstrate enhanced social skills, such as forming, maintaining and generalising friendly relationships (Van Mieghem et al., 2020). On the other hand, the benefits for students with typical development mainly involve increased understanding, acceptance and appreciation of diversity, forming meaningful friendships, reinforcing respect, preparing for an inclusive future society and opportunities to acquire social and cognitive skills through practice and teaching others (Ainscow, 2020).

In addition to the benefits, research also addresses various challenges associated with inclusive education. The most significant obstacle appears to be the negative attitude of society. Furthermore, there are physical barriers, such as the programme's inability to meet the needs of a wide range of students and the lack of sufficient training for educational faculty working in school settings (Finkelstein et al., 2021). It becomes evident that the significance of inclusion goes beyond the academic benefits for all students and that it also influences and shapes their social development.

THE SOCIAL DIMENSION OF INCLUSION

The term social dimension of inclusive education generally relates to the interaction, acceptance and relationship development amongst typical and atypical children, both within and outside the school context. Definitions of the social dimension of inclusive education may vary in content and formulation, as in many studies, a clear and analytical definition is not provided, or similar terms are used interchangeably, acquiring the same meaning (Qvortrup & Qvortrup, 2018). In relation to other terms, inclusion is considered the most general term, mainly when used in research related to education, referring to the process of coexistence and active participation of children with and without developmental and cognitive difficulties. Other researchers view the social dimension of inclusive education as the purpose achieved through various school practices, such as experiential techniques. Social inclusion is not just about placing students with special educational needs in mainstream schools; it also involves adequate human resources and the design and appropriate utilisation of educational materials, based on the individual needs of each student (Juvonen et al., 2019).

Some researchers clearly define the concept and content of the social dimension of inclusive education, considering specific aspects they deem essential. Hymel & Katz (2019) studied the social inclusion of atypical students in general education classes and identified three significant relevant aspects: social impact, social preference and social network affiliation. Social impact refers to the positive or negative effect a child's behaviour may have on the group or class. Social preference relates to the degree of social acceptance of a child with developmental and cognitive difficulties by their peers. The social network of affiliations, closely linked to a child's social preference and social impact, is described by the interactions a child develops, with whom and their perception of 'belonging' to a specific peer group.

Schwab (2015) also clearly defines the concept of the social dimension of inclusive education based on the acceptance of a student as a member of a group, the establishing of at least one mutual friendship and the active and equal participation in group activities. Furthermore, Schwab et al. (2015) point out that the social dimension of inclusive education refers to the ability to interact, form friendships and be accepted by peers.

In summary, the significant dimensions of the social aspect of inclusive education are: a) social interactions; b) social acceptance; and c) the development of friendships and relationships (Koster et al., 2009). Additionally, the social dimension of inclusive education in the context of secondary education may be subject to different interpretations by those involved (educators, students, parents), compared to the primary education context, as several characteristics of interactions during adolescence and the social environment of students change (Bossaert et al., 2013). More specifically:

a. The social interaction between children of typical and atypical development is an integral part of the social dimension of inclusive education. Many researchers consider interactions with peers as a fundamental criterion for evaluating the inclusion of children with developmental and cognitive difficulties, studying the frequency and nature of their social contacts and the development of positive social interactions amongst them (Krischler et al., 2019). Some researchers emphasise the study of peer social networks and social interactions, setting more qualitative criteria and comparing both the frequency of interaction and the patterns of behaviour that emerge (Paseka & Schwab, 2020). Furthermore, social interaction is examined to evaluate the social dimension of inclusive education within various activities, such as during lunch breaks at school (Bossaert et al., 2013). Additionally, certain studies explore the dual aspect of interaction by examining positive and negative interactions between students with and without developmental difficulties (Koster et al., 2009).

b. Other researchers focus on specific aspects of social interaction, such as social initiation, social bids and students' social behaviours. Social initiation refers to the involvement of children with developmental and cognitive difficulties in activities initiated by an adult or another child. It appears that children with developmental difficulties participate more in activities when an adult has initiated them or partakes in them, because they consider them more reliable than their peers and trust them more (Göransson & Nilholm, 2014). Social bids made by students and the responses they encounter from their peers differ in relationships between typically developing students and those with developmental difficulties. Students with cognitive difficulties seem to have a slight disadvantage and often do not respond adequately to social bids from students without cognitive difficulties. Researchers report that they do not have well-developed broader social behaviours, a fact that 'blocks' spontaneous interaction with peers (Stone et al., 2019). Moreover, children with developmental and cognitive difficulties demonstrate different social behaviours (e.g., behaviours adopted by adults) compared to children without difficulties, as they are more likely to interact socially with an adult than their peers. In contrast, children without difficulties direct their social behaviour more often towards their peers, thus interacting more with them and being more likely to receive social initiation from their peers (Camargo et al., 2014). Social acceptance or peer acceptance is a crucial dimension of the social aspect of inclusive education and refers to the acceptance of students with developmental and cognitive difficulties by their peers. Several researchers consider social acceptance to be at the core of the social dimension of inclusive education (Hymel & Katz, 2019). Schwab and her collaborators assessed the level of social inclusion of children with special educational needs in mainstream schools and explored the relationship between social inclusion and the self-concept of typical and atypical students. It is worth noting that the researchers evaluated social acceptance within the peer group using sociometric measures based on social preference and social rejection of students with developmental and cognitive difficulties, considering the study of the aforementioned variables as the most reliable predictor of the social acceptance of students with difficulties. Generally, social preference serves as a significant indicator of social acceptance and several researchers emphasise its importance, as it directly and accurately reflects students' evaluations of their peers (Avramidis, 2013).

It is noted that students with developmental and cognitive difficulties often display deficits in social skills, which can impact their social acceptance within the peer group. Therefore, intervention practices (such as encouraging communication) within group activities in the school setting are recommended to enhance social acceptance and acquire social skills that lead to social interaction, relationship building and friendly bonds (McCoy & Banks, 2012). Finally, the sense of 'belonging' that arises from the acceptance and equal participation of typically and atypically developing students in activities is also significant (Bossaert et al., 2013).

c. Friendly relationships are at the core of the study concerning the social dimension of inclusive education. Friends are an integral part of children's school life and without them, they cannot fully and actively participate in any school activity (Mamas, 2012). The ability of a child with cognitive difficulties to initiate or maintain equitable friendships is considered an indicator of their social development and integration in the school environment (Taylor & Houghton, 2008). In their research in Australia, using open-ended interviews with 48 participants (educators, high school students with general learning difficulties, parents), Taylor and Houghton focused on friendships to assess the degree of social inclusion of students with learning difficulties. According to their perspective, a child is deemed fully included if they have developed three or more friendships with their peers. The study's findings were interesting, as they revealed that, compared to the students themselves, educators and parents often perceive children with learning difficulties as more socially isolated and marginalised. This dimension of their perspectives could be attributed, on the one hand, to the excessive concern of the involved adults regarding the inclusion of students with difficulties, which makes them more 'sensitive' to instances of social rejection that may not solely concern students with developmental and cognitive challenges. On the other hand, it can be linked to these students' struggles in cognitive processing of social relationships and preferences within the school context, leading to erroneous conclusions about who is accepted and by whom (Hornby, 2011).

In conclusion, the term social dimension of inclusive education appears to be a specific concept describing social interaction, the development of social relationships and friendships, as well as the social acceptance of students with developmental and cognitive difficulties by their peers in mainstream schools (De Vroey et al., 2018). As observed, a precise and universally accepted definition cannot exist, because different contexts (e.g., different countries or educational policies) might associate it with different meanings. Koster et al. (2009) see positive connotations behind the concept of the social dimension of inclusive education, which refer to the coexistence of students with and without difficulties in mainstream schools, the co-creation of a common culture and the widespread use of the term by researchers and the educational community. The co-creation of a common culture is reflected in daily school life through the development and implementation of programmes that enhance the social dimension of inclusion.

PROGRAMMES FOR ENHANCING THE SOCIAL DIMENSION OF INCLUSION WITHIN THE SCHOOL CONTEXT

As mentioned, inclusive education calls upon educators to create a positive and supportive classroom environment, where all students play an active role, feel accepted and develop social relationships. In such an environment, students are able to further develop their social and emotional skills and become socially accepted (Vasileiadis et al., 2021). An inclusive school represents the school of the future. As a result, a significant portion of scientific research has focused on this field (Van Mieghem et al., 2020).

Whilst educational policies are becoming increasingly inclusive, social inclusion of students with developmental and cognitive difficulties remains a matter under deliberation (Klang et al., 2020). These specific students tend to have poor social participation in the framework of typical education. Studies indicate that students with developmental and cognitive difficulties are less accepted, have fewer friends and engage in fewer social interactions with peers compared to their non-disabled counterparts, spending less time with their typically developing peers during school breaks. Even if students with developmental and cognitive difficulties form some friendships, these relationships seem to be characterised of poorer quality, be less intimate and less stable than those reported by their non-disabled peers (Juvonen, et al., 2019).

Furthermore, students with difficulties express lower self-esteem and lower self-perception of social inclusion compared to their non-disabled peers (Toulia et al., 2022; Schwab, 2015). The way typically developing students perceive cognitive difficulties can influence the degree to which students with developmental and cognitive difficulties, who have access to special educational support (e.g., accommodations, modifications, etc.), are socially integrated or excluded. School-age students with developmental and cognitive difficulties tend to face difficulties establishing friendly relationships with their peers at school. The main obstacles are related to the negative behaviours exhibited by typically developing students towards their peers with developmental and cognitive difficulties. These negative attitudes towards developmental and cognitive difficulties jeopardise the very nature of inclusive education (Petry, 2018).

The main cause for the aforementioned findings is the lack of necessary skills for social interaction of students with developmental and cognitive difficulties, which can lead to their exclusion. For example, aggressive behaviour and difficulties in social skills have been identified as predictors of peer rejection. The behaviours of peers, classroom norms and the lack of support from educators contribute to the social exclusion of students with developmental and cognitive difficulties (Krischler et al., 2019).

Research data indicate that increased positive interactions amongst members of different social groups can reduce prejudices and increase positive attitudes amongst them (Toulia et al., 2022; Freer, 2021). A systematic review of 35 studies found a positive correlation between school-age children who have contact with students with developmental and cognitive difficulties and their attitudes towards them. Another recent study involving over 1,800 children supports the findings of the previous review and observes that the relation of contact to attitudes is influenced by empathy and anxiety about interacting with students who are different (Armstrong, et al., 2017).

In the case of students with special educational needs, based on their personal experiences after attending mainstream schools, it appears that their perceptions of social participation are closely related to their experiences within their learning environment. Research indicates that physical presence in a school does not guarantee the full engagement of students with developmental and cognitive difficulties. Their experiences in the school environment have shaped how they perceive themselves as learners and as group members. Furthermore, the interactions between students with developmental and cognitive difficulties and the educational, social, technical and physical aspects of the school environment have also influenced their emotions regarding inclusion and acceptance as active participants. The experiences and emotions of participating students regarding the school environment were often negative. They were less popular, had fewer friends, experienced feelings of fear, anger, disappointment and loneliness and exhibited limited involvement. Through their abilities (related to hobbies, motivations and academic or social strengths), students gained feelings of empowerment, capability and a sense of belonging (Vetoniemi & Kärnä, 2021).

Social support programmes for students with developmental and cognitive difficulties contribute to the development of all the factors that have been proved to hinder their social development. Toulia et al. (2022) report that structured programmes of Social Skills Training have focused exclusively on students with developmental and cognitive difficulties experiencing marginalisation, in order to enhance their social competence and facilitate their involvement in their classroom network. However, these specific programmes have been proved to be ineffective in teaching social skills and to consequently fail to foster social inclusion in regard to these students. The primary reason for their failure is that they are implemented in segregated learning environments rather than within the mainstream classroom setting, making it difficult to generalise and apply the teaching outcomes outside the learning contexts.

Literature also provides examples of more advanced interventions aiming to enhance the social participation of students with developmental and cognitive difficulties. Such interventions are implemented at the entire school level and modify certain fundamental systemic factors, such as the overall school culture and the attitudes of faculty and peers. This is achieved by promoting enhanced social interactions and developing positive peer relationships.

Lindsay and Edwards (2013) classified these interventions into five types:

1. social contact, where children without developmental and cognitive difficulties interact with students with developmental and cognitive difficulties;
2. simulation, in which children experience the challenges faced by individuals with developmental and cognitive difficulties in their everyday lives through simulation activities;
3. curriculum-based activities, which may include presentations, stories and exercises in the classroom focusing on a wide range of difficulties;
4. multimedia curriculum, including videos and online activities, in order to facilitate learning and promote classroom discussions about various types of difficulties;
5. multiple components, where different approaches are combined in multiple sessions.

Successful interventions are based on multi-component approaches that foster social interactions, which are implemented over a considerable period and are rigorously monitored with strict measures.

Specifically, there are three elements that can characterise a successful intervention (Toulia et al., 2022):

1. the development of student's social skills and social understanding;
2. teaching students about respect and appreciation for diversity;
3. improving students' abilities to create and maintain friendships.

In a research analysis and meta-analysis of 12 studies concerning the impact on typically developing students from their direct or indirect contact with students with developmental and cognitive difficulties, it was found that such contact effectively improves the behaviour of typically developing children towards individuals with developmental and cognitive challenges. All direct contact interventions included in the review were effective; therefore, schools should consider taking actions related to understanding and raising awareness of these specific difficulties. For example, they could invite an athlete or a student with developmental and cognitive difficulties to attend classes and discuss issues related to their impairment and engage in simulation activities. Extensive contact through reading relevant stories has been proved to be effective if this is not feasible. Furthermore, these interventions were successful after a one-off 45-minute session and when conducted by invited speakers, researchers or educators (Armstrong et al., 2017). Another study supported that two 45-minute interventions were more effective than a single 90-minute intervention (Freer, 2021).

Subsequently, the research review of 37 studies revealed that it is sensible for intervention programmes to provide students with meaningful contact opportunities with peers who have developmental and cognitive difficulties. Researchers designing interventions should avoid factors unrelated to positive attitudes towards developmental and cognitive difficulties. Simple awareness may not be sufficient to change students' attitudes towards these impairments. Thus, intervention developers should go beyond mere contact with developmental and cognitive difficulties, engaging in actions that require and produce different levels of knowledge and behavioural dimensions (Freer, 2021).

Fifty-six educators were randomly selected as intervention and control groups in a study aiming to investigate the impact of intervention programmes on students with and without developmental and cognitive difficulties in designing cooperative learning strategies. The educators received training and guidance on cooperative learning and implemented this approach three to four times per week for 15 weeks. The results showed a significant, albeit small, effect of cooperative learning on the social acceptance of children with developmental and cognitive difficulties, but no significant impact on children's friendships and perceptions of classroom relationships. The degree of cooperative learning implementation affected the social acceptance of children, but this effect was not consistent across all measurements of social acceptance. Therefore, it can be concluded that cooperative learning, as conducted during the duration and intensity of the present study, may not lead to substantial changes in the social inclusion of children with developmental and cognitive difficulties (Klang et al., 2020).

In the cooperative learning model, children work in small, heterogeneous groups structured to enhance the learning of all group members. An approach that has gained popularity in recent years is the 'Learning Together' strategy. This approach aims to promote group cohesion by structuring group work according to five principles based on the theory of social interdependence (Klang et al., 2020):

- Positive Interdependence: it ensures that all group members know they depend on each other's efforts to complete a task; an individual member cannot succeed unless all group members do their part.
- Individual Accountability: this means that all group members feel responsible for completing their share of the group workload.
- Promotive Interaction: the third principle provides opportunities for children to interact to promote group work by providing help, support and feedback to each other.
- Social Skills: the fourth principle involves explicitly teaching social skills and encouraging children to use them during group sessions.
- Group Processing: the final principle involves reflecting on the group's work to plan future group activities.

The educator's duty in approaching cooperative learning is to structure classroom activities based on the five principles mentioned above, as well as to introduce and monitor group work when needed.

In summary, international research indicates that students with developmental and cognitive difficulties are at higher risk of low social participation, despite increased attention to their social inclusion in recent years. The situation remains problematic, as evidenced by their low self-esteem regarding social inclusion, limited social acceptance, restricted interactions and scanty friendships. It appears that social inclusion is promoted more effectively in inclusive classrooms with the participation of a smaller number of students, compared to exclusively general education classrooms, and it is further enhanced through the systematic implementation of relevant school-based intervention programmes (Schwab, 2015).

REFERENCES

Ainscow, M. (2020). Promoting inclusion and equity in education: Lessons from international experiences. *Nordic Journal of Studies in Educational Policy*, *6*(1), 7–16. doi:10.1080/20020317.2020.1729587

Ainscow, M., Slee, R., & Best, M. (2019). The Salamanca Statement: 25 years on. *International Journal of Inclusive Education*, *23*(7-8), 671–676. doi:10.1080/13603116.2019.1622800

Akhmetova, D. Z., Chelnokova, T. A., & Morozova, I. G. (2017). Theoretical and Methodological Basis of Inclusive Education in the Researches of Russian Scientists in the First Quarter of 20th Century. *International Education Studies*, *10*(2), 174–179. doi:10.5539/ies.v10n2p174

Alkahtani, M. A. (2016). Review of the Literature on Children with Special Educational Needs. *Journal of Education and Practice*, *7*(35), 70–83.

Armstrong, M., Morris, C., Abraham, C., & Tarrant, M. (2017). Interventions utilising contact with people with disabilities to improve children's attitudes towards disability: A systematic review and meta-analysis. *Disability and Health Journal*, *10*(1), 11–22. doi:10.1016/j.dhjo.2016.10.003 PMID:27780687

Avramidis, E. (2013). Self-concept, social position and social participation of pupils with SEN in mainstream primary schools. *Research Papers in Education*, *28*(4), 421–442. doi:10.1080/02671522.2012.673006

Berghs, M., Atkin, K., Hatton, C., & Thomas, C. (2019). Do disabled people need a stronger social model: A social model of human rights? *Disability & Society*, *34*(7-8), 1034–1039. doi:10.1080/09687599.2019.1619239

Bossaert, G., Colpin, H., Pijl, S. J., & Petry, K. (2013). Truly included? A literature study focusing on the social dimension of inclusion in education. *International Journal of Inclusive Education*, *17*(1), 60–79. doi:10.1080/13603116.2011.580464

Broomhead, K. E. (2019). Acceptance or rejection? The social experiences of children with special educational needs and disabilities within a mainstream primary school. *Education 3-13*, *47*(8), 877-888. doi:10.1080/03004279.2018.1535610

Camargo, S. P. H., Rispoli, M., Ganz, J., Hong, E. R., Davis, H., & Mason, R. (2014). A review of the quality of behaviorally-based intervention research to improve social interaction skills of children with ASD in inclusive settings. *Journal of Autism and Developmental Disorders*, *44*(9), 2096–2116. doi:10.100710803-014-2060-7 PMID:24781498

Cobley, D. (2018). *Disability and international development: A guide for students and practitioners.* Routledge. doi:10.4324/9781315208558

De Bruin, K. (2019). The impact of inclusive education reforms on students with disability: An international comparison. *International Journal of Inclusive Education, 23*(7-8), 811–826. doi:10.1080/13603116.2019.1623327

De Vroey, A., Struyf, E., & Petry, K. (2016). Secondary schools included: A literature review. *International Journal of Inclusive Education, 20*(2), 109–135. doi:10.1080/13603116.2015.1075609

Dell'Anna, S., Pellegrini, M., & Ianes, D. (2021). Experiences and learning outcomes of students without special educational needs in inclusive settings: A systematic review. *International Journal of Inclusive Education, 25*(8), 944–959. doi:10.1080/13603116.2019.1592248

Finkelstein, S., Sharma, U., & Furlonger, B. (2021). The inclusive practices of classroom teachers: A scoping review and thematic analysis. *International Journal of Inclusive Education, 25*(6), 735–762. doi:10.1080/13603116.2019.1572232

Florian, L., Black-Hawkins, K., & Rouse, M. (2016). *Achievement and inclusion in schools*. Routledge. doi:10.4324/9781315750279

Florian, L., & Spratt, J. (2013). Enacting inclusion: A framework for interrogating inclusive practice. *European Journal of Special Needs Education, 28*(2), 119–135. doi:10.1080/08856257.2013.778111

Freer, J. R. R. (2021). Students' attitudes toward disability: A systematic literature review (2012–2019). *International Journal of Inclusive Education*, 1–19. doi:10.1080/13603116.2020.186668

Garrote, A., Dessemontet, R. S., & Opitz, E. M. (2017). Facilitating the social participation of pupils with special educational needs in mainstream schools: A review of school-based interventions. *Educational Research Review, 20*, 12–23. doi:10.1016/j.edurev.2016.11.001

Genova, A. (2015). Barriers to inclusive education in Greece, Spain and Lithuania: Results from emancipatory disability research. *Disability & Society, 30*(7), 1042–1054. doi:10.1080/09687599.2015.1075867

Göransson, K., & Nilholm, C. (2014). Conceptual diversities and empirical shortcomings–a critical analysis of research on inclusive education. *European Journal of Special Needs Education, 29*(3), 265–280. doi:10.1080/08856257.2014.933545

Graham, L. (Ed.). (2020). *Inclusive education for the 21st century: Theory, policy and practice*. Routledge. doi:10.4324/9781003116073

Hornby, G. (2011). Inclusive education for children with special educational needs: A critique. *International Journal of Disability Development and Education, 58*(3), 321–329. doi:10.1080/1034912X.2011.598678

Hymel, S., & Katz, J. (2019). Designing classrooms for diversity: Fostering social inclusion. *Educational Psychologist, 54*(4), 331–339. doi:10.1080/00461520.2019.1652098

Juvonen, J., Lessard, L. M., Rastogi, R., Schacter, H. L., & Smith, D. S. (2019). Promoting social inclusion in educational settings: Challenges and opportunities. *Educational Psychologist, 54*(4), 250–270. doi:10.1080/00461520.2019.1655645

Kefallinou, A., Symeonidou, S., & Meijer, C. J. (2020). Understanding the value of inclusive education and its implementation: A review of the literature. *Prospects, 49*(3-4), 135–152. doi:10.100711125-020-09500-2

Klang, N., Olsson, I., Wilder, J., Lindqvist, G., Fohlin, N., & Nilholm, C. (2020). A Cooperative Learning Intervention to Promote Social Inclusion in Heterogeneous Classrooms, Secondary. *Educational Psychology, 11*. doi:10.3389/fpstg.2020.586489

Koster, M., Nakken, H., Pijl, S. J., & Van Houten, E. (2009). Being part of the peer group: A literature study focusing on the social dimension of inclusion in education. *International Journal of Inclusive Education, 13*(2), 117–140. doi:10.1080/13603110701284680

Krischler, M., Powell, J. J., & Pit-Ten Cate, I. M. (2019). What is meant by inclusion? On the effects of different definitions on attitudes toward inclusive education. *European Journal of Special Needs Education, 34*(5), 632–648. doi:10.1080/08856257.2019.1580837

Lindner, K. T., Schwab, S., Emara, M., & Avramidis, E. (2023). Do teachers favor the inclusion of all students? A systematic review of primary schoolteachers' attitudes towards inclusive education. *European Journal of Special Needs Education*, 1–22. doi:10.1080/08856257.2023.2172894

Lindsay, S., & Edwards, A. (2012). A systematic review of disability awareness interventions for children and youth. *Disability and Rehabilitation, 35*(8), 623–646. doi:10.3109/09638288.2012.702850 PMID:22831703

Mamas, C. (2012). Pedagogy, social status and inclusion in Cypriot schools. *International Journal of Inclusive Education, 16*(11), 1223–1239. doi:10.1080/13603116.2011.557446

McCoy, S., & Banks, J. (2012). Simply academic? Why children with special educational needs don't like school. *European Journal of Special Needs Education, 27*(1), 81–97. doi:10.1080/08856257.2011.640487

Messiou, K. (2017). Research in the field of inclusive education: Time for a rethink? *International Journal of Inclusive Education, 21*(2), 146–159. doi:10.1080/13603116.2016.1223184

Messiou, K., & Ainscow, M. (2020). Inclusive Inquiry: Student–teacher dialogue as a means of promoting inclusion in schools. *British Educational Research Journal, 46*(3), 670–687. doi:10.1002/berj.3602

Meuser, S., Piskur, B., Hennissen, P., & Dolmans, D. (2023). Targeting the school environment to enable participation: A scoping review. *Scandinavian Journal of Occupational Therapy, 30*(3), 298–310. doi:10.1080/11038128.2022.2124190 PMID:36170879

Nilholm, C. (2021). Research about inclusive education in 2020–How can we improve our theories in order to change practice? *European Journal of Special Needs Education, 36*(3), 358–370. doi:10.1080/08856257.2020.1754547

Nteropoulou-Nterou, E., Zoniou-Sideri, A., Lampropoulou, N., & Tsermidou, L. (2017). Views and Perceptions of Senior Early Childhood Education Students Regarding Inclusive Education and Disability. *Mediterranean Journal of Social & Behavioral Research, 1*(1), 12–21.

Paseka, A., & Schwab, S. (2020). Parents' attitudes towards inclusive education and their perceptions of inclusive teaching practices and resources. *European Journal of Special Needs Education, 35*(2), 254–272. doi:10.1080/08856257.2019.1665232

Petry, K. (2018). The relationship between class attitudes towards peers with a disability and peer acceptance, friendships and peer interactions of students with a disability in regular secondary schools. *European Journal of Special Needs Education, 33*(2), 254–268. doi:10.1080/08856257.2018.1424782

Qvortrup, A., & Qvortrup, L. (2018). Inclusion: Dimensions of inclusion in education. *International Journal of Inclusive Education, 22*(7), 803–817. doi:10.1080/13603116.2017.1412506

Richards, S. B., Brady, M. P., & Taylor, R. L. (2014). *Cognitive and intellectual disabilities: Historical perspectives, current practices, and future directions.* Routledge. doi:10.4324/9780203508251

Schalock, R. L., & Luckasson, R. (2021). Intellectual disability, developmental disabilities, and the field of intellectual and developmental disabilities. In L. M. Glidden, L. Abbeduto, L. L. McIntyre, & M. J. Tassé (Eds.), *APA handbook of intellectual and developmental disabilities: Foundations* (pp. 31–45). American Psychological Association. doi:10.1037/0000194-002

Schalock, R. L., Luckasson, R., & Tassé, M. J. (2021). An overview of intellectual disability: Definition, diagnosis, classification, and systems of supports. *American Journal on Intellectual and Developmental Disabilities, 126*(6), 439–442. doi:10.1352/1944-7558-126.6.439 PMID:34700345

Schuelka, M. J. (2018). Social dimensions of inclusion in education of 4th and 7th grade pupils in inclusive and regular classes: Outcomes from Austria. *Research in Developmental Disabilities, 43*, 72–79. doi:10.1016/j.ridd.2015.06.005

Schwab, S., Gebhardt, M., Krammer, M., & Gasteiger-Klicpera, B. (2015). Linking self-rated social inclusion to social behaviour. An empirical study of students with and without special education needs in secondary schools. *European Journal of Special Needs Education, 30*(1), 1–14. doi:10.1080/08856257.2014.933550

Stone, B. G., Mills, K. A., & Saggers, B. (2019). Online multiplayer games for the social interactions of children with autism spectrum disorder: A resource for inclusive education. *International Journal of Inclusive Education, 23*(2), 209–228. doi:10.1080/13603116.2018.1426051

Toulia, A., Alves, S., Avramidis, E., Sanches-Ferreira, M., & Silveira-Maia, M. (2022). Qualitative evaluation of an intervention programme fostering students' social participation implemented by Greek and Portuguese elementary school teachers. *International Journal of Educational Research Open, 3*, 100205. Advance online publication. doi:10.1016/j.ijedro.2022.100205

Van Mieghem, A., Verschueren, K., Petry, K., & Struyf, E. (2020). An analysis of research on inclusive education: A systematic search and meta review. *International Journal of Inclusive Education, 24*(6), 675–689. doi:10.1080/13603116.2018.1482012

Vasileiadis, I., Koutras, S., & Stagiopoulos, P. (2021). Changing the attitudes of high school students towards intellectual disabilities: The contribution of a social coexistence programme. *Journal of Research in Special Educational Needs, 21*(1), 49–62. doi:10.1111/1471-3802.12498

Vetoniemi, J., & Kärnä, E. (2021). Being included–experiences of social participation of pupils with special education needs in mainstream schools. *International Journal of Inclusive Education, 25*(10), 1190–1204. doi:10.1080/13603116.2019.1603329

Vlachou, A., & Fyssa, A. (2016). 'Inclusion in practice': Programme practices in mainstream preschool classrooms and associations with context and teacher characteristics. *International Journal of Disability Development and Education, 63*(5), 529–544. doi:10.1080/1034912X.2016.1145629

Vlachou, A., & Papananou, I. (2018). Experiences and perspectives of Greek higher education students with disabilities. *Educational Research, 60*(2), 206–221. doi:10.1080/00131881.2018.1453752

Vygotsky, L. S. (2012). *Thought and language*. MIT press.

Chapter 2

Empowering Language:
Fostering Inclusion and Growth Through Assistive Intelligence for Students With Language Disorders

Efthymia Efthymiou
https://orcid.org/0000-0003-0411-1720
Zayed University, UAE

ABSTRACT

Language disorders, spanning challenges in comprehension, expression, and development, cast a profound influence on various aspects of students' educational experiences, affecting academic achievement, social interactions, and overall learning trajectories. This chapter delves into the complexities of language disorders, untangling their diverse manifestations, which include expressive, receptive, and mixed receptive-expressive language disorders. The implications ripple across academic domains, erecting barriers to reading, writing, and comprehension. Moreover, the socio-emotional domain is intertwined with these challenges, fostering isolation, self-doubt, and hindered communication. This comprehensive understanding of the multifaceted impacts of language disorders becomes the foundation upon which truly inclusive educational environments are forged. Guided by ethical imperatives and a commitment to equity, this chapter explores the potential of assistive intelligence technologies as a catalyst within inclusive education.

INTRODUCTION

This chapter delves into the powerful potential of assistive intelligence in fostering linguistic empowerment for students with language disorders within inclusive education. The concept of linguistic empowerment holds immense significance as it serves as a conduit for students to cultivate effective communication skills, self-expression, and meaningful engagement in their educational endeavors (Henry 2021). As language forms the substratum of learning, social interactions, and self-identity, the challenges faced by students grappling with language disorders in comprehending, utilizing, and comprehensively under-

DOI: 10.4018/979-8-3693-1982-6.ch002

standing language can have far-reaching implications on their academic journey and overall well-being. Recognizing linguistic empowerment as a pivotal objective within inclusive education, the aspiration is to equip students with language disorders with the requisite tools and support to unlock their untapped communicative potential, thus fostering a more equitable and enriching educational approach (Belda-Medina 2022). In this pursuit, the emergence of assistive intelligence emerges as a formidable ally, bearing the promise of great advancements. By identifying the capabilities of AI-driven technologies like speech recognition software, natural language processing applications, and text-to-speech synthesis tools, teachers can architect inclusive learning environments that not only nurture language development but also catalyze linguistic empowerment. These innovative technologies extend tailored assistance, offer alternative communication conduits, and augment students' capacity to comprehend, express, and engage with peers and teachers (Pegrum, Hockly & Dudeney 2022).

Inclusive education, a cornerstone of an equitable society, fervently seeks to offer equal opportunities to every student, irrespective of their unique needs and abilities (Medina-García, Doña-Toledo & Higueras-Rodríguez 2020). Amid this pursuit, students grappling with language disorders encounter distinctive obstacles that hinder their holistic participation and curtail their academic progress. Hindrances in communication, language assimilation, and self-expression profoundly impede their scholastic experiences (McGregor 2020). Yet, the rapid strides taken in the realm of Assistive Intelligence (AI) shine a beacon of hope, ushering in diverse solutions to champion and bolster these students. In the inclusive education paradigm, each student embodies distinct strengths, capabilities, and latent potential. The strategic integration of assistive intelligence, guided by ethical considerations, emerges as a catalyst to unearth these latent capabilities and ignite linguistic empowerment. It amplifies voices, and furnishes personalized interventions tailored to address the specific needs of students grappling with language disorders (Efthymiou 2023a). By embracing the latent metamorphic prowess of assistive intelligence, teachers can embolden students to navigate their educational odyssey with confidence, while actively contributing to the learning community.

This chapter embarks on a comprehensive exploration of the ethical underpinnings, pragmatic applications, and illustrative case studies that exemplify the catalytic role of assistive intelligence in nurturing language development and fostering profound linguistic empowerment. By underscoring the cardinal importance of linguistic empowerment and the agency wielded by assistive intelligence, our intention is to kindle inspiration among teachers, researchers, and policymakers to fully embrace these groundbreaking strides and orchestrate inclusive environments that not only nurture but also amplify the communicative potential inherent within every student grappling with language disorders.

THEORETICAL BACKGROUND

The intricate realm of education for students with language disorders reveals a landscape fraught with complexities, where the impact of these conditions resonates across every facet of their academic journey. These language disorders, spanning a spectrum of impediments in language comprehension, expression, and development, cast an indelible shadow over the educational experiences of these students, profoundly shaping their academic attainments, social interactions, and overall learning trajectories (Ziegenfusz et al. 2022). Delving into the heart of language disorders becomes an imperative foundational step in constructing inclusive environments adept at accommodating the unique needs of these students. Expressive language disorders, receptive language disorders, and mixed receptive-expressive language disorders represent the diverse challenges that these students grapple with (Rinaldi et al. 2021). Expressive language disorders constrain the articulation of thoughts and ideas, while receptive language disorders obstruct the assimilation of spoken or written language. The intersection of expressive and receptive language difficulties in mixed receptive-expressive language disorders further underscores the obscure mosaic of linguistic impairments.

Academic realms bear the brunt of these challenges, particularly in domains like reading, writing, and comprehension. The subtleties of linguistic constructs may erect insurmountable obstacles, hindering active engagement in classroom activities and fostering a disconnection from academic content (Thompson 2020). Consequently, students with language disorders often find themselves struggling with academic benchmarks, striving to attain their full scholarly potential. Beyond the scholastic sphere, the sway of language disorders extends its reach to social interactions and communication proficiencies, often fostering frustration, seclusion, and a tangible dent in self-assurance. The challenges in self-expression or deciphering others' speech can erect barriers, leading to strained social bonds, perplexed interpersonal exchanges, and hampered involvement in collaborative learning endeavors (Daniel & McLeod 2017). Beneath these overt repercussions, language disorders sow seeds of self-doubt and emotional well-being, engendering sentiments of inadequacy and exasperation that may flourish into diminished self-value, stifled motivation, and impeded educational experiences (Isaacs & Swartz 2022).

A holistic comprehension of the multifaceted impacts of language disorders on students' educational pursuits becomes the pivot for shaping genuinely inclusive educational environments. This nuanced understanding empowers teachers and experts to orchestrate targeted interventions, dispense personalized accommodations, and foster an inclusive classroom atmosphere (Efthymiou 2023a; Bryant, Bryant & Smith 2019). In the crucible of inclusive education, guided by ethical considerations and driven by an unwavering commitment to equity, the integration of assistive intelligence emerges as a catalyst. It could nurture linguistic empowerment that can cultivate resilience, self-advocacy, and academic prowess. By complementing the principles and aspirations of inclusive education with assistive intelligence, teachers wield the key to liberating students from the constraints of linguistic hurdles, engage fully, and script their own narratives within inclusive education.

Potential and Pitfalls of Integrating Assistive Intelligence

The potential of assistive intelligence (AI) technologies in revolutionizing language development and empowerment within inclusive education is a compelling proposition. In the context of students with language disorders, these technologies, fueled by AI algorithms, stand as allies that effectively address the intricate challenges associated with language comprehension and expression. By harnessing tools such as speech recognition software, natural language processing applications, and text-to-speech synthesis, teachers can meticulously craft environments that bridge the chasm between linguistic struggles and academic success (Miguel 2021). The integration of AI-driven mechanisms presents an opportunity to augment language comprehension, thereby propelling students toward more active and engaged participation in educational endeavors. For instance, the capability of speech recognition software to transmute spoken language into written text, accompanied by real-time transcription and feedback, empowers students to articulate their thoughts with increased fluency, leading to enhanced engagement in assignments and discussions. This innovation extends further, as natural language processing applications untangle the complexities of language, offering invaluable support in areas such as vocabulary enhancement, grammar correction, and reading comprehension (Eden 2020).

The impact of AI technologies on expressive language skills is equally profound, primarily through text-to-speech synthesis tools. These tools extend beyond aiding comprehension to bolstering written expression, allowing students to convey their ideas with newfound confidence and participate in collaborative projects and classroom dialogues (Toliao 2017). What sets AI-powered tools apart is their capacity for personalized interventions, which can be meticulously tailored to meet individual needs and learning styles. The integration of intelligent tutoring systems, infused with AI algorithms, facilitates targeted language instruction, adapting content delivery and pacing to cater to students' unique skill levels and progress. In essence, the synergy between AI and education not only fosters language development but also serves as the basis for an inclusive environment where diversity thrives (Caspari-Sadeghi 2023). The scope of assistive intelligence technologies extends to augmentative and alternative communication (AAC) systems, especially pertinent for students with pronounced challenges in verbal communication. Gesture recognition and computer vision technologies offer innovative pathways for non-verbal expression, translating gestures and signs into spoken language or text (Zdravkova 2022; Elsahar et al. 2019). This revolutionary approach empowers students to communicate meaningfully, bestowing upon them a sense of agency, active participation, and a profound feeling of belonging. These alternative communication methods break down barriers, ushering students into the folds of social inclusion while exemplifying the impact of assistive intelligence in shaping an inclusive educational environment (Efthymiou 2023a). These technologies offer more than mere solutions; they serve as vehicles of linguistic liberation. By democratizing language comprehension and expression, assistive intelligence technologies empower students to transcend their linguistic limitations and actively engage in their learning. The real-time feedback and personalized support afforded by these tools enable students to refine their language skills autonomously, cultivating a sense of agency and self-efficacy in their linguistic growth (Isaacs & Swartz 2022). Furthermore, the role of these technologies in augmenting social interactions and communication is pivotal. By providing alternative avenues for expression, such as converting gestures into language or synthesizing spoken words, students with language disorders are equipped with tools that amplify their voices and enable meaningful participation in social contexts (Efthymiou 2023b). This empowerment is rooted in the ability to transcend traditional barriers and connect with peers, teachers, and the broader educational community on an equal footing.

However, the integration of assistive intelligence technologies into language development and disorders is not without its drawbacks. One of the primary concerns revolves around accessibility and equity. Not all educational settings may have the necessary infrastructure and resources to provide equal access to AI-powered tools, potentially exacerbating existing disparities among students (Baudin et al. 2020). Moreover, reliance on AI technologies could inadvertently overshadow the importance of human interaction and interpersonal communication in language development. Students with language disorders may still benefit immensely from direct interactions with teachers, speech-language therapists, and peers to refine social communication skills, pragmatic abilities, and nuanced language understanding (Lloyd-Esenkaya, Russell & Clair 2020). The ethical dimensions of AI integration also warrant careful consideration. Issues related to data privacy, security, and algorithmic biases must be addressed to ensure that students' personal information is safeguarded and that the tools do not perpetuate inequalities (Wang, Xiong & Olya 2020). Furthermore, while AI-powered tools offer dynamic feedback, their efficacy could vary based on individual learning styles and preferences. Some students might thrive with these tools, while others may find them less effective or engaging, necessitating a balanced and inclusive approach (Borbajo, Malbas & Dacanay 2023).

Despite these potential drawbacks, the symbiotic integration of AI-powered tools into the educational framework for students with language disorders remains a promising endeavor. The benefits, including personalized interventions, real-time support, and alternative modes of comprehension and expression, empower students to surmount linguistic obstacles and actively contribute to their own learning experiences. As teachers continue to navigate this evolving approach, a thoughtful approach that combines technological advancements with human interaction and support is key to utilizing the full potential of assistive intelligence in inclusive education (Jiang 2023).

Case Studies That Demonstrate the Powerful Impact

In the realm of inclusive education, the integration of assistive intelligence technologies emerges as a force in addressing language comprehension and expression challenges faced by students with language disorders. These technologies, underpinned by sophisticated AI algorithms empower students with unique linguistic needs within educational contexts. By integrating tools such as speech recognition software, natural language processing applications, and text-to-speech synthesis, teachers can meticulously craft inclusive environments that bridge the gap between language barriers and the pursuit of educational excellence (Pegrum, Hockly & Dudeney 2022).

Examining specific case studies vividly highlights the efficacy of this approach in fostering linguistic empowerment. In a compelling instance, a student confronted hurdles in comprehending intricate texts and instructions due to a receptive language disorder. This manifested as challenges in text decoding, grappling with complex linguistic structures, and processing information at an optimal pace. These impediments consequently curtailed the student's active engagement with academic content and restricted their participation in classroom discourse. To overcome these obstacles, an AI-powered speech recognition tool was introduced. Through this technology, the student could vocalize their thoughts and queries pertaining to reading materials, which were instantaneously transcribed, enabling subsequent self-analysis and reflection. This real-time feedback mechanism facilitated error identification and self-correction, effectively augmenting the student's grasp of language complexities (Touretzky et al. 2019).

Similarly, a distinct case study centered on a student grappling with expressive language difficulties. Their challenges encompassed sentence structure complexities, vocabulary selection, and the coherent organization of ideas in written form. These hurdles significantly impeded the student's ability to articulate their thoughts fluently and cohesively in writing. The integration of a text-to-speech synthesis tool proved instrumental in addressing these issues. By converting written work into spoken language, the student could audibly engage with their own writing, facilitating error recognition, sentence structure refinement, and enhanced language use. This auditory reinforcement bolstered the student's learning experience, reinforcing comprehension of written materials (Toliao 2017).

In both case studies, the concept of linguistic empowerment emerges as a powerful narrative. The introduction of AI-driven technologies not only mitigates language-related challenges but also cultivates a sense of ownership and agency in students. The real-time feedback mechanisms and personalized interventions offered by these tools enable students to actively participate in their language development journey, fostering a heightened sense of control and self-confidence (Isaacs & Swartz 2022). This empowerment extends beyond the realm of academics, influencing social interactions and collaborative learning as well. Students equipped with assistive intelligence tools are better positioned to express themselves, engage with peers, and contribute meaningfully to classroom discussions, breaking barriers and embracing a more inclusive educational experience (Efthymiou 2023b). Thus, these case studies underline the potential of AI technologies in addressing linguistic challenges and in nurturing linguistic empowerment, amplifying students' voices, and propelling them toward holistic growth and success within inclusive educational environments.

Strategies for Effective Integration of AI Tools

The integration of assistive intelligence technologies for students with language disorders signifies a profound paradigm shift - a transition toward a more inclusive, equitable, and empowering approach to education. The rationale behind advocating these strategies is grounded in the remarkable potential of assistive intelligence to foster language development, and actively engage students in their own learning (De Klerk & Palmer 2022). By following these strategies, teachers can unlock the full capabilities of assistive intelligence technologies, rendering personalized interventions, instantaneous support, and alternative avenues for comprehension and expression (Caspari-Sadeghi 2023). At its core, the argument is that through the strategic execution of these methodologies, teachers can empower students to seize control of their language growth and become active architects of their learning experiences. In essence, these strategies assert that when thoughtfully intertwined with collaborative efforts, assistive intelligence technologies could reform the educational experiences for students with language disorders - ultimately nurturing comprehensive advancement, fostering inclusion, and facilitating achievement (Gargiulo & Metcalf 2022; Bryant, Bryant & Smith 2019).

This collective array of strategies forms a cohesive narrative aimed at guiding teachers on the effective utilization of assistive intelligence technologies. The crux here is that a meticulous grasp of students' language obstacles is essential prior to incorporating assistive intelligence technologies. Through collaboration with specialists, teachers ensure that these technologies are precisely calibrated to cater to the distinct linguistic requirements of each student (Hill 2017). The core contention features that proficiency in the use of these technologies is pivotal for both teachers and students. Teachers gain mastery through professional development, while students acquire confidence and competence via specialized training (Dunn, Hattie & Bowles 2019). The argument pivots on the inalienable principle of accessibility. By partnering with technology support personnel, teachers ensure that assistive intelligence technologies are universally accessible, irrespective of students' technological resources (Efthymiou 2023b). This strategy hinges on the synergy between teachers and specialists, ensuring the implementation of evidence-based practices and optimizing the impact on language development (Du 2021). The pivotal notion here is the recognition of diverse learning styles. By deploying an array of assistive intelligence technologies catering to individual preferences, teachers create a comprehensive intervention strategy (Barua et al. 2022). The focal point is on personalization - a dynamic adaptation of technology to accommodate unique needs, achieved by tailoring content delivery and offering customized support (Chen & Wang 2021). The heart of this strategy is the nurturing of not just language skills but also self-advocacy and autonomy among students with language disorders (Wehmeyer 2019). The central argument here is the continuous evolution of educational strategies. Through ongoing assessment and adaptation, teachers ensure that the integration remains responsive to the ever-evolving needs of students (Hooda et al. 2022). The central premise is that assistive intelligence technologies become a bridge that fosters collaboration and interaction, thus creating an inclusive classroom milieu (Archambault, Leary & Rice 2022). The core tenet is constant betterment. Teachers engage in reflective practices, continuously refining their integration approach based on feedback, technological advancements, and evolving student needs (McAleavy et al. 2018).

Collectively, these strategies advocate for the deliberate integration of assistive intelligence technologies as catalysts for inclusive, empowering education for students with language disorders. The crux of the argument rests on the notion that through the astute application of these strategies, teachers could foster language development, elevate communication skills, and craft a pedagogy through which students can flourish.

Considerations for Selecting and Implementing Appropriate AI Tools

The promotion of linguistic empowerment through inclusive education depends on the intelligent choice and efficient application of AI tools. These actions are essential in fostering an atmosphere in which students with language disorders not only overcome obstacles but also succeed in both their academic and linguistic endeavors. Success depends on how well AI technologies integrate with inclusive educational frameworks, pedagogical philosophies, ethical requirements, and the specific linguistic demands of students. The imperative for a comprehensive assessment reveals the complex layers of individual student needs, strengths, and aspirations. Collaborative efforts among teachers, speech-language therapists, and specialists converge to illuminate each student's linguistic profile, thereby enabling the pinpointing of specific language challenges and personalized interventions tailored to individual requirements (Tait 2020). Central to this synergy is the seamless integration of AI tools within the broader educational objectives of the inclusive classroom. These tools transcend mere technological aids; they are enablers of linguistic empowerment and academic advancement. The selected tools must intricately weave into the curriculum, teaching methodologies, and learning goals, contributing to the holistic blossoming of language skills and the active engagement of students in their learning (Du 2021). The canvas upon which these choices are painted is one of evidence and research. Teachers delve into a realm of empirical studies, evaluations, and systematic reviews that accentuate the efficacy of specific AI technologies in addressing language challenges. This evidence-based approach becomes the core where confidence and empowerment among students are nurtured, as these technologies substantiate their role in fostering linguistic growth (Barua et al. 2022).

Inclusive education's essence is encapsulated in its accessibility to all. Delving into the compatibility and accessibility of AI tools within diverse student learning environments becomes paramount. This entails evaluation of factors such as device availability, compatibility with existing technology infrastructure, user-friendliness, and provisions for technical support. The outcome is a coordinated technological ecosystem that transcends disparities, ensuring a universal avenue towards linguistic empowerment (Borbajo, Malbas & Dacanay 2023). The user experience becomes the cornerstone of integration. Teachers champion tools with intuitive interfaces that beckon both teachers and students to explore effortlessly. A symphony of lucid instructions, robust support resources, and customizable features engenders an environment fostering independent mastery, nurturing a sense of agency, and amplifying the pulse of control in students' linguistic development (Isaacs & Swartz 2022). AI tools do not stand in isolation; they find resonance within established pedagogical paradigms, teaching methodologies, and collaborative dynamics. This integration serves as the gateway for students to adopt AI technologies as extensions of their learning odyssey, cultivating a sense of familiarity and continuity (Gargiulo & Metcalf 2022). The ethical compass guides every step of AI's footprint. The selection leans toward tools fortified by robust privacy and data security protocols, ensuring the sanctuary of students' personal information. This conscientious approach not only upholds the sanctity of linguistic empowerment but also safeguards the privacy and security of sensitive data (Wang, Xiong & Olya 2020).

In envisioning a horizon beyond immediate gains, teachers chart the course toward the scalability and sustainability of chosen AI tools. This trajectory incorporates factors like licensing agreements, ongoing developer support, potential updates, and provisions for continuous professional development (Hooda et al. 2022). To realize this, teachers need to be equipped with comprehensive professional development opportunities. Through workshops, online courses, and a wealth of resources, teachers are fortified to navigate AI technologies with the assurance to orchestrate interventions that amplify language development and foster linguistic empowerment (Dunn, Hattie & Bowles 2019). Yet, linguistic empowerment is not a static destination; it's a dynamic process. The continuous assessment, nurtured by stakeholder feedback, data analysis, and introspective reflection, allows for a symbiotic relationship between AI tools and the ever-evolving needs of students. This cyclic process of refinement ensures that AI technologies remain finely tuned instruments, responsive to the nuances of linguistic growth, perpetuating a catalytic impact (McAleavy et al. 2018). This comprehensive, research-infused framework resonates beyond the classroom, in students' identities, trajectories, and aspirations (Jiang 2023).

Addressing Ethical Considerations

In the pursuit of linguistic empowerment within inclusive education, a robust framework emerges - one that is underpinned by ethical imperatives and resonates with the core argument of this chapter. The judicious selection and effective implementation of AI tools become not only strategic steps but ethical obligations, where the emphasis is on responsible and meaningful integration. By weaving together considerations of privacy, data security, fairness, informed consent, student involvement, training, goal setting, reflection, and advocacy, teachers manifest a synthesis that embodies the very essence of linguistic empowerment within AI-assisted inclusive education (Shneiderman 2020). The conscientious choice of AI tools that align with privacy regulations and unequivocal data protection policies upholds students' rights, ensuring that sensitive information is securely housed and only accessible to authorized individuals. Moreover, this ethical approach is manifested through transparent communication with students and their families, facilitating informed consent when the need arises (Wang, Xiong & Olya 2020). In addition, AI tools must be fortified with encryption and other robust security measures that fend off unauthorized access, breaches, or misuse, thereby fostering an environment where data are safeguarded with diligence (Baudin et al. 2020). The collaborative engagement with IT professionals for the establishment of stringent security protocols and continuous software updates forms a testament to the commitment to ensuring students' data security and privacy.

The specter of bias looms large in AI integration. Fairness and accuracy, particularly in the context of language comprehension, assessment, and feedback generation, become non-negotiable criteria for AI tool evaluation. Herein lies the responsibility to engage developers, researchers, and stakeholders to identify, rectify, and mitigate biases, thereby fortifying a foundation where equitable and unbiased support for students prevails (Burr & Leslie 2023). This framework cannot be complete without the active involvement of students. Empowerment unfurls its wings through informed consent, where students and their families are educated about the tools' purpose, potential risks, and benefits. By involving students in the decision-making process, teachers magnify their sense of agency, ownership, and empowerment, positioning them as co-pilots in their own linguistic development (Berendt, Littlejohn & Blakemore 2020). In this realm of empowerment, training becomes the torchbearer. Equipping students with the skills to navigate AI tools, understand their features, and harness their benefits is a formative aspect. It ensures that students become architects of their own linguistic growth, agents of their development, and explorers of their own linguistic potential (Dunn, Hattie & Bowles 2019). The bridge to empowerment is further illuminated by collaborative goal setting. By involving students in establishing individual linguistic development goals, AI tools are utilized as dynamic tools for progress monitoring and feedback. This self-reflective approach fosters language development and self-awareness, ownership, and empowerment within the learning process (Borbajo, Malbas & Dacanay 2023).

Beyond milestones lie conversations - rich, reflective discussions where students share their encounters, victories, and strategies in utilizing AI tools. These dialogues create a haven for expression, reinforce a sense of belonging, and foster a vibrant and inclusive learning community (Archambault, Leary & Rice 2022). Empowerment reaches its crescendo in self-advocacy. Students are not merely recipients of linguistic empowerment; they are architects of their journey, equipped to voice their needs, seek clarifications, and advocate for adjustments when required. These skills ripple beyond the classroom, shaping resilient individuals who navigate the world with confidence and agency (Wehmeyer 2019). In inclusive education, the responsible use of AI tools is an emblem of ethical practice and linguistic empowerment. By engraining considerations of privacy, security, fairness, consent, involvement, training, goal setting, reflection, and advocacy, teachers cultivate an environment that nurtures autonomy, respects students' rights, and kindles linguistic growth and success.

CONCLUSION

Assistive intelligence technologies within inclusive education stand as potent agents of change, holding the capacity to surmount the barriers that may impede linguistic empowerment, amplifying the voices that often go unheard, and profoundly elevating the development of language skills and communication proficiencies. Yet, this potential must be employed ethically and responsibly, a task that rests squarely on the shoulders of teachers. Teachers traverse a terrain marked by intricate considerations - privacy safeguards, data security fortifications, and the ever-watchful eye on algorithmic biases - critical elements that converge to ensure the judicious and equitable use of AI tools (Baudin et al. 2020; Shneiderman 2020). At the fulcrum of this change, teachers assume a role of unparalleled significance. To effectively integrate assistive intelligence into inclusive education settings, they must immerse themselves in a comprehensive understanding of the nuanced challenges that students with language disorders encounter. This profound understanding extends to discerning the junctures where AI tools could bridge linguistic gaps and foster communication breakthroughs. Within this educational endeavor, real-life case studies emerge as potent overtures, showcasing successes of implementation and articulating the language development strides achieved (Pegrum, Hockly & Dudeney 2022).

The chapter's final notes call for dedication to research and exploration in this dynamic arena. The horizon beckons with inquiry, including the tracing of the enduring impact of assistive intelligence through longitudinal studies (Archambault, Leary & Rice 2022). The realm of customization and personalization emerges, inviting investigations into the synchronization of AI algorithms with individual learning styles (Caspari-Sadeghi 2023). Professional development awaits further exploration, poised to reveal the most effective methods of equipping teachers with the ethical compass and technical skills required to integrate AI tools into inclusive education (Gargiulo & Metcalf 2022).

As the chapter unfolds, a trail of reflective questions accompanies the reader, inviting teachers to introspection. This process of critical self-evaluation empowers teachers to constantly refine and innovate their approaches to the integration of assistive intelligence (Dunn, Hattie & Bowles 2019). However, the march towards linguistic empowerment rests not solely on the shoulders of teachers; it flourishes in the fertile grounds of collaboration among teachers, researchers, and policymakers, united by discussions steeped in the ideals of equity, fairness, and respect - that lay the foundation for the ethical and effective implementation of assistive intelligence tools (Borbajo, Malbas & Dacanay 2023).

Reflective Questions and Activities

These reflective questions are designed to encourage readers to critically reflect on the content presented in the chapter and apply it to their own contexts. By engaging in self-reflection, teachers can deepen their understanding, refine their practices, and tailor the implementation of assistive intelligence technologies to meet the unique needs of their students with language disorders.

Reflective Questions

1. How can you integrate the discussed ethical considerations, such as privacy, data security, and algorithmic biases, into your own practice when implementing assistive intelligence technologies for students with language disorders?
2. In what ways can you promote student agency, and empowerment in the use of assistive intelligence technologies in your inclusive classroom? How can you involve students in the decision-making process and encourage their active participation?
3. Reflect on the potential challenges and benefits of using AI tools for language development and communication skills. How might these tools address the specific needs of your students with language disorders, and what potential limitations or considerations should be considered?
4. Consider the case studies presented in this chapter. How can you draw inspiration from these examples and apply similar strategies or interventions in your own inclusive classroom? What modifications or adaptations might be necessary based on your specific context?
5. Reflect on your current knowledge and understanding of assistive intelligence technologies. What additional professional development or training might you need to effectively integrate these tools into your instructional practices?
6. Think about ways to foster a collaborative and supportive classroom climate when implementing AI tools. How can you create opportunities for peer interaction, collaboration, and shared learning experiences that utilize assistive intelligence technologies?
7. Reflect on the potential impact of assistive intelligence technologies on student learning outcomes and engagement. How will you evaluate and measure the effectiveness of these tools in supporting the language development and communication skills of students with language disorders?
8. Consider your own beliefs and attitudes towards the integration of AI in inclusive education. How might these beliefs influence your decision-making process and implementation of strategies? How can you ensure a balanced and inclusive approach that considers both the benefits and potential risks of AI technologies?

Activities and Prompts for Further Exploration

1. **Design an Inclusive Lesson Plan:**

Imagine you are designing a lesson plan for a specific topic or skill in your content area that incorporates assistive intelligence tools to support students with language disorders. Consider the specific needs of your students and the goals of inclusive education. How can you integrate AI technologies to enhance language development and communication skills? Outline the objectives, activities, and assessments, and identify the specific AI tools that would be most beneficial for your lesson plan.

Sample Lesson Plan:

Subject: English Language Arts
Topic: Writing a Persuasive Essay
Grade Level: 8th grade
Duration: 3 class periods
Objective:

Students will be able to write a persuasive essay using assistive intelligence tools to support their language development and communication skills.

Activities:

1. Introduction (Class Period 1):
   - Engage students in a discussion about persuasive writing and its purpose.
   - Introduce the topic of the essay, such as 'Should students have longer recess?'
   - Provide examples of persuasive essays and discuss their structure and persuasive techniques.
   - Introduce the assistive intelligence tool: Speech Recognition Software.
2. Pre-Writing and Planning (Class Period 2):
   - Review the structure of a persuasive essay, including the introduction, body paragraphs, and conclusion.
   - Brainstorm persuasive arguments related to the essay topic as a class.
   - Demonstrate how to use the Speech Recognition Software to dictate ideas and outline the essay.
   - Allow students to practice using the tool to brainstorm and organize their thoughts.
3. Drafting and Revising (Class Period 3):
   - Instruct students to use the Speech Recognition Software to draft their persuasive essays.
   - Encourage them to focus on incorporating persuasive techniques and organizing their ideas effectively.
   - Provide guidance and feedback on their drafts, highlighting areas for improvement and clarity.
   - After revising their essays, ask students to self-edit using the software's real-time transcription feature.

Assessment:

- Students will submit their final persuasive essays.
- Evaluate the essays based on the clarity of arguments, use of persuasive techniques, and overall organization.
- Consider the effectiveness of the assistive intelligence tool in supporting students' language development and communication skills.

AI Tool:

- Speech Recognition Software: The Speech Recognition Software will enable students with language disorders to overcome barriers in writing by providing a means to dictate their thoughts and ideas. The tool will transcribe their speech into written form, supporting their writing process and promoting language development.

Note: Teachers should select and adapt the tools based on the specific needs and available resources in their own instructional contexts.

2. **Case Study Analysis:**

Select a case study or research study that explores the integration of assistive intelligence in inclusive education for students with language disorders. Analyze the study's findings, methodology, and implications. Reflect on the strengths and limitations of the study and consider how the findings can be applied to your own instructional practices. Discuss the potential benefits and challenges of implementing similar approaches in your classroom.

3. **Action Research Project:**

Conduct a small-scale action research project to explore the impact of using assistive intelligence tools in your inclusive classroom. Identify a specific research question or area of focus related to language development and communication skills. Design and implement interventions using AI technologies and collect data to assess the effectiveness of these tools on student outcomes. Reflect on the findings and share your insights with colleagues or through professional development forums.

These activities and prompts aim to engage readers in further exploration and practical application of the concepts discussed in the chapter. By actively participating in these activities, teachers can deepen their understanding, exchange ideas with peers, and implement innovative approaches in implementing assistive intelligence and promoting inclusive education for students with language disorders.

REFERENCES

Archambault, L., Leary, H., & Rice, K. (2022). Pillars of online pedagogy: A framework for teaching in online learning environments. *Educational Psychologist, 57*(3), 178–191. doi:10.1080/00461520.2022.2051513

Barua, P. D., Vicnesh, J., Gururajan, R., Oh, S. L., Palmer, E., Azizan, M. M., Kadri, N. A., & Acharya, U. R. (2022). Artificial intelligence enabled personalised assistive tools to enhance education of children with neurodevelopmental disorders—A review. *International Journal of Environmental Research and Public Health, 19*(3), 1192. doi:10.3390/ijerph19031192 PMID:35162220

Baudin, K., Mullersdorf, M., Sundstrom, A., & Gustafsson, C. (2020). The policies of provision of assistive and welfare technology - a literature review. *Societies (Basel, Switzerland), 10*(1), 22. doi:10.3390oc10010022

Belda-Medina, J. (2022). Promoting inclusiveness, creativity and critical thinking through digital storytelling among EFL teacher candidates. *International Journal of Inclusive Education*, *26*(2), 109–123. doi:10.1080/13603116.2021.2011440

Berendt, B., Littlejohn, A., & Blakemore, M. (2020). AI in education: Learner choice and fundamental rights. *Learning, Media and Technology*, *45*(3), 312–324. doi:10.1080/17439884.2020.1786399

Borbajo, M. N. M., Malbas, M. H., & Dacanay, L. R. (2023). Reforming Education: The Global Impact of Integrating Artificial Intelligence in the Classroom Environment. *American Journal of Language, Literacy and Learning in STEM Education (2993-2769)*, *1*(5), 16-27.

Bryant, D. P., Bryant, B. R., & Smith, D. D. (2019). *Teaching students with special needs in inclusive classrooms*. Sage Publications.

Burr, C., & Leslie, D. (2023). Ethical assurance: A practical approach to the responsible design, development, and deployment of data-driven technologies. *AI and Ethics*, *3*(1), 73–98. doi:10.100743681-022-00178-0

Caspari-Sadeghi, S. (2023). Artificial Intelligence in Technology-Enhanced Assessment: A Survey of Machine Learning. *Journal of Educational Technology Systems*, *51*(3), 372–386. doi:10.1177/00472395221138791

Chen, S. Y., & Wang, J. H. (2021). Individual differences and personalized learning: A review and appraisal. *Universal Access in the Information Society*, *20*(4), 833–849. doi:10.100710209-020-00753-4

Daniel, G. R., & McLeod, S. (2017). Children with speech sound disorders at school: Challenges for children, parents and teachers. *The Australian Journal of Teacher Education*, *42*(2), 81–101. doi:10.14221/ajte.2017v42n2.6

De Klerk, E. D., & Palmer, J. M. (2022). Technology inclusion for students living with disabilities through collaborative online learning during and beyond COVID-19. *Perspectives in Education*, *40*(1), 80–95. doi:10.18820/2519593X/pie.v40.i1.5

Du, X. (2021). *Technology and Special Education: Designing Effective Professional Development for Equitable and Inclusive Classrooms* [Doctoral dissertation, Teachers College, Columbia University].

Dunn, R., Hattie, J., & Bowles, T. (2019). Exploring the experiences of teachers undertaking Educational Design Research (EDR) as a form of teacher professional learning. *Professional Development in Education*, *45*(1), 151–167. doi:10.1080/19415257.2018.1500389

Eden, S. (2020). Technology Makes Things Possible. In *The Oxford handbook of deaf studies in learning and cognition* (p. 407). Oxford University Press.

Efthymiou, E. (Ed.). (2023a). *Inclusive Phygital Learning Approaches and Strategies for Students with Special Needs*. IGI Global. doi:10.4018/978-1-6684-8504-0

Efthymiou, E. (2023b). Examining Teachers' Perspectives on Equitable Digital Education: A Case Study on Delivering High-Quality and Inclusive Learning Experiences in Special Education. In E. Efthymiou (Ed.), *Inclusive Phygital Learning Approaches and Strategies for Students with Special Needs* (pp. 97–130). IGI Global. doi:10.4018/978-1-6684-8504-0.ch005

Elsahar, Y., Hu, S., Bouazza-Marouf, K., Kerr, D., & Mansor, A. (2019). Augmentative and alternative communication (AAC) advances: A review of configurations for individuals with a speech disability. *Sensors (Basel), 19*(8), 1911. doi:10.339019081911 PMID:31013673

Gargiulo, R. M., & Metcalf, D. (2022). *Teaching in today's inclusive classrooms: A universal design for learning approach*. Cengage Learning.

Henry, A. (2021). Motivational connections in language classrooms: A research agenda. *Language Teaching, 54*(2), 221–235. doi:10.1017/S0261444820000026

Hill, K. (2017). Role of Speech–Language Pathologists in Assistive Technology Assessments. In *Assistive technology assessment handbook* (pp. 301–324). CRC Press.

Hooda, M., Rana, C., Dahiya, O., Rizwan, A., & Hossain, M. S. (2022). Artificial intelligence for assessment and feedback to enhance student success in higher education. *Mathematical Problems in Engineering, 2022*, 2022. doi:10.1155/2022/5215722

Isaacs, D., & Swartz, L. (2022). "Stammering less so that I can be more of a man": Discourses of masculinities among young adult men in the Western Cape, South Africa, who stutter. *Psychology of Men & Masculinity, 23*(1), 74–85. doi:10.1037/men0000302

Jiang, M. (2023). The Impact and Potential of Educational Technology: A Comprehensive Review. *Research and Advances in Education, 2*(7), 32–49. doi:10.56397/RAE.2023.07.05

Lloyd-Esenkaya, V., Russell, A. J., & Clair, M. C. S. (2020). What are the peer interaction strengths and difficulties in children with developmental language disorder? A systematic review. *International Journal of Environmental Research and Public Health, 17*(9), 3140. doi:10.3390/ijerph17093140 PMID:32365958

McAleavy, T., Hall-Chen, A., Horrocks, S., & Riggall, A. (2018). Technology-Supported Professional Development for Teachers: Lessons from Developing Countries. Education Development Trust. Highbridge House. United Kingdom.

McGregor, K. K., Goffman, L., Van Horne, A. O., Hogan, T. P., & Finestack, L. H. (2020). Developmental language disorder: Applications for advocacy, research, and clinical service. *Perspectives of the ASHA Special Interest Groups, 5*(1), 38–46. doi:10.1044/2019_PERSP-19-00083

Medina-García, M., Doña-Toledo, L., & Higueras-Rodríguez, L. (2020). Equal opportunities in an inclusive and sustainable education system: An explanatory model. *Sustainability (Basel), 12*(11), 4626. doi:10.3390u12114626

Miguel, F. S. (2021). Assistive technology integration for children with specific learning disabilities: A systematic literature review perspective from Mexico. *African Journal of Emerging Issues, 3*(5), 40–49.

Pegrum, M., Hockly, N., & Dudeney, G. (2022). *Digital literacies*. Routledge. doi:10.4324/9781003262541

Rinaldi, S., Caselli, M. C., Cofelice, V., D'Amico, S., De Cagno, A. G., Della Corte, G., Di Martino, M. V., Di Costanzo, B., Levorato, M. C., Penge, R., Rossetto, T., Sansavini, A., Vecchi, S., & Zoccolotti, P. (2021). Efficacy of the treatment of developmental language disorder: A systematic review. *Brain Sciences, 11*(3), 407. doi:10.3390/brainsci11030407 PMID:33806938

Shneiderman, B. (2020). Bridging the gap between ethics and practice: Guidelines for reliable, safe, and trustworthy human-centered AI systems. [TiiS]. *ACM Transactions on Interactive Intelligent Systems*, *10*(4), 1–31. doi:10.1145/3419764

Tait, K. (2020). Preparing Educators to Collaborate with Professionals Who Work With Learners With Complex Conditions. In Oxford Research Encyclopedia of Education. doi:10.1093/acrefore/9780190264093.013.1204

Thompson, J. (2020). *Measuring Student Success Skills: A Review of the Literature on Complex Communication. 21st Century Success Skills*. National Center for the Improvement of Educational Assessment.

Toliao, P. S. (2017). *Underprepared, First-Year College Student Experiences with Academic Integration* [Doctoral dissertation, Northcentral University].

Touretzky, D., Gardner-McCune, C., Martin, F., & Seehorn, D. (2019, July). Envisioning AI for K-12: What should every child know about AI? *Proceedings of the AAAI Conference on Artificial Intelligence*, *33*(01), 9795–9799. doi:10.1609/aaai.v33i01.33019795

Wang, Y., Xiong, M., & Olya, H. (2020, January). Toward an understanding of responsible artificial intelligence practices. In *Proceedings of the 53rd Hawaii international conference on system sciences* (pp. 4962-4971). International Conference on System Sciences (HICSS). 10.24251/HICSS.2020.610

Wehmeyer, M. L. (2019). *Strengths-based approaches to educating all learners with disabilities: Beyond special education*. Teachers College Press.

Zdravkova, K. (2022). The potential of artificial intelligence for assistive technology in education. In Handbook on Intelligent Techniques in the Educational Process: Vol 1 Recent Advances and Case Studies (pp. 61-85). Cham: Springer International Publishing. doi:10.1007/978-3-031-04662-9_4

Ziegenfusz, S., Paynter, J., Flückiger, B., & Westerveld, M. F. (2022). A systematic review of the academic achievement of primary and secondary school-aged students with developmental language disorder. *Autism & Developmental Language Impairments*, *7*, 23969415221099397. doi:10.1177/23969415221099397 PMID:36382072

Chapter 3
Differentiated Teaching Practices of Physics in Inclusion Classes for Students With Learning Disabilities

Panagiotis F. Papalexopoulos
University of Thessaly, Greece & University of Nicosia, Greece

Vasia Karra
University of Athens, Greece

Theodoros Karakasidis
https://orcid.org/0000-0001-9580-0702
University of Thessaly, Greece

Denis Vavougios
University of Thessaly, Greece

ABSTRACT

In this chapter the authors present the educational framework that they believe the lower secondary school teacher of an inclusion class in Greece should know in order to help his/her students integrate into the physics class. This chapter will describe the legislative framework concerning the operation of the inclusion classes, the principles of differentiated pedagogy that can be exploited when teaching students with learning difficulties, the current and pilot physics curriculum, and present differentiated teaching practices in physics.

FUNCTIONING FRAMEWORK OF THE INCLUSION CLASSES

The World Congress on Special Education held in Salamanca, Spain (UNESCO 1994) gave a major international impetus to inclusive education and set the goal for schools in the future to be able to serve

DOI: 10.4018/979-8-3693-1982-6.ch003

all children, especially those with special educational needs. In Dakar, at the World Education Forum (UNESCO 1994), it was declared that 'Education for All' should take into account the diversity and different needs of people with disabilities and special educational needs, poor children and children and those in disadvantaged situations, including children of ethnic and linguistic minorities. Following the international agenda for inclusion, in Greece, students with mild educational needs, emotional disabilities and behavioral problems are allowed to participate in Inclusion Classes that operate within general schools.

According to the Greek Law 3699/2008, students with disabilities and students with special educational needs can attend Inclusion Classes, which have specialized teachers and special structures operating within general schools and vocational schools. Two types of curricula may be implemented in these cases: a) common and special programs for students with less severe special educational needs, b) special group or Individualized Education Program (IEP) of extended hours for students with more severe special educational needs, as defined by the Centres for Screening, Diagnosis and Support for Special Educational Needs [Kentra Diaforodiagnosis, Diagnosis kai Ypostirixis Eidikon Ekpaideytikon Anagkon (KEDDY)].

After the implementation of Law 3699 according to Law 4368/2016, Inclusion Classes' aim is the full integration of students with special educational needs and/or disabilities into the school environment through targeted educational interventions. Teachers in the Inclusion Classes (Ministerial Decision 27922/C6, 2007) collaborate with general classroom teachers to support students in the classroom environment, differentiate activities and teaching practices and adapt the teaching materials and the educational environment appropriately. When required, support is also provided in a face-to-face environment.

The Special Education teacher who teaches Physics in the Inclusion Class of Lower Secondary School should study the individual files of the students, should parents approve the attendance of their child in the Inclusion Class, and implement the IEP. The individual files of the students should contain the opinions-reports of the agencies competent for the diagnosis of the students' special needs, initially operating from 2008 and evolving later on. The relevant legislative framework for the operation of the Inclusion Classes and the agencies that published the reports is outlined in Ministerial Decision 27922/C6 (2007) and after a series of amendments up to the current Law 4823/2021.

Opinions-Reports for Students' Disabilities and IEP Design

Issued by KEDDY

According to Law 3699/2008, the special educational needs of students with disabilities and special educational needs were investigated and identified by the KEDDY, the Special Diagnostic Assessment Committee and last by pedagogical centers of other ministries authorized by the Ministry of Education and Religious Affairs (YPEPTH).

KEDDY had the mandate to cooperate with other health services to identify the educational needs of students with visual and/or hearing disability, chronic diseases and mental disorders, autism spectrum disorders and those on medication that may affect their ability to learn, and to design the IEPs. The assessment of students with disabilities and special educational needs in KEDDY was carried out by a scientific team of five experts: special education and training teachers (pre-school, primary and secondary), a paediatric psychiatrist or paediatric neurologist specialized in paediatric neurology, or a paediatric neurologist specialized in neurology, a social worker, a psychologist, and a speech therapist. Parents of students with disabilities and special educational needs could also be involved in the formulation of IEP, if invited for this purpose by the relevant service or provider, their views though are only advisory. Also, school units and examination boards for students with learning disabilities and special educational needs were required to implement the recommendations and proposals contained in the assessment reports drawn up by the competent services.

Law 3699/2008 stipulated that for each student with disabilities and special educational needs, an IEP had to be drawn up by the special education teacher in cooperation with the general classroom teacher, the special education adviser, the special education advisory teacher and the scientific team of the KEDDY. It was specified that for the implementation of an IEP the parent(s) of the student and the special educational staff of the special education school are involved, following a request from the KEDDY. These individualized educational programs were drawn up until 2018 when the operation of the KEDDY was officially terminated.

Issued by KESY

According to Law 3699/2008, the Education and Counselling Support Centres [Kentra Ekpaideytikis kai Symbouleytikis Ypostirixis (KESY)] were established. According to Law 4547/2018, the mission of the KESY was to support school units and laboratory centres in the areas of its jurisdiction, to ensure equal access to education for all students, without exception, and to promote their harmonious psychosocial development and progress. The responsibilities of the KESY are educational and include the assessment and identification of educational or other difficulties and needs of students of pre-school and school age (including students with disabilities and/or special educational needs) and the publication of relevant assessment reports. A basic competence also of the KESY for educational and psychosocial inclusion was the formulation of the basic elements of the IEP, as provided in Law 3699/2008.

The assessment report and the IEP are written by a three-member multidisciplinary team, which consist of a teacher specialized in special education, a social worker and a psychologist. The multidisciplinary team could also include a speech and language therapist or occupational therapist, on the recommendation of the tripartite multidisciplinary team. The teacher of the Inclusion Class who taught Physics had the task of implementing the IEP in collaboration with the general classroom teachers, making appropriate use of the teaching resources and general teaching support described in the opinion-report of the KESY. An additional possibility provided by Law 4547/2018 was for the teacher of the Inclusion Class to cooperate with the Interdisciplinary Evaluation and Support Committee (EDEAY) if the school unit he/she served belonged to a School Network of Scientific Support (SDEY). According to 4547/2018, the SDEY were consisted of school units and Laboratory Centres of primary and secondary general and vocational education, as well as special education. The SDEY aim was to strengthen and promote cooperation, as well as to coordinate the work of school units and laboratory centers, in order to ensure equal access to education for all students without exception.

In this context, a EDEAY was established in each school unit that belonged to a SDEY, as a competent body for the educational assessment and support of students and the school community. Each EDEAY should be composed of the following members: (a) the principal of the school unit in the role of coordinator, (b) a primary or secondary school teacher with specialization in special education serving in the school unit or in the SDEY, (c) a psychologist who worked at the SDEY, (d) a social worker who worked at the SDEY, (e) the teachers in charge of the sections of the student that need support. The EDEAY carried out assessments to identify the difficulties and educational, psychosocial, and other barriers to learning faced by certain students and, under certain circumstances, may recommend referral to the KESY for an assessment report - opinion.

The EDEAY also supported school teachers on issues of implementing differentiated teaching, interdisciplinary and multidisciplinary approaches, cooperative group teaching. The members of the EDEAY specified the main axes of the IEP, as defined by the KESY, in specific short and long-term objectives and were responsible for monitoring their implementation, in collaboration with the teachers of the student/s in need of support. The specific framework for the operation of the EDEAY could be used by the teacher of the Inclusion Class who taught Physics to further improve his/her differentiated practices and to integrate his/her students in the specific subject.

Issued by KEDASY

According to Law 3699/2008, the KESY, established by law 4547/2018, were renamed as Centres for Interdisciplinary Assessment, Counselling and Support (KEDASY) by law 4823. The aim of KEDASY is to ensure that all students have equal access to education without exclusion and to support them in order to have harmonious psychosocial development and progress. The responsibilities of the KEDASY inter alia include assessing the educational needs and barriers to learning of students with special educational needs, publishing the relevant individual assessment reports and the formulating of the basic axes of the IEPs according to Law 3699/2008. The implementation of the IEP for every student should be realised by the teacher of Physics in Inclusion Classes, in collaboration with the teachers of the school unit and the Interdisciplinary Support Committees [Epitropes Diepistimonikis Ypostirixis (EDY)].

According to law 4823/2021, School Education Support Networks [Sxolika Diktya Ekpaideytikis Ypostirixis (SDEY)] are reestablished. The purpose of the SDEY is to strengthen and coordinate the work of school units in order to respond to the educational needs of their students, to support the work of the Inclusion Classes and parallel support. Each SDEY can serve up to five school units accordingly and an Interdisciplinary Support Committee (EDY) is established in each of them. According to the operating regulations of the EDYs (Ministerial Decision 134960/D3, 2021), their purpose is to identify the educational needs and difficulties that hinder students' equal access to learning and to implement supportive measures for students with special educational needs in collaboration with the school units teachers. EDY consists of the Headmaster as chairperson, a special education teacher, a psychologist and a social worker. General classroom teachers supporting a student with learning disabilities participate in the meetings of the EDY with the right to vote. In the context of the functioning of the EDY and the SDEY, the teacher who teaches Physics in the Inclusion Class may collaborate with the members of the EDY serving in the same school and also with colleagues from other units of the SDEY to exchange experiences, improve teaching practices and, in general, to implement pedagogical interventions.

THEORETICAL APPROACHES OF DIFFERENTIATED TEACHING

Modern educational systems worldwide understand the importance of equity and inclusion in quality education and are ready to adopt the principles of differentiated instruction (DI). After all, to quote Thomas Jefferson, there is nothing more unequal than the equal treatment of unequals. In this context, 'leaving no one behind' is the core of the educational agenda, students are being offered choice and flexibility in how they learn, teachers personalize the process of learning (UNESCO 2020).

DI promotes greater social cohesion and aims to gradually change the whole education system so that every school, and every teacher can welcome students from all backgrounds (ethnic, educational, socio-economic), providing them with a good quality education alongside their peers. Tomlinson has described thoroughly the concept of differentiated instruction. In particular, teachers, based on student readiness, interest, or learning profile, can differentiate at least four classroom elements, in particular content (what the student needs to learn or how the student will get access to the information), process (activities in which the student engages in order to make sense of or master the content), product (culminating projects that ask the student to rehearse, apply, and extend what he or she has learned in a unit) and learning environment (Tomlinson, 2017).

As promising DI may seem, addressing different levels of student readiness, process skills, and product determination can be challenging for teachers. Bibliographical research has identified various barriers concerning DI's implementation. Teachers must often cater the diverse needs of the inclusive student population while simultaneously trying to meet the requirements of the mandated Curriculum, with predefined educational goals, not given initiative to modify the content or teaching method accordingly to their students' profile and needs. This lack of initiative affects teachers' sense of efficacy, resulting in pressure and hesitance to adopt differentiated learning techniques (Dixon, Yssel, McConnell & Hardin, 2014).

Moreover, the practice of DI is time-consuming in terms of lesson planning and evaluation and at the same time requires more learning time, making teachers feel uneasy and anxious (Nicolae, 2013). Teachers often complain that curricula should anticipate more learning time for DI implementation and that in-service training about DI is often circumstantial. Overall, curricular requirements, extensive teacher workload and lack of time, limited Curriculum resources, lack of administrative support and finally inadequate in-service training hinder the implementation of DI. Recognizing and then minimizing these barriers to learning is a prerequisite to achieve an available, accessible, acceptable, and adaptable education (Tomaševski, 2001).

DI in the subject of science is a very promising research field. Science teaching is correlated with scientific literacy, defined for the PISA 2015 as "the ability to engage with science-related issues and with the ideas of science as a reflective citizen" (Roberts & Bybee, 2014). In such a context, science teaching is linked with reasoning skills, such as problem-solving strategies, generating hypotheses, evaluating evidence, formulating conclusions under guided instruction, understanding the relationship between science, technology, and how that applies to society (Rott, 2018). Students gain scientific knowledge by building on pre-concepts and by "adding to, modifying and sometimes deleting elements from this complex of meanings and understandings" (Hodson, 2014).

In implementing subject-specific DI, modern curricula adopt differentiated teaching techniques and highlight the importance of scaffolding, interdisciplinary activities and mind mapping (Mastropieri & Scruggs, 2014). Teachers can draw on individual interests, preconceptions and experiences in order to make science relevant. They can also create a context that stimulates all learners to engage in science learning (Höft et al., 2019). Contexts, content and methods must support a deeper understanding of the natural world or be connected to everyday living (DeBoer, 2000). The very nature of science, though, implicates cognitive and affective barriers in DI implementation. Often, explanations of scientific phenomena involve assumptions about underlying processes that cannot be observed directly (Schneeweiß & Gropengießer, 2019). Another possible barrier is formed by the content itself or conception to be learnt. The level of abstraction in terms of content can discourage learners. Finally, students are unfamiliar with scientific terminology and linguistic features of scientific texts such as vocabulary complexity, polysemy and textual density, leading to cognitive overload and lack of students' motivation (Markic & Childs, 2016).

Considering the above mentioned barriers, science teaching should focus on investigating students' unique educational needs, exploiting students' former experience to stimulate their interest on Physics, then doing science, testing and applying scientific knowledge, so that all learners are offered different practical and theoretical ways to engage with scientific phenomena and objects. We should therefore emphasize to using methods and procedures of science to investigate phenomena, test and develop understanding, solve problems and follow interests.

PHYSICS CURRICULUM IN THE LOWER SECONDARY SCHOOL

The Special Education Physics teacher must follow the official Physics Curriculum in his/her Inclusion Classr, while at the same time adjusting it to the special needs of students with learning difficulties and developing IEP, as external organizations (such as KEDASY) and internal school commitees (such as EDY) recommend. According to Ministry's of Education programming, the newer approved Curriculum for Physics will be applied in all Greek schools in 2024-2005 and till that time, there is a possibility that the existent pilot program will be extended for the school year 2023-2024. In this context, the special education teacher, depending on the school type where he/she teaches (general/pilot schools), has the option to follow the 2003 Curriculum (Decision 21072b/C2, 2003) either the newest one approved in 2021 (Decision 149118/D2, 2021).

2003 Analytic Physics Curriculum (Interdisciplinary Unified Educational Frame, DEPPS)

In the 2003 Physics Curriculum, DI is not explicitly named, is though implicated through several recommended teaching techniques.

Students' Former Experiences

One of the basic parameters of DI, that is making advantage of students' former experiences, is mentioned in parts of the teaching methodology proposed by the Curriculum. To quote some characteristic phrases:

"*...While designing teaching activities, it should be noted that the understanding of concepts and the gain of essential knowledge is achieved when using students' former experiences....*»

"*...Teaching is more effective, if, before the introduction of concepts and relevant terminology, empirical knowledge is exploited, and the necessity of their introduction is explicitly explained. This can be done with appropriate examples or problems. Processing the concepts should be based on former knowledge and experience, so that the student can include the new knowledge in already acquired semantic schemes or create new concepts. Generalization should be supported by examples originating from students' environment and real- life experience....*»

"…Teaching through investigation and discovery is an important strategy for Physics, under the assumption that it exploits experience, it motivates students to observe, compare, measure, classify, generalize, and evaluate hypotheses.…»

Based on the above references, the Special Education Physics teacher is encouraged to exploit the real – life experience of students with learning disabilities. There are several examples of Physics phenomena and processes, that are already familiar to learners with disabilities. One characteristic example is the thermometer calibration, taught in 1st grade of Lower Secondary School. Students are likely to have used a thermometer at home and observed the difference of temperature during the day. Similarly, Lower Secondary School 3rd graders can easily understand the concept of electric current, as they have relevant experience at home with electric appliances, may have experienced static electricity while brushing their hair and have possibly discussed about electricity or relevant technological applications.

Students' Interests

The following quotes originate from the Curriculum's chapter named "Teaching methodology'" and highlight that Physics teachers should consider the second parameter of DI, students' interests.

"…Physics through its applications is linked with social environment and everyday life, and teachers can highlight this correlation, stimulating the interest of students, and leading to an active engagement (using the project method) on chosen themes from each scientific field…»

"…Homework and activities should be chosen, according to students' interests and constructed in such a way so that they can be gradually completed, engage the entire student team, inspiring interdisciplinary research.…»

In accordance with the Curriculum, the Special Education teacher who teaches Physics in the Inclusion Class can encourage students with learning disabilities to engage in projects organized by the general classroom Physics teacher, guiding them on choosing suitable project activities and helping them learn according to their interests.

Students' Needs

Regarding the third basic parameter of DI, that is students' needs, in several sections of the Curriculum, teachers are strongly advised to plan and implement their teaching based on their students' educational needs. Relevant references can be found in the teaching methodology section:

"… For PWD (People with disabilities), there should be special prevision for:

- *Flexibility, variety in assigned activities, corresponding to each student's learning profile*
- *A multisensory approach of learning aims, variety on teaching means and material*

- *Exploiting students' performance and learning level, applying individualized educational programs, since the use of a single teaching mean or method creates connotations but not concepts and limits drastically the semantic mechanism of generalization and knowledge transfer*
- *Choosing a scientific model and scientific concepts to be taught ...»*

In the above context the use of computational technology can also refresh the teaching of Physics. For example, measuring the oscillation time of a plain pendulum can be taught to Lower Secondary School 1st graders in the Inclusion Class by using material from the science lab, but also by simulation in a remote lab.

In the section of the Physics Curriculum entitled as "evaluation», it is stated that:

"... Exercise and problems should be in accordance with students learning abilities, be scaffolded, clear and scientifically exact and evaluate all skills originally planned for students to acquire (analysis, synthesis, critical evaluation, result presentation etc.)...»

In this concept, the special education teacher can collaborate with the general classroom teacher when designing exams or tests, so that evaluation overall is consistent with the individualized educational program for students with learning disabilities. Questions could be simplified in terms of language while maintaining their scientific correctness.

In the 'teaching material' section of the Curriculum can be found references for students' need, primarily addressed to the book writers, but also suggestions for Physics teachers. The special education teacher can help his/her students process material, by making adaptations and adjustments. In Physics lab guidebook teachers are given relevant guidelines, to address the needs of students with learning disabilities.

"... Especially for PWD.... teachers should be encouraged to create an individualized educational program according to students' needs, so that they are motivated and learn in the most effective way.

Guidelines for experiment implementation should be plain, exact, and informative about the secure way to use appliances and lab equipment. Furthermore, PWD must:

- *Be supported when participating in laboratory experiment and engage in a useful and safe way.*
- *Take part in alternative activities, use equipment in an appropriate manner, use new technology in laboratory exercises...»*

Likewise citations can be found in the rest of the book. In students book it is stated that:.

"..(the book) should be open to alternative teaching methods, in order to encourage the teacher to adjust his/her teaching, according to students' needs and particularities ...»

Contemporary Physics textbooks tend to include images, related to the theme to be taught. The special education teacher can make use of this material in various ways, in a multisensory approach. For instance, in the lesson of pressure, planned for 2nd Lower Secondary School graders, the photos of the ski athlete and truck wheels can help students understand the role of power and surface and grasp the concept of pressure.

Pilot Physics Curriculum 2021

According to 104671/CD4/2021 decision, the New Physics Curriculum was carried out as a pilot project during the school year 2021-22 in pilot schools by trained teachers. In April 2023 the Ministry of Education announced a call for participation in the evaluation and the integration of new approved textbooks into the official Textbook Repository. Until the process of delivery the new approved textbooks and accompanied material is complete, the special education teacher who teaches in an Inclusion Class can exploit the new possibilities granted by the New Curriculum, as well as the current student textbook and current workbook and lab guide.

In the New Curriculum there are several references to teaching tools and indirect reference to DI's basic parameters, as mentioned above. The teacher specialized in special education can use the experiences, interests of students with learning disabilities and consider their special needs in the context mentioned also for the current 2003 Curriculum.

In the section of "lesson planning", some phrases are characteristic:

"…To raise questions, inspire students to make hypotheses, engage in discussions, exploit former knowledge, investigate and make conclusions by cultivating skills such as teamwork, communication, intuition, rethinking, analytical thinking…»

Students' interests appear in:

A) the section of "aim setting":

"…the presentation of subjects that stimulate interest leads to a more appealing teaching, students' engagement to activities makes learning more effective »

B) the section of "lesson planning"

"…to motivate students with stimuli, such as timeliness, everyday phenomena, scientific or technological applications, extensions to society, art, civilization, so as to cultivate the skill of observation and encourage critical thinking …»

"…to increase student interest for each part of the educational process with stimuli such as everyday matter and life, natural or man-made related phenomena, scientific or technological breakthroughs. This way, students are urged to a deeper understanding of the natural word …"

For the students' needs there is a reference:

A) in the section "lesson profile"

"...The subject of Physics in Lower Secondary School is linked with the educational dimension of natural science, as adapted to the age level and educational needs of Lower Secondary School student, to understand and master concepts and phenomena. These adaptations consider student diversity, the teaching time available, infrastructure ...»

B) in the section of "aim setting"

"...the knowledge transfer and transformation of scientific content into intuitive knowledge take into account the students' developmental – age level and their ability to grasp and get familiar with scientific procedures..."

C) in the section "content – thematic fields"

"...According to this approach, thematic sections included to thematic- semantic fields, should be taught in such a sequence, so that they can be understood by students and in such a structure that concepts are gradually processed in terms of complexity and semantic depth".

And in the section of "evaluation" the needs and experiences of students are referred again:

"... Diagnostic- predictive evaluation, at the beginning of the school year or intermediately, when completing big thematic units, can be an important educational tool, as the teacher can assess preexistent knowledge, attitude and perception, performance and potential of his students, so as to apply at an early stage targeted and differentiated teaching tools and techniques....»

DIFFERENTIATED TEACHING PRACTICES FOR STUDENTS WITH LEARNING DISABILITIES

In this section the differentiated teaching practices of Physics that could be implemented during instruction according to the learning difficulties of their students are described. The difficulties that students with learning difficulties may encounter in Physics are a) misunderstanding of long texts, b) lack of concentration, c) mismatch of symbols with physical quantities, d) failure to identify data and issues in questions.

Misunderstanding of Long Texts

Students usually find difficulties during attending the class of Physics in understanding long texts of the questions and problems that they are asked to work on them. The differentiated teaching practices that could be exploited by the teacher are i) reading the question aloud to the students, ii) presentation of the question by software.

The following question is an example from the textbook of Physics (Antoniou et al, p. 61) that is taught in the 2nd grade of Lower Secondary School.

"According to legend, a horse knew Newton's laws. When he was told to drag a a cart, he refused in response: "if I force the cart forward, then according to Newton's third law, the cart will also exert a force of equal measure backwards. Therefore, the total force will be equal to zero, and according to Newton's first law, the total force will be equal to zero and the cart will remain stationary." What would you say to this rather strange horse?"

For this question the teacher of the Inclusion Class can apply the following differentiated teaching practices

Reading the Question Aloud to the Students

The question could be read by the teacher aloud once without interruption. To ensure that students do not misunderstand the text, the teacher may repeat the reading section by section or sentence by sentence and a hint between the sections may be suggested as it seems below.

- 1st section
  - According to legend, a horse knew Newton's laws. *(pause)*
  - When he was told to drag a a cart, he refused in response: *(pause) (Teacher: Do you remember Newton's laws?)*
- 2nd section
  - if I force the cart forward, then according to Newton's third law, *(pause) (Teacher: Write in your notebook Newton's third law)*
  - the cart will also exert a force of equal measure backwards. *(pause)*
  - Therefore, the total force will be equal to zero, and according to Newton's first law, *(pause) Teacher: Write in your notebook Newton's first law)*
  - the total force will be equal to zero and the cart will remain stationary." *(pause)*
- 3rd section
  - What would you say to this rather strange horse?

Presentation of the Question by Software

The question could be divided according to above mentioned plan in three slides of a software file of Power Point corresponding to the three sections. As for the two first slides the sentences of its slide could be appeared exploiting the motion effects of the software Power Point. For example, the 1st slide

- According to legend, a horse knew Newton's laws. (*it could be appeared by the motion effect of "gradually")*
- When he was told to drag a a cart, he refused in response: (*it could be appeared by the motion effect of "scheme")*

After the presentation of every slide the teacher could state a comment for the Newton´s laws or ask students to write them to their notebook. An alternative presentation of these sentences is to accompany them with relevant schemes drawn by the teacher or pictures of the textbook. An example is the following photo (see figure 1):

Figure 1. Image of a cart, related to Newton' s third law

Lack of Concentration

Usually students' with learning disabilities concentration is reduced during the task they have been asked to do, e.g. to solve an exercise or problem of Physics. The differentiated teaching practices that the teacher could implement are i) the students solve the exercise on the blackboard of the classroom ii) observation of the students' solution in their notebook iii) students dictate the solution to the teacher.

An example is the following exercise that is included in the textbook of Physics (Antoniou et al, p 61) of the 3rd grade of Lower Secondary School.

"A resistor has a resistance of 50 Ω. We connect the connectors of the resistor to the poles of a battery. We connect a voltmeter to the battery poles. The measurement of the voltmeter is 5 V.

a. Draw in your notebook the schematic representation of the circuit.
b. Draw the intensity of the electric current flowing through the resistor and the intensity of the current flowing through the source."

The differentiated practices that can be carried out by the teacher of the Inclusion Class are:

The Students Solve the Exercise on the Blackboard of the Classroom

The student could stand up at the blackboard and exploit the textbook of Physics in order to solve this exercise. When the teacher notices that the student's concentration is reducing may

- Read the phrase that contains the first request of the exercise "*Draw in your notebook the schematic representation of the circuit.*"
- Ask the student to define the data of the exercise and write them on the blackboard
- Ask the student to draw the schematic representation of the circuit on the blackboard
- Ask the student to draw the intensity of the electric current using marker pens with different colour in order to represent the current that flows through the resistor and through the source

Observation of the Students' Solution in Their Notebook

While the students are trying to solve the exercise in their notebook the teacher of the Inclusion Class can discreetly observe the actions they are recording. When the teacher becomes aware that the student they are observing loses concentration, he may take the following actions.

- reward him for the correct connections he has made up to that point in the circuit drawing in his notebook and thus to concentrate and continue to draw the direction of the current
- if he has drawn the connection of the voltmeter incorrectly
    - can describe how the ammeter is connected to the circuit so that the student can concentrate and ask himself how the voltmeter is correctly connected
    - ask him/her supportive questions to help him/her concentrate, e.g. how are the ammeter and the voltmeter connected to the electrical circuit?

Students Dictate the Solution to the Teacher

In case the teacher of the Inclusion Class observes that a student loses his/her concentration, he/she can bring him/her back by asking him/her to describe what he/she has done to solve the exercise and the teacher writes it on the classroom blackboard, provided that it is in the right direction. If there is a mistake, e.g. in the connection of the voltmeter, he can perform whichever of the above-mentioned actions he considers most appropriate.

Matching Symbols With Physical Quantities

Another difficulty encountered by students with learning difficulties concerns the correct matching of physical quantities with the symbols used in Physics. Thus, students with learning difficulties may not correctly identify the physical quantity represented by a Latin letter; for example, the Latin letter m in Physics may indicate a) the physical quantity of mass, b) the unit of measurement of length, c) the submultiples of one millimetre that may accompany units of measurement. Another example is the letter T which in Physics terminology can indicate a) temperature, b) friction, c) the period of oscillation. However, in addition to these multiple meanings of certain Physics symbols, pupils with learning difficulties may not correctly identify the physical quantity represented by a letter. For example, the Latin letter I corresponding to the intensity of an electric current may be recognised by students as the power P of an electric current when it appears in the mathematical relationship linking the two specific physical quantities P=VI

To overcome these difficulties the teacher of the Inclusion Class who teaches Physics can:

i) in collaboration with the students, make a table on the computer during the teaching time where the symbol is shown in one column and the meaning of the symbol in the other column (see table 1)

The board can be printed and posted in the classroom, for students to have it in their notebooks and, in collaboration with the general class teacher, be able to use it in the written tests until the final exams.

ii) ask the pupils to construct with paper-folding paper various geometrical polyhedra, each of which shows a different interpretation of the symbol, e.g. a pyramid, a cube, etc.
iii) in Powerpoint slides, to use the motion effects and show each interpretation differently, e.g. one interpretation of the symbol in steps, another interpretation by division, etc.

Failure to Identify Data and Issues in the Questions

Students with learning difficulties may find it difficult to distinguish between known physical quantities and those asked in Physics questions. The inclusion teacher can help them to work through some questions by highlighting the given physical quantities and the issues in different colours in a slide of Powerpoint. Below is an example of editing on a question from the first grade Physics textbook (Kalkanis et al, p. 5). Then the teacher can construct similar questions for the students to practice.

"Discuss with your classmates and write down your assumptions about the accuracy required in measuring time:

- *between two visits to the eye doctor:* ....
- *in a 100-meter race:* ....
- *one teaching "hour":* ....
- *creating a geological rock:* ...."

Table 1. Physics' symbol meaning

Symbol	Symbol Meaning
m	Mass
m	Metre
m	Milimetre
T	Friction
T	Temperature
T	Oscillation period
T	Rope tension

The data in the question are:

- between two visits to the eye doctor
- in a 100-meter race
- one teaching "hour"
- creating a geological rock

The issue of the question is the students to estimate the time needed for each of the above events to take place.

The question on a Powerpoint slide can take the following form after changing the colour to green for the data and blue for the issue

"Discuss with your classmates and write down your assumptions about the accuracy required in measuring time:

- between two visits to the eye doctor: ....
- in a 100-meter race: ....
- one teaching "hour": ....
- creating a geological rock: ...."

We believe that organizing the data and questions in a table, as shown below, will help students with learning difficulties to answer the question. Students can fill in their answers on the worksheet in the Physics textbook (see Table 2).

DISCUSSION

Teachers who are eligible to teach Physics in Inclusion Classes should a) be graduates of Physics Departments to teach it on a first assignment or graduates of other science departments to teach it on a second assignment, b) have acquired expertise in special education either through postgraduate and/or doctoral studies or through approved seminars. In the context outlined in this chapter, we believe that teachers who teach Physics at secondary level should come exclusively from the relevant departments in order to have the necessary level of scientific knowledge and skills needed to teach this subject. We also believe that it is necessary to train them in the issues developed in the chapter, i.e. in the context

Table 2. Exercise organizer graph

Data	Issue	Answer
between two visits to the eye doctor	measuring time	....
in a 100-meter race	measuring time	....
one teaching "hour"	measuring time	....
creating a geological rock	measuring time	....

of the functioning of the Inclusion Classes and in the possibility of exploiting differentiated teaching in the Physics concepts mentioned in the curricula.

REFERENCES

DeBoer, G. (2000). Scientific literacy: Another look at its historical and contemporary meanings and its relationship to science education reform. *Journal of Research in Science Teaching, 37*(6), 582–601. doi:10.1002/1098-2736(200008)37:6<582::AID-TEA5>3.0.CO;2-L

Decision 104671/CD4. (2021). Pilot Implementation of Curricula in Primary and Secondary Education. *Gazette of the Government of the Hellenic Republic* (4003/B/30-8-2021).

Decision 21072b/C2 (2003). Interdisciplinary Unified Framework of Curricula (D.E.P.P.S.) and Analytical Curricula (A.P.S.). *Gazette of the Government of the Hellenic Republic* (304/B/13-3-2003).

Dixon, F. A., Yssel, N., McConnell, J. M., & Hardin, T. (2014). Differentiated Instruction, Professional Development, and Teacher Efficacy. *Journal for the Education of the Gifted, 37*(2), 111–127. doi:10.1177/0162353214529042

Hodson, D. (2014). Learning Science, Learning about Science, Doing Science: Different goals demand different learning methods. *International Journal of Science Education, 36*(15), 2534–2553. doi:10.1080/09500693.2014.899722

Höft, L., Bernholt, S., Blankenburg, J. S., & Winberg, M. (2019). Knowing more about things you care less about: Cross-sectional analysis of the opposing trend and interplay between conceptual understanding and interest in secondary school chemistry. *Journal of Research in Science Teaching, 56*(2), 184–210. doi:10.1002/tea.21475

Kalkanis, G., Gkikopoulou, O., Kapotis, E., Gousopoulos, D., Patrinopoulos, M., Tsakonas, P., Dimitriadis, P., Papatsimpa, L., Mitzithras, K., Kapogiannis, A., Sotiropoulos, D., Politis, S. (2013). *Physics with experiments for the 1st grade of Lower Secondary School. [I Fysiki me Peiramata A΄ Gymnasiou].* Institute of Computer Technology and Publishing "Diophantus".

Law 3699 (2008). Special Education and Education of Persons with Disabilities or Special Educational Needs. [Eidiki Agwgi kai Ekpaidefsi atomwn me anapiria i me eidikes ekpaideftikes anagkes]. *Government Gazette 199*, Vol. A, 2-10-2008. (in Greek)

Law 4368 (2016). Measures to speed up government work and other provisions. [Metra gia tin epitaxynsi tou kyvernitikoy ergou kai alles diatakseis]. *Government Gazette 21,* Vol. A, 21-2-2016. (in Greek)

Law 4547 (2018). Reorganisation of primary and secondary education support structures and other provisions. [Anadiorganwsi twn domwn ypostiriksis tis prwtovathmias kai defterovathmias ekpaidefsis kai alles diatakseis]. *Government Gazette 102*, Vol. A, 12-6-2018. (in Greek)

Law 4823 (2021). School upgrading, teacher empowerment and other provisions. [Anavathmisi tou sxoleiou, endynamwsi twn ekpaideftikwn kai alles diatakseis]. *Government Gazette 136*, Vol. A, 3-8-2021. (in Greek)

Markic, S., & Childs, P. E. (2016). Language and the teaching and learning of chemistry. *Chemistry Education Research and Practice*, *17*(3), 434–438. doi:10.1039/C6RP90006B

Mastropieri, M. A., & Scruggs, T. E. (2014). *The inclusive classroom: Strategies for effective differentiated instruction* (5th ed.). Pearson.

Ministerial Decision 134960/D3. Unified regulation on the operation of the School Educational Support Networks (S.D.E.Y.) and the Interdisciplinary Support Committees (E.D.Y.) of general and vocational education school units and definition of the specific duties of their members. Government Gazette 5009, Vol. B, 27-10-2021. (in Greek)

Ministerial Decision 27922/C6. Tasks of integration teachers. No 3. Determination of the specific duties and responsibilities (a) The teaching staff, who serve as teachers working in special education units (SEU) primary and secondary education (special schools, integration departments), and in primary and secondary special education programmes (parallel support) and (b) special education staff and special auxiliary staff serving in school establishments of special education, primary and secondary schools. Government Gazette 449, Vol. B, 3-4-2007. (in Greek)

Ministry of Education and Religious Affairs 46978/ CD4 (2023). Call for expressions of interest for the submission of applications for participation in the process of evaluation and inclusion of textbooks in the Register of Textbooks and the Digital Library of Textbooks, 25-04-2023. (in Greek)

Nicolae, M. (2013). Teachers Beliefs as the Differentiated Instruction Starting Point: Research Basis. *Procedia: Social and Behavioral Sciences*, *128*, 426–431. doi:10.1016/j.sbspro.2014.03.182

Roberts, D. A., & Bybee, R. W. (2014). Scientific Literacy, Science Literacy, and Science Education. In N. G. Lederman & S. K. Abell (Eds.), *Handbook of Research on Science Education* (pp. 545–558). Routledge.

Rott, L., & Marohn, A. (2018). Choice2explore – a teaching concept for inclusive science education in primary schools. In: O. Finlayson, E. McLoughlin, S. Erduran, & P. Childs, (Eds.), Proceedings of the 12th *ESERA 2017 Conference, Research, practice and collaboration in science education* (pp. 2194-2202). Dublin: Dublin City University.

Schneeweiß, N., & Gropengießer, H. (2019). Organising Levels of Organisation for Biology Education: A Systematic Review of Literature. *Education Sciences*, *9*(3), 207. doi:10.3390/educsci9030207

Tomaševski, K. (2001). *Human rights obligations: making education available, accessible, acceptable and adaptable. (Right to Education Primers No. 3)*. Sida.

Tomlinson, C. (2017). *How to differentiate instruction in academically diverse class- rooms*. ASCD.

UNESCO. (1994). *The Salamanca Statement and Framework for Action on Special Needs Education.* World Conference on Special Needs Education: Access and Quality, Salamanca, Spain.

UNESCO. (2020). *Global education monitoring report, 2020: Inclusion and education: all means all.* UN. https://unesdoc.unesco.org/ark:/48223/pf0000373718

Chapter 4
Educational Challenges and Perspectives in Developmental Dyslexia

Afroditi Malisiova
https://orcid.org/0009-0005-0778-5028
Aristotle University of Thessaloniki, Greece

Vasiliki Folia
https://orcid.org/0000-0002-2159-7032
Aristotle University of Thessaloniki, Greece

ABSTRACT

The worldwide prevalence of students diagnosed with specific learning difficulties (SLD) has increased over the past few decades. Education systems strive to include students with SLD in general classrooms through the implementation of various educational methods and adjustments to the teaching process, although often with limited learning outcomes. This chapter focuses on developmental dyslexia (DD) and explores its primary characteristics while delving into the attitudes, misconceptions, and lack of training among teachers, as their approach significantly impacts the education of students with DD. By describing the key attributes of DD and identifying the resulting learning challenges for students, the chapter puts forth suggested teaching methods and practices based on the current literature. These approaches encompass differentiated instruction, implicit learning, the use of Information and Communication Technologies, multisensory teaching, and student-centered group work.

INTRODUCTION

General classrooms worldwide include a significant number of students with specific learning difficulties (SLD), with Developmental Dyslexia (DD) being a common diagnosis among them. The education systems, educators, and specialists in the field of SLD face challenges in integrating these students into the educational process and assisting them to overcome their learning difficulties and achieve their learn-

DOI: 10.4018/979-8-3693-1982-6.ch004

ing goals. Recent research on teaching students with DD has proposed various approaches, methods, practices, and teaching strategies, including Differentiated Instruction (D.I.), implicit learning, the use of Information and Communication Technologies (ICT), multisensory learning, and student-centered group and pair-work practices, aiming to establish a flexible, creative, and supportive educational environment. Despite these efforts, the number of students diagnosed with SLD is steadily increasing globally, while outdated educational policies continue to exist. This highlights the urgency of implementing more inclusive, updated, and student-friendly educational approaches in classrooms (Hallahan et al., 2020; Pham & Riviere, 2015). Furthermore, the attitudes, misconceptions, and inadequate training of teachers can impede the establishment of such classrooms, despite their dedication and significant efforts. Nevertheless, research has indicated that the integration of all the mentioned approaches, methods, and techniques in general schools can effectively support students with DD, provided there are updated educational policies, curricula, facilities, and efficient teacher training programs.

1. DEVELOPMENTAL DYSLEXIA: THE MOST COMMON LEARNING DIFFICULTY

The present chapter will primarily focus on DD since it stands as the most common SLD worldwide, irrespective of the students' social, cultural, economic, and educational background. Approximately 70-80% of students diagnosed with SLD exhibit dyslexia representing 5–10% of the global population and 5% - 15% of the school population (Forteza et al., 2018). Estimates suggest that there could be between one and five dyslexic students in every classroom (Knight, 2018).

Dyslexia is fundamentally characterized as a literacy difficulty (Elliott & Grigorenko, 2014). It arises from the intricate interplay between biological, cognitive, and behavioral factors, along with environmental and cultural factors, which significantly influence a dyslexic person's progress and academic achievements (Knight, 2018). Students with dyslexia are considered to have special educational needs and disabilities (SEND) (Knight, 2018). Different types of dyslexia have been reported, with the most common and intriguing one being Developmental Dyslexia (DD). DD is typically of genetic origin, present since birth, and is more frequently observed in boys (Stein, 2018). It can manifest as either "primary", indicating a genetically inherited condition, or "secondary" resulting from brain development issues during the early stages of a mother's pregnancy. Another subtype of dyslexia is acquired dyslexia which is less common and caused by traumatic brain injuries or diseases affecting the brain's language processing centers. Phonological dyslexia refers to difficulties in dividing words into syllables and sounds known as phonemes. Surface dyslexia, another subcategory, involves reading difficulties wherein students cannot recognize words by sight or read quickly and accurately (Newcombe & Marshall, 2017). Finally, deep dyslexia pertains to an acquired reading disorder caused most frequently by brain injuries and characterized by semantic errors and difficulty in reading functional words.

Furthermore, dyslexia can be classified into three primary types: the "P" (perceptual) type, which consists of learners who read relatively slowly and demonstrate fragmented reading, but are rather accurate in their reading; the "L" (linguistic) type, comprising learners who read quickly but produce a considerable number of errors, such as omissions and additions; and the "M" (mixed) type of learners, who read slowly and continue to make a significant number of errors (Pokrivčáková et al., 2015). Dyslexia has been frequently reported to co-occur with other developmental disorders, such as attention deficit hyperactivity disorder (ADHD), dyscalculia, dysgraphia, or dyspraxia (De Clercq-Quaegebeur et al., 2018).

1.1 Main Characteristics of Developmental Dyslexia Causing Learning Difficulties

DD is considered a SLD of neurological origin, related to impaired phonetic spelling strategy (Frith, 2017; Soriano-Ferrer & Echegaray-Bengoa, 2014; Stein, 2018). It affects students' ability to accurately, fluently, and easily recognize, spell, read, and write words, as well as achieve meaningful oral reading (prosody) and, consequently, reading comprehension (Eden & Moats, 2002; Lyon et al., 2003; Peterson & Pennington, 2012, 2015; Soriano-Ferrer & Echegaray-Bengoa, 2014; Stein, 2018). Although the cognitive abilities of students may not be affected, DD is considered a deficit in the phonological aspect of language, impeding vocabulary acquisition and the development of background knowledge (Soriano-Ferrer & Echegaray-Bengoa, 2014; Stein, 2018). DD is a significant reading difficulty, as students tend to read slowly, often avoid or fail in extensive reading activities, and face difficulties in producing written or spoken language, acquiring new vocabulary, and comprehending more complex grammar and syntactic structures. Former research has indicated impairments in implicit learning, meaning the acquisition of knowledge in a passive way without conscious awareness, (Folia et al., 2008; Jurchiş & Dienes, 2023; Pavlidou & Williams, 2014). Such weaknesses in implicit learning may be related to phonological acquisition and impaired reading skills, and hinder grapheme–phoneme correspondences, along with deficient mechanisms of automatization and phonology (Goswami et al., 2005; Pavlidou et al., 2010; Roodenrys & Dunn, 2007). However, there have been conflicting findings, indicating that implicit learning may be unimpaired in dyslexic individuals, despite their apparent difficulties in explicit learning tasks such as spelling, reading, and writing (Roodenrys & Dunn, 2007). Students with DD may even become confused while understanding questions, retrieving arithmetic facts in sequence, and distinguishing the left from the right (De Smedt & Boets, 2010).

It has also been suggested that the impairments in dyslexia across a wide variety of tasks are caused by deficits in the automatization of learning skills (Kelly et al., 2002). The most well-known and commonly found symptoms include impairments in visual processing, such as motion detection, temporal recall, choice reaction time, and executing actions automatically, as well as in skill acquisition processes (Nicolson & Fawcett, 1990, 1994). Consequently, tasks demanding skilled performance especially when conscious attentional resources are under pressure, become more challenging for students with dyslexia. However, concerning conscious compensation strategies, students with dyslexia appear to perform adequately, and no difficulties are indicated (Kelly et al., 2002). Former research also suggests a deficit in procedural abilities among students with dyslexia. Dyslexic readers were found to perform reading quite similarly to neurotypical students concerning the number of errors detected but at a slower pace (Vicary et al., 2005). Research findings indicate that limited procedural abilities are related to impairment in implicit learning processes, which are of significant importance in acquiring and performing cognitive, perceptual, and motor skills that support cognitive, speech, and sensory development (Vicary et al., 2005). Consequently, all the above impairments may lead to deficits in reading processes and automatization mechanisms necessary for reading acquisition and comprehension (Vicary et al., 2005). The phonological processing that appears to be impaired in dyslexics may also be influenced by the deficit in automatizing auditory and elementary articulatory skills (Marchetti et al., 2023; Vicary et al., 2005). There seems to be a connection among implicit learning, automatization, phonological failure, visual processing inadequacy, attentional deficits, and the development of successive abilities (Vicary et al., 2005). All the above impairments caused by dyslexia lead to difficulties in reading and writing, particularly in perceiving the different shapes of letters and relating them to specific sounds each letter represents as well as forming words by arranging letters in a specific order (Ohene-Djan & Begum, 2008; Vicary et al., 2005).

The main features of DD mentioned above have a negative impact on students' ability to acquire knowledge and succeed in current educational environments. This does not imply that students are incapable of learning or experiencing failure; rather, it highlights the failure of education systems to address these students' needs and include them effectively in the learning process (Banks, 2008; Kormos, 2020; Pfenninger, 2014). Subsequently, dyslexia can significantly impede students' cognitive and emotional development, leading to low self-esteem, behavioral issues, anxiety, stress, and, in some cases, social isolation (Lozano-Álvarez et al., 2023). Therefore, students often become demotivated, depressed, and hesitant, and may exhibit indifference towards the learning process. They may also be unwilling to participate, interact, and cooperate with their classmates, fearing embarrassment or exclusion due to the difficulties and low self-esteem caused by DD (Livingston et al., 2018).

2. TEACHERS' BELIEFS AND MISCONCEPTIONS CONCERNING DEVELOPMENTAL DYSLEXIA

Teachers' knowledge and beliefs regarding DD constitute one of the primary factors that determine the progress and inclusion of students with DD in the teaching process. Previous research has suggested that teachers' knowledge, skills, and training in SLD are insufficient hindering their ability to provide students with effective, creative, and motivating learning environments (Goldfus, 2012; Joshi et al., 2009; Malatesha et al., 2009; Soriano-Ferrer & Echegaray-Bengoa, 2014; Wadlington & Wadlington, 2005; Washburn et al., 2011). Teachers' beliefs about students with SLD are established early in their teaching careers and often persist despite accumulating teaching experience (Torff, 2011). Unfortunately, misconceptions create an even greater problem, leading teachers to have a blurred and often mistaken perception of the difficulties and abilities of students with DD, thus, underestimating their learning potential (Knight, 2018; Shaywitz, 2003; Vail, 2001). Students' progress and reading achievements are related to teachers' ability to be adequately trained to address the students' difficulties without displaying any negative or prejudiced attitude toward students (Hornstra et al., 2010).

Teachers lacking the ability to identify and comprehend DD and its characteristics due to limited, insufficient, or non-existent teacher training cannot effectively support and assist students in the learning process. Regrettably, this has resulted in biased or even contemptuous behaviors toward dyslexic students (Wadlington & Wadlington, 2005). Research has also suggested that teachers seem reluctant to differentiate their teaching, and adjust their methods, materials, and tasks to the students' needs, citing concerns about time consumption (Hertberg-Davis & Brighton, 2006). Despite teachers' considerable efforts to improve and upgrade their teaching and include students with DD in the classroom, lack of institutional support, rigid curricula that cannot be adjusted, and inadequate materials and facilities have negatively affected teaching conditions, especially in developing countries with limited funding for schools (Aftab, 2015). Thus, adequate teacher training is essential for teachers to understand the nature of DD as an LD and implement appropriate and efficient teaching methods, practices, and strategies. More importantly, it enables them to cultivate empathy and understanding and foster positive psychology and self-esteem in their students (Knight, 2018).

3. EDUCATIONAL SUGGESTIONS: TEACHING APPROACHES AND PRACTICES

Over the past few decades, research on educational perspectives in teaching students with dyslexia has yielded various innovative teaching practices and approaches. Implementing inclusive practices in teaching, such as Differentiated Instruction, implicit learning, the use of ICT, and multisensory and student-centered approaches, is fundamental to achieving inclusion and equity in the educational process for students with dyslexia (Kormos & Nijakowska, 2017).

3.1 Implementing Differentiated Instruction Practices in the Classroom

The implementation of Differentiated Instruction (D.I.) supports adjusting the teaching process according to the students' learning style, cognitive level, needs, interests, deficiencies, and abilities to create an educational context that is appropriate and highly productive for students with DD (Kotob & Abadi, 2019; Tomlinson, 2003; Tomlinson & Imbeau, 2010). Taking into account the students' learning pace, attitude, and skills aligns with the principles of D.I. and efficiently accommodates students with DD in terms of the behavioral and cognitive aspects of dyslexia. D.I. addresses the diverse needs of all learners, including those with SLD, providing them with an educational environment in which they can maximize their skills (Aftab, 2015; Thapliyal, 2022; Tomlinson, 1999).

D.I. refers to a technique that serves the purposes of Inclusive Education promoting the inclusion of all students regardless of their needs, preferences, cultural background, and especially their SLD (Ainscow, 2005). It suggests an organized yet flexible way of proactively planning the lessons, materials, contents, practices, and assessment methods according to the diverse needs of each classroom, meaning that the teaching process centers around the students' needs rather than solely adhering to a standardized curriculum (Kotob & Abadi, 2019; Tomlinson, 1999). Teachers need to modify and adjust their teaching methods, practices, and strategies according to the diverse needs of each classroom by conducting needs assessments. Thus, all students can set their personal goals, obtain knowledge, and achieve academically, albeit at a different pace and process according to their abilities (Aftab, 2015; Kotob & Abadi, 2019). As Tomlinson suggests (1995), continuous assessments of readiness levels and different grouping of students should take place in classrooms to promote collaboration among students and create more autonomous and independent learners who are responsible for their learning. Students are supported, guided, and supervised throughout the learning process by the teachers but set their own goals according to their interests, needs, cognitive level, and abilities (Tomlinson, 1995). D.I. is a technique that can assist all students in heterogeneous classes, especially those with DD, in gaining self-esteem by becoming more responsible, as independent learners who cooperate with their classmates and feel that despite their difficulties, they can contribute to their classroom by working in groups, exchanging ideas, and sharing knowledge (Aftab, 2015; Kotob & Abadi, 2019). This student-centered educational approach empowers students to be responsible for their learning and actively participate in lessons throughout the learning process (Tomlinson, 2001). The teaching process aims to trigger and maintain students' attention, commitment, and active engagement to achieve high educational standards and cognitive levels (Kotob & Abadi, 2019; Tomlinson, 2001). All of the above cannot be achieved unless teachers create a positive, productive, and collaborative classroom environment in which all students, especially the weaker ones or those with SLD can achieve their goals, feel proud and content about their skills, abilities, level of knowledge, and potential (Kotob & Abadi, 2019).

3.1.1 The Five Domains of Differentiated Instruction

The implementation of D.I. is based on five primary domains: content, process, product, affect, and learning environment (Aftab, 2015; Sousa & Tomlinson, 2011; Tomlinson, 2014). The domain of "content" or curriculum encompasses the knowledge, skills, and concepts taught, the timeline of each course, and the methods used to achieve the desired learning outcomes (Tomlinson & Imbeau, 2010). It is essential for students to grasp the content, particularly the key concepts known as enduring understandings, which add depth and significance to their learning experience (Tomlinson, 2014; Wiggins & McTighe, 2005). By understanding these key concepts students can apply their knowledge and skills effectively in various contexts (Kotob & Abadi, 2019; Wiggins & McTighe, 2005).

The "process" domain involves how students engage with the content (Kotob & Abadi, 2019). It includes the implementation of curricula through activities that engage students, provide necessary knowledge and skills, and assist them in reaching their learning goals (Kotob & Abadi, 2019; Sousa & Tomlinson, 2011; Tomlinson, 2014; Tomlinson & Imbeau, 2010; Tomlinson & Moon, 2013). The process (of learning) fosters "meaning and understanding" by incorporating various approaches, such as teacher instruction, pair/group work, or independent learning, tailored to the content, tasks, and students' needs (Kotob & Abadi, 2019). While teacher-directed instruction has its place, the focus should be on student-centered lessons that encourage interaction, collaboration, and autonomous learning (Holmes, 2008; Kotob & Abadi, 2019; Sousa & Tomlinson, 2011; Tomlinson, 2014; Tomlinson & Moon, 2013).

The "product" domain involves classroom assessment, which entails collecting and interpreting classroom information to guide teachers in decision-making regarding all aspects of teaching (Kotob & Abadi, 2019; Tomlinson & Moon, 2013). The "affect" domain refers to the influence of students' emotions and feelings on their learning which can enhance motivation, active participation, creativity, and commitment to their studies (Holmes, 2008). Establishing an appropriate learning environment is crucial in implementing D.I. This involves organizing the physical classroom to suit the needs of each class and grouping students based on tasks, time, or individual needs while providing teacher supervision and guidance. By fostering a student-centered approach and creating a pleasant, friendly, and creative learning environment, D.I. is effectively implemented (Sousa & Tomlinson, 2011; Tomlinson, 2014; Tomlinson & McTighe, 2006). Through collaboration with their peers and the teacher, students with DD will not only benefit cognitively but also experience improvements in their behavior gaining confidence and social-emotional health (Downes, 2007; Kotob & Abadi, 2019).

3.1.2 Assessment Methods in a Differentiated Classroom

In a differentiated classroom environment, instruction and assessment are closely interconnected. Therefore, assessment methods must be appropriate for their intended use, reliable, and objective while evaluating various aspects of students' performance, cognitive level, skills, needs/difficulties, and knowledge acquisition (Kotob & Abadi, 2019; Sousa &Tomlinson, 2011; Tomlinson, 2014). It is essential to employ both formal and informal or alternative assessment methods to accurately depict students' progress and provide essential information to the teacher (Johnson, 2010). Assessment can be categorized into diagnostic, formative, or summative approaches (Griva & Kofou, 2017; Kotob & Abadi, 2019). Diagnostic assessment refers to a pre-assessment process that identifies the cognitive level, knowledge, skills, and learning goals of each student before the beginning of a course/unit (Griva & Kofou, 2017; Kotob & Abadi, 2019). Formative assessment involves ongoing evaluation to track students' progress and determine whether the learning goals have been achieved or not. Various methods can be used, including traditional testing, self-assessment, peer assessment, or other alternative assessment methods including portfolios, diaries/journals, project-based assessment, classroom observation, descriptive assessment, and think-aloud protocols (Gregory & Chapman, 2012; Griva & Kofou, 2017). Finally, summative assessment occurs at the end of a unit/course/specific period to assess whether students have successfully met the learning goals set according to the curriculum (Griva & Kofou, 2017; Kotob & Abadi, 2019).

3.2 The "Implicit Learning" Approach

In contrast to extensive research suggesting phonological processing difficulty as a core feature of DD, the contribution of relevant cognitive processes in reading development remains unclear (for an overview refer to the chapter Folia et al., in this book). In addition to creating an optimal, creative, and supportive classroom environment for students with DD, as suggested by D.I., addressing the cognitive aspects of this difficulty related to phonological awareness, impaired reading and writing, and comprehension difficulties emphasizes the need for investigating both explicit and, more importantly, implicit learning approaches to support learners effectively. Given the cognitive aspects of DD and the challenges in explicit learning tasks reported by Roodenrys & Dunn (2007), it becomes essential to explore implicit learning approaches, especially since recent studies have started to view dyslexia as a deficit in implicit learning, particularly in the grapheme- to- phoneme mapping ability (Folia et al., 2008; Pennington & Bishop, 2009). Consequently, the reading difficulties experienced by dyslexic individuals may be linked to a deficit in implicit learning, prompting researchers to focus on implicit learning aptitude and reading-related development in children with RD (Lammertink et al., 2017). While numerous studies report implicit learning difficulties in individuals with dyslexia (e.g., Jiménez-Fernández et al., 2011), others do not find evidence for such a deficit (e.g. Rüsseler et al., 2006).

Early phonological and phoneme awareness (PA) skills can provide implications for a student's future reading ability (Boada & Pennington, 2006; Marchetti et al., 2023). Individuals with dyslexia, whether children or adults have been observed to exhibit deficits in implicit phonological representations, supporting the segmentation hypothesis (Bird & Bishop, 1992). Despite comparisons with reading or age-matched groups, research indicates that the dyslexic group lacks phoneme awareness although measuring this deficit has been challenging, leading to inconclusive findings (Boada & Pennington, 2006). Previous research suggested that dyslexics may not present major linguistic deficits and the development of underlying phonological representations is normal. However, explicit learning methods only provide limited assistance in reading and spelling, underscoring the need for combining implicit and explicit learning for improved learning outcomes (Boada & Pennington, 2006).

Test results have shown that individuals with DD have impaired implicit procedural learning of visual stimulus sequences (Vicari et al., 2005). However, these findings are specific to visual and not to auditory or multisensory stimuli, which might yield better outcomes for students with DD. Therefore, integrating multisensory teaching and learning practices into the educational process could potentially support explicit learning and offer students a more comprehensive, productive, and efficient learning environment. Additionally, research indicates that learning sequences do not necessarily rely on awareness of the sequence structure, suggesting that automatic skill learning remains intact in dyslexic individuals (Kelly et al., 2002). Similar patterns of implicit learning have been observed in university students with DD compared to normally reading students, although dyslexic students showed slower response times (Kelly et al., 2002). Thus, it is plausible that cognitive processes related to reading, have shown some recovery, especially for the most challenging skill for dyslexics, which is reading (Vicari et al., 2005). Various resources such as visual memory, verbal ability, use of context, and semantic knowledge available to students may compensate for the phonological impairment, suggesting that the difficulties faced by students with DD can be partially overcome by combining explicit and implicit learning with diverse teaching methods, strategies, materials, and practices (Vicari et al., 2005).

Emphasizing implicit learning through D.I., the use of ICT, and multisensory teaching practices integrated into innovative teaching pedagogies as suggested in this chapter, could potentially support students' behavioral, emotional, and cognitive growth in the classroom without the pressure and stress often associated with explicit learning strategies (Kelly et al., 2022).

3.3 The Integration of ICT in the Teaching Process

Practices and tasks that incorporate the use of ICT and multisensory learning, integrating both implicit and explicit learning, can offer alternative teaching methods to support cognitive and metacognitive knowledge (Roodenrys & Dunn, 2007). Recent research has highlighted the significance of integrating ICT in the teaching and learning process due to its ability to yield encouraging outcomes. ICT not only engages and motivates students to actively participate, but it also facilitates the creation and implementation of activities that help students overcome their LD through the use of multimodal texts, videos, interactive activities, sound, captivating images, diverse quizzes, and educational videogames (Irwin et al., 2022). Particularly, in educational environments with sufficient facilities to support one-to-one initiatives, where each student is provided with a personal device and access to technology, both students and teachers benefit significantly (Irwin et al., 2022; Zheng et al., 2016). The diversity of activities and tasks made possible by ICT, software programs, and devices can have a positive impact on the learning experience of students, especially those with DD who may find traditional educational methods uninteresting or even intimidating.

Emerging technologies, such as virtual reality and augmented reality, offer unique opportunities for tasks, activities, and learning experiences that can be particularly beneficial for students with dyslexia, fostering their participation and inclusion in the classroom (Lozano-Álvarez et al., 2023). ICT provides updated and enjoyable alternatives for practicing and acquiring knowledge engaging students in an attractive and interactive manner while also helping them and teachers identify and address LD. Moreover, virtual, and augmented reality creates a controlled, safe, and challenging learning environment, complementing traditional teaching methods like hands-on laboratory experiments, field trips, art-based projects, role-playing, internships, and interactive classroom games (Lozano-Álvarez et al., 2023). This diverse approach to teaching and learning, supported by the use of ICT, can also align with the flipped classroom pedagogical model and cater to students' interests and needs leading to increased concentration, improved performance, and significant progress (Lozano-Álvarez et al., 2023; Navarro-Haro et al., 2019). While research on virtual reality, especially through mobile devices, is still limited, it has shown promising results in offering enjoyable, playful, and implicit learning activities, and D.I. practices (Elias et al., 2021; Lozano-Álvarez et al., 2023; Navarro-Haro et al., 2019).

3.4 Multisensory Teaching Practices

In addition to implementing D.I. and using ICT, teaching practices may also involve engaging all of the students' senses. Multisensory teaching is considered one of the most effective approaches for learners with DD, as they often demonstrate adequate intelligence and intact sensory abilities despite their limited decoding and poor reading comprehension skills (Harrar et al., 2014; Peterson & Pennington, 2012, 2015). Using visuals, motion, body movement, and auditory elements in learning can lead to knowledge acquisition through implicit or/and explicit learning, proving to be an interesting, user-friendly, attractive, and supportive teaching approach (Ahmad et al., 2012). This approach, known as the visual, auditory, kinesthetic/tactile approach (VAKT), supports dyslexic students in various areas, including reading, writing, listening, speaking, phonology, spelling, syntax, morphology, semantics, and the organization of written and oral speech (Johnston, 2019). Research since the 1970s has indicated that using visual and auditory sensory modes can be more effective, creative, productive, and attractive in teaching than relying solely on one mode. Over the years, researchers investigating dyslexia have suggested various instructional methods to assist dyslexic students in developing reading, spelling, and writing skills (Vickery et al., 1987). Orton, Gillingham, and Monroe worked on a phonetic remedial curriculum for teaching dyslexic students and Gillingham and Stillman designed a multisensory approach based on this research, known as the Orton-Gillingham (OG), which is still used today. Research on multisensory teaching has indicated noticeable improvements in the language areas of the brain's left hemisphere after reading interventions with students with dyslexia (Johnston, 2019).

Regarding mixed-ability classrooms in general schools in which students with dyslexia attend multisensory practices and activities can engage all students and highlight the creativity and stronger sensory receptors (tactile/touch) that students with dyslexia are more confident in (Ohene-Djan & Begum, 2008). Online learning technology, applications, interactive games, and multisensory practices can emphasize students' strengths and minimize weaknesses in reading, writing, and math, providing an innovative assessment method (Ohene-Djan & Begum, 2008). Recent studies have emphasized the effectiveness of multisensory teaching for children with LD as it involves multisensory strategies and techniques that link eyes, ears, voice, and hand movements to symbolic learning engaging many sensory receptors in the learning process. Graphics and strong colors are used to create associations between shapes, letters, words, and numbers (Ahmad et al., 2012; Ohene-Djan & Begum, 2008). Tactile objects, different kinds of materials, and pictorial representations, including pictures or symbols, play an intrinsic role in multisensory teaching, helping students associate letters, words, numbers, and concepts - a particularly useful technique for students with DD (Ohene-Djan & Begum, 2008).

3.5 A Student-Centered Approach Based on Group Work

The entire teaching process should be student-centered, focusing on the students' interests, participation, and performance in class, as suggested by D.I., inclusive education, and recent pedagogies. One highly preferable and effective practice is assigning group or pair-work activities to students, as this allows the more advanced students to support and mentor their peers who may be struggling with LD and dyslexia. Encouraging collaboration and cooperation among students not only aids those with DD on a cognitive level but also positively impacts their behavior. Group work has been found to boost self-esteem, an area where dyslexic learners often experience challenges compared to typically developing students (Burton, 2004). Research involving groups of dyslexic and neurotypical students has shown that all students benefit from collaborative work and find it both enjoyable and productive (Burton, 2004). Peer and group work also fosters a friendly and trusting classroom atmosphere, as students discover shared perspectives and beliefs, exchange ideas, and empathize with each other's difficulties (Burton, 2004). By working together, students become more responsible and autonomous and display enthusiasm, commitment, and great effort to complete the tasks. Consequently, they gain self-confidence, acknowledge their strengths and weaknesses, and become more open to new experiences, knowing they have the support and help of their peers in the group/class (Burton, 2004). Importantly, this approach ensures that students feel included in the teaching process, and despite facing LD, disappointments, and obstacles they persist in striving to achieve both personal and group goals.

4. DISCUSSION

Implementing the aforementioned teaching approaches and practices by teachers, who understand, accept, and support the needs of students with DD, will lead to a creative and successful learning process for these students. Such educational perspectives, methods, and practices can create an educational environment that provides learning opportunities, encourages active participation, and offers innovative, constructive, and less stressful learning experiences for students with DD. To achieve this, institutional support, flexibility in curriculum implementation, materials, methodologies, and time are all essential for teachers and students striving for higher educational standards. Research has indicated that students' academic success is closely linked to the implementation of innovative teaching practices, thus, teachers need to include differentiated instructions to support students' needs and to implement multisensory methods and techniques to facilitate learning (Aftab, 2015; Khursheed & Ansari, 2012; Malik & Janjua, 2011). Creating an inclusive educational environment that provides learning opportunities, boosts learners' motivation, and positively influences their attitude can be achieved by integrating various teaching approaches. This includes using D.I. and implicit learning approaches alongside explicit ones, leveraging ICT, incorporating multisensory teaching practices, and fostering a student-centered teaching process enriched with group and pair-work activities and alternative assessment methods. All students, especially those with DD, who face various learning challenges, should be supported with these approaches and methods, and exposed to a flexible, friendly, and creative educational environment. This environment will allow them to optimize their full potential and develop their interests, skills, and abilities.

REFERENCES

Aftab, J. (2015). Teachers' Beliefs about Differentiated Instructions in Mixed Ability Classrooms: A Case of Time Limitation. *Journal of Education and Educational Development*, *2*(2), 94–114. doi:10.22555/joeed.v2i2.441

Ahmad, S. Z., Ludin, N. N. A. A. N., Ekhsan, H. M., Rosmani, A. F., & Ismail, M. H. (2012, December). Bijak Membaca—Applying Phonic Reading Technique and Multisensory Approach with interactive multimedia for dyslexia children. In *2012 IEEE Colloquium on Humanities, Science and Engineering (CHUSER)* (pp. 554-559). IEEE.

Ainscow, M. (2005). Developing inclusive education systems: What are the levers for change? *Journal of Educational Change*, *6*(2), 109–124. doi:10.100710833-005-1298-4

Banks, T. (2008). *Foreign Language Learning Difficulties and Teaching Strategies*. Online Submission.

Bird, J., & Bishop, D. V. M. (1992). Perception and awareness of phonemes in phonologically impaired children. *European Journal of Disorders of Communication*, *27*(4), 289–311. doi:10.3109/13682829209012042 PMID:1308694

Boada, R., & Pennington, B. F. (2006). Deficient implicit phonological representations in children with dyslexia. *Journal of Experimental Child Psychology*, *95*(3), 153–193. doi:10.1016/j.jecp.2006.04.003 PMID:16887140

Burton, S. (2004). Self-esteem groups for secondary pupils with dyslexia. *Educational Psychology in Practice*, *20*(1), 55–73. doi:10.1080/02667360420001 80410

De Clercq-Quaegebeur, M., Casalis, S., Vilette, B., Lemaitre, M. P., & Vallée, L. (2018). Arithmetic abilities in children with developmental dyslexia: Performance on French ZAREKI-R test. *Journal of Learning Disabilities*, *51*(3), 236–249. doi:10.1177/0022219417690355 PMID:28134569

De Smedt, B., & Boets, B. (2010). Phonological processing and arithmetic fact retrieval: Evidence from developmental dyslexia. *Neuropsychologia*, *48*(14), 3973–3981. doi:10.1016/j.neuropsychologia.2010.10.018 PMID:20965205

Downes, D. M. (2007). *Designing evaluation tools for the differentiated instruction staff development initiative* [Doctoral dissertation, Retrieved from ProQuest Dissertations & Theses Full Text]

Eden, G. F., & Moats, L. (2002). The role of neuroscience in the remediation of students with dyslexia. *Nature Neuroscience*, *5*(S11), 1080–1084. doi:10.1038/nn946 PMID:12403991

Elias, C. M., Vargas, S. I., & Castillo, K. V. B. (2021). La Realidad Virtual en la experiencia educativa de pregrado. *Delectus*, *4*(1), 139–145. doi:10.36996/delectus.v4i1.72

Elliott, J. G., & Grigorenko, E. L. (2014). *The dyslexia debate*. Cambridge University Press. doi:10.1017/CBO9781139017824

Folia, V., Uddén, J., Forkstam, C., Ingvar, M., Hagoort, P., & Petersson, K. M. (2008). Implicit learning and dyslexia. *Annals of the New York Academy of Sciences*, *1145*(1), 132–150. doi:10.1196/annals.1416.012 PMID:19076394

Forteza, D., Fuster, L., & Moreno-Tallón, F. (2018). Barriers to Learning and School Participation for Students with Dyslexia: Voices of Families. *Int. J. Educ. Soc. Justice*, *8*, 113–130.

Frith, U. (2017). Beneath the surface of developmental dyslexia. In *Surface dyslexia* (pp. 301–330). Routledge. doi:10.4324/9781315108346-18

Goldfus, C. (2012). Knowledge foundations for beginning reading teachers in EFL. *Annals of Dyslexia*, *62*(3), 204–221. doi:10.100711881-012-0073-5 PMID:22815105

Goswami, U., Ziegler, J. C., & Richardson, U. (2005). The effects of spelling consistency on phonological awareness: A comparison of English and German. *Journal of Experimental Child Psychology*, *92*(4), 345–365. doi:10.1016/j.jecp.2005.06.002 PMID:16087187

Gregory, G. H., & Chapman, C. (2012). *Differentiated instructional strategies: One size doesn't fit all*. Corwin.

Griva, E., & Kofou, I. (2017). *Alternative assessment in Language learning: Challenges and Practices*. Kyriakidis.

Hallahan, D. P., Pullen, P. C., Kauffman, J. M., & Badar, J. (2020). Exceptional learners. In Oxford Research Encyclopedia of Education.

Harrar, V., Tammam, J., Pérez-Bellido, A., Pitt, A., Stein, J., & Spence, C. (2014). Multisensory integration and attention in developmental dyslexia. *Current Biology*, *24*(5), 531–535. doi:10.1016/j.cub.2014.01.029 PMID:24530067

Hertberg-Davis, H., & Brighton, C. M. (2006). Support and sabotage: Principals' influence on middle school teachers' responses to differentiation. *Journal of Secondary Gifted Education*, *17*(12), 90–102. doi:10.4219/jsge-2006-685

Holmes, L. F. (2008). *Teachers' perceptions of a differentiated instruction professional development program*. The University of Alabama.

Hornstra, L., Denessen, E., Bakker, J., van den Bergh, L., & Voeten, M. (2010). Teacher attitudes toward dyslexia: Effects on teacher expectations and the academic achievement of students with dyslexia. *Journal of Learning Disabilities*, *43*(6), 515–529. doi:10.1177/0022219409355479 PMID:20445201

Irwin, D. A., Arslan-Ari, I., & Morris, W. (2022). Teachers' value beliefs and usage of one- to-one devices for students with dyslexia: A descriptive study. *Education and Information Technologies*. doi:10.100710639-022-11450-5 PMID:36438651

Jiménez-Fernández, G., Vaquero, J. M., Jiménez, L., & Defior, S. (2011). Dyslexic children show deficits in implicit sequence learning, but not in explicit sequence learning or contextual cueing. *Annals of Dyslexia*, *61*(1), 85–110. doi:10.100711881-010-0048-3 PMID:21082295

Johnson, E. (2010). *Improving students' academic achievement through differentiated instruction* [Doctoral dissertation, Retrieved from ProQuest Dissertations & Theses Full Text].

Johnston, V. (2019). Dyslexia: What reading teachers need to know. *The Reading Teacher*, *73*(3), 339–346. doi:10.1002/trtr.1830

Joshi, R. M., Binks, E., Graham, L., Dean, E., Smith, D., & Boulware-Gooden, R. (2009). Do textbooks used in university reading education courses conform to the instructional recommendations of the National Reading Panel? *Journal of Learning Disabilities, 42,* 458e463.

Jurchiş, R., & Dienes, Z. (2023). Implicit learning of regularities followed by realistic body movements in virtual reality. Psychonomic Bulletin & Review, 30(1), 269-279.

Kelly, M. L., Yeigh, T., Hudson, S., Willis, R., & Lee, M. (2022). Secondary teachers' perceptions of the importance of pedagogical approaches to support students' behavioural, emotional and cognitive engagement. *Australian Educational Researcher*, 1–23.

Kelly, S. W., Griffiths, S., & Frith, U. (2002). Evidence for implicit sequence learning in dyslexia. *Dyslexia (Chichester, England)*, *8*(1), 43–52. doi:10.1002/dys.208 PMID:11990224

Khursheed, F., & Ansari, U. (2012). Effects of innovative teaching strategies on students' performance. *Global Journal of Human Social science. Linguistics and Education, 12*(10), 46–54.

Knight, C. (2018). What is dyslexia? An exploration of the relationship between teachers' understandings of dyslexia and their training experiences. *Dyslexia (Chichester, England), 24*(3), 207–219. doi:10.1002/dys.1593 PMID:30019501

Kormos, J. (2020). Specific learning difficulties in second language learning and teaching. *Language Teaching, 53*(2), 129–143. doi:10.1017/S0261444819000442

Kormos, J., & Nijakowska, J. (2017). Inclusive practices in teaching students with dyslexia: Second language teachers' concerns, attitudes and self-efficacy beliefs on a massive open online learning course. *Teaching and Teacher Education, 68*, 30–41. doi:10.1016/j.tate.2017.08.005

Kotob, M. M., & Abadi, M. A. (2019). The influence of differentiated instruction on academic achievement of students in mixed ability classrooms. *International Linguistics Research, 2*(2), 8–28. doi:10.30560/ilr.v2n2p8

Lammertink, I., Boersma, P., Wijnen, F., & Rispens, J. (2017). Statistical learning in specific language impairment: A meta-analysis. *Journal of Speech, Language, and Hearing Research: JSLHR, 60*(12), 3474–3486. doi:10.1044/2017_JSLHR-L-16-0439 PMID:29149241

Livingston, E. M., Siegel, L. S., & Ribary, U. (2018). Developmental dyslexia: Emotional impact and consequences. *Australian Journal of Learning Difficulties, 23*(2), 107–135. doi:10.1080/19404158.2018.1479975

Lozano-Álvarez, M., Rodríguez-Cano, S., Delgado-Benito, V., & Mercado-Val, E. (2023). A Systematic Review of Literature on Emerging Technologies and Specific Learning Difficulties. *Education Sciences, 13*(3), 298. doi:10.3390/educsci13030298

Lyon, G. R., Shaywitz, S. E., & Shaywitz, B. A. (2003). A definition of dyslexia. *Annals of Dyslexia, 53*(1), 1–14. doi:10.100711881-003-0001-9 PMID:24234186

Malatesha, J. (2009). Do textbooks used in university reading education courses conform to the instructional recommendations of the National Reading Panel? *Journal of Learning Disabilities, 42*(5), 458–463. doi:10.1177/0022219409338739 PMID:19531632

Malik, S., & Janjua, F. (2011). Learning styles and teaching strategies: Creating a balance. *Language in India, 11*, 268–278.

Marchetti, R., Pinto, S., Spieser, L., Vaugoyeau, M., Cavalli, E., El Ahmadi, A., & Colé, P. (2023). Phoneme Representation and Articulatory Impairment: Insights from Adults with Comorbid Motor Coordination Disorder and Dyslexia. Brain Sciences, 13(2), 210.

Navarro-Haro, M. V., Modrego-Alarcón, M., Hoffman, H. G., Lopez-Montoyo, A., Navarro-Gil, M., Montero-Marin, J., García-Palacios, A., Borao, L., & García-Campayo, J. (2019). Evaluation of a mindfulness-based intervention with and without virtual reality dialectical behavior therapy mindfulness skills training for the treatment of generalized anxiety disorder in primary care: A pilot study. [CrossRef]. *Frontiers in Psychology, 10*, 55. doi:10.3389/fpsyg.2019.00055 PMID:30745888

Newcombe, F. R. I. E. D. A., & Marshall, J. C. (2017). Reading and writing by letter sounds. In *Surface dyslexia* (pp. 35–52). Routledge. doi:10.4324/9781315108346-4

Nicolson, R. I., & Fawcett, A. J. (1990). Automaticity: A new framework for dyslexia research? *Cognition, 35*(2), 159–182. doi:10.1016/0010-0277(90)90013-A PMID:2354611

Nicolson, R. I., & Fawcett, A. J. (1994). Comparison of deficits in cognitive and motor skills among children with dyslexia. *Annals of Dyslexia, 44*(1), 147–164. doi:10.1007/BF02648159 PMID:24234050

Ohene-Djan, J., & Begum, R. (2008). Multisensory games for dyslexic children. In *2008 Eighth IEEE International Conference on Advanced Learning Technologies* (pp. 1040-1041). IEEE. 10.1109/ICALT.2008.98

Pavlidou, E. V., Louise Kelly, M., & Williams, J. M. (2010). Do children with developmental dyslexia have impairments in implicit learning? *Dyslexia (Chichester, England), 16*(2), 143–161. doi:10.1002/dys.400 PMID:20440744

Pavlidou, E. V., & Williams, J. M. (2014). Implicit learning and reading: Insights from typical children and children with developmental dyslexia using the artificial grammar learning (AGL) paradigm. *Research in Developmental Disabilities, 35*(7), 1457–1472. doi:10.1016/j.ridd.2014.03.040 PMID:24751907

Pennington, B. F., & Bishop, D. V. (2009). Relations among speech, language, and reading disorders. *Annual Review of Psychology, 60*(1), 283–306. doi:10.1146/annurev.psych.60.110707.163548 PMID:18652545

Peterson, R. L., & Pennington, B. F. (2012). Developmental dyslexia. *Lancet, 379*(9830), 1997–2007. doi:10.1016/S0140-6736(12)60198-6 PMID:22513218

Peterson, R. L., & Pennington, B. F. (2015). Developmental dyslexia. *Annual Review of Clinical Psychology, 11*(1), 283–307. doi:10.1146/annurev-clinpsy-032814-112842 PMID:25594880

Pfenninger, S. (2014). Taking L3 learning by the horns: Benefits of computer-mediated intervention for dyslexic school children. *Innovation in Language Learning and Teaching*.

Pham, A. V., & Riviere, A. (2015). Specific learning disorders and ADHD: Current issues in diagnosis across clinical and educational settings. *Current Psychiatry Reports, 17*(6), 1–7. doi:10.100711920-015-0584-y PMID:25894357

Pokrivčáková, S. (2015). *Teaching Foreign Languages to Learners with Special Educational Needs: e-textbook for foreign language teachers*. Constantine the Philosopher University., doi:10.17846/SEN.2015.7-28

Roodenrys, S., & Dunn, N. (2007). Unimpaired implicit learning in children with developmental dyslexia. *Dyslexia (Chichester, England), 14*(1), 1–15. doi:10.1002/dys.340 PMID:17624907

Rüsseler, J., Gerth, I., & Münte, T. F. (2006). Implicit learning is intact in adult developmental dyslexic readers: Evidence from the serial reaction time task and artificial grammar learning. *Journal of Clinical and Experimental Neuropsychology, 28*(5), 808–827. doi:10.1080/13803390591001007 PMID:16723326

Shaywitz, S. (2003). *Overcoming dyslexia: A new and complete science-based program for reading problems at any level*. Alfred A. Knopf.

Soriano-Ferrer, M., & Echegaray-Bengoa, J. (2014). A Scale of Knowledge and Beliefs about Developmental Dyslexia: Scale Development and Validation. *Procedia: Social and Behavioral Sciences, 132*, 203–208. doi:10.1016/j.sbspro.2014.04.299

Sousa, D. A., & Tomlinson, C. A. (2011). *Differentiation and the brain: How neuroscience supports the learner-friendly classroom*. Solution Tree Press.

Stein, J. (2018). What is developmental dyslexia? *Brain Sciences, 8*(2), 26. doi:10.3390/brainsci8020026 PMID:29401712

Thapliyal, M., Ahuja, N. J., Shankar, A., Cheng, X., & Kumar, M. (2022). A differentiated learning environment in domain model for learning disabled learners. Journal of Computing in Higher Education, 34(1), 60-82.

Tomlinson, C. A. (1995). Deciding to differentiate instruction in middle school: One school's journey. *Gifted Child Quarterly, 39*(2), 77–87. doi:10.1177/001698629503900204

Tomlinson, C. A. (1999). Mapping a route toward differentiated instruction. *Educational Leadership, 57*, 12–17.

Tomlinson, C. A. (2001). *How to differentiate instruction in mixed-ability classrooms*. Ascd.

Tomlinson, C. A. (2003). *Differentiation into practice. A resource guide for differentiating curriculum, grades K-5*. Association for Supervision and Curriculum Development.

Tomlinson, C. A. (2014). *The differentiated classroom: Responding to the needs of all learners* (2nd ed.). Association for Supervision and Curriculum Development.

Tomlinson, C. A., & Imbeau, M. (2010). *Leading and managing a differentiated classroom*. ASCD.

Tomlinson, C. A., & McTighe, J. (2006). *Integrating differentiated instruction & understanding by design: Connecting content and kids*. Association for Supervision and Curriculum Development.

Tomlinson, C. A., & Moon, T. R. (2013). *Assessment and student success in a differentiated classroom*. Association for Supervision and Curriculum Development.

Torff, B. (2011). Teacher beliefs shape learning for all students. *Phi Delta Kappan, 93*(3), 21–23. doi:10.1177/003172171109300305

Vail, P. L. (2001). *Treating the whole person: emotion, denial, disguises, language, and connectedness. Dyslexia: theory and good practice*. Whurr Publishing.

Vicari, S., Finzi, A., Menghini, D., Marotta, L., Baldi, S., & Petrosini, L. (2005). Do children with developmental dyslexia have an implicit learning deficit? *Journal of Neurology, Neurosurgery, and Psychiatry, 76*(10), 1392–1397. doi:10.1136/jnnp.2004.061093 PMID:16170083

Vickery, K. S., Reynolds, V. A., & Cochran, S. W. (1987). Multisensory teaching approach for reading, spelling, and handwriting, Orton-Gillingham based curriculum, in a public school setting. *Annals of Dyslexia, 37*(1), 189–200. doi:10.1007/BF02648066 PMID:24234994

Wadlington, E. M., & Wadlington, P. L. (2005). What educators really believe about dyslexia. *Reading Improvement*, *42*(1), 16–33.

Washburn, E. K., Joshi, R. M., & Binks-Cantrell, E. S. (2011). Teacher knowledge of basic language concepts and dyslexia. *Dyslexia, 17,* 165e183.

Wiggins, G. P., & McTighe, J. (2005). *Understanding by design*. Association or Supervision and Curriculum Development.

Zheng, B., Warschauer, M., Lin, C. H., & Chang, C. (2016). Learning in one-to-one laptop environments: A meta-analysis and research synthesis. *Review of Educational Research*, *86*(4), 1052–1084. doi:10.3102/0034654316628645

Chapter 5
Fostering Inclusive Education:
Collaborative Strategies, Emerging Technologies, and Parental Engagement for Children With Language Disorders

Efthymia Efthymiou
https://orcid.org/0000-0003-0411-1720
Zayed University, UAE

Dimitra Katsarou
https://orcid.org/0000-0001-8690-0314
University of the Aegean, Greece

ABSTRACT

This book chapter forcefully delves into the paramount topic of inclusive education for children with language disorders, unearthing the undeniable efficacy and significance that lie in furnishing an equitable and buttressed learning environment. The imperative of early intervention and vigilant surveillance takes center stage, spotlighting the fundamental responsibility of pinpointing and redressing individual requisites within multifaceted classrooms. The call within the chapter is collaboration among teachers, speech-language therapists, parents, and invested stakeholders. Through a sweeping scrutiny of empirical investigations and research conclusions, the chapter exposes the resplendent influence of inclusive education on scholastic accomplishments, linguistic outcomes, and socio-emotional maturation in children beset by language disorders. It probes the formidable obstacles encountered, including paucity of resources and the clamor for specialized services.

1. INTRODUCTION AND CONTEXT SETTING

Amidst the diverse educational pursuits, the endeavor of fostering inclusive education for children with language disorders is of paramount significance. This chapter undertakes a comprehensive exploration of inclusive education that transcends conventional integration paradigms, casting a vision for an en-

DOI: 10.4018/979-8-3693-1982-6.ch005

riched environment that not only embraces diversity but also fosters the comprehensive linguistic and holistic development of each child. Rooted deeply in empirical research and practical application, this chapter divulges an inclusive education approach aligned with the principles of equity and unobstructed access to learning, particularly tailored for learners with language disorders (Salend, 2016; Artiles & Kozleski, 2016).

The terrain we traverse is marked by significant challenges, where the presence of language disorders can impede effective communication, impinge on academic advancements, and curtail the fluidity of social interactions. This discourse is grounded in a commitment to robust research and substantiated practice, revealing a multi-dimensional approach to inclusive education that transcends theoretical ideals and ventures into actionable strategies. This exploration revolves around the significance of equitable and supportive learning environments - a realm where education is not just dispensed, but where ecosystems are curated to enable children to prosper academically, socially, and emotionally (Smith et al., 2018).

Having laid this essential groundwork, our course naturally shifts towards the practical strategies that form the core of productive inclusive education. The pillars of early intervention and vigilant oversight propel us forward, championing the cause of effectively addressing the distinctive needs of children with language disorders. This juncture in our discourse bridges the chasm between theoretical paradigms and actionable endeavors. It heralds the need for rigorous collaborative efforts between teachers, parents, and specialists, who collectively undertake the task of identifying and assiduously addressing linguistic challenges. In early intervention and surveillance, we discuss the inherent capacity ingrained in language development and academic accomplishments. This exploration is guided by empirical insights (Smith et al., 2018; Scarborough, 2001).

As our discussion deepens, a recurring theme emerges; the coordinated collaboration among teachers, speech-language therapists, parents, and stakeholders. This motif forms the foundation - an eloquent testimony to united efforts in fostering inclusive methodologies. Weaving research-supported perspectives, we contemplate the outcomes of cooperative initiatives in exposing the capacity of inclusive education.

2. EARLY INTERVENTION AND SURVEILLANCE

The cornerstone of effective inclusive education for children with language disorders resides in the strategic deployment of early intervention and vigilant surveillance. This chapter examines how these fundamental pillars establish a foundation upon which tailored support can be integrated in diverse classrooms. Through empirical research and scholarly inquiries, we will elucidate the compelling rationale behind these practices and highlight their essential role in fostering successful inclusion.

Early intervention stands as a resounding testament to the adage “a stitch in time saves nine”. The critical juncture of a child’s formative years is where the seeds of development are sown, and intervention at this stage can alter the course of their educational journey. Empirical evidence consistently highlights the positive impact of early intervention on language acquisition, cognitive development, and adaptive behavior (Landa 2018). By identifying potential language disorders and addressing them promptly, teachers and specialists can effectively preempt learning gaps and promote positive outcomes for these children. It is a keystone practice that not only addresses developmental challenges promptly but also lays the groundwork for tailored support mechanisms within diverse classrooms (Smythe et al. 2021). The concept of early intervention is grounded in the recognition that the early years of a child’s life are a period of remarkable plasticity and rapid growth. Research in developmental psychology highlights that neural pathways related to language acquisition and cognitive functions are most malleable during these formative years (Noble 2021). As such, timely intervention can capitalize on this neuroplasticity, fostering more optimal outcomes for children facing language disorders.

Empirical evidence overwhelmingly demonstrates that early intervention significantly impacts language development (Elder et al. 2017). Numerous studies have shown that early identification and intervention can lead to substantial gains in language skills, communication abilities, and overall cognitive development (Bradshaw, Koegel & Koegel 2017; Guralnick 2017). By addressing language difficulties at an early stage, teachers and specialists can help mitigate the risk of academic underachievement and social isolation often experienced by children with language disorders. Moreover, the benefits of early intervention extend beyond the realm of language proficiency. Haft et al. (2019) revealed that early intervention positively influences social and emotional development, contributing to improved self-esteem, interpersonal relationships, and overall well-being. These findings highlight the cascading effects of early intervention, wherein nurturing language skills early on can lead to broader positive outcomes across various facets of a child's life.

In the context of inclusive education, early intervention assumes even greater significance. By proactively identifying language disorders and implementing targeted interventions, teachers can provide children with the scaffolding needed to access and engage with the curriculum effectively (Landa 2018; Guralnick 2017). This proactive approach levels the playing field, enabling children with language disorders to participate actively in classroom activities, interact with peers, and cultivate a sense of belonging. Landa (2018) mentions that as advancements in the field enable the earlier identification of autism spectrum disorders (ASD), the demand for evidence-based insights into early intervention continues to escalate. This comprehensive review delves into the literature of ASD early intervention (EI) over the last 15 years, focusing on efficacy studies. This analysis encompasses the neurodevelopmental context for early intervention, optimal initiation timing, predominant intervention approaches, and predictors of treatment outcomes. The collective evidence resoundingly underlines the efficacy of early interventions for young children with ASD. Notably, parents, through a parent-coaching intervention, acquire child-responsive engagement strategies that positively impact the child's developmental trajectory. Combining parent-mediated and direct clinician-implemented interventions emerges as a potent strategy to maximize developmental gains. Moreover, the central role of inclusive education amplifies the significance of early intervention. In the realm of inclusive education, the proactive identification of language disorders gains prominence. By promptly identifying these challenges and deploying targeted interventions, teachers become adept at providing the necessary scaffolding for children to proficiently access and engage with the curriculum. This proactive stance transcends mere accommodation; it empowers children with language disorders to actively participate in classroom activities, foster meaningful interactions with their peers, and cultivate an abiding sense of belonging within the educational context. However, the efficacy of early intervention hinges on timely and accurate identification. This highlights the importance of collaborative efforts between teachers, parents, and specialists. A comprehensive assessment process, informed by research-based tools and benchmarks, is essential for early detection. Once identified, the implementation of evidence-based interventions tailored to the unique needs of each child becomes paramount (Kansas State Department of Education 2018).

Vigilant surveillance, an integral companion to early intervention, amplifies the efficacy of tailored support. The astute monitoring of a child's linguistic progress allows teachers and stakeholders to dynamically adjust strategies, ensuring that interventions remain aligned with the evolving needs of each child. Research by Vietze & Lax (2020) substantiates that continuous assessment and surveillance lead to more precise and effective interventions. While the primary focus of the study pertains to ASD, parallels can be drawn between its findings and the concept of continuous assessment and surveillance in the context of language disorders. The study points out the significance of early intervention in addressing developmental challenges. This aligns with the broader perspective of identifying language disorders early in children's lives. Just as the study emphasizes timely intervention for ASD, this principle applies to language disorders as well. Continuous assessment and surveillance, integral components of both the ASD study and the discourse on language disorders, enable teachers and professionals to proactively monitor language development and identify potential issues. Moreover, the study's outcomes highlight the positive impact of targeted interventions on various developmental domains, including cognition, communication, and socio-emotional skills. This insight can be extrapolated to language disorders, underscoring the potential benefits of tailored interventions that directly address language challenges. The role of continuous assessment and surveillance becomes evident here, as they provide a nuanced understanding of each child's linguistic needs, guiding the implementation of effective interventions.

Vigilant surveillance serves as an ongoing monitoring and assessment process that informs tailored support strategies, ensuring that interventions remain attuned to the evolving needs of each individual student (Mitchell & Sutherland 2020). It operates on the premise that the learning trajectory of a child with a language disorder is not linear, but rather dynamic and subject to fluctuations. This understanding acknowledges that the challenges these children face can manifest differently over time, necessitating a flexible and adaptable approach to intervention. Studies have demonstrated that consistent and systematic monitoring of language development enables teachers and specialists to make timely adjustments to intervention plans, optimizing their effectiveness (Lipkin et al. 2020). This iterative process not only prevents stagnation but also capitalizes on moments of growth and progress, thus facilitating more meaningful and impactful learning experiences. Furthermore, vigilant surveillance acts as a diagnostic compass, guiding teachers and specialists to identify emerging difficulties, strengths, and areas of progress. Through regular assessments, practitioners gain insights into specific linguistic domains that require further attention, allowing them to tailor interventions with precision (Crothers et al. 2020). This individualized focus ensures that support efforts are concentrated where they are most needed, thus maximizing the potential for positive outcomes.

In the context of inclusive education, vigilant surveillance assumes heightened significance. The diverse classroom comprises students with varying learning profiles, necessitating a responsive and personalized approach. By monitoring the progress of children with language disorders within this context, teachers can ensure that interventions are aligned with the curriculum, accommodating individual needs while promoting active participation and engagement (Wilcox, Gray & Reiser 2020). Moreover, vigilant surveillance facilitates a proactive response to potential challenges. Should a student's progress plateau or regress, teachers can swiftly identify the factors at play and make necessary adjustments. This proactive stance is essential for preventing the entrenchment of learning gaps and ensuring that children with language disorders continue to make strides toward their educational goals (Brown 2017). However, the implementation of vigilant surveillance is contingent upon rigorous assessment tools and methodologies. Research-based instruments, such as standardized language assessments and developmental milestones, provide the quantitative data required to track progress accurately. Qualitative observations, coupled with ongoing communication between teachers, parents, and specialists, add a qualitative dimension to the surveillance process, enabling a comprehensive understanding of a child's linguistic development (Lal & Kishore 2020). By remaining attuned to the ebb and flow of linguistic progress, vigilant surveillance embodies the essence of inclusive education; a responsive, dynamic, and commitment to supporting every learner.

The potency of these foundational pillars reaches its zenith when synergized through collaborative efforts. Inclusive education is not a solitary endeavor; it thrives on the collaboration of various stakeholders. The dynamic interplay among teachers, speech-language therapists, parents, and invested stakeholders constitutes a potent force that reshapes the contours of education. Research conducted by Mugambi (2017) highlights collaborative work, demonstrating that coordinated efforts lead to more comprehensive and holistic support systems. Furthermore, this collaborative synergy engenders impact on the creation of an inclusive educational environment. It cultivates a context where expertise is pooled, insights are shared, and a holistic perspective is adopted to tailor education to individual needs. The cooperative engagement of stakeholders fosters an ecosystem that not only acknowledges diversity but actively celebrates it, thereby promoting a culture of inclusion that resonates beyond the confines of the classroom.

3. SYNERGISM FOR SUCCESSFUL INCLUSION

Advocating for collaborative efforts among teachers, speech-language therapists, parents, and stakeholders in fostering inclusion is a cornerstone of progressive educational practices. Ogletree et al. (2017) stress that the concept of collaborative efforts among teachers, speech-language therapists, parents, and stakeholders in fostering inclusion is a cornerstone of progressive educational practices. The study provides a detailed illustration of a case involving a child with severe disabilities, showcasing the significance of interprofessional collaboration in ensuring comprehensive and effective support for the child's development. According to Ogletree et al. (2017), the case study of Mary exemplifies the power of collaborative efforts among various professionals in the education and healthcare sectors. Teachers, speech-language therapists, parents, and other stakeholders are portrayed as integral members of a multidisciplinary team that works collectively to address the unique needs of the child. This collaborative approach goes beyond individual expertise and seeks to leverage the strengths of each team member to create a holistic and inclusive educational environment. Collaboration is not confined to a single professional discipline but extends to a diverse array of experts who contribute to the child's growth. Teachers, speech-language therapists, and parents are recognized for contributing to Mary's progress. Through regular communication, joint planning, and shared decision-making, the collaborative team ensures that Mary receives consistent and targeted support across various aspects of her development, including communication, academic achievements, and social interactions. Moreover, the study demonstrates that collaborative efforts transcend the boundaries of the classroom and encompass a broader ecosystem that includes families, service providers, and community members. By actively involving parents in the collaborative process, the team empowers them to become advocates and partners in their child's education. This approach enhances the quality of support Mary receives and fosters a strong sense of partnership and trust between school and home.

The collaboration between teachers and speech-language therapists offers a potent partnership that amplifies the impact of interventions. Speech-language therapists bring specialized expertise in understanding language disorders, assessing individual needs, and implementing evidence-based strategies. By working in tandem with teachers, they help tailor instruction and support that directly address the linguistic challenges faced by children with language disorders. This collaboration ensures that therapeutic efforts integrate into the classroom environment, promoting consistent language development across various settings (Valle & Connor 2019; Wilson, McNeill & Gillon 2017). The study conducted by Wilson, McNeill, and Gillon (2017) delves into the realm of inter-professional education (IPE), particularly focusing on the collaboration between student speech-language therapists (SLTs) and student teachers. Preliminary investigations into IPE have indicated the potential benefits of workshop-based applications in preparing participants for collaborative practice. This study seeks to expand upon these findings by exploring the integration of IPE into students' professional practice placements, aiming to develop attitudes, knowledge, and skills conducive to inter-professional collaboration. The primary aim of the study is to comprehend how student SLTs, and student teachers cultivate competence for collaborative practice while working together during professional practice placements, specifically in the context of supporting children's speech and literacy development. Through this investigation, the study endeavors to contribute to the advancement of knowledge concerning effective design and evaluation of inter-professional education initiatives, thereby shedding light on strategies that foster collaborative practice between SLTs and teachers in the pursuit of improving children's speech and literacy skills. The study's emphasis on inter-professional collaboration aligns with the importance of joint efforts between speech-language therapists and teachers to enhance the educational experiences and outcomes of children with language disorders.

Stakeholders, including administrators, policymakers, and professionals advocate for an inclusive educational environment. Their support in allocating resources, fostering a culture of acceptance, and implementing policies that prioritize inclusion creates an enabling atmosphere. Collaborative advocacy efforts ensure that the needs of children with language disorders are placed at the forefront of educational agendas, leading to systemic changes that benefit all students (McGregor 2020). Their support ensures that policies are designed to prioritize inclusion, and the necessary infrastructure is in place.

In addition, the role of parents in collaborative efforts cannot be understated. Research highlights that parental engagement is a pivotal factor in achieving positive outcomes for children with language disorders (Park & Holloway 2017). This collaborative engagement bolsters a sense of partnership between home and school, amplifying the impact of interventions (Đurišić & Bunijevac 2017). The study conducted by Park and Holloway (2017) delves into the intricate relationship between school-based parental involvement (PI) and its impact on academic achievement at both the child and elementary school levels. Within the context of school reform efforts, policymakers acknowledge the crucial role of PI, yet the evidence of its influence on student achievement remains inconclusive. Utilizing data from the Early Childhood Longitudinal Study-Kindergarten Cohort dataset, the study undertook a comprehensive exploration of the long-term effects of three distinct types of school-based PI: PI aimed at assisting an individual child (private-good PI), PI aimed at enhancing the school (public-good PI), and PI through peer networking. Through hierarchical linear modeling analyses, the study unearthed intriguing insights. All three types of school-based PI were found to positively impact student-level achievement in mathematics. However, only private-good PI demonstrated a connection with reading achievement. On a broader scale, both public-good PI and parent networking contributed to school-level achievement. Interestingly, the study highlighted that the effects of PI were not uniform across socioeconomic status (SES) groups. Both public-good and private-good PI exhibited a stronger association with student-level mathematics achievement for high SES students. Conversely, aggregated private-good PI showed a more pronounced correlation with school-level achievement in low-SES schools. These findings offer empirical evidence regarding the effectiveness of school-based PI in bolstering academic achievement. Importantly, the role of parents in collaborative efforts cannot be understated. Research highlights that parental engagement is a paramount factor in achieving positive outcomes for children with language disorders. Parents are integral members of the collaborative team, offering insights into their child's strengths, challenges, and preferences. Their involvement in goal setting, decision-making, and sharing of home-based strategies bridges the gap between home and school, reinforcing the child's language development and overall growth. The study's conclusions underline the multifaceted nature of parental involvement in educational contexts and emphasize its potential to influence academic outcomes at both the student and school levels.

4. EMPIRICAL INVESTIGATIONS AND RESEARCH FINDINGS

A comprehensive scrutiny of empirical research on the impact of inclusive education for children with language disorders reveals insights into the positive effects of inclusive practices on various aspects of their development. Inclusive classrooms have consistently been associated with enhanced academic achievements, improved language outcomes, and positive social-emotional growth for children with language disorders. The study by Kerch et al. (2020) delves into the language and social-emotional development of children, comparing those with disabilities to those without, within the context of a statewide pre-kindergarten program. The findings of this study suggest that an inclusive learning environment can have a positive impact on both language and social-emotional development for children with disabilities. The integration of children with disabilities alongside their typically developing peers appears to foster not only academic growth but also social interactions, contributing to a more holistic developmental trajectory. This underscores the significance of creating inclusive environments that cater to diverse learning needs and promote well-rounded development.

Research consistently highlights the academic benefits of inclusive education for these children. Studies have shown that when children with language disorders are educated in inclusive settings, they achieve greater academic progress compared to those in segregated environments. In the study conducted by Chen et al. (2020), which investigates the social networks of children with developmental language disorder in inclusive preschool programs, the findings shed light on the benefits of inclusive environments. The study highlights that children with developmental language disorders who are enrolled in inclusive preschool programs tend to have more diverse and extensive social networks compared to their peers in non-inclusive settings. This suggests that inclusive environments provide opportunities for children with developmental language disorders to interact and form connections with a broader range of peers. The presence of typically developing peers in these inclusive settings appears to facilitate social interactions and relationships, contributing to enhanced social integration and potentially mitigating the risk of social isolation often associated with language disorders. Moreover, inclusive classrooms offer exposure to a diverse range of instructional strategies and peer interactions, fostering language and cognitive development. This inclusive approach supports academic growth in various subjects, including reading, mathematics, and writing. Gargiulo and Metcalf (2022) emphasize the advantages of learning in inclusive environments for acquiring skills in various subjects. They highlight that inclusive classrooms where students with diverse abilities learn together, offer a conducive setting for fostering academic growth. The inclusive approach, guided by the principles of Universal Design for Learning (UDL), supports students with special needs and benefits typically developing students. The authors contend that in inclusive classrooms, students with disabilities are exposed to the same curriculum as their peers, and this exposure to grade-level content can lead to improved learning outcomes. By participating in the same instructional activities and assignments as their peers, students with disabilities could engage with challenging content and acquire subject-specific skills. This inclusive approach also encourages collaboration, peer learning, and shared problem-solving, promoting a supportive and enriching learning environment for all students. Furthermore, they suggest that inclusive education nurtures a sense of belonging and community among students, fostering positive attitudes towards diversity and reducing stigma. Students with disabilities who receive targeted support within the inclusive classroom setting are more likely to feel valued and empowered, leading to increased self-esteem and motivation. As a result, they are more likely to actively participate in academic tasks and exhibit greater perseverance in acquiring subject-related skills.

Language outcomes are also significantly impacted by inclusive education. Children with language disorders in inclusive classrooms benefit from consistent language-rich environments, peer models, and targeted interventions. These factors contribute to improved vocabulary acquisition, enhanced language comprehension, and more effective communication skills. The presence of typically developing peers provides a conducive setting for language learning, where children with language disorders have opportunities to engage in meaningful conversations and interactions. Archibald (2017) stresses that maintaining a language-rich environment within the inclusive classroom setting is pivotal. This approach ensures that children with language disorders are consistently exposed to a variety of vocabulary and language structures, which aids in enhancing their vocabulary acquisition and language comprehension skills. This enriched language environment provides ample opportunities for these students to engage in meaningful interactions and conversations, fostering their overall communication abilities. Secondly, the influence of peer models is noted as a significant contributor to the progress of children with language disorders. Inclusive classrooms often comprise a diverse group of students, including those with typical language development. Interactions with these peers serve as valuable opportunities for children with language disorders to observe and learn from their peers' language and communication skills. This process of observational learning can positively impact their language development and communication abilities, as they strive to emulate their peers' effective communication strategies. Lastly, collaborative efforts between speech-language pathologists (SLPs) and teachers play a crucial role in designing and implementing interventions. By addressing specific language challenges through evidence-based interventions, children with language disorders can experience improved language skills and enhanced communication abilities. The collaboration between SLPs and teachers ensures that interventions are integrated into the classroom context, maximizing their impact on the students' language development.

Moreover, inclusive education has a positive impact on the social-emotional development of children with language disorders. Brown (2019) highpoints the significance of inclusive classrooms in fostering positive peer interactions and promoting the development of essential social skills, e.g., empathy, and self-esteem. The study features that inclusive educational settings provide a unique platform for children with diverse abilities, including those with language disorders, to interact and collaborate with their peers in meaningful ways. According to Brown (2019), inclusive classrooms serve as environments where students of varying abilities work together, learn from one another, and build relationships. The interactions that take place within these classrooms provide valuable opportunities for children with language disorders to engage with their peers, share experiences, and communicate effectively. These positive peer interactions contribute to the development of essential social skills, such as cooperation, communication, and problem-solving, which are integral for successful social integration. Moreover, an inclusive environment nurtures empathy among all students, fostering a deeper understanding and appreciation of each other's strengths and challenges. As students collaborate and learn alongside their peers with language disorders, they gain insights into different communication styles and strategies. This firsthand experience enables them to develop empathy and sensitivity towards their peers' unique needs, creating a more inclusive and compassionate school climate. In addition, inclusive classrooms bolster the self-esteem of children with language disorders. When these students actively participate in classroom activities, contribute ideas, and engage in discussions, they experience a sense of accomplishment and validation. The acceptance and recognition from their peers and teachers contribute to a positive self-perception, boosting their confidence and overall self-esteem.

5. CHALLENGES AND OVERCOMING OBSTACLES

The implementation of inclusive education for children with language disorders is not devoid of challenges, as evidenced by research findings that highlight significant hurdles, including resource constraints and the demand for specialized services. Westwood (2018) recognizes the substantial challenge presented by resource constraints in the successful implementation of inclusive education. Within the context of inclusive classrooms, the acquisition of additional resources, spanning personnel, materials, and assistive technologies, becomes imperative. These resources play a focal role in effectively addressing the diverse and unique needs of children. The resource emphasizes the significance of allocating these resources to create an environment that fosters equitable access and quality education for all learners. In doing so, it aligns with the fundamental principles of inclusive education, striving to provide every child with the necessary support for meaningful learning and growth. However, limited budgets and inadequate funding can hinder schools from providing necessary accommodations and supports. This constraint can negatively impact the quality of education for all students, including those with language disorders, creating an urgent need for equitable resource allocation. The study conducted by Vincent and Chiwandire (2019) accentuates a critical aspect of inclusive education - the influence of financial constraints on its implementation. The research illuminates how limited budgets and insufficient funding can pose substantial barriers for educational institutions striving to provide necessary accommodations and supports for students with disabilities. This financial challenge not only hampers the ability to create an inclusive environment but also reverberates throughout the educational ecosystem, potentially compromising the quality of education for all students. In essence, the study highlights the intricate interplay between funding availability, equitable access, and the overall educational experience within the context of inclusive education.

The demand for specialized services further complicates the implementation of inclusive education. Children with language disorders often require targeted interventions and support from speech-language therapists, special teachers, and other professionals. However, the availability of these specialized services may be limited, leading to challenges in providing comprehensive and individualized support within inclusive classrooms. The scarcity of speech-language therapists and other experts can result in insufficient attention to the specific language needs of children with language disorders, impeding their progress. The study by Farquharson, Therrien, Barton-Hulsey, and Brandt (2022) underlines a critical aspect that has direct implications for the provision of inclusive education. Within the discourse of the shortage of qualified speech-language pathologists (SLPs) in public schools, the availability of specialized services becomes a focal point of concern. This scarcity of qualified professionals, such as SLPs and other experts, engenders challenges in offering comprehensive and individualized support within inclusive classrooms. The potential consequences of this scarcity highlight the limited availability of specialized professionals that lead to a shortfall in addressing the unique language needs of children with speech and language disorders. The broader context of inclusive education necessitates tailored interventions and focused attention to cater to the diverse needs of students, including those with language challenges. However, the shortage of specialized personnel can impede the delivery of such targeted services, potentially compromising the quality and efficacy of language support provided to these students. The scarcity of these specialized services serves as a pertinent reminder of the systemic challenges that must be addressed to ensure that every child receives the necessary and individualized support in an inclusive learning environment.

Addressing these challenges necessitates innovative approaches and strategic solutions. The work by Stepanova et al. (2018) aligns with the central themes emphasized in the discussion surrounding inclusive education for children with language disorders. Despite not directly addressing this specific group, the article underscores principles that hold relevance to the difficulties faced by these children. The call for advocacy in securing increased funding and resource allocation aligns with the need to ensure that inclusive classrooms have the necessary tools and support to effectively address the unique needs of children with language disorders. This resonates with the imperative to provide specialized services, assistive technologies, and tailored interventions that can facilitate language development and scholastic achievements in this population. Moreover, there is emphasis on collaboration among teachers, administrators, parents, and stakeholders reflecting a parallel effort to devise creative strategies and utilize available resources efficiently. This collaborative approach can extend to children with language disorders, involving speech-language therapists, parents, and teachers in a concerted effort to provide comprehensive support and create a truly inclusive learning environment. The importance of investing in professional development for teachers and specialists aligns with the expertise needed to effectively address the linguistic challenges faced by children with language disorders. This aligns with the necessity of equipping teachers and speech-language therapists with evidence-based strategies and interventions that promote language development and overall growth among these children.

Furthermore, collaborative resource-sharing models can alleviate the constraints posed by limited resources. Schools can partner with community organizations, speech-language therapy centers, and local universities to access expertise and resources that support children with language disorders. Collaborative efforts between teachers and external experts can enhance the quality of support provided and expand the range of available interventions. The findings of the study conducted by Biggs, Bumble, and Hacker (2022) resonate with the overarching principles discussed in this discourse on inclusive education for children with language disorders. While the study's focus is not explicitly on language disorders, it sheds light on the significance of collaborative networks in the context of special education and speech-language pathology. This aligns with the notion that educational institutions can extend their collaborations beyond traditional boundaries to enhance the support for children with language disorders. The study points out that schools can establish partnerships not only within their own faculty but also with external entities such as community organizations, speech-language therapy centers, and local universities. These partnerships can facilitate access to a wider range of expertise and resources that contribute to effective support for children with language disorders. Collaborative efforts, whether within the school environment or through external alliances, could enrich the quality of assistance provided to these children. Additionally, leveraging technology can offer cost-effective solutions, such as online professional development programs for teachers and remote support from speech-language therapists.

Strategic resource allocation also involves prioritizing the use of available resources to provide targeted support for children with language disorders. Implementing a tiered support system allows teachers to allocate resources based on the intensity of each student's needs. This approach ensures that students receive the level of intervention and assistance required for their optimal development. By focusing resources on evidence-based practices and interventions, teachers can maximize their impact on children's language skills and overall academic progress. The study conducted by Ahtiainen, Pulkkinen, and Jahnukainen (2021) offers valuable insights that parallel the concept of implementing a tiered support system, a vital approach in inclusive education for children with language disorders. While the study primarily delves into the broader context of inclusive and special education reforms in Finland, its emphasis on tiered support systems is inherently linked to the idea of allocating resources based on individual student needs, a crucial aspect for children facing language disorders. Inclusive education discourse advocates for tiered support systems, which involve tailoring interventions to match the varying intensities of students' needs. This notion strongly aligns with the findings of the study, as it explores the restructuring of support mechanisms within the Finnish education system. This kind of approach ensures that all students, including those with language disorders, receive the level of intervention and assistance necessary for their optimal growth and development. Moreover, the study's emphasis on evidence-based practices and interventions aligns with the principle of making the most of available resources to enhance students' language skills and overall academic progress. By aligning resources with strategies grounded in research, teachers can effectively address the specific linguistic challenges faced by students with language disorders, thereby contributing significantly to their comprehensive educational advancement.

Building upon the strategic allocation of resources and research-backed approaches discussed earlier, our exploration now shifts to Leveraging Emerging Technologies. This section delves into how technology, when integrated thoughtfully, can further enhance the learning experiences of students with language disorders.

6. LEVERAGING EMERGING TECHNOLOGIES

Inclusive education is undergoing a technological revolution, capturing the attention of teachers struggling with novel approaches to accommodate the intricate needs of children with language disorders. At the forefront of this change lie assistive technologies, to amplify the learning and communication capabilities of these students within inclusive classrooms. Augmentative and Alternative Communication (AAC) devices, including communication boards and speech-generating devices, emerge as focal instruments, enabling nonverbal students to assert their voices and actively partake in classroom dialogues. The implications are immense as students with limited verbal communication proficiency are propelled into the heart of academic engagements and social interactions. In this debate, Chambers' seminal work (2020) on assistive technology's role in fortifying inclusive education finds its resonance. At the vanguard stand AAC devices, exemplified by communication boards and speech-generating tools, offering a gateway for nonverbal students to articulate thoughts and actively shape classroom interactions. The resultant impact is significant, as these instruments empower children with restricted verbal communication abilities to embrace the dynamism of academic pursuits and social exchanges. The outcome is twofold, an elevation of overall engagement and a nurturing of language development among students with language disorders.

Virtual Reality (VR) and Augmented Reality (AR) technologies offer immersive and interactive learning experiences that can enhance the language skills and comprehension of children with language disorders. The insights gleaned from Li and Wong's (2021) comprehensive literature review resonate with the concept that Virtual Reality (VR) and Augmented Reality (AR) technologies could enrich language learning and development. These cutting-edge tools provide an avenue for not only immersive but also interactive learning experiences, offering an innovative approach to nurturing language skills and enhancing overall comprehension. These technologies come to life through virtual simulations, granting children the opportunity to engage in true-to-life scenarios, enabling them to practice authentic conversations and navigate social decisions within an environment that is both controlled and supportive. By embracing these innovative technologies, children with language disorders can effectively cultivate and refine their pragmatic language abilities, ultimately empowering them to navigate complex social interactions with greater confidence and efficacy, thereby contributing substantially to their holistic language development.

Furthermore, the relationship between personalized learning platforms and educational apps and the principles highlighted by Peng, Ma, and Spector (2019) substantiates a compelling argument. These platforms and apps possess the innate capacity to finely calibrate their features to cater to the specific requirements of children with language disorders, thereby heralding a new era of differentiated instruction and targeted interventions. The aspects of personalized adaptive learning, encapsulating the nuances of individual attributes, performance, development, and adaptability, find a vivid reflection in the design and functionality of these technologies. By integrating adaptive content and activities that dynamically respond to each child's progress and learning preferences, these tools establish an intricate connection with personalized adaptive learning. This dynamic interaction empowers children with language disorders to access learning materials that are attuned to their unique capabilities, ensuring that instruction unfolds at a pace and style aligned with their individual learning preferences. Thus, the confluence of personalized adaptive learning principles and the innovative capabilities of personalized learning platforms and educational apps stands as compelling evidence in shaping the learning experiences of children with language disorders.

Nonetheless, the successful integration of digital technologies in education necessitates comprehensive training for teachers to harness their potential within classroom settings. Ensuring the efficacy of these tools in catering to the diverse learning needs of children with language disorders within inclusive education environments hinges on several vital considerations. Accessibility, equitable access, and adherence to evidence-based practices are fundamental aspects that must be meticulously addressed. Drawing a parallel to Gabriel et al.'s (2022) exploration of digital education strategies worldwide, it becomes evident that while the infusion of technology holds promise, its effectiveness rests on the foundation of teacher preparedness and a commitment to addressing the unique needs of all learners. In both contexts, the convergence of technology and education points out the need for proactive measures while upholding the principles of inclusivity.

7. CULTIVATING INCLUSIVE SCHOOL CULTURE

Cultivating an inclusive school culture is essential for creating an environment that supports the academic, social, and emotional development of all students, including those with language disorders. An all-encompassing school culture that values diversity and fosters a sense of belonging is instrumental in supporting the holistic growth of children with language disorders. Ainscow's study (2020) on promoting inclusion and equity in education aligns with the ideals presented in the discourse of an inclusive school culture that nurtures the holistic development of all students, irrespective of their individual backgrounds or challenges. The inclusive school ethos characterized by values such as tolerance, enlightenment, and camaraderie among students, teachers, and stakeholders, echoes Ainscow's call for making education more inclusive and equitable. This convergence features the shared recognition of addressing challenges and ensuring equitable opportunities for diverse learners within the educational context. Furthermore, the principles articulated, encompassing the reduction of social isolation, enhancement of socio-emotional well-being, and cultivation of positive peer relationships, harmonize with the foundational principles underpinning Ainscow's perspective. The notion that fostering an inclusive educational environment, which values diversity, embraces inclusive practices, and places a strong emphasis on the overall growth and well-being of students, is a vital stride toward educational equity and enriched learning experiences.

However, cultivating an inclusive school culture requires deliberate efforts and ongoing commitment. The study conducted by Themane and Thobejane (2019) underpins the role of teachers as change agents in implementing inclusive education within challenging contexts. This echoes the notion that fostering an inclusive school culture requires deliberate and persistent efforts. The study's emphasis on teachers' resilience and commitment aligns with the idea that professional development opportunities are crucial for equipping teachers with the necessary skills to create an inclusive classroom and school environment. Moreover, the study's recognition of teachers' willingness to effect change and their collaboration with others mirrors the collaborative spirit necessary for cultivating inclusivity. Collaborating with families emerges as a key aspect highlighted by the study as well. This collaboration reinforces the partnership between schools and parents, promoting inclusivity both within the classroom and beyond. Furthermore, addressing challenges and achieving more through collaboration reduce social seclusion for children with language disorders. Creating a supportive environment that encourages collaboration and interaction provides opportunities for children's positive social interactions, meaningful friendships, and enhanced self-esteem.

Teachers play an instrumental role in facilitating social integration by promoting collaborative learning, group projects, and peer interaction activities. Peer buddy programs, where typically developing peers support children with language disorders in various activities, have proven effective in fostering social interactions and reducing feelings of seclusion. Addressing social seclusion also involves creating a classroom environment that values and respects individual differences. Teachers can implement activities that promote empathy, understanding, and appreciation of diverse abilities, fostering an inclusive culture where every student feels accepted and valued. Efthymiou (2023) emphasizes that teachers are essential in facilitating social integration through collaborative learning, group projects, and peer interactions. Timler's (2018) review of conversation intervention approaches for children and adolescents with autism spectrum disorder (ASD) sheds light on effective strategies that can be extended to support students with language disorders in inclusive education. While the focus of Timler's work is on individuals with ASD, the principles discussed hold valuable insights for fostering successful social interactions among all students. Timler emphasizes the significance of pragmatic language approaches, social skill approaches, and peer-focused approaches to enhance conversation skills. These approaches, which involve teaching verbal and nonverbal communication skills, initiating conversations, recognizing communication breakdowns, and engaging with peers, align closely with the objectives of inclusive education. Drawing from Timler's insights, teachers can leverage social skills instruction to explicitly teach children with language disorders the necessary skills for effective social interactions. By focusing on turn-taking, active listening, nonverbal communication cues, and initiating conversations, teachers empower these students to confidently navigate social situations and build meaningful connections with their peers. Incorporating strategies from Timler's review, teachers can create an inclusive classroom environment where students with diverse needs, including those with language disorders, acquire the skills essential for successful communication and social engagement. This proactive approach not only fosters a sense of belonging for these students but also contributes to a more cohesive and integrated classroom community. Exploring tangible lessons, the case study of Johann, a student with unique requirements, illustrates the dynamics of obstacles and achievements that children with language disorders experience within inclusive learning environments.

8. ILLUSTRATIVE CASE STUDY: JOHANN'S EXPERIENCE OF INCLUSIVE EDUCATION

The case study of Johann, sourced from the U.S. Department of State's website (Wiig 2004), provides a compelling illustration of the potential of inclusive education for children with language disorders. His experience encapsulates key takeaways, reinforcing the central themes discussed in this chapter.

Johann's developmental trajectory unfolded normally until concerns about his language abilities surfaced in kindergarten. Despite struggles with articulation and dysfluency, no language evaluation was conducted at the time, causing a delay in the timely intervention he required. By second grade, Johann's challenges became more pronounced, leading to a diagnosis of a language-based learning disability. While his Performance IQ was high, his Verbal IQ remained in the low-average range. Difficulties in decoding, reading comprehension, spelling, and writing were attributed to delays in vocabulary acquisition and sentence formulation. This diagnosis marked a turning point, prompting specialized services provided by speech-language pathologists and learning disabilities specialists within the school's resource room. Johann's linguistic strengths and weaknesses became evident as he faced language tests and tasks, revealing moderate-to-severe deficits in expressive language skills, auditory memory, and recall of spoken language. These challenges significantly impacted his academic progress, particularly within inclusive educational settings. An important moment in Johann's narrative unfolded when he was considered for admission to an international school. Language test results served as admission criteria, raising concerns about his ability to learn in English. This led to a temporary separation of Johann's family to facilitate education in his native language, enabling him to graduate high school and pursue engineering studies.

This case highlights the need for early intervention and comprehensive language assessment to promptly identify and address language disorders. Johann's story emphasizes the significance of tailored support services within inclusive classrooms, highlighting the crucial role of collaboration among teachers, specialists, and parents. A comprehensive assessment of Johann's linguistic strengths and weaknesses could have better supported his learning within an inclusive framework. This is a compelling testimony to the necessity of comprehensive assessment, early intervention, and collaborative efforts in creating an inclusive educational environment where all children, irrespective of their language challenges, can thrive academically, socially, and emotionally. Johann's case highlights the significance of collaborative efforts between teachers, specialists, and parents in guiding students towards successful academic and personal development. This leads us to another crucial aspect of inclusive education; the indispensable role of parental engagement and advocacy in shaping an effective and nurturing educational environment.

9. ROLE OF PARENTAL ENGAGEMENT AND ADVOCACY

The role of parents in inclusive education is critical, encompassing both active engagement and advocacy, as they collaborate with teachers and professionals to ensure the success of their children with language disorders. The study by Boonk, Gijselaers, Ritzen, and Brand-Gruwel (2018) provides valuable insights into the relationship between parental involvement and academic achievement. The study underlines certain indicators of parental involvement, such as reading at home, setting high expectations for academic achievement, maintaining effective communication with children about school, and providing encouragement and support for learning, correlate positively with academic outcomes. Research consistently shows that engaged parents who participate in school activities, communicate with teachers, and attend meetings often have children who exhibit motivation, positive behavior, and improved academic performance. This supports the idea that parental involvement is a key component in fostering success within inclusive education.

Engaged parents wield a significant influence when collaborating with teachers and specialists, actively participating in the formulation and review of Individualized Education Plans (IEPs) tailored to their child's specific language needs. The support offered by Dillon et al. (2021) robustly reinforces the role of engaged parents in fostering collaborative partnerships with teachers and specialists to craft and assess IEPs that are finely tuned to their children's language requirements. The study notably underscores the essential contribution of professionals who share their expertise and skills within the context of interdisciplinary collaboration - a sentiment that closely aligns with how engaged parents offer invaluable insights during IEP meetings, thereby shaping the development of impactful interventions based on their child's strengths, challenges, and preferences. This synergy between professionals' inputs and parents' contributions is further mirrored in the collaborative design of instructional strategies achieved through interdisciplinary teamwork within the IEP team. The reciprocal nature of this dynamic reinforces the notion that both professionals and parents play instrumental roles in coordinating comprehensive interventions for children with language disorders. The interconnectedness continues as the collaborative partnerships Dillon et al. (2021) highlight among professionals align with the collaborative partnerships that engaged parents foster with teachers, speech-language therapists, and school administrators. These partnerships, whether formed within the IEP team or between parents and educational stakeholders, share the common goal of driving changes that amplify inclusivity and bolster the triumph of children with language disorders.

Moreover, this holistic engagement of parents extends to effective communication channels established between parents and teachers - an additional cornerstone of parental empowerment. The establishment of open lines of dialogue serves as a conduit for the exchange of progress updates, challenges, and strategies, ensuring that parents remain well-informed and engaged participants in their child's overall well-being. As such, the intertwined aspects of collaborative IEP development, interdisciplinary teamwork, and parental engagement accentuate a cohesive narrative of collective efforts aimed at fostering an inclusive and educational environment. According to Darling-Hammond et al. (2018), the active involvement of parents translates into tangible benefits for students, encompassing improved school attendance, heightened engagement in learning activities, and increased self-assurance in their capabilities. However, the impact of parental empowerment in inclusive education reverberates on a systemic scale as well. Engaged and empowered parents could advocate for policies that champion inclusion, for equitable resource distribution, and bolster support structures within the broader educational framework.

10. CONCLUSION

The exploration of inclusive education for children with language disorders reveals interconnected factors that collectively contribute to their holistic growth and success within diverse educational settings. In fostering an inclusive environment, the essential role of teachers emerges prominently. Teachers stand as linchpins in cultivating an inclusive classroom culture, tapping into evidence-based strategies and interventions to address linguistic challenges head-on (Lal & Kishore 2020). By aligning resources with research-grounded methodologies, teachers can effectively tailor interventions to meet the unique linguistic needs of students with language disorders (Landa 2018). Emerging technologies have further broadened the horizons of inclusive education. Assistive technologies and virtual reality platforms offer transformative tools for enhancing language skills and social interaction capabilities among children with language disorders (Chambers, 2020). Leveraging augmented and virtual reality, teachers can create immersive learning experiences that bridge linguistic gaps and empower children to navigate complex social scenarios (Li & Wong, 2021).

However, the power of inclusive education transcends technological tools. The cornerstone of successful inclusion lies in the collaborative efforts of engaged parents, who collaborate with teachers to design and review Individualized Education Plans (IEPs) (Dillon et al., 2021). By actively participating in IEP meetings, parents provide invaluable insights that inform the development of tailored interventions, mirroring the interdisciplinary teamwork approach advocated by professionals (Timler, 2018). This collaborative ethos extends beyond IEPs to encompass the cultivation of an inclusive school culture. Engaged parents bolster their children's education by fostering an environment of acceptance, where diversity is valued, and empathetic attitudes are promoted (Themane & Thobejane 2019). By collaborating with teachers, parents establish an inclusive school culture that empowers children with language disorders to engage confidently in social interactions and peer relationships (Darling-Hammond et al. 2018; Timler, 2018).

In this endeavor, teachers, parents, and professionals converge to amplify the voices and perspectives of children with language disorders. The collective efforts of stakeholders, combined with advancements in technology and pedagogy, co-actively foster an inclusive education approach that transcends challenges and barriers. The path to inclusive education is one marked by collaboration, innovation, and commitment.

REFERENCES

Ahtiainen, R., Pulkkinen, J., & Jahnukainen, M. (2021). The 21st century reforms (re) shaping the education policy of inclusive and special education in Finland. *Education Sciences*, *11*(11), 750. doi:10.3390/educsci11110750

Ainscow, M. (2020). Promoting inclusion and equity in education: Lessons from international experiences. *Nordic Journal of Studies in Educational Policy*, *6*(1), 7–16. doi:10.1080/20020317.2020.1729587

Archibald, L. M. (2017). SLP-educator classroom collaboration: A review to inform reason-based practice. *Autism & Developmental Language Impairments*, *2*, 2396941516680369. doi:10.1177/2396941516680369

Biggs, E. E., Bumble, J. L., & Hacker, R. E. (2022). Professional networks of special educators and speech-language pathologists working with students who use augmentative and alternative communication. *Remedial and Special Education*, 07419325221128497.

Boonk, L., Gijselaers, H. J., Ritzen, H., & Brand-Gruwel, S. (2018). A review of the relationship between parental involvement indicators and academic achievement. *Educational Research Review, 24*, 10–30. doi:10.1016/j.edurev.2018.02.001

Bradshaw, J., Koegel, L. K., & Koegel, R. L. (2017). Improving functional language and social motivation with parent-mediated intervention for toddlers with autism spectrum disorder. *Journal of Autism and Developmental Disorders, 47*(8), 2443–2458. doi:10.100710803-017-3155-8 PMID:28536956

Brown, C. S. (2019). The importance and the challenges to ensuring an inclusive school climate. *Educational Psychologist, 54*(4), 322–330. doi:10.1080/00461520.2019.1655646

Brown, G. T. (2017). *Assessment of student achievement.* Routledge. doi:10.4324/9781315162058

Chambers, D. (2020). Assistive technology supporting inclusive education: Existing and emerging trends. *Assistive technology to support inclusive education*, 1-16.

Chen, J., Justice, L. M., Rhoad-Drogalis, A., Lin, T. J., & Sawyer, B. (2020). Social networks of children with developmental language disorders in inclusive preschool programs. *Child Development, 91*(2), 471–487. doi:10.1111/cdev.13183 PMID:30417944

Crothers, L. M., Hughes, T. L., Kolbert, J. B., & Schmitt, A. J. (2020). *Theory and cases in school-based consultation: A resource for school psychologists, school counselors, special educators, and other mental health professionals.* Routledge. doi:10.4324/9780429029974

Darling-Hammond, L., Cook-Harvey, C. M., Flook, L., Gardner, M., & Melnick, H. (2018). *With the whole child in mind: Insights from the Comer School Development Program.* ASCD.

Dillon, S., Armstrong, E., Goudy, L., Reynolds, H., & Scurry, S. (2021). Improving special education service delivery through interdisciplinary collaboration. *Teaching Exceptional Children, 54*(1), 36–43. doi:10.1177/00400599211029671

Đurišić, M., & Bunijevac, M. (2017). Parental involvement as an important factor for successful education. *Center for Educational Policy Studies Journal, 7*(3), 137–153. doi:10.26529/cepsj.291

Efthymiou, E. (2023). Amplifying Voices, Empowering Perspectives: Exploring the Experiences of Children with Disabilities in Inclusive Education During the Pandemic. In Inclusive Phygital Learning Approaches and Strategies for Students with Special Needs (pp. 1-32). IGI Global.

Elder, J. H., Kreider, C. M., Brasher, S. N., & Ansell, M. (2017). Clinical impact of early diagnosis of autism on the prognosis and parent–child relationships. *Psychology Research and Behavior Management, 10*, 283–292. doi:10.2147/PRBM.S117499 PMID:28883746

Farquharson, K., Therrien, M., Barton-Hulsey, A., & Brandt, A. F. (2022). How to recruit, support, and retain speech-language pathologists in public schools. *Journal of School Leadership, 32*(3), 225–245. doi:10.1177/1052684620966062

Gabriel, F., Marrone, R., Van Sebille, Y., Kovanovic, V., & de Laat, M. (2022). Digital education strategies around the world: Practices and policies. *Irish Educational Studies, 41*(1), 85–106. doi:10.1080/03323315.2021.2022513

Gargiulo, R. M., & Metcalf, D. (2022). *Teaching in today's inclusive classrooms: A universal design for learning approach*. Cengage Learning.

Guralnick, M. J. (2017). Early intervention for children with intellectual disabilities: An update. *Journal of Applied Research in Intellectual Disabilities*, *30*(2), 211–229. doi:10.1111/jar.12233 PMID:26764896

Haft, S. L., Chen, T., LeBlanc, C., Tencza, F., & Hoeft, F. (2019). Impact of mentoring on socio-emotional and mental health outcomes of youth with learning disabilities and attention-deficit hyperactivity disorder. *Child and Adolescent Mental Health*, *24*(4), 318–328. doi:10.1111/camh.12331 PMID:31649490

Kansas State Department of Education. (2018). *Kansas full-day kindergarten guide*. KSDE. https://files.eric.ed.gov/fulltext/ED598986.pdf

Kerch, C. J., Donovan, C. A., Ernest, J. M., Strichik, T., & Winchester, J. (2020). An exploration of language and social-emotional development of children with and without disabilities in a statewide pre-kindergarten program. *Education & Treatment of Children*, *43*(1), 7–19. doi:10.100743494-020-00002-6

Lal, R. S., & Kishore, M. T. (2020). Evidence-based Practices for Teaching Students with Learning Disabilities. In Oxford Research Encyclopedia of Education. doi:10.1093/acrefore/9780190264093.013.1222

Landa, R. J. (2018). Efficacy of early interventions for infants and young children with, and at risk for, autism spectrum disorders. *International Review of Psychiatry (Abingdon, England)*, *30*(1), 25–39. doi:10.1080/09540261.2018.1432574 PMID:29537331

Li, K. C., & Wong, B. T. M. (2021). A literature review of augmented reality, virtual reality, and mixed reality in language learning. *International Journal of Mobile Learning and Organisation*, *15*(2), 164–178. doi:10.1504/IJMLO.2021.114516

Lipkin, P. H., Macias, M. M., Norwood, K. W. Jr, Brei, T. J., Davidson, L. F., Davis, B. E., Ellerbeck, K. A., Houtrow, A. J., Hyman, S. L., Kuo, D. Z., Noritz, G. H., Yin, L., Murphy, N. A., Levy, S. E., Weitzman, C. C., Bauer, N. S., Childers, D. O. Jr, Levine, J. M., Peralta-Carcelen, A. M., ... Voigt, R. G. (2020). Promoting optimal development: Identifying infants and young children with developmental disorders through developmental surveillance and screening. *Pediatrics*, *145*(1), e20193449. doi:10.1542/peds.2019-3449 PMID:31843861

McGregor, K. K. (2020). How we fail children with developmental language disorder. *Language, Speech, and Hearing Services in Schools*, *51*(4), 981–992. doi:10.1044/2020_LSHSS-20-00003 PMID:32755505

Mitchell, D., & Sutherland, D. (2020). *What really works in special and inclusive education: Using evidence-based teaching strategies*. Routledge. doi:10.4324/9780429401923

Mugambi, M. M. (2017). Approaches to inclusive education and implications for curriculum theory and practice. *International Journal of Humanities Social Sciences and Education*, *10*(4), 92–106.

Noble, K. G. (2021). Early childhood: The opportunity to untap human potential. *The scale-up effect in early childhood and public policy: Why interventions lose impact at scale and what we can do about it*, 25-40.

Ogletree, B. T., Brady, N., Bruce, S., Dean, E., Romski, M., Sylvester, L., & Westling, D. (2017). Mary's case: An illustration of interprofessional collaborative practice for a child with severe disabilities. *American Journal of Speech-Language Pathology*, *26*(2), 217–226. doi:10.1044/2017_AJSLP-15-0065 PMID:28514476

Park, S., & Holloway, S. D. (2017). The effects of school-based parental involvement on academic achievement at the child and elementary school level: A longitudinal study. *The Journal of Educational Research*, *110*(1), 1–16. doi:10.1080/00220671.2015.1016600

Peng, H., Ma, S., & Spector, J. M. (2019). Personalized adaptive learning: An emerging pedagogical approach enabled by a smart learning environment. *Smart Learning Environments*, *6*(1), 1–14. doi:10.118640561-019-0089-y

Smythe, T., Zuurmond, M., Tann, C. J., Gladstone, M., & Kuper, H. (2021). Early intervention for children with developmental disabilities in low and middle-income countries–the case for action. *International Health*, *13*(3), 222–231. doi:10.1093/inthealth/ihaa044 PMID:32780826

Stepanova, G. A., Tashcheva, A. I., Stepanova, O. P., Menshikov, P. V., Kassymova, G. K., Arpentieva, M. R., & Tokar, O. V. (2018). The problem of management and implementation of innovative models of network interaction in inclusive education of persons with disabilities. *International journal of education and information technologies.*

Themane, M., & Thobejane, H. R. (2019). Teachers as change agents in making teaching inclusive in some selected rural schools of Limpopo Province, South Africa: Implications for teacher education. *International Journal of Inclusive Education*, *23*(4), 369–383. doi:10.1080/13603116.2018.1434690

Timler, G. R. (2018, April). Let's Talk: Review of Conversation Intervention Approaches for School-Aged Children and Adolescents with Autism Spectrum Disorder. [). Thieme Medical Publishers.]. *Seminars in Speech and Language*, *39*(02), 158–165. doi:10.1055-0038-1628367 PMID:29558770

Valle, J. W., & Connor, D. J. (2019). *Rethinking disability: A disability studies approach to inclusive practices*. Routledge. doi:10.4324/9781315111209

Vietze, P., & Lax, L. E. (2020). Early intervention ABA for toddlers with ASD: Effect of age and amount. *Current Psychology (New Brunswick, N.J.)*, *39*(4), 1234–1244. doi:10.100712144-018-9812-z

Vincent, L., & Chiwandire, D. (2019). Funding and inclusion in higher education institutions for students with disabilities. *African Journal of Disability*, *8*(1), 1–12. PMID:30899686

Westwood, P. (2018). *Inclusive and adaptive teaching: Meeting the challenge of diversity in the classroom*. Routledge. doi:10.4324/9781351061261

Wiig, E. (2004). Assessing Students for Successful Inclusion. In *Count Me In - Developing Inclusive International Schools*. Overseas Schools Advisory Council, Department of State, Washington, D.C. https://2009-2017.state.gov/m/a/os/45070.htm

Wilcox, M. J., Gray, S., & Reiser, M. (2020). Preschoolers with developmental speech and/or language impairment: Efficacy of the Teaching Early Literacy and Language (TELL) curriculum. *Early Childhood Research Quarterly*, *51*, 124–143. doi:10.1016/j.ecresq.2019.10.005

Wilson, L., McNeill, B., & Gillon, G. T. (2017). Inter-professional education of prospective speech–language therapists and primary school teachers through shared professional practice placements. *International Journal of Language & Communication Disorders*, *52*(4), 426–439. doi:10.1111/1460-6984.12281 PMID:27624388

Chapter 6
Language, Socio-Emotional Skills, and School Performance of Children and Adolescents With Developmental Language Disorder According to Parents' Perceptions

Asimina M. Ralli
National and Kapodistrian University of Athens, Greece

Maria Alexandri
National and Kapodistrian University of Athens, Greece

Maria Sofologi
https://orcid.org/0000-0003-0380-2220
University of Ioannina, Greece

ABSTRACT

The study investigates parents' perceptions of children and adolescents with DLD regarding their understanding of DLD, the developmental language history, their language, socio-emotional, and school performance profile, as well as to what extent oral language skills are associated with their school performance. One hundred parents of children with DLD completed a questionnaire. Most of the parents stated that their child started to communicate efficiently with others after four years of age. They defined DLD as articulation problems and language delay and they reported difficulties apart from articulation with expressive vocabulary, phonological awareness, syntax, etc. Most of the parents rated their child as extroverted with average self-esteem and good social relationships. They reported difficulties in oral lessons, spelling, writing, and reading. Significant relationships were found among oral language skills, narrative, writing, reading, and spelling. The results are discussed in terms of how parents understand DLD and their child's developmental profile.

DOI: 10.4018/979-8-3693-1982-6.ch006

INTRODUCTION

Developmental Language Disorder (DLD), previously known as Specific Language Impairment (SLI) is a common developmental disorder with unknown etiology characterized by a slow pace and deficits in language development (Bishop, 2015). Children with DLD present language problems that cannot be explained in terms of other cognitive, neurological, or perceptual deficits (Bishop et al., 2017; Bishop & Hayiou Thomas, 2008; Pennington & Bishop, 2009), while there is a discrepancy between their low oral language skills and a good index of non-verbal intelligence (Zarzo-Benlloch et al., 2017). Initially, it has been considered a childhood disorder, but research shows that it continues to affect individuals in adolescence and adulthood (Palikara et al., 2009).

From childhood and throughout adolescence parents play a key role in supporting their children's development. Parental awareness of their children's needs has been highlighted in previous studies (Adolf et al., 2017) in which it has also been found that the parents were frequently unaware of their children's difficulties. In parallel, according to Bishop et al., (2016), parents (when they are aware of their children's needs) are one of the main referral sources for identifying children with DLD before they start school (Bishop et al., 2016; Christopulos et al., 2020). A better understanding of parents' perceptions of their children with DLD could provide information that needs to be considered in the design of intervention programs for both parents and children in order to respond efficiently to their needs (Marshall, Harding, & Roulstone, 2017).

The last two decades, only a few studies have focused on investigating parents' perceptions of their children with DLD in different domains such as language, social and emotional skills, and school performance (Hobson et al. 2022; Lindsay et al., 2016; de Lopez et al., 2021; Pratt et al., 2006). Parents of children with DLD encounter a lack of familiarity with the terminologies used to characterize DLD and the possibility that the children's deficits may not be apparent (Forrest et al. 2018). Last, little is known about how parents understand the term DLD (Lopez et al. 2021), while their perspectives on the developmental language profile of those children is underinvestigated.

Therefore, the aim of the present study was to explore parents' perceptions regarding their understanding of DLD, the developmental language history, the oral language skills, and socioemotional profile as well as the school performance of their children with DLD in order to gain a holistic insight into the developmental profile of that group of children through the parents' lenses. Also, another aim of the study was to explore to what extent children's oral language skills are related to their school performance.

THE ORAL LANGUAGE PROFILE OF CHILDREN AND ADOLESCENTS WITH DEVELOPMENTAL LANGUAGE DISORDER ACCORDING TO THEIR PARENTS

In a significant epidemiological study, Tomblin et al., (1997) found that 70% of parents of kindergarten-aged children with DLD were ignorant of their child's language difficulties. Similar findings were found in two other studies with primary school children with DLD. In the first study, parents did not appear to be aware of their children's oral language difficulties (Hendricks et al., 2019) and in another study, parents reported no concerns about their child's speech and language, development (Adlof et al., (2017).

In a more recent research, Hobson et al., (2022), interviewed six parents of children with DLD regarding among others their child's language profile. One parent had been concerned about the child's early speech development but believed the problem would resolve later, and four out of the six parents had initially been concerned when their child was very young (between ages 1 and 2 years). One family, however, only became concerned when their child was around 7 years old (when it became apparent that his language lagged behind that of his younger sibling and younger sibling's peers). Three families (together with their experts) had first questioned if their child had DLD or other neurodevelopmental disorders before the age of 5 (between ages 2 and 4). Also, Auza, Murata & Penaloza (2023) found that parents of 4-6-year-old children with DLD were not accurate regarding the developmental language profile of their child mirroring the fact that parents may not always be aware of the developmental language milestones.

In contrast to the previous group of studies, de Lopez et al. (2021) interviewed ten parents of middle school-aged children with DLD from ten different countries and found that parents reported that their children face difficulties in semantics (e.g., cannot understand the difference between doctor and dentist), in communicating appropriately and maintaining the topic of a conversation in everyday situations. They also mentioned that their children had articulation difficulties.

It seems that in most of the few studies regarding the language profile of children with DLD, - except from de Lopez et al., (2021) the parents seem to be unaware of their child's difficulties, therefore among the aims of the present study was to further explore the above issues in the Greek setting.

THE SOCIO-EMOTIONAL SKILLS OF CHILDREN AND ADOLESCENTS WITH DEVELOPMENTAL LANGUAGE DISORDER ACCORDING TO THEIR PARENTS

Pratt et al., (2006) explored the characteristics and concerns of mothers of adolescents with a history of DLD, regarding their social interaction skills. The parents reported concerns about the adolescents' social behavior. They also mentioned that their adolescents expressed immature behavior, inability to control their anger, insecurity, hypersensitivity, and suffered from panic. It was also reported that they did not have many friends and they were at risk of bullying. In line with the above findings, in Harrison's et al., (2009) study, it was found that parents reported similar patterns of social difficulties for their elementary school children with DLD. In addition, they highlighted the difficulties of children participating and cooperating in working groups, a quite common educational practice in classroom settings.

Furthermore, according to Gough Kenyon et al., (2021), parents reported that their children with DLD had difficulties with social interaction and establishing long-lasting friendships. They also believed that this lack of social competence affected their children's quality of life in general. Furthermore, emotional and social difficulties as well as behavioral problems in comparison to their TD counterparts have been reported by the parents of children with DLD (Forrest et al., 2021; Burnley et al., 2023).

In the same line of results, Hobson et al., (2022) found that parents of children with DLD aged 7 to 17 years, with speech, language, and communication needs (SLCN) including parents of children with DLD reported that their children had a tough time expressing their feelings and reporting bad incidents, such as bullying, to adults. Hobson & Lee, (2022) in another study also found that parents of children 6 to 14 years old with DLD mentioned that their children with DLD used camouflaging or masked behaviors to achieve better conversational skills, such as relying on other people, avoiding choosing an environment where they need to use their language skills, using prosocial behaviors to be acceptable to others, choosing non-verbal communication, like smiling, or using disrupting behavior. These camouflaging behaviors were underlined by the parents of children with DLD as very exhausting tools for their children's emotional development.

Contradictory results to some extent for social relationships, were found by Lindsay et al., (2016) who investigated the perspectives of parents regarding the emotional and social needs of their children with DLD. The parents reported that their children, despite the language challenges they faced, occasionally had good relationships with their peers. Therefore, few and inconclusive findings exist regarding the socioemotional profile of children with DLD which may be related to the heterogeneity of the sample both on their language and socioemotional skills as well as their age and of course on the methodologies employed by the previous studies (interviews, questionnaires).

THE SCHOOL PERFORMANCE OF CHILDREN AND ADOLESCENTS WITH DLD ACCORDING TO THEIR PARENTS

Understanding and using both spoken and written language is an essential element for all the children in order to succeed in school (Adlof & Hogan, 2018; Conti-Ramsden et al., 2009). In addition to understanding and generating written language, children also learn through listening to and responding to their teacher's spoken language in the classroom (Adlof et al., 2017). In the last decades, only a few studies have investigated parents' perceptions about the school performance of their children with DLD (Adolf et al., 2017; Lindsay et al., 2016; McCabe, 2005; Pratt, 2006).

According to McCabe (2005), the parents of 6 years old children with DLD reported significant difficulties (a) in sustaining their attention during an ongoing school task, (b) in following instructions and rules, and (c) in completing homework tasks or any other task related to school. They also found that children with DLD were at a substantial risk of premature dropping out of school because they felt less "attached" to the school environment.

Also, Pratt et al., (2006) explored the characteristics and concerns of mothers of adolescents with a history of DLD, regarding among others, the school performance of their children. The parents reported concerns about the adolescents' educational achievement (e.g., reading), as well as their future. Lindsay et al., (2016) also examined the parents' perspectives of their elementary school children (8 and 9 years old) with language difficulties regarding their school performance. Parents reported difficulties in reading accuracy and reading comprehension and low levels of satisfaction regarding their children's educational progress. In another study, conducted by de Lopez et al., (2021) parents recognized also reading comprehension difficulties.

In contrast, Hendricks et al., (2019) found that a high percentage of parents of primary school children with DLD were unaware of their children's difficulties in reading accuracy and comprehension, while others were led by concerns of teachers due to children's low school performance.

The previous findings from this small group of studies demonstrate that children with DLD face difficulties with school performance, which are not always identified by their parents. Also, mainly reading has been examined and no other school subjects. There is a need to further examine how parents view their children's school performance in other domains apart from reading such as writing, spelling, narration, etc. in order to have a more holistic view of children's strengths and needs.

THE PRESENT STUDY

To the best of our knowledge, relatively little research has investigated the perceptions of parents of children and adolescents with DLD regarding their language profile, social-emotional skills, and school performance. Additionally, several earlier research has produced contradicting findings, such as those that concern children's friendships and social skills (Lindsay et al., 2016; Pratt et al., 2006; Sheila et al., 2021). Also, how parents understand the term DLD as well as the developmental language history of their children with DLD is under investigated.

The aim of the present study was to investigate how parents of children with DLD conceptualize DLD and the developmental language history of their children. Also, the multifaceted developmental profile of their children on language, socio-emotional skills, and school performance, was explored. Another aim of the study was to investigate possible relationships between oral language skills and school performance. We stated the following research questions: (a) What do parents know about DLD? (b) How do parents conceptualize the language, socio-emotional profile, and school performance, of their children with DLD? (c) To what extent children's oral language skills are correlated with their school performance?

METHODS

Participants

One hundred parents (69 mothers and thirty-one fathers) of 100 Greek-speaking children 3 to 18 years old, (39 were girls and sixty-one were boys), with DLD, participated in the study. Most of the parents (42%) were between 41-50 age years old, 38% were 31-40 years old, 11% were 21-30 years old 8% were 51-60 years old, and one participant was under 20 years old.

Most of the parents (43%) were university graduates, 31% of the parents had received a master's degree, 23% had attended Lyceum and 3% had attended mandatory education. Most of the children (77%) attended primary school (age range: 6-12 years old) while 14% of children attended high school (age range:12-18 years old) and 9% of the children were enrolled in kindergarten (age range:3-6 years old).

Measures

Parents completed an online questionnaire (Cronbach's a = 0.88), which was based on previous studies (Lindsay et al., 2016; Ralli et al., 2023). The questionnaire included six sections. Every section comprised of open-ended and Likert-type questions (*1= not good at all, 2= almost good, 3=good, 4=very good, 5=excellent).* The first section included questions concerning the demographic characteristics of the parents (*age, gender, and parents' educational level*) and their children (*age, gender, school grade, and diagnosis*). The second section included seven close-ended questions regarding the developmental language history of the children (e.g. *when their child began to talk, understand, and communicate, when the concerns about the child's language development began, who noticed the difficulties first*). The third section included an open-ended question regarding *parents' understanding of the term DLD*. The fourth section included two items concerning children's oral language skills. Parents were asked *if their child's oral language skills corresponded to those of their peers or not* in a close-ended question. Then they were asked *to evaluate the level of their child's oral language skills (receptive vocabulary, expressive vocabulary, conversation maintenance, articulation, change tone of voice, understanding of figurative language, syntax, grammar, phonological awareness)* on a five-point Likert scale. The fifth section included five close-ended questions about children's emotional and social skills (*whether parents considered their child to be extroverted or introverted, how would they describe his/her self-esteem, whether the child understands the difficulties he/she faces and how it feels about them, how would they describe their child's relationship with his/her peers*). In the last section, parents were asked *to evaluate their child's school performance in 5 domains*, narrative skills, reading, writing, spelling, and oral lessons on a basis of a five point-Likert scale (*1= not good at all, 2= almost good, 3=good, 4=very good, 5=excellent*),

Procedure

The research protocol for this study was approved by the Research Ethics Committee of the National and Kapodistrian University of Athens. The online questionnaire was created using Google Forms. Professionals working in public and private sectors in different geographical regions of Greece completed anonymously and voluntarily the online questionnaire. The link to the questionnaire was disseminated to the heads of educational and health services. The invitation explained the importance of collecting further information about DLD. In cases where the questionnaire was not completed, a reminder was sent to them two weeks later. The time needed for the completion of the questionnaire was approximately ten to fifteen minutes.

Results

The Developmental Language History of Children With DLD

Regarding the developmental language history of the children parents were asked to answer in about *what age range their children started to say their first words, comprehend language, and communicate efficiently with others, when they started to have concerns about their child's language and who was the first person who noticed the language difficulties.*

According to Figure 1, most of the parents (38%) reported that their child said his/her first word after the third year of age, 34% of the parents reported after the second year, 26% of the parents replied that their childr said the first words after their first year of age and 2% of the parents replied after the fourth year of age. Regarding the second question "*In about what age range did your child started to comprehend language,"* most of the parents (45%) replied that their child began to understand language after the second year of age, 32% after the first year of age, 21% after the third year of age and 2% after the fourth year of age.

As far as it concerns the third question "*In about what age range did your child started to communicate efficiently with others"* most of the parents (53%) replied after 4 years of age, 29% responded after 3 years of age, 12% of the parents reported that this happened after their child's 2nd birthday, and 6% of the parents answered after the 1st year of age. As it concerns "*when they started to have concerns about their child's language,"* most of the parents (60%) reported that they started to have concerns when their child was at the age of 3-4 years old, while 24% of the parents reported when their child was between 0-2 years of age. It is worth noting that 16% of parents started to have concerns when their child was 5-6 years old.

Regarding the question "*Who was the first person who noticed the language difficulties*" almost half of the sample (47%) replied that this was the mother, followed by the kindergarten teacher (16%), the pediatrician (15%), the father (9%), both parents (2%), the grandmother (1%) the nanny (1%), and the primary school teacher (1%).

Parents' Understanding of DLD

Parents were asked to report "*what do they think DLD is.*" Their responses were qualitatively analyzed and were grouped into 7 categories (a) *communication difficulties* (e.g. difficulty in the communication), (b) *language delay* (e.g. slow to learn to speak), (c) *general language difficulties* (e.g. difficulties in language development), (d) *comprehension difficulties* (e.g. not understanding language), (e) *difficulties in reading and writing* (e.g. they can't easily read and write), (f) *speech-articulation difficulties* (can't pronounce certain sounds, difficulties in speech) (g) *other* (immaturity, difficulties in school).

As it can be seen below in Figure 2, most of the parents (32%) think that DLD refers to "speech-articulation difficulties", while 31% of the parents thought that it is a "language delay". Furthermore, 27% of parents reported that DLD refers to "communication difficulties", 17% mentioned that DLD means "general language difficulties", 10% said that DLD refers to "comprehension difficulties", and 8% thought that DLD refers to "reading and writing difficulties". Last, 17% of parents reported "other answers", and 4% of the parents mentioned that they "did not know".

Figure 1. The developmental language history of the children with DLD

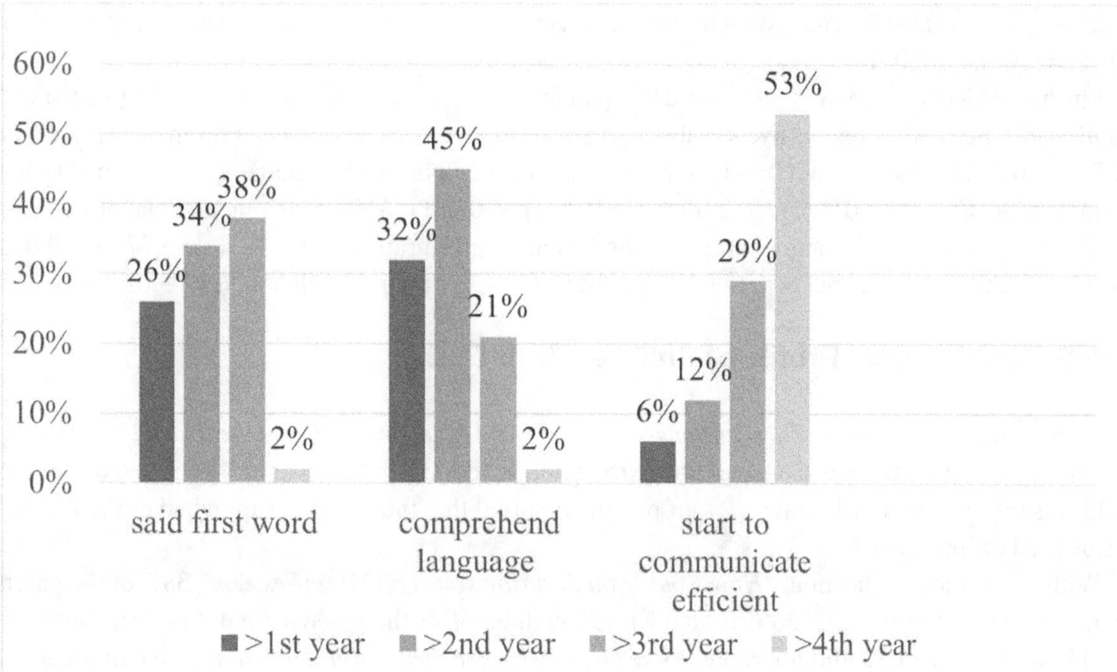

Figure 2. What do you think that DLD is?

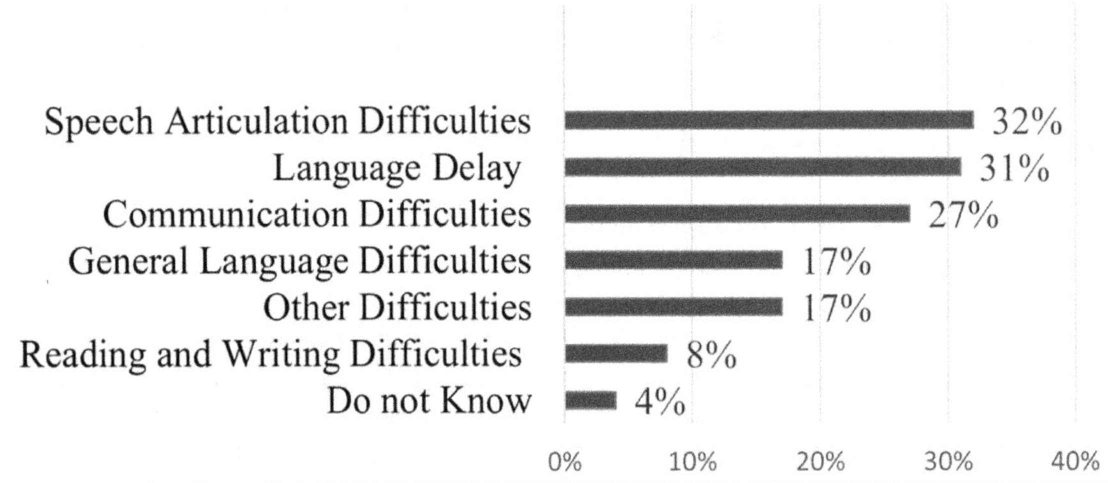

The Oral Language Profile of Children With DLD

Regarding the first question "*To what extent do parents think that their child's oral language skills were equivalent to his/her peers*," most of the parents (63%) acknowledged that their child's oral language skills were not equivalent to their peers.

When they were asked to evaluate the level of their child's oral language skills on a Likert-type scale (*1= not good at all, 2= almost good, 3-good, 4=very good, 5=excellent)*, receptive language and changing tone of voice were evaluated as "very good", while expressive vocabulary, conversation maintenance, and articulation, understanding of figurative language, syntax, grammar, and phonological awareness were rated as "good" (Table 1). According to the Friedman test, the differences were statistically significant ($x^2f(8)=170{,}71$ $p<0{,}001$).

Further, Wilcoxon comparisons showed that parents rated children's receptive vocabulary statistically significantly better than expressive vocabulary ($z= -4{,}40$, $p < 0{,}001$), conversation maintenance, ($z=-3{,}87$, $p < 0{,}001$), articulation, ($z= -5{,}29$, $p <0{,}001$), use of figurative language, ($z=-5{,}06$, $p < 0{,}001$), syntax, ($z=-6{,}47$, $p < 0{,}001$), and grammar, ($z=-6{,}54$, $p < 0{,}001$). Also, changing the tone of voice was rated as statistically significantly better than understanding figurative language, ($z=-3{,}77$, $p < 0{,}001$), and conversation maintenance was rated as significantly better than articulation, ($z= -3{,}01$, $p = 0{,}003$).

The Socioemotional Profile of Children With DLD

Regarding the first question "*Do you think that your child is introverted or extroverted?*" most of the parents (56%) characterized their child as extroverted while fewer parents (42%) answered that their child was introverted. Furthermore, 2% of parents reported that they are not sure whether their child is extroverted or introverted.

With respect to the question, "*How would you describe your child's self-esteem*" 38% of the parents evaluated this as "very good" 36% as "moderate", eighteen% of the parents rated it as "excellent", 5% rated it as "low", and 3% did not reply. As regards "*whether their child understands the language dif-*

Table 1. The oral language skills of the children with DLD according to their parents (1= not good at all, 2= almost good, 3-good, 4=very good, 5=excellent)

Oral language skills	N	Minimum	Maximum	Mean	Std. Deviation
Receptive vocabulary	100	1.00	5.00	3.62	0.92
Expressive vocabulary	100	1.00	5.00	3.31	0.88
Conversation maintenance	100	1.00	5.00	3.25	0.92
Articulation	100	1.00	5.00	2.92	0.97
Changing the tone of voice	100	1.00	5.00	3.51	0.95
Understanding of figurative Language	100	1.00	5.00	3.00	1.04
Syntax	100	1.00	5.00	2.53	1.18
Grammar	100	1.00	5.00	2.53	1.18
Phonological awareness	100	1.00	5.00	3.42	1.31

ficulties, he/she faces," 48% answered that they understand their language difficulties, whereas 31% replied that their child is not aware of their difficulties.

Concerning the question *"How does your child feel in relation to the language difficulties he/she faces,"* 32% of the parents mentioned that their child feels anxiety, 23% reported shame, 9% of the parents reported anger, and 5% mentioned fear. However, most (47%) of the parents answered that their child does not have any negative feelings. As it concerns the last question *"How you would evaluate your child's relationships with others,"* 35% of the parents characterized them as "very good", 28% as "excellent", 31% of the parents said they were "good", and 6% of the parents described the relationships with others as "not good".

The School Performance of Children With DLD

Regarding the school performance of children with DLD (Table 2), parents characterized their child's reading, spelling, and narrative skills at a "good" level, while the performance in oral lessons (e.g., history, geography, etc.) and writing were evaluated as "almost good. The differences were found to be statistically significant ($x^2f(4)=86,51$ $p<0,001$). Further Wilcoxon comparisons showed that parents rated children's performance in narrative skills to be statistically significantly better than in writing ($z=6,88$, $p < 0,001$) and in oral lessons, ($z= -5,79$, $p < 0,001$).

Relationship Between Oral Language Skills and School Performance

To determine if there is a correlation between children's oral language skills and their school performance a Spearman Rho correlation coefficient was used (Table 3). It was found that the narrative skills were statistically significantly correlated with receptive vocabulary [rho(100) = 0,63, p < 0,001], expressive vocabulary [[rho(100) = 0,61, p < 0,001], conversation maintenance [rho(100) = 0,69, p < 0,001], changing the tone of voice [rho(100) = 0,54, p < 0,001], understanding of figurative language [rho(100) = 0,53, p < 0,001], syntax [rho(100) = 0,43, p < 0,001], phonological awareness [rho(100) = 0,47, p < 0,001], grammar [rho(100) = 0,40, p < 0,001], and articulation [rho(100) = 0,32, p < 0,001].

Table 2. The school performance of children with DLD (1=not good at all, 2=almost good, 3=good, 4=very good, 5=excellent)

School performance	N	Minimum	Maximum	Mean	Std. Deviation
Narrative Skills	98	1.00	5.00	3.23	1.11
Writing	83	1.00	5.00	2.48	1.08
Reading	87	1.00	5.00	2.73	1.14
Spelling	85	1.00	5.00	2.56	1.10
Oral lessons	68	1.00	5.00	2.90	1.08

It was also found that writing was statistically significantly correlated with grammar [rho(100) = 0,66, p < 0,001], phonological awareness [rho(100) = 0,60, p < 0,001], the syntax [rho(100) = 0,65, p < 0,001], conversation maintenance [rho(100) = 0,50, p < 0,001], understanding of figurative language [rho(100) = 0,46, p < 0,001], expressive vocabulary [rho(100) = 0,43, p < 0,001], receptive vocabulary [rho(100) = 0,39, p < 0,001], articulation [rho(100) = 0,36, p < 0,001], and changing the tone of voice [rho(100) = 0,34, p < 0,001].

Reading was also found to be statistically significantly correlated with phonological awareness [rho(100) = 0,60, p < 0,001], grammar [rho(100) = 0,60, p < 0,001], syntax [rho(100) = 0,58, p < 0,001], articulation [rho(100) = 0,39, p < 0,001], understanding of figurative language [rho(100) = 0,36, p < 0,001], changing the tone of voice [rho(100) = 0,34, p < 0,001], conversation maintenance [rho(100) = 0,31, p < 0,001], expressive vocabulary [rho(100) = 0,27, p < 0,001], and receptive vocabulary [rho(100) = 0,18, p < 0,005].

Spelling was also statistically significantly correlated with grammar [rho(100) = 0,63, p < 0,001], phonological awareness [rho(100) = 0,60, p < 0,001], syntax [rho(100) = 0,59, p < 0,001], articulation [rho(100) = 0,39, p < 0,001], conversation maintenance [rho(100) = 0,33, p < 0,001], changing the tone of voice [rho(100) = 0,33 p < 0,001], understanding of figurative language [rho(100) = 0,28, p < 0,001], expressive vocabulary [rho(100) = 0,27, p < 0,005], and receptive vocabulary [rho(100) = 0,17, p < 0,005].

Last, statistically significantly correlations were found between oral lessons and grammar [rho(100) = 0,58, p < 0,001], syntax [rho(100) = 0,53, p < 0,001], phonological awareness [rho(100) = 0,47, p < 0,001], understanding of figurative language [rho(100) = 0,30, p < 0,001], conversation maintenance [rho(100) = 0,27, p < 0,001], articulation [rho(100) = 0,27, p < 0,001], expressive vocabulary [rho(100) = 0,24, p < 0,001], and receptive vocabulary [rho(100) = 0,21, p < 0,005].

DISCUSSION

The current study aimed to expand our knowledge on how parents of children and adolescents with DLD understand DLD, as well as the developmental language history of their children and their language, socioemotional skills, and school performance. Also, possible relationships between oral language skills and school performance were explored.

Concerning their children's developmental language history, a high percentage of parents stated that their child started: to speak after the third year, to understand language after the second year, to com-

Table 3. Correlations between oral language skills and school performance

	Narrative Skills	Writing	Reading	Spelling	Oral lessons
Receptive Vocabulary	0,63**	0,39**	0,18*	0,17*	0,21*
Expressive Vocabulary	0,61**	0,43**	0,27**	0,27*	0,24**
Conversation Maintenance	0,69**	0,50**	0,31**	0,33**	0,27**
Articulation	0,32**	0,36**	0,39**	0,39**	0,27**
Changing the tone of voice	0,54**	0,34**	0,34**	0,33**	0,14
Understanding of Figurative Language	0,53**	0,46**	0,36**	0,28**	0,30**
Syntax	0,43**	0,65**	0,58**	0,59**	0,53**
Grammar	0,40**	0,66**	0,60**	0,63**	0,58**
Phonological awareness	0,47**	0,60**	0,60**	0,60**	0,47**

*p < 0,05, **p < 0,01

municate effectively with others after the age of four. Furthermore, around the age of 3 to 4 years old, most parents began to worry about their child's language development. The current finding confirms a group of previous studies according to which parents recognized the delayed developmental language trajectories of their children as well as impairments in language, speech, and communication (Adlof et al., 2017; Lopez et al., 2021). Nevertheless, the present findings contradict with Auza et al., (2023) study who found that parents of 4-6-year-old children with DLD were not accurate regarding the developmental language profile of their child mirroring the fact that parents may not always be aware of language developmental milestones. Maybe these differences could be attributed to the diverse cultural contexts since the present results come from the Greek context, in which most of the parents are well educated while Auza et al., (2023) conducted their research in Mexico which is a developing country with limited resources. Additionally, in the present study, the mother was typically the first person to identify the language problems, which comes in accordance with Pratt et al., (2006).

Regarding parents' understanding of DLD, most of the participants defined it as "speech articulation difficulties" and as "a language delay." Fewer parents reported that DLD has to do with "communication difficulties," "general language difficulties," and "comprehension difficulties." It seems that parents define DLD as mostly language problems that can be easily seen, such as articulation problems, or language delay, when they probably compare their child's language performance with his/her peers. This hypothesis is also confirmed by the fact that in the current study, the parents acknowledged that their children's oral language skills were not at the same level as those of their peers.

Regarding parent's perceptions about their child's oral language skills, they reported that receptive language and changing tone of voice ranged in a better level than their expressive vocabulary, conversation maintenance, articulation, understanding of figurative language, syntax, grammar, and phonological awareness. Consequently, parents in the Greek setting seem to be aware of the language difficulties of their children. Similar results were also found by Adlof et al., (2017), however, another group of studies has found that a large number of parents are unaware of their child's difficulties with language (Hendricks et al., 2019; Tomblin et al., 1997). Maybe this could be attributed to the fact that Tomblin's study was conducted more than twenty years ago when all the research about DLD/SLI/SLCD was in the beginning and consequently, the parents were less aware of such difficulties.

When it comes to parents' perceptions regarding children's socioemotional skills half of the sample characterized their children as extroverted whereas the other half of the parents characterized them as introverted. Furthermore, most of the parents believed that their children have balanced self-esteem, while half of the participants reported that their child experiences fear, and anxiety due to language difficulties. Similar findings were reported by Forrest, Gibson, & St Clair, (2021) who showed that parents of adolescents with DLD reported more emotional difficulties in comparison to the parents with typically developing children. In the same line it has also been demonstrated by studies focusing on the children with DLD themselves, that they reported prominent levels of stress (Wadman et al., 2011).

Regarding the social relationships of their child with their peers a coherent pattern towards one or other direction was not evident since a large heterogeneity characterized the domain of social skills. The present findings confirm the heterogeneous profile of those children as well as the contradictory results from previous studies. For example, Lindsay et al. (2016) found that parents reported that their children, despite language challenges or difficulties had good relationships and interactions with their peers. Another group of studies have shown that children and adolescents with DLD, according to their parents have low social skills, poor social interaction that could exacerbate social problems by providing fewer opportunities to learn and practice social skills, as well as poor long-lasting relationships with their friends (Eadie et al., 2018; Burnley et al., 2023; Gough Kenyon et al., 2021; Hobson et al., 2022; Lopez et al., 2021; Mok et al., 2014; Voci et al., 2006).

Turning to school performance of children with DLD, parents characterized their child's reading, spelling, and narrative skills at an average level, while they reported more difficulties in oral lessons (e.g., history, geography, etc.) and writing. The above finding is consistent with previous studies, according to which oral expression is registering high percentages of difficulties for children with DLD diagnosis (e.g., Roello et al., 2015), due to impairments to short-term and working memory (Bishop et al., 2017). Additionally, young children with DLD often display poorer initial reading and writing skills and fail to catch up to their peers (Catts et al., 2006; Ralli et al., 2022).

Regarding the relationship between oral language skills and school performance, results revealed that narrative skills, writing, reading, and spelling were associated with vocabulary (receptive and expressive), conversation maintenance, syntax, phonological awareness, grammar, changing the tone of voice, understanding of figurative language and articulation. The above results confirm previous studies which show that oral language skills play a significant role in written text production (Ralli et al., 2022), that vocabulary, morphological and phonological skills predicts narrative speech in young children 5-7 years old (Ralli et. al.2021) as well as that reading is correlated with phonological awareness (Lara-Diaz et. al. 2021).

CONCLUSION

The purpose of the current study was to investigate parents' perceptions of children and adolescents with DLD regarding their understanding of DLD, the developmental language history of their children, their language, socio-emotional, and school performance profile. Also, the study explored to what extent children's oral language skills are associated with their school performance.

The information offered by parents is valuable and can help us understand language difficulties thoroughly through the parents' perspectives. Parents seem to acknowledge their child's language difficulties as well as potential problems in other developmental domains. They were also quite accurate about their child's oral language developmental history and thought that DLD has mainly to do with articulation difficulties and language delay. It is of vital importance to mention that this study was conducted for the first time in Greece, therefore future studies need to replicate and further explore parents' perceptions about DLD. Understanding the parents' views about the strengths and challenges of their children can contribute to a better understanding of the needs of both children and parents.

REFERENCES

Adlof, S. M., & Hogan, T. P. (2018). Understanding Dyslexia in the Context of Developmental Language Disorders. *Language, Speech, and Hearing Services in Schools*, *49*(4), 762–773. doi:10.1044/2018_LSHSS-DYSLC-18-0049 PMID:30458538

Adlof, S. M., Scoggins, J., Brazendale, A., Babb, S., & Petscher, Y. (2017). Identifying children at risk for language impairment or dyslexia with group-administered measures. *Journal of Speech, Language, and Hearing Research: JSLHR*, *60*(12), 3507–3522. doi:10.1044/2017_JSLHR-L-16-0473 PMID:29222567

Amin, M. S., & Harrison, R. L. (2009). Understanding Parents' Oral Health Behaviors for Their Young Children. *Qualitative Health Research*, *19*(1), 116–127. doi:10.1177/1049732308327243 PMID:18997150

Ash, A. C., Christopulos, T. T., & Redmond, S. M. (2020). "Tell me about your child": A grounded theory study of mothers understanding of language disorder. *American Journal of Speech-Language Pathology*, *29*(2), 819–840. doi:10.1044/2020_AJSLP-19-00064 PMID:32348158

Auza, B. A., Murata, C., & Penaloza, C. (2023). Predictive validity of a parental questionnaire for identifying children with developmental language disorders. *Frontiers in Psychology*, *14*, 14. doi:10.3389/fpsyg.2023.1110449

Bishop, D. V., & McDonald, D. (2009). Identifying language impairment in children: Combining language test scores with parental reports. *International Journal of Language & Communication Disorders*, *44*(5), 600–615. doi:10.1080/13682820802259662 PMID:19387886

Bishop, D. V. M., Snowling, M. J., Thompson, P. A., & Greenhalgh, T. (2017). Phase 2 of CATALISE: a multinational and multidisciplinary Delphi consensus study of problems with language development: Terminology. *Journal of Child Psychology and Psychiatry, and Allied Disciplines*, *58*(10), 1068–1080. doi:10.1111/jcpp.12721 PMID:28369935

Bishop, D. V. M., Snowling, M. J., Thompson, P. A., & Greenhalgh, T.Catalise Consortium. (2016). CATALISE: A multinational and multidisciplinary Delphi consensus study. Identifying language impairments in children. *PLoS One*, *11*(7), e0158753. doi:10.1371/journal.pone.0158753 PMID:27392128

Burnley, A., St Clair, M., Bedford, R., Wren, Y., & Dack, C. (2023). Understanding the prevalence and manifestation of anxiety and other socio-emotional and behavioral difficulties in children with DLD. *Journal of Neurodevelopmental Disorders*, *15*(17).

Catts, H., Adlof, S., & Ellis Weismer, S. (2006). Language Deficits in Poor Comprehenders: A Case for the Simple View of Reading. *Journal of Speech, Language, and Hearing Research: JSLHR*, *49*(2), 278–293. doi:10.1044/1092-4388(2006/023) PMID:16671844

Catts, H. W., Adlof, S. M., Hogan, T. P., & Weismer, S. E. (2005). Are specific language impairment and dyslexia distinct disorders. *Journal of Speech, Language, and Hearing Research: JSLHR*, *48*(6), 1378–1396. doi:10.1044/1092-4388(2005/096) PMID:16478378

Christopulos, T., & Kean, J. T. (2020). General education teachers' contribution to the identification of children with language disorders. *American Speech-Language Hearing Association*, *5*, 770–777. doi:10.1044/2020_PERSP-19-00166

Conti-Ramsden, G., & Botting, N. (2008). Emotional health in adolescents with and without a history of specific language impairment (SLI). *Journal of Child Psychology and Psychiatry, and Allied Disciplines*, *49*(5), 516–525. doi:10.1111/j.1469-7610.2007.01858.x PMID:18221347

Conti-Ramsden, G., & Botting, N. (2008b). Risk of affective disorders in adolescents with a history of SLI. *Journal of Child Psychology and Psychiatry, and Allied Disciplines*, *49*(5), 516–525. doi:10.1111/j.1469-7610.2007.01858.x PMID:18221347

Conti-Ramsden, G., Durkin, K., Simkin, Z., & Knox, E. (2009). Specific language impairment and school outcomes. Identifying and explaining variability at the end of compulsory education. *International Journal of Language & Communication Disorders*, *44*(1), 15–35. doi:10.1080/13682820801921601 PMID:18608604

Conti-Ramsden, G., Durkin, K., Toseeb, U., Botting, N., & Pickles, A. (2018). Education and employment outcomes of young adults with a history of developmental language disorder. *International Journal of Language & Communication Disorders*, *53*(2), 237–255. doi:10.1111/1460-6984.12338 PMID:29139196

Conti-Ramsden, G., Mok, P., Durkin, K., Pickles, A., Toseeb, U., & Botting, N. (2019). Do emotional difficulties and peer problems occur together from childhood to adolescence? The case of children with a history of developmental language disorder (DLD). *European Child & Adolescent Psychiatry*, *28*(7), 993–1004. doi:10.100700787-018-1261-6 PMID:30519863

Croteau, C., McMahon-Morin, P., Morin, C., Jutras, B., Trudeau, N., & Le Dorze, G. (2015). Life habits of school-aged children with specific language impairment as perceived by their parents and by school professionals. *Journal of Communication Disorders*, *58*, 21–34. doi:10.1016/j.jcomdis.2015.07.005 PMID:26342290

De Lopez, K. J., Feiberg, J., Baena, S., Lyons, R., & Harding, S. (2021). So I told him to look for friends" Barriers and protecting factors that may facilitate inclusion for children with Language Disorder in every day social settings: Cross-cultural qualitative interviews with parents. *Research in Developmental Disabilities*, 115.

Dubois, P., St-Pierre, M.-C., Desmarais, C., & Guay, F. (2020). Young Adults With Developmental Language Disorder: A Systematic Review of Education, Employment, and Independent Living Outcomes. *Journal of Speech, Language, and Hearing Research: JSLHR*, *63*(11), 3786–3800. doi:10.1044/2020_JSLHR-20-00127 PMID:33022192

Forrest, C. L., Gibson, J. L., Halligan, S. L., & St Clair, M. C. (2018). Longitudinal analysis of early language difficulty and peer problems on later emotional difficulties in adolescence: Evidence from the Millennium Cohort Study. *Autism & Developmental Language Impairments, 3*, 2396941518795392. doi:10.1177/2396941518795392

Forrest, C. L., Gibson, J. L., & St Clair, M. C. (2021). Social functioning as a mediator between Developmental Language Disorder (DLD) and emotional problems in adolescents. *International Journal of Environmental Research and Public Health, 18.*

Gough Kenyon, S. M., Palikara, O., & Lucas, R. M. (2021). Consistency of Parental and Self-Reported Adolescent Wellbeing: Evidence From Developmental Language Disorder. *Frontiers in Psychology, 12*, 12. doi:10.3389/fpsyg.2021.629577 PMID:33776852

Hendricks, A., Adlof, S., Alonzo, C., Fox, A., & Hogan, T. (2019). Identifying children at risk for developmental language disorder using a brief, whole-classroom screen. *Journal of Speech, Language, and Hearing Research: JSLHR, 62*(4), 1–13. doi:10.1044/2018_JSLHR-L-18-0093 PMID:30986146

Hobson, H., Kalsi, M., Cotton, L., Forster, M., & Toseeb, U. (2022). Supporting the mental health of children with speech, language and communication needs: The views and experiences of parents. *Autism & Developmental Language Impairments, 7.*

Lara-Díaz, M. F., Mateus-Moreno, A., & Beltrán-Rojas, J. C. (2021). Reading and Oral Language Skills in Children With Developmental Language Disorder: Influence of Socioeconomic, Educational, and Family Variables. *Frontiers in Psychology, 12*, 718988. doi:10.3389/fpsyg.2021.718988 PMID:34690876

Law, J., McBean, K., & Rush, R. (2011). Communication skills in a population of primary school-aged children raised in an area of pronounced social disadvantage. *International Journal of Language & Communication Disorders, 46*(6), 657–664. doi:10.1111/j.1460-6984.2011.00036.x PMID:22026567

Lindsay, G., & Dockrell, J. E. (2012). Longitudinal patterns of behavioral, emotional, and social difficulties and self-concepts in adolescents with a history of specific language impairment. *Language, Speech, and Hearing Services in Schools, 43*(4), 445–460. doi:10.1044/0161-1461(2012/11-0069) PMID:22826367

Lindsay, G., Ricketts, J., Peacey, L., Dockrell, J., & Charman, T. (2016). Meeting the educational and social needs of children with language impairment or autism spectrum disorder: The parents' perspectives. *International Journal of Language & Communication Disorders, 51*(5), 495–507. doi:10.1111/1460-6984.12226 PMID:26952185

Marshall, J., Harding, S., & Roulstone, S. (2017). Language development, delay and intervention—The views of parents from communities that speech and language therapy managers in England consider to be under-served. *International Journal of Language & Communication Disorders, 52*(4), 489–500. doi:10.1111/1460-6984.12288 PMID:27995697

McCabe, P. C. (2005). Social and behavioral correlates of preschoolers with Specific Language Impairment. *Psychology in the Schools, 42*(4), 373–387. doi:10.1002/pits.20064

Mok, P. L. H., Pickles, A., Durkin, K., & Conti-Ramsden, G. (2014). Longitudinal trajectories of peer relations in children with specific language impairment. *Journal of Child Psychology and Psychiatry, and Allied Disciplines, 55*(5), 516–527. doi:10.1111/jcpp.12190 PMID:24410167

Nilsson, K., & Jensen de López, K. (2016).Theory of mind in children with Specific Language Impairment: A systematic review and meta-analysis. *Child Development, 87* (1), 143 153, doi:10.1111/cdev.12462

Ottosson, S., Lorentzon, U. S., Kadesjo, B., Gillberg, C., & Miniscalco, C. (2022). Neurodevelopmental problems and quality of life in 6-year-olds with a history of developmental language disorder. *Acta Paediatrica (Oslo, Norway), 111*(1), 115–122. doi:10.1111/apa.16104 PMID:34516681

Palikara, O., & Ralli, A. M. (2013). Specific language impairment in childhood and adolescence: Educational and clinical implications. *Psychology (Irvine, Calif.), 20*, 243–266.

Radecki, L., Sand-Loud, N., O'Connor, K. G., Sharp, S., & Olson, L. M. (2011, July 01). Trends in the use of standardized tools for developmental screening in early childhood: 2002–2009. *Pediatrics, 128*(1), 14–19. doi:10.1542/peds.2010-2180 PMID:21708798

Ralli, A. M., Chrysochoou, E., Roussos, P., Diakogiorgi, K., Dimitropoulou, P., & Filippatou, D. (2021). Executive Function, Working Memory, and Verbal Fluency in Relation to Non-Verbal Intelligence in Greek-Speaking School-Age Children with Developmental Language Disorder. *Brain Sciences, 11*(5), 604. doi:10.3390/brainsci11050604 PMID:34066872

Ralli, A. M., Kalliontzi, E., & Kazali, E. (2022). Teachers views of children with Developmental Language Disorder in Greek mainstream schools. *Frontiers in Education, 7*, 832240. doi:10.3389/feduc.2022.832240

Ralli, A. M., Kazali, E., Kanellou, M., Mouzaki, A., Antoniou, F., Diamanti, V., & Papaioannou, S. (2021). Oral Language and Story Retelling During Preschool and Primary School Years: Developmental Patterns and Interrelationships. *Journal of Psycholinguistic Research, 50*(5), 949–965. doi:10.100710936-021-09758-3 PMID:33515178

Ramus, F., Marshall, C. R., Rosen, S., & van der Lely, H. K. (2013). Phonological deficits in specific language impairment and developmental dyslexia: Towards a multidimensional model. *Brain, 136*(2), 630–645. doi:10.1093/brain/aws356 PMID:23413264

Roello, M., Ferretti, M. L., Colonnello, V., & Levi, G. (2015). When words lead to solutions: Executive function deficits in preschool children with specific language impairment. *Research in Developmental Disabilities, 37*, 216–222. doi:10.1016/j.ridd.2014.11.017 PMID:25528081

Roulstone, S. (2015). Exploring the relationship between client perspectives, clinical expertise and research evidence. *International Journal of Speech-Language Pathology, 17*(3), 211–221. doi:10.3109/17549507.2015.1016112 PMID:25850604

Rudolph, J. M. (2017). Case history risk factors for specific language impairment: A systematic review and meta-analysis. *American Journal of Speech-Language Pathology, 26*(3), 991–1010. doi:10.1044/2016_AJSLP-15-0181 PMID:28672377

Silliman, E. R., & Berninger, V. W. (2011). Cross-disciplinary dialogue about the nature of oral and written language problems in the context of developmental, academic, and phenotypic profiles. *Topics in Language Disorders, 31*(1), 6–23. doi:10.1097/TLD.0b013e31820a0b5b

Sofologi, M., Kougioumtzis, G. A., & Koundourou, C. (2023). *Perspectives of Cognitive, Psychosocial, and Learning Difficulties From Childhood to Adulthood: Practical Counseling Strategies*. doi:10.4018/978-1-6684-8203-2

St Clair, M. C., Pickles, A., Durkin, K., & Conti-Ramsden, G. A. (2011). Longitudinal study of behavioral, emotional and social difficulties in individuals with a history of specific language impairment (SLI). *Journal of Communication Disorders*, *44*(2), 186–199. doi:10.1016/j.jcomdis.2010.09.004 PMID:20970811

Sultana, N., Wong, L. L. N., & Purdy, S. C. (2020). Natural language input: Maternal education, socioeconomic deprivation, and language outcomes in typically developing children. *Language, Speech, and Hearing Services in Schools*, *51*(4), 1049–1070. doi:10.1044/2020_LSHSS-19-00095 PMID:32755504

Tomblin, J. B., Records, N. L., Buckwalter, P., Zhang, X., Smith, E., & O'Brien, M. (1997). Prevalence of specific language impairment in kindergarten children. *Journal of Speech, Language, and Hearing Research: JSLHR*, *40*(6), 1245–1260. doi:10.1044/jslhr.4006.1245 PMID:9430746

Tomblin, J. B., Zhang, X., Buckwalter, P., & O'Brien, M. (2003). The stability of primary language disorder: Four years after kindergarten diagnosis. *Journal of Speech, Language, and Hearing Research: JSLHR*, *46*(6), 1283–1296. doi:10.1044/1092-4388(2003/100) PMID:14700355

Van den Bedem, N. P., Dockrell, J. E., van Alphen, P. M., Kalicharan, S. V., & Rieffe, C. (2018). Victimization, bullying, and emotional competence: Longitudinal associations in (Pre)adolescents with and without developmental language disorder. *Journal of Speech, Language, and Hearing Research: JSLHR*, *61*(8), 2028–2044. doi:10.1044/2018_JSLHR-L-17-0429 PMID:29998317

Vernon-Feagans, L., Bratsch-Hines, M., Reyonlds, E., & Willoughby, M. (2020). How early maternal language input varies by race and education and predicts later child language. *Child Development*, *91*(4), 1098–1115. doi:10.1111/cdev.13281 PMID:31317532

Wadman, R., Botting, N., Durkin, K., & Conti-Ramsden, G. (2011). Changes in emotional health symptoms in adolescents with specific language impairment. *International Journal of Language & Communication Disorders*, *46*(6), 641–656. doi:10.1111/j.1460-6984.2011.00033.x PMID:22026566

Chapter 7
Family Dynamics and Socio-Demographic Characteristics of Children With Spelling Difficulties

Assimina Tsibidaki
University of the Aegean, Greece

Stergoulla Treha
University of the Aegean, Greece

ABSTRACT

The present study aims to examine the correlation between students' performance on a family dynamics test and specific socio-demographic characteristics. The sample consisted of 225 children: 111 (49.3%) boys and 114 (50.7%) girls, with a mean age of 11.5 years. For data collection, the following were used: 1) A Self-administered Socio-demographic Questionnaire, 2) The Zachos Dictation Writing Test (DWT) and 3) The Family Dynamics Measure II Questionnaire (FDM II). The findings of the study indicated that most of the children produced a high number of spelling errors. They were found to have high scores on five of the six family dynamics dimensions, except for one. Statistical differences were found in four family dynamics dimensions in relation to demographic characteristics: Children's and parents' satisfaction with school performance, perceived difficulties in spelling, essay writing, arithmetic, oral and written tests, and leisure time utilization.

INTRODUCTION

Spelling is a basic academic skill that is essential for future successful participation in modern societies (Zarić et al., 2021). The ability to spell is a gradually developing, time-consuming, and complex process (Diamanti et al., 2014). The literature reports that many children experience great difficulty in learning

DOI: 10.4018/979-8-3693-1982-6.ch007

to spell. These children usually also have difficulties in learning to read as well. The family of these children plays a vital role in their efforts to master reading and writing (Treiman, 2017).

The family literacy environment is now an established predictor of children's language and literacy development (Hamilton et al., 2016; Shahaeian et al., 2018). The learning environment provided by parents at home has been well researched as a dimension and refers to the quality of language stimuli and behaviors that contribute to literacy development. For the development of children's language abilities, psycholinguists have long documented the influence of the family, in particular the mother (Gallaway & Richards, 1994). However, investigations of family variables likely to be associated with difficulties in spelling have mostly focused on environmental, genetic, and socioeconomic factors, and findings do not seem to respond well to the questions that have been raised over time (Puglisi et al., 2017).

In addition, no studies, both in Greek and international literature, can be identified that examine the association between spelling errors and family dynamics. Family dynamics refers to the patterns of interactions between family members, their relationships and roles, and the factors that shape these interactions. Interpersonal interactions between family members have an effect that is not temporary, it is long-lasting. Stable and supportive family relationships provide love, support, and care, whereas insecure and stressful family relationships bring about negative criticism, strain, and conflict. By implication, family dynamics and the quality of family relationships can have either a positive or negative impact on an individual's health, well-being, and overall development (Jabbari & Rouster, 2023). The family dynamics included by Barnhill (1979) in the "family health cycle" are defined as "the unique ways" in which family members relate.

Research on the family dynamics of children with difficulties in spelling is limited. Researchers point out that students' family dynamics are related to their performance in orthography. Besides, it has been shown that family cohesion, which constitutes one of the positive dimensions of family functioning, predicts positive or negative academic achievement, including spelling (Feldman et al., 2018).

The interaction between parents and children is an important interpersonal aspect of children's performance and school learning. Parental involvement influences children's success in school, with typical examples being, talking with the child about school, supervising homework, meeting with the teacher(s), or visiting the child's classroom. These behaviors have been shown to predict positive outcomes for children, including academic skills (Pomerantz et al., 2007). In addition, mothers and fathers have different roles in parenting, and these roles vary across countries (Newman et al., 2015).

The Present Study

The existing literature on learning environment conditions confirms the importance of adequate family functioning and the existence of a satisfactory family context for children's effective academic and literacy development (Briley et al., 2019; Erbeli et al., 2019; Kong et al., 2018). However, no studies have focused on the association between spelling errors and family dynamics, particularly the association between socio-demographic characteristics of children with difficulties in spelling and family dynamics.

The present study aims to examine the correlation between children's performance on a family dynamics test and specific socio-demographic characteristics, such as gender, father's and mother's occupation, help with homework, the degree of satisfaction with their school performance, their parents' degree of satisfaction with their school performance, difficulties they face in school subjects (reading, writing, arithmetic), essays, tests (oral and written), and use of leisure time. The hypotheses of the study were the following:

H_1= Children will score high on the spelling test.

H_2= Children will score high on each dimension of family dynamics.

H_3= Children's socio-demographic characteristics will be correlated with each dimension of family dynamics.

METHOD

This study presents the findings of the first phase of a larger study.

Participants

The sample consisted of 225 children: 111 (49.3%) boys and 114 (50.7%) girls. The average age of the children in the sample was 11.5 years, with the average age of the boys being only two months older than the girls. All children attended the 6th grade of primary school on the island of Rhodes: 50.2% of the children attended school in the city of Rhodes and 49.8% in the semi-urban and rural areas of the island.

Measures

Data were collected with 1) A Self-administered Socio-demographic Questionnaire, 2) The Zachos Dictation Writing Test (DWT) (Zachos & Zachos, 1998) and 3) The Family Dynamics Measure II Questionnaire (FDM II) (Lasky et al., 1985; White & Elander, 1992). More specifically:

1) The self-administered socio-demographic questionnaire of 14 questions was created to obtain socio-demographic information. In particular, questions 1–2 refer to the school (question 1) and the grade of attendance (question 2). Questions 3–4 focus on the date of birth (question 3) and the gender (question 4). Questions on family structure, birth order, and parental occupation follow, as the number of persons in the family (question 5), the child's birth order (question 6), the father's occupation (question 7), and the mother's occupation (question 8). The next questions, 9–12, deal with the child's school experience with studying. In more detail, who he/she receives help with homework from (question 9), how happy he/she is with his/her progress and grades at school (question 10), and whether his/her parents are happy with his/her school grades and performance (question 11). The next question (question 12) explores the child's perceived level of difficulty in specific school subjects. The last two questions examine leisure time utilization (question 13) and total time spent on activities (question 14).
2) The DWT is a dictation spelling test. It is an age-appropriate passage with morphological variety developed by Zachos and Zachos in 1998 (Zachos & Zachos, 1998). Errors are classified as grammatical/morphological, productive-synthetic, thematic, and phonetic-phonological. It includes a text that comprises a 49-word paragraph, suitable for the students of the 6th grade. Regarding the phonological composition of words, there are opportunities not only for skipping or replacing graphemes but also for simplifying or reversing two-digit graphemes. It also includes words that are inflected parts of speech with grammatical limitations in the spelling of the suffix, providing opportunities for morphological errors, as well as words with consonants that allow different writing of the subject and are limited only by their etymology, thus providing opportunities for visual

errors. Also, the text includes monosyllabic words that are stressed or not, as well as two-syllable, three-syllable, and polysyllabic words, thus providing opportunities for tonal errors. Punctuation marks are also included, and opportunities are provided for spelling mistakes as well as small-capital letter use errors (Zachos & Zachos, 1998).

3) The FDM II is a questionnaire of 66 questions, which are divided into six (6) dimensions. Scoring is in a 6-point Likert-type format (from "strongly agree" to "strongly disagree"). Each dimension has a different number of questions, which are in random order and are worded either positively or negatively. Each dimension has a negative and a positive pole. The dimensions are as follows: Dimension 1: Individualization - Enmeshment, Dimension 2: Reciprocity - Isolation, Dimension 3: Flexibility - Rigidity, Dimension 4: Stability - Disorganization, Dimension 5: Clear communication - Unclear communication and Dimension 6: Role reciprocity - Role conflict. Higher scores mean more positive family dynamics. The final scores of dimensions can be compared, as their structure does not provide a total score (Lasky et al., 1985; White & Elander, 1992).

Procedure and Analysis

Data collection took place in the school years 2017–20. The questionnaires were administered to the students by their teacher. Data analysis was based on descriptive statistics, and the non-parametric Kruskal-Wallis, the Mann-Whitney U tests for independent samples, and the Spearman rho tests.

FINDINGS

Children's Performance on Spelling Test

The analysis of the findings revealed (Table 1) that most of the students produced a high number of spelling errors and 46.7% of them made 3-15 spelling errors, and 26.7% of them made >=16 errors and <=2 errors respectively.

Family Dynamics

The children, as presented in Table 2, were found to score high on most of the family dynamics dimensions, except for the 3rd dimension: Flexibility-Rigidity where the mean (*Mdn*) was 3.37.

Table 1. Percentages (%) of the groups of all spelling errors in the DWT

Groups of number of spelling errors		n	Valid %
1	<=2 errors (1% - 25%)	60	26. 7
2	3-15 errors (26% - 74%)	105	46.7
3	>=16 errors (75% - 100%)	60	26.7

Table 2. Mean values of the dimensions of the family dynamics I (FDM II)

Dimensions of family dynamics	M
Dimension 1: Individuation - Enmeshment	4.00
Dimension 2: Mutuality - Isolation	5.07
Dimension 3: Flexibility - Rigidity	3.37
Dimension 4: Stability - Disorganization	4.47
Dimension 5: Clear - Unclear communication	4.67
Dimension 6: Role Reciprocity - Role conflict	4.55

Children's Socio-Demographic Characteristics and Family Dynamics

To examine the children's differences by socio-demographic characteristics on the variables related to family dynamics (FDM II), the Mann-Whitney non-parametric test was used. Statistical differences were found in four family dynamics dimensions (dimension 2: Mutuality-Isolation, dimension 4: Stability-Disorganization, dimension 5: Clear-Unclear Communication, and dimension 6: Role reciprocity-Role Conflict) in relation to demographic characteristics: Children's satisfaction with school performance, parents' satisfaction with school performance, perceived difficulties in reading, spelling, essay writing, arithmetic, oral and written tests, and leisure time utilization.

More specifically, the following were found:

a) Dimension 2: Mutuality - Isolation and
   - *children's satisfaction with school performance:* $H(6)=27.35$, $p=0.000<0.001$. Post hoc tests identified that children who had answered "Yes" ($Mdn=5.55$) had statistically significantly higher values than children who had answered "No": "I don't know" ($Mdn= 4.41$, $p=0.016<0.05$) and "I would like to have better grades" ($Mdn=4.59$, $p=0.014<0.05$).
   - *Parents' satisfaction with school performance:* $H(6)=34.90$, $p=0.000<0.001$). Post hoc tests identified that children who had answered "Yes" ($Mdn=5.55$) had statistically significantly higher values than children who had answered: "They say I don't study" ($Mdn=3.77$, $p=0.033<0.05$), "They would like me to study harder" ($Mdn=4.27$, $p=0.002<0.01$) and "I don't know" ($Mdn=4.36$, $p=0.024<0.05$).
   - *Perceived difficulties in reading:* $H(3)=18.37$, $p=0.000<0.001$. Post hoc tests identified that children who had answered "Not at all" ($Mdn=5.45$) had statistically significantly higher values than children who had answered: "A little" ($Mdn=4.82$, $p=0.006<0.01$) and "A lot" ($Mdn=3.82$, $p=0.021<0.05$).
   - Perceived difficulties in spelling*:* $H(3)=21.26$, $p=0.000<0.001$. Post hoc tests identified that children who had answered "Not at all" ($Mdn=5.45$) had statistically significantly higher values than children who had answered: "A little" ($Mdn=5.18$, $p=0.047<0.05$), "A lot" ($Mdn=4.27$, $p=0.005<0.01$) and "Very much" ($Mdn=3.67$, $p=0.026<0.05$).
   - *Perceived difficulties in essay writing:* $H(3)=24.02$, $p=0.000<0.001$. Post hoc tests identified that children who had answered "Not at all" ($Mdn=5.45$) had statistically significantly higher values than children who had answered "A lot" ($Mdn=4.36$, $p=0.001<0.01$) and "Very much" ($Mdn=3.64$, $p=0.009<0.01$).

- ◦ *Perceived difficulties in arithmetic:* $H(3)=30.04$, $p=0.000<0.001$. With the post hoc tests, we found that children who had answered: a) "Not at all" ($Mdn=5.55$) showed statistically significantly higher values than children who had answered: "A lot" ($Mdn=4.41$, $p=0.000<0.001$), "Very much" ($Mdn=3.46$, $p=0.002<0.01$), and b) "A little" ($Mdn=5.27$) showed statistically significantly higher values compared to children who had answered "A lot" ($Mdn=4.41$, $p=0.008<0.01$).
- ◦ *Perceived difficulties in oral tests:* $H(3)=25.67$, $p=0.000<0.001$. Post hoc tests identified that children who had answered "Not at all" ($Mdn=5.55$) had statistically significantly higher values than children who had answered: "A lot" ($Mdn=4.00$, $p=0.000<0.001$) and "Very much" ($Mdn=4.27$, $p=0.009<0.01$).
- ◦ *Perceived difficulties in written tests:* $H(3)=28.86$, $p=0.000<0.001$. Post hoc tests identified that children who had answered "Not at all" ($Mdn=5.55$) had statistically significantly higher values than children who had answered: "A little" ($Mdn=5.27$, $p=0.031<0.05$), "A lot" ($Mdn=4.59$, $p=0.000<0.001$) and "Very much" ($Mdn=3.91$, $p=0.002<0.01$).
- ◦ *Leisure time utilization:* Students who answered "No" on whether they stay at home ($Mdn=$ 5.36) seem to be statistically significantly different (higher values) from those who answered "Yes" ($Mdn=$ 5.18), the U-criterion value is 3865.50 with $p=0.017<0.05$ i.e., statistically significant and the effect size is -0.16.

b) Dimension 4: Stability-Disorganization and

- ◦ *children's satisfaction with school performance:* $H(6)=25.17$, $p=0.000<0.001$. Using post hoc tests, we found that children who had answered "Yes" ($Mdn=4.67$) had statistically significantly higher values than children who had answered: "I would like to be excellent" ($Mdn=4.22$, $p=0.048<0.05$) and "I would like to have better grades" ($Mdn=4.11$, $p=0.043<0.05$).
- ◦ *Parents' satisfaction with school performance:* $H((6)=30.64$, $p=0.000<0.001$). Post hoc tests identified that children who had answered "Yes" ($Mdn=4.67$) had statistically significantly higher values than children who had answered "No": "They say I don't study" ($Mdn=3.67$, $p=0.044<0.05$) and "They would like me to study harder" ($Mdn=4.00$, $p=0.006<0.01$).
- ◦ *Perceived difficulties in reading:* $H(3)=9.44$, $p=0.024<0.05$. With the post hoc tests, we did not find statistically significant differences between the children's respective responses (not at all, a little, a lot, very much).
- ◦ *Perceived difficulties in spelling:* $H((3)=12.41$, $p=0.006<0.01$. With the post hoc tests, we did not find statistically significant differences between the children's respective responses (not at all, a little, a lot, very much).
- ◦ Perceived difficulties in spelling: $H((3)=12.41$, $p=0.006<0.01$. Post hoc tests identified that children who had answered "Not at all" ($Mdn=4.61$) showed statistically significantly higher values than children who had answered "Very much" ($Mdn=3.67$, $p=0.019<0.05$).
- ◦ *Perceived difficulties in essay writing:* $H((3)=12.41$, $p=0.006<0.01$. Post hoc tests identified that children who had answered "Not at all" ($Mdn=4.78$) had statistically significantly higher values than children who had answered: "A little" ($Mdn=4.44$, $p=0.017<0.05$), "A lot" ($Mdn=4.22$, $p=0.005<0.01$) and "Very much" ($Mdn=3.67$, $p=0.008<0.01$).
- ◦ *Perceived difficulties in arithmetic:* Post hoc tests identified that children who had answered "Not at all" ($Mdn=4.67$) had statistically significantly higher values than children who had answered: "A lot" ($Mdn=4.06$, $p=0.018<0.05$) and "Very much" ($Mdn=4.06$, $p=0.009<0.01$.

- *Perceived difficulties in oral tests:* $H((3)=22.43$, $p=0.000<0.001$. With post hoc tests we found that children who had answered: "Not at all" (*Mdn*=4.67) showed statistically significantly higher values than children who had answered: "A lot" (*Mdn*=3.89, $p=0.000<0.001$), "Very much" (*Mdn*=3.94, $p=0.028<0.05$) and "A little" (*Mdn*=4.44) showed statistically significantly higher values compared to children who had answered "A lot" (*Mdn*=3.89, $p=0.006<0.01$).
- *Perceived difficulties in written tests:* $H((3)=26.27$, $p=0.000<0.001$. Post hoc tests identified that children who had answered "Not at all" (*Mdn*=4.78) had statistically significantly higher values than children who had answered: "A little" (*Mdn*=4.33, $p=0.002<0.01$), "A lot" (*Mdn*=4.00, $p=0.001<0.01$) and "Very much" (*Mdn*=3.89, $p=0.040<0.05$).
- Leisure time utilization: Children who answered "No" to whether they stay at home (*Mdn*= 4.56) seem to be statistically significantly different (higher values) from those who answered "Yes" (*Mdn*= 4.33), the *U*-criterion value is 3829.50 with $p=0.013<0.05$ i.e., statistically significant and the effect size is -0.17.

c) Dimension 5: Clear-Unclear Communication and
- *children's satisfaction with school performance:* $H(6)=31.96$, $p=0.000<0.001$. With post hoc tests we found that children who had answered "Yes" (*Mdn*=5.00) had statistically significantly higher values than children who had answered "I would like to have better grades" (*Mdn*=4.00, $p=0.000<0.001$).
- *Parents' satisfaction with school performance:* $H(6)=39.24$, $p=0.000<0.001$. Post hoc tests identified that children who had answered "Yes" (*Mdn*=5.00) had statistically significantly higher values than children who had answered: "They would like me to study harder" (*Mdn*=4.00, $p=0.001<0.01$) and "I would like to have better grades" (*Mdn*=4.18, $p=0.003<0.01$).
- *Perceived difficulties in reading:* $H(3)=13.30$, $p=0.004<0.01$. Post hoc tests identified that children who had answered "Not at all" (*Mdn*=4.91) had statistically significantly higher values than children who answered "A lot" (*Mdn*=3.67, $p=0.038<0.05$).
- perceived difficulties in spelling: $H(3)=33.81$, $p=0.000<0.001$. Post hoc tests identified that children who had answered "Not at all" (*Mdn*=5.00) had statistically significantly higher values than children who had answered: "A little" (*Mdn*=4.45, $p=0.000<0.001$), "A lot" (*Mdn*=4.00, $p=0.003<0.01$) and "Very much" (*Mdn*=3.45, $p=0.002<0.01$).
- *Perceived difficulties in essay writing:* $H(3)=23.81$, $p=0.000<0.001$. With the post hoc tests, we found that children who had answered: a) "Not at all" (*Mdn*=4.91) had statistically significantly higher values than children who had answered: "A lot" (*Mdn*=4.18, $p=0.002<0.01$) and "Very much" (*Mdn*=3.45, $p=0.002<0.01$), and b) "A little" (*Mdn*=5.00) showed statistically significantly higher values compared to children who had answered "Very much" (*Mdn*=3.45, $p=0.002<0.01$).
- *Perceived difficulties in arithmetic:* $H(3)=31.58$, $p=0.000<0.001$. Post hoc tests identified that children who had answered "Not at all" (*Mdn*=4.91) had statistically significantly higher values than children who had answered: "A little" (*Mdn*=4.73, $p=0.014<0.05$), "A lot" (*Mdn*=4.08, $p=0.000<0.001$) and "Very much" (*Mdn*=4.08, $p=0.001<0.01$).
- *Perceived difficulties in oral tests:* $H(3)=28.92$, $p=0.000<0.001$. Using post hoc tests we found that children who had answered: a) "Not at all" (*Mdn*=4.86) had statistically significantly higher values than children who had answered: "A lot" (*Mdn*=3.95, $p=0.000<0.001$)

and "Very much" (*Mdn*=3.77, *p*=0.005<0.01), and b) "A little" (*Mdn*=4.73) showed statistically significantly higher values compared to children who had answered: "A lot" (*Mdn*=3.95, *p*=0.003<0.01) and "Very much" (*Mdn*=3.77, *p*=0.042<0.05).

- *Perceived difficulties in written tests:* *H*(3)=34.17, *p*=0.000<0.001. Post hoc tests identified that children who had answered "Not at all" (*Mdn*=5.00) had statistically significantly higher values than children who had answered: "A little" (*Mdn*=4.64, *p*=0.001<0.01), "A lot" (*Mdn*=4.18, *p*=0.000<0.001) and "Very much" (*Mdn*=3.82, *p*=0.003<0.01).
- *Leisure time utilization:* Students who answered "No" to whether they stay at home (*Mdn*= 4.77) seem to be statistically significantly different (higher values) from those who answered "Yes" (*Mdn*= 4.55), the *U*-criterion value is 3883.50 with *p*=0.019<0.05 i.e., statistically significant and the effect size is -0.16.

d) Dimension 6: Role reciprocity-Role Conflict and

- *children's satisfaction with school performance:* *H*(6)=32.04, *p*=0.000<0.001. Post hoc tests identified that children who had answered "Yes" (*Mdn*=4.75) had statistically significantly higher values than children who had answered: "I would like to be excellent" (*Mdn*=4.17, *p*=0.005<0.01) and "I would like to have better grades" (*Mdn*=4.25, *p*=0.002<0.01).
- *Parents' satisfaction with school performance:* *H*(6)=42.29, *p*=0.000<0.001. With the post hoc tests, we found that children who had answered: a) "Yes" (*Mdn*=4.75) showed statistically significantly higher values than children who had answered: "They would like me to be excellent" (*Mdn*=4.33, *p*=0.013<0.05), "They would like me to study harder" (*Mdn*=3.92, *p*=0.001<0.01) and "They say I don't study at all" (*Mdn*=3.63, *p*=0.020<0.05), and b) "No" (*Mdn*=5.00) showed statistically significantly higher values than the children who had responded: "They would like me to study harder" (*Mdn*=3.92, *p*=0.024<0.05) and "They say I don't study at all" (*Mdn*=3.63, *p*=0.020<0.05).
- *Perceived difficulties in reading:* *H*(3)=14.46, *p*=0.002<0.01. Using post hoc tests, we found that children who had answered "Not at all" (*Mdn*=4.67) had statistically significantly higher values than children who had answered "A lot" (*Mdn*=3.67, *p*=0.015<0.05).
- *Perceived difficulties in spelling:* *H*(3)=20.65, *p*=0.000<0.001. Post hoc tests identified that children who had answered "Not at all" (*Mdn*=4.75) had statistically significantly higher values than children who had answered: "A little" (*Mdn*=4.50, *p*=0.011<0.05), "A lot" (*Mdn*=4.00, *p*=0.028<0.05) and "Very much" (*Mdn*=3.67, *p*=0.022<0.05).
- *Perceived difficulties in essay writing:* *H*(3)=25.60, *p*=0.000<0.001. With the post hoc tests, we found that children who had answered: a) "Not at all" (*Mdn*=4.75) showed statistically significantly higher values than children who had answered: "A lot" (*Mdn*=4.08, *p*=0.001<0.01) and "Very much" (*Mdn*=3.67, *p*=0.003<0.01), and b) "A little" (*Mdn*=4.50) showed statistically significantly higher values compared to children who had answered: "A lot" (*Mdn*=4.08, *p*=0.039<0.05) and "Very much" (*Mdn*=3.67, *p*=0.027<0.05).
- *Perceived difficulties in arithmetic:* *H*(3)=15.93, *p*=0.000<0.001. Using post hoc tests, we found that children who had answered "Not at all" (*Mdn*=4.67) had statistically significantly higher values than children who had answered "A lot" (*Mdn*=4.08, *p*=0.008<0.01).
- *Perceived difficulties in oral tests:* *H*(3)=24.55, *p*=0.000<0.001. Using post hoc tests, we found that children who had answered: a) "Not at all" (*Mdn*=4.71) had statistically significantly higher values than children who had answered "Very much" (*Mdn*=3.92,

$p=0.000<0.001$), and b) "A little" ($Mdn=4.50$) showed statistically significantly higher values compared to children who had answered, "A lot" ($Mdn=3.92$, $p=0.005<0.01$).

- *Perceived difficulties in written tests:* $H(3)=24.28$, $p=0.000<0.001$. With the post hoc tests, we found that children who had answered: a) "Not at all" ($Mdn=4.75$) showed statistically significantly higher values than children who had answered: "A lot" ($Mdn=4.04$, $p=0.000<0.001$) and "Very much" ($Mdn=3.67$, $p=0.040<0.05$), and "A little" ($Mdn=4.50$) showed statistically significantly higher values compared to children who had answered, "A lot" ($Mdn=4.04$, $p=0.021<0.05$).
- *Leisure time utilization*: Students who answered "No" on whether they live at home ($Mdn=$ 4.67) seem to be statistically significantly different (higher values) from those who answered "Yes" ($Mdn=$ 4.33), the *U*-criterion value is 3722.50 with $p=0.006<0.01$. i.e., statistically significant and the effect size is -0.18.

No statistically significant differences were found in terms of gender, number of family members, and occupation of parents (father and mother).

DISCUSSION

The present study aimed to examine the correlation between students' performance on a family dynamics test and specific socio-demographic characteristics.

Regarding the first hypothesis of the study "Children will score high on the spelling test", we notice that it is verified since the findings indicate that the majority of the children produced a high number of spelling errors in the KYG test. This finding is in line with a variety of research both in Greece (Spantidakis, 2009; Trecha & Tsibidaki, 2021, 2022; Triga-Mertika, 2010; Varsamidou & Spantidakis, 2007; Xanthi, 2017) and internationally (Puglisi et al., 2017; Tamboer et al., 2016).

In more detail, the literature research indicates that spelling is one of the most essential, long-standing problem areas for those who have difficulties in writing. Spelling errors are identified early in schooling and after the acquisition of reading. They also continue into secondary and tertiary education (Spantidakis, 2009; Triga-Mertika, 2010; Varsamidou & Spantidakis, 2007). Evidently, spelling ability is a gradually developing, time-consuming, and complex process, and difficulties in spelling are persistent and not always easy to overcome (Tamboer et al., 2016). While there is limited research investigating the development of spelling ability in individuals with and without LD, in recent years in Greece there has been attention to the linguistic factors related to the development of spelling ability as well as the analysis of spelling errors of students with and without LD (Anagnostopoulou & Kantartzi, 2008; Mouzaki & Protopapas, 2010; Pavlidis & Giannouli, 2003; Protopapas et al., 2013; Xanthi, 2017).

The findings related to the 2nd hypothesis "Children will score high on each dimension of family dynamics" indicated that the hypothesis is confirmed since children scored high on the majority of the family dynamics dimensions, except for the 3rd dimension: Flexibility - Rigidity. More specifically, on four of the six dimensions (2: Mutuality - Isolation, 4: Stability-Disorganization, 5: Clear - Unclear communication, and 6: Role Reciprocity - Role conflict) scores were well above average, on one was above average (1: Individuation - Enmeshment), and on one (3: Flexibility - Rigidity) was slightly lower. However, it was found that at the level of family functioning, 5 out of 6 indicators were positive and confirmed that children generally perceived their family functioning as healthy, fine, and effective, and the overall picture of family functioning has a positive aspect. Specifically, based on Barnhill's (1979) model, the fact that children scored high on these dimensions indicates they perceived that there was a good level of individuation of persons in the family and independence of thought, feelings, and judgment. They also had a sense of autonomy, personal responsibility, and individual boundaries. At the same time, they felt reciprocity, that is, a sense of emotional closeness and intimacy with other family members. They felt secure and consistent in their family interactions. In addition, regarding their family communication, there was a clear and successful exchange of information, and they felt free to ask questions to confirm the meaning and purpose of each exchange of information. Finally, they believed that there were agreed-upon patterns of behavior in their family, and whenever needed, one family member complimented another.

The above findings confirm that there were not very large differences between the dimensions, and this is consistent with Barnhill's (1979) theory, on which the questionnaire was based, that in families with healthy functioning, dimensions are interrelated and change in one domain reflects change in another, as in systems. Family dynamics are the unique ways in which family members relate to each other, and higher scores indicate areas of family functioning that are strong and should be maintained, while lower scores indicate areas that need attention and perhaps reinforcement and intervention. Therefore, the fact that the Flexibility - Rigidity dimension tended towards the negative pole indicates that children identified rigidity in family functioning, i.e., avoidance of change and stereotypical behavior with a lack of conciliatory behavior. These are the items that seem to be less adequate. It also confirms the lower scores in relation to the other 4 dimensions because dimension 1 of Individuation - Enmeshment, is closely related to dimension 3 of Flexibility - Rigidity. As Barnhill (1979) notes, individuation and mutuality are successfully achieved when they are together, suggesting both the need for more flexibility and joint role sharing in the family. It should of course be borne in mind here that dimensions (1 and 3) namely, Individuation - Enmeshment and Flexibility - Rigidity, in tests conducted showed lower reliability than the other dimensions and should be evaluated with caution.

At the same time, this particular finding, regarding the high scores on the majority of the family dynamics dimensions, is in line with various studies arguing that the Greek family as a system has a certain dynamic and functions effectively, despite the constant changes it undergoes (Tantaros, 2004). Basic characteristics of the Greek family are resilience, unity, and cohesion, and these are the elements that help it cope with the constant challenges and adversities (Tsibidaki, 2021).

Regarding the 3rd hypothesis "Children's socio-demographic characteristics will be correlated with each dimension of family dynamics", statistical differences were found in four dimensions (2, 4, 5, & 6) of family dynamics with respect to some demographic characteristics. As Robledo-Ramón et al. (2012) point out, the available research on learning and environmental conditions, such as socio-demographic characteristics, confirms the importance of adequate family functioning, as well as the existence of a satisfactory family environment for children's academic development. Studies show that children whose families help them and interact functionally with them use effective educational styles, and wherever there are few disagreements, children do better in school (Bodovski & Youn, 2010). However, in troubled or dysfunctional families, children receive fewer, and lower-quality stimuli, and their academic development is slower (Ghazarian & Buehler, 2010). In addition, research suggests that family structure is related to children's cognitive and academic achievement as well. Children living with two biological parents, in nuclear families, outperform in cognitive and academic skills those raised in other family structures, such as single-parent families (Abuya et al., 2019; Hampden-Thompson, 2013; Santín & Sicilia, 2016).

Research Applications

This work has a range of practical applications:

- ☐ It becomes clear that it is vitally important to understand family dynamics to recognize and address the needs of children with difficulties in spelling.
- ☐ Future educational practice in Greece needs to promote families as integral partners in the educational process of their children, especially those with difficulties in spelling.
- ☐ The adoption of supportive strategies to empower families is suggested, which may alleviate their burdened role, in conjunction with appropriate instruction and the reinforcement of children's spelling skills.

Consequently, the findings of the study confirm recent research findings suggesting the compelling need to focus on the family perspective and the familial experiences when working with children facing difficulties in learning spelling (Sahu et al., 2018).

Limitations

It is particularly important to highlight some limitations of the current study:

1. The survey data was collected based on children's statements, which may not always be accurate. However, the sufficient sample and the varied means of data collection allowed us to ensure a high degree of accuracy for these data.
2. The study did not examine the effect of different types of learning difficulties, nor did it look at the effect of children with a differential diagnosis.
3. The study relied only on quantitative data in terms of data collection and analysis. The combination of qualitative and quantitative research would enable us to gain an in-depth understanding of family dynamics.
4. While we acknowledge the above limitations, we do not believe that they prevent the generalization of the survey findings to a specific population of families with children with difficulties in learning spelling.

While we acknowledge the above limitations, we do not believe that they are such to prevent the generalization of the survey findings to a specific population of families with children with difficulties in learning spelling.

CONCLUSION

The present study revealed that most children showed a high number of spelling errors in the KYG spelling test. At the same time, the children scored high on most of the family dynamics dimensions in the FDM II questionnaire, specifically on five out of six dimensions (Individuation - Enmeshment, Mutuality - Isolation, Stability -Disorganization, Clear - Unclear communication, and Role reciprocity - Role conflict) except for the 3rd dimension: Flexibility - Rigidity. Finally, key demographic characteristics of children, such as children's satisfaction with school performance, parents' satisfaction with school performance, difficulties in reading, spelling, essay writing, arithmetic difficulties, oral and written tests difficulties, and leisure time utilization, are correlated with family dynamics (FDM II).

REFERENCES

Abuya, B. A., Mutisya, M., Onsomu, E. O., Ngware, M., & Oketch, M. (2019). Family structure and child educational attainment in the slums of Nairobi, Kenya. *SAGE Open*, *9*(2), 2158244019855849. doi:10.1177/2158244019855849

Anagnostopoulou, M., & Kantartzi, E. (2008). The spelling errors of primary school students in written expression. In A. Trillianos & I. Karaminas (Eds.), *Hellenic Pedagogical & Educational Research.* Conference Proceedings (*Vol. b*, pp. 995-1004). Atrapos. [in Greek]

Barnhill, L. R. (1979). Healthy family systems. *The Family Coordinator*, *28*(1), 94–100. doi:10.2307/583274

Bodovski, K., & Youn, M.-J. (2010). Love, discipline and elementary school achievement: The role of family emotional climate. *Social Science Research*, *39*(4), 585–595. doi:10.1016/j.ssresearch.2010.03.008

Briley, D. A., Livengood, J., Derringer, J., Tucker-Drob, E. M., Fraley, R. C., & Roberts, B. W. (2019). Interpreting behavior genetic models: Seven developmental processes to understand. *Behavior Genetics*, *49*(2), 196–210. doi:10.100710519-018-9939-6 PMID:30467668

Diamanti, V., Goulandris, N., Stuart, M., & Campbell, R. (2014). Spelling of derivational and inflectional suffixes by Greek-speaking children with and without dyslexia. *Reading and Writing*, *27*(2), 337–358. doi:10.100711145-013-9447-2

Erbeli, F., Hart, S. A., & Taylor, J. (2019). Genetic and environmental influences on achievement outcomes based on family history of learning disabilities status. *Journal of Learning Disabilities*, *52*(2), 135–145. doi:10.1177/0022219418775116 PMID:29790411

Feldman, D. B., Einav, M., & Margalit, M. (2018). Does family cohesion predict children's effort? The mediating roles of sense of coherence, hope, and loneliness. *The Journal of Psychology*, *152*(5), 276–289. doi:10.1080/00223980.2018.1447434 PMID:29652639

Gallaway, C., & Richards, B. J. (Eds.). (1994). *Input and interaction in language acquisition*. Cambridge University Press., doi:10.1017/CBO9780511620690

Ghazarian, S. R., & Buehler, C. (2010). Interparental conflict and academic achievement: An examination of mediating and moderating factors. *Journal of Youth and Adolescence*, *39*(1), 23–35. doi:10.100710964-008-9360-1 PMID:20091214

Hamilton, L. G., Hayiou-Thomas, M. E., Hulme, C., & Snowling, M. J. (2016). The home literacy environment as a predictor of the early literacy development of children at family-risk of dyslexia. *Scientific Studies of Reading*, *20*(5), 401–419. doi:10.1080/10888438.2016.1213266 PMID:28250707

Hampden-Thompson, G. (2013). Family policy, family structure, and children's educational achievement. *Social Science Research*, *42*(3), 804–817. doi:10.1016/j.ssresearch.2013.01.005 PMID:23521996

Jabbari, B., & Rouster, A. S. (2023). Family dynamics. In *StatPearls*. StatPearls Publishing. https://www.ncbi.nlm.nih.gov/books/NBK560487/

Kong, A., Thorleifsson, G., Frigge, M. L., Vilhjalmsson, B. J., Young, A. I., Thorgeirsson, T. E., Benonisdottir, S., Oddsson, A., Halldorsson, B. V., Masson, G., Gudbjartsson, D. F., Helgason, A., Bjornsdottir, G., Thorsteinsdottir, U., & Stefansson, K. (2018). The nature of nurture: Effects of parental genotypes. *Science, 359*(6374), 424–428. doi:10.1126cience.aan6877 PMID:29371463

Lasky, P., Buckwalter, K. C., Whall, A., Lederman, R., Speer, J., McLane, A., King, J. M., White, M. A., Woods, N. F., & Rees, B. L. (1985). Developing an instrument for the assessment of family dynamics. *Western Journal of Nursing Research, 7*(1), 40–57. doi:10.1177/0092055X8500700105 PMID:3850686

Mouzaki, A., & Protopapas, A. (2010) (Eds.). Orthography, learning and disorders. Gutenberg. [in Greek]

Newman, J., Gozu, H., Guan, S., Lee, J. E., Li, X., & Sasaki, Y. (2015). Relationship between maternal parenting style and high school achievement and self-esteem in China, Turkey and U.S.A. *Journal of Comparative Family Studies, 46*(2), 265–288. https://www.jstor.org/stable/43613115. doi:10.3138/jcfs.46.2.265

Pavlidis, G. Th., & Giannouli, V. (2003). Spelling errors accurately differentiate USA-English speakers from Greek dyslexics: Implications for causality and treatment. In R. M. Joshi, C. K. Leong, & L. J. Kaczmarek (Eds.), *Literacy acquisition: The role of phonology, morphology and orthography*. IOS Press.

Pomerantz, E. M., Moorman, E. A., & Litwack, S. D. (2007). The how, whom, and why of parents' involvement in children's academic lives: More Is not always better. *Review of Educational Research, 77*(3), 373–410. doi:10.3102/003465430305567

Protopapas, A., Fakou, A., Drakopoulou, S., Skaloumbakas, C., & Mouzaki, A. (2013). What do spelling errors tell us? Classification and analysis of errors made by Greek schoolchildren with and without dyslexia. *Reading and Writing, 26*(5), 615–646. doi:10.100711145-012-9378-3

Puglisi, M. L., Hulme, C., Hamilton, L. G., & Snowling, M. J. (2017). The home literacy environment is a correlate, but perhaps not a cause, of variations in children's language and literacy development. *Scientific Studies of Reading, 21*(6), 498–514. doi:10.1080/10888438.2017.1346660 PMID:29930486

Robledo-Ramón, P., García-Sánchez, J.-N., Robledo-Ramón, P., & García-Sánchez, J.-N. (2012). The family environment of students with learning disabilities and ADHD. In *Learning Disabilities*. IntechOpen. doi:10.5772/32507

Sahu, A., Bhargava, R., Sagar, R., & Mehta, M. (2018). Perception of families of children with specific learning disorder: An exploratory study. *Indian Journal of Psychological Medicine, 40*(5), 406–413. doi:10.4103/IJPSYM.IJPSYM_148_18 PMID:30275614

Santín, D., & Sicilia, G. (2016). Does family structure affect children's academic outcomes? Evidence for Spain. *The Social Science Journal, 53*(4), 555–572. doi:10.1016/j.soscij.2016.04.001

Shahaeian, A., Wang, C., Tucker-Drob, E., Geiger, V., Bus, A. G., & Harrison, L. J. (2018). Early shared reading, socioeconomic status, and children's cognitive and school competencies: Six years of longitudinal evidence. *Scientific Studies of Reading*, *22*(6), 485–502. doi:10.1080/10888438.2018.1482901 PMID:34108838

Spadidakis, I. (2009). *Difficulties of writing production of school-age children. Diagnosis - Assessment - Treatment* (8th ed.). Hellenic Letters. [in Greek]

Tamboer, P., Vorst, H. C. M., & Oort, F. J. (2016). Five describing factors of dyslexia. *Journal of Learning Disabilities*, *49*(5), 466–483. doi:10.1177/0022219414558123 PMID:25398549

Tantaros, S. (2004). Family and child and adolescent development: Theoretical approaches and considerations. In S. Tantaros (Ed.), *Human development and family* (pp. 15–34). [in Greek]

Trecha, S., & Tsibidaki, A. (2021). Spelling mistakes and performance on an intelligence assessment test. In V. Chiou, L. Geunis, O. Holz, N. O. Ertürk & F. Shelton (Eds), Voices from the classroom: A celebration of learning (pp. 385-397). Waxmann Verlag.

Trecha, S., & Tsibidaki, A. (2022). Correlation of spelling errors with intelligence and family dynamics of primary school students. In S. G. Soulis & M. Liakopoulou (Eds.), *Education in the 21st century: Contemporary challenges and concerns*. Proceedings of the International Scientific Conference (Vol. 2, pp. 54-67). Gutenberg. [in Greek]

Treiman, R. (2017). Learning to spell: Phonology and beyond. *Cognitive Neuropsychology*, *34*(3–4), 3–4. doi:10.1080/02643294.2017.1337630 PMID:28628367

Triga-Mertika, E. (2010). *Learning difficulties. General and specific learning difficulties - Dyslexia.* Gregory. [in Greek]

Tsibidaki, A. (2021). Resilience, meaning in life and self-efficacy in families with or without a member with special educational needs and disability during the COVID-19 pandemic. *Psychology: the Journal of the Hellenic Psychological Society*, *26*(3), 3. doi:10.12681/psy_hps.29161

Varsamidou, D., & Spadidakis, G. (2007). Relationship between written language production and comprehension. In M. Vlassopoulou, A., Giannetopoulou, M. Diamanti, L., Kirpotin, E., Levantis, E., Leftheri & G. Sakellariou (Eds.), Language difficulties and written language in the context of school learning (pp.377- 389). Grigoris. [in Greek]

White, M., & Elander, G. (1992). Translation of an instrument. *Scandinavian Journal of Caring Sciences*, *6*(3), 161–164. doi:10.1111/j.1471-6712.1992.tb00145.x PMID:1439377

Xanthi, S. (2017). Qualitative analysis of 4th - 6th grade students' errors in dictation and free writing spelling tasks. [in Greek]. *Research in Education*, *6*(1), 1–17.

Zachos, G. H., & Zachos, D. H. (1998). *Dyslexia. Treatment-Rehabilitation. Program implementation instructions*. Center for Psychological Studies.

Zarić, J., Hasselhorn, M., & Nagler, T. (2021). Orthographic knowledge predicts reading and spelling skills over and above general intelligence and phonological awareness. *European Journal of Psychology of Education*, *36*(1), 21–43. doi:10.100710212-020-00464-7

Chapter 8
A Family's Experiences of Raising a Child Diagnosed With ADHD:
Family Functioning and Organization, Sources of Support and Quality of Life – A Case Study

Kyriaki Tasiou
https://orcid.org/0000-0001-8144-8090
University of the Aegean, Greece

Eleni N. Nikolaou
https://orcid.org/0000-0003-1840-3433
University of the Aegean, Greece

ABSTRACT

Attention Deficit Hyperactivity Disorder (ADHD) affects people diagnosed with it and their families in many ways. Parents of children with ADHD are likely to face challenges in various aspects of parenting their children. This chapter describes a case study of a family of a child diagnosed with ADHD living permanently in Kos. The purpose of this study was to explore through in-depth structured interviews how parents perceive and manage the functioning and organisation of their family, the impact of the child's ADHD behaviour on their daily life, the sources of support they receive and their quality of life. The dominant themes identified were that parents perceive the disorder to affect family functioning and quality of life and seek support in order to cope with the difficulties of daily life. Understanding parents' own experiences is of paramount importance to clinical practice because the way a family functions and the sources of support available to them can have a significant impact on the child and the whole family system.

INTRODUCTION

Attention-deficit/hyperactivity disorder (ADHD) describes a disorder with a genetic and neurological

DOI: 10.4018/979-8-3693-1982-6.ch008

background (Olivier et al., 2009) and a significant impact on people's daily lives. The three main sub-categories of the disorder according to the Diagnostic and Statistical Manual of Mental Health (DSM-V) are ADHD with a predominantly inattentive type, ADHD with a predominantly hyperactive/impulsive type, and ADHD (combined type) (American Psychiatric Association, 2013). Children with ADHD often exhibit behaviour that parents find difficult to manage and as a result experience more distress compared to parents of children without some kind of disability (Ringer, 2019). This behaviour described as age-inappropriate occurs mainly in childhood possibly persisting through adolescence and adulthood (Sonna, 2005; Sue et al., 1994).

The environment plays a key role in the development of symptomatology (Howe, 2010). Parents who love, accept and protect their children essentially adopt a parenting style that reduces the distance between them. Communication, cooperation and involvement, warmth and tolerance towards the child with ADHD (Stamatis & Nikolaou, 2020) can be enhanced when there are clear parental roles, unity, consistency, discipline measures, appropriate parenting model and understanding of ADHD (Angenent, 1985). Parents of children with ADHD have been found to have reduced feelings of competence and satisfaction with their parenting style (Mash & Johnston 1983; Shelton et al., 1998).The impact of ADHD on the family unit permeates family functioning, reducing the quality of life of both children and their parents (Andrade et al., 2016; Dey et al., 2019).

The coexistence of additional problems such as those of self-regulation, emotional outbursts, lack of motivation, low self-esteem, difficulty in problem solving, hyperactivity, poor inhibition and poor impulse control are likely to be present, which contribute to the parent's difficulty in managing such behaviours (Aberson et al, 2007; Barkley, 2005; Rief, 2005; Tannock, 1998). In fact, given that Polanczyk et al. (2007) estimate that the prevalence rate of the disorder in children is close to 5.29% worldwide, there are many parents who have difficulties in raising their children with ADHD. The challenges faced by parents of children with ADHD prove to be significantly greater than those faced by parents of children without the disorder (Anastopoulos et al., 1992).

In order to understand the complex nature of ADHD, it is crucial to ''listen'' to the views and experiences of the parents themselves who are most affected by it (Firmin & Phillips, 2009). From parents, may emerge perspectives that are important for the implementation of supportive measures for the child (Podolski & Nigg, 2001).

Parents of Children With ADHD

Parenting involves attitudes, practices, or parenting styles (Cummings & Cummings, 2002). ADHD is a heterogeneous disorder resulting in parents having a variety of experiences to demonstrate (Taylor, 2009). Harrison & Sofronoff (2002) highlight how crucial the parental role and family functioning is to the future outcomes of the child with ADHD.

Pahlavanzadeh et al. (2018) set out to explore the needs of 27 caregivers of children with ADHD. They reported anxiety, inadequate information about the disorder, conflicting family environment, communication problems, reduced performance in parental and non-parental roles, discipline actions, marital conflict, parental resentment, and financial burdens as key problems as well as negative emotions and fear of stigmatization due to ADHD resulting in hiding the disorder and avoiding seeking care. They also reported parental depression, aggressive and inappropriate behaviours due to children's behaviours resulting from ADHD. The need for appropriate adjustment skills, anger management, problem solving, social and family support, clarity in child management was also shown.

ADHD and Family Functioning

A family's ability to problem-solve and encourage communication to meet the needs of their child with ADHD by utilizing family resources and other sources of support describes family functioning (Chen & Instone, 2008). In the study by Ching'oma et al. (2022), 16 parents of children with ADHD reported disruptions in family functioning and social interactions among family members due to the behavior of children with ADHD.

In families with children diagnosed with ADHD, higher rates of family dysfunction were noted due to problems in communication, relationships, and problem solving (Cunningham & Boyle, 2002), more conflict and lower levels of family organization, more mental health problems, and problems in interpersonal relationships were observed (Cappe et al., 2017; Mulligan et al., 2011). According to McIntyre & Hennessy (2012) it is not clear whether family dysfunction is the cause or the consequence of ADHD as it has been suggested that it may also cause it (Timimi & Taylor, 2004).

Wymbs & Pelham (2010) report that parent-child communication with a child diagnosed with ADHD is more negative and less positive. It has even been suggested that the behaviour of the child with ADHD has an apparent adverse effect on parental and interparental communication (Evans et al, 2013). Notably, children with ADHD are more prone to conflict with other family members than children without ADHD (Chang & Gau, 2017). In this regard, Hoag's (2014) qualitative study regarding parent-child communication found that mothers communicate with their child with ADHD in a different way than mothers communicate with their children without ADHD. This was attributed to the often unpredictable, negative and erratic nature that conversations with a child with ADHD can take on.

Parenting practices are parenting behaviours that are shaped by the socialization of children (Morris et al., 2007). They include warmth/engagement, behavioural (Lamborn et al., 1991) and psychological control (Barber, 1996). Parenting practices and parenting styles are distinct concepts, whereas the second relates to the parent's attitude towards the child, playing a role in shaping the emotional climate (Morris et al., 2007).

The study by McKee et al. (2004) found that parents overreact to impulsive behaviours, with frequent reprimands, underestimate the value of their children and often exert more control and criticism on them. They also often display coldness and higher levels of anxiety, and question their children's parenting ability. Inappropriate parenting styles adopted may exacerbate ADHD symptomatology (Molina & Musich, 2016; Ni & Gau, 2015). It has also been found that parents of children with ADHD are more directive, controlling and authoritarian compared to parents of children without ADHD (Barkley et al., 1991; Johnston & Mash, 2001; Lange et al., 2005). Research indicates that parents of children with ADHD might experience a phenomenon where effective parenting practices become gradually altered due to the ongoing caregiving demands and the behaviors associated with the disorder (McLaughlin & Harrison, 2006).

Emotional responsiveness is a dimension of parenting behavior and includes behaviors such as warmth, sensitivity and acceptance towards the child is demonstrated (Johnston et al., 2012). In Seipp & Johnston's (2005) study it was shown that mothers of children with ADHD and Oppositional Defiant Disorder showed less sensitivity and more hyperactivity compared to mothers of typically developing children.

Cohesive families are those characterized by warm and positive emotional relationships within and between family subsystems (Barber & Buehler, 1996). It has been observed that disruptive behaviors of children with ADHD appear to be reduced by the presence of parental unity in terms of decision making, rule setting in the home, and delegation of tasks (Sonna, 2005).

ADHD and Sources of Support

Social support describes the ability of a social network to provide psychological and material support to an individual to cope with stress (Cohen, 2004). A key source of support for many parents is grandparents who contribute emotionally, financially and practically. Friends, in particular friends with similar experiences, can be equally important sources of support, even reducing parents' stress through empathy, providing advice or strategies for adjustment (Thoits, 2011).

In Peters and Jackson's (2009) qualitative study, mothers reported receiving little practical support from family, friends or community services and expressed feelings of marginalization.

ADHD and Quality of Family Life

The World Health Organization defines quality of life as: "*an individual's perception of his or her place in life, in the context of the culture and value systems in which he or she lives and in relation to goals, aspirations, norms and concerns*" (Fitzgerald et al., 2001).

Overall, it is observed that ADHD affects the quality of life related to the health of a child and his/her family, as well as affecting family functioning (Peñuelas-Calvo et al., 2021). In this direction, Peasgood et al. (2020) concluded that the disorder has a multifaceted impact in terms of parents/caregivers' sleep hours and quality, leisure satisfaction and health-related quality of life. Similarly, Azazy et al. (2018) identified that most parents in addition to average quality of life, had dysfunctional families.

As the systematic literature review suggests, quantitative research has a greater resonance with parents of children with ADHD than qualitative research, resulting in a lack of knowledge from parents' experiences and perceptions (Ho et al., 2011). Qualitative exploration, within families, of the management of a child with ADHD becomes important as it will provide a literature base and contribute to the wider exploration of family theory. The aim of this study is to explore in depth the perceptions and experiences of two parents of a child with ADHD regarding specific aspects of parenting. The following research questions were explored: The perceptions of parents of a child with ADHD about family functioning, quality of life and the impact of the disorder on these and their experiences of the sources of support they have received.

METHODOLOGY

Participants-Place

This study is part of a larger study examining the experiences of parents of children diagnosed with ADHD. Participants are two parents who live permanently in Kos, in Dodecanese. The boy's mother (aged 12), a secondary school graduate and his stepfather a graduate of the Police School. The child was diagnosed with ADHD by a psychiatrist at a Mental Health Centre when he was 5 years old and there is no co-existing diagnosis or other disability. The child had been raised with the stepfather for at least eight consecutive years prior to receiving the diagnosis.

Procedure

Parents were invited to participate in a structured and thematically focused interview designed according to an interview guide. The specific type of interview was chosen because it gives the possibility of communication and intervention by the researcher, clarifying ambiguities that may arise (Mason, 2003), while a global view of the participants can be formed (Iosifidis, 2003). The interviews began with the researcher inviting the parents to talk about their experiences as parents of a child with ADHD. Among the questions asked were questions related to the child's diagnosis, the meaning of this diagnosis, child and family strengths and difficulties, sources of support and treatment, the impact of ADHD on family life, communication, relationships and family functioning and quality of life, and advice for other parents. Finally, they were also asked to answer a series of demographic-type questions.

Participants were assured that complete confidentiality and anonymity would be maintained in the handling of information, that the interview would be recorded, and signed a written informed consent form. The duration of the interviews ranged from 25-30 minutes.

Data Analysis

Qualitative Study Instruments

The interviews were transcribed verbatim and analyzed according to basic principles of thematic analysis (Braun & Clarke, 2006). The transcripts were coded by two coders, one of which has research-level reliability. The open approach was used as a data coding approach, where codes are extracted from the text (Blair, 2015).

Validity: Reliability

To ensure the consistency of the content, the transcripts were compared with the original text and audio files. There was frequent checking of the original transcripts to ensure that interpretations were based on the data, with the aim of maintaining validity. Questions were carefully evaluated for clarity, appropriateness and adequacy in order to enhance the reliability of the research (Guba & Lincoln, 1989). Cross-checks (Peräkylä, 2004) between researchers ensured that rubrics were consistently applied during data analysis. To establish the reliability of the study and to enhance objectivity, the process of categorizing, coding and identifying the individual themes was carried out independently by the second author-researcher and a high level of agreement of 95% was found, where minor modifications were made.

Data Analysis Process

Initially the researcher became familiar with the data through multiple readings of the texts, initial ideas and themes were noted. Systematic analysis of the data then began, through coding where initial codes were identified, which were drawn into possible themes and sub-themes. Key quotes from the data set were also identified. Three key themes were produced in line with the research questions. There was a review of the themes and coded data to check for possible overlap or similarity between codes, coded extracts and the data set (Braun, & Clarke, 2012). The key themes, subthemes, and codes that were generated are indicated in Figure 1.

Figure 1. Classification of findings into subjects, codes, and subthemes

SUBJECT	CODES	SUBTHEMES
1. Family organisation	a.General family function	a1.without planning a.2.anxiety, difficulty of control a3.feeling of effectiveness a4.feeling of inefficiency a5.parental emotional response
	b.Family dysfunction	b1.upset family & child with ADHD b2. anxiety, discomfort in member relationships, difficulty in predicting/controlling behaviour b3. family communication b4. problem solving b5. relationships between members
	c.Family practices	c1.limits, stability c2. communication, help from an expert c3.setting rules c4.absence of rules c5.existence of consequences c6.instability in determining consequences c7.different way of controlling behaviour
	d.Parental roles	d1.clarity of parental roles d2.conflict of parental roles
	e. Family cohesion, security and unity	e1.feeling of good connection between members e2.feeling of unity despite conflicts e3.feeling of security
	f.Decision-making	f. mother's decision making
	g. Emotional parental responsiveness	g1.frequent repetition of requests g2.open discussion g 3.help from experts
2. Sources of Support	a.Psychological Support	a1.no search for psychological support α2. child & mother psychotherapies
	b.Financial Support	b1.no search for financial support β2.financial support from parents-house accommodation
	c.Social Support	c. no social support
	d.Health care (treatments etc.)	d1.no search for access to health services d2. educational support
3. Quality of Life	a.Determinants of quality of life	a1.family love a2.health a3.economic factors a4.insufficient personal time
	b.Impact of ADHD on quality of life	b1.no impact of ADHD on quality of life b2.impact of ADHD on quality of life b3.insufficient personal time.

FINDINGS: RESULTS

The findings of the study relate to the perceptions and experiences of parents of a 12-year-old child diagnosed with ADHD, which are classified according to the questions asked. They include family organization, sources of support available, determinants that parents perceive as contributing to quality of life and the impact of the disorder on it. The main themes and subthemes that emerged are presented below.

Family Organization

The tensions and feelings of stress experienced by parents in managing daily life with a child with ADHD are highlighted. The extent to which participants perceive family dysfunctions on a daily basis is emphasized. Parenting practices and parental roles adopted are described, and the degree of family cohesion, unity and emotional responsiveness of parents is clarified.

General Family Functioning

Throughout the interview, parents highlighted the intense anxiety and the difficulty of controlling and predicting the behaviour of their child with ADHD, elements that characterize their role as parents and which they have to manage on a daily basis:

'' Under a lot of stress...there is no way, we will go somewhere and we will be heard. I'll be shouting all the time...if I go somewhere with friends to eat I'll always be anticipating not to be called snappy...not to be seen. I'm always ahead to pick him up a little, so he doesn't show it...Well, now that he's starting high school I won't be there...I think he'll get bullied, a lot...''(Mother)

The stepfather did not give a specific description of how the family is organized and concluded that most things are done instinctively. However, he stated greater confidence in its effectiveness. The mother, despite investing considerable time and energy in their son's well-being, expressed uncertainty about its effectiveness.

Family Dysfunctions

Both parents expressed the view that they experience family dysfunctions having a child with ADHD. These dysfunctions were identified in the relationships of the members:

''...he upsets in general. Where he's sometimes calm, then he gets caught up in his silliness, he gets upset, he upsets us all. He fights...he will fight with his sister, he will fight with his mother...and he fights with me...''(stepfather).

in their communication with each other:

''...we generally fight with his mum, because we fight for the reason that his mum...for the way she deals with this...'' (stepfather)

Parenting Practices

Among the practices parents use to manage their child's daily disruptive behaviors, they frequently mentioned words: "boundaries, rules, common line, patience, acceptance." The stepfather also emphasized the importance of stability in speech and actions.

''...Limits because if you don't set limits, you've lost it...Rules, rules definitely...What I have to say is common line...and patience...'' (Stepfather)

''...limits...parents should have patience...and accept...if you accept it and see it, I think it will happen later...There are many who do not accept it'' (Mother)

"We are Black and White."

Parents stated that everyone's role was clear, however different levels of clarity emerged. Indeed, they often conflict, with the father appearing absolute, firm and consistent and the mother more flexible.

Family Cohesion, Unity, and Decision-Making

Despite the difficulties, parents described a family environment characterized by cohesion and unity between members. In terms of decision making, the mother seemed to decide on most issues related to the child with ADHD.

Parental Emotional Response

As for her response to various disruptive behaviours of the child, the mother emphasized that frequent repetition of requests to the child, open discussion with the child with honesty and explanations, as well as help from experts, acted as a supportive factor in her efforts. In fact, after receiving the diagnosis she reported a change in her reactions and gained more empathy.

Sources of Support

Parents gave mixed accounts of their experiences of the sources of support they have sought to manage difficulties that have arisen due to ADHD. The mother even showed a willingness to praise schools and services. However, both converge on the fact that this support is very limited.

Psychological Support

The mother appeared more positive regarding the psychological support she received, although she commented on the transient nature of her contact with mental health services. She mentioned the need for additional therapies (speech and language therapy, occupational therapy) and expressed her difficulty in providing them due to financial difficulties and personal issues. The stepfather, on the other hand, argued that they do not often resort to the help of specialists.

Social, Financial, Family Support

Both parents underlined the limited social, economic and family support mainly due to circumstances (residence, divorce, etc.). The mother pointed out the financial help she received from her parents.

Quality of Life

Parents described different factors that they consider to contribute to quality of life. They mentioned the impact of the disorder on their daily life and on their quality of life.

Determinants of Quality of Life

As determinants of quality of life, parents mentioned financial factors, common family activities and carefree life, while the stepfather formulated the lack of personal time. Both agree that love and harmony in the family is the most important factor of quality of life.

Impact of ADHD on Quality of Life

The impact of ADHD on quality of life is evident from both reports. They certainly describe that they have seen improvements in their son's behaviour over the years, that they have become used to and accepted the situation and that they would not change anything in their lives. Despite the regular challenges they are forced to face, they both had positive aspects of their child with ADHD to describe. Their child was described as giving, kind-hearted, consistent, cooperative, autonomous, organized with empathy, and compassionate.

The stepfather even seemed to take a different, proactive approach to dealing with their son's ADHD:

''...it was just a kid, it will pass...because we don't deal with it like that at home. It is... a different kid. We don't deal with it somehow.''(Stepfather)

It is noteworthy that the mother's thinking reflects the need to change attitudes towards ADHD:

''...I have met parents...I often see...children with ADHD difficulties...I see them stressed at first and I tell them...and I'm okay, that's how I was...''(Mother)

Finally, regarding the limitations they may have felt in terms of reducing extra-familial activities due to the child's ADHD-related behaviours:

''...at parties, for example, that we have happened to not to go...I mean we have been one, two or three times, it has become an issue and to avoid making an issue we avoid parties...all these things picked me up a little bit too'' (Mother)

This was a point of contrast with the father's view that extra-familial activities have not been restricted.

SUMMARY: CONCLUSION

This study aims to explore aspects of the daily life of a family of a child with ADHD. The findings are broadly consistent with findings from previous research on family functioning issues, sources of support and quality of life for families. Parents interviewed indicated a high degree of involvement in their children's lives. Their willingness to devote time and resources to contribute to positive outcomes for their children is notable. They seemed quite familiar with clinical aspects of the disorder and with specific terminology ("heredity, ADHD"), and showed a good deal of understanding and acceptance of the condition and difficulties.

Throughout the interview, both parents, and more so the mother, expressed the intense anxiety with which even the simplest family functions were performed. The challenges faced by families raising a child with ADHD are great (Tasiou & Nikolaou, 2022; 2023). Indeed, research has found that parents of children with ADHD have increased levels of anxiety, decreased parental esteem and feelings of parental powerlessness (Deault, 2010; Johnston & Mash, 2001).

Gustafsson et al. (2008) report that in addition to behavioural problems they identify in their children with ADHD, parents find them to be sensitive and easily upset. For many families there was even the possibility that this upset and possible breakdown of the child could increase the tension levels of the whole family due to the constant vigilance in which the family members are under. This finding is confirmed by the present study as both parents reported several times situations where the child suddenly became upset and this tension was transferred to all members.

Regarding family functioning, observations in studies with ADHD children and their parents pointed to dysfunctional patterns of conflictual parent-child interaction and dysfunctional parenting styles (Cussen et al., 2012; Deault, 2010). Indeed, and according to parents' accounts, conflicts of the child with ADHD with all family members are neither few nor rare.

Although both reported that parental roles were clear and communication between them was good, they often stated that they were at odds over issues of managing the child with ADHD and issues related to parenting. This finding coincides with a study which found that marital conflict over care issues was common (Sollie, 2014). The stepfather in particular at several points pointed out mistakes by the mother in terms of her response to the child's behaviours, and the mother often mentioned that she was weak and therefore more resilient. It is documented in the literature that mothers being held responsible for disorder-related behaviors, documented or not, is not a rare occurrence (Jackson & Mannix, 2004).

The mother in this study expressed uncertainty about her effectiveness. The anxiety and self-efficacy that parents may feel about their role are key dimensions of their wellbeing. They even seem to have been negatively associated with the presence of a child with ADHD in the family (Lange et al., 2005; Podolski & Nigg, 2001). On the other hand, the stepfather stated that he or she felt largely effective. Practices followed by parents with higher perceived self-efficacy have been found to be significantly more effective compared to parents who feel less effective (McLaughlin & Harrison, 2006).

Insecurity was also expressed by the mother about the stability that may characterize her decision making on parenting issues and the setting of limits and rules, unlike the stepfather, who is more stable. If the child perceives parental inconsistency in parenting, he/she may perceive it as a lack of control over situations (Peñuelas-Calvo et al., 2021). Sonna (2005), states, when parents are united as they make decisions about setting rules and assigning tasks in the home, the child's ADHD behaviours are reduced. In Olivier et al.'s (2009) study, it was shown that parents who set rules independently of each other, children in order to achieve what they were aiming for may even manipulate one parent towards the other. From the stories of both parents in this study, it is evident from the different ways of dealing with the issue of boundaries, rules and consequences, although both admit that when there is ''common line'' the outcomes are better.

Olivier et al. (2009) suggest that clarity in boundaries is necessary because it guides children. Furthermore, they state that discipline in children with ADHD appeared effective, particularly by explaining the reasons for performing a task in a particular way. In the same study, parents found that one of the most difficult aspects to master was consistency, which is a safe guide for children, as repeated actions in a certain way are more effective in modifying behaviour (Pretorius, 1998).

The parents in this study seem to follow different practices. The mother, with a positive approach, constant communication, explanations, acceptance and empathy, tries to understand difficulties and manage ADHD-related behaviours, while the stepfather with rules, consequences and firm boundaries. For children with ADHD, it has been found that parenting practices characterized by warmth, responsiveness, appreciation, social acceptance, and better social skills have been associated with more favorable outcomes, particularly when the symptoms of the disorder are milder (Hurt et al., 2007; Keown, 2012). However, less family warmth and responsiveness and the use of authoritarian parenting styles are more common due to dealing with problems arising from the disorder (Harold et al., 2013; Tripp et al., 2007).

Regarding parental reactions to the child's disruptive behaviour, the mother in this study reports that she is often affected by emotion but with patience and open discussion tries to manage such situations, unlike the stepfather who usually takes the path of taking measures and setting limits. In the study by Ching'oma et al. (2022) some parents were concerned, others assigned activities to the child to release their energy, others applied discipline measures (scolding, use of corporal punishment).

The feeling of isolation from the community was a major concern expressed by the mother, who reported that she had avoided social interaction in the past due to negative experiences. Similarly, for the mothers who participated in Peters & Jackson's (2009) study, the exclusion and isolation for themselves and their children with ADHD often extended to their extended family, beyond their wider circle of social contacts. Chang et al. (2020) and Chou et al. (2020) agree that mothers of children with ADHD limit their social interactions and avoid contexts or environments that they seem inappropriate for their children.

It is understood that mothers of a child with ADHD may experience emotional distress due to self-blame, the blame they may receive for their child's disruptive behaviour and lack of family support (Harborne et al., 2004). Indeed, in this study, lack of support at all levels, social, family, socio-economic, is evident in both parents' narratives. The mother, reported that she received psychological support together with the child only during the first years of diagnosis and the stepfather did not seek any kind of help. It is very unlikely that fathers would seek coaching, as - unlike mothers - they do not consider their parenting skills to be in need of interventions to improve (Fabiano, 2007). In addition, the mother in this study identified the help her child received from special educators in schools as important support. This observation contradicts Peters & Jackson's (2009) finding where some mothers reported a lack of educational support and inadequate resources available at school to manage their children's behaviour and needs.

It is likely that ADHD has an impact on families' overall quality of life, with parents of children with ADHD being more likely to experience problems than parents of children without ADHD (Cussen et al., 2012). In the present study, the stepfather did not express concern about the social interactions of the child with ADHD, unlike the mother who expressed concern about the child's future in high school and the potential bullying he may experience. Also, avoidance of extra-familial activities appeared to be familiar to the mother. Throughout the interview she acknowledged her own anxiety about parenting.

The presence of anxiety in the family environment, and early on, can become chronic and have a negative impact on the well-being of parents, their children and the relationship between them (Deater et al., 1996). The stepfather on the other hand highlighted the absence of personal time.

In conclusion, it is both a challenge and a necessity for professionals who work with children who have diagnoses such as ADHD to consider family dynamics (Buschgens et al., 2008; Cunningham, 2007).

REFERENCES

Aberson, B., Shure, M. B., & Goldstein, S. (2007). Social problem-solving intervention can help children with ADHD. *Journal of Attention Disorders*, *12*(5), 391–393. doi:10.1177/1087054707299409 PMID:17606767

American Psychiatric Association. (2013). *Diagnostic and statistical manual of mental disorders* (5th ed.). American Psychiatric Association.

Anastopoulos, A. D., Guevremont, D. C., Shelton, T. L., & DuPaul, G. J. (1992). Parenting stress among families of children with attention deficit hyperactivity disorder. *Journal of Abnormal Child Psychology*, *20*(5), 503–520. doi:10.1007/BF00916812 PMID:1487593

Andrade, E. M., Geha, L. M., Duran, P., Suwwan, R., Machado, F., & Do Rosario, M. C. (2016). Quality of life in caregivers of ADHD children and diabetes patients. *Frontiers in Psychiatry*, *7*, 127. doi:10.3389/fpsyt.2016.00127 PMID:27504099

Angenent, H. (1985). *Opvoeding en persoonlijkheids ontwikkeling*. Nijkerk: Uitgevery Intro.

Azazy, S., Nour-Eldein, H., Mikhail, H., & Ismail, M. (2018). Quality of life and family function of parents of children with attention deficit hyperactivity disorder. *Eastern Mediterranean health journal=La revue de santé de la Méditerranée orientale=al-Majallah al-ṣiḥḥīyah li-sharq al-mutawassiṭ. 24*. 579-587.

Barber, B. K., & Buehler, C. (1996). Family cohesion and enmeshment: Different constructs, different effects. *Journal of Marriage and Family*, *58*(2), 433–441. doi:10.2307/353507

Barkley, R. (2005). *Taking Charge of AD/HD: The complete, authoritative guide for parents* (Rev.ed.). Guilford.

Barkley, R. A., Fischer, M., Edelbrock, C., & Smallish, L. (1991). The adolescent outcome of hyperactive children diagnosed by research criteria-III: Mother–child interactions, family conflicts and maternal psychopathology. *Journal of Child Psychology and Psychiatry, and Allied Disciplines*, *32*(2), 233–255. doi:10.1111/j.1469-7610.1991.tb00304.x PMID:2033106

Blair, E. (2015). A reflexive exploration of two qualitative data coding techniques. *Journal of Methods and Measurement in the Social Sciences*, *6*(1), 14–29. doi:10.2458/v6i1.18772

Braun, V., & Clarke, V. (2006). Using thematic analysis in psychology. *Qualitative Research in Psychology*, *3*(2), 77–101. doi:10.1191/1478088706qp063oa

Braun, V., & Clarke, V. (2012). *Thematic analysis*. American Psychological Association. doi:10.1037/13620-004

Buschgens, C., van Aken, M., Swinkels, S., Altin, M., Fliers, E., & Rommelese, N. (2008). Differential family and peer environmental factors are related to severity and comorbidity in children with ADHD. *Journal of Neural Transmission (Vienna, Austria)*, *115*(2), 177–186. doi:10.100700702-007-0838-x PMID:18200433

Cappe, E., Bolduc, M., Rouge, M. C., Saiag, M. C., & Delome, R. (2017). Quality of life, psychological characteristics, and adjustment in parents of children with attention- deficit /hyperactivity disorder. *Quality of Life Research: An International Journal of Quality of Life Aspects of Treatment, Care and Rehabilitation*, *26*(5), 1283–1294. doi:10.100711136-016-1446-8 PMID:27798755

Chang, C. C., Chen, Y. M., Liu, T. L., Hsiao, R. C., Chou, W. J., & Yen, C. F. (2020). Affiliate stigma and related factors in family caregivers of children with attention deficit/hyperactivity disorder. *International Journal of Environmental Research and Public Health*, *17*(2), 576. doi:10.3390/ijerph17020576 PMID:31963190

Chang, J. P. C., & Gau, S. S. F. (2017). Mother-child relationship in youths with attention-deficit hyperactivity disorder and their siblings. *Journal of Abnormal Child Psychology*, *45*(5), 871–882. doi:10.100710802-016-0218-9 PMID:27771825

Chen, J. Y., & Instone, S. L. (2008). *Family resilience and functioning in child with DMD: Functioning and resilience in families with children with Duchenne muscular dystrophy*. VDM Verlag Dr. Muller Aktiengesellschaft.

Ching'oma, C. D., Mkoka, D. A., Ambikile, J. S., & Iseselo, M. K. (2022). Experiences and challenges of parents caring for children with attention-deficit hyperactivity disorder: A qualitative study in Dar es salaam, Tanzania. *PLoS One*, *17*(8), e0267773. doi:10.1371/journal.pone.0267773 PMID:35921363

Chou, W. J., Liu, T. L., Hsiao, R. C., Chen, Y. M., Chang, C. C., & Yen, C. F. (2020). Application and perceived effectiveness of complementary and alternative intervention strategies for attention-deficit/hyperactivity disorder: Relationships with affiliate stigma. *International Journal of Environmental Research and Public Health, 17*, 1505.

Cummings, E. M., & Cummings, J. S. (2002). Parenting and Attachment. In M. H. Bornstein (Ed.), Handbook of Parenting: Vol. 5. *Practical Issues in Parenting* (pp. 35–58). Erlbaum.

Cunningham, C. E. (2007). A family-centered approach to planning and measuring the outcome of interventions for children with attention-deficit/hyperactivity disorder. *Ambulatory Pediatrics*, *7*(1), 60–72. doi:10.1016/j.ambp.2006.05.003 PMID:17261485

Cunningham, C. E., & Boyle, M. H. (2002). Preschoolers at risk for attention-deficit hyperactivity disorder: Family, parenting, and behavioral correlates. *Journal of Abnormal Child Psychology*, *30*(6), 555–569. doi:10.1023/A:1020855429085 PMID:12481971

Cussen, A., Sciberras, E., Ukoumunne, O. C., & Efron, D. (2012). Relationship between symptoms of attention-deficit/hyperactivity disorder and family functioning: A community-based study. *European Journal of Pediatrics*, *171*(2), 271–280. doi:10.100700431-011-1524-4 PMID:21743986

Deater-Deckard, K., & Scarr, S. (1996). Parenting stress among dual-earner mothers and fathers: Are there gender differences? *Journal of Family Psychology*, *10*(1), 45–59. doi:10.1037/0893-3200.10.1.45

Deault, L. C. (2010). A systematic review of parenting in relation to the development of comorbidities and functional impairments in children with attention-deficit/hyperactivity disorder (ADHD). *Child Psychiatry and Human Development*, *41*(2), 168–192. doi:10.100710578-009-0159-4 PMID:19768532

Dey, M., Castro, R. P., Haug, S., & Schaub, M. P. (2019). Quality of life of parents of mentally-ill children: A systematic review and meta-analysis. *Epidemiology and Psychiatric Sciences*, *28*(5), 563–577. doi:10.1017/S2045796018000409 PMID:30078381

Evans, S.W., Owens, J.S., & Bunford, N. (2013). Evidence-based psychosocial treatments for children and adolescents with attention deficit/hyperactivity disorder. *Journal of Clinical Child andvAdolescent Psychology*.

Fabiano, G. A. (2007). Father participation in behavioral parent training for ADHD: Review and recommendations for increasing inclusion and engagement. *Journal of Family Psychology*, *21*(4), 683–693. doi:10.1037/0893-3200.21.4.683 PMID:18179340

Firmin, M. W., & Phillips, A. (2009). A qualitative study of families and children possessing diagnoses of ADHD. *Journal of Family Issues*, *30*(9), 1155–1174. doi:10.1177/0192513X09333709

Fitzgerald, P. B., Williams, C. L., Corteling, N., Filia, S. L., Brewer, K., Adams, A., De Castella, A. R. A., Rolfe, T., Davey, P., & Kulkarni, J. (2001). Subject and observer-rated quality of life in schizophrenia. *Acta Psychiatrica Scandinavica*, *103*(5), 387–392. doi:10.1034/j.1600-0447.2001.00254.x PMID:11380309

Guba, E. G., & Lincoln, Y. S. (1989). *Fourth generation evaluation*. Sage.

Gustafsson, P., Thernlund, G., Besjakov, J., Karrlsson, M. K., Ericsson, I., & Svedin, C. G., & (2008). ADHD symptoms in primary school children. *Acta Paediatrica (Oslo, Norway)*, *97*(2), 233–238. doi:10.1111/j.1651-2227.2007.00608.x PMID:18177440

Harborne, A., Wolpert, M., & Clare, L. (2004). Making sense of ADHD: A battle for understanding parents' views of their children being diagnosed with ADHD. *Clinical Child Psychology and Psychiatry*, *9*(3), 327–339. doi:10.1177/1359104504043915

Harold, G. T., Leve, L. D., Barrett, D., Elam, K., Neiderhiser, J. M., Natsuaki, M. N., Shaw, D. S., Reiss, D., & Thapar, A. (2013). Biological and rearing mother influences on child ADHD symptoms: Revisiting the developmental interface between nature and nurture. *Journal of Child Psychology and Psychiatry, and Allied Disciplines*, *54*(10), 1038–1046. doi:10.1111/jcpp.12100 PMID:24007415

Harrison, C., & Sofronoff, K. (2002). ADHD and parental psychological distress: Role of demographics, child behavioural characteristics and parental cognitions. *Journal of the American Academy of Child and Adolescent Psychiatry*, *41*(6), 703–711. doi:10.1097/00004583-200206000-00010 PMID:12049445

Ho, S.-W., Chien, W., & Wang, L.-Q. (2011). Parents' perceptions of care-giving to a child with attention deficit hyperactivity disorder: An exploratory study. *Contemporary Nurse*, *40*(1), 41–56. doi:10.5172/conu.2011.40.1.41 PMID:22545905

Hoag, A. (2014). Mothers' perceptions of family communication patterns when having an ADHD child. In Family Relationships and Familial Responses to Health Issues (pp. 211-246). Emerald Group Publishing Limited.

Howe, D. (2010). The safety of children and the parent-worker relationship in cases of child abuse and neglect. *Child Abuse Review*, *19*(5), 330–341. doi:10.1002/car.1136

Hurt, E. A., Hoza, B., & Pelham, W. E. Jr. (2007). Parenting, family loneliness, and peer functioning in boys with attention-deficit/hyperactivity disorder. *Journal of Abnormal Child Psychology*, *25*(4), 413–424. doi:10.100710802-007-9111-x PMID:17333361

Iosifidis, T. (2003). *Qualitative data analysis in the social sciences*. Kritiki.

Jackson, D., & Mannix, J. (2004). Giving voice to the burden of blame: A feminist study of mothers' experiences of mother blaming. *International Journal of Nursing Practice*, *10*(4), 150–158. doi:10.1111/j.1440-172X.2004.00474.x PMID:15265225

Johnston, C., & Mash, E. J. (2001). Families of children with attention deficit/ hyperactivity disorder: Review and recommendations for future research. *Clinical Child and Family Psychology Review*, *4*(3), 183–207. doi:10.1023/A:1017592030434 PMID:11783738

Johnston, C., Mash, E. J., Miller, N., & Ninowski, J. E. (2012). Parenting in Adults with Attention-Deficit/Hyperactivity Disorder (ADHD). *Clinical Psychology Review*, *32*(4), 215–228. doi:10.1016/j.cpr.2012.01.007 PMID:22459785

Keown, L. J. (2012). Predictors of boys' ADHD symptoms from early to middle childhood: The role of father–child and mother–child interactions. *Journal of Abnormal Child Psychology*, *40*(4), 569–581. doi:10.100710802-011-9586-3 PMID:22038253

Lamborn, S., Mounts, N., Steinberg, L., & Dornbusch, S. (1991). Patterns of competence and adjustment among adolescents from authoritative, authoritarian, indulgent and neglectful families. *Child Development*, *62*(5), 1049–1065. doi:10.2307/1131151 PMID:1756655

Lange, G., Sheerin, D., Carr, A., Dooley, B., Barton, V., Marshall, D., Mulligan, A., Lawlor, M., Belton, M., & Doyle, M. (2005). Family factors associated with attention deficit hyperactivity disorder and emotional disorders in children. *Journal of Family Therapy*, *27*(1), 76–96. doi:10.1111/j.1467-6427.2005.00300.x

Mash, E. J., & Johnston, C. (1983). Parental perceptions of child behaviour problems, parenting self-esteem, and mothers' reported stress in younger and older hyperactive and normal children. *Journal of Consulting and Clinical Psychology*, *51*(1), 86–99. doi:10.1037/0022-006X.51.1.86 PMID:6826870

Mason, J. (2003). *Conducting qualitative research*. Hellenic Literature.

McIntyre, R., & Hennessy, E. (2012). 'He's just enthusiastic. Is that such a bad thing?' Experiences of parents of children with attention deficit hyperactivity disorder. *Emotional & Behavioural Difficulties*, *17*(1), 65–82. doi:10.1080/13632752.2012.652428

McKee, T. E., Harvey, E., Danforth, J. S., Ulaszek, W. R., & Friedman, J. L. (2004). The Relation Between Parental Coping Styles and Parent-Child Interactions Before and After Treatment for Children With ADHD and Oppositional Behavior. *Journal of Clinical Child and Adolescent Psychology*, *33*(1), 158–168. doi:10.1207/S15374424JCCP3301_15 PMID:15028550

McLaughlin, D. P., & Harrison, C. A. (2006). Parenting practices of mothers of children with ADHD: The role of maternal and child factors. *Child and Adolescent Mental Health, 11*(2), 82–88. doi:10.1111/j.1475-3588.2005.00382.x PMID:32811096

Molina, M.F., & Musich, F.M. (2016). Perception of parenting style by children with ADHD and its relation with inattention, hyperactivity/impulsivity and externalizing symptoms. *Ni*(5), 1656-1671.

Morris, A. S., Silk, J. S., Steinberg, L., Myers, S. S., & Robinson, L. R. (2007). The role of the family context in the development of emotion regulation. *Social Development, 16*(2), 361–388. doi:10.1111/j.1467-9507.2007.00389.x PMID:19756175

Mulligan, A., Anney, R., Butler, L., O'Regan, M., Richardson, T., Tulewicz, E. M., Fitzgerald, M., & Gill, M. (2011). Home environment: Association with hyperactivity/impulsivity in children with ADHD and their non-ADHD siblings. *Child: Care, Health and Development, 39*(2), 202–212. doi:10.1111/j.1365-2214.2011.01345.x PMID:22168816

Ni, H. C., & Gau, S. S. F. (2015). Co-occurrence of attention-deficit hyperactivity disorder symptoms with other psychopathology in young adults: Parenting style as a moderator. *Comprehensive Psychiatry, 57*, 85–96. doi:10.1016/j.comppsych.2014.11.002 PMID:25465651

Olivier, M. A., Gomes, A. M., & Greyling, A. J. (2009). Attention Deficit Hyperactivity Disorder (ADHD)—Dilemmas and Solutions. *Journal of Psychology in Africa, 19*(2), 237–241. doi:10.1080/14330237.2009.10820285

Pahlavanzadeh, S., Mousavi, S., & Maghsoudi, J. (2018). Exploring the needs of family caregivers of children with attention deficit hyperactivity disorder: A qualitative study. *Iranian Journal of Nursing and Midwifery Research, 23*, 149–154. PMID:29628964

Peasgood, T., Bhardwaj, A., Biggs, K., Brazier, J. E., Coghill, D., Cooper, C. L., & Sonuga-Barke, E. J. (2016). The impact of ADHD on the health and well-being of ADHD children and their siblings. *European Child & Adolescent Psychiatry, 25*(11), 1217–1231. doi:10.100700787-016-0841-6 PMID:27037707

Peñuelas-Calvo, I., Palomar-Ciria, N., Porras-Segovia, A., Miguélez-Fernández, C., Baltasar-Tello, I., Perez-Colmenero, S., & Baca-García, E. (2021). Impact of ADHD symptoms on family functioning, family burden and parents' quality of life in a hospital area in Spain. *European Journal of Psychiatry, 35*(3), 166–172. doi:10.1016/j.ejpsy.2020.10.003

Peräkylä, A. (2004). Conversation analysis. *Qualitative research practice,* 165-179.

Peters, K., & Jackson, D. (2009). Mothers' experiences of parenting a child with attention deficit hyperactivity disorder. *Journal of Advanced Nursing, 65*(1), 62–71. doi:10.1111/j.1365-2648.2008.04853.x PMID:19120583

Podolski, C. L., & Nigg, J. T. (2001). Parent stress and coping in relation to child ADHD severity and associated child disruptive behavior problems. *Journal of Clinical Child Psychology, 30*(4), 503–513. doi:10.1207/S15374424JCCP3004_07 PMID:11708238

Polanczyk, G., de Lima, M. S., Horta, B. L., Biederman, J., & Rohde, L. A. (2007). The worldwide prevalence of ADHD: A systematic review and metaregression analysis. *The American Journal of Psychiatry, 164*(6), 942–948. doi:10.1176/ajp.2007.164.6.942 PMID:17541055

Pretorius, J. W. M. (Ed.). (1998). *Sociopedagogics 2000*. Van Schaik Publishers.

Rief, S. F. (2005). *How to reach and teach children with ADD/ADHD: Practical Techniques, strategies and interventions* (2nd ed.). Jossey-Bass.

Ringer, N. (2019). Young people's perceptions of and coping with their ADHD symptoms: A qualitative study. *Cogent Psychology, 6*(1), 1608032. doi:10.1080/23311908.2019.1608032

Seipp, C. M., & Johnston, C. (2005). Mother-son interaction in families of boys with attention deficit/ hyperactivity disorder with and without oppositional behavior. *Journal of Abnormal Child Psychology, 33*(1), 87–98. doi:10.100710802-005-0936-x PMID:15759593

Shelton, T. L., Barkley, R. A., Crosswait, C., Moorehouse, M., Fletcher, K., Barrett, S., Jenkins, L., & Metevia, L. (1998). Psychiatric and psychological morbidity as a function of adaptive disability in preschool children with aggressive and hyperactive impulsive inattentive behaviour. *Journal of Abnormal Child Psychology, 26*(6), 475–494. doi:10.1023/A:1022603902905 PMID:9915654

Sollie, H. (2014). Struggling with and for A Grounded Theory of Parents Managing Life with Hard-to-Treat ADHD Teenagers. *The Grounded Theory Review, 13*(1), 3–15.

Sonna, L. (2005). *The everything parent's guide to children with ADD/ADHD*. Avon: F+W Publications.

Stamatis, P., & Nikolaou, E. (2020). *Communication and mental health promotion in early childhood education*. Nova Publishers. doi:10.52305/QXVD5566

Sue, D., Sue, D., & Sue, S. (1994). *Understanding abnormal behavior* (4th ed.). Houghton Miffin.

Tannock, R. (1998). Attention deficit hyperactivity disorder: Advantages in cognitive, neurobiological, and genetic research. *Journal of Child Psychology and Psychiatry, and Allied Disciplines, 39*(1), 65–99. doi:10.1111/1469-7610.00304 PMID:9534087

Tasiou, K., & Nikolaou, E. N. (2022). Resilience in Families with children with special needs. In P. I. Stamatis & E. N. Nikolaou (Eds.), *Counselling and communication in education* (pp. 271–295). Diadrasis.

Tasiou, K., & Nikolaou, E. N. (2023). The psychological resilience of families of children with attention deficit hyperactivity disorder. In D. B. Katsarou, C. Koundourou, & G. P. Reppa (Eds.), *New trends and approaches in child and adult psychopathology and mental health* (pp. 99–121). Gutenberg.

Taylor, E. (2009). Developing Adhd. *Journal of Child Psychology and Psychiatry, and Allied Disciplines, 50*(1-2), 126–132. doi:10.1111/j.1469-7610.2008.01999.x PMID:19076263

Thoits, P. A. (2011). Mechanisms linking social ties and support to physical and mental health. *Journal of Health and Social Behavior, 52*(2), 145–161. doi:10.1177/0022146510395592 PMID:21673143

Timimi, S., & Taylor, E. (2004). ADHD is best understood as a cultural construct. *The British Journal of Psychiatry, 184*(1), 8–9. doi:10.1192/bjp.184.1.8 PMID:14702221

Tripp, G., Schaughnecy, E. A., Langlands, R., & Mouat, K. (2007). Family interactions in children with and without ADHD. *Journal of Child and Family Studies*, *16*(3), 385–400. doi:10.100710826-006-9093-2

Wymbs, B. T., & Pelham, W. E. (2010). Child effects on communication between parents of youth with and without ADHD. *Journal of Abnormal Psychology*, *119*, 366–375. doi:10.1037/a0019034 PMID:20455609

Chapter 9
Migrant Mothers of ASD Children With Language Deficits in Greek Kindergarten Classrooms:
Barriers and Facilitators of School Involvement Through an Intersectional Lens

Emmanouela Vardis Seiradakis
Technical University of Crete, Greece & Hellenic Open University, Greece

ABSTRACT

Parental involvement especially in the early years of education significantly influences the academic and socioemotional development of children with disabilities. Nevertheless, findings suggest migrant parents with a lower socioeconomic positioning typically exhibit limited engagement with their children's schools. In Greece, research exploring parental involvement has largely focused on the dominant middle-class parent group within the general education context. Using an intersectional lens, this chapter shifts focus and explores the social interlocking barriers and facilitators of school involvement among low-income migrant mothers of ASD children with language deficits. Findings shed light to how these mothers' experiences are constructed at the intersections of their multiple marginalized identities within the highly-centralized Greek education system and the narrative of individual responsibilitization and have implications for educational policies and practices that will foster active engagement of mothers who lack cultural and economic privilege.

INTRODUCTION

Parental involvement especially in the early years of education significantly influences disabled children's later academic and socioemotional development (Reaves et al., 2022; Serpell & Mashburn, 2012).

DOI: 10.4018/979-8-3693-1982-6.ch009

Nevertheless, findings suggest migrant parents especially those with a lower socioeconomic positioning typically exhibit limited engagement with their children's schools due to a range of barriers they encounter in collaborating with teachers, special and auxiliary stuff in mainstream state schools (Antony-Newman, 2019). In Greece, although the student population is now rather diverse culturally and linguistically (Gkaintartzi et al., 2015; Samsari et al., 2022), research exploring parental school involvement is scarce (Antonopoulou et al., 2011; Koutroumpa et al., 2009; Tryfon et al., 2021) and has focused on the dominant middle-class parent group in general education. In an attempt to fill in this research gap the current work aims to investigate the lived experiences of migrant parents and more specifically the mothers of young children with autism spectrum disorders (ASD) with language deficits in Greek mainstream kindergartens. Mothers are the focus of this study for multiple reasons. Mothers in early childhood education are the "main education workers in ways that men traditionally are not" (Jamal Al-deen & Windle, 2017: 137). For migrant mothers in particular, schools constitute critical establishments as they usually are in charge of children's schooling as part of their gendered duties (Kibria & Beccerra, 2021). In fact children's well-being is commonly cited as the main reason of their migration (Antony-Newman, 2019, Kaya 2022). Compared to fathers, migrant mothers of disabled children usually bear more layers of obstacles when challenged with opposition which may disturb their engagement and advocacy skills in any authoritative context including schools, healthcare and disability services since they need to deal with sexism on top of the other "isms", i.e., ableism, classism, racism (Kibria & Beccerra, 2021).

We know from research conducted outside of Greece that migrant mothers of disabled children demonstrate low levels of school involvement due to a range of internal and external barriers which stretch beyond the typical obstacles mothers of disabled children encounter due to their added social complexities as migrants. The external barriers most commonly cited are related to financial struggles, migrant status, long hours of work, language difficulties, asymmetrical power relations, luck of a support network and lack of familiarity with the host country educational systems and disability services. Internal barriers are often related to discrimination, marginalization, micro-aggressions and social isolation (Antony-Newman, 2019; Bruhn, 2022; Jørgensen et al., 2021; Kibria & Beccerra, 2021). Yet, despite our declarative knowledge of the type of barriers migrant mothers encounter, little is known about the interconnected axes of marginalization that generate these obstacles and even less about potential enablers that could be translated into educational policies at the macrolevel.

I believe comprehending these mothers' daily experiences and struggles in navigating the Greek education system can offer valuable data for us as educators to design socially effective interventions within pre-primary education settings. More importantly, I believe that centring these mothers' voices is a small footstep towards holding Greek policymakers accountable for the quality of their school involvement experiences which is linked to their children's academic development and overall well-being. In this chapter I employ intersectionality (Collins, 2020; Crenshaw,1989) as a theoretical and interpretive tool for examining the hidden school involvement barricades these women encounter and highlight the intersections of their marginalized identities which have been downplayed in the Greek special education field as well as the facilitators which may potentially foster their involvement in Greek kindergartens. More specifically, I share findings from a qualitative interview-based study with four migrant mothers of ASD children with language deficits.

The questions leading the current work mirrored the intersectional lens used and the exploratory nature of the study: What are the barriers and facilitators of migrant mothers of ASD children with language deficits to school involvement in mainstream kindergartens? how can these barriers be targeted? What are the interactions between these migrant mothers' lived experiences and the intersections of social class, gender and immigration?

Involvement, Advocacy, and the Need for Intersectionality

Literature on parental involvement commonly focuses on how parents' demographic attributes and behaviors both at school and at home affect children's academic attainment and overall well-being. Parents are portrayed as school partners, as active learners who acquire skills and knowledge related to their child's education and as knowledgeable consumers (Baquedano-Lopez et al., 2013). Involvement assumes accountability, responsibility and providing tangible support to children and teachers both at home and at school. In other words, relevant literature sees "good" parents as those who have the capital both in terms of money and time to support, and implement schools' directives and norms (Matthiesen, 2017).

Epstein's (2001) well known model which encompasses six types of home and school-based engagement has been extensively used in the specific field. The majority of works using this model, after exploring parents and teachers' perspectives and practices present their findings and usually suggest a range of macro and micro level policies that should be put into place in order to facilitate different types of *home* engagements for example teachers training parents in implementing specific methodologies in order to supervise their children's homework or *school* engagements such as parents doing fundraising work (Antony-Newman, 2019). For minority parents however, especially those with multiple marginalized identities such as low-income migrants with disabled children, it is highly possible that this type of research and recommendations is simply irrelevant.

When it comes to mothers of children with disabilities, relevant literature is even more contradictive and puzzling. A well-established strand of school involvement and disability research argues that mothers, not educational systems, constitute the determining factor of the quality of education children receive. This scholarship is related to intensive mothering ideologies which responsibilize parents and specifically mothers as exclusively accountable for their children's accomplishments or failures (Nygreen, 2019). Mothers who are actively involved in schools and advocate for their children will be granted access to more resources, better therapies and their children will gain more attention from teachers (Morgan & Stahmer, 2020, Nevill et al., 2023, O'Hare et al., 2021; Tabatai, 2019). Mothers in this case, usually refer to middle class women who have the cultural, educational, psychological and most importantly the financial capital to invest time at school and simultaneously buy top-notch tutors and therapists privately when they are not satisfied by the quality of free services.

Corresponding narratives for working class migrant mothers portray the mother of a child with a disability as an active agent, a fighter who sacrifices herself and constantly battles authoritative educational institutions for her child's rights. The "Good Advocate Mother" (Kibria & Becerra, 2021) is strong, tireless, loud and dynamic. She studies scientific literature online about her child's condition, she constantly monitors her child's progress, she appreciates teachers and therapists who help her child but she's ready to question education experts if she thinks they jeopardize her child's interests, she has an active role in parent-teacher associations (PTAs), she attends seminars, workshops and she is active in all sorts of parent networks at school (Kibria & Becerra, 2021; Morgan & Stahmer, 2020; Rosetti et al., 2021; Sousa, 2011). This mother is a leader, she is the "Warrior-Hero" who fiercely fights "social and political forces to gain medical and educational interventions for [her] children despite the high personal and financial costs" (Sousa, 2011:220).

At school, these tireless mothers have a range of tactics in order to make sure teachers do not discriminate or neglect their children. They implement hyper-vigilance strategies, constantly showing up any time of the day to monitor teachers and make sure everything is done properly. In important meetings with the school or special education agencies they make use of attorneys, other healthcare professionals or even friends who are fluent in the host language "with no accent" because they know an accent functions as a "racialized signifier" (Kibria & Becerra, 2021:11), a weakness the system is going to take advantage of and undermine their children's educational needs due to their foreignness and their low socioeconomic status. Yet findings suggest that the tale of the migrant "super mother" takes a toll on the mothers who are unable to fit this idealistic concept and instead of nurturing empowerment and more active involvement at school, it triggers mother blaming and guilt to low-literate migrant mothers who bend under the immense daily demands of raising children with disabilities, catering for the whole family and having full-time jobs which are often low-pay and heavy (Kibria & Becerra, 2021; Rosetti et al., 2021, Sousa 2011). These findings show that reliance on mother advocacy rather than on public education systems may in fact constitute the main reproductive social mechanism of disability-related inequalities and injustice which makes the need for more fine-grained, bottom-up research imperative.

Intersectionality can contribute in exploring migrant mothers' unique lived experiences because no migrant mother is the same. Ethnicity, nationality, migrant status, class, religion, education, profession, type of a child's disability and the context within which all these identities operate create different forms of oppression and marginalization. The intersectional lens illuminates the interactions of social identities within various social contexts at the individual, relational, and organizational levels, which eventually emerge at the individual level (Collins, 2020). Using this lens can help us recognize the veiled systems of oppression these women encounter in kindergartens and shed light to the gap between what is described in Greek policymakers' rhetoric about inclusion and the reality of being a low-income migrant mother raising a child with disabilities in contemporary Greece.

METHOD

Context

In Greece, despite the existent comprehensive and detailed legislation for the implementation of educational policies for migrant children with disabilities, inclusion largely remains at a theoretical level with parents' daily reality in schools largely deviating from what is mandated on endless laws and regulations (Koutsoklenis & Papathanasiou, 2021; Sorkos & Hajisoteriou, 2021). In terms of parental involvement for migrant or non-migrant parents, Greece has a poor history in developing such policies with a serious of compartmentalized initiatives that have failed to establish systematic school-parent partnerships due to blurry and sometimes turbulent parent-teacher collaboration patterns, lack of school autonomy and accountability procedures, opposition by the unions and other pathogenies related to the highly-centralized education system (Rentzou & Ekine, 2017; Lazaridou & Gravani-Kassida, 2015). Up until now, parental involvement policies in Greek schools mandated the establishment of a Parent's Association and parent-teacher conferences at school. At the time of my study, the neoliberal government of Nea Dimokratia had launched two controversial reforms which are still fiercely fought by teachers' unions (Traianou, 2023a), a teacher evaluation and school evaluation system. The school evaluation scheme includes specific axes to evaluate teachers, headteachers and principals' actions on family engagement in K-12. More specifically, all state schools should report measures for i) developing communication channels with parents, ii) supporting and strengthening school-family cooperation and iii) supporting actions to inform parents/guardians on issues of common interest.

Participants, Instrument, and Data Analysis

I conducted this study with migrant mothers of ASD children with language deficits from four mainstream kindergartens at the suburbs of three medium-sized highly-touristic and affluent towns at the island of Crete, Greece. The student population in participants' schools was predominantly Greek white middle class with negligible populations of migrant students mostly from Albania, other Balkan countries and few from Syria. In-depth interviews in the form of an open conversation were conducted with four mothers whose children at the time were enrolled or had just finished the two compulsory years of kindergarten. The interviews focused on (i) mothers' perceptions and lived experiences of barriers to school involvement (ii) the connection of their identities to their experiences of school involvement barriers, and (iii) experiences which acted as involvement facilitators as well as suggested changes that could optimize involvement of migrant mothers of ASD children with language deficits in mainstream kindergartens. All of them reported their ethnicity as Albanian and they were all born outside Greece. Their age ranged in age from 28 to 34 years. Their language usage at home was in their heritage language, Albanian. All of them worked as domestic workers and as cleaners in hotels and Airbnb's during the touristic season. They were all married with two children or more. Elsa, Maria, Ana and Dina are the pseudonyms of the tireless yet exhausted mothers that gave me the opportunity to explore how a woman can juggle the strains of mothering and endless hours of work while navigating a fuzzy education system at a new country with no support network. Informed consent for interviews was obtained from all participants. Theoretical thematic analysis (Braun & Clarke, 2008) was employed in order to detect intersections of inequalities separately as well as concurrently (Bowleg, 2008).

RESULTS

Barriers

Three themes emerged from data analysis related to barriers including (a) Mothers silenced by the system, (b) Mothers silenced by teachers (c) Mothers silenced by other mothers.

Mothers Silenced by the System: Structural Barriers, Language Struggles, Financial Hardships and Microaggressions

The first theme covers participants' struggles triggered by structural barriers within the Greek kindergarten context. Data analysis revealed that social class and migrant status disturbed these mothers' involvement in numerous ways and triggered a myriad of obstacles in communicating with teachers and auxiliary stuff at school. All participants stated they would like to be more involved with their children's schools. They unanimously believed good parenting entails extensive school engagement, frequent communication with the teachers and volunteer work at school and felt guilty for their limited involvement. Lack of time however triggered by family-work balance struggles combined with the absence of a family support network prohibited them from adopting a more active presence.

Rigid school schedules and the time restrictions posed by headteachers and teachers in contact hours emerged as a major obstacle as these mothers were never able to be at school at the designated time due to their hectic work conditions. Two mothers described instances of special education teachers leaving school early and never having time for them which triggered a sense of devaluation for them and their children. Lack of frequent public transportation and school location also emerged as obstacles in being able to be at school on time. None of the participants owned a car or held a driving license and they all worked during daytime till late in the afternoon. All four of them described instances of microaggressions when they asked to see teachers at a time later in the day that would be more convenient for them. Constant change of teachers during the school year was another structural barrier which was mentioned by three mothers who thought this instability disturbs their engagement with the school but most importantly it harms their children's progress. Elsa's son for example changed three teachers during his first kindergarten year:

"They change all the time. Last year two of them came, they barely talked to me, they knew they would leave from the beginning and then the third one came, she was very young, stayed till the end of the year. I'm not sure if some of these teachers really want to work with children like my son. Some of them don't seem to understand how important they are for our children."

Participants described constant internal struggles and oppressions when interacting with the special education experts of the school i.e. support and integration class teachers and the psychologist who visited the school once a week, including multiple instances of prejudice and microaggressions which marginalized them and eliminated their opportunity to exercise their advocacy. All four mothers would like to have the power to object or at least have their opinion heard regarding their children's IEPs yet none of them dared to do so. Maria said she knew stories about other Greek mothers with ASD children who created tensions with special education teachers, headteachers, even with the Educational and Consulting Support Centre (ECSC) specialists and were able to change schools or teachers with whom they weren't satisfied. Reflecting on her experience with ECSC, she remembered herself and her husband feeling lost. She couldn't understand the technical jargon used by the committee of experts yet when asked whether she understood what they were telling her she kept nodding positively. She remembers they gave her a lot of papers, then they told her that the rest would be arranged by the school. Retrospectively, she was upset with herself for not having a higher Greek language knowledge, empowerment and confidence to speak up to defend her son's rights. She also felt jealous for the fact that as she said Greeks' children are luckier because they have parents who fight for them both by their voice and their money:

"Greek parents pay for everything they don't just stick to the peanuts we get for free...They pay psychiatrists, they get the best speech therapists, private support teachers...Then they go to the school and if they don't like something they shout or bring lawyers and get what they want. I don't blame them. I wish I could do the same for him (her son).".

Language-related difficulties in personal interactions with the special education teachers and auxiliary stuff were mentioned as a barrier by the other three mothers as well who felt that meaningful communication with the school remained at a theoretical level and no substantial measures were taken in order for them to be able to comprehend let alone collaboratively participate in their children's IEPs. Complex language and sophisticated special education terminology was perceived by Elsa as a strategy used by teachers to intimidate and silence her every time she would ask a question related to her son's IEP:

"...Some of them do it on purpose, to tell me indirectly, you are not educated, you don't speak Greek, you cannot understand and you cannot check up on us or make us do more work."

Language also emerged as a barrier in reading IEPs and school reports. Two mothers referred to the poor quality of these reports as they didn't reflect their sons' specialized needs and progress but seemed like copy-pasted paragraphs with no substance which they realized after friends translated the reports for them.

Mothers Silenced by Teachers: Lack of Information, Low Expectations, and Apathy

Mother participants further described they receive very little information regarding their children's daily activities. Their accounts indicated that support and integration teachers were solely responsible for their children's education whereas the general education teacher was in charge for the rest of the class. There was no collaboration whatsoever. Head teachers also seemed to reinforce this notion the few times they asked for information or encountered a problem. From her son's portfolio, the few things she was able to find out from teachers, her son himself and her other two children who are at the primary school within the same building as the kindergarten, Dina's son was mainly involved in low-complexity solitary free-play activities whereas engagement with the educational resources and mastery play was negligeable. Other mothers reflected on instances when support and integration class teachers' displayed indifference or unwillingness to devote time to their children and them which in turn disempowered and alienated them even more. For example, Ana referred to the communication book which was never used and Maria mentioned that the support teacher refused to escort her son to a school visit at the museum and as a result he ended up not going. Overall, these mothers felt that due to their class and migrant identities they were as Elsa said "easy targets" and school stuff strategically portrayed a fake picture of their children's progress in order to "get rid of them" constantly downplaying their concerns even during specific periods when their children were obviously struggling and didn't exhibit any progress at all:

"I could see he had more tantrums, he stopped saying words he used up until then but all I was getting was don't worry Mrs. Elsa everything is fine."

Different cultures related to parental involvement and teachers' seemingly low expectations of migrant children with disabilities also emerged. Elsa described how she felt that her son at the intersections of his migrant, class and disability identities receives similar education with the one he would be receiving in Albania. She thought that compared to EU countries, the Albanian educational system is dated, authoritarian and parents' traditional roles in schools are marginalized and restricted. She hoped that in Greece all her children would receive better education and she would be able to be more involved in it. Yet her experiences dashed her expectations. She thought school stuff in Greece appears more sophisticated and at the surface they encourage parental involvement and complain about uninvolved parents yet all the times she tried to make arrangements to see teachers at a later time during the day she was "put in her place" and was reminded about the legislation and school working hours. Maria's experiences related to teachers' attitudes was similar to the other participants but her account was even more enlightening as she highlighted teachers' own struggles which were also related to the intersections of their identities as women, mothers and teachers in cotemporary Greece:

"The integration class teacher has two children and is also alone here, she is from Athens. She also struggles, she is far from her husband. She never has time because she raises her children alone here and she works in the afternoon as a private tutor and her kids are alone at home. Where is she gonna find time for me?"

Mothers Silenced by Other Mothers: Mother Cliques and Isolation

Participants accounts revealed multiple oppressions which kept them silent and at time invisible or hyper visible simply because they deviated from the dominant middle-class Greek mother group of their respective schools. For example, Ana couldn't speak "proper Greek" in teacher-parent conferences so she opted to remain silent most of the time. She couldn't devote time at school as she had no "maternal leave" or a "flexible schedule" and no family support to help her with her other children so she could never be at school for organizing charity or social events and even if she could as she said she felt embarrassed to attend them simply because she lacked the financial capital to buy any of the items sold for fundraising purposes. Maria referred to feelings of embarrassment in teacher-parent conferences not only due to her poor Greek skills but also because of her appearance compared to other mothers and the teaching stuff of the school. At the intersection of being a woman, a cleaner and a mother to an ASD son she said:

"I'm a cleaner, I smell chlorine my clothes aren't like the other mothers' clothes, I need to go home, change and then go there. But there's no time for that, the teacher-parent conferences are at fixed times so I am always in a rush in the work clothes. I don't ask much especially in front of the other mothers, nobody really cares, I sit there for a while, then I run back to work."

None of the participants were active in parents' associations which in all four cases were constituted only from Greek middle-class women. Elsa describes how she felt as an outsider at a parents' association meeting at the school:

"It's weird, I cannot explain it exactly, I felt unwelcome, I felt like they felt sorry for me, they didn't say something specific, they were like "Hi, how are you?" and that's it and then they just ignored me and organized things for the school bazar, a yearbook, the food, they were talking about people I didn't know and so on. So I never went again."

Participants felt marginalized and oppressed by gossip, comments or even looks by other mothers who seemed to resend the existence of migrant children with support teachers and integration groups in mainstream kindergarten classrooms as they thought they "would hold their children back". Data analysis further revealed that silencing, exclusion and marginalization extended beyond the concrete school walls. Viber "mum groups" also occurred as a barrier for Maria who wasn't able to follow or react to discussions due to internalized oppressions related to her Greek language knowledge but also to her lack of self-confidence to state their opinion on any school issue. Attendance of social events at school and birthday parties where their children are never invited further reinforced feelings of isolation for Ana who however did by no means expect something different or cared:

"Everyone knows everyone, this is a small town, they become friends outside of the school, they invite their kids to each other's' parties, they organize events for the school with the teachers, they buy the teachers presents, they even write nice things about them in the local newspaper and so on...Every time I go to a school event, I sit at the back, other Albanians, Romanians do the same, we don't really hear much, some of us don't understand much in Greek in any case. It's logical, they (other mothers) have money, they have time, they have created bonds."

Facilitators of School Involvement

Perceived facilitators and changes that need to be implemented in order for migrant mothers of ASD children to become more involved in their children's schools included a) Solidarity and empathy b) Support, information and flexible communication c) Teacher stability and accountability.

Solidarity and Empathy

When asked about parental involvement facilitators, participants referred to a range of instances of school stuff but also women other than school stuff who helped them to gain confidence and engage more with their children's education. Elsa described how the support teacher of her son literally changed her life for the three months she was there and how her presence acted as an involvement facilitator yet as she remarked it was "pure luck" and lasted only for three months as she became pregnant and another teacher replaced her. For Dina, her anger towards the Greek education system which seemed to ignore her son's needs coupled with the helping hand provided by another woman-teacher for whom she worked as a domestic worker once a week acted as the driving force in enacting advocacy at her son's school where she was repeatedly ignored:

"She has given me specific things to do with him at home, she uses google translate and she gives me things in Albanian so that I can understand what she means and most importantly, she asks about him about his progress. She gave me strength and then I started asking more things at school and be less scared not that it changed anything but at least I feel a bit better."

All mother participants expressed their need for teachers and other experts in schools, to be patient, empathetic and less critical of them. They called for a more flexible, non-judgmental approach in communication that would lessen the stigma and the oppressions migrant mothers of children with disabilities often encounter in the wider contemporary Greek society.

Support, Information, and Flexible Communication

All mothers believed language, legal and emotional support should be provided to migrant parents of children with disabilities. Language support could be in the form of interpreters or translated documents especially for heritage languages of significant populations in their area. They also asked for information oral or written in a manner that could enable them to comprehend meaning. Participants also expressed their desire to have access to more frequent and more detailed and substantial information on their children's progress other than the standard progress reports which include theoretical information. Ana for example specifically mentioned that she would like the reports to include examples of her son's behavior and progress. Changes in contact hours and form of communication with special education teachers was mentioned by all participants. For example, Elsa said she would like to be able to call her son's support teacher if a problem comes up or if she has a question whereas Ana would like the school to be open once a week late in the afternoon so she can go to school in person:

. *"In an ideal world I would like to be able to talk to them without feeling we are in a rush in the afternoon. So for example, once a week from 7-8, I would like the school open. This is the time when both me and my husband are at home. He can stay with the other kids and I can go to school, clean and calm like a normal mother, sit down and talk... Parent-teacher conferences are not useful for me with all these people around."*

Teacher Stability and Accountability

All four mother participants thought that the recruitment process of special education teachers has to be changed despite the fact that they weren't able to provide alternative suggestions in terms of policies. Ana believed constant changes of teachers during the year jeopardizes children's academic and socioemotional progress especially when they get along and develop bonds with a particular teacher. Elsa believed all parents of children with any sort of a disability or disorder should have a say for their children's special education teachers:

"Somehow all mothers not just migrants have to have a say. They know their children, when a good support teacher for example comes along and cares about my child and they get on and she communicates well why does she have to change? This is taking the children back and makes parents' life hell."

CONCLUSION

This article explored the school involvement experiences of migrant mothers of ASD children with language deficits in Greek mainstream kindergartens using an intersectional lens. Findings indicate that much like most families in general education where the private shadow education system determines the quality of education students receive in K-12 (Bray, 2021), those with ASD children navigate Greek public education from unequal socioeconomical positionings with privileges and oppressions that pretrain and influence involvement and advocacy and reproduce social inequalities and injustice. Migrant mothers in particular, seem to bear more layers of oppressions as current findings reveal their involvement behaviors were deeply affected by unique interlocking social barricades constructed by the highly-centralized and underfinanced Greek educational system (Trainou, 2023a) combined with the narrative of individual responsibilization, intensive mothering and mother advocacy ideologies which essentially reinforce the notion that mothers are responsible for their children's education rather than the state (Nygreen,2019).

Contrary to the middle-class mothers of their schools, participants of the current work lacked the emotional, cultural, educational and economic privileges that would allow them to capitalize time and money in order to gain knowledge, get involved in their children's education and fight for the rights.

This finding agrees with other works in Europe, Australia and the US (Kibria & Becerra, 2021; Nevill et al., 2023; Jamal Al-deen & Windle, 2017; Sanderson, 2023) which also suggest that intersections of motherhood, disability, social class, migrant status and educational background influence the form and efficacy of involvement in daily school interactions and in IEP processes. The majority of these countries however have at least put in place a minimum of policies that aim to facilitate involvement of migrant parents with disabled children and despite the deficiencies, schools and special education agencies are obliged to implement specific strategies to reach out to them. In Greece, not only such policies are still absent from mainstream schools but systemic barriers related to constant teacher instability (Tryfon et al., 2021), lack of accountability procedures in kindergartens (Birbili & Myrovali, 2020), understaffed schools and special education agencies, poor special education stuff recruitment criteria, complex and time-consuming bureaucratic procedures for special education services (Koutsoklenis & Papathanasiou 2021)and lack of daycare create a labyrinth in which even parents with privileged identities and power frequently feel lost and overwhelmed (Tryfon et al., 2021).

Mother participants' accounts further showed that veiled social oppression forms interlocked between the school, the teachers but also the middle-class mothers who dominated local school culture. Based on their accounts, these mothers strategically used their soft skills stemming from their class, cultural and educational privileged identities in order to create bonds with teachers and headteachers to ensure better quality education and social networking for their children. Exclusion and isolation of migrant mothers, especially those with disabled children is in agreement with previous findings which suggest invisible mother cliques is a significant barrier that can minimize school engagement and in turn make migrant mothers of lower socioeconomic status be perceived as uninvolved by teachers (Stam, 2023)

Implications

Current work findings clearly show that the Greek educational system itself, not migrant mothers, ought to take on the burden of the advocacy to safeguard proper education for ASD children yet in order to reach this goal there are several macro and micro level policies and practices that should be implemented. Kindergartens and special education agencies must work together in order to achieve their common goals of ASD migrant children's well-being which however especially in early childhood education, assumes their mothers' involvement.

At the macro- level, developing inclusive school engagement policies for marginalized parent groups of ASD children in Greek state schools requires changes in pre-service teacher education curricula and ongoing training of in-service teachers, school leaders and other special education stuff and professionals on parental involvement strategies (de Bruïne et al., 2014; Smith & Sheridan, 2019). Centralized teacher and special education stuff recruitment procedures should also be reexamined as the current system functions as a hidden social mechanism which reproduces inequalities itself. Substitute special education teachers are commonly recruited later in the school year (Koutsoklenis & Papathanasiou 2021). Peculiar short-term mobility practices of the Greek Ministry of Education allowing thousands of teachers with permanent positions at rural areas to transfer in big cities further jeopardize teacher-student relationship continuity, school climate (Kougias & Efstathopoulos, 2020; Koutsoklenis & Papathanasiou 2021) and disturb parental involvement. This chaotic centralized system may result in having substitute teachers with an annual online training course and limited or non-existent experience in special education making complex diagnosis and designing IEPs at the ECSCs, the ministry's sole special education agency. Evaluation criteria and quality of formal special education qualifications based on which teachers are hired should also be reassessed as special education in Greece due to the extreme ten-year austerity and high-unemployment teacher rates became the "lifeboat for teacher employment" (Nteropoulou-Nterou & Slee, 2019:20) with desperate Greek teachers pursuing expensive yet fast and convenient postgraduate degrees in order to secure a state job (Nteropoulou-Nterou & Slee, 2019; Koutsoklenis & Papadimitriou, 2021). These pathogenies may not significantly affect middle class mothers of children with disabilities yet for working class migrant families such as the participants of the current study they seriously jeopardize their children's education and trigger mental distress.

Simplifying and accelerating procedures for diagnosis and therapies, providing mental health support and empowerment by stable in-school psychologists and social workers, are also of vital importance. Greek policymakers and academia should further examine migrant parents' representation in PAs across Greece since representation and even more so positions of power in local parent organizations can contribute in migrant parents' confidence and encourage their participation in decision making of their children's schools (Fleischmann, & de Haas 2016; Muro 2023).

Current findings indicate that communication modes presently used such as crowded parent-teacher conferences and emails may be time-efficient for the school but fail to offer migrant mothers of disabled children a truly open-door policy. Schools should provide more flexible parent-teacher individual contact hours, online meetings later in the afternoon or pay home visits. Information regarding children's daily activities and progress should be systematic, transparent, and easily accessible through multiple modes. Scheduled meetings but also informal contact and daily teacher-parent interactions are very important and particularly recommended for low-income migrant parents of children with disabilities (Horny & Blackwell, 2018; Kim, 2009; Rivera & Lavan 2012).

Oral language used by teachers should be simple and comprehensible and written documents should ideally be in the parents' heritage language or at least enriched with visuals and graphs comprehensible to a person with low Greek literacy. Translation services and applications can also be used to facilitate communication as language is one of the most important barrier migrant parents avoid school involvement (Rivera & Lavan, 2012; Stewart et al., 2022). Schools should also be able to provide migrant mothers' ongoing training on policies and legislation related to the Greek education system, their children's disabilities and the therapies they are entitled to. Flexible afternoon or online Greek language programs for migrant parents of disabled children should also be provided and schools should be able to direct parents to these programs (Stewart et al., 2022). Childcare during these activities is also required since many migrant mothers have no support or family networks.

In order to create truly inclusive schools, Greek policy makers other than "modernizing" once again the educational system on papers by implementing punitive teacher evaluation and accountability legislation (Traianou, 2023a), should devote financial resources and implement policies that truly support motherhood and women. This includes migrant mothers of children with disabilities and kindergarten teachers alike. Current findings show that teachers play a vital role in fostering or silencing involvement of migrant mothers in Greek kindergartens. In fact, participants of the current work seemed at times bitter and resentful towards their children's teachers for exhibiting apathy or indifference. Yet before putting the blame once again on teachers and on individual responsibility and accountability, we must take under consideration the working conditions and the extreme economic vulnerability teachers experience after the deep and painful ten-year Greek crisis and consecutive salary cuts (Traianou, 2023b). Around 40,000 teachers in Greece are currently on yearly substitute contracts with no tenure and commonly become domestic migrants themselves, moving from the mainland to expensive touristic islands like Crete in order to secure a state teaching job. Kindergarten teachers in particular, who are mostly women

(Androutsou & Tsafos, 2018) are often mothers with no support or family networks working extra jobs to make ends meet and cope with rocketing housing, electricity and childcare costs away from home. Making kindergartens truly inclusive and culturally responsive spaces assumes Greek policymakers also examine the visible and invisible oppressions Greek kindergarten teachers experience at the intersections of their gender and class identities triggered by recruitment procedures and extremely low-pay.

Limitations

Current work narratives functioned as spaces where these mothers, whose experience of school involvement deviates from the dominant middle class parent group offered a glimpse of their daily struggles in navigating the Greek educational system. The limited number of interviews offered abundant information on their own experiences yet the small size of participants, their age and their cultural backgrounds renders generalizations almost impossible.

REFERENCES

Alexopoulos, N. (2019). Resolving school staffing problems in Greece: A strategic management approach. *Frontiers in Education*, *4*, 1–14. doi:10.3389/feduc.2019.00130

Androusou, A., & Tsafos, V. (2018). Aspects of the professional identity of preschool teachers in Greece: Investigating the role of teacher education and professional experience. *Teacher Development*, *22*(4), 554–570. doi:10.1080/13664530.2018.1438309

Antonopoulou, K., Koutrouba, K., & Babalis, T. (2011). Parental involvement in secondary education schools: The views of parents in Greece. *Educational Studies*, *37*(3), 333–344. doi:10.1080/03055698.2010.506332

Antony-Newman, M. (2019). Parental involvement of immigrant parents: A meta-synthesis. *Educational Review*, *71*(3), 362–381. doi:10.1080/00131911.2017.1423278

Birbili, M., & Myrovali, A. (2020). Early childhood teachers' relationship with the official curriculum: The mediating role of professional and policy contexts. *Education Inquiry*, *11*(2), 110–125. doi:10.1080/20004508.2019.1687080

Bowleg, L. (2008). When Black+ lesbian+ woman≠ Black lesbian woman: The methodological challenges of qualitative and quantitative intersectionality research. *Sex Roles*, *59*(5-6), 312–325. doi:10.100711199-008-9400-z

Braun, V., & Clarke, V. (2008). Using thematic analysis in psychology. *Qualitative Research in Psychology*, *3*(2), 77–101. doi:10.1191/1478088706qp063oa

Bray, M. (2021). Shadow education in Europe: Growing prevalence, underlying forces, and policy implications. *ECNU. Review of Education*, *4*(3), 442–475.

Bruhn, S. (2022). Intersectional recognition: Immigrant motherhood in a gentrifying sanctuary city's schools. *Journal of Ethnic and Migration Studies*, 1–20.

Cheatham, G. A., & Lim-Mullins, S. (2018). Immigrant, bilingual parents of students with disabilities: Positive perceptions and supportive dialogue. *Intervention in School and Clinic, 54*(1), 40–46. doi:10.1177/1053451218762490

Collins, P. H., & Bilge, S. (2020). *Intersectionality*. John Wiley & Sons.

Crenshaw, K. (1989). Demarginalizing the intersection of race and sex: A black feminist critique of antidiscrimination doctrine, feminist theory and antiracist politics. *u. Chi. Legal f.*, 139.

Epstein, J. L. (2001). Introduction to the special section. New directions for school, family, and community partnerships in middle and high schools. *NASSP Bulletin, 85*(627), 3–6. doi:10.1177/019263650108562701

Gkaintartzi, A., Kiliari, A., & Tsokalidou, R. (2015). 'Invisible' bilingualism– 'invisible' language ideologies: Greek teachers' attitudes towards immigrant pupils' heritage languages. *International Journal of Bilingual Education and Bilingualism, 18*(1), 60–72. doi:10.1080/13670050.2013.877418

Jamal Al-deen, T., & Windle, J. (2017). 'I feel sometimes I am a bad mother': The affective dimension of immigrant mothers' involvement in their children's schooling. *Journal of Sociology (Melbourne, Vic.), 53*(1), 110–126. doi:10.1177/1440783316632604

Jørgensen, C. R., Dobson, G., & Perry, T. (2021). Migrant children with special educational needs in European schools–a review of current issues and approaches. *European Journal of Special Needs Education, 36*(3), 438–453. doi:10.1080/08856257.2020.1762988

Kibria, N., & Becerra, W. S. (2021). Deserving immigrants and good advocate mothers: Immigrant mothers' negotiations of special education systems for children with disabilities. *Social Problems, 68*(3), 591–607. doi:10.1093ocpropaa005

Kougias, K., & Efstathopoulos, J. (2020). The operational framework of the Greek educational system as an obstacle to the implementation of sustainable school. *Frontiers in Education, 5*, 1–11. doi:10.3389/feduc.2020.00142

Koutrouba, K., Antonopoulou, E., Tsitsas, G., & Zenakou, E. (2009). An investigation of Greek teachers' views on parental involvement in education. *School Psychology International, 30*(3), 311–328. doi:10.1177/0143034309106497

Koutsoklenis, A., & Papadimitriou, V. (2021). Special education provision in Greek mainstream classrooms: Teachers' characteristics and recruitment procedures in parallel support. *International Journal of Inclusive Education*, 1–16. doi:10.1080/13603116.2021.1942565

Nevill, T., Savage, G. C., & Forsey, M. (2023). It'sa diagnosis for the rich: Disability, advocacy and the micro-practices of social reproduction. *British Journal of Sociology of Education, 44*(2), 239–258. doi:10.1080/01425692.2022.2145931

Nteropoulou-Nterou, E., & Slee, R. (2019). A critical consideration of the changing conditions of schooling for students with disabilities in Greece and the fragility of international in local contexts. *International Journal of Inclusive Education, 23*(7-8), 891–907. doi:10.1080/13603116.2019.1623331

Nygreen, K. (2019). Neoliberal reform and family engagement in schools: An intersectional gender analysis. *Policy Futures in Education, 17*(2), 205–221. doi:10.1177/1478210318788416

Reaves, S., Martinez-Torteya, C., & Kosson, D. S. (2022). Understanding the relation between family engagement in education and preschoolers' socioemotional and behavioral functioning in a primarily Latinx sample. *Urban Education*, *57*(4), 630–661. doi:10.1177/0042085920974073

Rossetti, Z., Burke, M. M., Hughes, O., Schraml-Block, K., Rivera, J. I., Rios, K., & Lee, J. D. (2021). Parent perceptions of the advocacy expectation in special education. *Exceptional Children*, *87*(4), 438–457. doi:10.1177/0014402921994095

Samsari, E. P., Nikolaou, G., & Palaiologou, N. (2022). Multicultural diversity and special needs education: Small steps towards a successful inclusive environment in Greece. In *International Issues in SEND and Inclusion* (pp. 95–106). Routledge. doi:10.4324/9781003177135-12

Sanderson, K. A. (2023). "Be Prepared to Fight Like Hell": Parent Advice for IEP Meetings. *Exceptionality,* 1-18.

Serpell, Z. N., & Mashburn, A. J. (2012). Family–school connectedness and children's early social development. *Social Development*, *21*(1), 21–46. doi:10.1111/j.1467-9507.2011.00623.x

Stam, T., French, B., Lucassen, N., van Steensel, R., Godor, B., & Keizer, R. (2023). Not your cup of coffee? An ethnographic study on interparental dynamics during parental involvement activities in Dutch primary schools. *Ethnography and Education*, *18*(2), 159–182. doi:10.1080/17457823.2022.2158748

Traianou, A. (2023a). Evaluation and its politics: trade unions and education reform in Greece. *Education Inquiry*, 1-20.

Traianou, A. (2023b). The intricacies of conditionality: Education policy review in Greece 2015–2018. *Journal of Education Policy*, *38*(2), 342–362. doi:10.1080/02680939.2021.1986641

Tryfon, M., Anastasia, A., & Eleni, R. (2021). Parental perspectives on inclusive education for children with intellectual disabilities in Greece. *International Journal of Developmental Disabilities*, *67*(6), 397–405. doi:10.1080/20473869.2019.1675429 PMID:34925772

Chapter 10
The Role of Support Networks for Children and Adolescents With Language Developmental Problems

Zoi Siouti
National and Kapodistrian University of Athens, Greece

Georgios Kougioumtzis
https://orcid.org/0000-0002-2362-2094
National and Kapodistrian University of Athens, Greece

Anna Kaltsouda
University of Ioannina, Greece

Maria Theodoratou
https://orcid.org/0000-0003-4200-4643
Neapolis University, Pafos, Cyprus

ABSTRACT

This chapter presents the role of support networks for children and adolescents with language developmental problems. Support networks include family, school environment, community, and interpersonal relationships as well as digital networks. These networks can provide the necessary tools to children and adolescents with language developmental problems in order to overcome their problems and to be duly incorporated to the society. The assets provided to children and adolescents by the above-mentioned networks can be divided into two categories: external and internal. External assets include family support, empowerment, and proper set of boundaries and expectations. On the other hand, internal assets include proper motivation and school engagement, adaptation of positive values, evolution of social competences, and creation of a positive identity.

DOI: 10.4018/979-8-3693-1982-6.ch010

INTRODUCTION

Language developmental problems are a common indicator in the diagnosis and assessment of several genetic syndromes, including Down syndrome, Williams-Beuren syndrome, and Fragile X syndrome, as well as conditions such as autism, aphasia, and dyslexia. The term "language developmental problems" refers specifically to instances of language delay in children that are not due to an underlying medical condition and in which the child's cognitive intelligence (IQ) falls within the average range as defined by the American Psychological Association (APA, 1994 and noted by Clegg et al., 2005).

These challenges tend to emerge early in life and, in some cases, persist into adolescence and adulthood. At the same time, these language development problems can exacerbate the struggles associated with language disorders and contribute to increased levels of stress, anxiety, and depression in affected children.

In this context, children struggling with language developmental problems are at increased risk for both bullying in school and stereotyping. In addition, they often face a lack of social acceptance, which can further exacerbate their challenges (Holanda et al., 2015). In support of this, research by Locke et al. (2010) found that high school students with disabilities often struggle with feelings of loneliness, coupled with experiencing a lower quality of friendships and a lower social status compared to their peers (Locke, Ishijima, Kasari, & London, 2010).

In order to limit the above-mentioned situations, children with language developmental problems should be governed and mentored by support networks (such as family, school and society). These networks can help children with language developmental problems to be accepted by their peers, as well as to be incorporated by the society in a smoother way.

Social support is emerging as a critical factor in fostering successful interpersonal relationships among children and adolescents struggling with language development (Fernandez-Villardon et al., 2020) Evidence underscores the universal capacity of human environments to foster language acquisition by providing opportunities for communicative and social engagement. These communicative experiences, in turn, not only fuel the language acquisition process itself, but also help to shape the language model that serves as the foundation for this mechanism. In particular, differences in quality of life between individuals with and without disabilities are manifested across a wide range of dimensions. These include differences in the extent of social networks, opportunities to exercise autonomy, and the range of activities encountered (Sands & Kozleski, 1994).

Support networks include family (parents, siblings, caregivers, grandparents and wider family environment), school environment (teachers, supportive framework for language learning, individualized teaching, classmates), community and interpersonal relationships (neighborhood, city culture, awareness of social issues, friendships) as well as digital networks (computer media, social media, videogames) (Correa, Bonilla & Reyes-MacPherson, 2010).

According to research (Tunali & Power, 1993; Dubow & Ullman, 1989), support networks contribute to the strengthening of self-esteem, to the prevention of school bullying, to the reduction of stereotypes and to smoother adjustment of children and adolescents in adult life. Supportive networks play a crucial role in both increasing children's skills and strengthening their potentials; at the same time, supportive networks may be useful in the reduction of stress (Theodoratou et al., 2006, 2023a,2023b) and other psychological issues that children with language developmental problems may face. Moreover, supporting networks can strengthen emotional intelligence (e.g., empathy) as well as social intelligence (e.g., social skills) of children and adolescents with language developmental problems, thus shielding through the full development of their potentials. Family provides high levels of love and support, it the child and it monitors its compliance with social rules.

Thus, the purpose of this chapter is to present the challenges faced by the aforementioned networks, to delineate the pivotal role that these networks play in the construction of a robust support network of children with language developmental problems in both their educational and social spheres.

The Role of Family Support Networks for Children and Adolescents With Language Developmental Problems

Family-focused interventions place increasing emphasis on building on the strengths that already exist within families and fostering effective coping strategies while striving to cultivate positive family dynamics (Turnbull et al., 2005). This approach is based on the understanding that the functioning of a family is closely linked to the range of available supports available to each family and its members. Guided by this principle, family intervention practices have evolved. In particular, Dunst et al. (1988) contributed a widely recognized and adopted model of social support through their family systems assessment and intervention framework designed to promote positive family dynamics (Dunst, Trivette, & Deal, 1988).

According to family-focused interventions, the sources of support available to families of children with developmental language disorders can be effectively categorized into four primary groups: (1) the immediate family, which includes children, parents, and other household members; (2) the kinship network, which includes blood and marital relatives; (3) the informal network, which includes friends, neighbors, coworkers, and fellow church members; and (4) mental health professionals and professional organizations, which include physicians, early interventionists, and teachers. The optimal functioning of a family depends on a diverse array of supportive resources drawn from each of these groups. A lack of diversity within this support framework could indicate a deficiency in social support networks, potentially compromising the family's ability to access resources essential to their well-being (Horton and Wallander, 2001).

In addition, family support is critical in providing substantial levels of affection and positive communication. For example, young children often seek guidance and advice from their parents. In addition, family support includes the critical role of monitoring a child's behavior by setting boundaries. Within the sanctuary of the home, young people find a sense of security and view their parents as admirable role models (Benson, Leffert, Scales & Blyth, 1998).

The Role of School Environment Networks for Children and Adolescents With Language Developmental Problems

Furthermore, it is important to recognize that the instructional approach used by teachers can have a significant impact on the academic achievement of children and adolescents with language developmental disabilities (Danielsen et al., 2009; Torsheim & Wold, 2001). The Self-Determination Theory framework emphasizes the importance of fostering autonomy and academic competence in these individuals, thereby enhancing their self-regulation and learning experiences (Niemec & Ryan, 2009). Effective implementation of this theory can lead to notable improvements in academic achievement (Niemec & Ryan, 2009), provide students with essential motivation, ultimately reduce the incidence of dropout (Vallerand, Fortier & Guay, 1997), increase grades (Vansteenkiste et al., 2004), and curb instances of bullying and stress.

Preliminary research suggests that teacher support is associated with reduced academic stress among students (Raufelder et al., 2013; Vervoort et al., 2014), highlighting the potential for positive effects when self-determination theory is skillfully applied by educators.

It is evident that certain factors at school may cause stress to students. Some of these factors are unempathic and unsupportive teachers, poor classroom climate, poor relations between students and teachers. These factors can increase students' risk of developing mental health problems on the future. Hence, teachers should cooperate with doctors and school psychologists in order to understand the mechanism of stress, to identify stress factors and to reduce students' stress. A study has shown that school-based prevention programs have poor effects on the reduction of young persons' risk for the development of mental health issues on the future (Gerd Schulte-Körne, 2016).

The first wave of studies on the role of school environment networks for children and adolescents with language developmental problems was focused on the application of Self Determination Theory. The second wave of studies is focused on young children's "Theory of Mind". A recent longitudinal study has shown that Theory of Mind is closely linked to Self Determination Theory. As a matter of fact, the application of Theory of Mind in young children can help them develop the necessary skills in order to increase their autonomy and academic performance (Schneider, 2008). These findings are important for the appropriate functioning of the classroom. It is also worth noting that the role of the teacher is essential and crucial for the proper functioning of the classroom because he is like the maestro in the orchestra.

While the teacher undeniably plays a pivotal role, it's important to recognize that other factors also have a significant influence in cultivating an optimal school environment for children and adolescents with language development issues. These factors include the school principal, the parents of the students, the students themselves, and the educational policies of the state. In addition, it's important to recognize that a supportive school environment provides not only external support, characterized by a nurturing and motivating atmosphere, but also empowerment, as it creates a sense of security and provides students with meaningful roles within the academic environment.

In addition, a well-structured school environment establishes clear boundaries and sets appropriate expectations for children. The school's adherence to clear rules and consequences helps shape student behavior. In addition, the school environment efficiently allocates time for productive activities. This is exemplified by the allocation of time for instruction and practice in various arts disciplines, which allows young people to use their time in meaningful and enriching ways (Benson, Leffert, Scales & Blyth, 1998).

The Role of Community and Interpersonal Relationships for Children and Adolescents With Language Developmental Problems

In order to describe the role of the community on the development of children and adolescents with language developmental problems, it is necessary to identify the notion of "neighborhood". As a matter of fact, the mere definition of neighborhood varies from one person to another by both meaning as well as interpretation and is depended upon gender, race and generation (Burton & PriceSpratlen, 1999; Lee & Campbell, 1997). This definitional-conceptual problem of parents affects the definition of neighborhood that is given by children (Burton & Jarrett, 2000). By approaching the notion of "neighborhood" in terms of network, neighborhood can be described as a model of interpersonal relations in a local area (Burton & Jarrett, 2000). On the other hand, neighborhood has also got a cultural meaning: it is considered to be the geographic location where certain actions, beliefs, language and rituals take place on a daily basis (Burton & Jarrett, 2000). We should also mention that either way the neighborhood doesn't have strict and solid boundaries. Hence, the impact of it on children depends merely on the spatial diffusion of culture that identifies the above-mentioned social network complex (Burton & Jarrett, 2000).

An optimal community provides a number of external and internal assets for children and adolescents struggling with language development. Specifically, the community serves as a source of both psychological sustenance, as evidenced by nurturing neighborhoods where each child encounters caring neighbors, and empowerment. In cases where the community truly values its youth, young people find themselves with meaningful roles within the fabric of the community.

In addition, a thriving community plays a pivotal role in helping children and youth establish healthy boundaries and cultivate appropriate expectations. This is exemplified by adults who serve as positive role models for responsible behavior, while also taking responsibility for monitoring the behavior of young people. In this way, a healthy community environment contributes significantly to the growth and well-being of children and youth.

Conversely, the community also offers internal resources that have a profound impact on the development of children and youth. These include positive values that young people value, such as altruism, a commitment to equality, and the courage to stand up for their beliefs. These values, such as honesty, integrity and responsibility, are complemented by the cultivation of essential social skills. These competencies include skills such as effective planning and decision-making, skillful interpersonal interaction, cultural sensitivity, the ability to resolve conflict peacefully, and the resilience to withstand negative influences.

In addition, the community helps foster a positive identity in young people. This includes instilling a sense of personal empowerment, enhancing self-esteem, fostering a purposeful outlook on life, and promoting an optimistic view of one's future (Benson, Leffert, Scales & Blyth, 1998).

Given that a thriving community supports its members in their growth and development, the role of the community in the development of children and adolescents with language development challenges cannot be overstated. Nevertheless, it is imperative to emphasize the need to minimize incidents of bullying, as this is critical to fostering the necessary self-esteem that enables young people to integrate seamlessly into the social fabric and contextual milieu of their local community.

Friendship plays an important role in helping children navigate the challenges of language development. The impact of friendships is evident across cultures and is often profound (Hendrickson, Rosen & Aune, 2010). Friendships provide a variety of external and internal benefits to young people. For example, they provide a sense of empowerment, as these relationships create a space where a young person can find comfort and security. In addition, friendships serve as a means of establishing healthy boundaries, with a best friend often serving as a positive influence and role model. In addition, friendships contribute to the cultivation of positive values such as motivation and helping others, while also fostering important social skills such as planning and decision-making. In addition, friendships contribute to the development of a constructive sense of identity, enhance self-esteem, and promote resilience to peer pressure (Benson, Leffert, Scales & Blyth, 1998).

The Role of Digital Networks for Children and Adolescents With Language Developmental Problems

While conventional "traditional" media such as television, radio, and magazines provide users with a passive consumption experience, the modern digital media landscape empowers each user to not only consume content, but to actively generate it (Reid Chassiakos et al., 2016). Recent research has shown that engagement with modern digital platforms, particularly social media, can have positive outcomes for children and adolescents' socialization, communication, and learning skills (Hadjipanayis et al., 2019).

The use of digital media on children with language developmental problems may have a positive impact. Considering that, according to pedagogic theory, interaction improves learning, touchscreens that are used by modern digital devices are considered more educational for children (Reid Chassiakos et al., 2016). The use of digital media platforms by school children and adolescents benefits their communication skills and engagement, as well as it exposes them to new ideas and immersive learning experiences. Even though the use of digital interventions in children and adolescents with disabilities in order to improve their personal and social skills is proven extremely effective (Mazurek & Wenstrup, 2013; Mazurek et al., 2012; Tomopoulos et al., 2010), considering the fact that teenagers with autistic disorder suffer from higher rates of digital media abuse (Mazurek & Wenstrup, 2013; Mazurek et al., 2012), proper limits should be placed (Reid Chassiakos et al., 2016). As a matter of fact, proper limits considering the use of digital platforms should be placed, in order to avoid the negative effects of problematic media use by children and adolescents, such as cyberbullying, depression, anxiety or bad body image (Maurer & Taylor, 2020; Richards, Caldwell & Go, 2015).

Discussion

Children and adolescents with language development problems suffer from high levels of stress and anxiety as well as from poorer friendship quality and lower social status. They also fall victims to school bullying and stereotypes frequently. In order to extinguish the above-mentioned situations, children and adolescents who suffer from language developmental problems should be helped by support networks. These networks include family, school environment, community and digital networks.

First of all, in a family-focused intervention, the sources of support for children and adolescents can be categorized into four major categories (immediate family, kinship network, informal network and mental health professionals). A proper functioning family can provide children with the necessary love and positive communication, as well as it can monitor child's behavior by setting boundaries.

The school environment plays a pivotal role in providing essential support for children and adolescents with language developmental problems. Despite the potential stress-inducing factors present within schools, such as an unfavorable classroom atmosphere or strained student-teacher relationships, there exist specific programs that could empower these young individuals. These initiatives not only foster a sense of autonomy but also contribute to enhancing their academic achievements and forging stronger connections with both educators and peers.

Conversely, the community serves as a powerful influence in shaping healthy and constructive role models for children and adolescents, providing crucial psychological reinforcement and empowerment. Within a well-functioning community, the teaching of positive values such as honesty, integrity, and responsibility will be instrumental in fostering empathy in youth. In addition, the importance of friendship should not be underestimated. It serves as a source of empowerment, providing important lessons in setting healthy boundaries and fostering the development of positive values and a constructive sense of identity in children.

Finally, digital networks offer a valuable way for children and adolescents with language developmental problems to enhance their socialization, support their learning efforts, and engage in peer communication. However, caution must be exercised, as excessive or inappropriate use of digital media can lead to problematic patterns or even addiction. It should be emphasized that each of the aforementioned networks offers children and adolescents essential support in overcoming their barriers and integrating into society.

REFERENCES

American Psychiatric Association (Ed.). (2022). *Diagnostic and Statistical Manual of Mental Disorders* (Fifth Edition, Text Revision). American Psychiatric Publishing.

Benson, P. L., Leffert, N., Scales, P., & Blyth, D. A. (1998). Beyond the "Village" Rhetoric: Creating Healthy Communities for Children and Adolescents. *Applied Developmental Science*, *2*(3), 138–159. doi:10.12071532480xads0203_3

Burton, L. M., & Jarrett, R. L. (2000). In the Mix, Yet on the Margins: The Place of Families in Urban Neighborhood and Child Development Research. *Journal of Marriage and Family*, *62*(4), 1114–1135. doi:10.1111/j.1741-3737.2000.01114.x

Burton, L. M., & Price-Spratlen, T. (1999). Through the eyes of children: An ethnographic perspective on neighborhoods and child development. In A. Masten (Ed.), *Minnesota symposium on child psychology: Cultural processes in child development* (Vol. 29, pp. 77–96). Erlbaum.

Clegg, J., Hollis, C., Mawhood, L., & Rutter, M. (2005). Developmental language disorders – a follow-up in later adult life. Cognitive, language and psychosocial outcomes. *Journal of Child Psychology and Psychiatry, and Allied Disciplines*, *46*(2), 128–149. doi:10.1111/j.1469-7610.2004.00342.x PMID:15679523

Correa, V. I., Bonilla, Z. E., & Reyes-MacPherson, M. E. (2010). Support Networks of Single Puerto Rican Mothers of Children with Disabilities. *Journal of Child and Family Studies*, *20*(1), 66–77. doi:10.100710826-010-9378-3

Danielsen, A. G., Samdal, O., Hetland, J., & Wold, B. (2009). School-related social support and students' perceived life satisfaction. *The Journal of Educational Research*, *102*(4), 303–318. doi:10.3200/JOER.102.4.303-320

Dubow, E. F., & Ullman, D. G. (1989). Assessing Social Support in Elementary School Children: The Survey of Children's Social Support. *Journal of Clinical Child Psychology*, *18*(1), 52–64. doi:10.120715374424jccp1801_7

Dunst, C. J., Trivette, C. M., & Deal, A. (1988). *Enabling and empowering families: Principles & guidelines for practice*. Brookline Books.

Fernandez-Villardon, A., Alvarez, P., Ugalde, L., & Tellado, I. (2020). Fostering the Social Development of Children with Special Educational Needs or Disabilities (SEND) through Dialogue and Interaction: A Literature Review. *Social Sciences, 9*(6), 97. MDPI AG. doi:10.3390/socsci9060097

Hadjipanayis, A., Efstathiou, E., Altorjai, P., Stirs, T., Laliulis, A., Lonetzko, B., & Fonseca, H. (2019). Social Media and Children: What Is the Pediatrician's Role? *European Journal of Pediatrics, 178*(10), 1605–1612. doi:10.100700431-019-03458-w PMID:31468108

Hendrickson, B., Rosen, D., & Aune, R. K. (2010). An analysis of friendship networks, social connectedness, homesickness, and satisfaction levels of international students. *International Journal of Intercultural Relations, 15*, 1–15. doi:10.1016/j.ijintrel.2010.08.001

Holanda, C. M. A., Andrade, F. L. J. P., Bezerra, M. A., Silva Nascimento, J. P., Fonseca Neves, R., Alves, S. B., & Silva Ribeiro, K. S. Q. (2015). Support networks and people with physical disabilities: Social inclusion and access to health services. *Ciencia & Saude Coletiva, 20*(1), 175–184. doi:10.1590/1413-81232014201.19012013 PMID:25650611

Horton, T. V., & Wallander, J. L. (2001). Hope and social support as resilience factors against psychological distress of mothers who care for children with chronic physical conditions. *Rehabilitation Psychology, 46*(4), 382–399. doi:10.1037/0090-5550.46.4.382

Locke, J., Ishijima, E. H., Kasari, C., & London, N. (2010). Loneliness, friendship quality and the social networks of adolescents with high- functioning autism in an inclusive school setting. *Journal of Research in Special Educational Needs, 10*(2), 74–81. doi:10.1111/j.1471-3802.2010.01148.x

Maurer, B. T., & Taylor, L. C. (2020). The Effect of Digital Media on Children in Their Formative Years. *Journal of the American Academy of Physician Associates, 33*, 46–51. PMID:32345948

Mazurek, M. O., Shattuck, P. T., Wagner, M., & Cooper, B. P. (2012). Prevalence and correlates of screen-based media use among youths with autism spectrum disorders. *Journal of Autism and Developmental Disorders, 42*(8), 1757–1767. doi:10.100710803-011-1413-8 PMID:22160370

Mazurek, M. O., & Wenstrup, C. (2013). Television, video game and social media use among children with ASD and typically developing siblings. *Journal of Autism and Developmental Disorders, 43*(6), 1258–1271. doi:10.100710803-012-1659-9 PMID:23001767

Niemec, C. P., & Ryan, R. M. (2009). Autonomy, competence and relatedness in the classroom. Applying self-determination theory to educational practice. *Theory and Research in Education, 7*(2), 133–144. doi:10.1177/1477878509104318

Raufelder, D., Kittler, F., Braun, S. R., Lätsch, A., Wilkinson, R. P., & Hoferichter, F. (2013). The interplay of perceived stress, self-determination and school engagement in adolescence. *School Psychology International, 35*(4), 405–420. doi:10.1177/0143034313498953

Reid Chassiakos, Y., Radesky, J., Christakis, D., Moreno, M. A., Cross, C., Hill, D., Ameenuddin, N., Hutchinson, J., Levine, A., Boyd, R., Mendelson, R., & Swanson, W. S. (2016). Children and Adolescents and Digital Media. *Pediatrics, 138*(5), e20162593. doi:10.1542/peds.2016-2593 PMID:27940795

Richards, D., Caldwell, P. H. Y., & Go, H. (2015). Impact of Social Media on the Health of Children and Young People. *Journal of Paediatrics and Child Health, 51*(12), 1152–1157. doi:10.1111/jpc.13023 PMID:26607861

Sands, D. J., & Kozleski, E. B. (1994). Quality of life differences between adults with and without disabilities. *Education and Training in Mental Retardation and Developmental Disabilities, 29*, 90–101.

Schneider, W. (2008). The Development of Metacognitive Knowledge in Children and Adolescents: Major Trends and Implications for Education. *Mind, Brain and Education : the Official Journal of the International Mind, Brain, and Education Society*, *2*(3), 114–121. doi:10.1111/j.1751-228X.2008.00041.x

Schulte-Körne, G. (2016). Mental Health Problems in a School Setting in Children and Adolescents. *Deutsches Ärzteblatt International, 113*(11), 183–190. doi:10.3238/arztebl.2016.0183 PMID:27118666

Theodoratou, M., Farmakopoulou, I., Kougioumtzis, G., Kaltsouda, A., Siouti, Z., Gkintoni, E., Sofologi, M., Flora, K., & Tsitsas, G. (2023a). Emotion-focused coping, social support and active coping among university students: Gender differences. *J Psychol Clin Psychiatry, 14*(1), 5–9. doi:10.15406/jpcpy.2023.14.00720

Theodoratou, M., Kougioumtzis, G., Kaltsouda, A., Katsarou, D., Siouti, Z., Sofologi, M., Tsitsas, G., & Flora, K. (2023). Neuropsychological Aspects and Interventions for Internet Addiction in Adolescents with Asperger's Syndrome - Narrative Review. *Neurology & Neuroscience*, *4*(3), 1–10.

Theodoratou, M. M., Tafiadis, D., Mpekos, V., Euaggelatou, M., Kiritsi, B., Plitsi, A., & Pistola, D. (2006). Coping strategies of Greek students. *Annals of General Psychiatry*, *5*(S1, Suppl 1), S222. doi:10.1186/1744-859X-5-S1-S222

Tomopoulos, S., Dreyer, B. P., Berkule, S., Fierman, A. H., Brockmeyer, C., & Mendelsohn, A. L. (2010). Infant media exposure and toddler development. *Archives of Pediatrics & Adolescent Medicine, 164*(12), 1105–1111. doi:10.1001/archpediatrics.2010.235 PMID:21135338

Torsheim, T., & Wold, B. (2001). School-related stress, support, and subjective health complaints among early adolescents: A multilevel approach. *Journal of Adolescence*, *24*(6), 701–713. doi:10.1006/jado.2001.0440 PMID:11790051

Tunali, B., & Power, T. G. (1993). Creating Satisfaction: A Psychological Perspective on Stress and Coping in Families of Handicapped Children. *Journal of Child Psychology and Psychiatry, and Allied Disciplines, 34*(6), 945–957. doi:10.1111/j.1469-7610.1993.tb01100.x PMID:8408377

Turnbull, A. P., Turnbull, R., Erwin, E. J., & Soodak, L. C. (2005). *Families, professionals, exceptionality: Positive outcomes through partnership and trust* (5th ed.). Prentice Hall.

Vallerand, R. J., Fortier, M. S., & Guay, F. (1997). Self-determination and persistence in real life setting: Toward a motivational model of high school drop out. *Journal of Personality and Social Psychology, 72*(5), 1161–1176. doi:10.1037/0022-3514.72.5.1161 PMID:9150590

Vansteenkiste, M., Simons, J., Lens, W., Sheldon, K. M., & Deci, E. L. (2004). Motivating learning, performance, and persistence: The synergistic role of intrinsic goals and autonomy support. *Journal of Personality and Social Psychology*, *87*, 246–260. doi:10.1037/0022-3514.87.2.246 PMID:15301630

Vervoort, T., Logan, D. E., Goubert, L., De Clercq, B., & Hublet, A. (2014). Severity of pediatric pain in relation to school-related functioning and teacher support: An epidemiological study among school-aged children and adolescents. *Pain*, *155*(6), 1118–1127. doi:10.1016/j.pain.2014.02.021 PMID:24631587

Chapter 11
Understanding the Developmental Needs of Children With Developmental Language Disorder According to Professionals

Asimina M. Ralli
National and Kapodistrian University of Athens, Greece

Eleni Kalliontzi
https://orcid.org/0000-0001-9788-6626
National and Kapodistrian University of Athens, Greece

Elena Kazali
Univesrity of Ioannina, Greece

Olympia Palikara
https://orcid.org/0000-0003-3357-9736
University of Warwick, UK

ABSTRACT

The aim of the study was to explore professional understanding of the developmental needs of children with developmental language disorder (DLD), the diagnostic criteria that they apply, as well as the challenges they face when working with children with DLD. One hundred and fifty-four professionals (35 educational psychologists (EPs), 75 speech and language therapists (SLTs), and 44 special educational needs teachers (SEN teachers)) completed a questionnaire. Results showed that although most professionals were familiar with the term "DLD," they defined it differently. Most professionals reported that children with DLD have difficulties both in receptive and expressive language as well as socio-emotional problems. Regarding the diagnostic criteria, SLTs used mostly the discrepancy and the language deficits criteria. Last, participants identified different challenges according to their professional orientation. The results are discussed in terms of how they could better inform both training and practice to be able to respond more appropriately to children's developmental needs.

DOI: 10.4018/979-8-3693-1982-6.ch011

INTRODUCTION

DLD is a common developmental disorder that affects both across and within language domains such as phonology, semantics, morphology, grammar, syntax, pragmatics in both expressive and receptive level (Bishop, 2006; Leonard, 1998). DLD affects about 7% of the children at school entry (Tomblin et al, 1997; Norbury et al., 2016), while it is also persistent, since it can affect language abilities into adolescence or even into adulthood (Brizzolara et al., 2011). Children with DLD are also at risk for less successful academic outcomes as well as behavioral, emotional and social difficulties (Conti-Ramsden et al., 2009; St Clair et al., 2011).

Although DLD affects a substantial number of children and young people it has traditionally received much less research attention when compared to other developmental disorders (e.g. Autistic Spectrum Disorder, Attention Deficit and Hyperactivity Disorder, Bishop, 2010), whereas public awareness of the disorder and knowledge of its manifestations are still limited (Thordardottir et al, 2021). Additionally, to date, professionals' views about DLD have been studied mainly in English speaking countries by a small group of studies (Bishop et al., 2017) and there is a paucity of information concerning professionals' perspectives about DLD in other countries, such as Greece.

Previous studies have shown that professionals (SLTs, and Eps) have different views concerning the terminology and the criteria used for the diagnosis of DLD, the characteristics and difficulties experienced by children with DLD, (Dockrell et al., 2014; Glover et al., 2015; Palikara et al. 2007). Many reasons may account for this variation. For example, in the last four decades, there was a confusion resulting from differences in terminology (e.g., *Language Disorder*, *Specific Language Impairment*, *Speech and Language Deficits or Disorders*, *Primary Language Impairment*) (Reilly et al., 2014) or in the diagnostic criteria used by researchers and professionals worldwide to identify children with DLD (Bishop, 2014; Reilly et al., 2014). These reasons have raised barriers to the communication and collaboration among professionals that may also have an impact on raising public awareness about the specific disorder, on the process of activating the appropriate services providing support or choosing the most effective methods and programs for intervention (Hartas, 2004). At the same time, it is important to be aware of the professionals' understanding of the above issues as it is evidenced that their professionalism may have an impact on the implementation of programs and strategies enhancing children's learning, social and emotional wellbeing (St Clair et al., 2011).

Thus, the aim of the current study was to investigate Greek professionals' understanding of (a) DLD (terminology, provision of a definition), (b) the language and socio-emotional needs of children with DLD (c) the diagnostic criteria they apply as well as the challenges they face when working with children with DLD, given the fact that to our knowledge, no previous studies have been carried out in Greece, while very few studies have been conducted in this domain internationally (Dockrell et al., 2014; Glover et al., 2015; Palikara et al. 2007).

Professionals' Understanding of DLD: Previous Studies

Until recently, there was no agreed terminology for describing childhood language problems (Reilly et al., 2014). One reason for this was the fact that DLD is a complex and heterogeneous condition with no clear-cut boundaries from either typical development or other developmental disorders (Reilly et al., 2014). However, after the publication of DSM-5 (American Psychiatric Association, 2013), there has been considerable progress in the theoretical understanding of DLD which acknowledges that multiple mechanisms may work together to produce the range of profiles observed in children with DLD (Morton, 2004).

In this context, during the last two decades a group of studies have investigated the professionals' views about children with language difficulties (e.g. Dockrell & Howell, 2015; Dockrell et al. 2017). For example, Dockrell and Howell (2015) explored the views of experienced practitioners regarding children with speech, language and communication needs (SLCN). They reported that those practitioners used a range of terminology to refer to this group of children and they mentioned that literacy difficulties (reading decoding, reading comprehension, spelling, writing texts) were associated with language difficulties. They also mentioned a tendency for respondents to report that children with SLCN also experienced socio-emotional difficulties.

Dockrell et al. (2017) in another study compared the views of experienced education professionals and SLTs on children with SLCN. Education professionals were less familiar with terminology related to speech difficulties (e.g. articulation disorder, phonological disorder, oro-motor dyspraxia), but showed awareness of their academic (reading and writing) and behavior problems associated with language difficulties. SLTs reported to be confident in their understanding of the relevant DLD terminology but there was less clarity among them in the features that discriminated speech from language difficulties.

Thomas et al. (2019) explored SLTs views regarding assessment, diagnosis and characteristics of children with DLD. Regarding the diagnostic criteria, most of SLTs agreed on the inclusion of both language (e.g. syntax and grammar) and cognitive domains (e.g. phonological short-term memory and working memory); moreover, one third of the SLTs participating in their study reported that children with DLD may have difficulties with accessing the academic curriculum and their social relationships.

In Greece, SLTs are the professionals who mainly assess children with DLD. EPs participate in the assessment and diagnosis of children with language difficulties, particularly in relation to evaluation of their cognitive abilities and the presence or not of emotional difficulties. Teachers and mostly SEN teachers are the key persons for early identification and support of children with DLD in the Greek mainstream classroom. Child Psychiatrists, Child Neurologists and Developmental Pediatricians and SLTs working in public or private health and education services are those responsible for the ascription of DLD diagnosis. They are traditionally based on the DSM-5 and ICD-10 diagnostic criteria.

As it can be seen, only a limited number of studies have examined the perspectives of professionals' understanding of DLD, with most of the studies being conducted mainly in countries such as Great Britain or USA. To our knowledge only one study was recently conducted in Greece exploring preschool (KTs) and primary school teachers (PSTs) views of children with DLD in Greek mainstream schools (Ralli et. al. 2022). They found that half of the participants, did not know the term DLD, while among those who provided a definition for DLD most of them used a language-deficit focused definition. Both groups of professionals reported that children with DLD have vocabulary and syntactic difficulties in the receptive language. In the expressive language KTs identified more articulation and phonological difficulties, while PSTs referred vocabulary and grammatical difficulties. The majority of professionals mentioned additional difficulties such as emotional and behavioral problems. Both groups identified a variety of challenges while working with children with DLD. KTs focused mostly on children's emotional difficulties, while PSTs reported mostly their learning difficulties. Mapping the professionals views of DLD could contribute to a better understanding of the difficulties and challenges they face, in order to efficiently meet the children's needs.

The Present Study

The aim of the present study was to investigate Greek professionals' (EPs, SLTs and SEN teachers) understanding of (a) DLD (terminology and definition), (b) the language and socio-emotional needs of children with DLD. Also another aim was to explore the diagnostic criteria for DLD that the professionals use as well as the challenges they face when working with children with DLD. Therefore the following research questions were stated:

(1) To what extent understanding (terminology, definition) of DLD differ among the professionals? It was expected that EPs and SEN teachers to be less familiar than SLTs with current terminology and to provide less sufficient definitions for DLD (Dockrell & Howell, 2015; Dockrell et al., 2017).
(2) To what extent the views about the language and socio-emotional needs of children with DLD differ among the professionals? It was expected SLTs to have a more refined understanding of the wider linguistic needs of children with DLD (Dockrell and Howell, 2015; Dockrell et al., 2017), while for EPs and SEN teachers it was anticipated to have a better awareness of the socioemotional needs that are often experienced by the children with DLD (Dockrell and Lindsay, 2001).
(3) To what extent the perspectives about the diagnostic criteria for DLD as well as the challenges they face differ among the professionals? It was expected that EPs and SEN teachers to be less familiar than SLTs with the diagnostic criteria and to face different challenges than SLTs (Thomas et al., 2019).

Method

Participants

One hundred and fifty-four professionals (SLTs, EPs and SEN teachers) participated in the study (n=154; 87% female and 13% male). Thirty-five of them were EPs (22.7%), 75 SLTs (48.7%) and 44 SEN Teachers (28.6). Most of the professionals (SLTs, EPs and SEN teachers) aged between 31-40 years old, worked in private services for at least 6-10 years and had a postgraduate degree in Education (Table 1).

Materials

Participants responded to an online survey which was based on previous relevant studies (Dockrell and Lindsay, 2001; Dockrell and Howell, 2015; Dockrell et al., 2015, Dockrell et al., 2017; Ralli et al. 2022), the Greek curriculum and educational system. The questionnaire was piloted with a small group of twenty professionals (8 EPs, 5 SLTs and 7 SEN teachers) prior to the main study in order to ensure that the context of the questions was well understood as well as in order to evaluate the construct validity of the instrument. Changes in wording were made for this purpose considering professionals' (SLTs,' EPs' and SEN teachers') comments of the pilot version of the questionnaire. Regarding the validity of the questionnaire, there was a remarkably high percentage of agreement (>95%) among the professionals to the extent the questions were comprehensible for the readers as well as whether this questionnaire was in fact measuring what it was supposed to measure.

The final questionnaire consisted of three sections. In the first section, the respondents were asked to complete their demographic information, (gender, age, education, profession, working sector and

Table 1. Demographics of the professionals

	Educational Psychologists n (%)	Speech & Language Therapists n (%)	Special Educational Needs Teachers n (%)
Gender			
Female	34 (97%)	65 (87%)	35 (80%)
Male	1 (3%)	10 (13%)	9 (21%)
Age group			
20-30	9 (26%)	16 (21%)	14 (32%)
31-40	18 (51%)	34 (45%)	13 (30%)
41-50	6 (17%)	21 (28%)	13 (30%)
51-60	2 (6%)	3 (4%)	4 (9%)
>60	0 (0%)	1 (1%)	0 (0%)
Educational level			
Undergraduate degree	9 (26%)	37 (49%)	7 (16%)
Postgraduate degree	13 (37%)	31 (41%)	29 (66%)
PhD	13 (37%)	7 (9%)	8 (18%)
Where are you working now?			
Public sector	21 (60%)	14 (19%)	23 (52%)
Private sector	12 (34%)	57 (76%)	21 (48%)
Unemployed	2 (6%)	4 (5%)	0 (0%)
How many years have you been in this role?			
1-5	12 (34%)	15 (20%)	13 (30%)
6-10	13 (37%)	22 (29%)	7 (16%)
11-15	3 (9%)	20 (27%)	13 (30%)
> 16	7 (20%)	18 (24%)	11 (25%)

experience). The second section examined professionals' understanding of DLD. Using open-ended questions, professionals were asked whether they were familiar with the term DLD as well as to provide a definition for DLD. In this section, participants had to choose: (a) 3 out of 5 domains in receptive language (vocabulary, grammar, syntax, morphology, pragmatics) that preschool and school aged children with DLD present the most difficulties; (b) 3 out of 7 domains in expressive language (vocabulary, grammar, syntax, morphology, pragmatics, articulation and phonology) that children present the most difficulties, and (c) 3 out of 4 socio-emotional domains (emotional, behavioral, social problems, other) that they face difficulties.

The third section required from the professionals to identify the criteria for diagnosis by using an open-ended question. They were further asked about the challenges they face when working with children with DLD by choosing three among a list of six challenges (language issues, learning issues, emotional difficulties, behavioral issues, cooperation with parents, and cooperation with teachers).

Procedure

The research protocol for this study was approved by the Research Ethics Committee of National and Kapodistrian University of Athens, Greece. The questionnaire was created using Google Forms. Professionals working in public and private services in different geographical regions of Greece completed anonymously and voluntarily an online questionnaire. The link of the questionnaire was disseminated to the heads of educational and health services. The invitation explained the importance of collecting further information about DLD. In cases that the questionnaire was not completed, a reminder was sent to them two weeks later. The time needed for the completion of the questionnaire was ten to fifteen minutes.

RESULTS

Professionals' Understanding of Developmental Language Disorder

Professionals were asked whether they were *familiar with the term 'Developmental Language Disorder* and also *to provide a brief definition of DLD."* In total, the majority of the professionals reported that they were familiar with the term DLD.

The professionals were also asked *to provide a definition for DLD*. Answers had the form of quotes and through a content analysis conducted by the authors, codes and common themes emerged. These common themes became the options of new categorical variables that were used in the statistical analyses (see below in the results). Following a content analysis, the definitions provided were grouped into three categories: (a) *no answer:* when they didn't provide any answer (b) *insufficient definitions:* answers focusing only on language deficits, (answers like: "Difficulties in speech", "Congenital difficulties in oral speech") and (c) *sufficient definitions*: answers focusing on a discrepancy between nonverbal and language skills and / or additional difficulties, (answers like: "Difficulties in receptive and expressive language and / or the use of language despite typical development", "Difficulties in comprehension and expression which are not based on neurological or cognitive disorders"). The EPs and the SEN teachers provided statistically significant more "insufficient definitions," while the SLTs provided statistically significantly "no definitions."

Regarding the terminology that professionals used to refer to children with DLD, the EPs and SEN teachers used statistically significantly more the term "Speech and language difficulties" while the SLTs the term "DLD/SLI" in comparison to the other terms (Table 2).

Language Difficulties of Preschool and School Age Children With DLD

Professionals were also asked to identify the language modalities (receptive, expressive, or both) that preschool and school aged children with DLD have the greatest difficulties. Regarding the preschool children (Table 3) most of the EPs mentioned expressive language difficulties, while SLTs and SEN teachers reported both expressive and receptive language difficulties.

More specifically, regarding the receptive language difficulties of preschool children, all groups of professionals reported statistically significantly more difficulties with vocabulary than the other language domains. As it concerns the expressive language difficulties the EPs mentioned statistically significantly

Table 2. Professionals' understanding of DLD

	Educational Psychologists n (%)	Speech & Language Therapists n (%)	Special Educational Needs Teachers n (%)
Do you know the term DLD?			
Yes	32 (91%)	71 (95%)	36 (82%)
No	3 (9%)	4 (5%)	8 (18%)
	χ^2 (1)= 24.03, $p < 0.001$	χ^2 (1)= 59.85, $p < 0.001$	χ^2 (1)= 17.82, $p < 0.001$
Please provide a brief definition of the term DLD.			
No definition	8 (23%)	33 (44%)	15 (34%)
Insufficient definition	22 (63%)	23 (31%)	19 (43%)
Sufficient definition	5 (14%)	19 (25%)	10 (23%)
	χ^2 (2)= 14.11, $p = 0.001$	χ^2 (2)= 4.16, $p = 0.125$	χ^2 (2)= 2.77, $p = 0.250$
From the provided list which terminology do you use when you refer to the children with language difficulties?			
Developmental Language Disorder/ Specific Language Impairment	6 (17%)	32 (43%)	10 (23%)
Language Disorders	5 (14%)	13 (17%)	7 (16%)
Speech, Language and Communication Disorders	4 (11%)	7 (9%)	6 (14%)
Speech and Language difficulties	19 (54%)	23 (31%)	21 (48%)
	χ^2 (4)= 27.71, $p < 0.001$	χ^2 (3)= 19.45, $p < 0.001$	χ^2 (1)= 12.90, $p = 0.005$

more difficulties with articulation, while the SLTS and SEN teachers reported more difficulties with expressive vocabulary.

In respect to the school age children (Table 4) all groups of professionals mentioned difficulties both in the receptive and expressive modality. Regarding receptive and expressive language, all the professionals mentioned statistically significantly more difficulties in receptive and expressive vocabulary than the other domains. while in addition the SEN teachers reported difficulties with syntax.

Socio-Emotional Difficulties of Preschool and School Age Children With DLD

Professionals were also asked to identify from a given list the *three most important difficulties in the socio-emotional domain that children with DLD are constrained with.* For preschool children, the EPs mentioned statistically significantly more "difficulties in their relations with others," the SLTs reported mostly "behavior problems," while the SEN teachers referred mostly to "emotional difficulties." For school age children a change was evident, according to which each group of professionals referred to emotional difficulties as the most prominent difficulty of this age group (Table 5).

Professionals' Views About Diagnostic Criteria for DLD

Using an open-ended question, professionals were asked to report the diagnostic criteria for DLD that they usually employ. Professionals' responses were coded into the five following categories: (a)

Table 3. Language difficulties experienced by preschool children with DLD

	Educational Psychologists n (%)	Speech & Language Therapists n (%)	Special Educational Needs Teachers n (%)
Based on your experience, in which of the following domains *preschool children* with DLD have the greatest difficulties?			
Receptive language	1 (3%)	3 (4%)	1 (2%)
Expressive language	19 (54%)	26 (35%)	14 (32%)
Both	14 (40%)	46 (61%)	29 (66%)
	χ^2 (2)= 15.23, $p < 0.001$	χ^2 (2)= 37.04, $p < 0.001$	χ^2 (1)= 26.77, $p < 0.001$
Based on your experience, in which of the following domains of receptive language *preschool children* with DLD have the greatest difficulties?			
Syntax	2 (5%)	13 (17%)	5 (11%)
Morphology	6 (17%)	6 (8%)	5 (11%)
Vocabulary	19 (55%)	43 (57%)	28 (64%)
Grammar	2 (6%)	3 (4%)	0 (0%)
Pragmatics	6 (17%)	8 (11%)	6 (14%)
	χ^2 (4)= 28.00, $p < 0.001$		χ^2 (1)= 35.09, $p < 0.001$
Based on your experience, in which of the following domains of expressive language *preschool children* with DLD have the greatest difficulties?			
Syntax	3 (9%)	10 (13%)	2 (5%)
Morphology	2 (6%)	4 (5%)	3 (7%)
Vocabulary	5 (16%)	26 (35%)	16 (36%)
Grammar	1 (3%)	1 (1%)	4 (9%)
Pragmatics	2 (6%)	2 (3%)	1 (2%)
Articulation	15 (43%)	11 (15%)	9 (21%)
Phonology	6 (17%)	19 (25%)	9 (21%)
	χ^2 (6)= 28.58, $p < 0.001$	χ^2 (6)= 49.64, $p < 0.001$	χ^2 (6)= 27.27, $p < 0.001$

no answer, (b) *irrelevant answer*: no reference to a specific criterion, e.g. "I just report areas of difficulties", (c) *discrepancy criterion* between the performance in nonverbal IQ test and a standardized language test, e.g. "Low language skills and average nonverbal skills" (d) *language deficits only*: significant difficulties in several areas of receptive and expressive language, e.g. "Difficulties in receptive and expressive language and resistance to intervention", and (e) *expressive language, literacy and additional difficulties*, e.g. "Difficulties in expressive language, reading, writing, memory and self-esteem" (Table 6). Most of the professionals in each group did not provide an answer. From the answers provided, the SLTs used statistically significantly mostly the *discrepancy* and the *language deficits* criteria (Table 6).

Table 4. Language difficulties experienced by school-aged children with DLD

	Educational Psychologist n (%)	Speech & Language Therapist n (%)	Special Educational Needs Teachers n (%)
Based on your experience, in which of the following domains *school-aged children* with DLD have the greatest difficulties?			
Receptive language	3 (9%)	9 (12%)	4 (9%)
Expressive language	13 (37%)	24 (32%)	12 (27%)
Both	18 (51%)	42 (56%)	28 (64%)
	χ^2 (2)= 10.29, p = 0.006	χ^2 (2)= 21.84, p < 0.001	χ^2 (2)= 20.36, p < 0.001
Based on your experience, in which of **the following domains of receptive language *school-aged children* with DLD have the greatest difficulties?**			
Syntax	3 (9%)	9 (12%)	8 (18%)
Morphology	2 (6%)	7 (9%)	5 (11%)
Vocabulary	20 (57%)	42 (56%)	20 (46%)
Grammar	4 (11%)	5 (7%)	3 (7%)
Pragmatics	4 (11%)	8 (11%)	7 (16%)
	χ^2 (4)= 34.42, p < 0.001	χ^2 (4)= 68.64, p < 0.001	χ^2 (4)= 20.61, p < 0.001

Table 5. Socio-emotional difficulties experienced by preschool and school-aged children with DLD

	Educational Psychologists n (%)	Speech & Language Therapists n (%)	Special Educational Needs Teachers n (%)
Socio-emotional difficulties that *preschool children* with DLD face			
Emotional difficulties (e.g., stress)	13 (37%)	22 (29%)	21 (48%)
Behavioral problems (e.g., aggression)	6 (17%)	34 (45%)	8 (18%)
Difficulties in their relations with others	15 (43%)	15 (20%)	11 (25%)
Other	0 (0%)	1 (1%)	2 (5%)
I do not know	1 (3%)	3 (4%)	2 (5%)
	χ^2 (2)= 3.94, p = 0.139	χ^2 (4)= 54.87, p < 0.001	χ^2 (4)= 28.04, p < 0.001
Socio-emotional difficulties that *school-aged* children with DLD face			
Emotional difficulties (e.g., stress)	15 (43%)	31 (41%)	23 (52%)
Behavioral problems (e.g., aggression)	11 (31%)	23 (31%)	10 (23%)
Difficulties in their relations with others	8 (23%)	15 (20%)	9 (21%)
Other	0 (0%)	1 (1%)	0 (0%)
I do not know	1 (3%)	5 (7%)	2 (5%)
	χ^2 (2)= 2.17, p = 0.337	χ^2 (4)= 49.92, p < 0.001	χ^2 (2)= 8.71, p = 0.013

Table 6. Professionals' views about the diagnostic criteria for DLD

	Educational Psychologists n (%)	Speech & Language Therapists n (%)	Special Educational Needs Teachers n (%)
Based on your experience, which criteria do you use for the diagnosis of DLD?			
No answer	30 (85.7%)	36 (48%)	37 (84.09%)
Irrelevant answer	0 (0%)	8 (10.6%)	1 (2.27%)
Discrepancy	2 (5.71)	15 (20%)	2 (4.54%)
Language deficits only	0 (0%)	15 (20%)	1 (2.27%)
Expressive language and literacy and additional difficulties	3 (8.5%)	1 (1.3%)	3 (6.82)
	χ^2 (2)= 43.26, $p < 0.001$	χ^2 (4)= 45.73, $p < 0.001$	χ^2 (4)= 113.23, $p < 0.001$

Challenges Identified by Professionals Working With Children With DLD

Participants were also asked to report the challenges they experience while working with children with DLD by choosing three among a list of six challenges (language problems, learning difficulties, emotional difficulties, behavioral problems, cooperation with parents, and cooperation with teachers). EPs reported statistically significantly more "emotional difficulties" as the predominant challenge they experience while working with children with DLD in comparison to the other challenges. SLTs and SEN teachers referred notably to language problems, in comparison to the other types of challenges (Table 7).

DISCUSSION

The present study investigated for the first time Greek professionals' understanding of DLD, their views about the language and socioemotional difficulties of children with DLD, the diagnostic criteria they apply as well as the challenges they face when working with that group of children.

Table 7. Challenges identified by professionals working with children with DLD

	Educational Psychologists n (%)	Speech & Language Therapists n (%)	Special Educational Needs Teachers n (%)
Which is the greatest challenge you face when you work with children with DLD?			
Language problems	3 (9%)	32 (43%)	16 (36%)
Learning difficulties	4 (11%)	8 (11%)	7 (16%)
Emotional difficulties	9 (26%)	7 (12%)	5 (11%)
Behavioral problems	1 (3%)	9 (12%)	1 (2%)
Cooperation with parents	0 (0%)	5 (7%)	0 (0%)
Cooperation with teachers	1 (3%)	4 (5%)	0 (0%)
	χ^2 (4)= 12.00, $p = 0.017$	χ^2 (5)= 51.22, $p < 0.001$	χ^2 (4)= 25.33, $p < 0.001$

Professionals' Understanding of Developmental Language Disorder

The majority of the professionals reported that they were familiar with the term DLD, which was in contrast with our initial hypothesis. This may be due to the fact that in addition to SLTs, EPs and SEN teachers engage in the assessment and education of children with DLD in Greece. At the same time, differences were revealed among groups of professionals concerning the term they use and the way they define this specific disorder, confirming the initial hypothesis. More specifically, it was found that SLTs prefer to use the term *DLD/SLI* whereas EPs and SEN teachers feel more comfortable with the term *Speech and Language Difficulties*. Similar findings were reported by earlier studies in the field (Dockrell & Lindsay, 2001; Palikara et al., 2007). Reilly and colleagues (Reilly et al., 2014) reported that one interpretation for this may be the fact that DLD is a complex and heterogeneous condition that affects not only language but other developmental domains as well. Thus, they acknowledged that it is a challenging task for all the professionals involved in DLD to agree on the use of a single term, as each one of them needs to highlight a different aspect of the disorder. It is not, therefore, surprising that most of the SLTs used the term 'Developmental Language Disorder/ Specific Language Impairment' as they acknowledge the severity of language deficits that children with DLD have. On the other hand, EPs and SEN teachers may respectively preferred the term 'Speech and Language Difficulties' because it is a more comprehensible term focusing on difficulties that can be "easily seen."

Professionals also had major difficulties in providing a definition about DLD; It is surprisingly that most SLTS did not provide a definition in comparison to the other groups. This finding may indicate that SLTs have a lack of knowledge, or that they thought the question was too easy or they felt embarrassment if they gave a wrong answer. Whatever the reason, this should be further investigated. Also, most of EPs and SEN teachers provided insufficient definitions. These findings are consistent with previous research which suggests that professionals working in mainstream schools feel that they do not have the necessary knowledge for that group of children (Antoniazzi et al, 2010; Daniel & McLeod, 2017; Dockrell and Lindsay, 2001; Glover et al, 2015; McAllister et al., 2011). Overall, this finding revealed restricted knowledge regarding DLD among all the professionals, imposing the need for changes in educational-training institutions and policy makers (Dockrell and Howell, 2015)

Language and Socio-Emotional Difficulties Experienced by Children With DLD

Most of the SLTs and SEN teachers reported that preschool children with DLD have both receptive and expressive language difficulties, whereas EPs identified mostly expressive language difficulties. Regarding receptive language, all professionals (EPs, SLTs and SEN teachers) reported that preschool children with DLD experience marked difficulties in vocabulary. As far as expressive language is concerned, most SLTs and SEN teachers considered again vocabulary difficulties as the most prominent in preschool children, whereas EPs primarily mentioned articulation difficulties. This difference among professionals may suggest that EPs focus on difficulties that are more obvious during their interaction with children, like articulation problems, while SLTs and SEN teachers probably because of their training and involvement in the assessment procedure, can also identify difficulties in other domains not as much obvious as articulation (Hancock et al. 2023; Leonard, 2014). These differences among professionals also imply a lack of shared knowledge that can be related to limited opportunities for multidisciplinary experiences (Hancock et al., 2022). All professionals, however, identified that school aged children with DLD have difficulties in both receptive and expressive language, and mentioned that vocabulary was the most affected domain in both modalities (receptive and expressive). This is not surprising as previous research has found that language difficulties that persist in school age are more severe and obvious (Leonard, 2014).

Regarding the socio-emotional domain, all professionals mentioned that children with DLD face socio-emotional difficulties in general but focused on various aspects according to the age of children and probably because of their different professional roles (Atkinson et al., 2015). Thus, for preschool children EPs reported mostly difficulties in their relations with others; SLTs mentioned behavioral problems and SEN teachers focused mostly on emotional difficulties. Regarding school aged children, all professionals referred that emotional difficulties were the most prevalent difficulties that children have additionally to their language deficits. Research findings support the above results (e.g., Yew, & O'Kearney, 2013) as it has been found that different types of emotional or behavioral problems may be more obvious in different ages groups of children with DLD (St Clair et al., 2019) and also that behavioral problems and peer relation problems decline with age (Levickis et al., 2017) and emotional deficits become more obvious (Clair et al., 2011).

Diagnostic Criteria for DLD and Challenges Identified by Professionals Working With Children With DLD

The present study revealed that the majority of professionals had difficulties in reporting the criteria for the diagnosis of DLD as most of them avoided to provide a response to the specific question. From those who responded EPs and SEN teachers were less familiar than SLTs, a finding which agrees with our initial hypothesis. Also, it was found that SLTs applied mostly the criterion of *discrepancy* and the criterion of *language deficits*, whereas a limited number of EPs and SEN teachers reported the criterion of *deficits in expressive language, literacy and other skills*. The above findings concur with those of previous studies which reported that one of the main challenges that professionals working in schools have to deal with is their knowledge gap on DLD issues like diagnostic criteria (Dockrell et al, 1997; Dockrell & Howell, 2015; Dockrell & Lindsay, 2001).

Regarding the challenges the professionals face when working with children with DLD, EPs highlighted emotional difficulties whereas SLTs and SEN teachers referred notably to language difficulties. These different perspectives on the challenges they face may reflect that their different professional roles make them to focus on different developmental domains (Atkinson et al., 2015).

To our knowledge, this is the first study in Greece that has specifically examined the views of EPs, SLTs and SEN teachers concerning their knowledge about DLD. The findings of the current study shed some light on professionals understanding of DLD as well as the difficulties children face in different developmental domains, the diagnostic criteria professionals use and the challenges they face. However, the sample of professionals may be biased as those who responded to the survey may be the ones who were really interested in DLD. Nevertheless, the present study can form a basis for further research and allows for building evidence-based data concerning professionals' understanding of DLD and children's developmental needs.

CONCLUSION

The findings of the present study provided novel data on Greek professionals' (EPs' SLTs,' and SEN teachers') understanding of DLD. It was demonstrated that although all the professionals were familiar with the term DLD, they used different terminology, they faced different challenges when working with children with DLD and only SLTs were aware of the diagnostic criteria in comparison to the other groups of professionals. There is a need to further explore the previous findings in future studies since, such findings may indicate the need for further training of professionals (SLTs, EPs and SEN teachers) and increased awareness of the specificity of the challenges children with DLD face in the educational environment, in order for those working with that group of children to achieve a common ground of understanding and respond to the needs both of the children and their families.

ACKNOWLEDGMENT

The authors are extremely grateful to all the professionals (EPs, SLTs, and SEN teachers) who participated in this survey.

REFERENCES

Antoniazzi, D., Snow, P., & Dickson-Swift, V. (2010). Teacher identification of children at risk for language impairment in the first year of school. *International Journal of Speech-Language Pathology*, *12*(3), 244–252. doi:10.3109/17549500903104447 PMID:20433343

Atkinson, C., Dunsmuir, S., Lang, J., & Wright, S. (2015). Developing a competency framework for the initial training of educational psychologists working with young people aged 16–25. *Educational Psychology in Practice*, *31*(2), 159–173. doi:10.1080/02667363.2015.1004038

Bishop, D. V. (2006). What causes specific language impairment in children? *Current Directions in Psychological Science*, *15*(5), 217–221. doi:10.1111/j.1467-8721.2006.00439.x PMID:19009045

Bishop, D. V. (2010). Which neurodevelopmental disorders get researched and why? *PLoS One*, *5*(11), e15112. doi:10.1371/journal.pone.0015112 PMID:21152085

Bishop, D. V. (2014). Pragmatic language impairment: A correlate of SLI, a distinct subgroup, or part of the autistic continuum? In D. V. M. Bishop & L. Leonard (Eds.), *Speech and languageimpairments in children* (pp. 113–128). Psychology Press. doi:10.4324/9781315784878

Collis, J., & Bloch, S. (2012). Survey of UK speech and language therapists' assessment and treatment practices for people with progressive dysarthria. *International Journal of Language & Communication Disorders*, *47*(6), 725–737. doi:10.1111/j.1460-6984.2012.00183.x PMID:23121530

Consortium, A. (2017). Phase 2 of CATALISE: A multinational and multidisciplinary Delphi consensus study of problems withlanguage development: Terminology. *Journal of Child Psychology and Psychiatry, and Allied Disciplines*, *58*(10), 1068–1080. doi:10.1111/jcpp.12721 PMID:28369935

Conti-Ramsden, G., Durkin, K., Simkin, Z., & Knox, E. (2009). Specific language impairment and school outcomes. I: Identifying and explaining variability at the end of compulsory education. *International Journal of Language & Communication Disorders*, *44*(1), 15–35. doi:10.1080/13682820801921601 PMID:18608604

Daniel, G. R., & McLeod, S. (2017). Children with speech sound disorders at school: Challenges for children, parents and teachers. *The Australian Journal of Teacher Education*, *42*(2), 81–101. doi:10.14221/ajte.2017v42n2.6

Dockrell, J., Lindsay, G., Roulstone, S., & Law, J. (2014). Supporting children with speech, language and communication needs: An overview of the results of the Better Communication Research Program. *International Journal of Language & Communication Disorders*, *49*(5), 543–557. doi:10.1111/1460-6984.12089 PMID:24961589

Dockrell, J. E., George, R., Lindsay, G., & Roux, J. (1997). Professionals' understanding of specific language impairments: Implications for assessment and identification. *Educational Psychology in Practice*, *13*, 27–35.

Dockrell, J. E., & Howell, P. (2015). Identifying the challenges and opportunities to meet the needs of children with speech, language and communication difficulties. *British Journal of Special Education*, *42*(4), 411–428. doi:10.1111/1467-8578.12115

Dockrell, J. E., Howell, P., Leung, D., & Fugard, A. J. (2017). Children with speech language and communication needs in England: Challenges for Practice. [). Frontiers.]. *Frontiers in Education*, *2*, 35. doi:10.3389/feduc.2017.00035

Dockrell, J. E., & Lindsay, G. (2001). Children with specific speech and language difficulties—The teachers' perspective. *Oxford Review of Education*, *27*(3), 369–394.

Glover, A., McCormack, J., & Smith-Tamaray, M. (2015). Collaboration between teachers and speech and language therapists: Services for primary schoolchildren with speech, language and communication needs. *Child Language Teaching and Therapy*, *31*(3), 363–382. doi:10.1177/0265659015603779

Hancock, A., Northcott, S., Hobson, H., & Clarke, M. (2023). Speech, language and communication needs and mental health: The experiences of speech and language therapists and mental health professionals. *International Journal of Language & Communication Disorders*, *58*(1), 52–66. doi:10.1111/1460-6984.12767 PMID:36117337

Hartas, D. (2004). Teacher and speech-language therapist collaboration: Being equal. and achieving a common goal? *Child Language Teaching and Therapy*, *20*(1), 33–54. doi:10.1191/0265659004ct262oa

Leonard, L. B. (2014). Specific language impairment across languages. *Child Development Perspectives*, *8*(1), 1–5. doi:10.1111/cdep.12053 PMID:24765105

Leonard, L. B., & Bortolini, U. (1998). Grammatical morphology and the role of weak syllables in the speech of Italian-speaking children with specific language impairment. *Journal of Speech, Language, and Hearing Research: JSLHR*, *41*(6), 1363–1374. doi:10.1044/jslhr.4106.1363 PMID:9859891

M.(2011). Long-term reading and spelling outcome in Italian adolescents with a history of specific language impairment. *Cortex, 47*(8), 955-973.

McAllister, S., Lincoln, M., Ferguson, A., & McAllister, L. (2011). A systematic program of research regarding the assessment of speech-language pathology competencies. *International Journal of Speech-Language Pathology, 13*(6), 469–479. doi:10.3109/17549507.2011.580782 PMID:21846166

Morton, J. (2004). *Understanding developmental disorders: A causal modelling approach.* Blackwell Publishing. doi:10.1002/9780470773307

Norbury, C. F., Gooch, D., Wray, C., Baird, G., Charman, T., Simonoff, E., Vamvakas, G., & Pickles, A. (2016). The impact of nonverbal ability on prevalence and clinical presentation of language disorder: Evidence from a population study. *Journal of Child Psychology and Psychiatry, and Allied Disciplines, 57*(11), 1247–1257. doi:10.1111/jcpp.12573 PMID:27184709

Palikara, O., Lindsay, G., Cullen, M. A., & Dockrell, J. (2007). Working together?:the practice of educational psychologists and speech and language therapists with children with specific speech and language difficulties. *Educational and Child Psychology, 24*(4), 77–88. doi:10.53841/bpsecp.2007.24.4.77

Ralli, A. M., Kalliontzi, E., & Kazali, E. (2022). Teachers' Views of Children With Developmental Language Disorder in Greek Mainstream Schools. *Frontiers in Education, 7*, 832240. doi:10.3389/feduc.2022.832240

Reilly, S., Bishop, D. V., & Tomblin, B. (2014). Terminological debate over language impairment in children: Forward movement and sticking points. *International Journal of Language & Communication Disorders, 49*(4), 452–462. doi:10.1111/1460-6984.12111 PMID:25142092

Roulstone, S. E., Marshall, J. E., Powell, G. G., Goldbart, J., Wren, Y. E., Coad, J., & Coad, R. A. (2015). *Evidence based intervention for preschool children with primary speech and language impairments: Child Talk – An exploratory mixed-methods study*. NHS National Institute for Health Research.

St Clair, M. C., Pickles, A., Durkin, K., & Conti-Ramsden, G. (2011). Longitudinal study of behavioral, emotional and social difficulties in individuals with a history of specific language impairment (SLI). *Journal of Communication Disorders, 44*(2), 186–199. doi:10.1016/j.jcomdis.2010.09.004 PMID:20970811

Thomas, S., Schulz, J., & Ryder, N. (2019). Assessment and diagnosis of Developmental Language Disorder: The experiences of speech and language therapists. *Autism & Developmental Language Impairments, 4*, 4. doi:10.1177/2396941519842812

Thordardottir, E., & Topbaş, S. (2021). How aware is the public of the existence, characteristics and causes of language impairment in childhood and where have they heard about it? A European survey. *Journal of Communication Disorders, 89*, 106057. doi:10.1016/j.jcomdis.2020.106057 PMID:33279754

Tomblin, J. B., Records, N. L., Buckwalter, P., Zhang, X., Smith, E., & O'Brien, M. (1997). Prevalence of specific language impairment in kindergarten children. *Journal of Speech, Language, and Hearing Research: JSLHR, 40*(6), 1245–1260. doi:10.1044/jslhr.4006.1245 PMID:9430746

Watson, R. M., & Pennington, L. (2015). Assessment and management of the communication difficulties of children with cerebral palsy: A UK survey of SLT practice. *International Journal of Language & Communication Disorders, 50*(2), 241–259. doi:10.1111/1460-6984.12138 PMID:25652139

Yew, S. G. K., & O'Kearney, R. (2013). Emotional and behavioural outcomes later In childhood and adolescence for children with specific language impairments: Meta-analyses of controlled prospective studies. *Journal of Child Psychology and Psychiatry, and Allied Disciplines, 54*(5), 516–524. doi:10.1111/jcpp.12009 PMID:23082773

KEY TERMS AND DEFINITIONS

DLD: A difficulty in expressive and/or receptive language that some children exhibit during preschool age that are not explained by other biomedical conditions.

Educational Psychologists: Psychologists with license to practice and further academic training in special education.

Language Difficulties: Difficulties in all language domains in both receptive and expressive level; phonology, morphology, vocabulary, syntax, and pragmatics.

Preschool Age: Children aged from 4 to 6 years old.

School Age: Children aged from 6 to 12 years old.

Socioemotional Difficulties: Difficulties in relations with others and emotional difficulties (e.g., stress, anxiety, behavioral problems (e.g., aggression)

Special Educational Needs Teachers: Teachers with further academic training in special education.

Speech and Language Therapists: Speech and Language Therapists with license to practice.

Chapter 12
Counseling for Caregivers for Children and Adolescents With Developmental Language Disorders

Eirini Karakasidou
https://orcid.org/0000-0003-2946-8275
Panteion University, Greece

Anna Papadimitriou
Panteion University, Greece

Anastasios Stalikas
Panteion University, Greece

ABSTRACT

Caregivers are individuals who provide comprehensive care to those facing challenges and who are unable to manage daily demands independently. Due to the practical and emotional demands they face on a daily basis, it is crucial for them to prioritize self-care to effectively fulfill their caregiving role. Counseling plays a pivotal role in helping caregivers navigate the psychological impact of developmental disorders while also discovering purpose in their caregiving role. This chapter aims to explore the significance and benefits of counseling for parents caring for children with developmental language disorders. Counseling plays a pivotal role in supporting parent caregivers of children and adolescents with language developmental language disorders.

CAREGIVERS AND COUNSELING

The role of caregivers for children and adolescents with developmental language disorders is multifaceted, as outlined by Koch et al. (2021). In addition to their primary role as parents, caregivers also take on the responsibilities of a helper, a guide, and a friend. They bear full responsibility for the emotional,

DOI: 10.4018/979-8-3693-1982-6.ch012

psychological, practical, and financial aspects of caring for these children. Furthermore, caregivers act as mediators between the children, adolescents, and other professionals, including teachers, psychologists, speech therapists, and doctors. They embrace this role from the moment of diagnosis, and it continues to evolve over time, adapting to the different phases of the child's and adolescent's life and their changing needs (Koch et al., 2021).

Due to the intense workload that caregivers shoulder, it is crucial for them to integrate counseling into their lives, as highlighted by Carter (2023). Through counseling, caregivers gain a crucial understanding that their role in providing care should not be static or permanent. Instead, they learn to assess each situation based on the individual's needs and collaborate with professionals (Lafrance et al., 2020). This approach allows the care provided to be adjusted and adapted over time, ensuring that it remains effective and beneficial (Sullivan & Miller, 2015). In particular, Streisand et al. (2008) argue that parents should seek the support of a mental health professional from the moment of diagnosis, in order to manage the anxiety, depression, lack of self-efficacy, and pediatric parenting stress that they may face. By implementing counseling and seeking professional support, caregivers can better cope with the challenges they encounter and provide more effective care for children and adolescents with developmental language disorders. This support allows them to navigate the dynamic nature of their role and continue to provide the best possible care as the needs of the child or adolescent change over time.

Carl Rogers, often considered the father of counseling, defined counseling as a process in which the counselee takes an active role. With the help of the counselor and various techniques, the counselee is guided to search for solutions, self-awareness, and personal development with the aim of achieving positive changes in their life (Rogers, 1942). In counseling, the counselee bears the responsibility of finding a solution to their problem, as the counselor does not provide advice. However, the counselor may express an opinion within permissible limits without guiding the counselee. For counseling to be effective, establishing a good communication and therapeutic relationship is paramount. The counselee must feel safe and calm within the counseling framework to freely express their feelings, thoughts, concerns, and difficulties they face. On the other hand, the counselor, through an authentic and genuine attitude, unconditional acceptance, and empathy, helps the counselee in the search for their own reality (Corey, 2012). Counseling has been proven to help individuals manage everyday problems and difficulties. It aids the counselee in better managing anxiety and other negative emotions, and dealing with phobias, thus enabling them to build a life that aligns with their ideal standards (Thompson, 2015). Furthermore, counseling provides benefits in managing interpersonal relationship difficulties, leading to their improvement. The process also helps the person recognize and cultivate their strengths and skills, which in turn allows them to better manage difficulties, solve problems, and make wise decisions. Self-awareness and self-discovery are promoted through counseling, and the relationship built between the counselor and the counselee in a context of freedom and security serves as a positive and healthy relationship model (Sommers-Flanagan, J., & Sommers-Flanagan, R., 2018).

There are various types of counseling in which the counselor is trained to provide knowledge and assistance to individuals facing different challenges. People who encounter difficulties in their professional or educational field (Corey, 2012), social and emotional challenges, internal conflicts, or difficulties arising from their interactions with the environment (Thompson, 2015) are often referred for counseling. In counseling, the focus is not solely on the individual but also on how they interact with their environment (Thompson, 2015). One specific category of counseling is parent counseling. The primary goal of parent counseling is to support parents in their role by addressing challenges related to their interactions with their children and the issues they face. Parent counseling concentrates on three main aspects: knowledge, skills, and attitudes. Regarding knowledge, the aim is to provide information about the social, emotional, and psychological needs of children based on their developmental stage. Additionally, parents receive insights into the nature and specifics of the difficulties their children might be facing. Equipped with this knowledge, parents can recognize symptoms and challenges in their children and address them proactively. Through the counseling process, parents are empowered to enhance their abilities. The objective is for parents to recognize their strengths and improve their skills to better meet the needs of their children. Lastly, concerning attitudes, parent counseling strives to improve communication between parents and their children, as well as foster better communication between parents and socialization agencies (e.g., schools) and other professionals who interact with children (Metcalf, 2021). By engaging in parent counseling, caregivers can acquire the necessary tools to navigate the challenges of parenthood effectively and provide a supportive and nurturing environment for their children's growth and development.

Parent counseling can be conducted either individually or in a group setting. In a group context, common difficulties that children often face based on their age and developmental stage are discussed. This format allows parents to receive help through interactions with other parents, sharing information, and learning from others' experiences (Danino & Shechtman, 2012). Additionally, another type of counseling worth mentioning is "peer counseling" or "homilics." Peer counseling involves a process where individuals who have experienced similar situations offer support to others, demonstrating genuine empathy. The recommendation and establishment of peer counseling are based on the shared needs or common issues that individuals face (Tindall, 1989). For instance, a peer counseling group could be formed for parents with children having developmental language disorders. Due to their shared history and experiences, there is a greater level of empathy and the formation of strong and close bonds among group members. It is natural for people to seek support from those who are currently facing or have overcome similar difficulties in the past (Tindall, 1989).

The role of counseling goes beyond merely noting changes in attitudes, skills, and knowledge or sharing experiences and feelings. It is a highly personalized and complex process tailored to the specific needs of each individual. Particularly, when providing counseling to parents of children with developmental language disorders, who also take on the role of caregivers, the approach must address both the parent's needs and those of the child or adolescent. The objective of this chapter is to identify the needs of parent-caregivers of children and adolescents with developmental language disorders and demonstrate how counseling can benefit this population. The aim is to equip parent-caregivers with the tools to effectively respond to the needs of their children and adolescents while simultaneously enhancing their own well-being. Specific areas will be explored where counseling can benefit the caregiver as a whole, enabling them to better manage the day-to-day challenges they face due to the nature of developmental language disorders. This process will also emphasize how the caregiver can support the child and adolescent in meeting their demands and building a fulfilling everyday life. Moreover, the counseling process will recognize the individual's unique personal needs, empowering them to strengthen their personal aspects and ultimately improve their mental health and well-being, benefiting both the caregiver and the child or adolescent. By addressing the individualized needs of parent-caregivers through counseling, we can create a positive impact on their lives as well as the lives of the children and adolescents under their care.

Providing Knowledge and Improving Communication

Recognizing the symptoms of developmental language disorders and understanding the difficulties they cause in the daily life of children and adolescents on cognitive, emotional, behavioral, and social levels is a crucial tool for adapting to the disorder. Since parents are the primary caregivers of children and adolescents, it is essential to acknowledge their demands and needs. Psychoeducation about these needs serves as a key tool, helping parents gain a better understanding of the nature of the disorder and form realistic expectations (Patra et al., 2015; Suzuki et al., 2014). Depending on the child's age, parents can identify the challenges the child is likely to face in various areas, such as at school. Recognizing these difficulties enables parent-caregivers to better comprehend their children's emotions and the obstacles they encounter. Understanding their children's needs also fosters improved communication between parents and their children, leading to increased self-efficacy and better management of negative emotions, such as anxiety and depression (Zhou et al., 2019). It is important to note that comprehending the nature of developmental language disorders not only enhances parent-caregivers' communication with their children and adolescents but also improves their communication with other professionals who frequently, if not daily, interact with the child (Lin et al., 2022).

During the counseling process, it becomes evident that caregivers often grapple with feelings of inadequacy, which can stem from various reasons. For instance, they may feel uncertain due to their lack of familiarity with the symptomatology of the disorder. Communication challenges with the child or adolescent can also contribute to their sense of inadequacy. Moreover, caregivers may feel inadequate in their collaboration with other health and mental health professionals, leading to negative emotions (Zhou et al., 2019). Furthermore, caregivers may experience negative emotions driven by their fears concerning the future and development of the child or adolescent (Almansour et al., 2013; Gallagher et al., 2014; Kütük et al., 2021; Miodrag & Hodapp, 2010). At times, these negative emotions can be directed towards the children themselves (Wang et al., 2011). Parents often hold various beliefs about their children's development, such as the misconception that their children will never find happiness or succeed in life. Such beliefs can arise from a lack of emphasis on developmental language disorders in research, resulting in inadequate support for children with this specific disorder and perpetuation of myths (McGregor, 2020).

Having a thorough understanding of the nature of developmental language disorders is crucial for counselors as it enables them to collaborate effectively with caregivers and challenge any prevailing myths surrounding these disorders. Additionally, counselors should establish a strong network of collaboration with other health and mental health professionals, as well as relevant organizations, to ensure appropriate referrals. For instance, there might be financial benefits and assistance available for caregivers that they may not be aware of. The counselor's objective is not to provide immediate answers and solutions but rather to guide caregivers towards understanding their rights and where they can seek help and support (Ducharme, 2016).

Furthermore, a comprehensive understanding of the nature of the disorder facilitates effective communication between parents and various professionals, including teachers, health experts, and mental health practitioners, who frequently interact with and have direct contact with the child and adolescent experiencing the language disorder. A survey conducted in this context revealed a low level of agreement between caregivers and professionals concerning developmental issues, with the most significant disagreement observed in the cognitive domain. However, it was found that speech delay emerged as a significant predictor of behavioral, emotional, and cognitive problems. Researchers emphasize the crucial importance of collaboration between caregivers and professionals, accompanied by providing guidance to caregivers in these specific areas (Lin et al., 2022).

Parents typically take on the role of caregivers for children and adolescents with developmental language disorders. However, a significant challenge arises from their lack of specialized knowledge, as compared to professionals like nurses or speech therapists, which hampers their ability to provide specialized care for their children. As a result, it is crucial to encourage parents to undergo training in skills and strategies that can enhance their children's daily lives. Collaborating with healthcare and mental health professionals proves to be an effective means to acquire these strategies (Strömberg, 2013). Nevertheless, the literature suggests that cooperation often faces difficulties, leading parents as caregivers to encounter challenging situations and experience feelings of frustration (Aujoulat et al., 2002). Counseling for caregivers can play a crucial role in facilitating communication and cooperation between parents and various professionals, such as teachers, speech therapists, doctors, and psychologists, who regularly interact with the child or adolescent. School counselors, in particular, can play a vital role in addressing children's needs and bridging communication gaps between parents and teachers (Lee, 2001; Lin et al., 2022).

In a recent study conducted in rural South Africa, researchers focused on developing a web-based self-guided app to support caregivers of children with developmental disorders. The caregivers were divided into two groups: one group received hospital-based care alone, while the other group received the same intervention along with access to the web-based self-guided app. The evaluation included both the caregivers and the children involved. The results of the study revealed that caregivers in the second group reported a significant improvement in the children's communication abilities. Almost half of the children in the second group began to transition from using symbolic communication, such as crying, to verbal communication, using words. Additionally, caregivers in the second group reported overall improvements in the children's communication skills, even though some difficulties persisted. Notably, expressive communication showed substantial improvement in the second group of caregivers, which was not observed in the first group. These findings underscore the importance of utilizing relevant applications to enhance communication in children with developmental disorders (Romski et al., 2023).

Through the interaction between the counselor and the caregiver, the latter can develop and cultivate essential skills, such as empathy (Bell, 2018; Davis, 1990), which proves to be a valuable tool in their communication with the child and adolescent. In other words, counseling can also serve an educational function, helping caregivers to nurture these skills, which, in turn, strengthens their relationship with the child and adolescent. Consequently, the child or adolescent with developmental language disorders can navigate their difficulties and limitations more effectively, leading to an improved life course. As caregivers gain more understanding about the disorders, they can gradually step back, create space, and allow their children to take responsibility for their own life journey (Lee et al., 2015). Counseling plays a crucial role in empowering caregivers to motivate children with developmental language disorders to actively participate in their own care and take charge of various situations (Grunwald & McAbee, 2013; Sullivan & Miller, 2015).

Coping With Negative Emotions

Caregivers of children with developmental disorders often experience a range of negative emotions, including anxiety, depression (Almansour et al., 2013; Gallagher et al., 2014; Kütük et al., 2021), chronic stress, physical symptoms (Miodrag & Hodapp, 2010), burnout (Kütük et al., 2021), and compassion fatigue (Davenport & Zolnikov, 2022). Juggling multiple roles, facing daily demands, and coping with frustration contribute to a decline in their overall well-being. As a result, their physical and mental health, as well as their social life, are impacted. It is observed that individuals who provide care, such as psychotherapists, often neglect their own self-care (Figley, 2002). In recognition of this, many counseling intervention programs focus on enhancing the well-being of caregivers. These programs aim to cultivate coping strategies, reinforce personal strengths, and ultimately promote wellness among caregivers (Clarke et al., 2016).

The burden on caregivers' mental health can begin from the initial detection of their child's difficulties (e.g., speech delay) and intensify during the official diagnosis phase of the developmental language disorder. During this period, parents may experience negative emotions, such as sadness, fear, anxiety, and frustration (Jovanova & Radojichikj, 2013). Due to their limited knowledge about developmental language disorders, they may form myths and destructive scenarios about their children's development. The diagnosis phase brings about an upheaval of their previous beliefs, requiring adaptation to new circumstances, leading to constant agony while communicating with health and mental health professionals (Ducharme, 2016). A survey conducted on 31 parents of children with developmental disorders revealed that the moment of diagnosis and discovery of their child's disorder was reported as the most stressful throughout the course of the disorder (Jovanova & Radojichikj, 2013). Counseling can serve as a valuable companion for caregivers throughout their journey, from the moment of diagnosis and beyond. Therefore, it is important for doctors themselves, who inform parents about the results and diagnosis of the developmental language disorder, to refer them to a counselor, helping them better manage the negative emotions they experience. The acceptance process varies widely for each parent and is a deeply personal and unique experience. While some may reach the point of acceptance in a few months, it may take years for others (Jovanova & Radojichikj, 2013).

Research indicates that parents of children with developmental disorders experience more intense negative emotions, such as stress, anxiety, and depression (Merkaj et al., 2013), compared to parents of typically developing children. This heightened emotional response can be attributed to the fact that children with developmental disorders require more time and attention from their parents than children with typical development (Hassall et al., 2005). The stress and negative emotions are influenced by various factors, including the frustration of expectations, adaptation to a new reality that involves several aspects such as finding a suitable school environment, making home and routine adjustments, dealing with medical issues, collaborating with health and mental health professionals, and attending regular appointments. Additionally, special diets and related expenses may further strain the family budget, often leading parents, particularly mothers, to sacrifice their jobs to cope with the needs of the child and adolescent (Upadhyaya & Havalappanavar, 2008).

In addition to the challenges posed by the needs of the child or adolescent with developmental disorders and the significant changes in caregivers' lives after diagnosis, they also experience negative emotions stemming from the isolation they face within their family and social environment, often due to existing stigma. Stigma surrounding illnesses (Horsfield et al., 2020), mental disorders (Horsfield et al., 2020; Song et al., 2018), and developmental disorders (Song et al., 2018; Tekola et al., 2020; Tilahun et al., 2016) often leads to the isolation and marginalization of both individuals with the disorders and their families. The creation of stigma is primarily rooted in social factors, which may result from a lack of sufficient knowledge about the disorder and its symptoms, as well as the perpetuation of myths. As mentioned in the previous chapter, information plays a crucial role for everyone involved. Caregivers themselves may have incomplete knowledge about the disorder, and this lack of understanding can extend to the child or adolescent with the developmental disorder. Consequently, they may feel compelled to engage in self-isolation, self-rejection, and self-labeling (Horsfield et al., 2020). Addressing and combating stigma through education and awareness is essential to create a more inclusive and supportive environment for individuals and families affected by developmental disorders.

The relationship between stigma and mental health is bidirectional. People with mental health problems often face the burden of stigma surrounding mental illness, which, in turn, exacerbates their negative emotions. Research findings indicate that stigma acts as a strong predictive factor leading to distress, anxiety, and depression in individuals (Yokota et al., 2022).

Counseling plays a significant role in focusing on mental health and managing negative emotions, and its benefits are well-supported by research. For instance, a study conducted on parents caring for children with Smith-Magenis syndrome revealed that these parents experienced high levels of stress. However, those who attended counseling sessions reported better well-being compared to parents who did not seek counseling. Notably, mother caregivers tended to have worse mental health compared to father caregivers (Foster et al., 2010). Similar findings were observed in another study involving parents of children with autism, where mothers experienced more stress, anxiety, and depression compared to fathers, and overall, parents of children with autism had worse well-being compared to parents of typically developing children (Merkaj et al., 2013).

Counseling has proven to be highly beneficial for the well-being of caregivers. Through counseling, they learn to manage symptoms of anxiety and depression, improve sleep, enhance self-efficacy, and increase caregiver satisfaction (Foster et al., 2010). Merkaj et al. (2013) also emphasized the significance of counseling, including individual, family, and group counseling, to enhance the well-being of parent caregivers. Stress management techniques, such as relaxation techniques, were particularly highlighted as essential components of counseling. Additionally, it was underscored that not only psychologists but also other professionals, such as social workers and doctors interacting with the child, should be empathetic and aware of the stress experienced by parent caregivers due to the disorder (Merkaj et al., 2013).

The ultimate goal of counseling is to promote the acceptance of the child's and adolescent's developmental disorder. It appears that a key factor intensifying chronic stress in parents caring for children with developmental disorders is precisely the non-acceptance of the disorder. However, stress levels tend to decrease when parents reach a point of acceptance (Jovanova & Radojichikj, 2013). Furthermore, adaptation to the demands of developmental disorders also occurs through the recognition of the personal values of parental caregivers in light of their parental or caregiver role (Han et al., 2021; Márquez-González et al., 2010). In other words, when parents align their actions and decisions with their core values and beliefs, they can better navigate the challenges posed by developmental disorders in their children, leading to a more effective and fulfilling caregiving experience.

Building Relationships With Others

Good and positive social relationships are a crucial part of a person's life. It is not surprising that loneliness shows a positive relationship with depression, anxiety (Robb et al., 2020; Sarbarzeh et al., 2020), and stress (Sarbarzeh et al., 2020), as well as with addictions (Al-Kandari et al., 2021), while social support acts as a protective factor (Von Cheong et al., 2017). Especially during difficult times, we turn to people important to us to ease our pain and negative emotions (Hou et al., 2020). As previously mentioned, counseling equally focuses on the social domain of the person and explores their social network and how close they feel to the people around them when taking their history (Muarifah et al., 2019). The social network constitutes a person's social resources, which help them cope with difficulties and improve their mental health (Hou et al., 2020).

Due to the existing stigma, families of individuals with health, mental health, and disability problems often experience social isolation, which negatively impacts their mental health (Song et al., 2018;

Tekola et al., 2020; Tilahun et al., 2016). These families feel marginalized by society and excluded from groups and social events, either because of their own difficulties or those experienced by someone in their family. This isolation goes beyond just the inner loneliness caused by daily challenges; it also involves exclusion from others (Song et al., 2018; Tekola et al., 2020; Tilahun et al., 2016). In the context of counseling, great attention and importance are given to the cultivation of social skills and the improvement of individual socialization (Fazio-Griffith & Ballard, 2014). It is not uncommon for individuals themselves to withdraw socially due to the difficulties they face and attribute this situation to the behavior of others (Beck, 2002).

In counseling, it is equally important to mention couple counseling for several reasons. When problems arise within the family, they can also create turmoil in marital relationships, leading to higher divorce rates (Freedman et al., 2012). Therefore, counseling also focuses on improving marital relationships, as parents are equally caregivers for children and adolescents with developmental disorders, although one parent may be more burdened than the other. Whether in individual counseling or couple counseling, caregivers are trained to recognize and communicate their needs with their partner, express their feelings, and better manage negative emotions such as resentment, anxiety, and anger. The aim is to rebuild their relationship in a more supportive and cooperative manner and find quality time for themselves as a couple. Strong and healthy relationships within the couple are beneficial for improving mental health and better coping with difficulties and problems (Dattilio & Epstein, 2015). Additionally, positive relationships within the couple can extend to the wider family, creating a more harmonious environment for the child or adolescent with developmental language disorders. This sense of security and stability can positively influence their development and overall well-being.

Beyond marital relationships, counseling can also help individual caregivers strengthen their social environment and improve their friendships. Through counseling, caregivers are encouraged to find time for themselves to engage in activities such as hobbies and spending time with friends and loved ones (Muarifah et al., 2019). Stable, long-term, and positive friendships offer significant benefits to individuals, including improved mental health, greater life satisfaction, happiness, and acting as a buffer against negative life events (Güroğlu, 2022). It is often observed that people who share common experiences are more likely to form friendships with each other (Ellis & Zarbatany, 2007). For example, caregivers of children and teenagers with developmental disorders may find support and connection by interacting with each other, and peer counseling can be beneficial in such cases. However, it is also important for caregivers to be encouraged to have friendly relationships with other parents or individuals, so they can step out of their role as caregivers and engage in conversations about other aspects of life. For instance, as schools become more inclusive, it can be helpful for parents of children and adolescents with developmental disorders to socialize with parents of typically developing children (Beveridge, 2013). This broader social interaction can provide a sense of belonging and enhance their overall well-being.

Therefore, counseling takes into account thel support network of caregivers, recognizing its importance in improving mental health, and encourages caregivers to be open to forming both old and new friendships without being limited by specific criteria (e.g., only seeking peer friendships). By expanding their social circle and building social resources, caregivers can experience positive emotions (Fredrickson, 2004). A noteworthy study highlights the significance of social support in the context of stigma surrounding developmental disorders (Song et al., 2018; Tekola et al., 2020; Tilahun et al., 2016). In a survey conducted in Ethiopia on parents of children with developmental disorders, most parents reported experiencing severe stigma and feeling pressured to internalize it. However, they mentioned that having a support network played a protective role against internalizing stigma. When parents perceived acceptance of the disorder from their family and social environment and felt supported, they reported experiencing less stigma and were less likely to internalize it (Tekola et al., 2020). This study underscores the importance of social support in mitigating the negative effects of stigma and highlights how having a supportive network can significantly impact the well-being of caregivers and parents of children with developmental disorders.

Taking Care of Yourself

A key focus of counseling is to recognize the needs of caregivers, moving away from the context of obligations and what parent caregivers should do for their children (Kepic et al., 2019). It is crucial for caring parents to make space for their personal well-being and, through the counseling process, develop self-care, recognizing it as a priority rather than a luxury (Kepic et al., 2019).

Caregivers, due to their constant exposure and interactions, are at risk of developing compassion fatigue (Lynch et al., 2018). This condition manifests through symptoms of burnout and secondary traumatic stress (Stamm, 2005). Research conducted on caregivers has shown the protective role of self-compassion against burnout (Gerber & Anaki, 2012). Self-compassion refers to an individual's caring attitude towards oneself during difficult times. It involves recognizing that difficulties and pain are universal human experiences and acknowledging one's thoughts and feelings in the present moment (Neff, 2003). Counseling offers a new perspective and a means for individuals to prioritize self-care. Although there is no specific treatment solely focused on self-compassion, it can be integrated into treatment approaches. Various exercises can enhance self-compassion, such as writing a self-compassion letter, practicing self-compassion breaks, changing the inner voice from judgmental to compassionate, and viewing oneself through the eyes of a compassionate other (Karakasidou et al., 2020). Compassion Focused Therapy is the therapeutic approach most closely related to self-compassion. It falls under the category of third-wave therapies and encourages individuals to understand their difficulties as part of their evolutionary journey. The therapy emphasizes being aware of one's thoughts and feelings in the present moment and cultivating compassionate actions (Gilbert, 2010).

Compassion-focused therapy primarily targets an individual's judgmental attitude. It acknowledges that self-shame and self-criticism are prevalent in humans, especially in individuals with mental health conditions such as depression, anxiety disorders, eating disorders, post-traumatic stress disorder, and personality disorders (Gilbert, 2010). The therapy places significant emphasis on creating a safe therapeutic relationship that serves as a role model, enabling the person to develop a compassionate self-relationship when faced with difficulties. It focuses on fostering self-connection and promoting compassionate interactions with others (Gilbert, 2010). The positive effects of self-compassion on caregivers have been demonstrated through research. Studies in this field have shown that self-compassion acts protectively against caregiver burden (Lloyd et al., 2019; Xu et al., 2020), depression (Xu et al., 2020), and the adoption of dysfunctional coping strategies (Lloyd et al., 2019).

Caregivers often neglect their own personal care while focusing on providing care to others (Sullivan & Miller, 2015). However, prioritizing self-care is crucial for caregivers to meet the daily demands and prevent burnout and other health and mental health issues (Sullivan & Miller, 2015). The problems caregivers face are not solely due to the act of caregiving itself but rather stem from the lack of self-care. The multidisciplinary care model, commonly used for patients with chronic diseases, is also recommended for caregivers. This model suggests various strategies, including accepting help and support, engaging in social activities, practicing self-care, receiving psychoeducation about the specific disorder, acknowledging and sharing emotions, and participating in local organizations (Sullivan & Miller, 2015). Socialization, in particular, is highly important, as social support acts as a protective factor against caregiver burden, along with fostering an internal locus of control through a good understanding of the disorder (Strömberg, 2013).

Resilience and Post-Traumatic Growth

Individual counseling, according to research conducted on caregivers, has been shown to enhance resilience compared to participants who did not receive counseling (Doungyota et al., 2010). This is because the counseling experience helps caregivers build resources and empowerment, which, in turn, contributes to the development of resilience. Resilience refers to the ability to adapt and overcome difficulties and challenges in life (Masten, 2018). The presence of resilience in caregivers has been demonstrated to foster positive perceptions surrounding the disorder (Bekhet et al., 2012) and promote adjustment, while reducing burden and stress (Palacio et al., 2019).

A related concept to that of resilience is post-traumatic growth. As the name suggests, post-traumatic growth refers to the growth and positive changes that occur through the process of trauma and difficulties faced by an individual (Tedeschi & Calhoun, 2004). Through post-traumatic growth, people who have experienced adversity begin to value life differently and modify their priorities. They focus on creating more positive and close relationships while recognizing the new possibilities they have acquired, along with their personal strengths (Tedeschi & Calhoun, 2004).

Post-traumatic growth is highly beneficial for the adaptation and acceptance of developmental disorders and has been associated with several advantages based on research conducted on parent-caregivers. According to studies, post-traumatic growth is linked to hope (Nouzari et al., 2019), self-compassion, and distress management (Chan et al., 2020). It occurs when there is an acceptance of the disorder, and building positive perceptions around it plays a significant role. Contrary to the myth that parents of children with developmental disorders only experience difficulties, research by Taunt and Hastings (2002) revealed that parents identified several positive aspects of their child's developmental disorder. They found satisfaction in caring for the child, experiencing the child as a source of joy and happiness, having opportunities to share positive feelings with the child, and feeling free from self-criticism. Additionally, they derived satisfaction from doing their best to support their child's smooth development and developed new skills to respond to their child's needs. Furthermore, the experience of parenting a child with a developmental disorder strengthened family and marital bonds, deepened spirituality, increased socialization, and created more opportunities for the child's development and learning. Parents' perspectives on life and priorities also changed, leading to personal growth and the development of positive character traits, such as increased empathy and reduced selfishness. They set new goals, lived more mindfully, built self-confidence, and felt empowered through their child's developmental disorder (Taunt & Hastings, 2002). Through the counseling process, emphasis can be placed on changing the perspective of the child's disorder, and these positive perspectives can serve as tools and strategies to help the parent-caregiver respond more effectively to the demands and needs of their child (Hastings & Taunt, 2002). By fostering post-traumatic growth and promoting positive perceptions, counseling can facilitate the caregiver's journey towards better adaptation and acceptance of their child's developmental disorder.

Finding Meaning

Individual events do not inherently affect people emotionally, but the meaning attributed to them determines how individuals think and feel about a situation (Beck, 2020). Frustration often arises in parents and caregivers of children and adolescents with developmental disorders due to the challenges they face in assuming the caregiver role. They are required to adapt their daily routines and lives around the needs of the child and adolescent, which can lead them to experience burnout (Kütük et al., 2021) and compassion fatigue (Davenport & Zolnikov, 2022).

Through the counseling process, parent-caregivers can discover a new meaning and perspective on their situation. Counseling helps them recognize new values in their role as caregivers, enabling them to better respond to this role and experience positive emotions and positive interactions (Han et al., 2021; Márquez-González et al., 2010; Schlebusch et al., 2022). Recognizing the positive elements of their caregiving role enhances their self-efficacy in responding to the challenges of the disorder and increases their overall well-being (Hastings & Taunt, 2002; Taunt & Hastings, 2002). Additionally, finding meaning in the caregiving process becomes a new self-discovery for parents, revealing strong elements of their character, leading to improved well-being. As a result, depression and negative emotions decrease, and life satisfaction increases (Schutte & Malouff, 2019). Moreover, counseling fosters self-awareness (Oden et al., 2009), and through interactions with the counselor, caregivers discover new aspects and possibilities for personal growth and positive change.

Counseling, particularly through psychoeducation, can assist caregivers in challenging and reconstructing distorted beliefs and fears they may have about managing the situation and their ability to cope with their children's needs (Gallagher-Thompson & Coon, 2007). The counseling process helps them understand and accept their weaknesses, but from a more compassionate and less critical perspective. This allows them to mobilize and work towards overcoming those weaknesses. Through self-awareness, caregivers not only discover their strengths but also acknowledge their weaknesses, viewing themselves as a whole rather than selectively focusing only on their weaknesses. This approach helps them avoid reinforcing feelings of inadequacy, guilt, and moving away from their caregiving role (Gallagher-Thompson & Coon, 2007).

Counseling also places emphasis on the caregiver's interaction with the child and adolescent, aiming to help the caregiver discover what they are learning from this experience. As mentioned earlier, through their role as caregivers, parents can uncover new aspects of themselves, which can aid them in coping better with the demands and, at the same time, enhance their personal well-being (Hastings & Taunt, 2002; Taunt & Hastings, 2002).

The positive contribution of finding meaning in caregiving has also been supported by research, indicating that counseling can play a significant role in helping caregivers discover meaning in the process of caring for children and adolescents with developmental language disorders. A survey conducted on caregivers revealed that those who approach their caring role by recognizing positive aspects tend to experience better overall well-being (Quinn et al., 2012). It has been observed that caregivers who derive a higher sense of meaning from their caregiving activities tend to spend more time providing care, have stronger religious beliefs, exhibit a high sense of competence, possess intrinsic and extrinsic motivation, enjoy better relationship quality, and feel less trapped in their caregiving role (Quinn et al., 2012).

Zhang and Lee (2017) argue that caregivers often experience negative emotions, burnout, and a sense of being trapped in their caregiving role due to external pressures from social norms, others' expectations, and moral and religious imperatives. However, finding meaning in caregiving cannot be solely created through these external factors; rather, it comes from a subjective perception about caregiving. Caregivers can find meaning in what they do by moving away from external pressures and expectations and placing more emphasis on values such as reciprocity, love, and hope (Zhang & Lee, 2017). Counseling can support caregivers in this process of finding personal meaning and value in their caregiving role.

Through counseling, caregivers can discover the values that guide them in their roles as caregivers and parents. Drawing upon principles from Acceptance and Commitment Therapy, caregivers can recognize empowering values and commit to actions and activities related to the care of children and adolescents with developmental language disorders. They learn to accept without self-criticism the emotional distress arising from external factors, such as the diagnosis and the difficulties faced by the child and adolescent, as well as the internal emotional distress arising from negative thoughts, feelings, and psychological symptoms, which fosters greater psychological flexibility (Márquez-González et al., 2010). Research from a systematic review and meta-analysis confirms that Acceptance and Commitment Therapy helps reduce anxiety, stress, and depression, while improving the quality of life in caregivers (Han et al., 2021). Thus, counseling plays a crucial role in focusing on the personal values of caregivers, enabling them to find meaning in their caregiving role and cope effectively with the associated challenges and psychological discomfort arising from internal and external situations.

For instance, a survey was conducted on caregivers of children with developmental disorders in rural South Africa, where an intervention using Acceptance and Commitment Therapy techniques was employed. The intervention focused on enhancing mindfulness, flexibility, recognition of thoughts and feelings, and commitment to behaviors aligned with caregivers' values. Following the completion of the three-session intervention, caregivers reported improvements in their mental health and overall well-being. They also demonstrated increased abilities to effectively care for their children with developmental disorders (Schlebusch et al., 2022).

It is important to note that the process of finding meaning in caregiving is not immediate but occurs gradually and is reshaped according to the needs of the child and adolescent, as well as the caregiver's own needs in a personal and family context, as the dynamics within the family change (Lee et al., 2015). Interviews with mothers who were caregivers of children aged 6 to 35 with disabilities revealed that the acceptance of disability came gradually, and the meaning of caregiving was developed through their growing maturity in their role as caregivers, as well as through the process of finding effective solutions to help their children respond and have a better everyday life (Lee et al., 2015).

Finding meaning helps parent caregivers build resilience, which enables them to cope with challenges. This process promotes resilience as it combats distress and rumination (Ostafin & Proulx, 2020). Finding meaning and hope are equally linked to resilience, which is why counselors are suggested to not only focus on risk factors and psychopathology but also emphasize the support network, personal resources, and the development of meaning in life and hope in order to enable caregivers to cope with difficulties and challenges (Kim et al., 2005).

CONCLUSION

This chapter identified the key aspects on which counseling for parents of children and adolescents with developmental language disorders can focus, aiming to empower them and better respond to their children's needs. It is crucial for parents to participate in individual, group, or family counseling, as it can help them effectively manage the stress resulting from the nature of developmental disorders (Kim et al., 2005; Merkaj et al., 2013). Moreover, counseling can help parents focus on the positive perspectives that developmental disorders bring and what they can gain through caring for their children and adolescents (Hastings & Taunt, 2002; Taunt & Hastings, 2002).

In conclusion, it is important to note that the existing literature primarily focuses on studying the psychological effects experienced by caregivers, particularly spouses, of individuals with dementia or Alzheimer's disease. In contrast, research regarding parents of children and adolescents with developmental disorders, including language disorders, is relatively limited. However, some studies have explored specific contexts such as suicidal ideation (Leyenaar et al., 2022), neuromotor disorders (Marsico et al., 2021), and autism (Haakonsen Smith et al., 2018; Hens et al., 2016). Despite this, there is a lack of specialized research specifically focused on language disorders. As developmental language disorders belong to the broader category of developmental disorders, it is crucial to conduct more research that exclusively focuses on developmental language disorders and the needs of children, adolescents, and their parents-caregivers.

Counseling has demonstrated beneficial effects for caregivers, positively impacting both the care recipients (children and adolescents with developmental language disorders) and the caregivers themselves. However, to develop effective intervention and counseling programs, a comprehensive assessment of the needs of both the children/adolescents and the caregivers is necessary. This will enable the creation of appropriate interventions aimed at improving the well-being of both groups.

REFERENCES

Al-Kandari, Y. Y., & Al-Sejari, M. M. (2021). Social isolation, social support and their relationship with smartphone addiction. *Information Communication and Society, 24*(13), 1925–1943. doi:10.1080/1369118X.2020.1749698

Almansour, M. A., Alateeq, M. A., Alzahrani, M. K., Algeffari, M. A., & Alhomaidan, H. T. (2013). Depression and anxiety among parents and caregivers of autistic spectral disorder children. *Neuroscience Journal, 18*(1), 58–63. https://nsj.org.sa/content/nsj/18/1/58.full.pdf PMID:23291799

Aujoulat, I., Libion, F., Bois, H., Martin, F., & Deccache, A. (2002). Communication difficulties of healthcare professionals and family caregivers of HIV infected patients. *Patient Education and Counseling, 47*(3), 213–222. doi:10.1016/S0738-3991(01)00197-5 PMID:12088599

Beck, A. T. (2002). Cognitive models of depression. In R. Leahy & T. Dowd (Eds.), *Clinical advances in cognitive psychotherapy: Theory and application* (pp. 29–61). Springer Publishing Company.

Beck, J. S. (2020). *Cognitive behavior therapy: Basics and beyond.* Guilford Publications.

Bekhet, A. K., Johnson, N. L., & Zauszniewski, J. A. (2012). Effects on resilience of caregivers of persons with autism spectrum disorder: The role of positive cognitions. *Journal of the American Psychiatric Nurses Association, 18*(6), 337–344. doi:10.1177/1078390312467056 PMID:23139377

Bell, H. (2018). Creative interventions for teaching empathy in the counseling classroom. *Journal of Creativity in Mental Health, 13*(1), 106–120. doi:10.1080/15401383.2017.1328295

Beveridge, S. (2013). *Children, families and schools: Developing partnerships for inclusive education*. Routledge. doi:10.4324/9780203464700

Carter, R. (2023). *Helping yourself help others: A book for caregivers*. University of Arkansas Press. doi:10.2307/jj.2354066

Chan, B. S. M., Deng, J., Li, Y., Li, T., Shen, Y., Wang, Y., & Yi, L. (2020). The role of self-compassion in the relationship between post-traumatic growth and psychological distress in caregivers of children with autism. *Journal of Child and Family Studies*, *29*(6), 1692–1700. doi:10.100710826-019-01694-0

Clarke, P. B., Adams, J. K., Wilkerson, J. R., & Shaw, E. G. (2016). Wellness-based counseling for caregivers of persons with dementia. *Journal of Mental Health Counseling*, *38*(3), 263–277. doi:10.17744/mehc.38.3.06

Corey, G. (2012). *Theory and practice of counseling and psychotherapy*. Cengage learning.

Danino, M., & Shechtman, Z. (2012). Superiority of group counseling to individual coaching for parents of children with learning disabilities. *Psychotherapy Research*, *22*(5), 592–603. doi:10.1080/10503307.2012.692953 PMID:22694319

Dattilio, F. M., & Epstein, N. B. (2015). Cognitive-behavioral couple and family therapy. In *Handbook of family therapy* (pp. 89–119). Routledge. doi:10.4324/9780203123584-6

Davenport, S., & Zolnikov, T. R. (2022). Understanding mental health outcomes related to compassion fatigue in parents of children diagnosed with intellectual disability. *Journal of Intellectual Disabilities*, *26*(3), 624–636. doi:10.1177/17446295211013600 PMID:34027745

Davis, C. M. (1990). What is empathy, and can empathy be taught? *Physical Therapy*, *70*(11), 707–711. doi:10.1093/ptj/70.11.707 PMID:2236214

Doungyota, T., Prasoetsuk, T., Kirdpitak, P., & Pinyoanuntapong, B. (2010). A study and development of resilience of psychiatric patient caregivers through individual counseling. *Journal of Behavioral Science*, *16*(2), 51.

Ducharme, S. M. (2016). *Childhood speech and language disorders: Supporting children and families on the path to communication*. Rowman & Littlefield.

Ellis, W. E., & Zarbatany, L. (2007). Explaining friendship formation and friendship stability. The role of children's and friends' aggression and victimization. *Merrill-Palmer Quarterly*, *53*(1), 79–104. https://www.jstor.org/stable/23096292. doi:10.1353/mpq.2007.0001

Fazio-Griffith, L. J., & Ballard, M. B. (2014). Cognitive behavioral play therapy techniques in school-based group counseling: Assisting students in the development of social skills. *Vistas online, 18*, 1-14.

Figley, C. R. (2002). Compassion fatigue: Psychotherapists' chronic lack of self care. *Journal of Clinical Psychology*, *58*(11), 1433–1441. doi:10.1002/jclp.10090 PMID:12412153

Foster, R. H., Kozachek, S., Stern, M., & Elsea, S. H. (2010). Caring for the Caregivers: An Investigation of Factors Related to Well-Being Among Parents Caring for a Child with Smith-Magenis Syndrome. *Journal of Genetic Counseling*, *19*(2), 187–198. doi:10.100710897-009-9273-5 PMID:20151318

Fredrickson, B. L. (2004). The broaden–and–build theory of positive emotions. *Philosophical Transactions of the Royal Society of London. Series B, Biological Sciences*, *359*(1449), 1367–1377. doi:10.1098/rstb.2004.1512 PMID:15347528

Freedman, B. H., Kalb, L. G., Zablotsky, B., & Stuart, E. A. (2012). Relationship status among parents of children with autism spectrum disorders: A population-based study. *Journal of Autism and Developmental Disorders*, *42*(4), 539–548. doi:10.100710803-011-1269-y PMID:21590433

Gallagher, S., & Hannigan, A. (2014). Depression and chronic health conditions in parents of children with and without developmental disabilities: The growing up in Ireland cohort study. *Research in Developmental Disabilities*, *35*(2), 448–454. doi:10.1016/j.ridd.2013.11.029 PMID:24361813

Gallagher-Thompson, D., & Coon, D. W. (2007). Evidence-based psychological treatments for distress in family caregivers of older adults. *Psychology and Aging*, *22*(1), 37–51. doi:10.1037/0882-7974.22.1.37 PMID:17385981

Gerber, Z., & Anaki, D. (2021). The Role of Self-compassion, Concern for Others, and Basic Psychological Needs in the Reduction of Caregiving Burnout. *Mindfulness*, *12*(3), 741–750. doi:10.100712671-020-01540-1 PMID:33224308

Gilbert, P. (2010). *Compassion focused therapy: Distinctive features*. Routledge. doi:10.4324/9780203851197

Grunwald, B. B., & McAbee, H. (2013). *Guiding the family: Practical counseling techniques*. Routledge. doi:10.4324/9780203768143

Güroğlu, B. (2022). The power of friendship: The developmental significance of friendships from a neuroscience perspective. *Child Development Perspectives*, *16*(2), 110–117. doi:10.1111/cdep.12450

Haakonsen Smith, C., Turbitt, E., Muschelli, J., Leonard, L., Lewis, K. L., Freedman, B., Muratori, M., & Biesecker, B. B. (2018). Feasibility of coping effectiveness training for caregivers of children with autism spectrum disorder: A genetic counseling intervention. *Journal of Genetic Counseling*, *27*(1), 252–262. doi:10.100710897-017-0144-1 PMID:28879629

Han, A., Yuen, H. K., & Jenkins, J. (2021). Acceptance and commitment therapy for family caregivers: A systematic review and meta-analysis. *Journal of Health Psychology*, *26*(1), 82–102. doi:10.1177/1359105320941217 PMID:32659142

Hassall, R., Rose, J., & McDonald, J. (2005). Parenting stress in mothers of children with an intellectual disability: The effects of parental cognitions in relation to child characteristics and family support. *Journal of Intellectual Disability Research*, *49*(6), 405–418. doi:10.1111/j.1365-2788.2005.00673.x PMID:15882391

Hastings, R. P., & Taunt, H. M. (2002). Positive perceptions in families of children with developmental disabilities. *American Journal of Mental Retardation*, *107*(2), 116–127. doi:10.1352/0895-8017(2002)107<0116:PPIFOC>2.0.CO;2 PMID:11853529

Hens, K., Peeters, H., & Dierickx, K. (2016). Genetic testing and counseling in the case of an autism diagnosis: A caregivers perspective. *European Journal of Medical Genetics*, *59*(9), 452–458. doi:10.1016/j.ejmg.2016.08.007 PMID:27544064

Horsfield, P., Stolzenburg, S., Hahm, S., Tomczyk, S., Muehlan, H., Schmidt, S., & Schomerus, G. (2020). Self-labeling as having a mental or physical illness: The effects of stigma and implications for help-seeking. *Social Psychiatry and Psychiatric Epidemiology*, *55*(7), 907–916. doi:10.100700127-019-01787-7 PMID:31641830

Hou, T., Zhang, T., Cai, W., Song, X., Chen, A., Deng, G., & Ni, C. (2020). Social support and mental health among health care workers during Coronavirus Disease 2019 outbreak: A moderated mediation model. *PLoS One*, *15*(5), e0233831. doi:10.1371/journal.pone.0233831 PMID:32470007

Jovanova, N. C., & Radojichikj, D. D. (2013). Parents of children with developmental disabilities: Stress and support. *Journal of Special Education and Rehabilitation*, *14*(1-2), 7–19. doi:10.2478/v10215-011-0029-z

Karakasidou, E. Yotsidis, & Papadimitriou, A. (2020). Self-compassion: The technique to take care of myself. In A. Stalikas, V. Yotsidis & E. Karakasidou (Eds.) Conquering prosperity (pp. 197-215). Topos.

Kepic, M., Randolph, A., & Hermann-Turner, K. M. (2019). Care for caregivers: Understanding the need for caregiver support. *Adultspan Journal*, *18*(1), 40–51. doi:10.1002/adsp.12068

Kim, T. H., Lee, S. M., Yu, K., Lee, S., & Puig, A. (2005). Hope and the meaning of life as influences on Korean adolescents' resilience: Implications for counselors. *Asia Pacific Education Review*, *6*(2), 143–152. doi:10.1007/BF03026782

Koch, A., Kozhumam, A. S., Seeler, E., Docherty, S. L., & Brandon, D. (2021). Multiple roles of parental caregivers of children with complex life-threatening conditions: A qualitative descriptive analysis. *Journal of Pediatric Nursing*, *61*, 67–74. doi:10.1016/j.pedn.2021.03.017 PMID:33780717

Kütük, M. Ö., Tufan, A. E., Kılıçaslan, F., Güler, G., Çelik, F., Altıntaş, E., Gökçen, C., Karadağ, M., Yektaş, Ç., Mutluer, T., Kandemir, H., Büber, A., Topal, Z., Acikbas, U., Giray, A., & Kütük, Ö. (2021). High depression symptoms and burnout levels among parents of children with autism spectrum disorders: A multi-center, cross-sectional, case–control study. *Journal of Autism and Developmental Disorders*, *51*(11), 1–14. doi:10.100710803-021-04874-4 PMID:33459915

Lafrance, A., Henderson, K. A., & Mayman, S. (2020). *Emotion-focused family therapy: A transdiagnostic model for caregiver-focused interventions*. American Psychological Association. doi:10.1037/0000166-000

Lee, C. C. (2001). Culturally responsive school counselors and programs: Addressing the needs of all students. *Professional School Counseling*, *4*(4), 257.

Lee, Y. J., Park, H. J., & Recchia, S. L. (2015). Embracing each other and growing together: Redefining the meaning of caregiving a child with disabilities. *Journal of Child and Family Studies*, *24*(12), 3662–3675. doi:10.100710826-015-0175-x

Leyenaar, J. K., Tolpadi, A., Parast, L., Esporas, M., Britto, M. T., Gidengil, C., Wilson, K. M., Bardach, N. S., Basco, W. T. Jr, Brittan, M. S., Williams, D. J., Wood, K. E., Yung, S., Dawley, E., Elliott, A., Manges, K. A., Plemmons, G., Rice, T., Wiener, B., & Mangione-Smith, R. (2022). Collaborative to increase lethal means counseling for caregivers of youth with suicidality. *Pediatrics*, *150*(6), e2021055271. doi:10.1542/peds.2021-055271 PMID:36321386

Lin, L. Y., Yu, W. H., Lin, W. P., Chen, C. C., & Tu, Y. F. (2022). Agreement Between Caregivers' Concerns of Children's Developmental Problems and Professional Identification in Taiwan. *Frontiers in Pediatrics, 10*, 804427. doi:10.3389/fped.2022.804427 PMID:35295704

Lloyd, J., Muers, J., Patterson, T. G., & Marczak, M. (2019). Self-compassion, coping strategies, and caregiver burden in caregivers of people with dementia. *Clinical Gerontologist, 42*(1), 47–59. doi:10.1080/07317115.2018.1461162 PMID:29723129

Lynch, S. H., Shuster, G., & Lobo, M. L. (2018). The family caregiver experience–examining the positive and negative aspects of compassion satisfaction and compassion fatigue as caregiving outcomes. *Aging & Mental Health, 22*(11), 1424–1431. doi:10.1080/13607863.2017.1364344 PMID:28812375

Márquez-González, M., Romero-Moreno, R., & Losada, A. (2010). Caregiving issues in a therapeutic context: New insights from the acceptance and commitment therapy approach. In N. A. Pachana, K. Laidlaw, & B. Knight (Eds.), *Casebook of clinical geropsychology: International perspectives on practice* (pp. 33–53). Oxford University Press. doi:10.1093/med/9780199583553.003.0003

Marsico, P., Graser, J. V., & van Hedel, H. J. (2021). Effectiveness of Facilitation, Arrangement of Task and Situation,(Non-) verbal Communication, and Counseling of Caregivers in Children with Neuromotor Disorders: A Systematic Review. *Advances in Neurodevelopmental Disorders, 5*(4), 1–21. doi:10.100741252-021-00220-y

Masten, A. S. (2018). Resilience theory and research on children and families: Past, present, and promise. *Journal of Family Theory & Review, 10*(1), 12–31. doi:10.1111/jftr.12255

McGregor, K. K. (2020). How we fail children with developmental language disorder. *Language, Speech, and Hearing Services in Schools, 51*(4), 981–992. doi:10.1044/2020_LSHSS-20-00003 PMID:32755505

Merkaj, V., Kika, M., & Simaku, A. (2013). Symptoms of stress, depression and anxiety between parents of autistic children and parents of tipically developing children. *Academic Journal of Interdisciplinary Studies, 2*(2), 345–352. doi:10.5901/ajis.2013.v2n2p345

Metcalf, L. (2021). *Counseling toward solutions: A practical, solution-focused program for working with students, teachers, and parents*. Routledge. doi:10.4324/9781003122128

Miodrag, N., & Hodapp, R. M. (2010). Chronic stress and health among parents of children with intellectual and developmental disabilities. *Current Opinion in Psychiatry, 23*(5), 407–411. doi:10.1097/YCO.0b013e32833a8796 PMID:20592593

Muarifah, A., Widyastuti, D. A., & Fajarwati, I. (2019). The effect of social support on single mothers' subjective well-being and its implication for counseling. *Jurnal Kajian Bimbingan dan Konseling, 4*(4), 143-149. doi:10.17977/um001v4i42019p143

Neff, K. (2003). Self-compassion: An alternative conceptualization of a healthy attitude toward oneself. *Self and Identity, 2*(2), 85–101. doi:10.1080/15298860309032

Nouzari, R., Najafi, S. S., & Momennasab, M. (2019). Post-traumatic growth among family caregivers of cancer patients and its association with social support and hope. *International Journal of Community Based Nursing and Midwifery, 7*(4), 319–328. doi:10.30476/IJCBNM.2019.73959.0 PMID:31641681

Oden, K. A., Miner-Holden, J., & Balkin, R. S. (2009). Required counseling for mental health professional trainees: Its perceived effect on self-awareness and other potential benefits. *Journal of Mental Health (Abingdon, England)*, *18*(5), 441–448. doi:10.3109/09638230902968217

Ostafin, B. D., & Proulx, T. (2020). Meaning in life and resilience to stressors. *Anxiety, Stress, and Coping*, *33*(6), 603–622. doi:10.1080/10615806.2020.1800655 PMID:32755239

Palacio, G. C., Krikorian, A., Gómez-Romero, M. J., & Limonero, J. T. (2020). Resilience in caregivers: A systematic review. *The American Journal of Hospice & Palliative Care*, *37*(8), 648–658. doi:10.1177/1049909119893977 PMID:31830813

Patra, S., Arun, P., & Chavan, B. S. (2015). Impact of psychoeducation intervention module on parents of children with autism spectrum disorders: A preliminary study. *Journal of Neurosciences in Rural Practice*, *6*(04), 529–535. doi:10.4103/0976-3147.165422 PMID:26752898

Quinn, C., Clare, L., & Woods, R. T. (2012). What predicts whether caregivers of people with dementia find meaning in their role? *International Journal of Geriatric Psychiatry*, *27*(11), 1195–1202. doi:10.1002/gps.3773 PMID:22334416

Robb, C. E., De Jager, C. A., Ahmadi-Abhari, S., Giannakopoulou, P., Udeh-Momoh, C., McKeand, J., Price, G., Car, J., Majeed, A., Ward, H., & Middleton, L. (2020). Associations of social isolation with anxiety and depression during the early COVID-19 pandemic: A survey of older adults in London, UK. *Frontiers in Psychiatry*, *11*, 591120. doi:10.3389/fpsyt.2020.591120 PMID:33132942

Rogers, C. R. (1942). *Counseling and psychotherapy*. Houghton Mifflin.

Romski, M. A., Sevcik, R. A., King, M., DeLeo, G., Branum-Martin, L., & Bornman, J. (2023). Using a self-guided app to provide communication strategies for caregivers of young children with developmental disorders: A pilot investigation. *Journal of Policy and Practice in Intellectual Disabilities*, *20*(1), 73–88. doi:10.1111/jppi.12436

Sarbarzeh, P. A., Karimi, S., Jalilian, M., & Mosafer, H. (2020). Depression, anxiety, stress and social isolation in hepatitis patients. *SciMedicine Journal*, *2*(4), 225–233. doi:10.28991/SciMedJ-2020-0204-5

Schlebusch, L., Chambers, N., Rosenstein, D., Erasmus, P., & de Vries, P. J. (2022, November 09). WHO CST Team, & de Vries, P. J. (2022). Supporting caregivers of children with developmental disabilities: Findings from a brief caregiver well-being programme in South Africa. *Autism*. doi:10.1177/13623613221133182 PMID:36352758

Schutte, N. S., & Malouff, J. M. (2019). The impact of signature character strengths interventions: A meta-analysis. *Journal of Happiness Studies*, *20*(4), 1179–1196. doi:10.100710902-018-9990-2

Sommers-Flanagan, J., & Sommers-Flanagan, R. (2018). *Counseling and psychotherapy theories in context and practice: Skills, strategies, and techniques*. John Wiley & Sons.

Song, J., Mailick, M. R., & Greenberg, J. S. (2018). Health of parents of individuals with developmental disorders or mental health problems: Impacts of stigma. *Social Science & Medicine*, *217*, 152–158. doi:10.1016/j.socscimed.2018.09.044 PMID:30333078

Stamm, B. H. (2005). *The ProQOL Manual: The Professional Quality of Life Scale: Compassion satisfaction, burnout & compassion fatigue/secondary trauma scales*. Sidran Press.

Streisand, R., Mackey, E. R., Elliot, B. M., Mednick, L., Slaughter, I. M., Turek, J., & Austin, A. (2008). Parental anxiety and depression associated with caring for a child newly diagnosed with type 1 diabetes: Opportunities for education and counseling. *Patient Education and Counseling*, *73*(2), 333–338. doi:10.1016/j.pec.2008.06.014 PMID:18692342

Strömberg, A. (2013). The situation of caregivers in heart failure and their role in improving patient outcomes. *Current Heart Failure Reports*, *10*(3), 270–275. doi:10.100711897-013-0146-8 PMID:23857163

Sullivan, A. B., & Miller, D. (2015). Who is taking care of the caregiver? *Journal of Patient Experience*, *2*(1), 7–12. https://journals.sagepub.com/doi/pdf/10.1177/237437431500200103. doi:10.1177/237437431500200103 PMID:28725810

Suzuki, M., Yamada, A., Watanabe, N., Akechi, T., Katsuki, F., Nishiyama, T., ... Furukawa, T. A. (2014). A failure to confirm the effectiveness of a brief group psychoeducational program for mothers of children with high-functioning pervasive developmental disorders: A randomized controlled pilot trial. *Neuropsychiatric Disease and Treatment*, *10*, 1141–1153. doi:10.2147/NDT.S60058 PMID:25061301

Taunt, H. M., & Hastings, R. P. (2002). Positive impact of children with developmental disabilities on their families: A preliminary study. *Education and Training in Mental Retardation and Developmental Disabilities*, 410–420. https://www.jstor.org/stable/23880074

Tedeschi, R. G., & Calhoun, L. G. (2004). Posttraumatic growth: Conceptual foundations and empirical evidence. *Psychological Inquiry*, *15*(1), 1–18. doi:10.120715327965pli1501_01

Tekola, B., Kinfe, M., Girma, F., Hanlon, C., & Hoekstra, R. A. (2020). Perceptions and experiences of stigma among parents of children with developmental disorders in Ethiopia: A qualitative study. *Social Science & Medicine*, *256*, 113034. doi:10.1016/j.socscimed.2020.113034 PMID:32446155

Thompson, R. A. (2015). *Counseling techniques: Improving relationships with others, ourselves, our families, and our environment*. Routledge. doi:10.4324/9781315886114

Tilahun, D., Hanlon, C., Fekadu, A., Tekola, B., Baheretibeb, Y., & Hoekstra, R. A. (2016). Stigma, explanatory models and unmet needs of caregivers of children with developmental disorders in a low-income African country: A cross-sectional facility-based survey. *BMC Health Services Research*, *16*(1), 1–12. doi:10.118612913-016-1383-9 PMID:27117326

Tindall, J. A. (1989). *Peer counseling: An in-depth look at training peer helpers*. Muncie Accelerated Development Inc.

Upadhyaya, R. G., & Havalappanavar, N. B. (2008). Coping in parents of the mentally challenged. *Journal of the Indian Academy of Applied Psychology*, *34*(2), 221–225.

Von Cheong, E., Sinnott, C., Dahly, D., & Kearney, P. M. (2017). Adverse childhood experiences (ACEs) and later-life depression: Perceived social support as a potential protective factor. *BMJ Open*, *7*(9), e013228. doi:10.1136/bmjopen-2016-013228 PMID:28864684

Wang, P., Michaels, C. A., & Day, M. S. (2011). Stresses and coping strategies of Chinese families with children with autism and other developmental disabilities. *Journal of Autism and Developmental Disorders*, *41*(6), 783–795. doi:10.100710803-010-1099-3 PMID:20859670

Xu, S., Zhang, H., & Wang, J. (2020). Caregiver burden and depression among Chinese family caregivers: The role of self-compassion. *Mindfulness*, *11*(7), 1647–1654. doi:10.100712671-020-01378-7

Yokota, R., Okuhara, T., Okada, H., Goto, E., Sakakibara, K., & Kiuchi, T. (2022). Association between stigma and anxiety, depression, and psychological distress among Japanese women undergoing infertility treatment. *Health Care*, *10*(7), 1300. doi:10.3390/healthcare10071300 PMID:35885826

Zhang, J., & Lee, D. T. (2017). Meaning in stroke family caregiving: A literature review. *Geriatric Nursing*, *38*(1), 48–56. doi:10.1016/j.gerinurse.2016.07.005 PMID:27671537

Zhou, Y., Yin, H., Wang, M., & Wang, J. (2019). The effect of family-focused psychoeducational therapy for autism spectrum disorder children's parents 'on parenting self-efficacy and emotion. *Archives of Psychiatric Nursing*, *33*(1), 17–22. doi:10.1016/j.apnu.2018.08.002 PMID:30663619

Chapter 13
Associations Between Language Impairments and Behavioral Problems in Childhood:
Neurocognitive Mechanisms and Future Implications

Antonios I. Christou
https://orcid.org/0000-0003-2981-1651
University of Thessaly, Greece

Ioanna-Dimitra Karachristou
University of Thessaly, Greece

Stella Tsermentseli
https://orcid.org/0000-0003-3622-0171
University of Thessaly, Greece

ABSTRACT

Language development has a significant impact on healthy emotional functioning throughout the lifespan. There is increasing evidence highlighting the existence of specific language deficits on distinct developmental diagnoses, which posits difficulties in various aspects of language, such as language processing deficits, vocabulary and verbal fluency, and pragmatic language impairment. In particular, separate lines of research have unveiled that language problems may exist in conduct disorder, oppositional defiant disorder, and also in populations posing elevated callous unemotional traits. The scope of the present chapter is to summarize key evidence in this area of inquiry, by focusing on the underlying neurocognitive mechanisms involved in language problems. Conducting such analysis will aid in a better understanding of the key behaviours, cognitive mechanisms, and biological signatures of such difficulties that may assist future research in this area of research and designation of more tailored educational and therapeutic interventions.

DOI: 10.4018/979-8-3693-1982-6.ch013

INTRODUCTION

Poor linguistic performance in young children has been shown to present a unique predictive value as per the occurrence of conduct issues during the same or a subsequent time period (Petersen & LeBeau, 2021). There is mounting evidence to suggest that atypical language acquisition patterns and aggression share an underlying bond. Clinical cases that are classified under the category of language present behavioral manifestations as well, such as the case of Developmental Language Disorder (DLD). This connection is also vastly denoted in the context of conduct difficulties, such as Conduct Disorder (CD), Oppositional Defiant Disorder (ODD) and Callous-Unemotional (CU) traits, where frequent linguistic implications are reported. The literature has described this relationship as bidirectional, though studies that have simultaneously examined both directions have concluded that language affects later behavior more robustly than the reverse (Petersen & LeBeau, 2021). The present chapter aims to summarize key evidence on the association between language deficits and such behavioural problems in development, highlighting that possible underlying neurocognitive mechanisms may have significant implications on early accurate diagnosis, intervention approaches, and long-term outcomes.

Communication Disorders

Communication disorders form a distinct area of the Diagnostic Statistical Manual – V (DSM; APA, 2023) which incorporates clinical sub-conditions where the process of communication is impaired, while other neurological factors remain intact. Language acquisition and use are compromised, and reflect pervasive and persistent problems in every element of the process of communication: language acquisition, language comprehension and production, as well as speech processing. These effects present as cross-modal, which means that they can affect verbal, written, and sign communication (Cummings, 2023). Communication disorders can disrupt the mechanisms that promote encoding and decoding of the linguistic material, a condition that leads to a language disorder. They are subdivided into five clinical entities: developmental language disorder (DLD), speech sound disorder, childhood-onset fluency disorder (stuttering), social (pragmatic) communication disorder, and unspecified communication disorder (Flickinger et al., 2022).

The prevalence of communication disorders in the general population is high, but the exact rate varies across studies. In the United States, the prevalence is estimated nearly one out of ten school-aged children, whereas in South India and Spain the percentage falls to 4.29% and 1% respectively (Cummings, 2023). By the time children reach the first grade, a 5% presents with a diagnosable communication deficit. A percentage of 28% - 60% of the children with a communication disorder have a parent and/or a sibling who is also affected (Glasby et al., 2022).

The impact of a communication disorder is pervasive in every aspect throughout development. Emotion regulation, social adjustment, and learning outcomes are immediately affected, whereas, in the absence of proper psychological treatment during childhood, the condition can lead to mental health problems, such as depression and anxiety disorders (Stransky et al., 2020). The initial focus of the present chapter is on Developmental Language Disorder (DLD) as a distinct clinical entity and its relation to behavioral problems.

DLD: Characteristics and Prevalence

Developmental Language Disorder (DLD) refers to the serious and ongoing difficulty in receiving and expressing linguistic material, while other neurological or intellectual deficits are absent. In DSM - V it is placed beneath the spectrum of communication disorders, as it affects the comprehension and/or production of spoken, written, and sign language, or other forms of language (Sheng et al., 2023). Semantics, pragmatics, verbal memory, grammar, phonology, and discourse can be areas of impairment manifestation (Bishop et al., 2017). The severity ranges from mild to profound and it interferes tremendously with everyday functioning (Nudel et al., 2023). Other circumstantial parameters, like lack of exposure to language or socioeconomic factors, should be absent for such a diagnosis to be assigned (Ricketts, 2011). In addition, DLD is expected to present a high risk for poor learning outcomes and mental health concerns (Ghandour et al., 2018).

The diagnostic term 'DLD' was formed and proposed by a panel of experts during a consensus study in 2017 (CATALISE Consortium; Bishop et al., 2017). The incorporation of the heterogenous clinical manifestations into one specific clinical entity served the purpose of public recognition and concise communication between experts. A significant number of researchers in this area consider DLD as overlapping or synonym to the previously established term Specific Language Impairment (SLI). According to the CATALISE panel the term DLD is the only accurate term as it accommodates adequately the pure linguistic nature of the condition (Kraljevic, 2023).

DLD has a strong genetical influence and tends to show patterns of co-occurrence between close relatives (Bishop et al., 2017). Of course, every known genotype is an outcome of the long-term and complex interplay between genetic and environmental factors. Low-weight birth and premature infants face a greater risk of developing DLD (Vernes et al., 2008). The primary criterion for diagnosing DLD is a general inadequacy in language usage, regardless of modality. Reported problems are reduced vocabulary, morphological abnormalities, and poor pragmatics. The overall linguistic capacity appears to be significantly below the age-appropriate level and this impacts social participation, learning outcomes, and functional communication. Assessment must contain both types of linguistic domains, expressive and receptive for the determination of the exact level of severity. Diagnosing DLD can be challenging because children who face difficulties in one cognitive demeanor may find ways to work around them almost efficiently. Using context is a well-known strategy for children with language difficulties (Gillam et al., 2021).

The prevalence as revealed by epidemiological studies, is estimated roughly as one out of fifteen school-aged children (Norbury et al., 2016). Szukiel et al., (2017) states that DLD affects the 3.6% of the population, and a longitudinal study reported that children with DLD constitute 1.5 to 7% of the preschool-aged population (Leonard, 2014). Yet it is believed that the vast majority of the cases remain undiagnosed or misdiagnosed (Kuvac Kraljevic, 2023). In addition, gender ratio is 4:1, with boys being more vulnerable than girls, though it has been argued that girls might have analogous difficulties which do not receive the same level of attention (McGregor, 2020).

Deficits can occur in all areas of language comprehension and production. Children who could potentially receive the diagnosis face crucial impediments while expressing their thoughts verbally. They could seem forgetful of what has been previously said, inattentive, or can be characterized as slow readers and writers (Larson et al., 2023). They could also present as merely unsuccessful when they follow instructions or answer questions. Grammar skills can be also seriously affected: production may lack proper prefixes, suffixes, verb endings, syntax, and morphology, whereas comprehension is weak regarding differences in wording, grammatical interpretation, word placement and slight linguistic cues (Gillam et al., 2021). Contextual interpretation, or "pragmatics", and selection of a reply appropriate to the setting is another area of adversity for children with DLD. Phonological awareness, and the acoustic distinction between similar sounds are also compromised, posing an additional burden on emergent literacy skills. Verbal memory both at the word and sentence level is exposed in flaws like errors and or delays, as a function of length and complexity (e.g., Larson et al., 2023).

Neurocognitive Implications of DLD

It is widely accepted that linguistic problems often co-occur with neurocognitive deficits, affecting procedural memory, motor control and executive functions (Marini et al., 2020). Neurocognitive deficits have also been reported for children with DLD. Speed of processing, attention, and working memory have been previously identified as areas of restricted competence in DLD. There is a complex and robust relationship between executive functions and DLD, and is currently receiving a growing amount of interest in the field. Marini and her colleagues (2020) investigated the relationship between two components of executive functions, inhibition and updating, and the linguistic and narrative skills of 16 preschoolers diagnosed with DLD, matched with 24 typically-developing counterparts. Findings revealed that DLD preschoolers, compared to their TD peers, face serious impediments in executive tasks (Marini et al., 2020). Nowadays, the notion that children with linguistic problems may face executive functioning deficits is widely acknowledged.

Executive functioning at its core encompasses discrete components: continuous monitoring (sustained attention), updating (working memory), shifting (flexibility), and inhibition. The components of executive functioning share a common underlying neural substrate, but they do not emerge simultaneously, but rather in a hierarchical manner (Larson et al., 2023). Sustained attention is the first executive component to emerge early during development. It enables and guides the development of the other components and plays a significant role in cognitive development in general. Part of linguistic development relies on emerging executive functioning. Children with DLD appear to have difficulties maintaining their focus both in verbal and non-verbal stimuli, in phonological working memory, in inhibitory control, and in cognitive flexibility. Message production and comprehension require multistage processes that involve distinct executive components, like constant monitoring of the communicative flow, shifting, updating of the information that is being exchanged or transmitted, inhibition of the irrelevant or competitive semantic elements (Kalliontzi et al., 2022; Mozeiko et al., 2011). Interestingly, several studies have revealed evidence for impaired haptic perception in children with DLD, which means that haptic recognition of objects and integration of somatosensory information and symbolic representation of the respective objects is impaired (Müürsepp et al., 2014; Tseng & Hsu, 2023). Such associations could not be explained by working memory or executive deficits, but they rather reflect another set of deficits in the motor domain (Tseng & Hsu, 2023).

In a similar vein, there is increasing neuroimaging evidence to highlight the existence of neurophysiological mechanisms involved in the manifestation of language deficits and disorders during development. More specifically, left motor and language areas have been shown to have reduced white matter in individuals with DLD (Ullman et al., 2020). Connectivity beneath language areas and between these regions and basal ganglia follow abnormal patterns, as revealed by DTI studies (Krishnan et al., 2022). Examining the local brain circuits, children with DLD appear to have focal myelin decreases in the left striatum and Broca's area. All these structural data reveal a key role for basal ganglia in DLD (Lee et al., 2020), although the laterality of the abnormalities has been questioned, as studies have revealed a symmetrical pattern of alterations (Guerreiro et al., 2002 ; Herbert et al., 2003). Perisylvian areas have been also shown to be significant to the symptomatology of DLD (Guerreiro et al., 2002). The aforementioned brain areas have been consistently associated with the Procedural circuit Deficit Hypothesis (PDH), which posits that abnormalities of brain structures underlying procedural memory (learning and memory that relies on the basal ganglia and associated circuitry) can explain numerous brain and behavioral characteristics, across learning and processing, in multiple disorders, especially the ones associated with language deficits (Ullman et al., 2020).

DLD and Behavior

Early social interactions, which often serve as a strong mental health indicator, are severely restricted for children with language disorders, because their difficulties limit their opportunities for participation. One of the most common behavioral manifestations in preschool children with receptive and/ or expressive language difficulties is physical aggression (Girard et al., 2016). DLD diagnosis is often linked to severe social and often clinically important, behavioral problems, whereas several studies reveal that a vast number of children, adolescents, and young adults with psychiatric problems have an undiagnosed language deficit. Emotional problems, peer rejection, depression, and anxiety are the most commonly reported problems, which progressively proceed to more complex situations as a function of age (Willinger et al., 2003).

Comorbidities Associated With DLD

DLD often co-occurs with other clinical entities. ADHD is a commonly met comorbidity, as well as specific learning disorders (SLD), namely dyscalculia and dyslexia. Regarding the relationship between DLD and dyslexia, as they both are neurodevelopmental language disorders of language and reading (Ghandour et al., 2018 ; Nitin et al., 2022), two distinct dimensions should be considered in order to shed light on the developmental course of both disorders. Dyslexia comes with poor phonological skills, whereas DLD contains a significant difficulty in comprehension, but poor phonology doesn't apply in all cases (Snowling et al., 2020). Poor phonological awareness is associated with speech production deficits, and it has been argued that working memory mediates this relationship (Torres et al., 2020). It has been stated that dyslexia lies beneath the spectrum of DLD (Guerreiro et al., 2002).

Moreover, disruptive conditions like conduct disorder and oppositional defiant disorder, delayed milestones, coordination and motor deficits, and disorders of the acoustic nerve have been found to accompany DLD. Children with DLD are 6 times more likely to report emotional difficulties and clinically significant anxiety (Im-Bolter & Cohen, 2007). With the progression of age, as a child with DLD reaches adolescence, emotional implications become more prominent and obtain a more robust clinical significance. The results of the long-term complex interplay between linguistic communication, social functionality, and poor learning outcomes come into light as low self-esteem, depressive symptomatology, aggressiveness, low social cognition and emotional regulation competence, which in turn can serve as a fertile soil for the development of further adversities (Arts et al., 2022). Emotional problems arise as a byproduct, an indirect effect of the DLD condition, which is mediated by the level of social functioning, according to the "social mediation hypothesis" by (Forrest et al., 2021). The objective of this study was to unravel the underlying pathways that link emotional problems, namely anxiety and depression, and the language deficits of DLD. Social functioning and emotional outcomes of 27 adolescents with DLD were measured using self and parent reports and were compared to their neurotypical counterparts (TD). Results revealed minor differences between TD and DLD subjects regarding self-reports, but a concrete divergence was reported in parent reports (Forrest et al., 2021).

Furthermore, a careful and thorough investigation should be completed in order to differentiate DLD from other neurodevelopmental disorders with a similar clinical phenotype. Pragmatic discrepancies are a common feature between certain ASD profiles and DLD cases and should be actively addressed during a differential diagnosis (McGregor, 2020). Similarly to ASD, reading comprehension is much more impaired than word recognition for DLD than for dyslexia, which is another point that differentiates these disorders (Ricketts, 2011).

Emotion and behavior dysregulation problems are possible to occur throughout the childhood, from preschool years to early adolescence. Low self-esteem and self-concept combined with restricted social functioning constitute robust determinants for a poor prognosis (Im-Bolter & Cohen, 2007). The impact of the inability to self-expression affects tremendously the competence and quality of life (Rinaldi et al., 2021). Adolescence and early adult life can pose novel challenging objectives. DLD cases in puberty, experience adverse emotions, low quality of social interactions, low employability (Tsou et al., 2023). Lack of self-regulation and aggression appear as substitutes for the lack of propped skills and competencies. Social deprivation and low social status are common problems faced by adults with DLD, that might give rise to psychopathology (Forrest et al., 2021). Therefore, identifying effective interventions early on the course of life of a person with DLD is imperative.

Behavioral Challenges and Language Problems Early in Life: Conduct Disorder, Oppositional Defiant Disorder and Callous Unemotional Traits

There are cases where aggression or behavioral dysregulation stands out as the problem that gets primarily referred and assessed, whereas language impairments as seen as comorbid. Most notably, Conduct Disorder (CD), Oppositional Defiant Disorder (ODD), Callous Unemotional Traits (CU) are a distinct category of childhood psychiatric conditions that appear to be strongly connected with impaired language skills. Studies have shown that an atypical course of language acquisition may exist before the behavioral manifestations. Inner or private speech is the root of self-regulation, inhibition and behavioral organization (Awadalla et al., 2023). Children that fall under these diagnostic categories are at risk for further language impairments and poor academic performance during the subsequent years due to their difficulties in social interaction. Especially for CU and ODD, conflicting evidence has been reported as per what was there first. Symptoms like lack of empathy and remorse, dominance seeking, and deception can be present during early childhood and contribute to verbal and learning problems through two paths: the maladaptive presence in the school environment and the structural inability to process the subtle pragmatics of the linguistic material, especially when it portrays emotional connotations (Helland et al., 2014).

Conduct Disorder: Characteristics and Prevalence

Conduct Disorder is a behavioral and emotional disorder that typically manifests in childhood or adolescence and is characterized by a repetitive pattern of behaviors that violate the basic rights of others or major societal norms and rules. Lack of empathy and remorse appear as a function of age, along with aggression towards people, animals, properties, deceitfulness and further disrespectfulness of social rules (SAMSHA, 2016). There is a distinction between two types of this disorder, depending on the developmental stage of onset, which differentiates the qualitative characteristics, the prognosis, and overall estimated damage. The "childhood onset" type refers to cases with onset before the age of ten. This type is linked to more pervasive and consolidated effects compared to the "adolescence onset type", with the disorder onset after 10 years of age, which is linked to more restricted impairments. Continuity between disorders has been revealed repetitively by research, in a way such that conduct disorder is often given as a diagnosis to children previously diagnosed with oppositional defiant disorder. Adults with antisocial personality disorder had been diagnosed with conduct disorder as children, or they presented a psychological record that would possibly meet the criteria (Woodward et al., 2023 ;Lu et al., 2023).

A CD diagnosis would take into account the existence of a persistent pattern of disruptive behaviors and violation of age-appropriate societal norms and rules. More specifically, according to DSM-V, an individual needs to exhibit characteristics such as aggression toward people and/or animals, destruction of property, deceitfulness or theft, and serious violations of rules. The impact of the behavior must cause clinically significant impairment in social, academic, or occupational functioning. The global prevalence of conduct disorder is approximately 5% and represents one of the most frequent standalone reasons for referral to mental health services. The gender ratio appears to be rather burdensome for boys, as it ranges from 4:1 to 12:1 (Wu et al., 2022 ; Mohammadi et al., 2021).

Interestingly, ADHD and learning disability have been reported as common comorbidities with CD during childhood. In a study by Konrad and colleagues, girls from 9 to 18 years old with CD exhibited higher rates of major depression, anxiety disorders and borderline personality disorder, whereas boys with CD had higher rates of ADHD. According to the study's results girls with CD reported as facing more lifetime psychiatric comorbidities. Girls are more likely to have the adolescence onset type, whereas boys are affected mostly during childhood for the first time. Although childhood onset entails a worse prevalence, girls present significant psychopathological traits, similar to boys (Konrad et al., 2022). In addition to comorbidities, gender differences have been associated with the presence of callous-unemotional traits, that are primarily associated with limited prosocial emotions. Girls with CD, typically, tend to have lower callous unemotional traits compared to boys with CD (Ackermann et al., 2019). Girls with CD and higher levels of CU are more likely to display reactive aggression, whereas boys are more likely to display proactive and physical aggression, bullying, and delinquency combined with lower level of internalizing problems (Colins et al., 2015). It has been argued that the presence of differences in comorbidities may be linked to different developmental pathways of the disorder (Konrad et al., 2022). The current evidence supports the idea that CD severity is associated with greater psychiatric impact only in the female side of the population, and can be explained by the "gender paradox" which states that lower occurrence rates of a disease or a disorder in a particular gender is often associated with greater severity in that gender (Kwilas et al., 2015).

Language Problems in CD

There is increasing evidence to confirm that early effective acquisition of language and communication skills are paramount for the establishment of social interaction and behavioral skills (Hollo et al., 2014). Separate lines of research in childhood have previously highlighted considerable overlaps between language impairments and behavioral problems (Hartas, 2012). For instance, children with poorer vocabulary, may experience difficulties communicating their emotions which, as a result, may lead to emotion dysregulation and peer rejection. In addition, children with social communication difficulties may be challenged to interpret social situations and interactions due to deficits in understanding other's emotions (Salmon et al., 2016). Especially in relation to CD, there is mounting evidence to point to the existence of links between conduct problems and language problems (Barker et al., 2011). Such difficulties have been mainly associated with deficits in engaging in private speech, which is considered a paramount skill for organization, regulation, and inhibition of behavior (Lazaratou et al., 2018).

Interestingly, children with CD has also shown to exhibit language processing deficits, including receptive language skills (comprehension) and expressive language skills (verbal expression) (Moffitt, 2006). Additional difficulties include vocabulary and verbal fluency, where children with Conduct Disorder may have limited vocabulary and difficulties with verbal fluency (e.g., (Bourke et al., 2005). Pragmatic Language Impairments, which refers to the social use of language, including understanding and using appropriate language in different social contexts has also been found in children with conduct disorder (Moffitt, 2006). Social communication deficits have also been reported in children with Conduct Disorder (Gilmour et al., 2004).

Furthermore, there is evidence to highlight the existence of neurocognitive mechanisms in the language deficits observed in CD. There is evidence coming from investigations with neurocognitive tasks to show that youths with CD exhibit deficits in facial (Fairchild et al., 2009) and vocal (Stevens et al., 2001) emotion recognition, and also show deficits in affective empathy (Martin-Key et al., 2017), decision-making and reinforcement learning (Fanti et al., 2016). Furthermore, youth with CD have been shown to be influenced by potential rewards and less influenced by punishment than controls (Sonuga-Barke, 2016). Interestingly, such decision-making biases have been shown more recently, to be more pronounced in males with CD (Sidlauskaite et al., 2018). Most notably, executive functioning deficits, such as difficulties with inhibitory control, working memory, and cognitive flexibility, have been consistently observed in children with CD (Barnett, 2009); for a review see (Willcutt E. G.-1., 2005). While executive functions are not specific to language, they play a crucial role in language processing, organization, and regulation. In a similar vein, CD is associated with impairments in social cognition, including deficits in empathy, perspective-taking, and emotion recognition (e.g., (Sebastian, 2012) (Marsh A. A., 2013). Language processing is intertwined with social cognitive processes, and disruptions in social cognitive functioning may impact the effective use and comprehension of language.

Oppositional Defiant Disorder: Characteristics and Prevalence

Another developmental disorder that will be examined in the present chapter in relation to documented language difficulties is Oppositional Defiant Disorder (ODD), which is a behavioral disorder characterized by a pattern of defiant, disobedient, and hostile behavior towards authority figures. ODD is listed under the Disruptive, impulse, and conduct disorders in DSM-V and refers to a clinical symptomatology consisting of irritability, argumentative and defiant behavior, or vindictiveness targeted towards peers or authority figures, like parents and teachers. It has a significant resemblance to CD, but the main difference is that CD's main characteristic is aggression, but ODD'S primary sign is the deliberate provocation (Pardini & Fite, 2010).

In order for a diagnosis to be established, the pattern of negativity and irritable mood, argumentative or defiant behavior and vindictiveness has to last for at least 6 months and has to be present with at least one individual who is not a sibling. The behavioral pattern causes distress and despair in the immediate family and social environment and impacts tremendously academic, professional, and social adjustment and outcomes (Caserini et al., 2023).

The prevalence of ODD varies as a function of the parameters of each study, variables included and timing of the diagnosis. ODD is estimated to often be misdiagnosed as CD or age-appropriate behavioral issues. The estimated range of prevalence is 2% to 11%. Males tend to get diagnosed quiet more often compared to girls 1.4:1, however this difference does not apply during adolescents or adulthood (Barry et al., 2013).

Language Problems in ODD

Poor language skills are widely considered to be a shared risk factor for disruptive behavior disorders (DBDs), including ODD (for a review see Gremillion and Martel, 2014). Poor language skills are also closely associated with social withdrawal, academic underachievement, and problems in impulse regulation and attention (van Daal, Verhoeven, & van Balkom, 2007). Interestingly, some studies have reported associations between DBDs and language (e.g., Gurevitz, Geva, Varon, & Leitner, 2012) while others have not observed such associations (e.g., Whitehouse, Robinson, & Zubrick, 2011). Further, normal variation in language skills and its association with DBD is understudied.

Language deficits in children with ODD include pragmatic language difficulties. Such deficits involve difficulties in the appropriate use of language in social contexts and impaired communication skills which generate difficulties to effectively convey their thoughts and emotions, leading to communication breakdowns and increased frustration. Such difficulties have been also associated with the manifestation of specific neurocognitive mechanisms such as executive functioning abilities (i.e., inhibitory control, working memory, and cognitive flexibility; for a review see (Willcutt E. G., 2005). A separate line of neurophysiological research has suggested that abnormalities in brain regions involved in emotional processing and regulation, such as the amygdala and prefrontal cortex, may contribute to emotional and behavioral dysregulation in children with ODD (e.g., (Blair, 2003), and theory of mind deficits involving the medial prefrontal cortex and temporoparietal junction (Sebastian et al., 2012).

Callous Unemotional Traits: Characteristics and Prevalence

An additional focus of the present chapter is the presence of language problems observed in children with Callous-Unemotional (CU) traits. CU traits are characterized by a lack of empathy, shallow affect, and a disregard for others' feelings. Callous Unemotional Traits (CU traits) are set of psychopathic traits which include lack of guilt, remorse, empathy, callousness and unemotional traits (Portnoy et al., 2020). It's characterized by shallow or deficient affect (Raschle et al., 2018). Law parental attachment, negative parenting behaviors and attitude, childhood maltreatment, inconsistent discipline, reduced maternal sensitivity and monitoring have been linked to the emergence of CU traits (Portnoy et al., 2020; (Robinson et al., 2016). This identification has been used for typing and dividing conduct disorder cases into low CU traits and high CU traits. DSM-V lists CU traits as a specifier for CD named "limited prosocial emotions", and encompasses the following characteristics: lack of remorse or guilt, shallow or deficient affect, lack of empathy, lack of concern with performance and flat reactions to traumatic events. Three categories are formed to fit these characteristics: callous, which reflect ruthlessness, uncaring (passive disregard for others). These attributes resemble to the core characteristics of the adult psychopathy (Wendt et al., 2017).

Research has documented deficits in verbal reasoning and comprehension skills for children with high CU traits (e.g., (Ciucci, 2014). Children with callous-unemotional traits may also experience difficulties in pragmatic language skills, such as understanding social cues, using appropriate language in different contexts, and displaying appropriate conversational turn-taking skills (Willoughby, 2014). Interestingly, neuroimaging studies have shown that children with high levels of CU traits exhibit differences in brain regions involved in emotional processing and empathy, such as the amygdala and prefrontal cortex. These differences may contribute to reduced emotional responsiveness and difficulties in understanding and expressing emotions through language (Marsh A. F., 2013). Associations between neural connectivity and language processing difficulties in children with CU traits have also been reported. More specifically, studies have found altered functional connectivity patterns and neural activation during language processing tasks in children with CU traits. These differences may affect the integration of language-related brain regions and contribute to language deficits observed in this population (e.g., (Decety, 2012).

CU traits can be found as a standalone constellation of features without CD In this case they are linked to a higher risk for disruptive behaviors. Nevertheless, they are thought to be precursors of psychopathic traits in adulthood (Vasconcelos et al., 2021). When co-existing with CD, they represent a more seriously affected cohort who displays a more stable and resistant to therapy set of symptoms. They are also more likely to engage in long term and serious aggressive behaviors, especially boys (Pardini & Fite, 2010). CU traits have been described as moral dysfunction, though this isn't completely accurate, as CU traits cases are competent in forming cognitive judgments about morality, but they rather have a limited propensity for resonating with other' s emotions (Fang et al., 2020). Even though cognitive aspects of CU traits are present during first years of childhood, they seem to soften as children acquire cognitive empathy, due to the intact verbal abilities (Waller et al., 2020).

There is cumulative evidence that CU traits in adulthood can be divided into two variants with different etiologies and developmental courses. The first variant is high in CU traits and low in anxiety. It is thought to be an implicit, temperamental characteristic or a genetic difficulty to process emotion. The second variant is high in CU traits and high in anxiety and can be the consequence of childhood abuse and exposure to trauma (Michielsen et al., 2022). Thus, CU traits cases are a significantly heterogenous population, a fact that renders studying youth psychopathy a rather challenging task. Exact prevalence rate estimations vary significantly, but it's roughly suggested that a 13% to 46% of the antisocial youth would meet the diagnostic criteria (Kahn et al., 2012). In order to address the issue of measurement, researchers evaluated psychopathy taking into account two distinct perspectives: the strong correlation between conduct disorders and severe antisocial behavior, which led to the formation of a 41-item psychometric tool named Child-Psychopathy Scale, which evaluates behavioral problems, attention and hyperactivity-impulsivity. The second perspective in studying youth psychopathy focuses on the combination of narcissism, impulsivity and deficits in emotion experiencing and processing. A second 20-item instrument was created in order to combine these two perspectives, the Antisocial Screening Device, but after the identification of its validity flaws in its CU traits factor, a subsequent instrument named Inventory of Callous Unemotional Traits was produced (Arango-Tobon et al., 2022). Interestingly, there is evidence that conduct problems, CU traits, and ADHD co-occur (Saunders et al., 2019) and that they share common underlying neural mechanisms (Zhang et al., 2021), though the heterogeneity of the clinical population allows only a small space for such inference.

In terms of the neurocognitive mechanisms associated with the presence of CU traits the literature has been mixed. Whereas some studies have found no significant associations with CU traits (e.g., Fanti et al., 2016), other research suggests that CU traits are associated with better executive functioning (Rydell & Brocki, 2019). Importantly, the studies varied greatly in their measurement of executive functioning, including types of tasks used and the specific functions of executive functioning measured. Interestingly, previous studies did not find associations between CU traits and response inhibition or selective attention. However, a study did find that CU traits were associated better sustained attention (Rydell & Brocki, 2019). Thus, further research is needed to clarify the extent to which CU traits may be characterized by deficits in specific components of executive function and the contribution to potential language and communication deficits.

Language Problems in CU Traits

As CU traits are considered as a dimension of psychopathy, the literature for childhood age is scarce. Studies begin to investigate CU traits from the age of adolescence, and usually the subjects have been implicated in events that yield the existence of such personality psychopathology. Moreover, CU traits are mostly examined under the light of an existing disorder as comorbid. These are the reasons why the studies regarding CU traits per se are very few and refer to ages beyond childhood. Psychopathy in general has been previously connected to above-average oral language skills both in adolescents and young adults, though they appear to present systematic subtle deficits in higher order linguistic processes (Anderson et al., 2022). Reported evidence suggests that high psychopathic individuals possess slightly superior semantic and phonological skills versus the low psychopathic (Selenius & Strand, 2015). However, persistent pragmatic deficits are reported in high psychopathic adolescents (Nilsen & Bacso, 2017). Language lateralization has been found weaker in this population, yielding different patterns or cognitive resources available during language production (Hiatt et al., 2002). Taking this relationship further on, CC traits are seen as a mediator between psychopathy and language when predicting violent delinquency: individuals with high CC traits and high verbal skills report greatest violent delinquency and the lowest skin conductance reactivity during experimental provocation (Muñoz et al., 2008).

Future Implications

Taken together, investigating the current evidence, models and approaches to language deficits in various developmental disorders and conditions may shed light on the current understanding of the neurocognitive mechanisms of such difficulties. Especially taking into account the strong evidence suggesting high cooccurrence between the disorders and traits of interest, increasing our current understanding of this area can help elucidate the underlying mechanisms, including genetic, neurological, and environmental factors that contribute to the development and maintenance of both callous-unemotional traits and aggressive behaviors. Such investigation adheres to the Research Domain Criteria (RDoC) that highlight the importance of studying how developmental processes give rise to psychopathology, which can lead to novel discoveries to identify, prevent, and treat mental health problems across the lifespan.

Furthermore, taken the increasing evidence highlighting that language deficits can be an early indicator of developmental psychopathology, further studying language deficits above and beyond diagnoses and characteristics, researchers can identify risk factors and early markers that can facilitate early identification and intervention, leading to improved outcomes for children with developmental psychopathology. Understanding the specific language profiles associated with different disorders can aid in distinguishing between overlapping conditions, reducing misdiagnosis, and ensuring appropriate interventions.

In addition, the present chapter may aid in the future refinement of diagnostic criteria for the studied developmental disorders and behavioural manifestations. By identifying specific neurocognitive markers and risk factors that are language and communication-specific, researchers can enhance diagnostic tools and assessments, leading to more accurate identification and classification of individuals with these conditions. Such refinement can contribute to the development and evaluation of targeted interventions for individuals by identifying effective evidence-based strategies for managing and reducing maladjustment early in life. Especially in relation to DLD, interventions should target social, linguistic, cognitive and mental health problems. Early diagnosis is key to the design of an adequate support plan both in school and in the family environment.

CONCLUSION

Taken the specific focus of the present chapter on the evidence investigating the neurocognitive mechanisms of language deficits in developmental psychopathology, the work can provide insights into the current understanding of the underlying cognitive, neural, and genetic mechanisms involved in developmental psychopathology. Further research in this area can aid the uncovering of specific language-related processes that are impaired in different disorders, shedding light on the core cognitive and neural impairments that contribute to these conditions. Finally, taken the increasing understanding that language deficits early in life may have long-lasting effects on academic achievement, social integration, and overall quality of life, the present work may aid current and future research to gain insights into the long-term outcomes and trajectories of individuals with developmental psychopathology, informing interventions and support services that promote positive developmental trajectories.

REFERENCES

Ackermann, K., Kirchner, M., Bernhard, A., Martinelli, A., Anomitri, C., Baker, R., Baumann, S., Dochnal, R., Fernandez-Rivas, A., Gonzalez-Madruga, K., Herpertz-Dahlmann, B., Hervas, A., Jansen, L., Kapornai, K., Kersten, L., Kohls, G., Limprecht, R., Lazaratou, H., McLaughlin, A., & Freitag, C. M. (2019). Relational Aggression in Adolescents with Conduct Disorder: Sex Differences and Behavioral Correlates. *Journal of Abnormal Child Psychology*, *47*(10), 1625–1637. doi:10.100710802-019-00541-6 PMID:30949882

Anderson, S. A. S., Hawes, D. J., & Snow, P. C. (2022). Oral language skills, callous and unemotional traits and high-risk patterns of youth offending. *European Child & Adolescent Psychiatry, 0123456789*. doi:10.100700787-022-01980-1 PMID:35403912

Arango-Tobon, O. E., Pinilla-Monsalve, G. D., Grisales-Aguirre, A. M., Gómez-Tabare, A. S., & Carmona-Cardona, C. A. (2022). Consistency and validity of the inventory of callous- unemotional traits in a multi-centric community sample. *Heliyon*, *8*(6), e09789. doi:10.1016/j.heliyon.2022.e09789 PMID:35800728

Arts, E., Orobio de Castro, B., Luteijn, E., Elsendoorn, B., & Vissers, C. T. W. M. (2022). Improving social emotional functioning in adolescents with Developmental Language Disorders: A mini review and recommendations. *Frontiers in Psychiatry*, *13*(1), 966008. Advance online publication. doi:10.3389/fpsyt.2022.966008 PMID:36569624

Awadalla, E. N., Khattab, A. N., & El-ella, E. I. A. (2023). Language Profile In Conduct Disorder Children Aged Between 7 To 12 Years Old. *74*, 143–152.

Barker, E. D., Tremblay, R. E., van Lier, P. A., Vitaro, F., Nagin, D. S., Assaad, J. M., & Séguin, J. R. (2011). The neurocognition of conduct disorder behaviors: Specificity to physical aggression and theft after controlling for ADHD symptoms. *Aggressive Behavior*, *37*(1), 63–72. doi:10.1002/ab.20373 PMID:21046606

Barnett, R. M., Maruff, P., & Vance, A. (2009). Neurocognitive function in attention-deficit-hyperactivity disorder with and without comorbid disruptive behaviour disorders. *The Australian and New Zealand Journal of Psychiatry*, *43*(8), 722–730. doi:10.1080/00048670903001927 PMID:19629793

Barry, T. D., Marcus, D. K., Barry, C. T., & Coccaro, E. F. (2013). The latent structure of oppositional defiant disorder in children andadults. *Journal ofPsychiatric Research*, *47*(12), 1932–1939. doi:10.1016/j.jpsychires.2013.08.016 PMID:24075326

Bishop, D. V. M., Snowling, M. J., Thompson, P. A., Greenhalgh, T., Adams, C., Archibald, L., Baird, G., Bauer, A., Bellair, J., Boyle, C., Brownlie, E., Carter, G., Clark, B., Clegg, J., Cohen, N., Conti-Ramsden, G., Dockrell, J., Dunn, J., Ebbels, S., & Whitehouse, A. (2017). Phase 2 of CATALISE: a multinational and multidisciplinary Delphi consensus study of problems with language development: Terminology. *Journal of Child Psychology and Psychiatry, and Allied Disciplines*, *58*(10), 1068–1080. doi:10.1111/jcpp.12721 PMID:28369935

Blair, R. J. (2003). Neurobiological basis of psychopathy. *The British Journal of Psychiatry*, *182*(1), 5–7. doi:10.1192/bjp.182.1.5 PMID:12509310

Bourke. (2005). *Journal of Child Psychology and Psychiatry*, 1200–1210.

Caserini, C., Ferro, M., Nobile, M., Scaini, S., & Michelini, G. (2023). Shared genetic influences between depression and conduct disorder in children and adolescents: A systematic review. *Journal of Affective Disorders, 322*(July 2022), 31–38. doi:10.1016/j.jad.2022.11.001

Ciucci, E. B. (2014). *The association between callous-unemotional traits and behavioral and academic adjustment in children: Further validation of the Inventory of Callous-Unemotional Traits.*

Colins, O. F., Andershed, H., & Pardini, D. A. (2015). Psychopathic traits as predictors of future criminality, intimate partner aggression, and substance use in young adult men. *Law and Human Behavior*, *39*(6), 547–558. doi:10.1037/lhb0000148 PMID:26301710

Cummings, L. (2023). Communication disorders: A complex population in healthcare. *Language and Health*, (June). doi:10.1016/j.laheal.2023.06.005

Decety, J. M., Michalska, K. J., & Kinzler, K. D. (2012). The contribution of emotion and cognition to moral sensitivity: A neurodevelopmental study. *Cerebral Cortex (New York, N.Y.)*, *22*(1), 209–220. doi:10.1093/cercor/bhr111 PMID:21616985

Fairchild, G., Van Goozen, S. H. M., Calder, A. J., Stollery, S. J., & Goodyer, I. M. (2009). Deficits in facial expression recognition in male adolescents with earlyonset or adolescence-onset conduct disorder. *Journal of Child Psychology and Psychiatry, and Allied Disciplines*, *50*(5), 627–636. doi:10.1111/j.1469-7610.2008.02020.x PMID:19432683

Fairchild, G. P., Passamonti, L., Hurford, G., Hagan, C. C., von dem Hagen, E. A. H., van Goozen, S. H. M., Goodyer, I. M., & Calder, A. J. (2011). Brain structure abnormalities in early-onset and adolescent-onset conduct disorder. *The American Journal of Psychiatry*, *168*(6), 624–633. doi:10.1176/appi.ajp.2010.10081184 PMID:21454920

Fang, J., Wang, X., Yuan, K. H., & Wen, Z. (2020). Childhood psychological maltreatment and moral disengagement: A moderated mediation model of callous-unemotional traits and empathy. *Personality and Individual Differences*, *157*(January), 109814. doi:10.1016/j.paid.2020.109814

Fanti, K. A., Kimonis, E. R., Hadjicharalambous, M. Z., & Steinberg, L. (2016). Do neurocognitive deficits in decision making differentiate conduct disorder subtypes? *European Child & Adolescent Psychiatry*, *25*(9), 989–996. doi:10.100700787-016-0822-9 PMID:26832949

Flickinger, T. E., Waselewski, M., Tabackman, A., Huynh, J., Hodges, J., Otero, K., Schorling, K., Ingersoll, K., Tiouririne, N. A. D., & Dillingham, R. (2022). Communication between patients, peers, and care providers through a mobile health intervention supporting medication-assisted treatment for opioid use disorder. *Patient Education and Counseling*, *105*(7), 2110–2115. doi:10.1016/j.pec.2022.02.014 PMID:35260260

Forrest, C. L., Gibson, J. L., & St Clair, M. C. (2021). Social functioning as a mediator between developmental language disorder (Dld) and emotional problems in adolescents. *International Journal of Environmental Research and Public Health*, *18*(3), 1–17. doi:10.3390/ijerph18031221 PMID:33572993

Ghandour, H., Eldin, S., Sallam, Y., & Mahmoud, S. (2018). Associated comorbidities of specific language impairment. *Benha Medical Journal*, *35*(2), 115. doi:10.4103/bmfj.bmfj_155_17

Gillam, S. L., Holbrook, S., & Kamhi, A. G. (2021). Developmental Language Disorder. The Handbook of Language and Speech Disorders, 171–191. Dld, doi:10.1002/9781119606987.ch9

Girard, L. C., Pingault, J. B., Doyle, O., Falissard, B., & Tremblay, R. E. (2016). Developmental Associations Between Conduct Problems and Expressive Language in Early Childhood: A Population-Based Study. *Journal of Abnormal Child Psychology*, *44*(6), 1033–1043. doi:10.100710802-015-0094-8 PMID:26496905

Glasby, J., Graham, L. J., White, S. L. J., & Tancredi, H. (2022). Do teachers know enough about the characteristics and educational impacts of Developmental Language Disorder (DLD) to successfully include students with DLD? *Teaching and Teacher Education*, *119*, 103868. doi:10.1016/j.tate.2022.103868

Greenberg, M. T., Speltz, M. L., & Deklyen, M. (1993). The role of attachment in the early development of disruptive behavior problems. *Development and Psychopathology*, *5*(1-2), 191–213. doi:10.1017/S095457940000434X

Gremillion, M. L., & Martel, M. M. (2014). Merely misunderstood? Receptive, expressive, and pragmatic language in young children with disruptive behavior disorders. *Journal of Clinical Child and Adolescent Psychology*, *43*(5), 765–776. doi:10.1080/15374416.2013.822306 PMID:23924073

Guerreiro, M. M., Hage, S. R. V., Guimarães, C. A., Abramides, D. V., Fernandes, W., Pacheco, P. S., Piovesana, A. M. S. G., Montenegro, M. A., & Cendes, F. (2002). Developmental language disorder associated with polymicrogyria. *Neurology*, *59*(2), 245–250. doi:10.1212/WNL.59.2.245 PMID:12136065

Gurevitz, M., Geva, R., Varon, M., & Leitner, Y. (2012). Early markers in infants and toddlers for development of ADHD. *Journal of Attention Disorders*. PMID:22751678

Hartas, D. (2012). Children's social behavior, language, and literacy in early years. *Oxford Review of Education*, *38*(3), 357–376. doi:10.1080/03054985.2012.699748

Helland, W. A., Lundervold, A. J., Heimann, M., & Posserud, M. B. (2014). Stable associations between behavioral problems and language impairments across childhood - The importance of pragmatic language problems. *Research in Developmental Disabilities*, *35*(5), 943–951. doi:10.1016/j.ridd.2014.02.016 PMID:24642228

Herba, C. M. (2004). Annotation: Developmental psychopathology: The role of emotion regulation in the development of psychopathology. *Journal of Child Psychology and Psychiatry, and Allied Disciplines*.

Herbert, M. R., Ziegler, D. A., Makris, N., Bakardjiev, A., Hodgson, J., Adrien, K. T., Kennedy, D. N., Filipek, P. A., & Caviness, V. S. (2003). Larger brain and white matter volumes in children with developmental language disorder. *Developmental Science*, *6*(4), 11–22. doi:10.1111/1467-7687.00291

Hiatt, K. D., Lorenz, A. R., & Newman, J. P. (2002). Assessment of emotion and language processing in psychopathic offenders: Results from a dichotic listening task. *Personality and Individual Differences*, *32*(7), 1255–1268. doi:10.1016/S0191-8869(01)00116-7

Hollo, A., Wehby, J. H., & Oliver, R. M. (2014). Unidentified language deficits in children with emotional and behavioral disorders: A meta-analysis. *Exceptional Children*, *80*(2), 169–186. doi:10.1177/001440291408000203

Im-Bolter, N., & Cohen, N. J. (2007). Language Impairment and Psychiatric Comorbidities. *Pediatric Clinics of North America*, *54*(3), 525–542. doi:10.1016/j.pcl.2007.02.008 PMID:17543908

Kahn, R. E., Frick, P. J., Youngstrom, E., Findling, R. L., & Youngstrom, J. K. (2012). Diagnosis of Conduct Disorder. *Journal of Child Psychology and Psychiatry, and Allied Disciplines*, *53*(3), 271–282. doi:10.1111/j.1469-7610.2011.02463.x PMID:21950481

Kalliontzi, E., Ralli, A. M., Palikara, O., & Roussos, P. (2022). Examining the relationship between oral language skills and executive functions: Evidence from Greek-speaking 4–5-year-old children with and without Developmental Language Disorder. *Research in Developmental Disabilities*, *124*(March), 104215. doi:10.1016/j.ridd.2022.104215 PMID:35298958

Kempes, M. M., Matthys, W., de Vries, H., & van Engeland, H. (2005). Reactive and proactive aggression in children: A review of theory, findings and the relevance for child and adolescent psychiatry. *European Child & Adolescent Psychiatry, 14*(1), 11–19. doi:10.100700787-005-0432-4 PMID:15756511

Konrad, K., Kohls, G., Baumann, S., Bernhard, A., Martinelli, A., Ackermann, K., Smaragdi, A., Gonzalez-Madruga, K., Wells, A., Rogers, J. C., Pauli, R., Clanton, R., Baker, R., Kersten, L., Prätzlich, M., Oldenhof, H., Jansen, L., Kleeven, A., Bigorra, A., & Freitag, C. M. (2022). Sex differences in psychiatric comorbidity and clinical presentation in youths with conduct disorder. *Journal of Child Psychology and Psychiatry, and Allied Disciplines*, *63*(2), 218–228. doi:10.1111/jcpp.13428 PMID:34008879

Krishnan, S., Cler, G. J., Smith, H. J., Willis, H. E., Asaridou, S. S., Healy, M. P., Papp, D., & Watkins, K. E. (2022). Quantitative MRI reveals differences in striatal myelin in children with DLD. *eLife*, *11*, 2020–2022. doi:10.7554/eLife.74242 PMID:36164824

Kuvac Kraljevic, J. (2023). Can prevalence data help us identify developmental language disorder? *The Lancet Regional Health. Western Pacific*, *34*(February), 100714. doi:10.1016/j.lanwpc.2023.100714 PMID:37283974

Kwilas, A. R., Donahue, R. N., Tsang, K. Y., & Hodge, J. W. (2015). 乳鼠心肌提取 HHS Public Access. *Cancer Cell*, *2*(1), 1–17. doi:10.1111/jora.12170.Gender

Larson, C., Mathée-Scott, J., Kaplan, D., & Weismer, S. E. (2023). Cognitive processes associated with working memory in children with developmental language disorder. *Journal of Experimental Child Psychology*, *234*, 105709. doi:10.1016/j.jecp.2023.105709 PMID:37285760

Lazaratou, H., Kalogerakis, Z., Petroutsou, A., Bali, P. P., Konsta, A., Pirlympou, M., & Dikeos, D. (2018). Differences in verbal and performance IQ in conduct disorder: Research findings from a Greek sample. *Journal of Psychiatry and Behavioral Science*, *2*(2), 1–6. doi:10.33582/2637-8027/1010

Lee, J. C., Nopoulos, P. C., & Tomblin, J. B. (2020). Procedural and declarative memory brain systems in developmental language disorder (DLD). *Brain and Language*, *205*(February), 104789. doi:10.1016/j.bandl.2020.104789 PMID:32240854

Leonard, L. B. (2014). Specific language impairment across languages. *Child Development Perspectives*, *8*(1), 1–5. doi:10.1111/cdep.12053 PMID:24765105

Lu, F., Guo, Y., Luo, W., Yu, Y., Zhao, Y., Ni, S., Chen, J., Cai, X., Shen, C., Wang, X., He, J., Yang, G., Gao, Q., He, Z., & Zhou, J. (2023). Disrupted functional networks within white-matter served as neural features in adolescent patients with conduct disorder. *Behavioural Brain Research*, *447*(January), 114422. doi:10.1016/j.bbr.2023.114422 PMID:37030546

Marini, A., Piccolo, B., Taverna, L., Berginc, M., & Ozbič, M. (2020). The complex relation between executive functions and language in preschoolers with developmental language disorders. *International Journal of Environmental Research and Public Health*, *17*(5), 1–14. doi:10.3390/ijerph17051772 PMID:32182903

Marsh, A. F., Finger, E. C., Fowler, K. A., Adalio, C. J., Jurkowitz, I. T. N., Schechter, J. C., Pine, D. S., Decety, J., & Blair, R. J. R. (2013). Empathic responsiveness in amygdala and anterior cingulate cortex in youths with psychopathic traits. *Journal of Child Psychology and Psychiatry, and Allied Disciplines*, *54*(8), 900–910. doi:10.1111/jcpp.12063 PMID:23488588

Martin-Key, N., Brown, T., & Fairchild, G. (2017). Empathic accuracy in male adolescents with conduct disorder and higher versus lower levels of callous-unemotional traits. *Journal of Abnormal Child Psychology*, *45*(7), 1385–1397. doi:10.100710802-016-0243-8 PMID:28032270

McGregor, K. K. (2020). How we fail children with developmental language disorder. *Language, Speech, and Hearing Services in Schools*, *51*(4), 981–992. doi:10.1044/2020_LSHSS-20-00003 PMID:32755505

Michielsen, P. J. S., Habra, M. M. J., Endendijk, J. J., Bouter, D. C., Grootendorst-van Mil, N. H., Hoogendijk, W. J. G., & Roza, S. J. (2022). Callous-unemotional traits and anxiety in adolescents: A latent profile analysis to identify different types of antisocial behavior in a high-risk community sample. *Child and Adolescent Psychiatry and Mental Health*, *16*(1), 1–12. doi:10.118613034-022-00493-8 PMID:35854316

Moffitt, T. E.-l. –5. (2006). Life-course-persistent versus adolescence-limited antisocial behavior. In D. Cicchetti & D. J. Cohen (Eds.), Developmental psychopathology, Vol. 3: Risk, disorder, and adaptation (pp. 570–598). John Wiley & Sons.

Mohammadi, M. R., Salmanian, M., & Keshavarzi, Z. (2021). The global prevalence of conduct disorder: A systematic review and meta-analysis. *Iranian Journal of Psychiatry*, *16*(2), 205–225. doi:10.18502/ijps.v16i2.5822 PMID:34221047

Mozeiko, J., Le, K., Coelho, C., Krueger, F., & Grafman, J. (2011). The relationship of story grammar and executive function following TBI. *Aphasiology*, *25*(6–7), 826–835. doi:10.1080/02687038.2010.543983

Muñoz, L. C., Frick, P. J., Kimonis, E. R., & Aucoin, K. J. (2008). Verbal ability and delinquency: Testing the moderating role of psychopathic traits. *Journal of Child Psychology and Psychiatry, and Allied Disciplines*, *49*(4), 414–421. doi:10.1111/j.1469-7610.2007.01847.x PMID:18081757

Müürsepp, I., Aibast, H., Gapeyeva, H., & Pääsuke, M. (2014). Sensorimotor function in preschool-aged children with expressive language disorder. *Research in Developmental Disabilities*, *35*(6), 1237–1243. doi:10.1016/j.ridd.2014.03.007 PMID:24685939

Nilsen, E. S., & Bacso, S. A. (2017). Cognitive and behavioural predictors of adolescents' communicative perspective-taking and social relationships. *Journal of Adolescence*, *56*(1), 52–63. doi:10.1016/j.adolescence.2017.01.004 PMID:28157666

Nitin, R., Shaw, D. M., Rocha, D. B., Walters, C. E. Jr, Chabris, C. F., Camarata, S. M., Gordon, R. L., & Below, J. E. (2022). Association of Developmental Language Disorder with Comorbid Developmental Conditions Using Algorithmic Phenotyping. *JAMA Network Open*, *5*(12), E2248060. doi:10.1001/jamanetworkopen.2022.48060 PMID:36580336

Norbury, C. F., Gooch, D., Wray, C., Baird, G., Charman, T., Simonoff, E., Vamvakas, G., & Pickles, A. (2016). The impact of nonverbal ability on prevalence and clinical presentation of language disorder: Evidence from a population study. *Journal of Child Psychology and Psychiatry, and Allied Disciplines*, *57*(11), 1247–1257. doi:10.1111/jcpp.12573 PMID:27184709

Nudel, R., Christensen, R. V., Kalnak, N., Schwinn, M., Banasik, K., Dinh, K. M., Consortium, D. G., Erikstrup, C., Pedersen, O. B., Burgdorf, K. S., Ullum, H., Ostrowski, S. R., Hansen, T. F., & Werge, T. (2023). Developmental language disorder – a comprehensive study of more than 46,000 individuals. *Psychiatry Research, 323*(October 2022), 115171. doi:10.1016/j.psychres.2023.115171

Pardini, D. A., & Fite, P. J. (2010). Symptoms of conduct disorder, oppositional defiant disorder, attention-deficit/hyperactivity disorder, and callous-unemotional traits as unique predictors of psychosocial maladjustment in boys: Advancing an evidence base for DSM-V. *Journal of the American Academy of Child and Adolescent Psychiatry*, *49*(11), 1134–1144. doi:10.1097/00004583-201011000-00007 PMID:20970701

Petersen, I. T., & LeBeau, B. (2021). Language ability in the development of externalizing behavior problems in childhood. *Journal of Educational Psychology*, *113*(1), 68–85. doi:10.1037/edu0000461

Portnoy, J., Cui, N., Raine, A., Frazier, A., Rudo-Hutt, A. S., & Liu, J. (2020). Autonomic nervous system activity and callous-unemotional traits in physically maltreated youth. *Child Abuse and Neglect, 101*(November 2019), 104308. doi:10.1016/j.chiabu.2019.104308

Raschle, N. M., Menks, W. M., Fehlbaum, L. V., Steppan, M., Smaragdi, A., Gonzalez-Madruga, K., Rogers, J., Clanton, R., Kohls, G., Martinelli, A., Bernhard, A., Konrad, K., Herpertz-Dahlmann, B., Freitag, C. M., Fairchild, G., De Brito, S. A., & Stadler, C. (2018). Callous-unemotional traits and brain structure: Sex-specific effects in anterior insula of typically-developing youths. *NeuroImage: Clinical, 17*(November 2017), 856–864. doi:10.1016/j.nicl.2017.12.015

Ricketts, J. (2011). Research Review: Reading comprehension in developmental disorders of language and communication. *Journal of Child Psychology and Psychiatry, and Allied Disciplines*, *52*(11), 1111–1123. doi:10.1111/j.1469-7610.2011.02438.x PMID:21762147

Rinaldi, S., Caselli, M. C., Cofelice, V., D'Amico, S., De Cagno, A. G., Della Corte, G., Di Martino, M. V., Di Costanzo, B., Levorato, M. C., Penge, R., Rossetto, T., Sansavini, A., Vecchi, S., & Zoccolotti, P. (2021). Efficacy of the treatment of developmental language disorder: A systematic review. In Brain Sciences, 11(3). doi:10.3390/brainsci11030407

Robinson, B. A., Azores-Gococo, N., Brennan, P. A., & Lilienfeld, S. O. (2016). The Roles of Maternal Psychopathic Traits, Maternal Antisocial Personality Traits, and Parenting in the Development of Child Psychopathic Traits. *Parenting, Science and Practice*, *16*(1), 36–55. doi:10.1080/15295192.2016.1116894

Rydell, A.-M., & Brocki, K. C. (2019). Cognitive and emotional profiles of CU traits and disruptive behavior in adolescence: A prospective study. *Journal of Abnormal Child Psychology*, *47*(6), 1039–1051. doi:10.100710802-018-0496-5 PMID:30523475

Salmon, K., O'Kearney, R., Reese, E., & Fortune, C.-A. (2016). The role of language skill in child psychopathology: Implications for intervention in the early years. *Clinical Child and Family Psychology Review, 19*(4), 352–367. doi:10.100710567-016-0214-1 PMID:27678011

SAMSHA. (2016). *DSM-5 Changes: Implications for Child Serious Emotional Disturbance (unpublished internal documentation).* APA. www.ncbi.nlm.nih.gov/books/NBK519712/table/ch3.t8/

Saunders, M. C., Anckarsäter, H., Lundström, S., Hellner, C., Lichtenstein, P., & Fontaine, N. M. G. (2019). The Associations between Callous-unemotional Traits and Symptoms of Conduct Problems, Hyperactivity and Emotional Problems: A Study of Adolescent Twins Screened for Neurodevelopmental Problems. *Journal of Abnormal Child Psychology, 47*(3), 447–457. doi:10.100710802-018-0439-1 PMID:29728890

Sebastian, C. L., Fontaine, N. M. G., Bird, G., Blakemore, S.-J., De Brito, S. A., McCrory, E. J. P., & Viding, E. (2012). Neural processing associated with cognitive and affective theory of mind in adolescents and adults. *Social Cognitive and Affective Neuroscience, 7*(1), 53–63. doi:10.1093can/nsr023 PMID:21467048

Selenius, H., & Strand, S. (2015). Superficiality in forensic psychiatric patients is related to superior phonological, semantic and syntactic skills. *Nordic Journal of Psychiatry, 69*(5), 392–396. doi:10.3109/08039488.2014.994031 PMID:25592288

Sheng, L., Yu, J., Su, P. L., Wang, D., Lu, T. H., Shen, L., Hao, Y., & Lam, B. P. W. (2023). Developmental language disorder in Chinese children: A systematic review of research from 1997 to 2022. *Brain and Language, 241*(June 2022), 105268. doi:10.1016/j.bandl.2023.105268

Sidlauskaite, J., González-Madruga, K., Smaragdi, A., Riccelli, R., Puzzo, I., Batchelor, M., Cornwell, H., Clark, L., Sonuga-Barke, E. J. S., & Fairchild, G. (2018). Sex differences in risk-based decision making in adolescents with conduct disorder. *European Child & Adolescent Psychiatry, 27*(9), 1133–1142. doi:10.100700787-017-1024-9 PMID:28688012

Snowling, M. J., Hayiou-Thomas, M. E., Nash, H. M., & Hulme, C. (2020). Dyslexia and Developmental Language Disorder: Comorbid disorders with distinct effects on reading comprehension. *Journal of Child Psychology and Psychiatry, and Allied Disciplines, 61*(6), 672–680. doi:10.1111/jcpp.13140 PMID:31631348

Sonuga-Barke, E. J., Cortese, S., Fairchild, G., & Stringaris, A. (2016). Annual research review: Transdiagnostic neuroscience of child and adolescent mental disorders — differentiating decision making in attention-deficit/ hyperactivity disorder, conduct disorder, depression, and anxiety. *Journal of Child Psychology and Psychiatry, and Allied Disciplines, 57*(3), 321–349. doi:10.1111/jcpp.12496 PMID:26705858

Stevens, D., Charman, T., & Blair, R. (2001). Recognition of emotion in facial expressions and vocal tones in children with psychopathic tendencies. *The Journal of Genetic Psychology, 162*(2), 201–211. doi:10.1080/00221320109597961 PMID:11432605

Stransky, M. L., Oshita, J. Y., & Morris, M. A. (2020). Prevalence of Behavioral Health Problems among Adults with and without Communication Disabilities. *Journal of the American Board of Family Medicine, 33*(6), 934–941. doi:10.3122/jabfm.2020.06.200216 PMID:33219072

Szukiel, B., Górska, M., & Kruk, U. (2017). Differential Diagnosis of Specific Language Impairment-Sli. *Pol. J. Appl. Sci*, *3*, 5–10.

Torres, F., Fuentes-López, E., Fuente, A., & Sevilla, F. (2020). Identification of the factors associated with the severity of the speech production problems in children with comorbid speech sound disorder and developmental language disorder. *Journal of Communication Disorders, 88*(June 2019). doi:10.1016/j.jcomdis.2020.106054

Tseng, Y. T., & Hsu, H. (2022, October). jen. (2023). Not only motor skill performance but also haptic function is impaired in children with developmental language disorder. *Research in Developmental Disabilities*, *134*, 104412. doi:10.1016/j.ridd.2022.104412 PMID:36638673

Tsou, Y. T., Wiefferink, C. H., Broekhof, E., & Rieffe, C. (2023). Short report: Longitudinal study on emotion understanding in children with and without developmental language disorder. *Research in Developmental Disabilities, 137*(January 2022), 104493. doi:10.1016/j.ridd.2023.104493

Ullman, M. T., Earle, F. S., Walenski, M., & Janacsek, K. (2020). The neurocognition of developmental disorders of language. *Annual Review of Psychology*, *71*(1), 389–417. doi:10.1146/annurev-psych-122216-011555 PMID:31337273

Van Daal, J., Verhoeven, L., & van Balkom, H. (2007). Behavior problems in children with language impairment. [PubMed: 17995490]. *Journal of Child Psychology and Psychiatry, and Allied Disciplines*, *48*(11), 1139–1147. doi:10.1111/j.1469-7610.2007.01790.x PMID:17995490

Vasconcelos, M., Viding, E., Sebastian, C. L., Faria, S., Almeida, P. R., Gonçalves, Ó. F., Gonçalves, R. A., Sampaio, A., & Seara-Cardoso, A. (2021). Callous-Unemotional Traits Moderate Anticipated Guilt and Wrongness Judgments to Everyday Moral Transgressions in Adolescents. *Frontiers in Psychiatry*, *12*(March), 1–11. doi:10.3389/fpsyt.2021.625328 PMID:33762977

Vernes, S. C., Newbury, D. F., Abrahams, B. S., Winchester, L., Nicod, J., Groszer, M., Alarcón, M., Oliver, P. L., Davies, K. E., Geschwind, D. H., Monaco, A. P., & Fisher, S. E. (2008). A Functional Genetic Link between Distinct Developmental Language Disorders. *The New England Journal of Medicine*, *359*(22), 2337–2345. doi:10.1056/NEJMoa0802828 PMID:18987363

Wakschlag, L. S. (2005). Disruptive behavior disorders: Developmental pathways to conduct disorder. In D. Cicchetti & D. J. Cohen (Eds.), *Developmental psychopathology*. Developmental psychopathology.

Waller, R., Wagner, N. J., Barstead, M. G., Subar, A., Petersen, J. L., Hyde, J. S., & Hyde, L. W. (2020). A meta-analysis of the associations between callous-unemotional traits and empathy, prosociality, and guilt. *Clinical Psychology Review, 75*(April 2019), 101809. doi:10.1016/j.cpr.2019.101809

Wendt, G. W., Bartoli, A. J., & Arteche, A. (2017). Dimensions of youth psychopathy differentially predict concurrent pro- and antisocial behavior. *Revista Brasileira de Psiquiatria (Sao Paulo, Brazil)*, *39*(3), 267–270. doi:10.1590/1516-4446-2016-2143 PMID:28813114

Whitehouse, A. J., Robinson, M., & Zubrick, S. R. (2011). Late talking and the risk for psychosocial problems during childhood and adolescence. [PubMed: 21727106]. *Pediatrics*, *128*(2), e324–e332. doi:10.1542/peds.2010-2782 PMID:21727106

Willcutt, E. G., Doyle, A. E., Nigg, J. T., Faraone, S. V., & Pennington, B. F. (2005). Validity of the executive function theory of attention-deficit/hyperactivity disorder: A meta-analytic review. *Biological Psychiatry, 57*(11), 1336–1346. doi:10.1016/j.biopsych.2005.02.006 PMID:15950006

Willcutt, E. G., Doyle, A. E., Nigg, J. T., Faraone, S. V., & Pennington, B. F. (2005). Validity of the executive function theory of attention-deficit/hyperactivity disorder: A meta-analytic review. *Biological Psychiatry, 57*(11), 1336–1346. doi:10.1016/j.biopsych.2005.02.006 PMID:15950006

Willinger, U., Brunner, E., Diendorfer-Radner, G., Sams, J., Sirsch, U., & Eisenwort, B. (2003). Behaviour in Children with Language Development Disorders. *Canadian Journal of Psychiatry, 48*(9), 607–614. doi:10.1177/070674370304800907 PMID:14631881

Willoughby, M. T.-K. (2014). Measuring callous unemotional behaviors in early childhood: Factor structure and the prediction of stable aggression in middle childhood. *Journal of Psychopathology and Be.*

Woodward, D., Wilens, T. E., Yule, A. M., DiSalvo, M., Taubin, D., Berger, A., Stone, M., Wozniak, J., Burke, C., & Biederman, J. (2023). Examining the clinical correlates of conduct disorder in youth with bipolar disorder. *Journal of Affective Disorders, 329*(February), 300–306. doi:10.1016/j.jad.2023.02.119 PMID:36863464

Wu, J., Chen, L., Li, X., Yue, S., Huang, X., Liu, J., Hou, X., & Lai, T. (2022). Trends in the prevalence of conduct disorder from 1990 to 2019: Findings from the Global Burden of Disease Study 2019. *Psychiatry Research, 317*(May 2021), 114907. doi:10.1016/j.psychres.2022.114907

Zelazo, P. D. (1996). Impulse control in aggressive children. *Aggressive Behavior*, 1098–2337.

Zhang, R., Bashford-Largo, J., Lukoff, J., Elowsky, J., Carollo, E., Schwartz, A., Dobbertin, M., Bajaj, S., Blair, K. S., Leibenluft, E., & Blair, R. J. R. (2021). Callous-Unemotional Traits Moderate the Relationship Between Irritability and Threatening Responding. *Frontiers in Psychiatry, 12*(November), 1–12. doi:10.3389/fpsyt.2021.617052 PMID:34867494

Chapter 14
Case Study:
Communication Abilities of a Child With Leukoencephalopathy (LBSL)

Ourania Veneti
University of Nicosia, Greece

Pineio Christodoulou
University of Nicosia, Greece

Foteini Christopoulou
University of Ioannina, Greece

Anastasia Barbouni
https://orcid.org/0000-0003-4145-2233
University of West Attica, Greece

ABSTRACT

The present study aims to implement an intervention program on a 2.5-year-old boy with a rare metabolic syndrome, Leukoencephalopathy with brainstem and spinal cord involvement and lactate elevation (LBSL). Although the recorded cases of the syndrome are unknown, there are aproximately100 patients worldwide that undergo treatment. This specific syndrome refers to a genetic biological disorder in expression. An attempt was made to investigate the outcome of an intervention program involving projects based on play therapy for the development of deficit communication skills. The ESCS was used as an approved psychometric scale of communication skills. The results showed that there was a quantitative and qualitative increase in the early communication skills of the child, and also the emergence of a more complex type of play.

DOI: 10.4018/979-8-3693-1982-6.ch014

INTRODUCTION

LBSL syndrome is a genetic metabolic syndrome that falls into the category of Leukodystrophy, in the spectrum of Leukoencephalopathies. Leukodystrophies are rare, metabolic, evolving and mainly inherited diseases, which can be inherited either be being autosomal, in a residual or predominant way or in a sex-linked way. However, leukodystrophies may also be due to random mutations. They were so named from the "white" substance-myelin, which insulates protecting structures of the nervous system, ensuring the high speed of the propagation of nerve signals. Leukodystrophies disrupt the growth or maintenance of myelin, which is due to a multitude of mutations in various genes. Depending on the gene and its' mutation, there are many categories of leukodystrophies.

LBSL is caused by an abnormal variant in the DARS2 gene (Van Berge et al., 2014; Shimojima et al., 2017; Rathore et al., 2017). The people who are affected people are affected in the white matter of the brain (leukoencephalopathy). Without the existence of myelin, signals between nerve cells cannot be properly transmitted, resulting in the development of basic neurological deficits and also having a negative effect on overall nerve development (Stevens & Iowe, 1993). Due to the fact that there have been only 100 reported or recognized cases of the syndrome worldwide there is a lack of the clinical trials that could be made. Having in mind that many combinations of mutation types can cause this syndrome make it difficult to develop a complete picture of symptoms and prognosis (A cure for Ellie, 2023).

LBSL syndrome can cause symptoms that develop either before birth with serious complications throughout infancy or early in childhood which disappear within the first two years of life. However, some people may not show obvious symptoms until school age or adulthood and these symptoms may remain mild for many years. The onset, progression, and severity of symptoms vary. The most common symptoms are spasticity or stiffness of the muscles and cerebellar ataxia, which is the difficulty of coordinating walking and performing fine motor skills (Uziel et al., 2011).

There is no cure for LBSL, nor has any standard treatment protocols or guidelines for affected individuals and treatment efforts focus on addressing each individual's specific symptoms been found. Individuals who are affected may benefit from physical therapy and rehabilitation, as well as the use of assistive devices (e.g. orthotics and wheelchairs), speech therapy, and additional medical, social and in some cases occupational services may be needed, including special education (mdahellas.gr).

Regarding the correlation between playing and the neurodevelopmental level of the child, there has been evidence that there is a positive effect on the child's nervous development when playing (Cozolino, 2010; Levy, 2011; Stewart et al., 2016). More specifically, during the game there is an increase in the levels of the hormone oxytocin (Stewart et al., 2016), as well as activation of mirror neurons (Levy, 2011). These neurodevelopmental challenges have behavioral manifestations in the individual, such as: stimulating the feeling of trust, reducing fear, benefits of the recognition of the feelings for the person involved in the play (Stewart et al., 2016), understanding and response of the therapist to the child's feelings during play time all with the help of the biological process of mirror neurons (Levy, 2011).

The psychoanalytic view of the action of playtime is a theoretical pillar used for the present research. More specifically, the classical psychoanalyst Winnicott (1971) defines a developmental path of psychographic stages for the child's play. Based on the child's interaction with the play object and the presence of the nurturer to provide the child the opportunity for reality. Subsequently, the object exists in the next stage between acceptance and denial as "objectively perceived". And the nurturer acts by participating in the return of what is rejected (Winnicott, 1971). In the present study, the participant is at this stage, in terms of play, and based on this, his attitude to the play was determined by the educator-researcher.

So that there is a physical transition to the next stage- goal stage for the study -where the child can play alone, in the presence of an adult, with the latter reflecting this play. The final stage of achieving a play is the joint play (Winnicott, 1971).

The present intervention was based on the techniques of play therapy, which have Freud as a starting point, already from the case of Little Hans (Freud, 1905/2014), and similar psychoanalytic applications of play therapy by his daughter, A. Freud (Freud, 1965). It also relied on similar Klein applications (Landreth, 2012). In the 1980s and 1990s, play therapy approaches flourished (Bratton et al., 2005), the most important of which are systemic play therapy, Adlerian play therapy, released play therapy (Levy, 1939), and non-directed child-centered play therapy (Axline, 1969; Landreth, 2012). In particular, regarding released therapy, it is a structured intervention that aims with specific materials to help the child release the stressful event and thus achieve purgation. The therapist reflects on the child's verbal and non-verbal expressions (Menassa, 2009; Landreth, 2002). In the symbolic play project that was applied in the present study, the dialogue between the educator-researcher and the participant, which took place after a demanding physiotherapy session for the participant, has the view of released therapy.

The fundamental elements of the non-directed child-centered approach concern principles such as the child's indisputable ability to self-manage events, the approach of the child's developmental stages in terms of naturalness, and the perspective of a developmental path to maturity. The same tendency for maturity is approached as exclusively internal to the child and not hetero-determined (Landreth, 2002).

According to previous research, deficits in communication skills harm the further emotional and social development of the individual (Astramovich et al., 2015). Specifically, in syndromes accompanied by deficits in communication behavior - such as ASD - a deficit in Joint Attention Behaviors (JBA) at 3 or 4 years old is identified (Wetherby et al., 2007). In many studies, this behavior is associated with language proficiency (Cochet & Byrne, 2017; Monn, 2015; Charman et al., 2003; Sigman et al., 1999). Regarding the kinetic discount, which is the main deficit for LBSL, there seems to be a general connection with the communication level. According to Leonard et al. (2013), in children with communication deficits, there is a deficit in the kinesiological level, without a cause-and-effect relationship that has been identified yet (Leonard et al., 2013).

In the present study, play is intended to be a self-healing framework for a child (Landreth, 2002), and the therapist's main goal is to bring the patient out of the condition of not being able to play to the one who is fit to play (Winnicott, 1971). The "project" was also used, as it is a fundamental tool in the interdisciplinary approach and a tool of significant utility for every pedagogical need. In addition, it is a teaching method (Bender, 2012) in which each topic is studied in depth, enabling children to participate in it and events in the immediate environmdnt (Gliaou, Christodoulou, 2002). The projects were organized based on pedagogical expediency and experiential involvement.

PURPOSE OF THE RESEARCH

The purpose of this study was to investigate the effectiveness of the implementation of an interdisciplinary approach and play therapy intervention program regarding the improvement of communication skills and play behaviors in a case of a child with LBSL syndrome.

RESEARCH QUESTIONS

The research questions of the study are recorded as follows:

1. Can the interdisciplinary approach and play therapy intervention program contribute to the quantitative and qualitative development of communication skills in the case of a child with LBSL?
2. Do play therapy techniques framed in interdisciplinary projects have a positive effect on the appearance of more complex play in the case of a child with LBSL?

IMPORTANCE OF THE RESEARCH

This research study is original on a global scale, without any previous relevant references to the exact pedagogical subject for this syndrome. Therefore, there is a research gap, as it is a recently recorded syndrome, in 2004 (A cure for Ellie, 2023). Also, the importance lies in the successful outcome of this intervention program, which positively affected communication skills, according to the ESCS.

MATERIAL AND METHODS

Participant

The participant of this intervention is a boy aged 2.5 years, at the beginning of the intervention. It is noted that the researcher who performed the intervention was the caregiver of the participant on a daily 8-hour basis, from the age of 9 months of the participant. Regarding the participant's profile, he developed LBSL genetic syndrome in the 6th month of his infancy, after his parents observed a delay in the onset of developmental stages, confirmed by subsequent specialized examinations (Whole Exome Sequencing-WES). He is the only child in the family; the parents have high educational and financial levels and scientific backgrounds. The family lives in a big city in Greece.

Due to the condition of leukodystrophy, the participant manifests the following symptoms: he shows extensive hypotension. For the symptom of hypotension, it should be noted that at the age of 9 months, it was difficult for him to stay awake for 30 minutes continuously. Gradually, with increasingly long-lasting play activities and his neurological development, at the age of 2 years, the symptom of hypotension has been significantly alleviated. There is now a significantly shorter total sleep duration; however, the low intensity of activity remains. Before the start of the program, although he remained awake for most of the day, he had rarely reacted enthusiastically to an activity.

Furthermore, the participant in infancy participates in an individualized physiotherapy program. So, at the age of 2.5 years, he is in the kinesiological developmental stage of the first 2-3 months. However, with proper support, he performs a crawl position, upright posture, lifting the lower limbs for gait and gait. He also shakes hands and head, which intensifies in a state of discomfort or euphoria and with proper management-comfort in the arms, removal of provocation, caress-returns to a calmer state.

In addition, he has deficits in communication skills and visual difficulties, as although the anterior organ of vision is not defective, visual processing in the corresponding part of the brain seems to be deficient. Until the start of the intervention program, he made random, instantaneous eye contact at close range of caregiver-infant at a frequency of 0-2 seconds during the activity. He reacted to visual stimuli with visual contact for 0-6 seconds at a random frequency. Also, he did not perform Joint Attention Behaviors at a remarkable frequency and did not show significant and spontaneous interest in play.

However, at the age of 11 months of infancy, after the systematic placement of a baby harmonium in front of him and the direction of the participant's hands to hit the keys by the caregiver initially passively, he began to respond at some point with a mechanical keystroke. Finally, he showed enthusiasm for the first time in Christmas traditional music at 1.5 years old and thus gave the trigger to the caregiver for the organization and implementation of this intervention.

Measure

The ESCS was used in the pedagogical intervention (Early Social Communication Scales, Mundy, et al., 2003/2013). The ESCS is a psychometric tool for structured video surveillance, and this edition assesses non-verbal communication points, as manifested in the behavior of infants 8-30 months or older children with a mental age in this range. It has a total duration of about 15 to 25 minutes.

Early Social Communication Behaviors (ESCB) are assessed by the ESCS, where the classification of these behaviors is determined by whether any Early Social Communication Behavior started as a request for admission of the child (IJA, IBR, ISI) or if a response started as a request of the researcher (RJA, RBR, RSI).

They are classified as: Initiating Joint Attention-IJA refers to the frequency with which a child uses eye contact, pointing, and showing to initiate shared attention to objects or events; Responding to Joint Attention-RJA refers to the child's skill in following the tester's line of regard and pointing gestures (Mundy et al., 2003/2013).

Initiating Behavioral Requests-IBR refers to the child's skill in using eye contact, reaching, giving, or pointing to elicit aid in obtaining an object, or object-related event; Responding to Behavioral Requests-RBR refers to the child's skill in responding to the tester's gestural or verbal simple commands to obtain an object or action from the child (Mundy et al., 2003/2013).

Initiating Social Interaction-ISI refers to the chil's skill at initiating turn-taking sequences and the tendency to tease the tester; Responding to Social Interaction-RSI refers to the frequency of eye contact, gestures, and turns-taking exhibited by a child in response to turn-taking interactions initiated by the tester (Mundy et al., 2003, 2013).

The ESCS was used in three phases to assess the participant's early communication skills. It was applied before the intervention, as a threshold for the entry of the participant in the intervention program-initial evaluation, and then it was applied after the end of 6 weeks of the program's implementation-formative evaluation and at the end of the intervention program-final evaluation. The psychometric tool is free to use and for its credibility, a double blind translation was conducted. However, it has not been weighed into the Greek population.

In terms of ethics, permission and approval was given from the child's parents for the video recording and the use of the data for research purposes. Also, the principles of voluntary participation, informed consent, confidentiality, and communication of results were respected.

Content of the Intervention Program

To investigate the effect of an individualized intervention program-based on the interdisciplinary approach of projects and play therapy-the following program was organized and implemented with 4 projects, total duration 15-25 minutes. These projects were attempted to be implemented daily for a period of 12 weeks, however, on some days due to the participant's hypotension, it was not possible to carry out all the projects.

The 1st music project (6-11 minutes) was implemented as follows: At the beginning, after playing 4 seconds of a familiar rattle, music of a different kind of music per week is heard. The researcher uses play therapy techniques, mirroring, and verbalization for any expressive movement of the participant. For example, "I see you frowned (and the corresponding expression of imitation)" or The participant now laughs and I laugh (laughs). In other words, the researcher's response does not occur only for typical communicative behavioral manifestations, because the repertoire of communication points is significantly limited for the participant. The next developmental stage occurs naturally in the non-directed child-centered approach of play therapy and is based on the importance of the intimate relationship - according to Winnicott (1971). The above is the basis of all types of projects.

Then there is a creative pause of music for 2 seconds. The first 4 weeks are given percussion instruments in front of the participant and the pedagogue-researcher plays with the element of animation and motivation for the participant. In the next 4 weeks, the educator-researcher plays, making regular pauses for a deliberate investigation of the participant's response, i.e. in a possible continuation of the play during the educator pause, the latter to encourage the participant with verbal verbalization and intensity of the mirroring: "You like it, you play the drum loudly with your hands!". While in case the participant stops playing, the pedagogue-researcher starts a new style of playing, expecting the participant to follow. For the last 4 weeks, while the instruments are being shared, the educator-researcher has been waiting for the participant to express himself as he wishes. However, in informal expressive movements, there will be no mirroring by the teacher, but there will be verbal verbalization: "And now you frowned, you probably do not like this music", and suggest a typical communicative behavior, instead of the informal one-i.e. a smile instead of a nod. The unpredictable and successful result was that the participant in his way-rhythm-based movement, relative arm extension-showed a desire to dance, and was done repeatedly after the 6th week.

The 2nd story-tale project (2-4 minutes) was implemented as follows: Each week a fairy tale of progressive difficulty is read. It is preceded by a 4 seconds playing of a familiar rattle and immediately afterwards about half of the story is read. In the middle of the story and until the end, the teacher pauses saying: "And now I become your mirror, as long as I read this story what you do I will do like a real mirror!". The narration continues with mirroring. At the end of the story, the teacher for relaxation makes a constant bow/nod and says: "The mirror is over and we continue because the nice games now begin".

The 3rd project of visual stimulus-image-painting with two colors (3-5 minutes) consists of 3 stages. Initially, the project consisted of images of adapted difficulty with patterns. However, after the participant's regular visit to the ophthalmologist, it was recommended that the visual stimuli be simple (monochrome or bicolor), where yellow and red were recommended. Therefore, the project was reorganized: instead of a patterned image, a cardboard with a color was presented in front of the participant, to investigate the visual and communicative response. Due to the existing visual difficulty of the participant, play therapy techniques for communication skills were not developed, as in the rest of the projects. The colors used were yellow, red, green, and blue, in a circular process. And here the project begins with listening to 2 seconds of a familiar rattle.

In the 2nd stage, the educator-researcher takes a large white paper supported by a solid frame and a marker of a different color each time. She places it in front of her and front of the participant and leaves in front of him a marker of the same color. She then paints a shape as a frame and she involves the participant saying: "Let's paint together!" and supports the participant to participate. The hand of the educator-researcher follows the hand of the participant by withdrawing step-by-step the force, so that the participant takes more and more initiative in the movement, in the context of the theory of scaffolding (Verenikina, 2003).

In the 3rd stage, the researcher planned to use printed Kandinsky paintings. However, following the doctor's specific recommendations the stage was reorganized and each time the final phase of this project was a yellow cardboard.

The 4th symbolic play project (3-6 minutes) consists of 2 parts and was implemented as follows: The dialogues in the symbolic play project were drawn from the daily routine of the participant, in the context of individualization, as defined in the context of differentiated teaching. As tools were used two symbolic figures-glove dolls, the same for the whole project-consolidation of security frame-of different sizes, symbolizing the mom and the child.

Before Part A of this project starts, the sound of the same and familiar to the participant rattle is heard for 4 seconds. It is noted that imitation applies, i.e. any expressive or kinesiological movement of the participant will be encouraged by the educator with the corresponding movement by herself (mirroring). The observation technique is also used. In Part B the dialogues are enhanced by the technique of verbalization in addition to the observation and the mirroring mentioned in Part A. These dialogues are drawn from the daily games of the participant and from moments that feed communication and psycho-emotional shapes for him.

Observation and Recording of Audio-Visual Data

The researcher observed and recorded the audiovisual data that she videotaped for 12 weeks. She kept notes of all communicative behaviors observed, as defined by the ESCS. The coding of the videotaped data was based on the procedure mentioned in the manual ESCS (ESCS, Mundy et al., 2003/2013). It is noted that log tables and numerical coding tables are provided for the ESCB being examined.

Measurement Procedure

The layout of the room when applying ESCS is as follows: a table must be located between the researcher and the child. In case the child cannot sit independently in a chair, as in the case investigated here, his parent can hug him, as long as the child's legs are not obstructed by the height of the table. The researcher sits opposite and discreetly on the side so that all the expressions of the child, as well as the profile of the researcher, are adequately videotaped.

The toys used in ESCS are a hat, a pair of glasses, a comb, three small wind-up mechanical toys, three hand-operated toys, a book with large distinct pictures on its pages, a balloon, a small car, a ball that will roll easily across the table and a clear plastic jar with two additives clockwork toys that fit inside the jar.

RESULTS

Table 1. ESCB from ESCS's initial, formative, and final evaluations

ESCB	1st evaluation	2nd evaluation	3rd evaluation
IJA	2	9	9
RJA	6	10	11
IBR	7	7	16
RBR	1	4	2
ISI	0	1	3
RSI	2	6	5
Total score ESCB	18	37	46

Note *[1]The numbers represent the successful corresponding ESCB, as defined by the ESCS.

**[2] ESCB=Early Social Communication Behaviors, ESCS= Early Social Communication Scales, IJA= Initiating Joint Attention, RJA= Responding to Joint Attention, IBR= Initiating Behavioral Requests, RBR= Responding to Behavioral Requests, ISI= Initiating Social Interaction, RSI= Responding to Social Interaction

ESCB was detected through videotaped observation and data were recorded and processed as indicated in the ESCS manual (ESCS, Mundy et al., 2003/2013). The sum of the total ESCB for each of the 3 evaluations of the scale was found and the results are presented in Table 1. According to Table 1, the highest score of successful corresponding ESCB was achieved in the third evaluation (total score=46).

The percentage increase between the total scores of the ESCB between the 3 evaluations of the scale was then calculated. Specifically, between the 1st and 2nd evaluations of the scale, there was a percentage increase per aver1-2 ESCS = 105.5556%, and between the 2nd and 3rd evaluations of the scale, there was a percentage increase per aver 2-3 ESCS = 24.3243%. It is observed that with the implementation of the intervention program, the ESCB in the mid-term evaluation increased by 105.5556% from the initial evaluation. This high rate of improvement demonstrates the value of implementing the intervention program (Table 1)

Table 2. Initiating and responding ESCB

ESCB	1st evaluation	2nd evaluation	3rd evaluation
IJA+IBR+ISI	9	17	28
RJA+RBR+RSI	9	20	18
ISI+RSI	2	7	8

Note *[1]The numbers represent the successful initiating and responding ESCB, as defined by the ESCS.

**[2] ESCB=Early Social Communication Behaviors, IJA= Initiating Joint Attention, RJA= Responding to Joint Attention, IBR= Initiating Behavioral Requests, RBR= Responding to Behavioral Requests, ISI= Initiating Social Interaction, RSI= Responding to Social Interaction

The ESCB is divided into initiating and responding behaviors. Thus, the sum of successful initiating communication behaviors (IJA+IBR+ISI) and the sum of successful responding communication behaviors (RJA+RBR+RSI) were calculated: summit ESCS1= 9, sumresp ESCS1= 9, suminit ESCS2=17, sumresp ESCS2=20 and suminit ESCS3=28, sumresp ESCS3=18. Then, the percentage increase between the above sums was calculated and it emerged that from the 1st to the 2nd evaluation the percentage change is = 88.89%, and from the 2nd to the 3rd evaluation is 64.70% for the initiating communication behaviors. For responding communication behaviors the corresponding values are 122.22% and -10%, respectively. It is observed that with the implementation of the intervention program, the initiating and responding communication behaviors, in the interim evaluation increased by 88.89% and 122.22%, respectively, from the initial evaluation. However, during the final evaluation, the responding communication behaviors showed a negative sign (Table 2).

The sum of successful social interaction behaviors (initiating and responding) for each evaluation of the scale was calculated and obtained: 1st ISI+RSI =2, 2nd ISI+RSI=7, 3rd ISI+RSI=8. Then, the percentage increase between the above sums was calculated and it emerged that from the 1st to the 2nd evaluation the percentage change is 250% and from the 2nd to the 3rd evaluation is 14.2857%. It is observed that with the implementation of the intervention program, the successful social interaction behaviors, in the formative evaluation increased by 250% from the initial evaluation, which is a very high percentage, demonstrating the high rate of improvement (Table 2).

Table 3. Averages and average percentage changes of ESCB for four projects

1º PROJECT	2º PROJECT	3º PROJECT	4º PROJECT
Average of total ESCB	Average of total ESCB	Average of total ESCB	Average of total ESCB
187	78	74	100
Average of total ESCB 1-6 weeks	Average of total ESCB 1-6 weeks	Average of total ESCB 1-6 weeks	Average of total ESCB 1-6 weeks
112	86	72	111
Average of total ESCB 7-12 weeks	Average of total ESCB 7-12 weeks	Average of total ESCB 7-12 weeks	Average of total ESCB 7-12 weeks
247	67	76	88
Average-> Percent. Change total ESCB 1-6 weeks	Average-> Percent. Change total ESCB 1-6 weeks	Average-> Percent. Change total ESCB 1-6 weeks	Average-> Percent. Change total ESCB 1-6 weeks
16.7215%	111.0217%	210.2613%	44.50244%
Average-> of all Percent. Change total ESCB 7-12 weeks	Average->of all Percent. Change total ESCB 7-12 weeks	Average-> of all Percent. Change total ESCB 7-12 weeks	Average-> of all Percent. Change total ESCB 7-12 weeks
20.2460%	37.6517%	39.1605%	138.8261%
Average ESCB INIT	Average ESCB INIT	Average ESCB INIT	Average ESCB INIT
86	50	22	41
Average ESCB RESP	Average ESCB RESP	Average ESCB RESP	Average ESCB RESP
101	27	52	57
Average-> of all percent change ESCB INIT	Average-> of all percent change ESCB INIT	Average-> of all percent change ESCB INIT	Average-> of all percent change ESCB INIT
11.3526%	59.56014%	78.9936%	101.5792%
Average-> of all percent change ESCB RESP	Average-> of all percent change ESCB RESP	Average-> of all percent change ESCB RESP	Average-> of all percent change ESCB RESP
54.6136%	66.55256%	296.9024%	138.0066%
Average ISI+RSI 1-6 weeks	Average ISI+RSI 1-6 weeks	Average ISI+RSI 1-6 weeks	Average ISI+RSI 1-6 weeks
85	66	53	65
Average ISI+RSI 7-12 weeks	Average ISI+RSI 7-12 weeks	Average ISI+RSI 7-12 weeks	Average ISI+RSI 7-12 weeks
263	50	56	84
Percent. Change -> Average ISI+RSI (1-6) - (7-12) weeks	Percent. Change -> Average ISI+RSI (1-6) - (7-12) weeks	Percent. Change -> Average ISI+RSI (1-6) - (7-12) weeks	Percent. Change -> Average ISI+RSI (1-6) - (7-12) weeks
209.4118%	-24.2424%	5.6604%	29.2308%

Note *[1]The numbers represent the successful corresponding ESCB, as defined by the ESCS.
**[2] ESCB=Early Social Communication Behaviors, IJA= Initiating Joint Attention, RJA= Responding to Joint Attention, IBR= Initiating Behavioral Requests, RBR= Responding to Behavioral Requests, ISI= Initiating Social Interaction, RSI= Responding to Social Interaction

In particular, in the 1st music project, an average percentage increase was observed: aver-> per. chan.

proj. 1 = 18.5490%, from day to day, and the average of the total score values concerning the sum of the successful ESCB of each day of project implementation was calculated: average-> total score ESCB project. 1 = 187. Also, the average of the sums of successful ESCB of each day of project implementation for the period 1-6 weeks was calculated: ESCB project. 1, 1-6 w = 112, and for the period 7-12 weeks: average-> total score ESCB proj 1, 7-12 w = 247 (Table 3).

Following the same procedure, the average percentage increase from day to day of project implementation, for initiating communication behaviors (IJA+IBR+ISI): average => percentage change total ESCB init, proj 1 = 11.3526% and responding communication behaviors (RJA+RBR+RSI): average => percentage change total ESCB resp, proj 1 = 54.6136%. As well as the average from the sums of scores of successful initiating and responding ESCB was calculated, respectively: average total ESCB init, proj 1 = 112, and average total ESCB resp, proj 1 = 247 (Table 3). Furthermore, for each project were calculated the social interaction behaviors (ISI+RSI). Specifically, the average score of successful ISI+RSI, for the periods 1-6 weeks and 7-12 weeks for the 1st project was calculated: average-> total isi & rsi, 1-6 w, 1 pr = 85 and average-> total isi & rsi, 7-12 w, 1 pr = 263, respectively.

Following the same procedure for the other 3 projects, the results are obtained, as shown in Table 3. As can be seen from the results, the 1st music project yielded the most benefits (average of total ESCB = 187).

From the observation of the audiovisual data, for the 1st music project, it was observed that the child's social interaction behavior increased with significant duration (up to 30 seconds) and moments of genuine eye communication, while before the intervention was fragmentary and not integrated into a social context (Joint Attention Behavior integrated with Social Interaction Behavior according to ESCS). The progress in the emergence of joint attention behaviors showed a significant quantitative increase after the 5th week, from 8 to 16 successful joint attention behaviors, and the increase in their duration (from 3 to 10 seconds). As already from the 3rd week, babbling, laughter-expressions of pleasure-as well as prolongation of these behaviors were added, until the end of the intervention.

At the same time, there was a transition of the above playful acts and communication behaviors to the active act of a dance movement of social interaction by the participant, on the second day of the 3rd week, to a musical listening of the classical opera of M.Callas. The next day, while shaking like a dancing movement again, the researcher-educator spread his arms, and then the dancing movement became more intense and was accompanied by the laughter of excitement and babbling, along with eye contact and joint attention behaviors (Social Interaction Behavior). The same move often took place in the following weeks in listening to various pieces of music, with a faint preference for music with a more intense rhythm (Greek traditional music, Scottish and African). In the following weeks, the participant often asked for a dance, moving himself until the researcher-educator held his hands. Gradually on the outstretched hands of the researcher-educator and in the instruction: "Give me your hands to dance" at a frequency of 4/10 times he touched or clapped his hands on the outstretched hands of the researcher-educator (Social Interaction Behavior).

From the 10th week onwards, the participant achieved what in play therapy is defined as a non-directed child-centered play therapy practice. He defined, in his way, this musical game, with nods, facial expressions, movements, laughter, and babbling. Depending on these communication behaviors of enthusiasm or dislike, either the dance continued, the playing with the instruments began or stopped, or the mirroring for the participant intensified. Finally, when the participant was in another part of the house or another context, but with the same music, he asked for a dance, by starting to swing like the above. On the outstretched hands of the educator-researcher he also extended his arms and as he was shaking vigorously, the educator supported him standing and danced in an upright position for a few minutes, leaning on the hands of the educator (Initiating Social Interaction).

In the 2nd fairy tale project, from the 2nd week, the participant seemed to examine the educator-researcher during the mirroring. In the 6th week, on the 2nd day, while reading the story, he approached the educator, laughing with him. In the 7th week, on the last day, during the mirroring, he started stroking the hand of the educator and in the 11th week again in a quest for intimacy, the participant fell into the arms of the educator (Initiating Social Interaction and Initiating Behavioral Requests).

In the 3rd visual stimulus-image-painting with two colors, initially, the child's ophthalmologist gave yellow as the color of choice and then red. The participant had more eye contact with an object in blue, followed by green, yellow, and red. The joint attention behaviors were more successful in the 1st week of the project, 8 times in red, with a similar performance in the 10th week in blue. During the middle phase, where there was an attempt for joint painting, the participant increased in duration the eye contact, the visual contact with an object, and the joint attention behaviors, up to 10 seconds more.

In the 4th symbolic play project, no active interaction was expected in the context of a typical symbolic play, but the early social communication behaviors benefited, too.

CONCLUSION AND DISCUSSION

Based on the results, it was found that the intervention program of an interdisciplinary approach and play therapy direction can contribute to the quantitative and qualitative development of communication skills in the case of a child with LBSL. Also, it was found that play therapy techniques framed in interdisciplinary projects have a positive effect on the appearance of more complex play in the case of a child with LBSL.

The intervention program had more benefits on the child's joint attention behaviors. In addition, it turned out that the music project had the most benefits in the communication behavior of the child with LBSL. According to Carmichael & Atchinson (1997), music plays a catalytic role in situations where the child does not show interest in play but seems to enjoy music. Similarly, the participant had shown interest in moments with music, before the intervention (piano-first game/Christmas music), but also during the intervention, in moments with music, showed the greatest progress in achieving early social communication behaviors. In general, music also aids cognitive function (Rose et al., 2018).

In an overall assessment of the intervention, it appears that after the 6th week of the program, there was a significant increase in the score of all early social; communication behaviors in all 4 types of projects. This result is in line with the research of Stagnitti & Casey (2011), according to which, during the 7th week of play therapy sessions, significant and obvious benefits begin to emerge. Although no formal play therapy sessions are used in this intervention, the results seem to confirm that the framework of the pedagogical relationship developed between participant and caregiver, who later became an educator-researcher, is close to the course of a therapeutic alliance. Moreover, McGarry & Russo (2011) confirm that the pre-existing relationship of trust between an adult and a child is an important precursor to any benefits of the intervention/treatment. However, in this case, the participant does not show obvious signs of a typical attachment bond with any person. However, this does not mean that trust does not play a key role, as in moments of anxiety the participant was always calmer in the arms of familiar people.

Furthermore, the results show that the participant is aware of the social stimulus and in fact, in the course of the intervention begins to prefer it. In particular, he prefers to dance holding hands, rather than hitting the percussion. Also, he shows a greater communicative response to joint painting in the visual stimulus-image-painting project, than at the moment of simple visual stimulation. Although the benefits of early social communication behaviors are increased and/or consolidated, he is not yet explicitly involved in a symbolic play, or mimetically in an experiential storytelling. Other research by Vivanti et al. (2017) confirms that similar social stimulus awareness skills are significantly disadvantaged in ASD, but not in other developmental syndromes such as Williams syndrome.

According to Schietecatte et al. (2012), joint attention behavior requires skills such as social preference, abstract attention, and understanding motivation. In the present condition, the severely disadvantaged joint attention behavior in a free context, which seems to be manifested in a structured context from the beginning, to be established in the course of the intervention and then be transformed into a more genuine social interaction, implies the acquisition of the above skills by the participant. Indeed, the data from the videotaped observation showed that the behavior of social preference (to dance instead of playing instruments, to perform an act of joint attention behavior to social stimulus), of abstract attention (to combine music with movement, as well as he responds to both separately and in parallel) and of understanding motivation (expression of curiosity in the technique of mirroring).

According to Wetherby & Prutting (1984), children with ASD use Initiating Behavioral Requests but do not use Responding to Behavioral Requests with equal frequency. From the distinction between early social communication behaviors in input and response, in the present study, almost the same frequency emerged in behavioral input and response requests (IBR and RBR).

As mentioned above, Winnicott (1971) considers that the therapist's purpose is to bring the patient from the condition he cannot play to the one he is playing. Based on this, the initial purpose for the participant seems to have been achieved, as judging by the progress of the complexity of the participant's early social communication behaviors, he participated in the complex intervention program, showing moments of genuine interest and enthusiasm; a valuable element given his profile.

LIMITATIONS OF RESEARCH

The lack of previous literature on the effort to improve the communication skills of a child with LBSL, through individualized intervention programs is a limitation of the present study. The present study examined other disorders and syndromes that show communication deficits, such as ASD and Williams Syndrome. The sample consists of one participant satisfying the purpose of this research but limits the generalization of the results.

SUGGESTIONS FOR PRACTICAL APPLICATION AND FUTURE RESEARCH

This study provides practical ground for the organization of similar intervention programs, for the same syndrome or for other syndromes that suffer from communication deficits. It would be interesting to conduct a repetitive measurement to investigate whether the benefits of the intervention program are maintained. In addition, an attempt could be made to use this intervention on participants with the same syndrome, to investigate whether the results of the present study can be generalized. This syndrome may be extremely rare to date, but it is still a life struggle for those who deal with it, as well as a trigger for further research.

ACKNOWLEDGEMENTS

I would like to warmly thank the family of the participant for their cooperation and participation in this research.

REFERENCES

Astramovich, R. L., Lyons, C., & Hamilton, J. N. (2015). Play Therapy for ChildrenWith Intellectual Disabilities. *Journal of Child and Adolescent Counseling*, *1*(1), 27–36. doi:10.1080/23727810.2015.1015904

Axline, V. M. (1969). *Play Therapy: The inner Dynamics of Childhood.* Houghton Miffli.

Bender, W. N. (2012). *Project-based learning: Differentiiated instruction for the 21st century.* Corwin.

Bratton, S. C., Ray, D., Rhine, T., & Jones, L. (2005). The Efficacy of Play Therapy with Children: A Meta-Analytic Review of Treatment Outcomes. *Professional Psychology, Research and Practice*, *36*(4), 376–390. doi:10.1037/0735-7028.36.4.376

Carmichael, K. D., & Atchinson, D. H. (1997). Music in Play Therapy: Playing my feelings. *International Journal of Play Therapy*, *1*(6), 63–72. doi:10.1037/h0089414

Charman, T., Baron-Cohen, S., Swettenham, J., Baird, G., Drew, A., & Cox, A. (2003). Predicting Language Outcome in Infants with Autism and Pervasive Developmental Disorder. *International Journal of Language & Communication Disorders*, *38*(3), 265–285. doi:10.1080/136820310000104830 PMID:12851079

Cochet, H., & Byrne, R. W. (2016). Communication in the second and third year of life: Relationships between nonverbal social skills and language. *Infant Behavior and Development*, *44*, 189–198. doi:10.1016/j.infbeh.2016.07.003 PMID:27450099

Cole, M., & Cole, S. R. (2002). *The development of children, the beginning of life, pregnancy, childbirth and infancy*. Typothito/Dardanos.

Cozolino, L. (2010). *The neuroscience of psychotherapy: Healing the social Brain* (2nd ed.). Norton.

Freud, A. (1965). *Normality and Pathology in Childhood International.* Universities Press.

Freud, S. (2008). *The Ego and the Id* (N. Mylonas, Trans.). Nikas. (Original work published 1923)

Freud, S. (2014). *Five medical histories* (K. Liaptsi & A. Anagnostou, Trans.). Epikouros. (Original work published 1905)

Gliaou, Christodoulou, N. (2002). Project method, the importance of the method, what is the final project, the project method in kindergarten. *Modern Kindergarten*, *25*, 14–19.

Landreth, G. (2002, 2012). Play therapy: The art of relationship. Brunner-Routledge.

Leonard, N. R., Jha, A. P., Casarjian, B., Goolsarran, M., Garcia, C., Cleland, C. M., Gwadz, M. V., & Massey, Z. (2013). Mindfulness training improves attentional task performance in incarcerated youth: A group randomized controlled intervention trial. *Frontiers in Psychology*, *4*, 792. doi:10.3389/fpsyg.2013.00792 PMID:24265621

Levy, A. J. (2011). Neurobiology and the Therapeutic Action of Psychoanalytic Play Therapy with Children. *Clinical Social Work Journal*, *39*(1), 50–60. doi:10.100710615-009-0229-x

Levy, D. (1939). Release therapy. *The American Journal of Orthopsychiatry*, *9*(4), 713–736. doi:10.1111/j.1939-0025.1939.tb05641.x

McGarry, L. M., & Russo, F. A. (2011). Mirroring in Dance/Movement Therapy: Potential mechanisms behind empathyenhancement. *The Arts in Psychotherapy*, *38*(3), 178–184. doi:10.1016/j.aip.2011.04.005

MDAhellas. (2023). *Leukodystrophies*. MD Ahellas. https://mdahellas.gr/leukodystrophies/?lang=en

Menassa, B. M. (2009). 2018). Theoretical Orientation and Play Therapy: Examining Therapist Role, Session Structure, and Therapeutic Objectives. *Journal of Professional Counseling, Practice, Theory, & Research*, *37*(1), 13–26. doi:10.1080/15566382.2009.12033852

Monn, E. R. (2015). *Social Communication Across Language Environments in Nonverbal Children with ASD from English and non-English Speaking Families*. [Doctoral dissertation, University of Minnesota]. ProQuest Dissertations and Theses Global.

Mundy, P., Delgado, C., Block, J., Venezia, M., Hogan, A., & Seibert, J. (2003/2023). *A manual for the Abridged Early Social Communication Scales (ESCS)*. Coral Gables, FL: University of Miami. http://www.ucdmc.ucdavis.edu/mindinstitute/ourteam/faculty_staff/ escs.pdf

Non profit organization for research into LBSL. (2023). *About LBSL*. A cure for Ellie. http://acureforellie.org/

NORD-National Organization for Rare Disorders. (2023). *Leukoencephalopathy with Brain Stem and Spinal Cord Involvement and Lactate Elevation*. NORD. https://rarediseases.org/rare-diseases/leukoencephalopathy-brain-stem-spinal-cord-involvement-lactate-elevation/

Rathore, G., Star, L., Larsen, P., & Rizzo, W. (2017). Novel mutation of DARS2 gene leads to a rare and aggressive presentation of leukoencephalopathy with brainstem and spinal cord involvement and lactate elevation (LBSL). *Neurology*, *88*(16 Supplement) P4.174 https://n.neurology.org/content/88/16_Supplement/P4.174/tab-article-info

Rose, D., Bartoli, A. J., & Heaton, P. (2018). Learning a Musical Instrument can benefit a Child with Special Educational Needs. Psychomusicology: Music, Mind, and Brain. *American Psychological Association, 28*(2), 71-81. doi:10.1037/pmu0000209

Schietecatte, I., Roeyers, H., & Warreyn, P. (2012). Exploring the nature of joint attention impairments in young children with autism spectrum disorder: Associated social and cognitive skills. *Journal of Autism and Developmental Disorders*, *42*(1), 1–12. doi:10.100710803-011-1209-x PMID:21360019

Shimojima, K., Higashiguchi, T., Kishimoto, K., Miyatake, S., Miyake, N., Takanashi, J. I., Matsumoto, N., & Yamamoto, T. (2017). A novel *DARS2* mutation in a Japanese patient with leukoencephalopathy with brainstem and spinal cord involvement but no lactate elevation. *Human Genome Variation*, *4*(1), 17051. doi:10.1038/hgv.2017.51 PMID:29138691

Sigman, M., Ruskin, E., Arbeile, S., Corona, R., Dissanayake, C., Espinosa, M., Kim, N., López, A., & Zierhut, C. (1999). Continuity and change in the social competence of children with autism, Down syndrome, and developmental delays. *Monographs of the Society for Research in Child Development*, *64*(1), 1–114. doi:10.1111/1540-5834.00002 PMID:10412222

Stagnitti, K., O'Connor, C., & Sheppard, L. (2012). Impact of the Learn to Play program on play, social competence and language for children aged 5-8 years who attend a specialist school. *Australian Occupational Therapy Journal*, *59*(4), 302–311. doi:10.1111/j.1440-1630.2012.01018.x PMID:22934903

Stevens, A., & Iowe, J. (1993). *Histology*. Paschalidis.

Stewart, A. L., Field, T. A., & Echterling, L. G. (2016). Neuroscience and the Magic of Play Therapy. *International Journal of Play Therapy*, *25*(1), 4–13. doi:10.1037/pla0000016

Uziel, G., Ghezzi, D., & Zeviani, M. (2011). Infantile Mitochondrial Encephalopathy. Seminars in Fetal & Neonatal Medicine. *Elsevier, 16*(4), 205- 215. https://doi.org/ doi:10.1016/j.siny.2011.04.003

Verenikina, I. (2003). Vygotsky' s Socio-Cultural Theory and the Zone of Proximal Development. In H. M. Hasan, I. M. Verenikina, & E. L. Gould (Eds.), *Expanding the Horizon. Information Systems and Activity Theory* (pp. 4–14). University of Wollongong Press.

Vivanti, G., Fanning, P. A. J., Hocking, D. R., Sievers, S., & Dissanayake, C. (2017). Social Attention, Joint Attention and Sustained Attention in Autism Spectrum Disorder and Williams Syndrome: Convergences and Divergences. *Journal of Autism and Developmental Disorders*, *47*(6), 1866–1877. doi:10.100710803-017-3106-4 PMID:28349363

Wetherby, A. M., & Prutting, C. A. (1984). Profiles of communicative and cognitive-social abilities in autistic children. *Journal of Speech and Hearing Research*, *27*(3), 364–377. doi:10.1044/jshr.2703.364 PMID:6482406

Wetherby, A. M., Watt, N., Morgan, L., & Shumway, S. (2007). Social communication profiles of children with autism spectrum disorders late in the second year of life. *Journal of Autism and Developmental Disorders*, *37*(5), 960–975. doi:10.100710803-006-0237-4 PMID:17066310

Winnicott, D. W. (1971). *Playing and Reality*. Penguin Books.

Chapter 15
Using the Language Environment Analysis (LENA) System to Investigate Language Input in Greek Speaking Children

Paris Binos
Cyprus University of Technology, Cyprus

Loukia Taxitari
Neapolis University Pafos, Cyprus

ABSTRACT

This study sought to assess the effectiveness of the language environment analysis integrating wearable audio recording with automated voice analysis, within the context of Greek-speaking families, aiming to discern evolving patterns of child-directed speech in typically developing children. Audio data from children aged 6-46 months were recorded during home interactions. The LENA Pro software calculates parameters like conversational turn count, child vocalizations, and adult word count. The findings underscored a pronounced duration of silence-background noise and distant sounds. Strong correlations also emerged between parental linguistic input, adult-child conversational exchanges, child vocalizations, and meaningful interactions between children and adults. An inverse association between electronic device engagement and child vocalizations was also observed. LENA demonstrates its power in effectively mapping non-English linguistic environments, such as Greek, offering invaluable insights to stakeholders on refining language inputs for optimal language development.

DOI: 10.4018/979-8-3693-1982-6.ch015

INTRODUCTION

Language development in early childhood is a crucial aspect of cognitive and social development. The ability to communicate effectively lays the foundation for various cognitive processes and social interactions. Language acquisition research frequently relies on the use of short recordings of children's spontaneous or semi-spontaneous speech and interactions, periods of in-person observations (Keller et al., 2007) or questionnaires filled by adults (Fenson et al., 1994). Although these methods offer valuable insights into the language development process, they do not come without their drawbacks. Recordings can be laborious and time-consuming in terms of data collection and analysis (Keller et al., 2007), while questionnaires and observations can be subjective, especially when younger children are concerned (Oliver, Schofield & Kolt, 2007). The challenges associated with these traditional methodologies are particularly evident for speech-language pathologists who often face practical limitations due to the costs and logistical constraints involved.

To address these challenges, technological advancements have provided alternative approaches for studying language acquisition. For instance, the use of electronic devices and innovative software has facilitated more efficient data collection and analysis methods. One such tool is the Language Environment Analysis (LENA) system, a revolutionary device designed to objectively analyse and assess the linguistic environment of young children. LENA combines wearable audio recorders with automated vocal analysis (Cristia, Bulgarelli, & Bergelson, 2020). This system allows for the seamless monitoring and quantification of language input in naturalistic environments, offering researchers and speech-language pathologists a more practical and streamlined approach to studying language acquisition (Cristia, Bulgarelli, & Bergelson, 2020). By incorporating these technological advancements and remote data collection methods, researchers and speech-language pathologists can overcome the limitations associated with traditional methodologies, making language acquisition research more feasible, cost-effective, and accessible for both researchers and practitioners in the field (VanDam & Yoshinaga-Itano, 2019).

The revolutionary software known as the Language Environment Analysis (LENA) system acts as a "talk pedometer," which combines a wearable audio recorder with automated vocal analysis (LENA Research Foundation, 2014). It consists of a small recording device, known as a "LENA recorder," worn by the child. The recorder captures and analyzes verbal interactions and sounds from the child's surrounding environment, offering insights into the quality and quantity of language exposure. The LENA software then processes the recorded data to provide comprehensive reports on the child's language environment, including the number of adult words, child vocalizations, conversational turns, and the duration of audio input. Its primary objective is to enable adults, teachers, and clinicians to effortlessly monitor the quantity and quality of language input that children receive (Binos, Papastefanou & Psillas, 2021).

The LENA system has garnered considerable attention due to its unique functionality. By utilizing a wearable audio recorder, LENA records the linguistic exchanges occurring in the child's natural environment. The software subsequently employs automated vocal analysis algorithms to decipher and quantify the amount and quality of language input (Cristia et al., 2021). This valuable information equips adults, teachers, and clinicians with vital insights into the child's language exposure and provides a basis for optimizing language development strategies (Duncan et al., 2023).

The LENA system has been instrumental in identifying language gaps and disparities in children's language exposure. Research has shown that children from low-income families often have less exposure to rich language environments compared to their more affluent peers (Hart & Risley, 1999). These findings underscore the importance of targeted interventions to bridge this language gap and ensure equitable language development opportunities. LENA-generated feedback has led to increased parental awareness of the importance of conversational interactions. Adults who receive regular LENA reports are more likely to engage in responsive and meaningful conversations with their children, which in turn positively impacts language and cognitive development (Ferjan Ramirez, Lytle, Fish, Kuhl, 2019; Ferjan Ramirez, Lytle, Kuhl, 2020; McGillion et al., 2017; Wang, Williams, Dilley & Houston, 2020; Wong et al., 2020).

Moreover, studies utilizing LENA data have revealed the strong correlation between early language exposure and cognitive development. Children exposed to a more linguistically stimulating environment during their formative years tend to exhibit enhanced cognitive abilities, including better problem-solving skills, critical thinking, and academic performance (Adams et al., 2018; Gilkerson et al., 2018; Weisleder & Fernald, 2013). LENA's data-driven insights have highlighted the importance of linguistic diversity in early childhood education. The system has showcased how exposure to multiple languages, when appropriately managed, can contribute to advanced cognitive and linguistic skills, including better multitasking abilities and metalinguistic awareness (Ferjan Ramirez, Weiss, Sheth & Kuhl, 2023).

In the current study, families from Cyprus were selected as the focus group, marking the first exploration of its kind within the Greek-speaking context. The objective was to gain comprehensive knowledge about various aspects of the linguistic behaviour concerning interactions between adults and their children, since language-specific lexical entities is far from uniform across languages. By employing the LENA system, researchers aimed to observe and document the trends and tendencies prevalent in these specific families' day-to-day lives. Studies of language development in Greek, including Cypriot-Greek, have mainly focused on the use of parental questionnaires (Taxitari et al., 2017) or recordings of spontaneous speech (Stephany & Voeikova, 2009; Stephany & Aksu-Koc, 2021). However, these methods focus on limited time durations or subjective judgements by parents. The use of the LENA software is expected to provide a more complete picture of parent-child early interactions, and their relationship with children's language development.

The purpose, therefore, of this study was to record, analyse and reveal conversational turns, input and participant vocalisations in Cypriot Greek-speaking families using the computerised LENA software for the first time ever in Greek language in general. Additionally, the study aimed to identify any unique cultural and contextual factors influencing the language environment within Greek-speaking families (Piot, Havron & Cristia, 2022).

METHOD

Four Cypriot Greek-speaking families participated in this study, each with typically developing children. The children were between 6 and 46 months and were born full-term without any neurodevelopmental or hearing disorders. To this study, these participating families were given explicit instructions.

Families were instructed to incorporate the wearable audio recorders into the natural flow of their daily activities and routines. This would allow for an authentic capture of the linguistic exchanges and interactions that naturally occurred within the familial setting of their homes. The recorded data was then collected, analysed, and subjected to rigorous examination. To conduct a thorough analysis, the LENA software required recordings of at least 10 hours in duration. Four natural interaction sessions were recorded for each child, for a total of 214 hours. Although data were collected for several hours each day, in the final dataset the data from 7am to 9pm were included as children were asleep before and after that time slot. This decision was rooted in the observation that children were typically in a state of rest or sleep before and after this designated time frame. Incorporating data outside of this window would inadvertently skew results, introducing a bias. This would lean heavily towards periods of silence which aren't representative of a child's active hours and might mislead any interpretation of the holistic data picture. The inclusion of the data would, therefore, create a bias towards more silent time which does not occur during children's waking hours and could give the wrong impression in the overall picture.

The Language Environment Analysis (LENA) system, born out of research highlighting the advantages of early language enrichment, is a tool designed to quantify the oral language and auditory milieu (including TV, electronic sounds, noise, and silence) in the lives of infants and young children (Ganek & Eriks-Brophy, 2018b). It is composed of a digital language processor and voice recognition software, operating much like an audio pedometer. This compact wearable recording device, powered by low-energy processors akin to those in hearing aids, can record for as long as 16 hours.

The audio data collected is processed via automated voice recognition software on the cloud and classified using the LENA Pro software, which categorizes sounds into eight distinct categories. These categories include:

- adult word count (AWC), representing words spoken by an adult to or in proximity to the child,
- conversational turn count (CTC), which are the adult-child back-and-forths occurring when one responds to the other within a 5-second interval.
- child vocalization count (CVC), consisting of words, babbling, and isolated sounds;
- and an automatic vocalization assessment (AVA) that encompass *meaningful interactions*, *distant sounds, electronic devices* (various electronic devices, such as cell phones, tablets, TV, radio etc.), *noise* and *silence and background sounds* (Ganek, Smyth, Nixon & Eriks-Brophy, 2018).

AVA provides calculations of the various parameters in minutes. However, to have a clearer idea of the amount of time spent for each of these parameters daily, AVA parameters were calculated for three four-hour time slots: 7-11am, 12-16pm and 17-21pm.

Moreover, the LENA system can differentiate and selecting between segments of meaningful speech (the number of minutes or hours that a child is exposed to distinguishable vocalizations such as babbling, protophones, words etc. during the recorded time), non-speech, and distant speech. Advanced algorithms within the cloud processing system, trained to distinguish adult speech from child speech and TV/electronic noise, are used to acquire these metrics (Magimairaj et al., 2022). These algorithms can also separate the child's speech (LENA user) from other children's speech and non-speech sounds like crying. Not the actual words spoken, but the frequencies of speech sounds and intervals between sounds are used by the software to generate data representing the child's auditory environment's talk volume. The efficacy of the LENA system has been validated across five languages (www.lena.org) (Magimairaj et al., 2022).

The children's performance and language input conformed to the standard scores of the LENA system for typically developing children. The system, however, has its limitations as it classifies these vocals as one CV when a child produces prelinguistic vocalisation in a sequence or a single breath. To identify specific vocalisations in word or syllable structure, human coding is necessary since the software is incapable of calculating shorter recordings of less than 10 hours that may be helpful in language acquisition research (Ganek & Eriks-Brophy, 2017).

RESULTS

Daily Interactions Between Adults and Children

Figure 1 shows the overall distribution of the AVA parameters across the waking hours of children, while Figure 2 shows the mean minutes spent per every 2-hour time slot for the five aspects of the AVA as provided by LENA for children's waking hours. The time spent on Silence & Background seems to be the most prominent interaction in all time slot, followed by Distand sounds. Meaningful interactions seem to be next, although much less than the first two, followed by Noise and Electronic Devices. Figure 2 presents the same for AWC, CTC and CVC. As expected, AWC are most sounds captured by the device, while CTC and CVC are much less. These observations do not seem to differ considerably across time slots.

To confirm these observations, univariate ANOVAs were conducted with all LENA parameters as a dependent variable and time slot as a fixed factor. There were no significant effects for any of the parameters (ps > .05), except Distant sounds ($F(2,190) = 3.44$, $p < .05$). Post-hoc tests revealed a significant difference between the second and third time slots ($p < .05$) and a marginal difference between the first and second (.08). Also, a univariate ANOVA was conducted with Time as a dependent variable and AVA Parameters as a fixed factor. The latter showed a significant effect of AVA parameters on Time ($F(4,1345) = 27.12$, $p < .01$). Post-hoc tests showed that, overall, Silence & Background was higher than all the other parameters ($p < .01$), while Distant Sounds were significantly higher than all other parameters except Silence & Background from which it was lower ($ps < .01$).

Figure 1. Distribution of the AVA parameters across children's waking hours

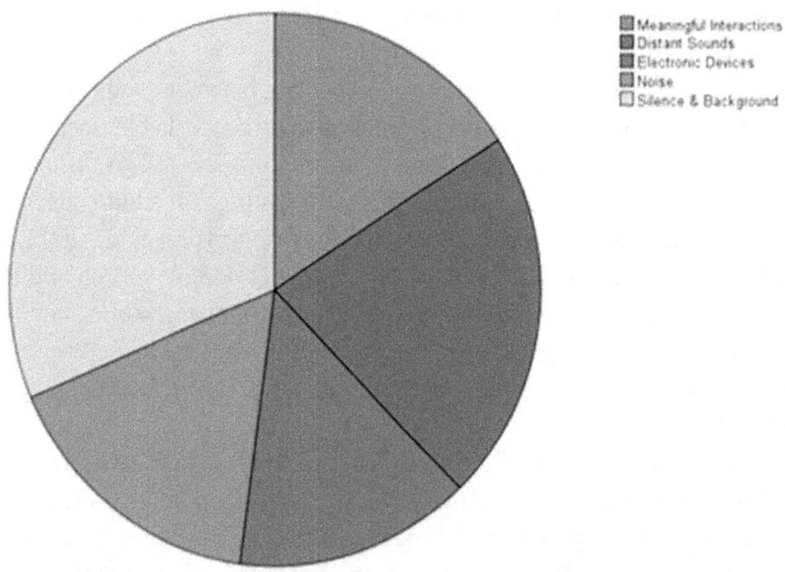

Additionally, univariate ANOVAs were run with AWC, CTC and CVC as dependent variable and Time Slot as fixed factor, separately for each LENA parameter. These analyses revealed only a marginally significant main effect of Time Slot for AWC ($F(2,224) = 2.81, p = .06$, but not for the other two measures (CTC:: $F(2,224) = 1.16, p = .31$ and CVC:: $F(2,224) = 2.24, p = .09$) (Figures 3 and 4). Post-hoc tests showed a significant increase in AWC from time slot 1 to time slot 2 ($p < .05$) and a trend between time slot 1 and time slot 3 ($p = .08$). Time slots 2 and 3 did not significantly differ from each other ($p = .64$).

Moreover, univariate ANOVAs were run for each Time Slot separately, with Time as a dependent variable and AVA parameter as a fixed factor (Figure 2). For all Time Slots, there was a highly significant effect of AVA Parameter on Time (Time Slot 1: $F(4,373) = 8.93, p < .01$/ Time Slot 2: $F(4,373) = 10.14, p < .01$/ Time Slot 3: $F(4,371) = 29.43, p < .01$). For Time Slot 1, post hoc tests showed that Silence & Background was significantly higher than all the rest of the parameters ($ps < .01$), and Time for Distant Sounds was significantly higher from Time with Electronic Devices ($p < .05$). For Time Slot 2, post hoc tests showed that Silence & Background as well as Distant Sounds were significantly higher than all the rest of the parameters ($ps < .01$), except from each other. For Time Slot 3, post hoc tests showed that all parameters differed from each other except Meaningful Interactions from Electronic Devices ($p = .10$), with a marginal difference between Electronic Devices and Noise ($p = .07$).

Figure 2. Descriptive communication environment input analysis per 2-hour time slots for the AVA parameters

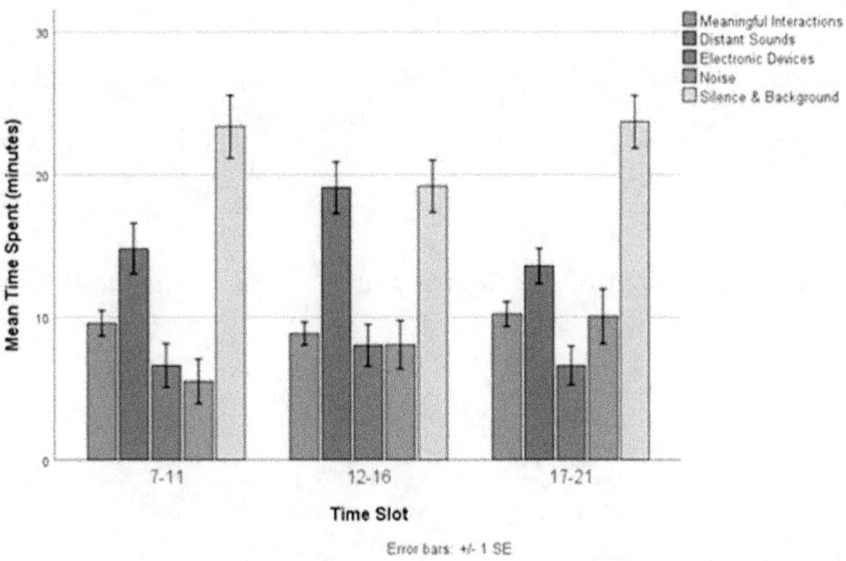

Figure 3. Mean number of turn-taking events and child vocalizations for the three four-hour time slots for the AVA parameters

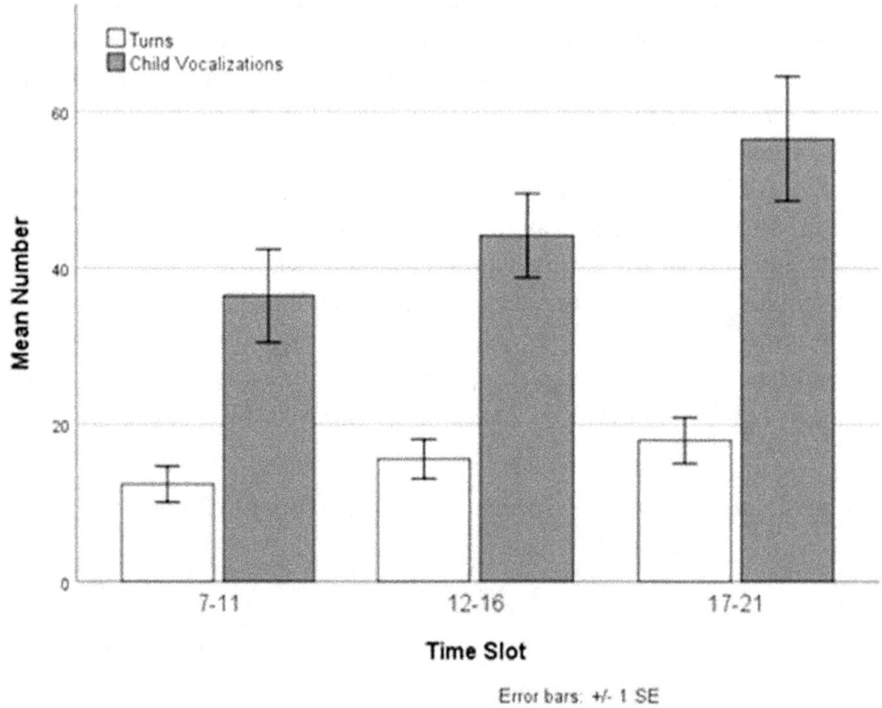

Figure 4. Mean Adult Word Count (AWC) for the three four-hour time slots for the AVA parameters

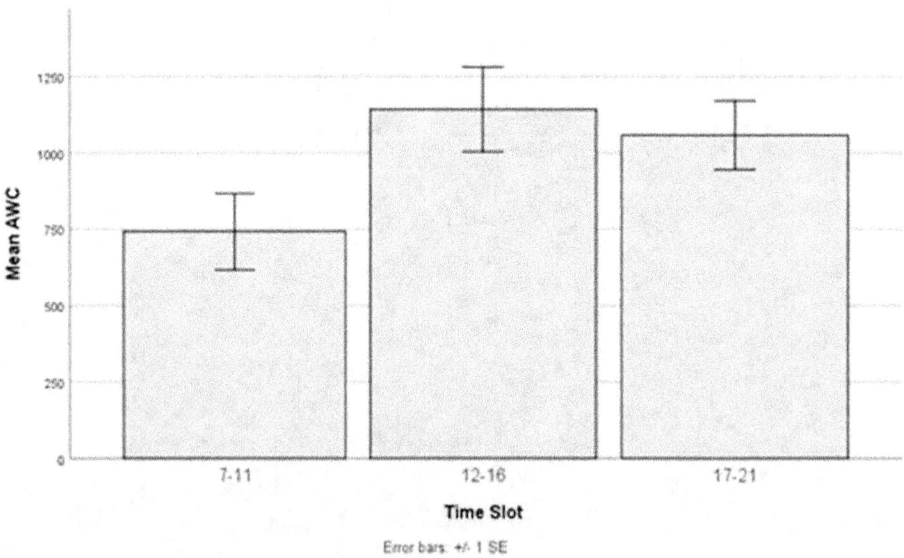

Relationship Between LENA Parameters

In order to test the relationship between the different parameters provided by Lena, Pearson r correlations were conducted for all parameters. This analysis of the recorded data revealed strong correlations (r > .06) between the amount of parental language, turn-taking between adults and children, child vocalizations and Meaningful interaction (Table 1), suggesting that adult speech has a significant impact on the quantity of the child's own verbal productions. Also, weak correlations were found between Silence & Background and each of the above.

Table 1. Pearson r correlation analysis between the LENA parameters

	Number of Adult Words	Turns	Child Vocalizations	Meaningful	Distant	Electronic Devices	Noise	Silence & Background
Number of Adult Words		.784**	.617**	.914**	.143*	-.028	.109	.345**
Turns	.784**		.870**	.766**	.088	-.090	.089	.272**
Child Vocalizations	.617**	.870**		.676**	.159**	-.081	.116	.259**
Meaningful	.914**	.766**	.676**		.197**	-.017	.136*	.412**
Distant	.143*	.088	.159**	.197**		-.204**	-.003	.014
Electronic Devices	-.028	-.090	-.081	-.017	-.204**		.010	-.080
Noise	.109	.089	.116	.136*	-.003	.010		.103
Silence & Background	.345**	.272**	.259**	.412**	.014	-.080	.103	

Finally, to further test the relationship of these parameters, adding a predictive dimension to it, linear regression models with AWC, CVC and CTC as the dependent variable and the parameters of AVA as independent variables were run. All three models were highly significant with the AWC model explaining the greatest degree of variability in the data ($R^2 = .80$, $F(5, 154) = 120.17$, $p < .001$), while the CTC model also showed high significance ($R^2 = .55$, $F(5, 154) = 37.11$, $p < .001$). The CVC model was also significant, but the regression did not explain the variability in a high degree ($R^2 = .35$, $F(5, 154) = 16.29$, $p < .001$). It was found that Meaningful Interactions significantly predicted all three variables (β = [β-value], *ps* < .001). Meaningful Interactions were shown to be the most important variable in explaining the variability in all dependent variables (Figures 5 and 6). Interestingly, the use of electronic devices also explained the variability in CVC ($p < .05$) but in a negative way: the more the use of electronic devices, the less child vocalizations were produced (Figure 7).

Figure 5. Positive relationship between AWC and meaningful interactions

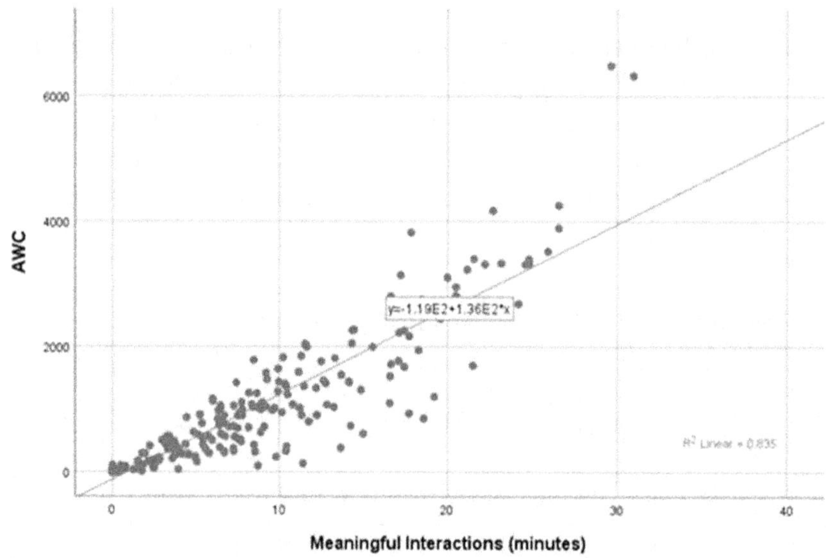

Figure 6. Positive relationship between CTC and meaningful interactions

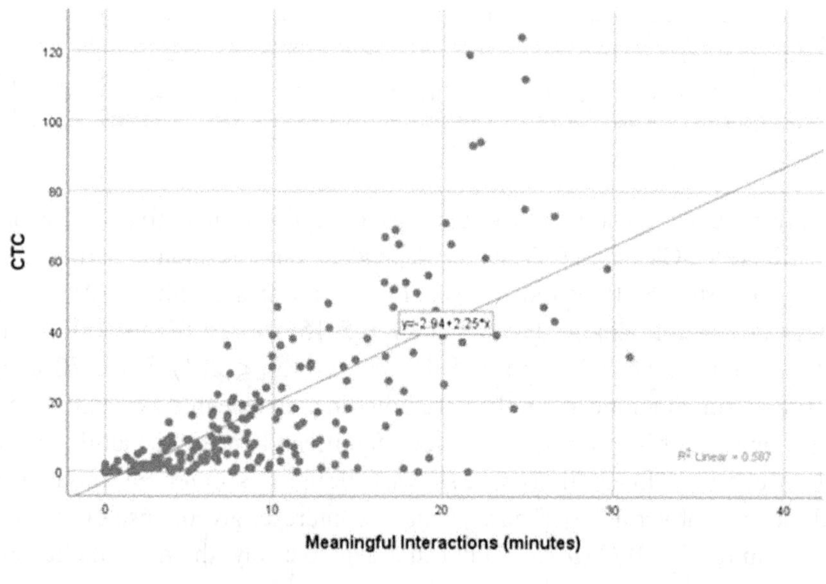

Figure 7. Negative relationship between CTC and the use of electronic devices

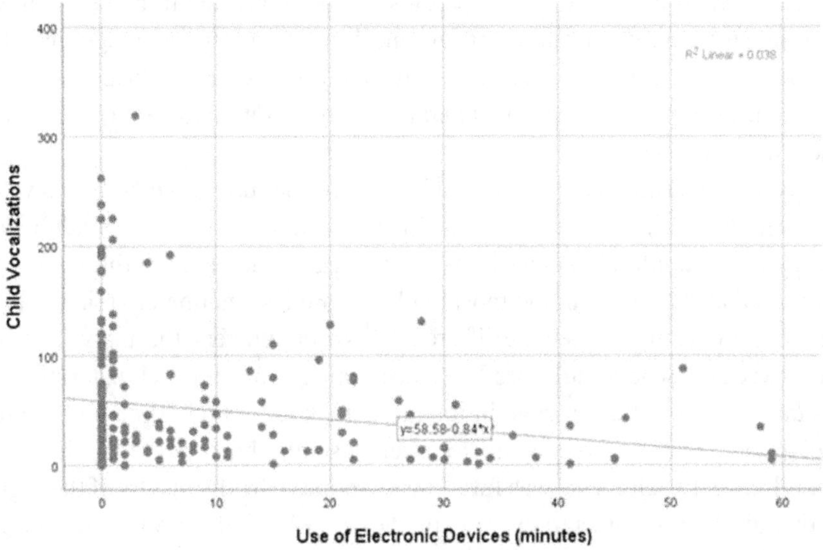

DISCUSSION

The aim of the current study was to shed light into the daily communicative interactions between adults and their young children in Greek-speaking Cyprus and to uncover relationships between the different parameters involved using the LENA device. Indeed, the latter seems to provide very interesting data concerning child and adults' speech practices, which can feed the academic and clinical community with valuable information. Using data from LENA recordings, clinicians can provide parents with recommendations to enhance the child's learning environment.

The first aim of the study, concerning communicative interactions between adults and children, was investigated with an overall analysis of the AVA parameters, and revealed that throughout the day the most prominent sounds involve Silence and Background noises, as well Distant Sounds. The number of Meaningful Interactions between adults and children did not differ from the use of Electronic Devices or Noise. This suggests that over the course of the day, children are only involved in communicative interactions with adults for a small percentage of their waking hours which in fact does not differ from the amount of time they spent in the presence of electronic devices. The division of the children's day in three time slots confirmed the patterns above, with Silence and Background noises being prominent in all three time slots, followed by Distant Sounds. This outcome about the percentage of Distant Sounds can be explained by the fact that the caregivers carried the recorder around near the child, however, not always close enough for the LENA system to record input as meaningful (i.e. close proximity speech). Parents reported that their children occasionally reacted with hesitation to wearing the LENA vest. Similar recording conditions have been reported in literature (Charron et al., 2016) to explain why distant speech is much more elevated than meaningful speech. Also, Levin-Asher et al. (2023) reported a similar longer duration for Distant Sounds for Hebrew speech instead of Arabic. The patterns of Background Noises and Silence can be also explained by the fact that parents of this pilot study never received training regarding the importance of enriching the auditory input by reducing background noise. The data imply that the children's learning environments are not optimal, given that there is potential for enhancing the parents' performance. With this information, parents can be motivated to make the most of these time periods, offering plentiful significant interactions and imparting new language knowledge, including vocabulary and grammatical constructs. The rest of the parameters did not differ between them except in the third time slot, the evening hours, when all parameters were found to be different except Meaningful Interactions and Electronic Devices.

A similar analysis concerning AWC, CTC and CVC for the three time slots showed no differences across the day, except for a slight increase in AWC with morning production of adult words being at its lowest. This suggests that adult talk is less in the morning and increases in the afternoon and evening, which might suggest that caregivers in the morning hours are less inclined to talk to children than later.

Concerning the relationship between the different LENA parameters, the analysis showed a high positive correlation between the words adults produce, turn-taking and child vocalizations. This suggests that the more adults talk, the more they engage in interactions with their children and the more sounds the children themselves produce. All three parameters were also highly correlated with Meaningful Interactions between children and adults. This was further corroborated by the results of the regression analyses which showed that all three parameters were explained at a large degree by Meaningful Interactions. Interestingly, Child Vocalizations were also explained to a large extend using Electronic Devices, but in a negative manner: the more the use of electronic devices, the less the Child Vocalizations. This result aligns with findings from other studies in the literature. Notably, Sosa (2016) strongly asserted that the more time a child dedicates to electronic devices, the less language input they receive. Furthermore, this engagement not only affects the quantity but also the quality of language input, both necessary components of language development (Christakis et al., 2009; Richards et al., 2017). Therefore, parents are advised to limit the use of electronic devices and instead encourage play with traditional toys or reading books.

The role of input to young children has been shown in several studies in the past. The quantity of the adult input, as well as the quality impact clinical outcomes since environmental input, such as spoken language conversation must be delivered to the auditory cortex during periods of optimal plasticity (Cardon, Campbell & Sharma, 2012). It is very important to note the three-way relationship between number of adult words, turn-taking and child vocalizations. Adult words do not contribute solely to interactions with the child, but they encourage the child to produce linguistic output even in the absence of the adult or in the absence of an interaction with the adult, as evident by the relationship between AWC and CVC.

An environmental element, the exposure to language at an early age, is indicative of children's linguistic, cognitive capabilities, and subsequent schǒlastic success. Conversational turn-taking involves a rich experience of high linguistic quality, social and attentional features (Rowe, 2012). The connection between language input, turns and brain structure remains less explored. Through assessing the everyday language exposure of children aged between 4- and 6-years Leonard et al. (2018) found that enhanced adult-child conversational interactions (turn-taking), unaffected by socio-economic status or the pure volume of adult speech, correlate with more robust and consistent neural connections in the left arcuate and superior longitudinal fasciculi. This is particularly evident near their anterior endpoint at the Broca's region located in the left inferior frontal cortex.

Evidently, the results of this study provide valuable insights into the language dynamics within Cypriot Greek-speaking families and highlight the importance of adult speech in shaping the language development of children. By uncovering these correlations and highlighting the impact of various aspects of the audio environment, this study provides a foundation for designing effective interventions and strategies to support language acquisition and development in Cypriot Greek-speaking children. The findings underscore the importance of promoting rich and meaningful language interactions in the home environment while minimizing exposure to electronic devices. Such knowledge can guide adults, educators, and clinicians in creating language-rich environments that optimize children's linguistic growth and overall development (Cristia, Boulgarelli & Bergelson, 2020), through tailored language intervention programs and educational approaches to suit the specific needs and circumstances of this population.

From the current study and previous studies with the LENA system, it appears that the latter offers several benefits that contribute to a deeper understanding of language development and to the facilitation of early language skills. Traditional methods of assessing language exposure, such as parent questionnaires, seem to be more subject to biases and inaccuracies, especially in the early stages of lexical development (Houston-Price, Mather & Sakkalou, 2007; Styles and Plunkett, 2008). The LENA system provides objective and quantifiable measurements of a child's language environment, reducing potential sources of error. The system offers a quantitative and unbiased measurement of the child's linguistic environment, minimizing potential inaccuracies and biases associated with subjective assessments.

Additionally, the LENA reports offer valuable feedback to adults and caregivers about their child's language environment. This information empowers them to make informed decisions about language-rich activities and interactions that can foster language development. Several studies have explored the practical implications of the LENA system for language development. For instance, a study by Caskey et al. (2014) examined the impact of the LENA system on promoting responsive parenting behaviours in mothers of preterm infants and found that mothers who received LENA-based feedback were more likely to engage in conversational interactions with their infants, leading to improved language outcomes.

The LENA system can also be used by researchers to study language development patterns across diverse populations, leading to a better understanding of the factors that influence language acquisition. By analyzing large datasets obtained from diverse populations, researchers can uncover patterns and trends that shed light on language acquisition across cultures, socioeconomic backgrounds, and linguistic variations. This wealth of information informs the development of evidence-based interventions and educational policies. Educators and speech-language therapists can use LENA reports to tailor their interventions and teaching strategies, ensuring that they align with the child's specific linguistic needs. Importantly, by identifying language deficits early on, the LENA system can allow timely interventions. Children at risk of language delays can receive targeted support to bridge the gap and enhance their language skills before entering formal education.

More specifically, in the area of developmental language disorders (DLD) LENA can help in the early identification which is crucial for timely interventions that can mitigate the long-term impact of these disorders. LENA-generated data offer insights into the language exposure and conversational interactions of children with DLD. Comparing these patterns with typically developing peers enables researchers to pinpoint deviations in language environments, facilitating targeted intervention strategies that focus on language-rich interactions. Wang et al. (2017) investigated the feasibility of using LENA-generated data as a screening tool for identifying children at risk of DLD, language disorders, and/or effects of economic disadvantage. Law et al. (2009) posited that language deficits and delays are intrinsically linked to early literacy competencies, preparedness for school, and subsequent academic advancement. Consequently, advanced electronic instruments like LENA, underpinned by intricate software, become indispensable tools for assessing linguistic progression. The study demonstrated that LENA data, combined with other clinical assessments, could effectively identify children who may benefit from further diagnostic evaluations and early interventions.

LENA can also quantify language exposure by providing metrics such as adult word count, child vocalizations, conversational turns, and noise levels. Studies utilizing LENA data have revealed that children with DLD often experience reduced exposure to adult language compared to their peers. A study by Thordardottir et al. (2015) utilized LENA data to explore the impact of early language exposure on the language outcomes of children with DLD. The study found that children with DLD had significantly lower language exposure, fewer conversational turns, and reduced adult-child interaction compared to typically developing peers. Such findings highlight the need for interventions that enhance linguistic input for children at risk of DLD.

LENA-generated data can offer researchers the opportunity to characterize specific language deficits in DLD. For instance, the system can highlight whether the deficits predominantly involve expressive or receptive language, enabling a more nuanced understanding of the disorder's underlying mechanisms. Additionally, it can help distinguish between different types of language disorders which is essential for accurate diagnosis and intervention planning. LENA data can help differentiate between expressive and receptive language disorders by analyzing conversational dynamics, response patterns, and overall language engagement.

In a more recent study, Romeo et al. (2020) utilized LENA data to examine the relationship between language exposure in early childhood and later language outcomes in children with DLD. The researchers found that children with more optimal language environments during early years demonstrated better language development trajectories over time, suggesting that LENA can identify and support language development in both typical and atypical populations, offering researchers, adults, clinicians, and educators' valuable data for their child's current language and for improved outcomes over time.

Ultimately, the Language Environment Analysis system has opened new possibilities for understanding and optimizing language development in children. By enabling the monitoring and analysis of language input, this innovative technology empowers adults, teachers, and clinicians to play a more active role in supporting and promoting optimal language acquisition. Through the exploration of Cypriot-Greek speaking families' linguistic behaviour, this study marks an important step towards fostering effective language interventions and positively impacting children's language outcomes.

The Language Environment Analysis (LENA) system can revolutionize the study of developmental language disorders (DLD). By objectively quantifying language exposure, analysing conversational dynamics, and characterizing language deficits, LENA can provide researchers with a powerful tool to unravel the complexities of DLD. Through recent studies, valuable insights have been offered into the role of the language environment in shaping language outcomes for children with DLD. As the potential of the LENA system is further unveiled in different language environments, we can move closer to more effective early identification, tailored interventions, and improved quality of life for individuals affected by developmental language disorders. Broadening the recordings to encompass language input under multiple auditory settings beyond the home environment will allow for a data analysis that better reflects typical daily activities. This is another constraint of this initial study. It would therefore be useful to replicate our outcomes on a larger scale and with a more diverse sample in future studies.

REFERENCES

Adams, K. A., Marchman, V. A., Loi, E. C., Ashland, M. D., Fernald, A., & Feldman, H. M. (2018). Caregiver talk and medical risk as predictors of language outcomes in full term and preterm toddlers. *Child Development, 89*(5), 1674–1690. doi:10.1111/cdev.12818 PMID:28452393

Binos, P., Papastefanou, T., & Psillas, G. (2023). Socio-Economic Status and Language Development in Hearing Loss: A Critical Appraisal. *Audiology Research, 13*(1), 151–159. doi:10.3390/audiolres13010015 PMID:36825953

Cardon, G., Campbell, J., & Sharma, A. (2012). Plasticity in the developing auditory cortex: Evidence from children with sensorineural hearing loss and auditory neuropathy spectrum disorder. *Journal of the American Academy of Audiology, 23*(6), 396-411(16). doi:10.3766/jaaa.23.6.3

Caskey, M., Stephens, B., Tucker, R., & Vohr, B. R. (2014). Adult talk in the NICU with preterm infants and developmental outcomes. *Pediatrics, 133*(3), e578–e584. doi:10.1542/peds.2013-0104 PMID:24515512

Charron, C., Fitzpatrick, E. M., & McSweeney, E. (2016). Language ENvironment Analysis (LENA) with children with hearing loss: A clinical pilot. *CJSLPA, 40*, 93–104.

Christakis, D. A., Gilkerson, J., Richards, J. A., Zimmerman, F. J., Garrison, M. M., Xu, D., Gray, S., & Yapanel, U. (2009). Audible television and decreased adult words, infant vocalizations, and conversational turns. *Archives of Pediatrics & Adolescent Medicine, 163*(6), 554. doi:10.1001/archpediatrics.2009.61 PMID:19487612

Cristia, A., Bulgarelli, F., & Bergelson, E. (2020). Accuracy of the language environment analysis system segmentation and metrics: A systematic review. *Journal of Speech, Language, and Hearing Research: JSLHR, 63*(4), 1093–1105. doi:10.1044/2020_JSLHR-19-00017 PMID:32302262

Cristia, A., Lavechin, M., Scaff, C., Soderstrom, M., Rowland, C., Räsänen, O., Bunce, J., & Bergelson, E. (2021). A thorough evaluation of the Language Environment Analysis (LENA) system. *Behavior Research, 53*(2), 467–486. doi:10.375813428-020-01393-5 PMID:32728916

Duncan, R. J., Anderson, K. L., King, Y. A., Finders, J. K., Schmitt, S. A., & Purpura, D. J. (2023). Predictors of Preschool Language Environments and Their Relations to Children's Vocabulary. *Infant and Child Development, 32*(1), e2381. doi:10.1002/icd.2381

Fenson, L., Dale, P. S., Reznick, J. S., Bates, E., Thal, D. J., Pethick, S. J., Tomasello, M., Mervis, C. B., & Stiles, J. (1994). Variability in early communicative development. *Monographs of the Society for Research in Child Development, 59*(5), 1–185. doi:10.2307/1166093 PMID:7845413

Ferjan Ramirez, N., Lytle, S. R., Fish, M., & Kuhl, P. K. (2019). Parent coaching at 6 and 10 months improves language outcomes at 14 months: A randomized controlled trial. *Developmental Science, 22*(3), e12762. doi:10.1111/desc.12762 PMID:30318708

Ferjan Ramirez, N., Lytle, S. R., & Kuhl, P. K. (2020). Parent coaching increases conversational turns and advances infant language development. *Proceedings of the National Academy of Sciences of the United States of America, 117*(7), 3484–3491. doi:10.1073/pnas.1921653117 PMID:32015127

Ferjan Ramírez, N., Weiss, Y., Sheth, K. K., & Kuhl, P. K. (2023). Parentese in infancy predicts 5-year language complexity and conversational turns. *Journal of Child Language*, 1–26. doi:10.1017/S0305000923000077 PMID:36748287

Ganek, H., & Eriks-Brophy, A. (2017). Language ENvironment analysis (LENA) system investigation of day long recordings in children: A literature review. *Journal of Communication Disorders*, *72*, 77–85. doi:10.1016/j.jcomdis.2017.12.005 PMID:29402382

Ganek, H., Smyth, R., Nixon, S., & Eriks-Brophy, A. (2018). Using the Language Environment Analysis (LENA) System to Investigate Cultural Differences in Conversational Turn Count. *Journal of Speech, Language, and Hearing Research: JSLHR*, *61*(9), 2246–2258. doi:10.1044/2018_JSLHR-L-17-0370 PMID:30076420

Gilkerson, J., Richards, J. A., Warren, S. F., Oller, D. K., Russo, R., & Vohr, B. R. (2018). Language experience in the second year of life and language outcomes in late childhood. *Pediatrics*, *142*(4), e20174276. doi:10.1542/peds.2017-4276 PMID:30201624

Hart, B., & Risley, T. R. (1999). *The social world of children: Learning to talk*. Brookes Publishing Company.

Hoff, E., Core, C., Place, S., Rumiche, R., Señor, M., & Parra, M. (2012). Dual language exposure and early bilingual development. *Journal of Child Language*, *39*(1), 1–27. doi:10.1017/S0305000910000759 PMID:21418730

Houston-Price, C., Mather, E., & Sakkalou, E. (2007). Discrepancy between parental reports of infants' receptive vocabulary and infants' behaviour in a preferential looking task. *Journal of Child Language*, *34*(4), 701–724. doi:10.1017/S0305000907008124 PMID:18062356

Law, J., Rush, R., Schoon, I., & Parsons, S. (2009). Modeling developmental language difficulties from school entry into adulthood: Literacy, mental health, and employment outcomes. *Journal of Speech, Language, and Hearing Research: JSLHR*, *52*(6), 1401–1416. doi:10.1044/1092-4388(2009/08-0142) PMID:19951922

LENA Research Foundation. (2015). *User Guide LENA Pro*. LENA. http://www.lenafoundation.org/

Levin-Asher, B., Segal, O., & Kishon-Rabin, L. (2023). The validity of LENA technology for assessing the linguistic environment and interactions of infants learning Hebrew and Arabic. *Behavior Research Methods*, *55*(3), 1480–1495. doi:10.375813428-022-01874-9 PMID:35668342

McGillion, M., Pine, J. M., Herbert, J. S., & Matthews, D. (2017). A randomised controlled trial to test the effect of promoting caregiver contingent talk on language development in infants from diverse socioeconomic status backgrounds. *Journal of Child Psychology and Psychiatry, and Allied Disciplines*, *58*(10), 1122–1131. doi:10.1111/jcpp.12725 PMID:28429816

Oliver, M., Schofield, G. M., & Kolt, G. S. (2007). Physical activity in preschoolers. *Sports Medicine (Auckland, N.Z.)*, *37*(12), 1045–1070. doi:10.2165/00007256-200737120-00004 PMID:18027993

Oller, K. (2000). *The Emergence of the Speech Capacity*. Lawrence Erlbaum Associates. doi:10.4324/9781410602565

Piot, L., Havron, N., & Cristia, A. (2022). Socioeconomic status correlates with measures of Language Environment Analysis (LENA) system: A meta-analysis. *Journal of Child Language*, *49*(5), 1037–1051. doi:10.1017/S0305000921000441 PMID:34180383

Richards, J. A., Xu, D., Gilkerson, J., Yapanel, U., Gray, S., & Paul, T. (2017). Automated assessment of child vocalization development using LENA. *Journal of Speech, Language, and Hearing Research: JSLHR*, *60*(7), 2047–2063. doi:10.1044/2017_JSLHR-L-16-0157 PMID:28609511

Romeo, R. R., Leonard, J. A., Robinson, S. T., West, M. R., Mackey, A. P., Rowe, M. L., ... Gabrieli, J. D. E. (2020). Beyond the 30-Million-Word Gap: Children's conversational exposure is associated with language-related brain function. *Psychological Science*, *31*(5), 586–598. doi:10.1177/0956797617742725 PMID:29442613

Romeo, R. R., Segaran, J., Leonard, J. A., Robinson, S. T., West, M. R., Mackey, A. P., Yendiki, A., Rowe, M. L., & Gabrieli, J. D. E. (2018). Language Exposure Relates to Structural Neural Connectivity in Childhood. *The Journal of Neuroscience : The Official Journal of the Society for Neuroscience*, *38*(36), 7870–7877. doi:10.1523/JNEUROSCI.0484-18.2018 PMID:30104336

Rowe, M. L. (2012). A longitudinal investigation of the role of quantity and quality of child-directed speech in vocabulary development. *Child Development*, *83*(5), 1762–1774. doi:10.1111/j.1467-8624.2012.01805.x PMID:22716950

Sosa, A. V. (2016). Association of the type of toy used during play with the quantity and quality of parent-infant communication. *JAMA Pediatrics*, *170*(2), 132–137. doi:10.1001/jamapediatrics.2015.3753 PMID:26720437

Stephany, U., & Aksu-Koç, A. (Eds.). (2021). Development of Modality in First Language Acquisition: A Cross-Linguistic Perspective (Studies on Language Acquisition 54). Berlin & Boston: De Gruyter Mouton.

Stephany, U., & Voeikova, M. (Eds.). (2009). Development of Nominal Inflection in First Language Acquisition: A Cross-Linguistic Perspective (Studies on Language Acquisition 30). Berlin & New York: Mouton de Gruyter.

Styles, S. J., & Plunkett, K. (2008). What is 'word understanding' for the parent of a one-year-old? Matching the difficulty of a lexical comprehension task to parental CDI report. *Journal of Child Language*, *36*(4), 895–908. doi:10.1017/S0305000908009264 PMID:19079845

Taxitari, L., Floros, G., Kambanaros, M., & Grohmann, K. K. G. (2017). Early language development in a bilectal context: The Cypriot adaptation of the MacArthur-Bates CDI. In E. Babatsouli, D. Ingram, & N. Müller (Eds.), *Crosslinguistic encounters in language acquisition: Typical and atypical development* (pp. 145–171). Multilingual Matters. doi:10.21832/9781783099092-010

Thordardottir, E., Ellis Weismer, S., & Evans, J. L. (2015). Continuity in lexical and morphosyntactic development from 2;6 to 21. *Journal of Speech, Language, and Hearing Research: JSLHR*, *58*(3), 587–602. doi:10.1017/S0305000900009302

VanDam, M., & Yoshinaga-Itano, C. (2019). Use of the LENA Autism Screen with Children who are Deaf or Hard of Hearing. *Medicina*, *55*(8), 495. doi:10.3390/medicina55080495 PMID:31426435

Wang, Y., Hartman, M., Aziz, N. A., Arora, S., Shi, L., & Tunison, E. (2017). A Systematic Review of the Use of LENA Technology. *American Annals of the Deaf, 162*(3), 295–311. doi:10.1353/aad.2017.0028 PMID:28824021

Wang, Y., Williams, R., Dilley, L., & Houston, D. (2020). A meta-analysis of the predictability of LENA automated measures for child language development. *Developmental Review, 57*, 100921. Advance online publication. doi:10.1016/j.dr.2020.100921 PMID:32632339

Weisleder, A., & Fernald, A. (2013). Talking to children matters: Early language experience strengthens processing and builds vocabulary. *Psychological Science, 24*(11), 2143–2152. doi:10.1177/0956797613488145 PMID:24022649

Wong, K., Thomas, C., & Boben, M. (2020). Providence talks: A citywide partnership to address early childhood language development. *Studies in Educational Evaluation, 64*, 100818. doi:10.1016/j.stueduc.2019.100818

Zimmerman, F. J., Gilkerson, J., Richards, J. A., Christakis, D. A., Xu, D., Gray, S., & Yapanel, U. (2009). Teaching by listening: The importance of adult-child conversations to language development. *Pediatrics, 124*(1), 342–349. doi:10.1542/peds.2008-2267 PMID:19564318

Chapter 16
The Human Side of Dyslexia:
An Exploration of Children's Self-Esteem and Potential Interventions

Fani Nasika
Hellenic Open University, Greece

Theodosia Thoma
Ministry of Education, Greece

ABSTRACT

This chapter explores self-esteem and dyslexia and potential holistic interventions. Despite the increased interest from different scientific disciplines, dyslexia remains a complex construct. Moreover, dyslexia and self-esteem constitute a field of limited research. Evidence suggests that dyslexia tends to negatively affect academic self-esteem, although it may not be necessarily associated with negative global self-esteem. Research has produced mixed findings regarding factors that may affect the self-esteem of children with dyslexia, such as placement and diagnosis. Yet, it has been supported that intervention on self-esteem may improve self-perception and academic performance. In this respect, there is also strong evidence about the positive contribution in the intervention of significant others such as a supportive family, teachers, and peers. Therefore, it is important to supplement literacy instruction interventions with counselling services and socio-emotional support to promote the development of students' self-concept, self-advocacy, coping and emotional regulation skills.

INTRODUCTION

Over the past decades, dyslexia has intrigued the interest of experts from various disciplines such as medicine, psychology, linguistics, pedagogy and social sciences assessing all its different facets (Helland, 2020). However, research has been mainly conducted within the strand of linguistic theory (Uppstad & Tønnessen, 2007) and has focused upon issues of etiology and remediation, neglecting the human side of dyslexia, that is the personal and socio-emotional needs of children with dyslexia (Burden, 2005). In fact, there has been a paucity of research on dyslexia and self-esteem (Burden, 2008; Glazzard, 2010),

DOI: 10.4018/979-8-3693-1982-6.ch016

although self-esteem is suggested to play a significant role in children's psychological wellbeing, social functioning and cognitive development (Paulus et al., 2018). Both children's and adults' performance on different tasks (e.g., work, school) tend to be related to their self-perceptions (Cvencek et al., 2018). Education has set the boosting of students' self-concept as a goal and a desirable outcome, since it may act as mediator facilitating academic achievement (Shavelson & Bolus, 1982). Therefore, the intention of the present paper is to discuss the emotional aspects of dyslexia in association with children's self-perceptions. More specifically, the paper will provide an overview of recent literature analysing the notion of dyslexia, the notions of global self-esteem and specific-domain self-concepts, the relationship between dyslexia and children's self-perceptions and feelings towards themselves, as well as proposed interventions.

The Concept of Dyslexia

Although over the last years dyslexia has received increased attention by experts from different disciplines (Helland, 2020), it remains vaguely defined (Paradice, 2001). The field has not managed so far to develop a universally accepted and precise operational definition. Even worse, a variety of related terms have been employed and used interchangeably and synonymously to the term dyslexia (Elliot & Grigorenko, 2014). The discrepancy definition of dyslexia, which was initially employed, argued that there is a distinction between actual reading ability and expected reading ability based on intelligence measures. However, it received criticism because it failed to identify the reading differences between children with dyslexia and children with general learning difficulties and perceived dyslexia solely in terms of poor reading (Snowling et al., 2020). More recently, the Diagnostic and Statistical Manual (DSM-V) of the American Psychiatric Association (APA, 2013) categorizied dyslexia (or specific learning disorder with impairment in reading) to specific learning disorders. More specifically, it defined dyslexia as "an alternative term used to refer to a pattern of learning difficulties characterized by problems with accurate or fluent word recognition, poor decoding, and poor spelling abilities" (APA, 2013, p. 67). DSM-V definition was perceived as progress; the identification criteria provide a detailed report of the difficulties in reading, writing or mathematics and acknowledge that, besides childhood, dyslexia may affect adulthood (Maia et al., 2017). Yet, DSM-V has received criticisms, because it relies on Response to Intervention (RTI) for documenting difficulties and this may lead to late diagnosis or even underdiagnosis in cases of children with dyslexia who perhaps have been working hard and have average attainment levels (Cunnigham, 2021).

Interestingly, most definitions tend to attribute difficulties of dyslexia solely to within-person characteristics. However, dyslexia-type difficulties have become a disability due to the huge emphasis placed upon literacy and the implications of being "illiterate" in modern societies (Riddick, 2001). According to Frith (1999), dyslexia is a neuro-developmental difficulty, but individuals with dyslexia suffer in contexts where literacy is a priority, especially in languages with complex orthographies. The acknowledgment of societal and cultural factors in defining dyslexia would perhaps provide a more holistic understanding and eliminate potential burdens.

Regarding the prevalence of dyslexia, it is considered to be the commonest learning disability among school children; however, the rates are uncertain and existing data is limited and outdated (Barbiero et al., 2012). Although literature suggests dyslexia ranges between less than 5% to 20%, a definite rate may be elusive because of the uncertainty surrounding the cut-off points for identification on the continuous distribution, differences in operational definitions and unreliabilities in the diagnostic processes (Wagner et al., 2020). Moreover, there seems to be rate variability across different nationalities which may be attributed to language differences. For instance, reading disabilities tend to be infrequent in Japan and countries of southern Europe in comparison to countries of northern Europe and North America (Vlachos et al., 2013). Generally, logographic systems and shallow orthographic systems have been seen as more "dyslexia-friendly". However, Yang et al. (2022) suggest non-significant differences in the dyslexia prevalence across different writing systems and orthographic depths, but in boys it was considerably higher than girls.

As far as etiology is concerned, a variety of theories have been suggested mainly lying within the neurobiological and cognitive disciplines. For instance, following neurobiological approaches, research has shown that dyslexia is inherited within families by 40% to 80% (Schumacher et al., 2007). Specific genes (such as DYX1-DYX9, FOXP2, etc.) have also been associated with dyslexia (Rahul & Ponniah, 2021). Moreover, neuroanatomical evidence has shown subtle abnormalities in perisylvian regions of the left hemisphere in individuals with dyslexia (Galaburda, 1993). Regarding cognitive approaches, deficits in the information processing, speech processing, and motor or temporal processing mechanisms have been postulated (Frith, 2002). Furthermore, it is assumed that there is a working memory deficit, affecting the phonological, orthographic and morphological loop (Roitsch & Watson, 2019). In this respect, the phonological deficit theory is considered the predominant theory in the field (Riddick, 1996) and claims that impaired phonological awareness skills impede reading accuracy. Other explanations of dyslexia have been proposed by the double-deficit hypothesis, the auditory and visual processing hypotheses, the magnocellular theory, the automaticity account and the attentional deficit (Stein, 2018).

There have also been attempts to synthesize different theories and develop a more holistic explanation of dyslexia. In this context, Frith (2002) suggested the three-levels framework as a causal model for developmental disorders, including dyslexia. In this model, three distinct levels (the biological, the cognitive and the behavioural level) interact with the environmental factor, which includes adequate teaching methods, the socio-cultural context and stances about dyslexia, along with the type of language system and socioeconomic factors. This model considers dyslexia as part of a system of potential causal factors, interacting with each other, and takes into consideration individual variability, developmental changes, differences in severity and personality. In addition, it approaches dyslexia diagnosis and, consequently, intervention holistically and multi-dimensionally.

The main characteristics of dyslexia include slow and effortful reading, errors in decoding graphemes to phonemes, omissions or transpositions of letters, difficulties with phonological awareness, spelling errors, etc.. These difficulties may vary based on the transparency level of the writing system of each language and its grapheme-to-phoneme mapping (Peterson & Pennington, 2012; APA, 2013). Research suggests that although dyslexia characteristics mainly manifest in learning, dyslexia implications are evident in individuals in far-reaching ways than that of learning (Nalavany et al., 2018) and can have persisting emotional effects on individuals' lives placing them at a risk of unsatisfactory life outcomes (Cunningham, 2021). For instance, learners with dyslexia may also exhibit anxiety, depression, disruptive behaviours, low self-esteem, and difficulties in emotional regulation. Furthermore, dyslexia may lead to low academic achievement, school drop-out, unemployment and low income (Lithari, 2019; Boyes et al., 2020). Moreover, dyslexia might affect negatively students' social interactions and experiences as well as their self-advocacy skills (Ross, 2021). It also seems that students may develop feelings of inferiority, frustration, and stigmatization resulting in learned helplessness, apprehension towards school and low motivation (Lithari, 2019). In addition, Boyes et al. (2020) suggested that children with dyslexia might show behavioural and emotional problems that can be externalized or internalized. Yet, characteristics should be perceived within a spectrum of individuality, since all people with dyslexia are different and unique.

Self-Related Concepts

Over the last years, research in educational psychology has established a positive correlation between a child's behaviour and achievements and one's feelings towards self (Lawrence, 2006). Therefore, prior to proceeding to the exploration of the self-aspects in dyslexia, it seems important to define self-related terms such as self-concept, self-image and self-esteem. This though emerges as a demanding task; until recently such terms tended to be used interchangeably to describe the same notion (Lawrence, 2006), although they have interrelated but distinct meanings (Riddick, 1996). Such lack of consensus reflects upon the variety of theoretical self-esteem conceptualizations proposed by researchers, ranging from one-dimensional to multidimensional and hierarchical models (Rentzsch et al., 2016).

Initially, the main body of research adopted one-dimensional models that perceive self-esteem as a single general entity - a global evaluation of the self - without differentiating between the facets of self-concept - these are one's specific evaluations of personal abilities in certain areas (Brunner et al., 2010). Early research received criticism for lacking theoretical grounding, appropriate measurement instruments, methodological soundness and consistent results (Marsh, 1990). Therefore, over the last decades, writers focused on multidimensional conceptualisations which consider the sub-factors of self-esteem (Rosenberg, 1995; Brunner et al., 2010). In fact, a person may demonstrate negative self-concept in one area but a positive self-concept in another area and so, instruments of global self-esteem tend to be ineffective for specific-domain self-concepts (Marsh & Hau, 2003). As a result, many theories and measurement instruments have been generated, varying in terms of specificity and the number of the included self-concept sub-domains (Coelho et al., 2020).

Shavelson's et al. (1976) multidimensional hierarchical model is considered the most influential in research (Rentzsch et al., 2016). As they broadly defined, self-concept is individuals' perceptions of themselves. Such perceptions are created through interactive experiences with the environment, and they are particularly affected by significant others' evaluations and reinforcement. A reciprocal relationship has been suggested, between self-perceptions and one's actions. The model indicates that self-esteem is the general level of self-concept, which comprises academic self-concept and three facets of non-academic self-concept: social, emotional and physical self-concept. General academic self-concept is further differentiated into specific school-subject domains (e.g., English, history, math) (Shavelson et al., 1976). Given that the model explores academic achievement, it has been considered useful in research regarding the relationship between attainment and self-concept (Köller & Baumert, 2006). Finally, general self-concept is considered firm, yet it becomes progressively situation-specific when moving down the hierarchy and increasingly multi-faceted as a person moves towards adulthood (Shavelson et al., 1976).

Lawrence (2006) proposed a differed hierarchical model according to which self-concept is an overarching entity which embraces self-image, ideal-self and self-esteem. Self-concept has been defined "as the sum total of an individual's mental and physical characteristics and his/her evaluation of them" (Lawrence, 2006, p.2). Self-image is one's understanding of their mind and body traits. It starts at an early age and develops with environmental experiences. Ideal-self relates to the human one would wish to become. As a child grows up, there is a realization that there are certain standards in terms of behavior and skills that are highly valued. Such standards derive from family, school, peers and media, but become less influential as a person matures. Finally, the deviation between the ideal-self and self-image forms one's self-esteem; it is considered a normal phenomenon, but in case there is a huge discrepancy between the two entities regarding a valued skill, this may provoke negative feelings (Lawrence, 2006).

In line with modern hierarchical conceptions of self-esteem, Humphrey (2002) has provided a different model which conceptualises self (or self-perception) as a wide notion at the apex of the hierarchy, embracing self-concept, ideal-self and self-esteem and describing their relationship. Self-perception is more than a simplistic sum of the consisting schemas, involving individuals' sentiments, thoughts, beliefs and stances. Finally, in this model, self-esteem derives from the associations between ideal-self and self-concept.

Based on the models previously mentioned, it has been made apparent that different researchers conceptualise self-related notions variously. Arens et al. (2021) provided a thorough review of key academic self-esteem models (e.g., higher-order factor model, bifactor exploratory structural equation model, Marsh/Shavelson model, nested Marsh/Shavelson model, and first-order factor model). However, the present study does not provide a systematic analysis of all models that have been developed to address self-esteem, because its intention is mainly to clarify key terms and highlight the complexity of the phenomenon as reflected in the variety of conceptualisations.

Since the focus of this study is on dyslexia, academic self-concept emerges as a key issue demanding clarification. Academic self-concept includes personal evaluations of one's ability generally as well as regarding certain skills in specific academic subjects (Shavelson et al., 1976). In the academic context, a distinction between specific academic self-concept areas and global self-esteem is significant (Köller & Baumert, 2006), as achievement in certain academic areas (e.g., math) seems to be less inter-related to global self-esteem than to corresponding academic self-concepts (Marsh & Craven, 2006). Academic self-concept is multidimensional and hierarchically organised, with global self-concept at the top of the hierarchy and domain-specific academic self-concepts at a lower level (Arens et al., 2021). There is still debate regarding the direction of influences between academic attainment and academic self-concepts, however reciprocal effects have been mentioned (Köller & Baumert, 2006). Moreover, the extent of change in academic self-concepts seems uncertain, since longitudinal studies have produced mixed results (Sherrer & Preckel, 2019). Yet, it is important that academic self-concept is open to change and can possibly be promoted by educational interventions (O'Mara et al., 2006).

Ultimately, multiple factors affect self-esteem. Among these factors, family characteristics, such as intimacy during childhood and parental care, seem to be strongly connected to adolescents' self-esteem (Chen & Ma, 2023). A secure attachment relationship is assumed to have a positive impact upon the perception of self and upon the relationships with others (Paulus et al., 2018). Paulus et al. (2018) indicated that the child's social self-concept can be predicted by mothers' early sensitivity. Apparently, individuals' self-concept reflects how they are evaluated by significant others (Lachowicz-Tabaczek & Śniecińska, 2011). Moreover, school climate and relationships with teachers play a significant role in adolescents' self-esteem (Chen & Ma, 2023; Scherrer et al., 2022). Interpersonal relationships can also affect self-esteem; adolescents who have close friendships during school years obtain a higher self-esteem as opposed to those who may have only a few friends (Chen & Ma, 2023). Finally, research has also suggested that self-esteem has a genetic basis (Neiss et al., 2005). The variety of factors affecting self-esteem implies the complexity surrounding the phenomenon. From another perspective though, it could be seen as an opportunity for multiplicity of interventions on all sorts of levels.

Dyslexia and Self-Esteem

The contribution of self-esteem in children's psychological, social and cognitive development is significant (Paulus et al., 2018). Yet, research on self-esteem and dyslexia is limited (Burden, 2008; Glazzard, 2010). The present review will explore dyslexia in relation to the major aspects of self, such as global self-esteem, academic self-concept and social self-concept. Moreover, among the multiplicity of factors that influence self-esteem, the role of educational context and diagnosis will be mostly discussed because they constitute areas of possible educational modifications.

As far as global self-esteem is concerned, a recent review of relevant research examining the association between self-esteem and dyslexia reveals that findings are mixed (Gibby-Leversuch et al., 2021). Some studies advocate that there is clearly a negative association between dyslexia and children's self-concept and self-esteem (e.g., Humprey, 2002; Humphrey & Mullin, 2002). University students with dyslexia presented lowered general self-esteem and reported increased anxiety (Riddick et al., 1999). However, meta-analytic reviews have shown insignificant differences in global self-esteem for students with or without dyslexia, which suggests that literacy difficulties and dyslexia are not associated straightforwardly with low global self-esteem (Gibby-Leversuch et al., 2021; Zeleke, 2004). In fact, reduced levels of learned helplessness and depression, more interestingly, high levels of locus of control, self-efficacy, and engagement to effort as a required strategy for learning have been mentioned by children with dyslexia attending specialised educational contexts (Burben & Burdett, 2005). Academic self-concept tends to be lowered for children with dyslexia, but it does not inevitably influence general self-esteem (Gibby-Leversuch et al., 2021; Kloomak & Cosden, 1994; Terras et al., 2009). Supportive family, positive social relations with teachers and peers as well as success recognition in other domains are protective factors of positive self-esteem, while differences in research results can be explained by the employment of different definitions and measurement instruments for self-esteem (Gibby-Leversuch et al., 2021). Moreover, it has been proposed that instruments of global self-esteem cannot describe it efficiently - and can even be misleading about one's feelings (Burden, 2008) and self-concept in specific domains (Marsh & Hau, 2003).

Since dyslexia is primarily an educational issue, it is likely to have implications on academic self-concept, which may also influence the child's learning identity (Burden, 2005). Zeleke's (2004) review indicated that approximately 89% of the examined studies reported significantly more negative academic self-concept for children with learning difficulties compared to their peers. Children and young people with dyslexia or literacy difficulties have more possibilities of developing negative self-concepts in domains which are directly associated with their difficulties such as reading, writing and academic achievement (Gibby-Leversuch et al., 2021). Research in Greek students with dyslexia suggested consistently lower academic self-concept in all domains, apart from practical ability, in comparison to their high achieving peers (Polychroni et al., 2006). Seen from another perspective though, lower academic self-concept implies a realistic perception of academic ability. Once children with dyslexia learn to manage their difficulties, it is assumed that academic self-concept will be enhanced; if they do not receive appropriate assistance, academic self-concept will possibly remain stable or deteriorate (Burden, 2008). The way children with dyslexia perceive their learning ability can be affected by their attributional style and the factors they consider responsible for their academic success and/or failure, the quality of the relationships they have with parents and peers and their stand towards dyslexia (Gibby-Leversuch et al., 2019). The multiplicity of involved factors may make self-esteem enhancement complex and a challenge for designing appropriate intervention programmes.

The development of social identity and positive social self-concept is a procedure of social learning (Humphrey, 2002) and it is an area impacted by social interactions, expectations, and experiences. It also seems to be influenced by significant others, including parents, peers, and teachers. These relationships and interactions can have variable effects on self-concept, especially when it comes to comparisons against peers regarding academic performance. There have been concerns about the impact of dyslexia on social relations, leading to isolation and behavioural difficulties (Burden, 2008). Children with learning difficulties are likely to face difficulties in social relationships with peers (Terras et al., 2009), be less accepted and experience bullying (Eaude, 1999; Glazzard, 2010). School and academic matters can contribute to feelings of loneliness and exclusion, with these becoming more evident in mainstream settings (Humphrey & Mullin, 2002). Given that academic achievement supports social life significantly, failing academically can threaten children's social integration (Rohmer et al., 2022). However, Burden (2008) suggests there is inadequate proof of an association between dyslexia and low social self-concept and Zeleke's (2004) meta-analalysis of social self-concept indicates that 70% of the analyzed studies did not present differences between children with and without learning difficulties. Similarly, Gibby-Leversuch et al. (2021) suggested that there is no link between dyslexia and perceptions about social / peer acceptance. However, interestingly, when children with dyslexia have a supportive family context and their parents present a positive approach towards dyslexia, children tend to demonstrate higher self-esteem (Terras et al., 2009).

Although research in the field is limited (Gibby-Leversuch et al., 2021), placement in educational settings is a significant issue to consider when exploring self-concept (Humphrey & Mullins, 2002). Chapman's (1988) review of research revealed no correlation between self-concept and context for children with learning difficulties. In fact, children with dyslexia attending mainstream schools did not demonstrate higher self-concepts than those attending specialist units and vice versa. However, other research suggests lower self-esteem for children with dyslexia attending mainstream settings (Crozier et al., 1999). Casserly (2013) found fair or negative socio-emotional feelings and self-esteem on entry to specialist settings. Yet, most teachers and parents mentioned that self-esteem increased in the specialised reading settings and remained unchanged on return to mainstream. In Humphrey's (2002) research, students with dyslexia attending mainstream settings reported significantly lowered levels of self-esteem in reading and writing compared to both the specialist unit students with dyslexia and the control group. Contradictory though, teachers' reports showed that most inappropriate behaviours manifest in the specialist unit. Moreover, although Burden (2005) indicated that initially students with dyslexia attending specialist schools demonstrated more negative academic self-concepts than the standardisation sample attending the mainstream school, gradually their academic self-concept increased. It can be assumed that specialised instruments and resources, special teachers paying attention and providing space for realistic comparisons between personal achievements and peers' attainment perhaps explain the phenomenon (Humphrey, 2002). In fact, students attending the specialised unit reported their teachers had been more supportive, spending time and paying more attention than teachers at mainstream schools (Humphrey & Mullins, 2002).

Although definite conclusions cannot be drawn due to limited research in the field, the research conducted so far provides some evidence of the features of a supportive educational setting (Gibby-Leversuch et al., 2021). Caring and acceptive contexts that provide clear understanding of dyslexia and high-quality specialist educational provision seem to foster self-esteem for students with dyslexia (Gibby-Leversuch et al., 2021). According to parents' views, children with dyslexia benefit from positive relationships with teachers, praise, reinforcement and faith in students' abilities, as well as constructive relations with peers with alike struggles and academic progress (Casselry, 2013). “Children and young people with dyslexia thrive when they are accepted and have their needs understood, something that is not unique to any setting, or to those with dyslexia” (Gibby-Leversuch et al., 2021, p.5608).

Teachers should provide increased attention especially to teenage girls with dyslexia to support them foster their self-esteem (Alexander-Passe, 2006). Data from Alexander-Passe’s (2006) study suggested that males scored better than females across all self-esteem sub-domains, including global and academic self-esteem. Moreover, females employed more emotional and avoidant copying strategies and demonstrated higher levels of depression than the male participants. Contrarily, Sucheta (2020) found significant gender differences in children with specific learning difficulties, with girls scoring significantly higher than boys on general, social, academic, and parental self-concept, as well as on overall self-esteem. Apparently, there is a paucity of literature exploring the links between self-esteem and gender in individuals with learning difficulties and research conducted so far has come up with conflicting findings (Emam & Saad Abu-Serei, 2014).

The role of diagnosis needs also to be explored in more depth in relation to self-esteem, since there is evidence that positive dyslexia diagnosis constitutes the most significant factor in self-esteem enhancement, even more important than relationships with significant others (Glazzard, 2010). Participants in Glazzard’s (2010) study suggested that diagnosis provided an explanation for their difficulties, which were no longer understood as related to their intelligence. Similarly, research by Riddick (1995) suggested that 90% of the children with dyslexia perceived positively the label of dyslexia because it suggested they were not unintelligent, while it generally helped them, providing an understanding of their difficulties and making them realize that other students face similar difficulties. However, the review by Gibby-Leversuch et al. (2021) reached mixed findings; some individuals mentioned dyslexia was a positive alternative to negative terms (e.g., lazy) while others that received diagnosis at late adolescence felt that labelling was stigmatizing, uninstructive, and unsupportive. Mixed results suggest that all professionals involved in the child’s treatment need to take into consideration their uniqueness and provide precise information about dyslexia to eliminate stigma or negative attributions so that learners can cautiously decide if the label will have a positive effect on their self-conception (Gibby-Leversuch et al., 2021).

Interventions

Regarding intervention in dyslexia, the main approaches involve RTI, Multi-tiered Systems of Support (MTSS), multi-sensory approaches, and phonological awareness and phonics instruction. For an intervention to be effective, it should be based on a detailed learner’s profile and should be structured, systematic and multisensory, including training in phonological awareness skills, grapheme-to-phoneme correspondences, vocabulary, orthographic and morphophonological rules as well as reading comprehension, narration, oral production, and metacognitive skills (Hulme & Snowling, 2016; Galuschka et al., 2020). However, taking into consideration that learners with dyslexia might experience low self-esteem, anxiety and/or frustration, intervention should become more holistic, involving empowering learners towards academic achievement and critical thinking, creating enhanced learning environments, along with a whole-school approach to promote academic, emotional and social wellness. Finally, it has been suggested that counselling on self-esteem and training on study, coping and self-advocacy skills can complement reading and spelling interventions and maximize their efficacy (Piit & Soni, 2017; Kirwan & Leather, 2011; Alexander-Passe, 2006).

More specifically, dyslexia interventions at literacy level can be targeting reading and/or writing skills. The reading interventions involve explicit instruction of phonological awareness and phonics skills, while they can also aim at improving reading fluency, through the development of oral language skills, and reading comprehension by teaching specific strategies (e.g., visualization, inferencing, etc.). These interventions are mostly effective when they focus on explicit literacy instruction and provide guided practice, modelling, and scaffolding along with small group teaching and multisensory techniques (Otaiba et al., 2018). As far as the writing interventions are concerned, these target handwriting, spelling and/or written production at the sentence and text level. Explicit instruction is used along with multisensory methods and strategies such as self-monitoring, mnemonics, writing strategies, etc. (Otaiba et al., 2018).

Although research has shown that effective dyslexia interventions seem to involve explicit and systematic instruction of reading, spelling and/or writing skills, scaffolding, modelling, and frequent opportunities for practice along with contingent, timely and constructive feedback, and the use of multisensory methods (Otaiba et al., 2018), interventions can also benefit from incorporating overlearning, metacognitive awareness skills and study, organization and memory strategies. Metacognitive skills, specifically, play a significant role in learning as students become aware of their learning style and can select their preferred learning strategies and techniques to promote self-efficacy and gradually become autonomous learners (Rahul & Ponniah, 2021).

Taking into consideration the three-level framework suggested by Frith (2002) and the fact that dyslexia difficulties are not limited to literacy skills, intervention should follow a more holistic approach, thus targeting the environmental level as well, considering the individual variability along with personality traits and socio-emotional parameters. In this respect, structured literacy interventions are suggested to be complemented by counselling (Alexander-Passe, 2006) and emotional support provision (Rahul & Ponniah, 2021). In addition, since self-esteem plays a significant role in individuals' psychological, social and cognitive development, educational systems should prioritise the enhancement of students' self-concept (Shavelson & Bolus, 1982). Not only teachers but also parents and therapists should focus on the enhancement of self-esteem because it is assumed to be a source of positive results (Baumeister et al., 2003).

According to O'Mara et al. (2010), dyslexia intervention should also aim at improving academic self-concept and academic skills. Thus, interventions could use systematic praise and feedback and combine them with specific skills training (Marsh & Craven, 2006) as well as focusing on specific areas of self-concept. The enhancement of self-concept can result in improved academic achievement, emotional regulation, social interaction and overall well-being. Moreover, interventions that incorporate self-esteem enhancement and positive thinking, emotion recognition and regulation training, as well as social-interpersonal skills training seem to promote mental health (Boyes et al., 2020). In addition, intervention schemes that were based on group work and aimed at enhancing self-esteem through self-awareness, motivation, self-adequacy and self-appreciation intervention resulted in increased self-confidence, empowerment and self-advocacy, more positive thinking and motivation, better self-monitoring and self-evaluation skills, and improved self-perceptions (Burton, 2004). Furthermore, interventions can be supplemented with attribution retraining programmes since this can have a positive effect upon students' motivation and academic attainment (Gibby-Leversuch et al., 2019). Research has also shown that interventions combining self-perception and literacy skills goals can be effective as well as those which target self-efficacy, which result in enhanced self-concept (Griffin & Murtagh, 2015).

As far as the role of the teachers is concerned, it can have an impact on students' self-esteem (Humphrey, 2003). Thus, they need to be aware of what dyslexia entails and show acceptance and understanding along with counselling skills. Apart from teaching basic literacy skills, they need to train their students in metacognitive, organizational and critical thinking skills as well as enhancing their self-esteem. Teachers need to show empathy, both cognitively and emotionally, and build a trusting relationship with their students, showing that they believe in their abilities. They should also be conscious of the effect of their behaviour on their students' self-perceptions. Thus, feedback need to be contingent, constructive and encouraging while praise should be systematic (Jayasree, 2016). Moreover, teachers should create a supportive, understanding and inclusive environment and provide differentiated teaching of high quality. In addition, students need to experience success at the various stages of learning and receive positive reinforcement (Casserly, 2013). Teachers could also promote positive self-referent statements and make the students feel accepted, respected and important. Furthermore, the role of the teacher is also significant in the management of bullying incidents. The teacher can offer coping strategies such as assertion and social skills training. Finally, the teacher can promote peer support for students with dyslexia through listening, befriending, mediation, peer tutoring and mentoring (Humphrey, 2003).

CONCLUSION

The aim of the present paper was to explore the human aspects of dyslexia and more specifically dyslexia and self-esteem. Although research in the field is limited and findings contradictory, dyslexia seems to affect primarily academic self-concept and not necessarily global self-esteem. A multiplicity of factors have also been suggested to be involved such as significant others, school setting and diagnosis; yet, answers are far from definite, and further research is essential. Moreover, interventions should be seen within the spectrum of multiplicity and differentiality, based on an individual's idiosyncrasy and personal circumstances. Therefore, interventions should not be limited to literacy treatment but involve self-esteem enhancement programmes, as well as modifications at the environmental level. Supportive parents, encouraging teachers, dyslexia-friendly school ethos as well as positive interpersonal relationships can foster self-perceptions and promote emotional and social well-being for students with dyslexia.

REFERENCES

Alexander-Passe, N. (2006). How Dyslexic Teenagers Cope: An Investigation of Self-esteem, Coping and Depression. *Dyslexia (Chichester, England)*, *12*(4), 256–275. doi:10.1002/dys.318 PMID:17152342

American Psychiatric Association. (2013). Neurodevelopmental Disorders. In Diagnostic and statistical manual of mental disorders (5th ed.).

Arens, A. K., Jansen, M., Preckel, F., Schmidt, I., & Brunner, M. (2021). The structure of academic self-concept: A methodological review and empirical illustration of central models. *Review of Educational Research*, *91*(1), 34–72. doi:10.3102/0034654320972186

Armstrong, D., & Humphrey, N. (2009). Reactions to a Diagnosis of Dyslexia Among Students Entering Further Education: Development of the 'resistance-Accommodation' Model. *British Journal of Special Education*, *36*(2), 95–102. doi:10.1111/j.1467-8578.2008.00408.x

Barbiero, C., Lonciari, I., Montico, M., Monasta, L., Penge, R., Vio, C., Tressoldi, P. M., Ferluga, V., Bigoni, A., Tullio, A., Carrozzi, M., & Ronfani, L. (2012). The Submerged Dyslexia Iceberg: How Many School Children Are Not Diagnosed? Results from an Italian Study. *PLoS One*, *7*(10), 1–9. doi:10.1371/journal.pone.0048082 PMID:23118930

Baumeister, R. F., Campbell, J. D., Krueger, J. I., & Vohs, K. D. (2003). Does high self-esteem cause better performance, interpersonal success, happiness, or healthier lifestyles? *Psychological Science in the Public Interest*, *4*(1), 1–44. doi:10.1111/1529-1006.01431 PMID:26151640

Boyes, M. E., Leitão, S., Claessen, M., Badcock, N. A., & Nayton, M. (2020). Correlates of externalising and internalising problems in children with dyslexia: An analysis of data from clinical casefiles. *Australian Psychologist*, *55*(1), 62–72. doi:10.1111/ap.12409

Boyes, M. E., Tebbutt, B., Preece, K. A., & Badcock, N. A. (2018). Relationships between reading ability and child mental health: Moderating effects of self-esteem. *Australian Psychologist*, *53*(2), 125–133. doi:10.1111/ap.12281

Brunner, M., Keller, U., Dierendonck, C., Reichert, M., Ugen, S., Fischbach, A., & Martin, R. (2010). The structure of academic self-concepts revisited: The nested Marsh/Shavelson model. *Journal of Educational Psychology*, *102*(4), 964–981. doi:10.1037/a0019644

Burden, R. (2005). *Dyslexia and self-concept*. Whurr Publishers.

Burden, R. (2008). Is dyslexia necessarily associated with negative feelings of self-worth? A review and implications for future research. *Dyslexia (Chichester, England)*, *14*(3), 188–196. doi:10.1002/dys.371 PMID:18646275

Burden, R., & Burdett, J. (2005). Factors Associated with Successful Learning in Pupils with Dyslexia: A Motivational Analysis. *British Journal of Special Education*, *32*(2), 100–104. doi:10.1111/j.0952-3383.2005.00378.x

Casserly, A. M. (2013). The socio-emotional needs of children with dyslexia in different educational settings in Ireland. *Journal of Research in Special Educational Needs*, *13*(1), 79–91. doi:10.1111/j.1471-3802.2011.01227.x

Chapman, J. W. (1988). Cognitive-motivational characteristics and academic achievement of learningdisabled children: A longitudinal study. *Journal of Educational Psychology*, *80*(3), 357–365. doi:10.1037/0022-0663.80.3.357

Chen, X., & Ma, R. (2023). Adolescents' Self-Esteem: The Influence Factors and Solutions. J*ournal of Education. Humanities and Social Sciences*, *8*, 1562–1566.

Coelho, V. A., Bear, G. G., & Brás, P. (2020). A Multilevel Analysis of the Importance of School Climate for the Trajectories of Students' Self-concept and Self-esteem Throughout the Middle School Transition. *Journal of Youth and Adolescence*, *49*(2), 1793–1804. doi:10.100710964-020-01245-7 PMID:32356038

Cvencek, D., Fryberg, S. A., Covarrubias, R., & Meltzoff, A. N. (2018). Self-Concepts, Self-Esteem, and Academic Achievement of Minority and Majority North American Elementary School Children. *Child Development*, *89*(4), 1099–1109. doi:10.1111/cdev.12802 PMID:28386954

Eaude, T. (1999). *Learning Difficulties: dyslexia, bullying and other issues*. Letts Educational.

Elliott, J., & Grigorenko, E. L. (2014). *The Dyslexia Debate*. Cambridge University Press. doi:10.1017/CBO9781139017824

Emam, M. M., & Saad Abu-Serei, U. (2014). Family Functioning Predictors of Self-Concept and Self-Esteem in Children at Risk for Learning Disabilities in Oman: Exclusion of Parent and Gender Contribution. *International Education Studies*, *7*(10), 89–99. doi:10.5539/ies.v7n10p89

Frith, U. (1999). Paradoxes in the Definition of Dyslexia. *Dyslexia (Chichester, England)*, *5*(4), 192–214. doi:10.1002/(SICI)1099-0909(199912)5:4<192::AID-DYS144>3.0.CO;2-N

Frith, U. (2002). Resolving the paradoxes of dyslexia. *Dyslexia and Literacy. Theory into Practice*, 69–83.

Galaburda, A. M. (1993). Neuro anatomic basis of developmental dyslexia. *Neurologic Clinics*, *11*(1), 161–173. doi:10.1016/S0733-8619(18)30175-0 PMID:8441368

Galuschka, K., Görgen, R., Kalmar, J., Haberstroh, S., Schmalz, X., & Schulte-Körne, G. (2020). Effectiveness of spelling treatment approaches for learners with dyslexia – A meta-analysis and systematic review. *Educational Psychologist*, *55*(1), 1–20. doi:10.1080/00461520.2019.1659794

Gibby-Leversuch, R., Hartwell, B. K., & Wright, S. (2021). Dyslexia, literacy difficulties and the self-perceptions of children and young people: A systematic review. *Current Psychology (New Brunswick, N.J.)*, *40*(11), 5595–5612. doi:10.100712144-019-00444-1

Glazzard, J. (2010). The impact of dyslexia on pupils' self-esteem. *Support for Learning*, *25*(2), 63–69. doi:10.1111/j.1467-9604.2010.01442.x

Griffin, C. P., & Murtagh, L. (2015). Increasing the sight vocabulary and reading fluency of children requiring reading support: The use of a precision teaching approach. *Educational Psychology in Practice*, *31*(2), 186–209. doi:10.1080/02667363.2015.1022818

Helland, T. (2022). Trends in Dyslexia Research during the Period 1950 to 2020 - Theories, Definitions, and Publications. *Brain Sciences*, *12*(10), 1323. doi:10.3390/brainsci12101323 PMID:36291256

Hulme, C., & Snowling, M. J. (2016). Reading disorders and dyslexia. *Current Opinion in Pediatrics*, *28*(6), 731–735. doi:10.1097/MOP.0000000000000411 PMID:27496059

Humphrey, N. (2002). Teacher and pupil ratings of self-esteem in developmental dyslexia. *British Journal of Special Education*, *29*(1), 29–36. doi:10.1111/1467-8527.00234

Humphrey, N. (2003). Facilitating a positive sense of self in pupils with dyslexia: The role of teachers and peers. *Support for Learning*, *18*(3), 130–136. doi:10.1111/1467-9604.00295

Humphrey, N., & Mullins, P. M. (2002). Self-concept and self-esteem in developmental dyslexia. *Journal of Research in Special Educational Needs*, *2*(2). http://www3.interscience.wiley.com/cgi-bin/fulltext/120188296/

Jayasree, K. (2016). A Holistic Approach to Learning: Remedial Intervention for Students with Learning Disabilities (Dyslexia). *International Journal of New Technology and Research*, *2*(11), 60–61.

Kirwan, B., & Leather, C. (2011). Students' voices: A report of the student view of dyslexia study skills tuition. *Support for Learning*, *26*(1), 33–41. doi:10.1111/j.1467-9604.2010.01472.x

Kloomak, S., & Cosden, M. (1994). Self-concept in children with learning disabilities: The relationship between global self-concept, academic 'discounting', non-academic self-concept and perceived social support. *Learning Disability Quarterly*, *17*(2), 140–153. doi:10.2307/1511183

Köller, O., & Baumert, J. (2006). Self-Esteem, Academic Self-Concept, and Achievement: How the Learning Environment Moderates the Dynamics of Self-Concept. *Journal of Personality and Social Psychology*, *90*(2), 334–349. doi:10.1037/0022-3514.90.2.334 PMID:16536654

Lachowicz-Tabaczek, K., & Śniecińska, J. (2011). Self-concept and self-esteem: How the content of the self-concept reveals sources and functions of self-esteem. *Polish Psychological Bulletin*, *42*(1), 24–35. doi:10.2478/v10059-011-0005-y

Lawrence, D. (2006). *Enhancing self-esteem in the classroom*. SAGE Publications Ltd. doi:10.4135/9781446213513

Lithari, E. (2019). Fractured academic identities: Dyslexia, secondary education, self-esteem and school experiences. *International Journal of Inclusive Education*, *23*(3), 280–296. doi:10.1080/13603116.2018.1433242

Long, M., Wood, C., Littleton, K., Passenger, T., & Sheehy, K. (2011). *The Psychology of Education* (2nd ed.). Routledge.

Maia, L., Simões, F., Rodrigues, P., Santos, B., Monteiro, F., Castanho, L., Magalhães, M., Mendes, P., Augusto, T., & Eusébio, A. (2017). Dyslexia how it survived (or not) to classification alterations all over the years Implications to assessment and intervention. *Cuadernos de Neuropsicología / Panamerican. Journal of Neuropsychology*, *11*(3), 151–165. doi:10.7714/CNPS/11.3.209

Marsh, H. W. (1990). A Multidimensional, Hierarchical Model of Self-Concept: Theoretical and Empirical Justification. *Educational Psychology Review*, *2*(2), 77–172. doi:10.1007/BF01322177

Marsh, H. W., & Craven, R. G. (2006). Reciprocal effects of self-concept and performance from a multidimensional perspective: Beyond seductive pleasure and unidimensional perspectives. *Perspectives on Psychological Science, 1*(2), 133–163. . 1745- 6916. 2006. 00010.x doi:10.1111/j

Marsh, H. W., & Hau, K. T. (2003). Big-fish-little-pond effect on academic self-concept. A cross-cultural (26-country) test of the negative effects of academically selective schools. *The American Psychologist*, *58*(5), 364–376. doi:10.1037/0003-066X.58.5.364 PMID:12971085

Marsh, H. W., & O'Mara, A. (2008). Reciprocal effects between academic self-concept, self-esteem, achievement, and attainment over seven adolescent years: Unidimensional and multidimensional perspectives of self-concept. *Personality and Social Psychology Bulletin*, *34*(4), 542–552. doi:10.1177/0146167207312313 PMID:18340036

Nalavany, B. A., Logan, J. M., & Carawan, L. W. (2018). The relationship between emotional experience with dyslexia and work self-efficacy among adults with dyslexia. *Dyslexia (Chichester, England)*, *24*(1), 17–32. doi:10.1002/dys.1575 PMID:29230916

Neiss, M. B., Stevenson, J., Sedikides, C., Kumashiro, M., Finkel, E. J., & Rusbult, C. E. (2005). Executive self, self-esteem, and negative affectivity: Relations at the phenotypic and genotypic level. *Journal of Personality and Social Psychology*, *89*(4), 593–606. doi:10.1037/0022-3514.89.4.593 PMID:16287421

O'Mara, A. J., Marsh, H. W., Craven, R. G., & Debus, R. L. (2006). Do Self-Concept Interventions Make a Difference? A Synergistic Blend of Construct Validation and Meta-Analysis. *Educational Psychologist*, *41*(3), 181–206. doi:10.120715326985ep4103_4

Otaiba, A. S., Rouse, A. G., & Baker, K. (2018). Elementary grade intervention approaches to treat specific learning disabilities, including dyslexia. *Language, Speech, and Hearing Services in Schools*, *49*(4), 829–842. doi:10.1044/2018_LSHSS-DYSLC-18-0022 PMID:30458544

Paradice, R. (2001). An Investigation into the Social Construction of Dyslexia. *Educational Psychology in Practice*, *17*(3), 213–225. doi:10.1080/02667360120072747

Paulus, M., Licata, M., Gniewosz, B., & Sodian, B. (2018). The impact of mother-child interaction quality and cognitive abilities on children's self-concept and self-esteem. *Cognitive Development*, *48*, 42–51. doi:10.1016/j.cogdev.2018.07.001

Peterson, R. L., & Pennington, B. F. (2012). Developmental dyslexia. *Lancet*, *379*(9830), 1997–2007. doi:10.1016/S0140-6736(12)60198-6 PMID:22513218

Pitt, S., & Soni, A. (2017). Students' experiences of academic success with dyslexia: A call for alternative intervention. *Support for Learning*, *32*(4), 387–405. doi:10.1111/1467-9604.12182

Polychroni, F., Koukoura, K., & Anagnostou, I. (2006). Academic self-concept, reading attitudes and approaches to learning of children with dyslexia: Do they differ from their peers? *European Journal of Special Needs Education*, *21*(4), 415–430. doi:10.1080/08856250600956311

Rahul, D. R., & Ponniah, J. (2021). Educational Insights into Dyslexia. *Rupkatha Journal on Interdisciplinary Studies in Humanities*, *13*(4), 1–12. doi:10.21659/rupkatha.v13n4.35

Rentzsch, K., Wenzler, M. P., & Schütz, A. (2016). The structure of multidimensional self-esteem across age and gender. *Personality and Individual Differences*, *88*, 139–147. doi:10.1016/j.paid.2015.09.012

Riddick, B. (1995). Dyslexia: Dispelling the myths. *Disability & Society*, *10*(4), 457–473. doi:10.1080/09687599550023453

Riddick, B. (1996). *Living With Dyslexia: The social and emotional consequences of specific learning difficulties/ disabilities* (1st ed.). Routledge. doi:10.4324/9780203432600

Riddick, B. (2001). Dyslexia and Inclusion: Time for a Social Model of Disability Perspective? *International Studies in Sociology of Education*, *11*(3), 223–236. doi:10.1080/09620210100200078

Riddick, B., Sterling, C., Farmer, M., & Morgan, S. (1999). Self-Esteem and Anxiety in the Educational Histories of Adult Dyslexic Students. *Dyslexia (Chichester, England)*, *5*(4), 227–248. doi:10.1002/(SICI)1099-0909(199912)5:4<227::AID-DYS146>3.0.CO;2-6

Rohmer, O., Doignon-Camus, N., Audusseau, J., Trautmann, S., Chaillou, A. C., & Popa-Roch, M. (2022). Removing the academic framing in student evaluations improves achievement in children with dyslexia: The mediating role of self-judgement of competence. *Dyslexia (Chichester, England)*, *28*(3), 309–324. doi:10.1002/dys.1713 PMID:35623893

Roitsch, J., & Watson, S. M. (2019). An overview of dyslexia: Definition, characteristics, assessment, identification, and intervention. *Science Journal of Education*, *7*(4), 81–86. doi:10.11648/j.sjedu.20190704.11

Rosenberg, M., Schooler, C., Schoenbach, C., & Rosenberg, F. (1995). Global Self-Esteem and Specific Self-Esteem: Different Concepts, Different Outcomes. *American Sociological Review*, *60*(1), 141–156. doi:10.2307/2096350

Ross, H. (2021). 'I'm Dyslexic but What Does That Even Mean?': Young People's Experiences of Dyslexia Support Interventions in Mainstream Classrooms. *Scandinavian Journal of Disability Research*, *23*(1), 284–294. doi:10.16993jdr.782

Scherrer, V., & Preckel, F. (2019). Development of Motivational Variables and Self-Esteem During the School Career: A Meta-Analysis of Longitudinal Studies. *Review of Educational Research*, *89*(2), 211–258. doi:10.3102/0034654318819127

Schumacher, J., Hoffman, P., Schmaeil, C., Schulte-Korne, G., & Nothen, M. (2007). Genetics of dyslexia: The evolving landscape. *Journal of Medical Genetics*, *44*(5), 289–297. doi:10.1136/jmg.2006.046516 PMID:17307837

Shavelson, R. J., & Bolus, R. (1982). Self concept: The interplay of theory and methods. *Journal of Educational Psychology*, *74*(1), 3–17. doi:10.1037/0022-0663.74.1.3

Shavelson, R. J., Hubner, J. J., & Stanton, G. C. (1976). Self-Concept: Validation of Construct Interpretations. *Review of Educational Research*, *46*(3), 407–441. doi:10.3102/00346543046003407

Snowling, M. J. (2013). Early identification and interventions for dyslexia: A contemporary view. *Journal of Research in Special Educational Needs*, *13*(1), 7–14. doi:10.1111/j.1471-3802.2012.01262.x PMID:26290655

Stein, J. (2018). What is developmental dyslexia? *Brain Sciences*, *8*(2), 26. doi:10.3390/brainsci8020026 PMID:29401712

Sucheta (2020). Gender differences on self-esteem in children with specific learning disability. *International Journal of Advances in Engineering and Management (IJAEM)*, *2*(7), 593-599.

Terras, M., Thompson, L. C., & Minnis, H. (2009). Dyslexia and psycho-social functioning: An exploratory study of the role of self-esteem and understanding. *Dyslexia (Chichester, England)*, *15*(4), 304–327. doi:10.1002/dys.386 PMID:19384920

Uppstad, P. H., & Tønnessen, F. E. (2007). The notion of 'phonology' in dyslexia research: Cognitivism—and beyond. *Dyslexia (Chichester, England)*, *13*(3), 154–174. doi:10.1002/dys.332 PMID:17624910

Vlachos, F., Avramidis, E., Dedousis, G., Chalmpe, M., Stalla, I., & Giannakopoulos, M. (2013). Prevalence and Gender Ratio of Dyslexia in Greek Adolescents and its Association with Parental History and Brain Injury. *American Journal of Educational Research*, *1*(1), 22–25. doi:10.12691/education-1-1-5

Wagner, R. K., Zirps, F. A., Edwards, A. A., Wood, S. G., Joyner, R. E., Becker, B. J., Liu, G., & Beal, B. (2020). The prevalence of dyslexia: A new approach to its estimation. *Journal of Learning Disabilities*, *53*(5), 354–365. doi:10.1177/0022219420920377 PMID:32452713

Yang, L., Li, C., Li, X., Zhai, M., An, Q., Zhang, Y., Zhao, J., & Weng, X. (2022). Prevalence of developmental dyslexia in primary school children: A systematic review and metaanalysis. *Brain Sciences*, *12*(2), 240. doi:10.3390/brainsci12020240 PMID:35204003

Zeleke, S. (2004). Self-concepts of students with learning disabilities and their normally achieving peers: A review. *European Journal of Special Needs Education*, *19*(2), 145–170. doi:10.1080/08856250410001678469

Chapter 17
Learning Difficulties and Children's Drawing

Christos Charmpatsis
https://orcid.org/0009-0007-8122-766X
University of Ioannina, Greece

Dimitrios Sarris
University of Ioannina, Greece

Panagoula Papadimitropoulou
University of Patras, Greece

Dimitra V. Katsarou
https://orcid.org/0000-0001-8690-0314
University of the Aegean, Greece

ABSTRACT

The major purpose of this research study was to detect the significant differences in human figure drawing between the students with learning difficulties and the students without learning difficulties. Moreover, this scientific research aimed to detect the differences between students of different genders with and without learning difficulties. The sample of this study consisted of 80 students who attended elementary school. The 40 were students with learning disabilities and the other 40 were students without learning disabilities. The main research tool used was the Goodenough-Harris drawing test (GH), which was assessed in 20 points. The results showed that the children without learning disabilities outperform children with learning disabilities. The drawing of students without learning difficulties is more detailed and they display more often in their drawing both proportions and symmetries in comparison with students with learning difficulties. Similar results are also observed in the drawings between the two sexes, as girls outperform boys of the same chronological age.

DOI: 10.4018/979-8-3693-1982-6.ch017

1. INTRODUCTION

The child's drawings are one of the most essential factors that the teacher considers when evaluating the student's mental, emotional, and social development (Brooks, 2009). The human form is a frequent point of reference, particularly in children's drawing and in "human figure drawing," because the subject needs both a living body (Anzieu, 1993) and an unconscious body (Piaget, 1965) in order to stand in the environment around him. We consider the human's drawing as a test of a mental type since the other drawings, such those for the family or the house, refer to the child's emotional surroundings. Like all assessments, the "human figure drawing" test captures the symbolic personality that children exhibit through their expressiveness (Luquet, 1927-1967). According to Piaget (1950, 1964), every element of a child's expressive world is a mental image and a symbolic language. By dividing the symbol into a signifier and a signified through imitation and drawing, drawing, in accordance with his theory, acts as a bridge between the earliest form of representation and representational thought (Vygotsky, 1978). According to Piaget, symbolic play is a prerequisite for the transition to representational thinking since it enables both typically developing and non-typically developing children to mentally reproduce reality (Winnicott, 1975). Progressively, children's drawing tends to be delineated between play and mental imagery (Giannouli, Sarris, & Bannou, 2019; Satrazemi, Mpakagianni, Sarris, Vergou, & Zakopoulou, 2017).

2. RESEARCH METHODOLOGY

2.1. Objectives, Research Questions, and Research Hypotheses

The main objective of this research study is to detect the differences in human figure drawing between students with and without learning disabilities, as well as the differences between students of different sexes with and without learning disabilities.

Based on the objectives of our research, the following research questions are formulated:

(a) Is there a significant difference in human figure drawing between students with and without learning disabilities?
(b) Is there a significant difference in human figure drawing between students of different genders with and without learning disabilities?

The findings of the relevant literature revies grant us the possibility to hypothesize that students with learning disabilities will be at a disadvantage in the human figure drawing compared to students without learning disabilities. Last but not least, the recent literature review shows that there are differences between boys and girls in human figure design.

2.2. Procedure and Participants

The main objective of this research is to detect how students with and without learning difficulties differ in terms of their basic drawing, as well as how students of different genders differ from each other. 80 students participated in the study. The 40 were students with special educational needs attending the inclusion section of their school, while the remaining 40 were students in the respective general classes in which the students with special educational needs attended. The second grade had 24 students, third grade had 36, and fourth grade had 20. 33 girls and 47 boys participated in this study. The primary research instrument was the 20-point Goodenough's-Harris Drawing Test.

3. RESULTS

According to the study's findings, there were statistically significant differences between the means of students with and without learning disabilities regarding the limbs and the facial details, or more specifically, the way that the points are mapped: arms and legs in the right position of the torso, appearance of the neck, nose, nostrils, hair, clothes etc..

Table 1 shows the distribution of frequencies for the 20 points of the human figure drawing given to us by the children from the entire sample. The frequencies in Table 1 are presented in absolute values and in percentages (%). As shown in Table 1, all children (80) drew heads, legs, eyes and mouth. The differences concern the remaining parts of the human body. For instance, the great majority of drawings are lacking of nostrils, ears, eye details, jaw and forehead.

Table 2 shows the frequency distributions according to the class of the students. Table 3 shows the frequency distributions according to the gender of the students, while Table 4 shows the frequency distributions according to whether the students have learning difficulties or not.

Table 1. Human figure drawing: Frequencies of values in the total sample

	Yes f (%)	No f (%)
Head	80 (100)	–
Eyes	80 (100)	-
Eyelids, Eyebrows	17 (21,2)	63 (78,8)
Eye pupil	33 (41,2)	47 (58,8)
Ears	8 (10)	72 (90)
Nose	44 (55)	36 (45)
Nostrils	13 (16,2)	67 (83,8)
Mouth	80 (100)	-
Neck	18 (22,5)	62 (77,5)
Jaws, Forehead	5 (6,2)	75 (93,8)
Hair	41 (51,3)	39 (48,7)
Torso	77 (96,3)	3 (3,7)
Arms	71 (88,7)	9 (11,3)
Fingers	46 (58)	34 (42)
Legs	80 (100)	–
Clothes	27 (33,7)	53 (66,3)
Arms and Legs placed on the Torso	76 (95)	4 (5)
Correct Placement of Arms and Legs	55 (68,8)	25 (31,2)
Two Dimensions of Arms and Legs	24 (30)	56 (70)
Correct Placement of Head Sections	52 (65)	28 (35)

Table 2. Human figure drawing: Frequencies by class

		CLASS		
		2nd grade	3rd grade	4th grade
Head	Yes	24	36	20
Eyes	Yes	24	36	20
Eyelids, Eyebrows	No	20	26	17
	Yes	4	10	3
Eye pupil	No	14	21	12
	Yes	10	15	8
Ears	No	23	32	17
	Yes	1	4	3
Nose	No	11	17	8
	Yes	13	19	12
Nostrils	No	21	30	16
	Yes	3	6	4
Mouth	Yes	24	36	20
Neck	No	20	27	15
	Yes	4	9	5
Jaws, Forehead	No	24	33	18
	Yes	0	3	2
Hair	No	13	19	7
	Yes	11	17	13
Torso	No	2	1	0
	Yes	22	35	20
Arms	No	3	4	2
	Yes	21	32	18
Fingers	No	11	15	8
	Yes	13	21	12
Legs	Yes	24	36	20
Clothes	No	16	24	11
	Yes	8	10	9
Arms and Legs placed on the Torso	No	2	1	1
	Yes	22	35	19
Correct Placement of Arms and Legs	No	8	10	7
	Yes	16	26	13
Two Dimensions of Arms and Legs	No	17	26	13
	Yes	7	10	7
Correct Placement of Head Sections	No	9	13	6
	Yes	15	23	14

Table 3. Human figure drawing: Frequencies by sex

		Sex	
		Boy	**Girl**
Head	Yes	47	33
Eyes	Yes	47	33
Eyelids, Eyebrows	No	38	25
	Yes	9	8
Eye pupil	No	24	23
	Yes	23	10
Ears	No	43	29
	Yes	4	4
Nose	No	22	14
	Yes	25	19
Nostrils	No	41	26
	Yes	6	7
Mouth	Yes	47	33
Neck	No	36	26
	Yes	11	7
Jaws, Forehead	No	44	31
	Yes	3	2
Hair	No	22	17
	Yes	25	16
Torso	No	3	0
	Yes	44	33
Arms	No	5	4
	Yes	42	29
Fingers	No	21	13
	Yes	26	20
Legs	Yes	47	33
Clothes	No	35	18
	Yes	12	15
Arms and Legs placed on Torso	No	2	2
	Yes	45	31
Correct Placement of Arms and Legs	No	17	8
	Yes	30	25
Two Dimensions of Arms and Legs	No	34	22
	Yes	13	11
Correct Placement of Head Sections	No	17	11
	Yes	30	22

Table 4. Human figure drawing: Frequencies according to whether students have learning difficulties or not

		Students without Learning Difficulties	Students with Learning Difficulties
Head	Yes	40	40
Eyes	Yes	40	40
Eyelids, Eyebrows	No	25	38
	Yes	15	2
Eye pupil	No	26	37
	Yes	14	3
Ears	No	30	39
	Yes	10	1
Nose	No	7	24
	Yes	33	16
Nostrils	No	35	40
	Yes	5	0
Mouth	Yes	40	40
Neck	No	23	35
	Yes	17	5
Jaws, Forehead	No	36	40
	Yes	4	0
Hair	No	12	23
	Yes	28	17
Torso	No	1	3
	Yes	39	37
Arms	No	2	8
	Yes	38	32
Fingers	No	17	20
	Yes	23	20
Legs	Yes	40	40
Clothes	No	21	34
	Yes	19	6
Arms and Legs placed on the Torso	No	1	5
	Yes	39	35
Correct Placement of Arms and Legs	No	4	19
	Yes	36	21
Two Dimensions of Arms and Legs	No	23	38
	Yes	17	2
Correct Placement of Head Sections	No	11	17
	Yes	29	23

Table 5 presents the results from the comparison of the means of the human figure drawing of the students according to their gender, using the t-test for two independent samples. It should be noted that only the statistically significant results are presented, at a statistical significance level of $p<0.05$. Statistically significant differences between boys and girls were found for the following points: head (t= -2.098, df= 42.00, p= 0.037), arms and legs placed on the torso (t= -2.765, df= 45.00, p= 0.048), torso (t= -2.466, df= 38.025, p= 0.027) and hands (t= -2.789, df= 49.876, p= 0.01). In these points, girls outperform boys, as can be noted in Table 6, which shows the averages of boys and girls for the respective points mentioned above.

Table 5. T test: Gender

	t	***df***	**Sig. (2-tailed)**	**Mean Rank**	**Standard Error**
Head	-2,098	42,000	0,037	-0,187	0,041
Arms and Legs placed on the Torso	-2,765	45,000	0,048	-0,134	0,056
Torso	-2,466	38,025	0,027	-0,456	0,167
Arms	-2,789	49,876	0,010	-0,322	0,188

Table 6. Human figure drawing: Sex means, standard deviation and standard error of the mean

	Sex	**N**	**Mean Rank**	**Standard Deviation**	**Standard Error**
Head	Boy	47	0,93	0,363	0,051
	Girl	33	1,00	0,000	0,000
Arms and Legs placed on the Torso	Boy	47	0,49	0,407	0,068
	Girl	33	0,93	0,000	0,000
Torso	Boy	47	0,77	0,356	0,058
	Girl	33	1,00	0,000	0,000
Arms	Boy	47	0,66	0,603	0,088
	Girl	33	0,81	0,299	0,081

Table 7 presents the results from the comparison of the averages of the human figure drawing of the students according to whether or not they have learning difficulties, using the t-test for two independent samples. It should be noted that only the statistically significant results are presented, at a statistical significance level of $p<0.05$. Statistically significant differences between students with learning disabilities and students without learning disabilities were found for the points: eyebrows-eyelids (t= 4,233, *df*= 32,786, p= 0,002), eye pupil (t= 7,689, *df*= 39,187, *p*= 0,03), ears (t= 2,699, *df*= 27,888, p= 0,018), nose (t= 2,693, *df*= 55,873, *p*= 0,014), neck (t= 2,456, *df*= 52,089, *p*= 0,035), hair (t= 3,564, *df*= 54,687, *p*= 0,001), torso (t= 2,124, *df*= 54,175, *p*= 0,039), arms(t= 3,902, df= 38,358, p= 0,005), fingers (t=

2,610, *df*= 56,621, *p*= 0,061), correct placement of arms and legs (t= 4,099, *df*= 43,792, *p*= 0,002), two dimensions of arms and legs (t= 4,122, *df*= 38,304, *p*= 0,005).

In these points, students without learning difficulties outperform students with learning difficulties, as can be noted in Table 8, which presents the averages for the aforementioned points.

Table 7. T test: Students with and without learning difficulties

	T	df	Sig. (2-tailed	Mean	Standard Error
Eyelids, Eyebrows	4,233	32,786	0,002	0,393	0,096
Eye pupil	7,689	39,187	0,030	0,655	0,087
Ears	2,699	27,888	0,018	0,235	0,069
Nose	2,693	55,873	0,014	0,432	0,143
Neck	2,456	52,089	0,035	0,521	0,171
Hair	3,564	54,687	0,001	0,378	0,114
Torso	2,124	54,175	0,039	0,267	0,122
Arms	3,902	38,358	0,005	0,544	0,099
Fingers	2,610	56,621	0,061	0,201	0,139
Correct Placement of Arms and Legs	4,099	43,792	0,002	0,555	0,118
Two Dimensions of Arms and Legs	4,122	38,304	0,005	0,431	0,099

Table 8. Human figure drawing: Means of students with and without learning difficulties, standard deviation and standard error of the mean

	Without LD and with LD	N	Mean	Standard Deviation	Standard Error
Eyelids, Eyebrows	No	40	0,43	0,356	0,048
	Yes	40	0,03	0,518	0,098
Eye pupil	No	40	0,82	0,581	0,094
	Yes	40	0,12	0,397	0,067
Ears	No	40	0,26	0,475	0,079
	Yes	40	0,05	0,515	0,081
Nose	No	40	0,76	0,486	0,076
	Yes	40	0,42	0,112	0,023
Neck	No	40	0,39	0,477	0,081
	Yes	40	0,17	0,515	0,092
Hair	No	40	0,52	0,567	0,095
	Yes	40	0,23	0,449	0,076
Torso	No	40	0,75	0,550	0,086
	Yes	40	0,54	0,617	0,094
Arms	No	40	0,47	0,564	0,093
	Yes	40	0,05	0,177	0,039
Fingers	No	40	0,78	0,434	0,087
	Yes	40	0,49	0,223	0,055
Correct Placement of Arms and Legs	No	40	0,96	0,267	0,091
	Yes	40	0,65	0,523	0,016
Two Dimensions of Arms and Legs	No	40	0,43	0,477	0,087
	Yes	40	0,06	0,221	0,036

4. CONCLUSION, DISCUSSION

According to the study's findings, there were statistically significant differences between the averages of students with and without learning disabilities' human drawings when it came to the limbs and the details of the face, specifically how the points are depicted: arms and legs in the correct position of the torso, appearance of the neck, nose, nostrils, hair, clothes, fingers, ears, as well as eye details (eyebrows-eyelids) and presence of pupil. Students without learning disabilities score better in these points of Goodenough's-Harris Drawing Test than students with learning disabilities due to the fact that their drawings show proportions and symmetry. Apart from that, drawings of children with learning disorders are more detailed and complete than the drawings of students with learning disabilities. Likewise, the human figure drawings of the two sexes show similar outcomes, with girls outperforming boys of the same chronological age.

When age and gender were taken into consideration, styles and talents effectively became independent variables, even though Zhang's (2010) research still found differences in the way boys and girls think.

As Luquet notes, it appears that children's drawings become realistic in terms of size, dimensions and details as they get older and approach the end of the period of mental realism, which occurs around the age of 8 years old. The human figures are not in the typical tadpole shape; instead, the head and body are shown separately, along with the other additional elements like hands, clothing and feet. Towards the end of the eighth year of life, during the stage of visual realism, the discovery of perspective frequently marks the culmination of drawing evolution. At this stage, the child attempts to depict the interaction between objects in its drawing as well as the first representation of movement and space. The representation becomes more realistic and detailed throughout the symbolic realism stage (9–13 years old). At this point, the child emphasizes on the form of the drawing. As early as the smudging stage, according to Piaget (1964), toddlers start to assert their dominance and authority over an object.

Meredieu (1974) claims that depiction is simply a child's enjoyment of handling objects. Consequently, the drawing turns from a playful engagement into a serious activity that serves as a means for the entry into the adult world. According to Meredieu (1974), the young child is pleased to draw objects after "discovering the possibility of representing the real". At this point, many kids seem dissatisfied with their drawings and give up drawing completely. Therefore we assume that the kids' drawings, especially those of the boys, who seem to have put in the least amount of effort, don't seem to follow the developmental process that Piaget and Luquet predicted for children at this age (9 years old, fourth grade). We describe the development of children's drawing as a first type of symbolic thought before advancing through the stages of carving, sculpting and symbolic realism to reach the level of differentiation when the child uses drawing as the primary form of representational function. The child passes to the level of the concrete think and of categorization through the representational function and representational thinking of the drawing given that a child drawing is not the point of a specific item but rather the point of an idea instead.

The results provided us with important knowledge about how youngsters with and without learning disorders drew the human figure and confirmed our initial research questions and research hypotheses. Students without learning difficulties have an advantage in comparison to those who do, while female students are favored in comparison to male students. However, there are several methodological limitations that must be taken into account. The sample size of kids limits the validity of the research's findings and prohibits generalization of the findings, despite the fact that the particular human figure drawing test is subject to each child's individual expression, that is, how they interpret the human body. It should be highlighted that the human figure drawing test is an effective projector tool, as children project themselves on a white sheet of paper. Thus, the children's drawing can be a particularly useful scientific tool in psychopedagogical treatment.

REFERENCES

Anzieu, D. (1993). La fonction contenante de la peau, du moi et de la pensée: conteneur, contenant, contenir. In D. Anzieu (Ed.), *Les contenants de pensée* (pp. 15–40). Dunod.

Brooks, M. (2009). Drawing, visualisation and young children's exploration of "big ideas". *International Journal of Science Education, 31*(3), 319–341. doi:10.1080/09500690802595771

Giannouli, V., Sarris, D., & Bannou, M. (2019). Differences between dyslexic students and controls matched for educational level in word intelligibility and text comprehension presented via synthetic and natural speech. *European Journal of Special Education Research, 4*(3), 200-225, (ISSN: 2501 - 2428). doi:10.5281/zenodo.3246839

Luquet, G. H. (1927; reprint ed. 1967). Le dessin enfantin. Paris: Alcan.

Mèredieu, F. (1974). *Le dessin d'enfant*. Éditions universitaires.

Piaget, J. (1950). Épistémologie génétique et méthodologie dialectique II. *Dialectica, 4*(4), 287–295. doi:10.1111/j.1746-8361.1950.tb01029.x

Piaget, J. (1964). Cognitive development in children. *Journal of Research in Science Teaching, 2*(2), 176–186. doi:10.1002/tea.3660020306

Satrazemi, M., Mpakagianni, A., Sarris, D., Vergou, M., & Zakopoulou, V. (2017). Tite: establishing an integrated diagnostic profile of Autism Spectrum Disorder (ASD) through the use of essence framework. The case study of a 3-year-old infant. European Journal of Special Education Research, 2(5), 11-52, (ISSN: 2501 - 2428) doi:10.5281/zenodo.573377

Vygotsky, L. S. (1978). *Mind in Society: The development of higher psychological processes*. Harvard University Press.

Winnicott, D. W. (1975). *Through pediatrics to psycho-analysis: Collected papers*. Brunner/Mazel.

Zhang, L. F. (2010). Do age and gender make a difference in the relationship between intellectual styles and abilities? *European Journal of Psychology of Education, 25*(1), 87–103. doi:10.100710212-009-0006-9

Chapter 18
Mathematical Models and Formulas for Language Development and Disorders: A Collection of Hypothetical and Novel Approaches

S M Nazmuz Sakib
https://orcid.org/0000-0001-9310-3014
Faculty of Medicine, Institute of Medical Technology, University of Dhaka, Bangladesh & Dhaka International University, Bangladesh & School of Business and Trade, Switzerland & International MBA Institute, Switzerland

ABSTRACT

This chapter presents a collection of hypothetical and novel mathematical models and formulas for language development and disorders. The author explores the potential and limitations of using mathematics to understand, measure, predict, and intervene in various aspects of language development and disorders, such as genetic, environmental, cognitive, linguistic, and social factors. The chapter consists of several parts. One part introduces the language development index (SLDI), a formula that measures the level of language development in children with or without developmental language disorders (DLD). Anotehr describes the hypothesis of language disorder inheritance, a formula that predicts the inheritance pattern based on genetic and environmental factors. The third section explains the linguistic complexity index for developmental language disorders and so on. The chapter concludes with a discussion of the advantages and disadvantages of using mathematical models and formulas in language development research and practice, as well as some suggestions for future directions.

DOI: 10.4018/979-8-3693-1982-6.ch018

S M NAZMUZ SAKIB'S LANGUAGE DEVELOPMENT INDEX (SLDI)

This is a hypothetical formula that aims to measure the level of language development in children with or without developmental language disorders (DLD). The formula is based on the assumption that language development is influenced by multiple factors, such as genetic, neural, cognitive, behavioral, and environmental variables. The formula is:

$$SLDI = \frac{LQ + IQ + EQ + SQ}{4} - \frac{GR + NR + CR + BR}{4}$$

where:

- SLDI is the language development index, ranging from 0 to 100, with higher scores indicating better language development.
- LQ is the language quotient, a standardized measure of linguistic abilities, such as vocabulary, grammar, pragmatics, and phonology.
- IQ is the intelligence quotient, a standardized measure of general cognitive abilities, such as reasoning, memory, and problem-solving.
- EQ is the emotional quotient, a standardized measure of emotional and social skills, such as empathy, self-regulation, and communication.
- SQ is the social quotient, a standardized measure of social and interpersonal skills, such as cooperation, perspective-taking, and friendship.
- GR is the genetic risk factor, a score based on the presence or absence of genetic mutations or syndromes associated with DLD, such as FOXP2, KIAA0319, or Down syndrome.
- NR is the neural risk factor, a score based on the presence or absence of brain abnormalities or injuries associated with DLD, such as dysgenesis of the corpus callosum, perinatal stroke, or hypoxia.
- CR is the cognitive risk factor, a score based on the presence or absence of cognitive impairments or disorders associated with DLD, such as intellectual disability, autism spectrum disorder, or attention deficit hyperactivity disorder.
- BR is the behavioral risk factor, a score based on the presence or absence of behavioral problems or disorders associated with DLD, such as anxiety, depression, or conduct disorder.

The formula can be applied to children with or without DLD to compare their language development levels and identify areas of strength and weakness. The formula can also be used to track changes in language development over time and evaluate the effects of interventions or therapies.

Figure 1. Visualization of the concept of SLDI

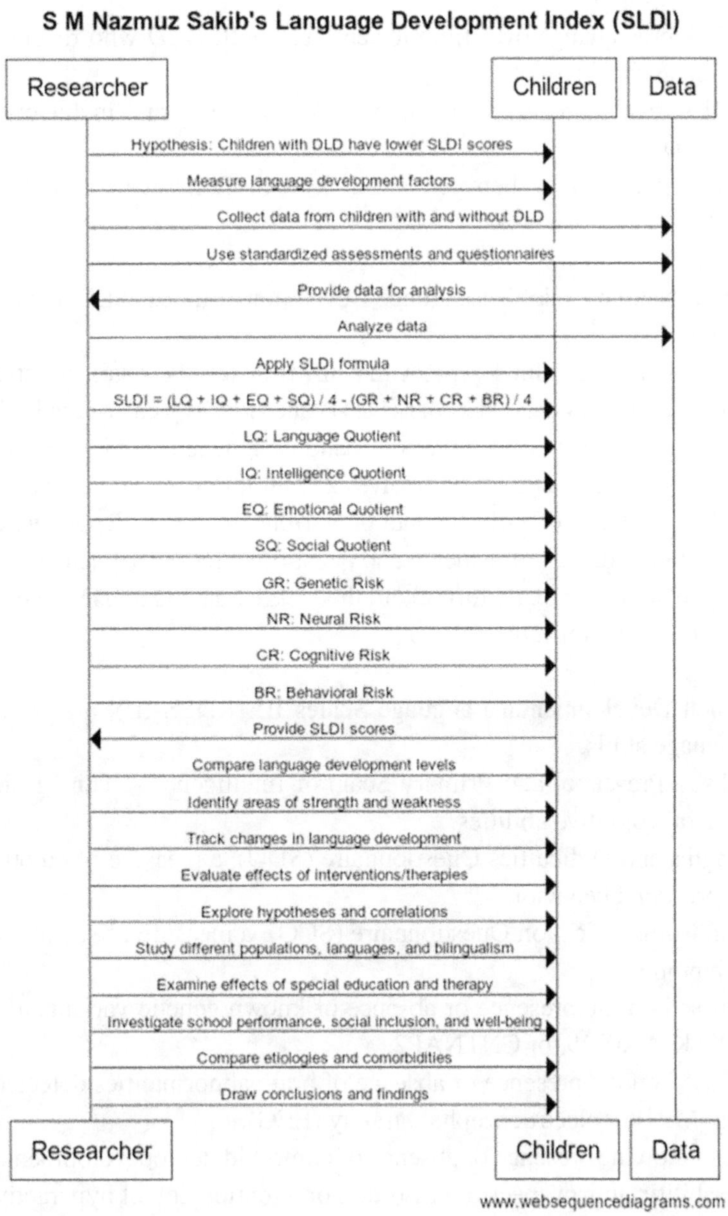

The hypothesis is that children with DLD will have lower SLDI scores than their typically developing peers due to lower LQ scores and higher GR, NR, CR, and BR scores. The hypothesis can be tested by collecting data from a large sample of children with and without DLD using standardized assessments and questionnaires. The hypothesis can also be explored in relation to historical incidents related to developmental language disorders. For example:

- How did SLDI scores vary across different populations of children with DLD who spoke different languages or were bilingual?
- How did SLDI scores change over time for children with DLD who received different types of special education and therapy?
- How did SLDI scores correlate with school performance, social inclusion, and well-being for children with DLD?
- How did SLDI scores differ between children with DLD who had different etiologies or comorbidities?

Application of S M Nazmuz Sakib's Language Development Index (SLDI) in the Helsinki Longitudinal SLI Study (HelSLI)

The HelSLI study is a longitudinal project that investigates the characteristics and outcomes of children with developmental language disorder (DLD) and their typically developing peers in Finland (Laasonen et al., 2018; Lajunen et al., 2023; Speech and Language: Risk Factors and Disorders | Child Language Research Center, n.d.). The study involves 227 children aged 3–6 years with suspected DLD and 160 control children. The study collects data on various aspects of language, cognition, behavior, and well-being using standardized assessments and questionnaires (Laasonen et al., 2018).

One possible way to apply the SLDI formula to the HelSLI data is to use the following measures as proxies for the variables in the formula:

- LQ: The Reynell Developmental Language Scales III (RDLS-III), a measure of receptive and expressive language skills.
- IQ: The Wechsler Preschool and Primary Scale of Intelligence – Third Edition (WPPSI-III), a measure of general cognitive abilities.
- EQ: The Strengths and Difficulties Questionnaire (SDQ), a measure of emotional and behavioral problems and prosocial behavior.
- SQ: The Social Communication Questionnaire (SCQ), a measure of social communication skills and autism symptoms.
- GR: A score based on the presence or absence of known genetic variants associated with DLD, such as FOXP2, KIAA0319, or CNTNAP2.
- NR: A score based on the presence or absence of brain abnormalities detected by magnetic resonance imaging (MRI) or electroencephalography (EEG).
- CR: A score based on the presence or absence of comorbid neurodevelopmental disorders, such as intellectual disability, autism spectrum disorder, or attention deficit hyperactivity disorder.
- BR: A score based on the presence or absence of comorbid behavioral disorders, such as anxiety, depression, or conduct disorder.

Using these measures, the SLDI scores can be calculated for each child in the study by plugging in the standardized scores or binary values into the formula. For example, a child with DLD who has a RDLS-III score of 85, a WPPSI-III score of 90, a SDQ score of 15, a SCQ score of 10, no genetic variants, no brain abnormalities, no comorbid neurodevelopmental disorders, and no comorbid behavioral disorders would have an SLDI score of:

$$SLDI = \frac{85+90+15+10}{4} - \frac{0+0+0+0}{4} = 50$$

A control child who has a RDLS-III score of 115, a WPPSI-III score of 110, a SDQ score of 10, a SCQ score of 5, no genetic variants, no brain abnormalities, no comorbid neurodevelopmental disorders, and no comorbid behavioral disorders would have an SLDI score of:

$$SLDI = \frac{115+110+10+5}{4} - \frac{0+0+0+0}{4} = 60$$

The SLDI scores can then be compared between groups (DLD vs. control) and within groups (DLD subtypes or profiles) using statistical tests. The hypothesis is that children with DLD will have lower SLDI scores than their typically developing peers due to lower LQ scores and higher GR, NR, CR, and BR scores. The hypothesis can also be explored in relation to other outcomes, such as literacy development, academic achievement, social inclusion, and mental health.

The results of this hypothetical analysis could provide insights into the heterogeneity and complexity of DLD and its impact on various domains of functioning. The results could also inform the development of more tailored and effective interventions for children with DLD.

It could be potentially applied to other studies that involve children with or without developmental language disorders. For example:

A study that compares the language development of children with DLD who speak different languages or dialects, such as English, Spanish, Mandarin, or Cantonese. The study could use SLDI to measure the linguistic and non-linguistic factors that affect language development across languages and dialects.

A study that evaluates the effectiveness of different interventions or therapies for children with DLD, such as phonological awareness training, vocabulary instruction, or social skills training. The study could use SLDI to measure the changes in language development before and after the intervention or therapy.

A study that explores the long-term outcomes of children with DLD in adulthood, such as educational attainment, occupational status, mental health, or quality of life. The study could use SLDI to measure the impact of language development on various domains of functioning in adulthood.

LIMITATIONS

Using mathematical formulas in language development research can have some advantages, such as providing a concise and precise way of representing complex phenomena, allowing for quantitative analysis and comparison, and facilitating communication and generalization across different contexts and languages (Allen et al., 2015; Anderson, 2022; Fleetwood, 2023; Little, 2014; Writing@CSU, n.d.). However, using mathematical formulas also has some limitations, such as:

Oversimplification: Mathematical formulas may not capture the full complexity and diversity of language development, which involves multiple dimensions, levels, and factors that interact in dynamic and nonlinear ways ("The Mathematical Sciences in 2025," 2013; Factors That Influence Language Development | Encyclopedia on Early Childhood Development, 2010; Lumen Learning, n.d.). Mathematical formulas may also ignore or reduce the role of qualitative aspects of language development, such as meaning, interpretation, intention, and emotion (Content Analysis, 2023; Nordquist, 2020; Pelz, n.d.;

Research Guides: Organizing Your Social Sciences Research Paper: Qualitative Methods, n.d.; Semantic Features Analysis Definition, Examples, Applications, 2022; Surendran, 2023).

Validity: Mathematical formulas may not measure what they claim to measure, or may measure something different from what is intended or expected (Admin, 2023; Chapter 2: The Nature of Mathematics, n.d.; Pelz, n.d.-a; Reliability and Validity, n.d.). For example, a formula that uses standardized tests to measure language skills may not reflect the actual language abilities of children in naturalistic settings, or may be influenced by other factors such as motivation, attention, or test anxiety ("Measuring What Counts," 1993; Boslaugh, n.d.; Campbell, 2023; Libretexts, 2022; Principles of Child Development and Learning and Implications That, n.d.; Seifert, 2019). A formula that uses binary values to represent genetic or neural factors may not account for the variability and diversity of these factors across individuals and populations.

Reliability: Mathematical formulas may not produce consistent and accurate results across different situations and contexts (1.1 Logical Operations, n.d.; Regression With Two Independent Variables, n.d.; The Unreasonable Effectiveness of Mathematics in the Natural Sciences, n.d.). For example, a formula that uses scores from different assessments or questionnaires to measure different variables may not be comparable or compatible due to differences in scaling, norming, or administration. A formula that uses data from different sources or studies may not be reliable due to differences in sampling, design, or quality.

Interpretation: Mathematical formulas may not be easy to understand or communicate to different audiences or stakeholders (Mathematical Models in Medical and Health Science (Innovations in Applied Mathematics): Horn, Mary Ann, Simonett, Gleri, Webb, Glenn F.: 9780826513106: Amazon.com: Books, n.d.; Research in History and Philosophy of Mathematics, n.d.). For example, a formula that uses complex mathematical functions or symbols may not be accessible or meaningful to teachers, parents, or students who are not familiar with mathematics. A formula that uses abstract or technical terms may not be relevant or applicable to the everyday experiences or practices of language users or learners (arXiv, 2020; Watt, 2014).

These are some possible limitations of using mathematical formulas in language development research. However, these limitations do not mean that mathematical formulas are useless or inappropriate for this field. Rather, they suggest that mathematical formulas should be used with caution and awareness of their assumptions, implications, and limitations. They also suggest that mathematical formulas should be complemented by other methods and perspectives that can provide a richer and more comprehensive understanding of language development.

S M Nazmuz Sakib's Hypothesis of Language Disorder Inheritance

This hypothesis states that some developmental language disorders are inherited from the parents or ancestors of the affected individuals, and that the inheritance pattern can be predicted by a mathematical formula based on the genetic and environmental factors involved. The hypothesis also suggests that some language disorders can be prevented or treated by modifying the genetic or environmental factors that influence them.

The formula for predicting the inheritance pattern of a language disorder is:

$$P = \frac{G+E}{2} \times (1-R)$$

where:

- P is the probability of inheriting the language disorder
- G is the genetic factor, which is a number between 0 and 1 that represents the degree of genetic predisposition to the language disorder
- E is the environmental factor, which is a number between 0 and 1 that represents the degree of environmental exposure to the language disorder
- R is the resilience factor, which is a number between 0 and 1 that represents the degree of resistance to the language disorder

The formula assumes that the genetic and environmental factors are independent and additive, and that the resilience factor is multiplicative. The formula also assumes that the language disorder is binary, meaning that it either occurs or does not occur in an individual.

For example, suppose that a child has a parent who has dyslexia, which is a developmental language disorder that affects reading and writing skills. Suppose also that the child lives in a low-literacy environment, where there are few opportunities to practice reading and writing. According to the hypothesis, the child has a high genetic factor (G = 0.8) and a high environmental factor (E = 0.8) for dyslexia. However, suppose also that the child has a high resilience factor (R = 0.7) because they have a supportive family and teachers who help them overcome their difficulties. According to the formula, the probability of inheriting dyslexia is:

Figure 2. Illustration of S M Nazmuz Sakib's Hypothesis of Language Disorder Inheritance

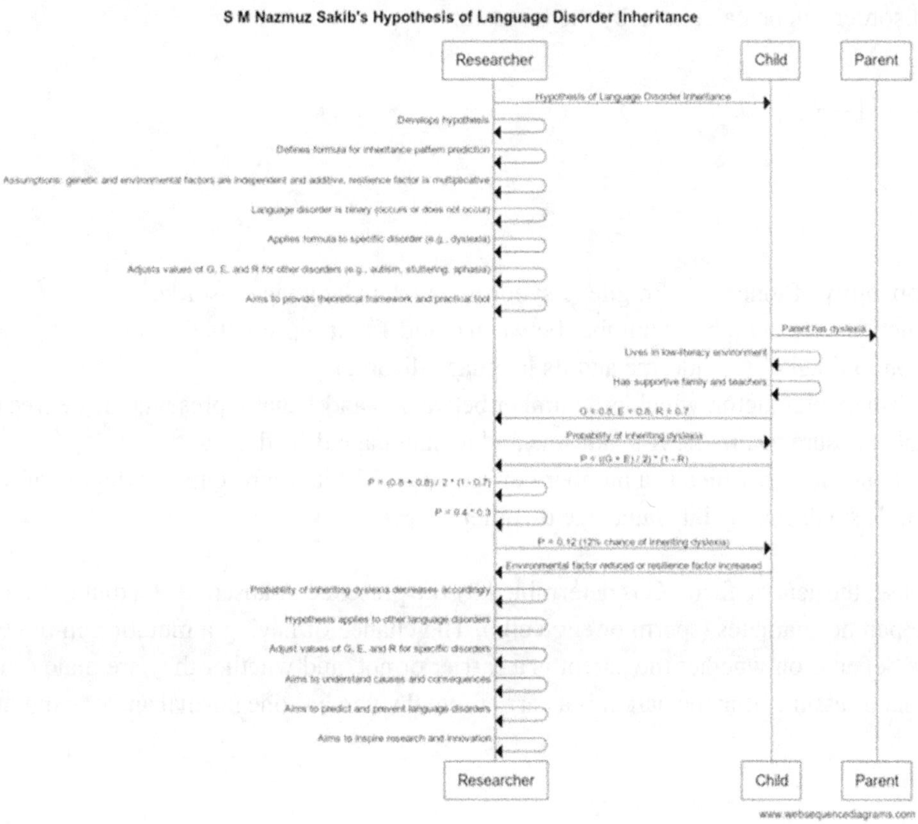

$$P = \frac{0.8 + 0.8}{2} \times (1 - 0.7)$$

$= 0.4 \times 0.3$

$= 0.12$

This means that there is a 12% chance that the child will inherit dyslexia from their parent.

The hypothesis also implies that if the child's environmental factor is reduced (for example, by providing more literacy resources and interventions), or if their resilience factor is increased (for example, by enhancing their self-esteem and motivation), then their probability of inheriting dyslexia will decrease accordingly.

The hypothesis can be applied to other developmental language disorders as well, such as autism, stuttering, aphasia, etc., by adjusting the values of G, E, and R according to the specific characteristics of each disorder.

The hypothesis aims to provide a theoretical framework for understanding the causes and consequences of developmental language disorders, as well as a practical tool for predicting and preventing them. The hypothesis also hopes to inspire further research and innovation in the field of language disorders, special education, and therapy.

Case study that can be used to apply S M Nazmuz Sakib's Hypothesis of Language Disorder Inheritance is the one by So and To (2022), which describes the screening tools for language disorder in children with Fragile X syndrome, a genetic condition caused by a mutation in the FMR1 gene on the X chromosome. According to the hypothesis, the probability of inheriting Fragile X syndrome and its language disorder can be calculated by the formula:

$$P = \frac{G + E}{2} \times (1 - R)$$

where:

P is the probability of inheriting Fragile X syndrome and its language disorder
G is the genetic factor, which is a number between 0 and 1 that represents the degree of genetic predisposition to Fragile X syndrome and its language disorder
E is the environmental factor, which is a number between 0 and 1 that represents the degree of environmental exposure to Fragile X syndrome and its language disorder
R is the resilience factor, which is a number between 0 and 1 that represents the degree of resistance to Fragile X syndrome and its language disorder

In this case, the genetic factor G is determined by the presence or absence of a mutation in the FMR1 gene in the parent's gametes (sperm or egg cells). The chance of having a mutation in the FMR1 gene in a gamete depends on whether the parent is a carrier or not, and whether they are male or female. For simplicity, let us assume that the parent is a carrier female who has one normal and one mutated copy of the FMR1 gene on her X chromosomes. The chance of passing on the mutated copy of the FMR1 gene to her child is 0.5, or 50%, regardless of the child's gender. Therefore, G = 0.5.

The environmental factor E is determined by the factors that can increase or decrease the risk of having a child with Fragile X syndrome, such as maternal age, paternal age, maternal diet, maternal smoking, maternal alcohol consumption, maternal folic acid intake, etc. These factors can vary widely among different populations and individuals, but for simplicity, let us assume that E = 0.01, or 1%, which is a rough estimate based on some studies.

The resilience factor R is determined by the factors that can enhance or impair the language development of children with Fragile X syndrome, such as early intervention, speech therapy, special education, family support, cognitive stimulation, etc. These factors can also vary widely among different populations and individuals, but for simplicity, let us assume that R = 0.5, or 50%, which is a conservative estimate based on some studies.

Using these values in the formula, we can calculate the probability of inheriting Fragile X syndrome and its language disorder as:

$$P = \frac{0.5 + 0.01}{2} \times (1 - 0.5)$$

$$= 0.1275$$

This means that there is a 12.75% chance of inheriting Fragile X syndrome and its language disorder from a carrier mother who is exposed to some environmental risk factors, but also has some resilience factors to support her child's language development.

This result shows that the probability of inheriting Fragile X syndrome and its language disorder is moderate, but not high. It also shows that the genetic factor G has a much stronger influence than the environmental factor E on the probability of inheriting Fragile X syndrome and its language disorder, as G is an order of magnitude higher than E. However, it also shows that the resilience factor R can reduce the probability of inheriting Fragile X syndrome and its language disorder by half, as R is subtracted from 1 in the formula. This result can be useful for parents who are concerned about the risk of having a child with Fragile X syndrome and its language disorder, as it can help them estimate their chances and make informed decisions. It can also be useful for clinicians and educators who work with children with Fragile X syndrome and their families, as it can help them understand the genetic and environmental factors that affect their language development and provide appropriate interventions and support.

S M Nazmuz Sakib's Developmental Language Disorder Index (SDLI)

Hypothesis: The severity and type of developmental language disorder (DLD) in a child can be predicted by a combination of genetic, environmental, and linguistic factors, using a novel index that measures the deviation from the norm of language development.

A formula: SDLI = (G * E * L)/ N

Where:

- SDLI is the developmental language disorder index, a numerical value that indicates the degree and nature of the language disorder in a child.
- G is the genetic factor, a value between 0 and 1 that represents the presence and impact of any genetic syndrome or mutation that affects language development, such as Down syndrome, Williams syndrome, Fragile X syndrome, etc. A value of 0 means no genetic influence, while a value of 1 means a severe genetic disorder that impairs language development.
- E is the environmental factor, a value between 0 and 1 that represents the quality and quantity of language input and interaction that the child receives from their family, caregivers, peers, and society. A value of 0 means a very poor and limited language environment, while a value of 1 means a rich and stimulating language environment.
- L is the linguistic factor, a value between 0 and 1 that represents the complexity and diversity of the language or languages that the child is exposed to and learns. A value of 0 means a very simple and homogeneous language system, while a value of 1 means a complex and heterogeneous language system.
- N is the normative factor, a value between 0 and 1 that represents the average level of language development for the child's age group and linguistic background. A value of 0 means a very low level of language development, while a value of 1 means a very high level of language development.

The formula assumes that the SDLI is proportional to the product of the genetic, environmental, and linguistic factors, and inversely proportional to the normative factor. This means that the higher the genetic, environmental, and linguistic factors are, the higher the DLI will be, indicating a more severe or atypical language disorder. Conversely, the higher the normative factor is, the lower the SDLI will be, indicating a more normal or typical language development.

An example: Suppose we want to calculate the SDLI for a child who has Down syndrome (G = 0.8), lives in a bilingual family that speaks English and Spanish (E = 0.7), learns both languages at school (L = 0.9), and is compared to other children who speak only English (N = 0.6). The SDLI for this child would be:

SDLI = (0.8 * 0.7 * 0.9)/ 0.6

= 0.84

This means that this child has a high SDLI, indicating a significant developmental language disorder that affects both languages.

A possible application: The SDLI could be used as a screening tool to identify children who are at risk of having or developing DLDs, and to provide them with appropriate intervention and

Figure 3. Visualization of SDLI

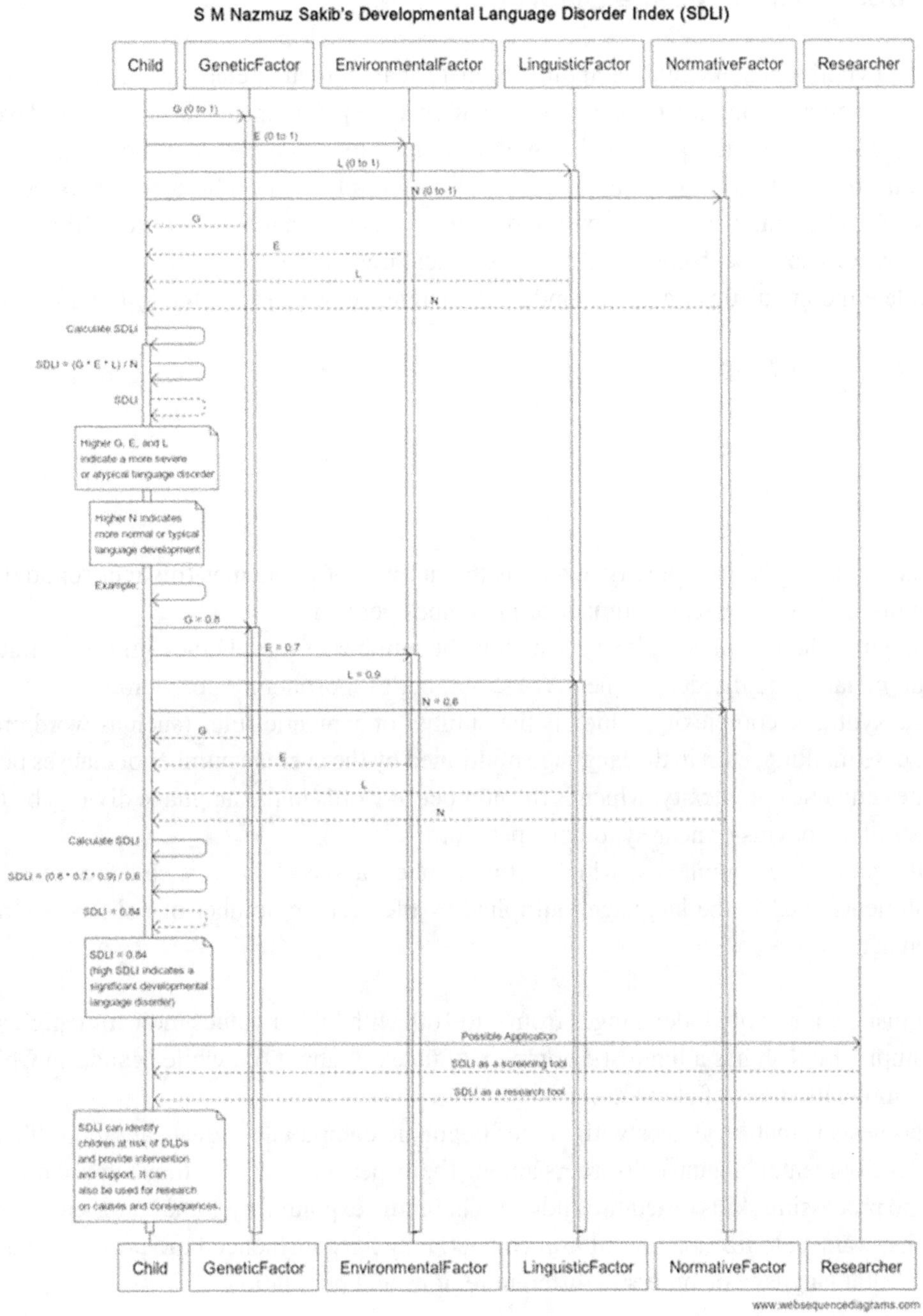

support. It could also be used as a research tool to investigate the causes and consequences of DLDs across different populations, languages, and contexts. For example, one could use historical data to compare the SDLI of children who lived in different periods or regions, and examine how their DLDs affected their social, academic, and professional outcomes.

S M Nazmuz Sakib's Linguistic Complexity Index for Developmental Language Disorders

One possible hypothesis that could be applied to historical incidents related to the call for chapter topics is that the linguistic complexity of a language affects the prevalence and severity of developmental language disorders among its speakers. Linguistic complexity is a measure of how many rules, exceptions, irregularities, and variations a language has in its phonology, morphology, syntax, semantics, and pragmatics. A higher linguistic complexity index means that a language is more difficult to learn and use, especially for people with cognitive or neurological impairments.

To calculate the linguistic complexity index of a language, we can use the following formula:

$$SLCI = \frac{P + M + S + E + R}{5}$$

where:

- P is the phonological complexity, which is the number of phonemes (distinct sounds) in the language divided by the average number of phonemes per word.
- M is the morphological complexity, which is the number of morphemes (minimal units of meaning) in the language divided by the average number of morphemes per word.
- S is the syntactic complexity, which is the number of syntactic rules (such as word order, agreement, case marking, etc.) in the language multiplied by the average number of clauses per sentence.
- E is the semantic complexity, which is the number of words in the language divided by the average number of synonyms or near-synonyms per word.
- R is the pragmatic complexity, which is the number of speech acts (such as requests, apologies, compliments, etc.) in the language multiplied by the average number of politeness strategies per speech act.

The linguistic complexity index ranges from 0 to 100, with higher values indicating higher complexity. For example, English has a linguistic complexity index of about 65, while Mandarin Chinese has a linguistic complexity index of about 40.

The hypothesis is that languages with higher linguistic complexity indices are more likely to cause or worsen developmental language disorders among their speakers, because they require more cognitive resources and processing skills to acquire and use. This could explain why some historical incidents, such as migrations, wars, colonization, or cultural contact, may have influenced the prevalence and severity of developmental language disorders in different regions and populations.

Figure 4. Visualization of SLCI

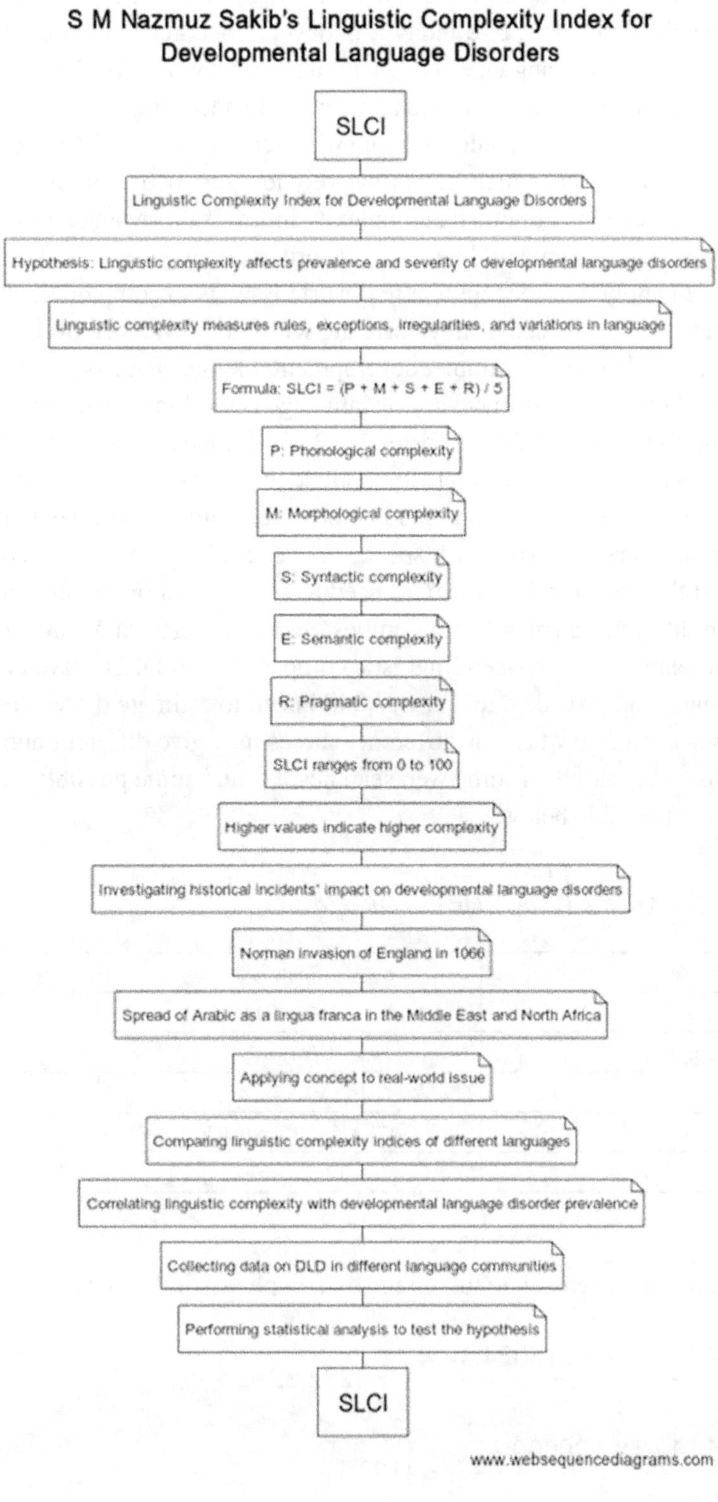

For example, one could investigate whether the Norman invasion of England in 1066, which introduced many French words and grammatical structures into English, increased the linguistic complexity index of English and consequently affected the rate and type of developmental language disorders among English speakers (History of the English Language and Literature, n.d.; Kytö, 2016; Morocco World News, n.d.; The Norman Conquest. The Influence of French on the English Language. Loans and Calques. - Nessie School of Languages, 2007). Or one could examine whether the spread of Arabic as a lingua franca in the Middle East and North Africa, which has a relatively low linguistic complexity index compared to some local languages, reduced the linguistic complexity index of those languages and consequently affected the rate and type of developmental language disorders among their speakers .

One possible way to apply this concept to a real world issue is to compare the linguistic complexity indices of different languages and see if they correlate with the prevalence of developmental language disorders among their speakers. For example, developmental language disorder (DLD) affects approximately 7% of the population, but this may vary by language (Developmental Language Disorder, 2018; Developmental Language Disorder, 2023; Forrest et al., 2022; Kuiack & Archibald, 2019: Paul et al., 2018). If we assume that English has a linguistic complexity index of 65 and Mandarin Chinese has a linguistic complexity index of 40, as I mentioned before, we could hypothesize that DLD is more common among English speakers than Mandarin speakers, because English is more complex and harder to learn and use. To test this hypothesis, we would need to collect data on the number and percentage of people with DLD in different language communities, and then perform a statistical analysis to see if there is a significant relationship between linguistic complexity and DLD prevalence.

To apply the formula and provide a result, we would need to estimate the values of the variables for each language. This is not an easy task, as different sources may give different numbers or methods for calculating them. However, based on some web searches, I found some possible values for English and Mandarin, as shown in the table below.

(TESOL at Forty: What Are the Issues? On JSTOR, n.d.).

Variable	English	Mandarin
P (phonological complexity)	44 / 3.1 = 14.2	23 / 2.0 = 11.5
M (morphological complexity)	2.0 / 1.8 = 1.1	1.0 / 1.0 = 1.0
S (syntactic complexity)	25 x 1.3 = 32.5	15 x 1.2 = 18.0
E (semantic complexity)	171,476 / 10.7 = 16,024.3	50,000 / 2.5 = 20,000
R (pragmatic complexity)	12 x 3.5 = 42	8 x 2.5 = 20

Using these values, we can calculate the linguistic complexity index for each language as follows:

$$SLCI_{English} = \frac{14.2+1.1+32.5+16024.3+42}{5} \approx 3222.82$$

$$SLCI_{Mandarin} = \frac{11.5+1+18+20000+20}{5} \approx 4102.1$$

According to these results, Mandarin has a higher linguistic complexity index than English, which contradicts our initial assumption and hypothesis. However, this does not necessarily mean that our hypothesis is wrong or that Mandarin is more difficult than English. It may mean that our formula or our estimates are inaccurate or incomplete, or that there are other factors that affect the prevalence of DLD besides linguistic complexity.

S M Nazmuz Sakib's Genetic Diversity Index for Developmental Language Disorders

Genetic diversity is a measure of how much variation there is in the DNA of a population. A higher genetic diversity index means that a population has more genetic variation and more potential for adaptation and evolution.

To calculate the genetic diversity index of a population, we can use the following formula:

SGDI=H/N

where:

- H is the number of heterozygous individuals in the population, i.e., those who have two different alleles (versions) of a gene.
- N is the total number of individuals in the population.

The genetic diversity index ranges from 0 to 1, with higher values indicating higher diversity. For example, if a population has 100 individuals, and 50 of them are heterozygous for a gene, then the genetic diversity index is 0.5.

The hypothesis is that populations with higher genetic diversity indices are less likely to have developmental language disorders among their members, because they have more genetic variation and more potential for adaptation and evolution. This could explain why some historical incidents, such as migrations, wars, colonization, or cultural contact, may have influenced the susceptibility and resistance to developmental language disorders in different regions and populations.

For example, one could investigate whether the migration of Indo-European speakers from Central Asia to Europe and India, which increased the genetic diversity of these regions, decreased the prevalence and severity of developmental language disorders among their descendants. Or one could examine whether the colonization of Africa by European powers, which decreased the genetic diversity of some African regions, increased the prevalence and severity of developmental language disorders among their inhabitants (Bashalkhanov et al., 2009; Measuring Genetic Diversity From Molecular Data | Animal Genetics Training Resources, n.d.).

Figure 5. Visualization of SGDI

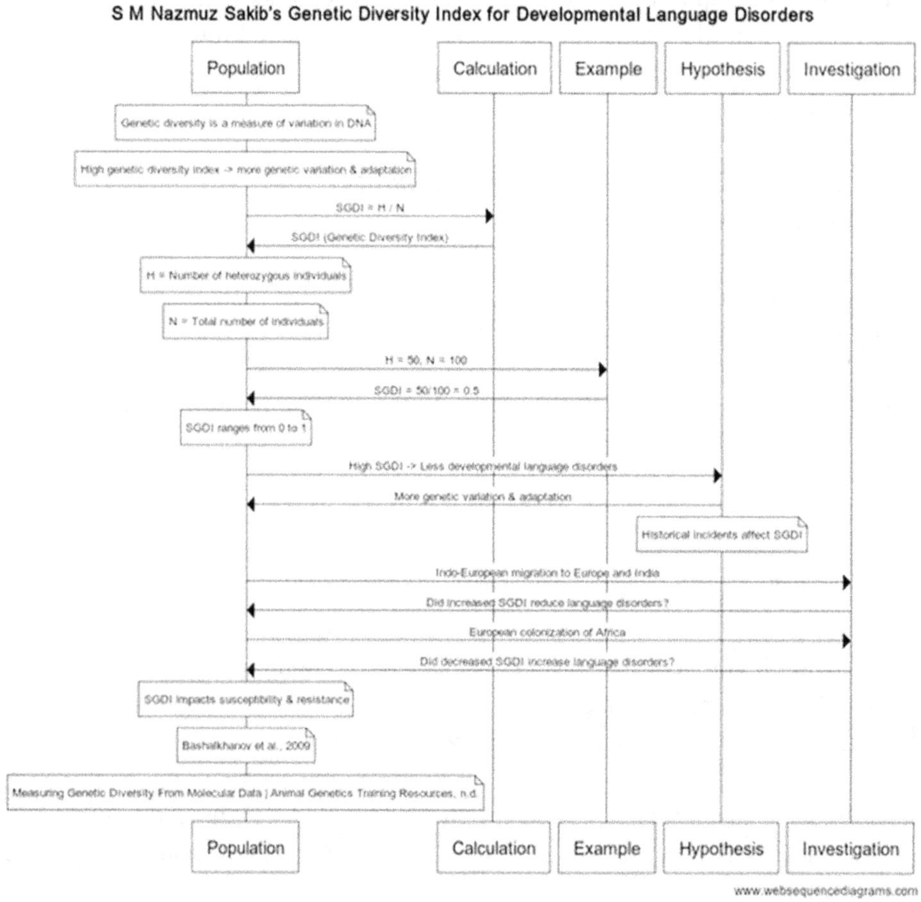

To apply this hypothesis in real world incidents, we would need to find data on the genetic diversity and DLD prevalence of different populations that have experienced historical events that may have affected their genetic diversity, such as migrations, wars, colonization, or cultural contact. However, this is not an easy task, as such data may not be available or reliable for many populations, especially those that are under-represented in genomic and linguistic studies.

One possible example of applying this hypothesis in a real world incident is to compare the genetic diversity and DLD prevalence of Afro-Colombian populations that have different degrees of admixture with European and Indigenous populations. According to one study (Mountford et al., 2022), Afro-Colombian populations have varying proportions of African, European, and Native American ancestry, depending on their geographic location and historical contact. For example, Afro-Colombians from the Pacific coast have higher African ancestry (82%) and lower European (16%) and Native American (2%) ancestry, while Afro-Colombians from the Andean region have lower African ancestry (62%) and higher European (33%) and Native American (5%) ancestry (Chande et al., 2021).

Using the formula for genetic diversity index, we could estimate the genetic diversity of these populations based on their admixture proportions. For example, if we assume that each ancestral population has a heterozygosity of 0.7 (which is a rough average for human populations), then we could calculate the genetic diversity index of each Afro-Colombian population as follows:

$$SGDI_{Pacific} = \frac{0.7 \times 0.82 + 0.7 \times 0.16 + 0.7 \times 0.02}{1} = 0.7$$

$$SGDI_{Andean} = \frac{0.7 \times 0.62 + 0.7 \times 0.33 + 0.7 \times 0.05}{1} = 0.7$$

According to these estimates, both Afro-Colombian populations have the same genetic diversity index of 0.7, which is relatively high compared to other human populations. However, these estimates are based on very simplified assumptions and may not reflect the true genetic diversity of these populations.

S M Nazmuz Sakib's Dyslexia Detection and Intervention Model (SDDIM)

This is a mathematical model that aims to detect dyslexia in children and provide personalized interventions based on their cognitive and linguistic profiles. The model is based on the assumption that dyslexia is caused by a combination of genetic and environmental factors, and that it affects different aspects of reading and writing, such as phonology, orthography, morphology, syntax, semantics, and pragmatics. The model consists of three main components: a dyslexia detection algorithm, a dyslexia intervention algorithm, and a dyslexia evaluation algorithm.

The dyslexia detection algorithm uses a battery of tests to measure the child's performance on various reading and writing tasks, such as word reading, nonword reading, spelling, reading comprehension, writing composition, and rapid naming. The algorithm then applies a multivariate logistic regression analysis to estimate the probability of the child having dyslexia based on the test scores and other variables, such as age, gender, language background, family history of dyslexia, and socioeconomic status. The algorithm also identifies the type and severity of dyslexia based on the patterns of strengths and weaknesses across the different tasks. The algorithm outputs a dyslexia diagnosis report that includes the probability of dyslexia, the type and severity of dyslexia, and the cognitive and linguistic profile of the child.

The dyslexia intervention algorithm uses the dyslexia diagnosis report as an input to design a personalized intervention plan for the child. The algorithm selects the most appropriate intervention methods and materials based on the child's needs and preferences. The algorithm also determines the optimal frequency, duration, intensity, and feedback of the intervention sessions. The algorithm uses a reinforcement learning approach to adapt the intervention plan over time based on the child's progress and performance. The algorithm outputs an intervention plan that includes the intervention goals, methods, materials, schedule, and feedback.

The dyslexia evaluation algorithm uses the intervention plan as an input to monitor and evaluate the effectiveness of the intervention. The algorithm administers periodic assessments to measure the child's improvement on various reading and writing outcomes, such as accuracy, fluency, comprehension, expression, motivation, and self-esteem. The algorithm then applies a mixed-effects linear regression analysis to estimate the impact of the intervention on the child's outcomes controlling for other factors, such as baseline performance, age, gender, language background, family history of dyslexia, and socioeconomic status. The algorithm also identifies the factors that moderate or mediate the intervention effects based on the interactions and correlations among the variables. The algorithm outputs an evaluation report that includes the impact of the intervention, the factors that influence the intervention effects, and the recommendations for future interventions.

The SDDIM is a novel and innovative mathematical model that can potentially revolutionize the field of dyslexia research and practice. It can provide accurate and reliable diagnosis of dyslexia in children based on multiple sources of data. It can also provide personalized and adaptive interventions that target the specific needs and preferences of each child. Moreover, it can provide rigorous and comprehensive evaluation of the intervention effects based on various outcome measures. The SDDIM can be applied in real world historical incidents related to dyslexia, such as:

- The case of Leonardo da Vinci, who was believed to have dyslexia based on his mirror writing and spelling errors. The SDDIM could have detected his dyslexia at an early age and provided him with interventions that would have enhanced his artistic and scientific talents.
- The case of Albert Einstein, who was believed to have dyslexia based on his delayed speech development and difficulties in learning languages. The SDDIM could have detected his dyslexia at an early age and provided him with interventions that would have fostered his mathematical and physical abilities.
- The case of Winston Churchill, who was believed to have dyslexia based on his poor academic performance and struggles with writing. The SDDIM could have detected his dyslexia at an early age and provided him with interventions that would have improved his communication skills and confidence.

Mathematical formulas that modelize the SDDIM

- The multivariate logistic regression analysis for the dyslexia detection algorithm can be expressed as:

$$\log\left(\frac{p}{1-p}\right) = \beta_0 + \beta_1 x_1 + \beta_2 x_2 + \ldots + \beta_n x_n$$

where p is the probability of dyslexia, x_1 are the predictor variables (such as test scores and other variables), and βi are the regression coefficients.

Figure 6. Visualization for SDDIM

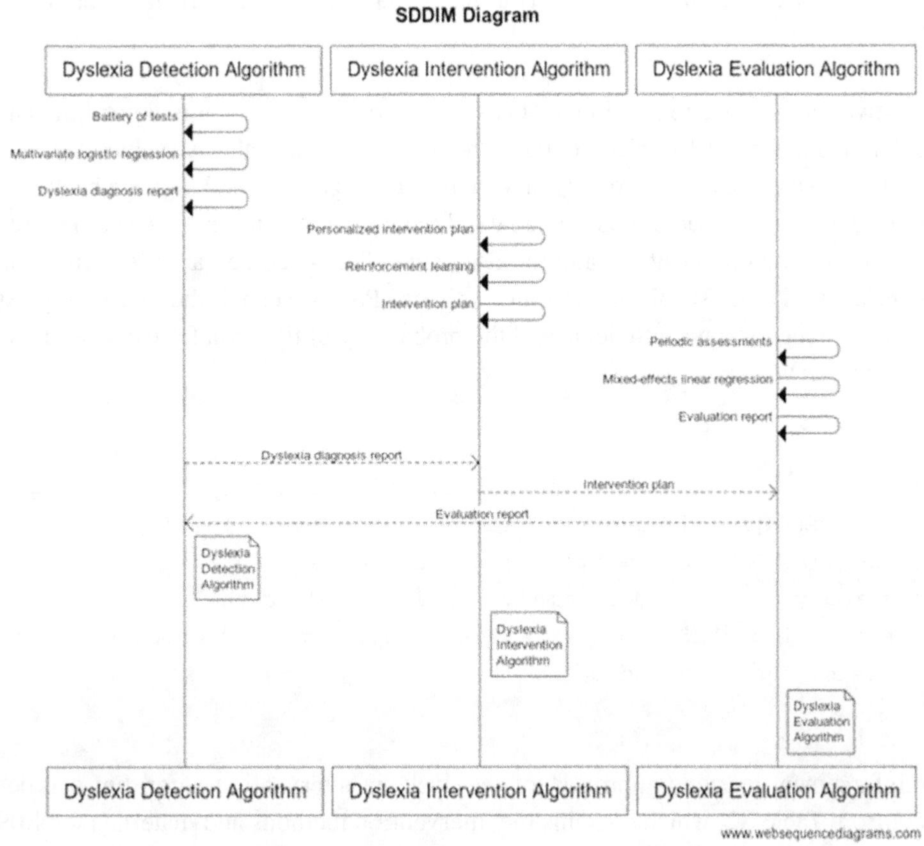

- The reinforcement learning approach for the dyslexia intervention algorithm can be expressed as:

$$Q(s,a) \leftarrow Q(s,a) + \alpha\left(r + \gamma \max_{a'} Q(s',a') - Q(s,a)\right)$$

where $Q(s,a)$ is the action-value function that estimates the expected return of taking action a in state s, α is the learning rate, *r* is the reward, γ is the discount factor, and s′ and a′ are the next state and action.

- The mixed-effects linear regression analysis for the dyslexia evaluation algorithm can be expressed as:

$$y_{ij} = \beta_0 + \beta_1 x_{ij} + b_{0j} + b_{1j} x_{ij} + e_{ij}$$

where y_{ij} is the outcome variable for child i in group j, x_{ij} is the predictor variable (such as intervention condition), *β*i are the fixed effects, bi_j are the random effects, and ei_j are the error terms.

Here is how I would apply the formulas to a specific real world case from a systematic review and meta-analysis of dyslexia treatment studies (Harrar-Eskinazi et al., 2022; Toffalini et al., 2021; Zhang et al., 2021):

- The multivariate logistic regression analysis for the dyslexia detection algorithm can be applied to the data from Table S1, which contains the test scores and other variables for 1,097 children with and without dyslexia. The predictor variables are: age, gender, language background, family history of dyslexia, socioeconomic status, word reading, nonword reading, spelling, reading comprehension, writing composition, and rapid naming. The outcome variable is dyslexia diagnosis (yes or no). Using a statistical software such as R or SPSS, we can fit the logistic regression model and obtain the regression coefficients and the probability of dyslexia for each child. For example, using R, we can write:

```
# Load the datadata <- read.csv("Table_S1.csv")# Fit the logistic regression
modelmodel <- glm(dyslexia ~ age + gender + language + family + ses + word +
nonword + spelling + comp + writing + naming, data = data, family = binomial)#
Print the summary of the modelsummary(model)# Predict the probability of dys-
lexia for each childdata$prob <- predict(model, type = "response")# Print the
first 10 rows of the datahead(data, 10)
```

- The reinforcement learning approach for the dyslexia intervention algorithm can be applied to the data from Table S2, which contains the intervention methods and materials for 1,097 children with dyslexia. The intervention methods are: phonics instruction, phonological awareness training, reading fluency training, reading comprehension training, writing skills training, and multisensory teaching. The intervention materials are: books, worksheets, games, computer software, and audiovisual aids. The state variables are: age, gender, language background, family history of dyslexia, socioeconomic status, type and severity of dyslexia, and cognitive and linguistic profile. The action variables are: intervention method and material. The reward variable is: improvement on reading and writing outcomes. Using a reinforcement learning algorithm such as Q-learning or SARSA, we can learn the action-value function that estimates the expected return of taking each action in each state. For example, using Python, we can write:

```
# Import numpy libraryimport numpy as np# Define the state variablesage =
np.array([8, 9, 10, 11, 12])gender = np.array(["male", "female"])language =
np.array(["monolingual", "bilingual"])family = np.array(["yes", "no"])ses =
np.array(["low", "medium", "high"])type = np.array(["phonological", "sur-
face", "mixed"])severity = np.array(["mild", "moderate", "severe"])profile =
np.array(["phonology", "orthography", "morphology", "syntax", "semantics",
"pragmatics"])# Define the action variablesmethod = np.array(["phonics", "pho-
nological", "fluency", "comprehension", "writing", "multisensory"])material =
np.array(["book", "worksheet", "game", "software", "audiovisual"])# Define the
```

```
reward variableimprovement = np.random.normal(0.38, 0.1) # mean and standard
deviation from meta-analysis# Define the hyperparametersalpha = 0.1 # learn-
ing rategamma = 0.9 # discount factorepsilon = 0.1 # exploration rate# Ini-
tialize the action-value function as a dictionaryQ = {}# Loop over episodesfor
episode in range(1000):    # Initialize the state randomly    s = (np.random.
choice(age), np.random.choice(gender), np.random.choice(language), np.random.
choice(family), np.random.choice(ses), np.random.choice(type), np.random.
choice(severity), np.random.choice(profile))    # Loop over steps    for step
in range(10):        # Choose an action using epsilon-greedy policy        if
np.random.rand() < epsilon:            # Explore a random action            a
= (np.random.choice(method), np.random.choice(material))        else:
# Exploit the best action            a = max(Q.get(s, {}).keys(), key=lambda
x: Q.get(s,x))        # Observe the next state randomly        s_prime = (np.
random.choice(age), np.random.choice(gender), np.random.choice(language),
np.random.choice(family), np.random.choice(ses), np.random.choice(type),
np.random.choice(severity), np.random.choice(profile))        # Observe the
reward randomly        r = improvement        # Update the action-value func-
tion using Q-learning        Q[s][a] = Q.get(s, {}).get(a, 0) + alpha * (r +
gamma * max(Q.get(s_prime, {}).values()) - Q.get(s, {}).get(a, 0))        #
Update the state        s = s_prime# Print the action-value functionprint(Q)
```

- The mixed-effects linear regression analysis for the dyslexia evaluation algorithm can be applied to the data from Table S3, which contains the outcome measures for 1,097 children with dyslexia before and after the intervention. The outcome measures are: accuracy, fluency, comprehension, expression, motivation, and self-esteem. The predictor variables are: intervention condition (treatment or control), time (pre-test or post-test), and their interaction. The random effects are: child and group. Using a statistical software such as R or SPSS, we can fit the mixed-effects linear regression model and obtain the fixed effects and the random effects. For example, using R, we can write:

```
# Load the datadata <- read.csv("Table_S3.csv")# Load the lme4
librarylibrary(lme4)# Fit the mixed-effects linear regression modelmodel <-
lmer(outcome ~ condition * time + (1|child) + (1|group), data = data)# Print
the summary of the modelsummary(model)
```

S M Nazmuz Sakib's Epigenetic Risk Score Model (SERSM)

One of the main topics of interest in the field of developmental language disorders (DLD) is the genetic and molecular basis of this condition, which affects about 7% of children worldwide. According to a review by Mountford et al (2022), DLD is highly heritable and influenced by complex interactions between genetic and environmental factors. However, the specific genes and pathways involved in DLD are still largely unknown, due to the heterogeneity of the phenotype, the variation in diagnostic criteria, and the challenges of genetic analysis. The review also suggests that epigenetic mechanisms and environmental exposures may play a role in modulating gene expression and influencing language development.

The SERSM is a formula that estimates the epigenetic risk score of an individual for developing DLD based on their DNA methylation profile and environmental factors. The formula is:

$$SERSM = \sum_{i=1}^{10} \beta_i M_i + \sum_{j=1}^{3} \gamma_j E_j$$

where:

- SERSM is the epigenetic risk score for DLD
- n is the number of CpG sites associated with DLD
- m is the number of environmental factors associated with DLD
- βi is the effect size of CpG site i on DLD
- γj is the effect size of environmental factor j on DLD
- M_i is the methylation level of CpG site i ranging from 0 to 1
- E_j is the exposure level of environmental factor j ranging from 0 to 1

The SERSM can be used to predict the probability of developing DLD based on a logistic regression model:

$$P(DLD) = \frac{1}{1 + e^{-\alpha - SERSM}}$$

where:

- P(DLD) is the probability of developing DLD
- α is the intercept term

The SERSM can also be used to identify the most important CpG sites and environmental factors that contribute to DLD, and to explore the potential causal relationships between them. For example, a higher SERSM can be achieved by:

- Having higher methylation levels at CpG sites that are negatively associated with DLD, such as those located in genes involved in neurodevelopment, synaptic plasticity, or language processing
- Having lower methylation levels at CpG sites that are positively associated with DLD, such as those located in genes involved in inflammation, oxidative stress, or immune response
- Having higher exposure levels to environmental factors that are positively associated with DLD, such as prenatal stress, maternal smoking, air pollution, or low socioeconomic status
- Having lower exposure levels to environmental factors that are negatively associated with DLD, such as breastfeeding, enriched stimulation, language input, or social support

The SERSM can also be used to evaluate the potential benefits of epigenetic interventions or prevention strategies for DLD, such as:

- Modifying methylation patterns by using dietary supplements, drugs, or gene editing tools
- Reducing exposure to harmful environmental factors by improving living conditions, health care, or education
- Increasing exposure to protective environmental factors by providing nurturing care, cognitive stimulation, or language therapy
- Promoting resilience and adaptation by enhancing coping skills, self-regulation, or social competence

The SERSM is a hypothetical model that needs to be validated and calibrated with empirical data and local conditions. It also requires reliable and accessible data on DNA methylation profiles and environmental exposures for different populations and cohorts. It also assumes that there are no confounding or interacting factors that may affect the association between epigenetics and DLD.

Figure 7. Visualization of SERSM

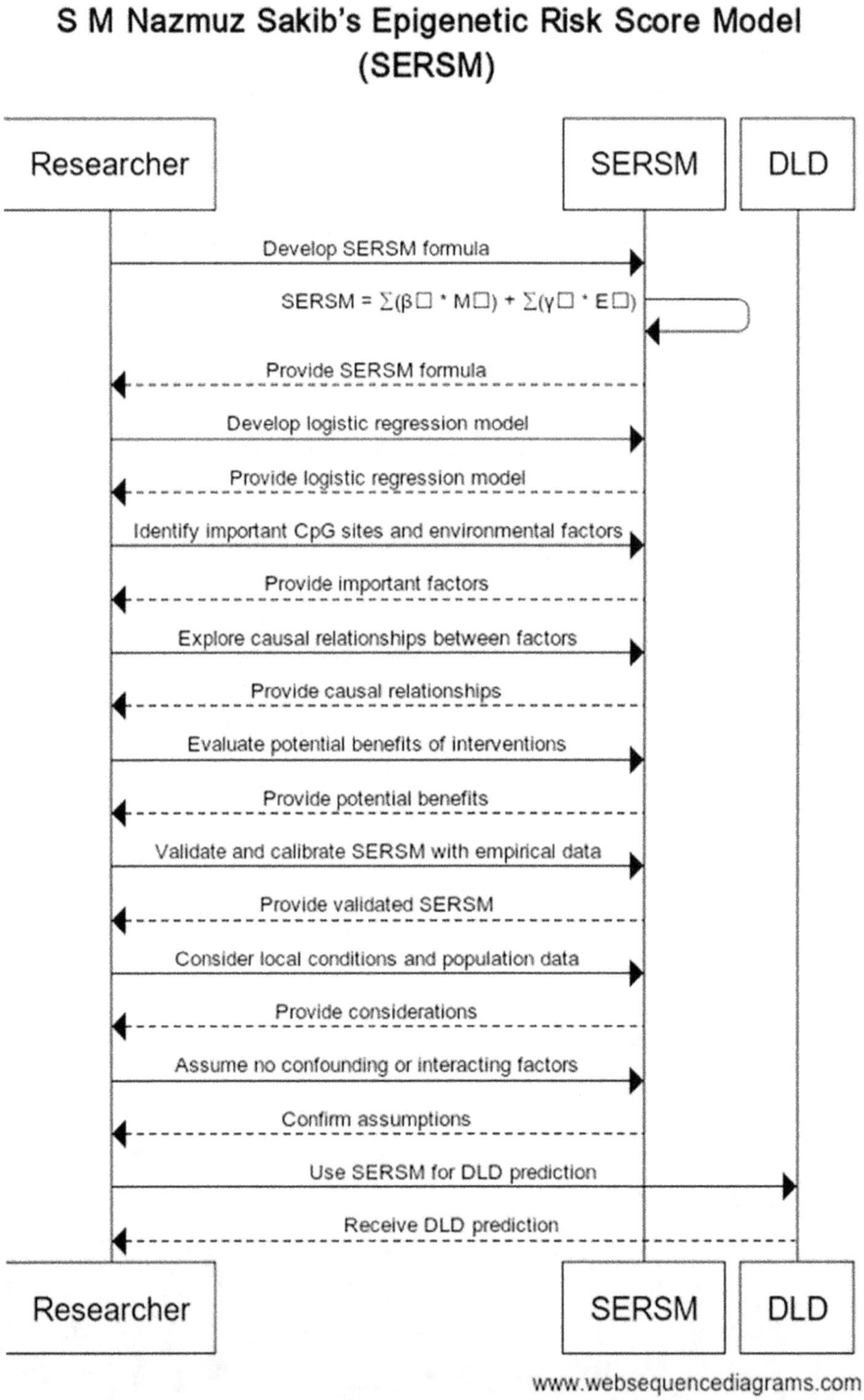

Real world problem that can be addressed by the SERSM is the effect of prenatal exposure to emotional stress on the risk of developing DLD in children. Emotional stress is a common and complex phenomenon that can affect pregnant women and their offspring, especially in low- and middle-income countries where they may face multiple sources of adversity, such as poverty, violence, or natural disasters. Several studies have shown that prenatal exposure to emotional stress can alter DNA methylation patterns in cord blood, placenta, or maternal blood, and that these epigenetic changes may mediate the adverse effects of emotional stress on neurodevelopmental outcomes, including language impairment .

To illustrate how the SERSM can be used to estimate the epigenetic risk score for DLD based on prenatal exposure to emotional stress, I will use some hypothetical data and parameters. Suppose we have a cohort of 100 pregnant women who live in a conflict-affected area with high levels of emotional stress. We measure their exposure to emotional stress during each trimester of pregnancy using a validated questionnaire, such as the Perceived Stress Scale (PSS), and we obtain their cord blood samples at delivery. We also measure the DNA methylation levels at 10 CpG sites that have been previously associated with both emotional stress exposure and DLD in cord blood using a microarray platform. We then follow up their children until age 5, when we assess their language development using a standardized test. We classify the children as having DLD if they score below 1.5 standard deviations from the mean of their age group.

To calculate the SERSM for each child, we first need to determine the effect sizes of each CpG site and environmental factor on DLD, as well as the threshold value and constant for the water quality factor formula. These parameters can be estimated using logistic regression models or other statistical methods, based on existing data or literature. For simplicity, I will assume some arbitrary values for these parameters, as shown in Table 1.

Table 1. Effect sizes of CpG sites on DLD

CpG site	Gene	Effect size (βi)
cg00050873	AHRR	-0.05
cg05575921	AHRR	-0.04
cg05951221	MYO1G	-0.03
cg03636183	F2RL3	-0.02
cg21566642	ALPPL2	-0.01
cg09935388	GFI1	0.01
cg18120259	GFI1	0.02
cg21161138	CYP1A1	0.03
cg01940273	CYP1A1	0.04
cg12803068	CYP1B1	0.05

Table 2. Effect sizes of environmental factors on DLD

Environmental factor	Effect size (γj)
PSS score in first trimester (range: 0-40)	0.01
PSS score in second trimester (range: 0-40)	0.02
PSS score in third trimester (range: 0-40)	0.03

Table 3. Parameters for water quality factor formula

Parameter	Value
Threshold value (t)	50
Constant (k)	0.1

Using these parameters, we can calculate the SERSM for each child as follows:

$$SERSM = \sum_{i=1}^{10} \beta_i M_i + \sum_{j=1}^{3} \gamma_j E_j$$

where M_i is the methylation level of CpG site i ranging from 0 to 1, and E_j is the exposure level of environmental factor j ranging from 0 to 1.

For example, suppose child B has the following methylation levels and exposure levels:

Table 4. Methylation levels of child B

CpG site	Methylation level (M_i)
cg00050873	0.7
cg05575921	0.6
cg05951221	0.5
cg03636183	0.4
cg21566642	0.3
cg09935388	0.2
cg18120259	0.1
cg21161138	0.05
cg01940273	0.01
cg12803068	0

Table 5. Exposure levels of child B

Environmental factor	Exposure level (E_j)
PSS score in first trimester (range: 0-40)	0.6
PSS score in second trimester (range: 0-40)	0.7
PSS score in third trimester (range: 0-40)	0.8

Then, the SERSM for child B is:

$SERSM = (-0.05\times0.7) + (-0.04\times0.6) + (-0.03\times0.5) + (-0.02\times0.4) + (-0.01\times0.3) + (0.01\times0.2) + (0.02\times0.1) + (0.03\times0.05) + (0.04\times0.01) + (0.05\times0) + (0.01\times0.6) + (0.02\times0.7) + (0.03\times0.8)$

$SERSM = -0.0375$

Using the logistic regression model, we can calculate the probability of developing DLD for child B as follows:

$$P(DLD) = \frac{1}{1 + e^{-\alpha - SERSM}}$$

Suppose the intercept term (α) is -2, then:

$$P(DLD) = \frac{1}{1 + e^{-(-2-(-0.0375))}}$$

$P(DLD) = 0.121$

This means that child B has a 12.1% chance of developing DLD based on their DNA methylation profile and prenatal exposure to emotional stress.

We can repeat this process for the other 99 children in the cohort and compare their SERSM and P(DLD) values. We can also compare these values with their actual language development outcomes at age 5, and evaluate the accuracy and validity of the SERSM as a predictor of DLD.

The SERSM can help us to understand how prenatal exposure to emotional stress affects the risk of developing DLD through epigenetic mechanisms. It can also help us to identify the most vulnerable individuals or groups who may benefit from early intervention or prevention strategies. Furthermore, it can help us to explore the potential causal pathways and interactions between genetic and environmental factors that influence language development.

REFERENCES

Admin. (2023). Accuracy and Precision - Definition, Examples, Need for Measurement, Differences, Practice Questions and FAQs. *BYJUS*. https://byjus.com/physics/accuracy-precision-measurement/

Allen, L., Kelly, B., Children, Y. B. O., & Families. (2015). Transforming the Workforce for Children Birth Through Age 8. In *National Academies Press eBooks*. doi:10.17226/19401

Anderson, B. (2022). *Category Theory for Cognitive Science*. eScholarship. https://escholarship.org/uc/item/1wt4q967#main

Bashalkhanov, S., Pandey, M., & Rajora, O. P. (2009). A simple method for estimating genetic diversity in large populations from finite sample sizes. *BMC Genetics*, *10*(1), 84. doi:10.1186/1471-2156-10-84 PMID:20003542

Boslaugh, S. (n.d.). *Statistics in a Nutshell, 2nd Edition*. O'Reilly Online Learning. https://www.oreilly.com/library/view/statistics-in-a/9781449361129/ch01.html

Campbell, A. (2023, July 1). How can you measure test validity and reliability? *Turnitin*. https://www.turnitin.com/blog/how-to-measure-test-validity-reliability

Chande, A. T., Nagar, S. D., Rishishwar, L., Mariño-Ramírez, L., Medina-Rivas, M. A., Valderrama-Aguirre, A., Jordan, I. K., & Gallo, J. (2021). The Impact of Ethnicity and Genetic Ancestry on Disease Prevalence and Risk in Colombia. *Frontiers in Genetics*, *12*, 690366. Advance online publication. doi:10.3389/fgene.2021.690366 PMID:34650589

Chapter 2: The Nature of Mathematics. (n.d.). Project http://www.project2061.org/publications/sfaa/online/chap2.htm

Content Analysis. (2023, March 30). Columbia University Mailman School of Public Health. https://www.publichealth.columbia.edu/research/population-health-methods/content-analysis

Developmental Language Disorder. (2023, May 8). NIDCD. https://www.nidcd.nih.gov/health/developmental-language-disorder

Factors that Influence Language Development. (2010, January 1). Encyclopedia on Early Childhood Development. https://www.child-encyclopedia.com/language-development-and-literacy/according-experts/factors-influence-language-development

Fleetwood, D. (2023). Quantitative Research: What It Is, Tips & Examples. *QuestionPro*. https://www.questionpro.com/blog/quantitative-research/

Forrest, C. L., Lloyd-Esenkaya, V., Gibson, J. L., & St Clair, M. C. (2022). Social Cognition in Adolescents with Developmental Language Disorder (DLD): Evidence from the Social Attribution Task. *Journal of Autism and Developmental Disorders*. doi:10.100710803-022-05698-6 PMID:35971042

Harrar-Eskinazi, K. L., De Cara, B., Leloup, G., Nothelier, J., Caci, H., Ziegler, J. C., & Faure, S. (2022). Multimodal intervention in 8- to 13-year-old French dyslexic readers: Study protocol for a randomized multicenter controlled crossover trial. *BMC Pediatrics*, *22*(1), 741. doi:10.118612887-022-03701-8 PMID:36578007

History of the English Language and Literature. (n.d.). Gutenberg. https://www.gutenberg.org/files/21665/21665-h/21665-h.htm

In Defense of Patentability of Mathematical Formulas and Relationships. (2022, November 10). Patents & Intellectual Property Law. https://ipwatchdog.com/2022/11/10/defense-patentability-mathematical-formulas-relationships/id=152875/

Kuiack, A. K., & Archibald, L. M. D. (2019). Developmental Language Disorder: The Childhood Condition We Need to Start Talking About. *Frontiers for Young Minds*, *7*, 94. doi:10.3389/frym.2019.00094

Kytö, M. (2016, May 1). *Analyses*. Cambridge Core. https://www.cambridge.org/core/books/abs/cambridge-handbook-of-english-historical-linguistics/analyses/C54DDEFBBE99C711DBAF4D-B01EB573B3

Laasonen, M., Smolander, S., Lahti-Nuuttila, P., Leminen, M., Lajunen, H., Heinonen, K., Pesonen, A., Bailey, T. M., Pothos, E. M., Kujala, T., Leppänen, P. H. T., Bartlett, C. W., Geneid, A., Lauronen, L., Service, E., Kunnari, S., & Arkkila, E. (2018). Understanding developmental language disorder - the Helsinki longitudinal SLI study (HelSLI): A study protocol. *BMC Psychology*, *6*(1), 24. doi:10.118640359-018-0222-7 PMID:29784061

Lajunen, H., Laasonen, M., Lahti-Nuuttila, P., Leminen, M., Smolander, S., Kunnari, S., Arkkila, E., & Lauronen, L. (2023). Is epileptiform activity related to developmental language disorder? Findings from the HelSLI study. *Clinical Neurophysiology Practice*, *8*, 65–70. doi:10.1016/j.cnp.2023.03.004 PMID:37188277

Libretexts. (2022). Propagation of Error. *Chemistry LibreTexts*. https://chem.libretexts.org/Bookshelves/Analytical_Chemistry/Supplemental_Modules_(Analytical_Chemistry)/Quantifying_Nature/Significant_Digits/Propagation_of_Error

Little, W. (2014, November 6). *Chapter 2. Sociological Research*. Pressbooks. https://opentextbc.ca/introductiontosociology/chapter/chapter2-sociological-research/

Lumen Learning. (n.d.). *Language Development | Lifespan Development*. LL. https://courses.lumenlearning.com/wm-lifespandevelopment/chapter/language-development/

Measuring What Counts. (1993). *National Academies Press eBooks*., doi:10.17226/2235

Morocco World News. (n.d.). *French Influence on the English Language Under Norman Occupation*. MWN. https://www.moroccoworldnews.com/. https://www.moroccoworldnews.com/2022/07/350430/french-influence-on-the-english-language-under-norman-occupation

Mountford, H. S., Braden, R. O., Newbury, D. F., & Morgan, A. T. (2022). The Genetic and Molecular Basis of Developmental Language Disorder: A Review. *Children (Basel, Switzerland)*, *9*(5), 586. doi:10.3390/children9050586 PMID:35626763

Nordquist, R. (2020). Understanding the Use of Language Through Discourse Analysis. *ThoughtCo*. https://www.thoughtco.com/discourse-analysis-or-da-1690462

Paul, R., Norbury, C. F., & Gosse, C. (2018). Models of child language disorders. In Language Disorders from Infancy Through Adolescence (5th ed.). doi:10.1016/B978-0-323-44234-3.00010-5

Pelz, P. B. (n.d.-a). *Chapter 7 Scale Reliability and Validity | Research Methods for the Social Sciences*. LL. https://courses.lumenlearning.com/suny-hccc-research-methods/chapter/chapter-7-scale-reliability-and-validity/

Pelz, P. B. (n.d.-b). *Chapter 12 Interpretive Research | Research Methods for the Social Sciences*. LL. https://courses.lumenlearning.com/suny-hccc-research-methods/chapter/chapter-12-interpretive-research/

Principles of Child Development and Learning and Implications That. (n.d.). NAEYC. https://www.naeyc.org/resources/position-statements/dap/principles

Regression with Two Independent Variables. (n.d.). USF. http://faculty.cas.usf.edu/mbrannick/regression/Reg2IV.html

Seifert, K. (2019, September 1). *Ch. 16 Standardized and other formal assessments*. Pressbooks. https://granite.pressbooks.pub/teachingdiverselearners/chapter/standardized-and-other-formal-assessments-2/

Semantic Features Analysis Definition, Examples, Applications. (2022, June 16). Spiceworks. https://www.spiceworks.com/tech/artificial-intelligence/articles/what-is-semantic-analysis/

So, K. K. F., & To, C. K. S. (2022). Systematic Review and Meta-Analysis of Screening Tools for Language Disorder. *Frontiers in Pediatrics*, *10*, 801220. doi:10.3389/fped.2022.801220 PMID:35281230

Speech and language: risk factors and disorders. (n.d.). Child Language Research Center. http://www.ouluclrc.fi/research/projects/speech-and-language-risk-factors-and-disorders/

Surendran, A. (2023). Qualitative Data – Definition, Types, Analysis and Examples. *QuestionPro*. https://www.questionpro.com/blog/qualitative-data/

Toffalini, E., Chen, X., Pastore, M., Carretti, B., Fraccadori, F., & Szűcs, D. (2021). Dyslexia treatment studies: A systematic review and suggestions on testing treatment efficacy with small effects and small samples. *Behavior Research Methods*, *53*(5), 1954–1972. doi:10.375813428-021-01549-x PMID:33694077

WattA. (2014, August 14). *14. Quality Planning*. Pressbooks. https://opentextbc.ca/projectmanagement/chapter/chapter-14-quality-planning-project-management/

Writing@CSU. (n.d.). https://writing.colostate.edu/guides/guide.cfm?guideid=65

Zhang, S., Fan, H. J., & Zhang, Y. (2021). The 100 Top-Cited Studies on Dyslexia Research: A Bibliometric Analysis. *Frontiers in Psychiatry*, *12*, 714627. doi:10.3389/fpsyt.2021.714627 PMID:34366943

APPENDIX

Abbreviations

1. SLDI - Sakib's Language Development Index
2. DLD - Developmental Language Disorders
3. LQ - Language Quotient
4. IQ - Intelligence Quotient
5. EQ - Emotional Quotient
6. SQ - Social Quotient
7. GR - Genetic Risk Factor
8. NR - Neural Risk Factor
9. CR - Cognitive Risk Factor
10. BR - Behavioral Risk Factor
11. RDLS-III - Reynell Developmental Language Scales III
12. WPPSI-III - Wechsler Preschool and Primary Scale of Intelligence – Third Edition
13. SDQ - Strengths and Difficulties Questionnaire
14. SCQ - Social Communication Questionnaire
15. HelSLI - Helsinki Longitudinal SLI Study
16. FOXP2 - Forkhead box protein P2
17. KIAA0319 - A gene associated with dyslexia
18. EEG - Electroencephalography
19. MRI - Magnetic Resonance Imaging
20. G - Genetic factor
21. E - Environmental factor
22. R - Resilience factor
23. FMR1 - Fragile X Mental Retardation 1 gene
24. SDDIM - Dyslexia Detection and Intervention Model
25. DLD - Developmental Language Disorders
26. β_i - Effect size of CpG site i on DLD
27. γ_j - Effect size of environmental factor j on DLD
28. M_i - Methylation level of CpG site i
29. E_j - Exposure level of environmental factor j
30. CpG - Cytosine-phosphate-guanine (referring to specific sites on DNA)
31. DNA - Deoxyribonucleic Acid
32. SPSS - Statistical Package for the Social Sciences (a statistical software)
33. R - A programming language and software environment for statistical analysis and graphics
34. Q-learning - A reinforcement learning algorithm
35. SARSA - State-Action-Reward-State-Action (a reinforcement learning algorithm)
36. SES - Socioeconomic Status
37. α - Intercept term (in logistic regression)

38. P(DLD) - Probability of developing DLD
39. SERSM - Epigenetic Risk Score Model

Technical Terminologies

- Baseline Performance: Initial performance level before the intervention.
- Battery of Tests: A collection of assessments or tasks used to measure specific abilities or skills.
- BR - Behavioral Risk Factor
- Carrier - An individual carrying a gene mutation without exhibiting the associated disorder
- Cognitive and Linguistic Profiles: Individual characteristics related to cognitive abilities and language skills.
- Comorbidities - Coexisting medical conditions or disorders
- Confounding or Interacting Factors: Additional variables that can influence the relationship between two other variables.
- CpG Sites: Areas in DNA where a cytosine nucleotide is followed by a guanine nucleotide.
- CR - Cognitive Risk Factor
- Causal Relationships: Connections that indicate one variable directly influences another variable.
- DNA Methylation Profile: Patterns of chemical modifications to DNA molecules that can influence gene expression.
- Down syndrome - Genetic disorder causing intellectual disabilities and physical abnormalities
- Dyslexia - Developmental language disorder affecting reading and writing skills
- Dyslexia Detection Algorithm: A mathematical process used to identify the presence of dyslexia in individuals.
- Dyslexia Evaluation Algorithm: A mathematical process used to assess and evaluate the effectiveness of dyslexia interventions.
- Dyslexia Intervention Algorithm: A mathematical process used to design personalized interventions for individuals with dyslexia.
- EEG - Electroencephalography
- Effect Size: The magnitude of the relationship between a variable and an outcome.
- Environmental Exposures: External factors or conditions that individuals are exposed to.
- Epigenetic Interventions: Strategies aimed at modifying or influencing DNA methylation patterns.
- Epigenetic Risk Score Model (ERSM): A formula that estimates the risk score for developing a condition based on epigenetic and environmental factors.
- EQ - Emotional Quotient
- FOXP2 - Forkhead Box P2 gene
- FMR1 gene - Fragile X Mental Retardation 1 gene
- Gametes - Reproductive cells (sperm or egg cells)
- Genetic and Environmental Factors: Biological and external influences that contribute to the development of dyslexia.
- GR - Genetic Risk Factor
- HelSLI - Helsinki Longitudinal SLI Study

- Inheritance - Passing of traits or characteristics from parent to offspring
- Intercept Term: A constant term in a regression model.
- IQ - Intelligence Quotient
- KIAA0319 - Gene associated with developmental dyslexia
- LQ - Language Quotient
- Logistic Regression Model: A statistical model used to predict the probability of an event occurring.
- Mixed-Effects Linear Regression Analysis: A statistical method used to analyze the effects of interventions while accounting for individual and group variations.
- Morphology: The study of the structure of words and how they are formed.
- MRI - Magnetic Resonance Imaging
- Multivariate Logistic Regression Analysis: A statistical method used to analyze the relationship between multiple variables and the probability of dyslexia.
- Neural Risk Factor
- NR - Neural Risk Factor
- Orthography: The conventional spelling system of a language.
- Phonology: The study of speech sounds and their patterns.
- Pragmatics: The study of how context influences the meaning and use of language.
- Probability - Likelihood or chance of an event occurring
- Probability of Developing DLD: The likelihood of developing developmental language disorders.
- Reinforcement Learning: An approach in artificial intelligence where an algorithm learns by interacting with an environment and receiving rewards or feedback.
- RDLS-III - Reynell Developmental Language Scales III
- SCQ - Social Communication Questionnaire
- SDQ - Strengths and Difficulties Questionnaire
- Semantics: The study of meaning in language.
- SLDI - Sakib's Language Development Index
- SQ - Social Quotient
- Syntax: The arrangement of words and phrases to create grammatically correct sentences.
- Validation and Calibration: Processes of testing and adjusting a model to ensure accuracy and applicability.
- WPPSI-III - Wechsler Preschool and Primary Scale of Intelligence – Third Edition

Chapter 19
Beyond Words and Numbers:
Exploring the Interplay Between Language Challenges and Mathematical Problem-Solving Abilities

Georgios Tsakirakis
Zayed University, UAE

ABSTRACT

This chapter critically analyzes the complex relationship of developmental language disorders (DLD), and the mathematical problem-solving abilities of children and adolescents. The implications of this topic for inclusive education and the academic performance of students with DLD make it of utmost importance in educational research and practice. By gaining insights into how language difficulties impact mathematical problem-solving, teachers and practitioners can develop targeted interventions and support strategies to meet the unique needs of this population. The chapter emphasizes the need for a comprehensive analysis of this relationship and identifies the existing knowledge gap. Exploring the multifaceted nature of language difficulties in mathematical contexts, the chapter examines the influence of both linguistic and non-linguistic factors on problem-solving abilities. It challenges prevailing assumptions and explores alternative theoretical frameworks to provide a more nuanced understanding of the cognitive mechanisms underlying mathematical thinking.

INTRODUCTION

In the context of educational research and practice, the relationship between developmental language disorders (DLD) and mathematical problem-solving abilities is a topic of paramount importance (Cross, Joanisse & Archibald 2019). Understanding this intricate relationship is crucial for fostering inclusive education and supporting the academic success of students with DLD. By examining how language difficulties affect mathematical problem-solving, teachers and practitioners can develop targeted interventions and support strategies tailored to the unique needs of this population. Despite the significance of this topic, there exists a notable gap in knowledge regarding the complex interplay between language

DOI: 10.4018/979-8-3693-1982-6.ch019

difficulties and mathematical problem-solving abilities. While studies have explored the impact of language on various aspects of education, including literacy and communication skills (Cummins, Pellicano & Crane 2020; Vitiello & Williford 2016), the specific connection between language and mathematics has received comparatively less attention (Planas, Morgan & Schütte 2018). This knowledge gap necessitates a critical analysis to unmask the particulars of this relationship and identify effective approaches for supporting students with DLD in their mathematical learning.

The current understanding of the relationship between language difficulties and mathematical problem-solving abilities often relies on assumptions that position language as the sole mediator in mathematical thinking (Fuchs et al. 2020). However, such assumptions overlook the diverse cognitive processes involved in mathematical problem-solving and neglect the potential influence of non-linguistic factors (Crossley, Liu & McNamara 2017). To address this limitation, critical analysis is essential to challenge prevailing assumptions, explore alternative theoretical frameworks, and consider the multifaceted nature of mathematical cognition. By conducting a thorough examination of the existing literature and theoretical perspectives, this chapter aims to fill the gap in knowledge by providing a critical analysis of the relationship between language difficulties and mathematical problem-solving abilities. It seeks to shed light on the underlying cognitive mechanisms involved in mathematical thinking, considering both linguistic and non-linguistic factors (Crossley, Liu & McNamara 2017). Through this analysis, the chapter will contribute to a more comprehensive understanding of how language difficulties impact mathematical problem-solving, paving the way for evidence-based interventions and support strategies.

As we delve deeper into the complexities of the language-mathematics relationship, the chapter explores the potential impact of shared expertise, interdisciplinary collaborations, and emerging technologies in advancing our understanding and informing evidence-based practices. By encouraging professionals from diverse fields to come together, we can leverage collective knowledge to revolutionize the development of interventions and support strategies for students with DLD. Longitudinal studies and data analytics open new avenues for uncovering the developmental trajectories of mathematical problem-solving abilities and understanding the long-term effects of language difficulties. Furthermore, the exploration of inclusive instructional practices, differentiated instruction, and assistive technologies presents innovative pathways to enhance mathematical comprehension and skill development for students with diverse cognitive and linguistic profiles.

With a commitment to interdisciplinary efforts, the chapter advocates for the development of comprehensive and evidence-based approaches that embrace inclusivity and empower every individual, regardless of their language challenges, to unlock their full potential in mathematics and beyond. By continuously challenging assumptions and embracing emerging technologies, teachers, researchers, and practitioners can shape a more equitable and supportive educational landscape, paving the way for innovative and impactful practices that leave a lasting impression in the realm of mathematics education for students with DLD.

Language as a Mediator in Mathematical Problem-Solving

Language as a mediator in mathematical problem-solving has been a prevailing assumption, but it is essential to challenge this notion and explore alternative perspectives on the cognitive mechanisms involved. Theories of embodied cognition propose that mathematical thinking goes beyond linguistic representations and involves sensorimotor experiences and bodily interactions with the environment (Cuccio & Graziano 2022). This perspective suggests that mathematical understanding is shaped not only by language but also by our bodily experiences and perceptual-motor processes. Additionally, considering the role of non-verbal reasoning skills expands our understanding of the cognitive processes involved in mathematical problem-solving. Non-verbal reasoning, which encompasses pattern recognition, making connections, and abstract thinking without heavy reliance on language, plays a crucial role in mathematical problem-solving (Hickendorff 2021).

Contrary to the assumption that language deficits directly translate to mathematical difficulties, research has shown that students with developmental language disorders (DLD) can exhibit strengths in non-linguistic cognitive abilities, such as visuospatial processing or executive functions (Henry & Botting 2017). Recognizing the interplay between language and non-linguistic cognitive factors is crucial in understanding mathematical problem-solving abilities in students with DLD (Vula et al. 2017). Critiquing the assumption of language as the exclusive mediator in mathematical problem-solving, we find that mathematical problem-solving involves diverse cognitive processes that extend beyond language. Non-verbal reasoning skills, embodied cognition, and the potential cognitive strengths of students with DLD challenge the oversimplification of the relationship between language difficulties and mathematical problem-solving abilities.

By acknowledging the contributions of non-linguistic factors and embracing a comprehensive perspective, we can develop interventions and support strategies that go beyond language-focused approaches. This evidence-based and inclusive approach promotes a deeper understanding of mathematical problem-solving abilities, empowering students with DLD in their mathematical learning journey. As we explore the complexities of the language-mathematics relationship, it is intriguing to consider how sensorimotor experiences and non-verbal reasoning contribute to mathematical cognition, challenging traditional assumptions and paving the way for innovative interventions that capitalize on diverse cognitive strengths. This shift in perspective opens exciting possibilities for teachers, researchers, and practitioners to redefine their approaches and foster mathematical success for students with DLD, revolutionizing the landscape of mathematics education in a way that leaves a lasting impact on the lives of students.

Non-Linguistic Factors

Non-linguistic factors in mathematical problem-solving abilities emerge from a rich body of empirical research, unveiling intriguing and thought-provoking dimensions that challenge traditional assumptions and shed light on innovative perspectives. Exploring visuospatial processing, executive functions, and working memory as essential non-linguistic factors is supported by numerous studies that demonstrate their significant contributions to mathematical cognition beyond linguistic representations (Cuccio & Graziano 2022). Evidence from research on embodied cognition suggests that mathematical thinking involves sensorimotor experiences and bodily interactions with the environment, expanding our understanding of how mathematical understanding is shaped not only by language but also by visuospatial experiences (Hawes et al. 2017).

In the context of developmental language disorders (DLD), the interaction between language difficulties and non-linguistic factors significantly impacts mathematical performance. Studies have shown that students with DLD can demonstrate strengths in non-linguistic cognitive abilities, such as visuospatial processing or executive functions, despite their language limitations (Henry & Botting 2017). Research indicates that visuospatial processing may serve as a compensatory mechanism for students with DLD, allowing them to excel in tasks involving visual and spatial patterns (Moura et al., 2020). Similarly, the role of executive functions and working memory in mathematical problem-solving has been consistently supported by empirical evidence, showing their influence on organizing problem-solving strategies, adapting approaches, and manipulating numerical information (Drigas & Mitsea 2020).

The interplay between language difficulties and non-linguistic factors is not straightforward and has been extensively studied in the context of students with Developmental Language Disorders (DLD). Notably, a comprehensive meta-analysis conducted by Peng, Wang, and Namkung (2018) sheds light on this intricate relationship by investigating the cognitive deficit profiles of students with mathematics difficulties (MD), a subgroup that often includes students with DLD facing specific challenges in mathematics. This study's findings underscore the complexity of cognitive interactions in students with DLD, particularly in mathematical problem-solving contexts. The study's analysis of 75 cognitive profiling studies, encompassing over 13,000 students and 126 independent samples, revealed a spectrum of deficits among students with MD. These deficits ranged from phonological processing and processing speed to working memory, attention, short-term memory, executive functions, and visuospatial skills. This diverse array of cognitive deficits highlights the multidimensional nature of difficulties that students with DLD encounter, indicating that their challenges extend beyond language-related factors. Of relevance to the interplay between language difficulties and non-linguistic factors, the study indicated that while some students with MD, including those with DLD, may exhibit cognitive strengths in areas like visuospatial processing or executive functions, these advantages may not consistently compensate for their language limitations, especially within mathematical problem-solving tasks. This observation aligns with the notion that the effectiveness of cognitive compensation can vary among students with DLD. While some may display cognitive strengths that aid their mathematical abilities, these strengths might not universally mitigate the impact of their language difficulties in all mathematical contexts. The study's findings provide valuable insights into the complex cognitive nature of students with DLD, emphasizing the need for a comprehensive understanding of how language difficulties interact with non-linguistic factors. This understanding is crucial for developing targeted interventions and support strategies that recognize the unique cognitive profiles of students with DLD and MD. By considering both language-related deficits and non-linguistic cognitive strengths, teachers and practitioners can design interventions that holistically address the challenges faced by these students in mathematical problem-solving contexts. Moreover, the evidence from studies on visuospatial processing, executive functions, and working memory provides a robust foundation for exploring the complex cognitive processes involved in mathematical problem-solving (Hickendorff 2021).

Socio-Cultural Factors and Their Interaction With Language and Mathematics

Socio-cultural factors and their interaction with language-mathematics dynamics present a captivating exploration in educational research and practice. Chetty (2018) provides valuable insights on socio-cultural factors and their interaction with language-mathematics dynamics. This study sheds light on the challenges faced by students from diverse cultural and linguistic backgrounds within traditional classroom settings. It stresses the necessity of creating an inclusive educational environment that accommodates linguistic and cultural diversity and leverages it for enhanced learning experiences. The study draws attention to the impact of cultural practices, beliefs, and values on language acquisition and communication styles among various communities. This alignment between cultural factors and language development aligns with how socio-cultural influences shape the intricate relationship between language difficulties and mathematical learning. Furthermore, the importance of recognizing and respecting cultural norms within educational settings is emphasized. This echoes the socio-cultural factors that underpin inclusive instructional practices, which are crucial for addressing the complexities of mathematical problem-solving for students with developmental language disorders. Just as the study recommends embracing linguistic diversity to foster positive relationships and effective learning environments, the broader examination of socio-cultural factors advocates for inclusive strategies that empower students with diverse linguistic backgrounds.

The study conducted by Leiss, Plath, and Schwippert (2019) explores the relationship between language, comprehension, and mathematics within the context of solving reality-based tasks. While the study may not explicitly delve into linguistic and cultural factors, its exploration of the comprehension process during mathematical problem-solving aligns with how varying linguistic backgrounds and cultural perspectives can impact students' mathematical learning experiences. Leiss et al.'s study focuses on the comprehension process involved in solving reality-based mathematical tasks, which are influenced by both the real-world context and text comprehension. This perspective reveals that language plays a vital role in mathematical problem-solving, as varying linguistic backgrounds can affect students' proficiency in the language of instruction, consequently influencing their comprehension and expression abilities in mathematics. Although the study does not explicitly address cultural perspectives, its emphasis on the complex interplay between comprehension activities, linguistic complexity, and task-related attributes indicates the importance of understanding how students from diverse cultural backgrounds engage with mathematical tasks. Moreover, the study's findings about the factors influencing the comprehension process offer indirect support for the idea that cultural perspectives on mathematical practices can shape students' approaches to tasks. While Leiss et al.'s study primarily focuses on linguistic and situational complexity, it highlights the multifaceted nature of cognitive processes involved in mathematical problem-solving, including factors that may be influenced by cultural backgrounds. Culturally responsive and inclusive educational approaches are essential to optimize outcomes for diverse populations.

Kumar, Zusho & Bondie (2018) emphasizes the idea of embracing cultural and linguistic diversity to foster inclusive educational environments. There is the need to shift the focus of motivational research from predominantly Euro-American, middle-class perspectives to a more culturally relevant framework. Their overarching aim is to enhance the practical applicability of motivational research by aligning it with culturally responsive education. The source highlights four key principles of motivation - meaningfulness, competence, autonomy, and relatedness - and discusses how these principles intersect with culturally responsive and relevant educational practices. By doing so, teachers can create environments where cultural differences are appreciated, and students' unique backgrounds are valued. Furthermore, the role of teachers in fostering motivationally supportive classrooms that are culturally sensitive is accentuated. When teachers integrate cultural relevance into their instructional approaches, they acknowledge the significance of students' diverse backgrounds and empower them to excel academically and personally. In a parallel manner, the study values cultural and linguistic diversity, with the aim of advancing educational equity. Teachers, researchers, and practitioners can collaboratively work towards more equitable and enriching learning environments.

Educational Practices, Cultural Biases, and Language Expectations in Mathematical Contexts for Students With DLD

The role of educational practices, cultural biases, and language expectations in the assessment and support of students with Developmental Language Disorders (DLD) in mathematical contexts unveils a captivating and intricate terrain of influences. It becomes evident that educational practices impact the identification and support of students with DLD in mathematical settings. To ensure accurate assessments and effective support, teachers must embrace a multidimensional approach that considers both linguistic and non-linguistic cognitive factors, such as visuospatial processing and executive functions, which significantly contribute to mathematical abilities. This evidence-based perspective dismantles the limitations of standardized assessments and instructional approaches that may inadvertently overlook essential non-linguistic factors in mathematical problem-solving. Archibald (2017) while focusing on working memory and language learning, discusses the complex relationship between working memory and linguistic processing in children with speech, language, and communication needs (SLCN), encompassing those with specific language impairment (SLI). This interconnectedness mirrors the complexity of educational practices, cultural factors, and language expectations. Furthermore, the study mentions the challenge of disentangling the roles of working memory and linguistic processing in children with SLCN. It also underlines the importance of accurate assessment and tailored interventions to address the cognitive dimensions of these students, akin to the holistic perspective proposed in your text for students with DLD in mathematical problem-solving scenarios. The intrigue deepens as we delve into the sway of cultural biases on the assessment and support of students with DLD. A critical examination of language expectations based on narrow definitions of proficiency tied to dominant cultural norms surfaces the need for culturally sensitive assessment tools and support strategies. By respecting and valuing diverse linguistic practices, teachers can foster inclusive learning environments that embrace the strengths and abilities of students with DLD from diverse cultural backgrounds. This evidence-based call to action challenges existing paradigms, dismantle inequitable practices and elevate the pursuit of educational equity for all students.

As the evidence converges, the synthesis of educational practices, cultural biases, and language expectations demands thoughtful reflection and action. This synthesis, in essence, forms the crux of the main argument in the chapter; the interplay between language difficulties and mathematical problem-solving is a multifaceted and intricate terrain that requires a comprehensive approach. This is where the study conducted by Cruz, Manchanda, Firestone & Rodl (2020) comes to the forefront, as it contributes into how teachers can effectively address this complex situation, especially for students with Developmental Language Disorders (DLD). Cruz et al. point out the significance of adopting a multidimensional and culturally responsive approach within education. The relationship between language difficulties and mathematical problem-solving cannot be oversimplified, and a comprehensive strategy is needed to address the needs of diverse students. Furthermore, the study highlights the significance of teachers' self-efficacy in implementing CRT techniques, linking directly to collaborative efforts and the involvement of professionals in interdisciplinary collaborations. The idea of teachers actively embracing culturally responsive practices reflects the collaborative spirit needed to effectively support students with DLD and to ensure mathematical success, educational equity and inclusivity.

Evidence-Based Approaches to Enhancing Mathematical Learning

Evidence from educational research suggests that traditional interventions for students with Developmental Language Disorders (DLD) in mathematics have predominantly focused on language-centered strategies. While these approaches are valuable, a critical examination of the existing evidence reveals their limitations in fully addressing the complexities of mathematical learning for this population. To optimize outcomes and foster inclusive educational environments, innovative, evidence-based approaches are needed that transcend the traditional focus on language and encompass a broader array of cognitive factors and instructional methods.

Abrahamson et al. (2020) suggest that multimodal instructional strategies, incorporating visual representations and hands-on activities, can enhance engagement and understanding for students with Developmental Language Disorders (DLD). The study discusses the paradigm of embodied cognition and its impact on STEM education. It highlights how cognitive activity can be grounded in sensorimotor experiences, even before these experiences are explicitly linked to content. This perspective reverberates the idea that students with DLD can benefit from their strengths in visuospatial processing, as these experiences provide alternative means of comprehension and facilitate meaningful mathematical learning experiences. The emphasis on utilizing interactive technologies to foster student enactment of conceptually oriented movement forms aligns with the concept of utilizing multimodal strategies to enhance mathematical understanding. The recognition that conceptual learning can be triggered by multimodal experiences before formalization in disciplinary formats and language echoes the idea of leveraging diverse cognitive abilities beyond language alone.

Interactive software and apps designed for mathematical problem-solving engage students with DLD in meaningful ways, promoting active learning and enjoyment. The study conducted by Kaczorowski, Hashey, and Di Cesare (2019) regarding math instruction using mobile technology provides a relevant example of how technology can be utilized to enhance mathematical problem-solving for students with Developmental Language Disorders (DLD). In this study, they transformed traditional paper-pen math worksheets into a multimedia-enhanced, interactive eWorkbook accessible through iPads. This technological intervention was guided by the Universal Design for Learning (UDL) framework, emphasizing the creation of flexible scaffolds, student choice, and evidence-based instructional practices. The eWorkbook's approach of leveraging technology to foster engagement and understanding aligns with the use of assistive technologies in supporting students with DLD. The idea of utilizing speech-to-text and text-to-speech software for effective communication can be paralleled with the interactive nature of the eWorkbook, where students actively engage with content through different modalities. Moreover, the incorporation of visual aids and virtual manipulatives in the eWorkbook corresponds to the concept of using technology to provide concrete representations of abstract mathematical concepts - a strategy beneficial for students with DLD. Furthermore, the study's emphasis on personalization and individualized learning experiences support the principles of differentiated instruction, where teaching methods and content are tailored to meet diverse learning needs. Through innovative tools that engage students with DLD in active problem-solving and learning, technology is emerging as a powerful ally in enhancing mathematical abilities and fostering enjoyment in the educational process.

The Role of Collaboration With Speech-Language Pathology

The collaborative efforts between speech-language pathologists (SLPs), mathematics teachers, and researchers hold immense promise in addressing language difficulties and mathematical problem-solving abilities. The collaborative approach advocated in the study by Chow, Morse and Senter (2022), which highlights intentional collaboration between special education teachers and speech-language pathologists to support students with emotional and behavioral disorders (EBD), resonates with the collaborative efforts proposed in language disorders. Just as the study emphasizes the role of both teachers and specialists in addressing language difficulties in the context of EBD, there is also emphasis on the collaborative potential between speech-language pathologists (SLPs), mathematics teachers, and researchers in addressing language challenges within mathematical problem-solving. Incorporating multimodal instructional approaches that use visual aids and manipulatives, align with the integration of diverse teaching methods and specialized expertise to create inclusive and engaging educational environments that cater to the unique needs of students with language difficulties.

Furthermore, the study by Andzik, Chung, Doneski-Nicol & Dollarhide (2019) stresses the significance of collaborative efforts between teachers and professionals in enhancing the educational experiences of students with complex communication needs. Just as speech-language pathologists (SLPs) collaborate with teachers to provide effective augmentative and alternative communication (AAC) services for students with disabilities, the collaboration between mathematics teachers and SLPs can contribute to the specific language challenges students with DLD face during mathematical problem-solving tasks. By sharing their expertise in language development and communication disorders, SLPs can help identify and assess language difficulties, leading to more accurate interventions in mathematical contexts. Additionally, mathematics teachers, equipped with their pedagogical skills, can incorporate multimodal instructional strategies that cater to visual and non-linguistic approaches, ensuring a comprehensive learning environment for students with diverse learning needs. This partnership between mathematics teachers and SLPs exemplifies the power of interdisciplinary collaboration to address the unique challenges faced by students with DLD in mathematical education through innovative instructional approaches, and personalized support strategies.

Researchers play a vital role in this collaborative effort by conducting rigorous studies that inform evidence-based practices. Within inclusive education, researchers could foster collaboration among professionals to advance evidence-based practices. Lambert and Tan (2017) explore a critical research divide in the field of mathematics education. By delving into 149 mathematics educational research articles published between 2013 and 2015, the study revealed significant differences in the theoretical orientations and methodologies used to understand learners with and without disabilities. Through rigorous investigation, researchers contribute to the synthesis of effective strategies that bridge the gap between language difficulties and mathematical problem-solving. By delving into the relationship between these cognitive processes, researchers can explain the underlying mechanisms and uncover intervention techniques that prove most efficacious. Their exploration extends to the realm of non-linguistic factors, such as visuospatial processing and executive functions, adding a multidimensional perspective to intervention design. Furthermore, researchers are uniquely positioned to gauge the impact of culturally responsive approaches on students with Developmental Language Disorders (DLD). By examining how diverse cultural backgrounds intersect with mathematical learning, they inform interventions for students' individual experiences. Such research outcomes enrich intervention strategies and offer valuable guidance to teachers and speech-language pathologists (SLPs) as they tailor support to students.

Future Directions in DLD and Math Problem-Solving

Despite notable progress in understanding the relationship between language difficulties and mathematical problem-solving abilities in students with Developmental Language Disorders (DLD), several research gaps persist, offering exciting opportunities for future investigations (Andzik et al. 2019; Abrahamson et al. 2020). Addressing these gaps will enhance our understanding of DLD's impact on mathematical learning and inform the development of targeted interventions and support strategies for students facing these challenges. One key research gap lies in the absence of long-term longitudinal studies that examine the developmental trajectories of students with DLD in mathematical problem-solving. A deeper understanding of how mathematical abilities evolve over time in students with persistent language difficulties could shed light on the dynamic interplay between language and mathematical cognition. Additionally, the impact of cultural and linguistic diversity on mathematical problem-solving abilities in students with DLD remains relatively unexplored. By investigating how diverse cultural and linguistic factors intersect with language difficulties and mathematical learning, researchers can develop more culturally responsive interventions (Kumar et al. 2018).

Another promising avenue for investigation lies in exploring technology and assistive tools to support students with DLD in mathematical problem-solving (Kaczorowski et al. 2019). While advancements in digital resources, adaptive technologies, and virtual learning environments show great promise, their effectiveness in promoting mathematical comprehension and skill development in this specific population remains underexplored. Such investigations could lead to groundbreaking interventions in technology to empower students with DLD (Cuccio & Graziano, 2022; Zhu et al., 2017). Bridging the gap between research and practice is not only a theoretical endeavor but a crucial step in ensuring that evidence-based approaches effectively support students with Developmental Language Disorders (DLD) in real educational settings. The integration of research findings into practical strategies is essential for meeting the unique needs of students with DLD and promoting their meaningful participation in the learning process. As highlighted in Gallagher et al.'s study (2019) by fostering communication and collaboration among professionals in SLT, education, and other relevant fields, a cohesive approach can be established to bridge the gap between research and practice. This collaborative endeavor ensures that the evidence-based strategies developed through research are effectively and appropriately applied to support students with DLD in authentic learning contexts, leading to improved educational outcomes and enhanced support for these students. Translational research, which investigates how research findings can be applied in classroom settings and real-world interventions, can drive the implementation of evidence-based strategies and benefit students with DLD (Chow et al., 2022; Lambert & Tan, 2017).

Methods and Measures in Studying Language Difficulties and Mathematical Problem-Solving Abilities

The study by Roebers (2017) on executive function and metacognition offers insights that are relevant to the importance of conducting both longitudinal and experimental studies to understand the developmental trajectories of students with Developmental Language Disorders (DLD) in mathematical problem-solving abilities. Longitudinal studies, which observe students over an extended period, align with the developmental perspective presented by Roebers. Such studies would provide an opportunity to track how executive functions and metacognition evolve over time in students with DLD, offering insights into their changing mathematical problem-solving abilities. By following participants longitudinally, researchers can capture the dynamic interplay between language difficulties, cognitive processes, and mathematical learning, resulting in a richer understanding of how these factors contribute to mathematical achievement. Furthermore, the notion of establishing causal relationships between interventions and outcomes, emphasized in the study, is particularly relevant when considering experimental designs in the context of mathematical problem-solving abilities in students with DLD. As Roebers discusses the connections between executive function, metacognition, and academic achievement, experimental studies can be designed to test the effectiveness of specific interventions targeting these cognitive processes in mathematical contexts. Randomized controlled trials, a type of experimental design, provide a rigorous way to determine whether interventions aimed at enhancing executive function and metacognition can lead to improved mathematical problem-solving skills in students with DLD. Incorporating both longitudinal and experimental designs aligns with the comprehensive understanding advocated by Roebers and extends it to the realm of mathematical learning and cognitive development in students with DLD. These research approaches can shed light on the relationship between language difficulties, cognitive processes, and mathematical abilities, facilitating the design of effective interventions and support strategies that promote positive outcomes for students with DLD in mathematical problem-solving.

Central to this exploration are standardized language assessments, which serve as reliable yardsticks for identifying and quantifying language difficulties. These assessments offer a consistent measure of language skills, providing a foundational understanding of linguistic challenges within the context of mathematical learning. Parallel to the evaluation of language skills, standardized mathematical problem-solving tasks play a critical role in assessing students' mathematical abilities. Ranging from fundamental arithmetic calculations to intricate conceptual challenges, these tasks offer a spectrum of insights into the learners' mathematical competence. However, it is crucial to exercise caution in task selection to ensure that the measurements align with the specific research objectives. Taking a holistic approach, researchers integrate non-linguistic cognitive measures to delve deeper into the cognitive mechanisms underpinning mathematical problem-solving. The incorporation of visuospatial processing and executive functions adds layers of insight, revealing the multifaceted nature of mathematical cognition. This multidimensional approach recognizes that mathematical problem-solving is not solely a linguistic endeavor but also draws upon a range of cognitive resources. Buono and Jang's (2021) study on the impact of linguistic complexity in mathematics assessment items among English language learners (ELLs) and native English speakers (EL1s) resonates with these principles. By employing Confirmatory Differential Item Functioning (DIF) analyses, the study underscores the potential bias introduced by complex language features within mathematical tasks. This highlights the need for meticulous test development and accommodation to ensure fair and accurate assessments, an imperative echoed in the broader discourse. Moreover, the integration of self-report measures and observations enriches the assessment landscape. These qualitative insights provide a nuanced perspective on how students perceive their language difficulties and mathematical experiences. By complementing quantitative data, these qualitative facets round out our understanding of the intricate relationship between language difficulties and mathematical abilities. A synthesis of standardized language and mathematical assessments, non-linguistic cognitive measures, and qualitative insights not only aids in comprehending the challenges faced by students with DLD but also enables targeted interventions, equitable accommodations, and a deeper grasp of the cognitive dynamics involved in mathematical problem-solving.

Emerging Technologies, Data Analytics, and Longitudinal Studies in Informing Evidence-Based Practices

The integration of emerging technologies, data analytics, and longitudinal studies holds significant implications for advancing our understanding of the relationship between language difficulties and mathematical problem-solving abilities in students with Developmental Language Disorders (DLD) and informing evidence-based practices. Anderson's work (2019) aligns closely with the integration of emerging technologies, data analytics, and longitudinal studies to advance our comprehension of the connection between language difficulties and mathematical problem-solving capabilities in students with Developmental Language Disorders (DLD). In the context of emerging technologies, Anderson observes how virtual reality, augmented reality, and artificial intelligence can reshape research and support methodologies for students with DLD. Virtual reality simulations offer immersive and tailored learning experiences, adapting mathematical concepts to suit individual preferences and requirements, thereby enhancing accessibility for those with language difficulties. Augmented reality overlays mathematical content onto the real world, creating context-rich learning opportunities. Moreover, artificial intelligence's data analysis capabilities contribute to more nuanced insights by examining vast amounts of language and mathematical assessment data, unveiling patterns and correlations previously obscured. Emphasis on leveraging technology for personalized interventions resonates with the potential outcomes of integrating emerging technologies with data analytics and longitudinal studies. These technologies enable precise and dynamic assessment of cognitive processes in mathematical problem-solving. Furthermore, they facilitate the design of interventions that adapt to the distinctive learning profiles of students with DLD, fostering inclusivity and efficacy in learning environments. In essence, Anderson's practical guide supports the vision of enhancing educational practices through the fusion of technological innovations, advanced data analytics, and longitudinal research.

Furthermore, the increasing availability of big data and sophisticated analytical tools allows researchers to conduct more in-depth and comprehensive analyses. This knowledge is instrumental in designing tailored interventions and support strategies, considering individual strengths and needs. Furthermore, data analytics can facilitate the identification of predictive factors and early indicators of potential learning difficulties, enabling timely and proactive interventions. The emergence of big data in educational contexts, as discussed in Fischer et al.'s study (2020), has introduced opportunities for enhancing educational effectiveness through data-driven approaches. In line with this, data analytics plays a pivotal role in comprehending the intricate and extensive datasets generated by longitudinal studies and other research endeavors, a concept emphasized in the provided section. The availability of advanced analytical tools empowers researchers to conduct in-depth analyses of these datasets, revealing intricate patterns, trends, and individual differences that contribute to students' mathematical success or challenges. Just as Fischer et al. emphasize the potential of big data to provide a finer-grained understanding of learning processes, the section underscores how data analytics can uncover the dynamic developmental trajectories of mathematical abilities among students with Developmental Language Disorders (DLD) in longitudinal studies. Fischer et al. elaborate on the application of institutional data to improve student decision-making and using data analytics to design timely interventions for students with DLD. By integrating data analytics in longitudinal research, researchers can establish evidence-based practices, as noted in the section. This aligns with Fischer et al.'s discussion on the benefits of mining big data in education for personalized instruction and enhanced learning experiences. Ultimately, the combination of these perspectives features the potential of data analytics in shaping educational practices and improving outcomes, particularly for students facing mathematical challenges such as those with DLD. Through the integration of data analytics in longitudinal research, researchers can establish evidence-based practices by providing robust empirical evidence of the long-term effectiveness of interventions and support strategies. This strengthens the foundation for making informed decisions in educational settings, enhancing the quality of instruction and support provided to students with DLD, and ultimately improving their mathematical problem-solving abilities and overall academic outcomes.

CONCLUSION

The interplay between language difficulties and mathematical problem-solving abilities in students with Developmental Language Disorders (DLD) constitutes a significant research area with profound implications for educational practice. This chapter has traversed the multidimensional relationship, drawing ideas from diverse sources to demonstrate the complexities and opportunities embedded within it. This exploration began with an understanding of the foundational role of language in mathematical cognition (Archibald, 2017; Leiss et al., 2019). As students develop mathematical problem-solving, the convergence of linguistic processes with executive functions and visuospatial processing comes to the forefront (Cristofori et al., 2019; Drigas & Karyotaki, 2019). However, these interactions are not uniform, as linguistic and cognitive factors can lead to divergent trajectories of mathematical development (Cross et al., 2019; Hickendorff, 2021).

Guided by the vision of evidence-based interventions, the chapter ventured into diverse methodologies and collaborative frameworks that bridge research with practice. The partnerships between speech-language pathologists, mathematics educators, and researchers hold immense promise, epitomizing the convergence of specialized knowledge to create innovative strategies (Chow et al., 2022; Crossley et al., 2017; Vitiello & Williford, 2016). These partnerships align with the overarching goal of creating inclusive learning environments through multimodal strategies, assistive technologies, and personalized interventions (Andzik et al., 2019; Kaczorowski et al., 2019; Vula et al., 2017).

Longitudinal studies, the backbone of developmental research, emerged as crucial conduits for understanding the trajectories of mathematical growth and the intricate dance between language and mathematics (Cummins et al., 2020; Zhu et al., 2017). Such studies, when fortified with data analytics, transcend the confines of cross-sectional snapshots and instead reveal the dynamic unfolding of cognitive processes (Fischer et al., 2020; Roebers, 2017). The integration of emerging technologies, such as virtual reality, augmented reality, and artificial intelligence, marks a paradigm shift in research and support strategies. These technologies enable immersive, individualized learning experiences that bridge linguistic gaps (Anderson, 2019). The holistic utilization of data analytics, longitudinal research, and technological innovations offers unprecedented potential to reshape educational paradigms, forging a future where evidence-based interventions are not just the exception but the norm.

This chapter echoes the sentiment that the relationship between language difficulties and mathematical problem-solving abilities in students with DLD transcends a mere academic endeavor. It is a pursuit that fuels advancements in education, fostering equity, and inclusivity.

REFERENCES

Abrahamson, D., Nathan, M. J., Williams-Pierce, C., Walkington, C., Ottmar, E. R., Soto, H., & Alibali, M. W. (2020, August). The future of embodied design for mathematics teaching and learning. []. Frontiers Media SA.]. *Frontiers in Education*, *5*, 147. doi:10.3389/feduc.2020.00147

Anderson, A. (2019). *Virtual reality, augmented reality and artificial intelligence in special education: A practical guide to supporting students with learning differences*. Routledge. doi:10.4324/9780429399503

Andzik, N. R., Chung, Y. C., Doneski-Nicol, J., & Dollarhide, C. T. (2019). AAC services in schools: A special educator's perspective. *International Journal of Developmental Disabilities*, *65*(2), 89–97. doi:10.1080/20473869.2017.1368909 PMID:34141328

Archibald, L. M. (2017). Working memory and language learning: A review. *Child Language Teaching and Therapy*, *33*(1), 5–17. doi:10.1177/0265659016654206

Baddeley, A. (2020). Working memory. In *Memory* (pp. 71–111). Routledge. doi:10.4324/9780429449642-4

Buono, S., & Jang, E. E. (2021). The effect of linguistic factors on assessment of English language learners' Mathematical ability: A differential item functioning analysis. *Educational Assessment*, *26*(2), 125–144. doi:10.1080/10627197.2020.1858783

Casey, B. M., & Fell, H. (2018). Spatial reasoning: A critical problem-solving tool in children's mathematics strategy toolkit. *Visualizing mathematics: The role of spatial reasoning in mathematical thought*, 47-75.

Chow, J. C., Morse, A., & Senter, R. (2022). Intentional collaboration with speech-language pathologists to support language outcomes of students with emotional and behavioral disorders. *Beyond Behavior*, *31*(3), 140–150. doi:10.1177/10742956221108350

Cristofori, I., Cohen-Zimerman, S., & Grafman, J. (2019). Executive functions. *Handbook of Clinical Neurology*, *163*, 197–219. doi:10.1016/B978-0-12-804281-6.00011-2 PMID:31590731

Cross, A. M., Joanisse, M. F., & Archibald, L. M. (2019). Mathematical abilities in children with developmental language disorder. *Language, Speech, and Hearing Services in Schools*, *50*(1), 150–163. doi:10.1044/2018_LSHSS-18-0041 PMID:30950775

Crossley, S., Liu, R., & McNamara, D. (2017, March). Predicting math performance using natural language processing tools. In *Proceedings of the Seventh International Learning Analytics & Knowledge Conference* (pp. 339-347). ACM. 10.1145/3027385.3027399

Cruz, R. A., Manchanda, S., Firestone, A. R., & Rodl, J. E. (2020). An examination of teachers' culturally responsive teaching self-efficacy. *Teacher Education and Special Education*, *43*(3), 197–214. doi:10.1177/0888406419875194

Cuccio, V., & Graziano, M. (2022). A Two-Level Model of Embodied Mathematical Thinking. Body Schema, Body Image and Language. In *Metaphors and Analogies in Sciences and Humanities: Words and Worlds* (pp. 87–113). Springer International Publishing. doi:10.1007/978-3-030-90688-7_5

Cummins, C., Pellicano, E., & Crane, L. (2020). Autistic adults' views of their communication skills and needs. *International Journal of Language & Communication Disorders*, *55*(5), 678–689. doi:10.1111/1460-6984.12552 PMID:32618026

Drigas, A., & Karyotaki, M. (2019). Executive Functioning and Problem Solving: A Bidirectional Relation. *Int. J. Eng. Pedagog.*, *9*(3), 76–98. doi:10.3991/ijep.v9i3.10186

Drigas, A., & Mitsea, E. (2020). The 8 pillars of metacognition. [iJET]. *International Journal of Emerging Technologies in Learning*, *15*(21), 162–178. doi:10.3991/ijet.v15i21.14907

Fuchs, L. S., Fuchs, D., Seethaler, P. M., & Craddock, C. (2020). Improving language comprehension to enhance word-problem solving. *Reading & Writing Quarterly*, *36*(2), 142–156. doi:10.1080/10573569.2019.1666760 PMID:32542068

Gallagher, A. L., Murphy, C. A., Conway, P., & Perry, A. (2019). Consequential differences in perspectives and practices concerning children with developmental language disorders: An integrative review. *International Journal of Language & Communication Disorders*, *54*(4), 529–552. doi:10.1111/1460-6984.12469 PMID:30945410

Hawes, Z., Moss, J., Caswell, B., Naqvi, S., & MacKinnon, S. (2017). Enhancing children's spatial and numerical skills through a dynamic spatial approach to early geometry instruction: Effects of a 32-week intervention. *Cognition and Instruction*, *35*(3), 236–264. doi:10.1080/07370008.2017.1323902

Henry, L. A., & Botting, N. (2017). Working memory and developmental language impairments. *Child Language Teaching and Therapy*, *33*(1), 19–32. doi:10.1177/0265659016655378

Hickendorff, M. (2021). The demands of simple and complex arithmetic word problems on language and cognitive resources. *Frontiers in Psychology*, *12*, 727761. doi:10.3389/fpsyg.2021.727761 PMID:34733206

Kaczorowski, T. L., Hashey, A. I., & Di Cesare, D. M. (2019). An exploration of multimedia supports for diverse learners during core math instruction. *Journal of Special Education Technology*, *34*(1), 41–54. doi:10.1177/0162643418781298

Khatin-Zadeh, O. (2022). How does representational transformation enhance mathematical thinking? *Axiomathes*, *32*(S2, Suppl 2), 283–292. doi:10.100710516-021-09602-2

Kumar, R., Zusho, A., & Bondie, R. (2018). Weaving cultural relevance and achievement motivation into inclusive classroom cultures. *Educational Psychologist*, *53*(2), 78–96. doi:10.1080/00461520.2018.1432361

Lambert, R., & Tan, P. (2017). Conceptualizations of students with and without disabilities as mathematical problem solvers in educational research: A critical review. *Education Sciences*, *7*(2), 51. doi:10.3390/educsci7020051

Leiss, D., Plath, J., & Schwippert, K. (2019). Language and mathematics-key factors influencing the comprehension process in reality-based tasks. *Mathematical Thinking and Learning*, *21*(2), 131–153. doi:10.1080/10986065.2019.1570835

Peng, P., Wang, C., & Namkung, J. (2018). Understanding the cognition related to mathematics difficulties: A meta-analysis on the cognitive deficit profiles and the bottleneck theory. *Review of Educational Research*, *88*(3), 434–476. doi:10.3102/0034654317753350

Planas, N., Morgan, C., & Schütte, M. (2018). Mathematics education and language: Lessons and directions from two decades of research. *Developing research in mathematics education. Twenty years of communication, cooperation and collaboration in Europe*, 196-210.

Roebers, C. M. (2017). Executive function and metacognition: Towards a unifying framework of cognitive self-regulation. *Developmental Review*, *45*, 31–51. doi:10.1016/j.dr.2017.04.001

Vitiello, V., & Williford, A. P. (2016). Relations between social skills and language and literacy outcomes among disruptive preschoolers: Task engagement as a mediator. *Early Childhood Research Quarterly*, *36*, 136–144. doi:10.1016/j.ecresq.2015.12.011

Vula, E., Avdyli, R., Berisha, V., Saqipi, B., & Elezi, S. (2017). The impact of metacognitive strategies and self-regulating processes of solving math word problems. *International Electronic Journal of Elementary Education*, *10*(1), 49–59. doi:10.26822/iejee.2017131886

Zhu, M., Cai, D., & Leung, A. W. (2017). Number line estimation predicts mathematical skills: Difference in grades 2 and 4. *Frontiers in Psychology*, *8*, 1576. doi:10.3389/fpsyg.2017.01576 PMID:28955282

Chapter 20
Navigating Dysphagia in Child Developmental Communication Disorders Using Telepractice Methods

Soultana L. Papadopoulou
University of Ioannina, Greece

Eugenia I. Toki
University of Ioannina, Greece

ABSTRACT

Childhood and adolescence are crucial periods for physical and cognitive development, and dysphagia can negatively impact growth and development. Telepractice offers accessibility, convenience, and flexibility for pediatric dysphagia patients, allowing parents to engage with healthcare professionals from home while promoting a familiar setting and reducing travel. However, technical obstacles, limited physical assessment, and privacy concerns must be addressed. The aim of this chapter is to thoroughly pinpoint modern diagnostic and intervention methods performed by trained specialists to ensure accurate diagnosis and aid in the development of an individualized rehabilitation program in the era of telepractice. Critical considerations for the current and future usage of telepractice in pediatric dysphagia services are mainly presented in this chapter. Prioritizing feeding and swallowing problems are essential for survival and social engagement, making telepractice an innovative and sustainable solution for children with developmental communication disorders.

INTRODUCTION

Feeding and swallowing are vital physiological functions necessary for the human body's survival, that affect growth, health, and socialization across the lifespan. Feeding and swallowing have an important social function as they set the occasion for social interactions. For example, participation in meals (e.g.,

DOI: 10.4018/979-8-3693-1982-6.ch020

eating with family and/or friends) is extremely widespread among different cultures and is an important aspect of both daily and social life. These processes accompany a series of socialization events, during which the individual can develop dialogue and share thoughts, knowledge, feelings, stories, and experiences. In its social dimension, feeding enables the individual to integrate into society, to develop psychologically, culturally, and emotionally, and thus lead a better quality of life (Wilkinson et al., 2021).

Swallowing is a complex neuromuscular, dynamic, semi-autonomous sensorimotor, and cognitive process. As a physiological function, swallowing ensures the provision of adequate nutrition and hydration, through the simultaneous execution of the following three vital functions: a) airway protection, b) nourishment, and c) hydration, while significantly contributing to the maintenance of the human body (Rosenbek & Jones, 2007; Shaker et al., 2012).

1.1. Feeding and Swallowing Difficulties

As vital functions, feeding and swallowing require constant neurological control as well as the coordinated action of 30 muscle groups (mouth, pharynx, oesophagus, larynx), 5 cranial nerves, and 4 cervical nerves from the central nervous system (CNS) (Perlman & Schulze-Delrieu, 1996). Normal swallowing is a safe, efficient, pleasant, and smooth process and is related to organic, socio-cultural, psychological, and environmental factors. Swallowing is typically a safe, comfortable, and efficient process, affected by various organic, socio-cultural, psychological, and environmental factors. However, individuals may develop dysphagia if the anatomical integrity and function of the structures involved in swallowing are affected by any dysfunction, damage, or disorder.

During the initial developmental stage, newborns are typically fed through either breastfeeding or bottle-feeding. As infants reach their third month, their brainstem reflexes, such as the sucking reflex, disappear. Around six months of age, they begin to chew and consume different types of food with varying consistencies. This process helps in strengthening their oral muscles. Starting from the oral cavity, as infants and children grow and develop, the absolute and relative size and shape of oral and pharyngeal structures change, and chewing matures. The "adult" swallowing pattern is typically established during adolescence once all the necessary anatomical structures involved in swallowing have fully formed (van den Engel-Hoek et al., 2015).

1.1.1. Dysphagia

The term dysphagia is derived from the synonyms of the ancient Greek words "dis" + "efagon" meaning "difficulty" + "eat", respectively. In its synthesis the word "dysphagia" describes any difficulty or inability to effectively and safely manage and transfer saliva, food of any consistency (liquids, semi-liquid, solids), and drugs/medication from the oral cavity, into the pharynx, the esophagus and finally into the stomach. The terms dysphagia, swallowing disorder, and deglutition disorder/dysfunction are frequently used interchangeably to describe the same condition (Paik & Kim, 2021; Perren et al., 2019).

According to Taber's Cyclopedic Medical Dictionary, dysphagia can be classified into five subcategories 1. Constricta - disorder of swallowing due to narrowing of the pharynx or the esophagus 2. Lusoria - swallowing disorder due to the compression of the esophagus by the right subclavian artery 3. Oropharyngeal dysphagia - difficulty transferring food from the mouth to the esophagus 4. Paralytica - swallowing disorder due to paralysis of the muscles of the mouth, pharynx, or esophagus 5. Spastica - swallowing disorder that arises from spasms of the pharynx or esophagus (Davis, 1993). However, in clinical practice, only oropharyngeal dysphagia from this classification is used with any frequency (Groher & Crary, 2020). Furthermore, in the tenth revision of the International Classification of Diseases (ICD-10), the World Health Organization (WHO) assigned the code R13.12 to dysphagia, oropharyngeal phase (World Health Organization (WHO), 1993).

In the case of oropharyngeal dysphagia, the oral preparatory, oral propulsive and/or pharyngeal phases of swallowing are afflicted. If the esophageal phase is disturbed, esophageal dysphagia is present. Both types of dysphagia may influence the other; therefore, dysphagia makes the comprehensive evaluation of the aerodigestive tract from the oral cavity to the stomach necessary.

It is important to distinguish the following terms:

- Pediatric feeding disorder (PFD) - defined as impaired oral intake that is not age appropriate and is associated with at least one dysfunctional domain: medical; nutritional; feeding skills; and psychosocial. Symptoms of PFD must be present daily for at least two weeks. PFD can be classified into acute (< 3 months' duration) and chronic (≥ 3 months' duration) (Goday et al., 2019). Feeding disorders may or may not include problems with swallowing, and while pica and rumination can be associated with PFD, their presence alone does not constitute PFD (Uher & Rutter, 2012).
- Avoidant/Restrictive Food Intake Disorder (ARFID) – which is an eating or a feeding disturbance (e.g., apparent lack of interest in eating or food, avoidance based on the sensory characteristics of food, concern about aversive consequences of eating), as manifested by persistent failure to meet appropriate nutritional and/or energy needs associated with one (or more) of the following: significant weight loss (or failure to achieve expected weight gain or faltering growth in children) significant nutritional deficiency dependence on enteral feeding or oral nutritional supplements marked interference with psychosocial functioning without body image or weight concerns (American Psychiatric Association, 2015). ARFID and PFD may exist separately or concurrently.
- Eating disorders (e.g., neurogenic anorexia, bulimia nervosa) - patients with an eating disorder present with body image disturbances and restriction of energy intake leading to significantly low body weight.
- Swallowing disorders or dysphagia - which was previously analyzed, can lead to avoidance of food intake and consequently a feeding disorder (Dharmaraj et al., 2023).

Feeding disorders are usually observed in the first one to three years of life when a child has poor weight gain, decreased oral intake, and/or delayed development of feeding skills. They often present with signs and symptoms such as malnutrition, refusal to eat and drink, food pocketing, disruptive feeding behavior, slow feeding (>30 min to finish), food selectivity or rigid food preferences, limited appetite, and delayed feeding milestones (Dharmaraj et al., 2023).

1.1.2. Prevalence

Feeding and swallowing disorders, as mentioned above, affect a large proportion of the clinical population, usually secondary to a disease, trauma, or disorder. Estimated reports of the incidence and prevalence of pediatric feeding and swallowing disorders vary widely due to many factors including variations in the conditions and populations sampled; how PDF, ARFID, and/or swallowing impairment are defined; and the assessment methods utilized (Arvedson, 2008; Lefton-Greif, 2008).

The incidence of pediatric dysphagia is estimated to be approximately 1% but is thought to be higher in at-risk clinical populations (e.g., children with cerebral palsy, traumatic brain injury, and airway malformations) (Bhattacharyya, 2015; Horton et al., 2018; Kakodkar & Schroeder, 2013; Prasse & Kikano, 2009; Raol et al., 2018; Svystun et al., 2017). More specifically, swallowing disorders, including oropharyngeal and esophageal dysphagia, affect 0.9% ± 0.1% of children in the US each year (Bhattacharyya, 2015). According to more recent findings, the annual prevalence of PDFs in the US was 1 in 23-37 children under the age of five (Kovacic et al., 2021). In addition, approximately 50% of parents report that their otherwise healthy children have feeding problems (Borowitz & Borowitz, 2018).

As our ability to care for patients with extreme prematurity and complex medical conditions, such as cerebral palsy, bronchopulmonary dysplasia, and cardiac anomalies improves, the incidence of swallowing disorders, increases (Kakodkar & Schroeder, 2013). A large, population-based cohort study found the prevalence of feeding problems in premature infants born at less than 37 weeks' gestation to be 10.5%, increasing to 24.5% among those born with a very low birth weight of less than 1500 g. (Motion et al., 2001). In addition, oropharyngeal dysphagia and/or feeding dysfunction in children with cerebral palsy is estimated to be 19.2%–99.0%, while rates increase with greater severity of cognitive impairment and decline in gross motor function (Benfer et al., 2014, 2017; Calis et al., 2008; Erkin et al., 2010; Speyer et al., 2019).

Regarding specific clinical populations, among children with communication disorders aged 3–10 years, the prevalence of swallowing problems is 4.3%. The prevalence rises to 14.5% in 11- to 17-year-olds with communication disorders. The odds of having a feeding problem increase by 2–5 times in children with autism spectrum disorder (ASD) compared with children who do not have ASD (Seiverling et al., 2018; Sharp et al., 2013). Additionally, up to 80% of children with developmental delays may have difficulties feeding (Borowitz & Borowitz, 2018), and 33%–83% of children with craniofacial disorders present with oral dysphagia (Caron et al., 2015; De Vries et al., 2013; Reid et al., 2006). Further it has been reported that approximately 20%–50% of children who are typically developing can experience feeding difficulties, while feeding difficulties can affect 70%–89% of children who have developmental delays (Patel et al., 2023).

1.1.3. Etiology of Dysphagia

Several etiologies have been attributed to feeding and swallowing difficulties and require further investigation. A variety of disorders, conditions, and diseases of the central and peripheral nervous system, including developmental disability, prematurity, autoimmune diseases, cardiopulmonary, neurological, and gastroesophageal disorders, anatomic malformations (abnormalities), and/or genetic syndromes, inflammation, infections, neoplasms, congenital diseases, trauma, iatrogenic and psychogenic causes as well as drugs may disrupt the typical development of feeding and swallowing skills in pediatric patients. These factors are considered the most common underlying causes of dysphagia (see Table 1) (McCarty & Chao, 2021; Park, 2021).

Additionally, in the pediatric population factors such as behavioral disorders, impairments in sensorimotor function, delayed development of feeding skills, delayed feeding developmental milestones, and impairments regarding eating pragmatics, i.e., the social behaviors required during eating, should be considered. Any delay can result in communication difficulties, dysfunctional feeding, and in severe cases it may negatively affect children's growth, and overall health and well-being (Mourão et al., 2017). The causes of dysphagia in children are varied and often multifactorial (Lawlor & Choi, 2020).

Table 1. Etiology of dysphagia in the infant and child population

Etiology	Causes	Allied complications
Neurological conditions	Related to CNS damage or musculoskeletal disorders	Birth asphyxia and Cerebral palsy, Microcephaly, Hydrocephalus, Intraventricular hemorrhage, Periventricular leukomalacia, Acquired brain injuries, Seizures
Syndromes	Associated birth defects or anomalies with dysphagic symptoms.	Down Syndrome, Pierre Robin sequence, Cornelia de Lange syndrome, Cri-du-chat.
Gastrointestinal abnormalities or dysfunction	Gastro-esophageal reflux is often a significant factor in eating and drinking difficulties.	Food allergies and intolerances, Necrotizing enterocolitis, Eosinophilic esophagitis, Gastroschisis, Hirschsprung's disease, Gastroesophageal reflux disease (GERD), Tracheoesophageal fistula and esophageal atresia, Congenital diaphragmatic hernia
Facial and Oral structural abnormalities	Anatomical and functional abnormalities related to feeding and swallowing due to structural and anatomical orofacial deficits.	Cleft lip and/or palate, Tethered tissues (e.g., tongue tie)
Respiratory problems and Cardiac disorders	They are associated with diseases that cause weakening of the cardiovascular system such as congenital heart defects.	Faltering weight and growth, Apnea of the newborn, Bronchopulmonary dysplasia (chronic lung disease), Laryngo-/tracheo-/bronchomalacia, Cyanotic and acyanotic heart defects Respiratory distress syndrome
Prematurity	Babies born before 37 weeks, weighing less than 2.5 kg	May be accompanied by comorbidities associated with prematurity
Metabolic disorders	Associated with metabolic diseases that interfere with normal feeding patterns, such as Niemann-Pick and Gaucher diseases	Can lead to brain damage and phenylketonuria
Caustic esophageal injury	Acidic or alkaline substances (e.g., cleaning substances)	Oral and tongue edema, drooling, and vomiting may occur. Upper airway edema can cause vocal alterations, stridor, and respiratory difficulty in some patients. If vessel erosion has occurred hematemesis may be present
Sensory-motor integration disorders	Sensory loss can lead to dysphagia in the absence of main motor impairment. To enhance diagnosis, sensory dysphagia should be defined as a distinct type of swallowing motility disease	Raising awareness and establishing proper assessment methods could help to progress dysphagia care
Emotional and psychological issues	Patients with developmental disabilities and comorbid feeding disorders	Difficulties arise as a result of psycho-emotional and social factors
Iatrogenic complications and medication side effects	Unintended unfavorable complications or side effects of treatment. Iatrogenic consequences such as dysphagia, pneumonia, disorientation, and falls may be caused by medications, and are often neglected	Medications, Tube feeding, Tracheostomy, Intubation, Respiratory support

1.1.4. Signs and Symptoms of Dysphagia in the Pediatric Population

As a common finding, dysphagia can affect people of all ages, races, and it can occur at any stage of swallowing - including oral (preparatory and propulsive), pharyngeal, and oesophageal. However, there are many differences in the manifestation of dysphagia between different patients. Symptoms vary based on the phase(s) affected, the child's developmental level, the cause(s) of dysphagia, and the child's medical history (Lawlor & Choi, 2020; Moroco & Aaronson, 2022).

Some common signs and symptoms of dysphagia include (ASHA, n.d.; Lawlor & Choi, 2020; Lefton-Greif & Arvedson, 2007):

- cough and/or choking during or after swallowing
- frequent pauses due to difficulties in the successive movements of the suck-swallow-breathe pattern
- gagging
- loss of food/fluids from the mouth when eating
- posturing, such as back arching and neck extension
- nasal regurgitation, and frequent congestion, especially after meals
- noisy or wet voice (murmur) during and after feeding
- taking small amounts of food, filling and storing food in their mouth (pocketing)
- vomiting
- difficulty chewing foods whose texture may be age-appropriate (may spit out, retain, or swallow partially chewed food)
- difficulty in managing secretions (including saliva secretions not related to teething)
- difficulty initiating the swallowing process
- crying during feeding
- food refusal (certain brands, colors, textures, etc.)
- decreased responsiveness during feeding
- prolonged feeding time (> 30 minutes per meal)
- signs of discomfort, such as grimaces, spreading their fingers in front of the mouth, turning their head in the opposite direction, and/or away from the food
- stillness
- changes in the normal rhythms of the heartbeat (bradycardia/tachycardia) in relation to feeding
- hypoxia (reduction of oxygen)
- increased respiratory rate during feeding
- skin discoloration (cyanosis)
- recurrent respiratory tract infections due to aspiration or silent aspiration
- dehydration
- weight loss or failure to achieve expected weight

Consequently, the symptoms above harm the achievement of developmental milestones, resulting in communication difficulties. Developmental language difficulties in childhood and adolescence are primarily impacted by swallowing difficulties, particularly in acquiring language skills such as speech and writing, as well as non-verbal expressions (Moroco & Aaronson, 2022). Communication disorders are frequently observed in children who experience challenges with feeding and swallowing. These difficulties are commonly attributed to pathology, syndrome, or disease. Communication difficulties become evident when a youngster cannot effectively communicate to transmit intended messages to their conversational partner. In this particular scenario, a suitable mode of communication is selected, frequently employing assistive technology (Newman et al., 2001). The ability to communicate and the choice of reinforcement mode are influenced by factors such as age, gross motor function, and manual dexterity. Adolescents of advanced age tend to employ supportive communication strategies with greater frequency. According to research findings, communication effectiveness increases as unsupported communication decreases (Reilly et al., 1996).

1.1.5. Pediatric Feeding and Swallowing Evaluation

In children with feeding and swallowing disorders, a comprehensive swallowing assessment is necessary to provide adequate management and recommendations for efficient and safe feeding.

The World Health Organization has defined the International Classification of Functional Disability and Health (ICF) as a possible framework for categorizing functional status and developing a uniform, standardized language for the description and study of health and health-related domains. The ICF could be very useful for speech and language pathologists (SLPs) working with feeding and swallowing issues in the pediatric population. More specifically, it is a recognized instrument that can help estimate the incidence and effect of pediatric feeding and swallowing difficulties by classifying information on the functional status of swallowing disorders and other health-related issues. Furthermore, it could help the evaluation of intervention results as well as the identification of healthcare needs, allowing expenses to be met from available resources on an evaluative basis (Lefton-Greif & Arvedson, 2007). Through the ICF clinicians can assess information related to a child's participation during mealtimes, as well as their neuromotor development, neuromuscular conditions, and motor skills (Arvedson, 2008; Kostanjsek, 2011).

The feeding and swallowing evaluation process is structured along the following three axes: a) obtaining a thorough medical and feeding & swallowing history (comprehensive review of medical/clinical records and interviews with the family and health care professionals), b) assessing the child's developmental level, and c) examining their feeding skills (eating and drinking boluses of various textures and consistencies), their preferred feeding method(s), and the means used. Neuromotor development and oral motor skills are also assessed (ASHA, n.d.; van den Engel-Hoek et al., 2015).

If there are any concerns regarding the efficiency and safety of swallowing a videofluoroscopic swallow study (VFSS) or a fiberoptic endoscopic evaluation of swallowing (FEES) should be undertaken (Lefton-Greif & Arvedson, 2007; Logemann, 1995). Determining the appropriate procedure to use depends on what needs to be visualized and which procedure will be best tolerated by the child. The child's responsiveness (e.g., acceptance of oral stimulation or tastes on the lips without signs of distress) and the potential for medical complications, are also considered. For example, the VFSS may be appropriate for a child who is currently NPO or has never eaten by mouth.

Descriptions of pediatric FEES routines were recently published (AB-SSD Task Force-Pediatric Group: et al., 2023; Harrington & Maybee, 2022; Miller et al., 2020; Miller & Willging, 2020). Additionally, a practical algorithm was proposed to guide the evaluation and management of pediatric dysphagia (Lawlor & Choi, 2020).

During the clinical instrumental examination, the following elements are usually assessed: lip closure, chewing, bolus preparation, propulsion, and transfer, tongue movement, control and tongue base retraction, initiation of the pharyngeal phase of swallowing, elevation, and retraction of the soft palate, laryngeal elevation, anterior displacement of the hyoid bone, laryngeal closure, pharyngeal stripping wave, and construction, pharyngeal segment opening, and esophageal clearance (Robbins et al., 2008).

Parameters such as skin colour, oxygen requirements, respiratory and heart rate (for more than 60 seconds), quality of phonation, oxygen saturation, management of secretions, tolerance of feeding, and the child's state (alertness or drowsiness) provide important information to the clinician regarding the child's safety, adequacy, and quality of feeding. These parameters must be carefully assessed as criteria for both the initiation of feeding and its progression, since they can determine and at the same time, could be indicators for safe swallowing and feeding.

Assessment of dysphagia is usually completed by an SLP, often in conjunction with radiologists or another specialist e.g., otolaryngologist (Lefton-Greif & Arvedson, 2017). Evaluation by a multidisciplinary team can facilitate accurate diagnosis and guide dysphagia treatment (Lawlor & Choi, 2020).

In children with difficulty swallowing esophageal inflammation, which may be caused by gastroesophageal reflux, eosinophilic esophagitis, or a variety of other etiologies, should be suspected. Significant inflammation of the esophagus may lead to odynophagia, and an ongoing fear of swallowing, which can also result in reduced intake. Therefore, if these conditions are present, they must be timely and effectively assessed (e.g., through a 24-hour pH monitoring, an esophagogastroduodenoscopy etc.), and managed by a pediatric gastroenterologist (Dharmaraj et al., 2023).

1.1.6. Treatment of Pediatric Swallowing Disorders

Following clinical and instrumental assessment, recommendations can be made regarding changes in feeding and hydration pathways, specific dietary guidelines, safe feeding, and head and trunk support. For example, the consistency/and or texture of food and the method and timing of its administration can be modified (Arvedson, 1998).

Appropriate management depends on the cause of dysphagia (Lawlor & Choi, 2020). The main target is to focus on the child's holistic well-being, including their social, physical, and emotional health (e.g., ensuring their safety, comfort, and enjoyment). Moreover, clinicians should be aware that oral feeding isn't always the best treatment option.

It is well known that appropriate nutritional intake is essential for the rapid growth and development that occurs during infancy and childhood (Dodrill & Gosa, 2015). Therefore, even a small boost in basic nutrition and hydration can enhance growth, as well as recovery (Ekberg et al., 2002; Farri et al., 2007). Consequently, this can significantly improve the child's overall quality of life and improve communication skills, adding value to the treatment, care, or rehabilitation services provided (Kumin et al., 2001).

Several evidence-based intervention methods can be applied following individualized protocols to achieve primary intervention goals. These usually include:

- Eliminating the possibility of aspiration or laryngeal penetration by eliminating their cause,
- Assisting in the establishment of a diet that will progressively contribute to adequate nutrition and hydration of the body, thereby making feeding a pleasurable experience.
- Exploring feeding skills and encouraging self-feeding so that the process of feeding becomes effortless and functional.
- Optimizing the child's quality of life by facilitating an enjoyable and safe feeding experience (either individually or in a social setting e.g., eating with family) (Ongkasuwan & Chiou, 2018).

The complex causes and consequences of dysphagia cross traditional boundaries between professional disciplines. Thus, managing dysphagia necessitates the involvement of a team of specialists from different fields. The composition of the dysphagia interprofessional team may differ depending on the setting (Logemann, 1995). The patient's team of medical professionals may consist of various specialists, such as the attending physician, an SLP who is typically the swallowing specialist, a physical therapist, an

Figure 1. Family dynamics in pediatric dysphagia

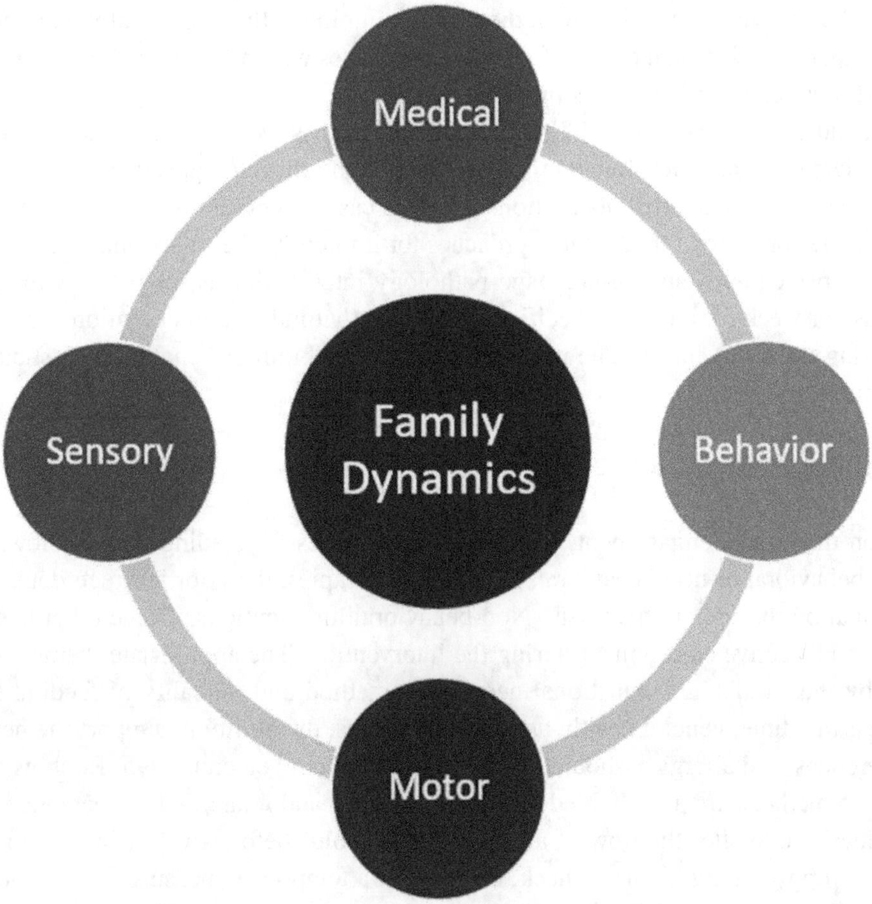

occupational therapist, a dietitian, a gastroenterologist, an otolaryngologist, a neurologist, a pharmacist, etc. Additional medical and rehabilitation specialists may be included, depending on the professional expertise needed, and the specific population being served.

SLPs play an integral role in a) the assessment and treatment of children with swallowing disorders, b) educating children and their families to prevent complications related to feeding and swallowing disorders, and c) recommending a safe swallowing and feeding plan for the individualized family service plan (IFSP) or individualized education program (IEP) (ASHA, n.d.) Specialist hospital clinics, intensive care units, subacute and emergency units, and rehabilitation clinics are the usual structures that accommodate patients with feeding and swallowing disorders. However, many children with feeding and swallowing disorders receive services in their own homes.

Basic principles clinicians should consider while developing a treatment plan are (ASHA, n.d.; Robbins et al., 2008):

- The primary goals of feeding and swallowing intervention for children are to support safe and adequate nutrition and hydration; determine the optimal feeding methods and techniques to maximize swallowing safety and feeding efficiency; collaborate with the family to incorporate dietary preferences; achieve age-appropriate eating skills in the most natural setting and manner possible (i.e., eating meals with peers in the preschool, mealtime with the family); minimize the risk of pulmonary complications; maximize the quality of life; and prevent future feeding issues with positive feeding-related experiences to the extent possible, given the child's medical situation.

- Young children with feeding and swallowing disorders, as well as some older children with concomitant intellectual disabilities, frequently require intervention techniques that do not require them to follow simple verbal or nonverbal instructions. In these cases, intervention may take the form of environmental changes or indirect treatment approaches for improving the safety and efficiency of feeding.
- The basic principle of speech-language pathology intervention is for patients to receive one to three sessions per week for a period specified by metrics that indicate intervention success and can be modified during the intervention. The responsiveness of the brain or behavioral plasticity determines the rate and intensity.

1.1.7. Therapeutic Approaches

Depending on the child's engagement, therapeutic approaches for feeding and swallowing issues are classified as behavioral or non-behavioral. Behavioral therapies, direct or indirect, demand the child's motor participation throughout treatment. Non-behavioral interventions, on the other hand, take place without the child's active engagement during the intervention. The appropriate therapeutic strategy is determined by the child's age, nutritional needs, and method and modality of feeding (e.g., utensils used). At the same time, general health, and co-morbidities, the ability to support the head and trunk, dietary preferences, and allergies, should also be considered (Logemann, 1995; Robbins et al., 2008).

Therapeutic methods are also divided into compensatory and rehabilitative techniques. Compensatory approaches aim to alter the flow of a food or liquid bolus before swallowing, by modifying their consistency or repositioning the head, neck, or body, as a temporary measure to facilitate safer eating and drinking. In contrast, rehabilitative interventions aim to improve swallowing physiology, through swallowing exercises that focus on muscle strength, resistance training or skill training, oral sensory stimulation, and/or swallowing maneuvers (Duncan et al., 2020).

Treatment techniques often applied by SLPs include postural and positioning techniques (adjusting the child's posture or position to establish central alignment and stability for safe feeding), postural/position techniques (to redirect the movement of the bolus in the oral cavity and pharynx and modify pharyngeal dimensions. These techniques may be used prior to or during the swallow e.g., head tilt), diet modifications (altering the viscosity, texture, temperature, portion size, or taste of a food or liquid to facilitate safety and ease of swallowing e.g., pureeing solid foods), using Adaptive equipment and utensils e.g., weighted forks and spoons, maneuvers (used to change the timing or strength of movements of swallowing e.g., supraglottic swallow), and oral-motor treatments (stimulation to—or actions of—the lips, jaw, tongue, soft palate, pharynx, larynx, and respiratory muscles, they range from passive e.g., tapping, stroking, and vibration to active e.g., range-of-motion activities, resistance exercises, or chewing and swallowing exercises) (ASHA, n.d.; Logemann, 1995; Robbins et al., 2008).

1.2. Telepractice

Current technological trends offer various opportunities to upgrades clinical practices. An important advancing modality to deliver clinical procedures is telepractice. Telepractice, or telehealth or telemedicine, involves using information and communication technologies to provide remote healthcare services (Becker & Gillespie, 2021). These terms are frequently employed synonymously, although they possess distinct conceptual delineations. Precisely, "telehealth" is a term that was used to describe the use of information and communication technologies to obtain health care (Achenbach, 2020). Telehealth refers to the process of electronically sending medical information, delivering, and facilitating clinical care between different locations, and involves a broader range of services, extending beyond clinical care to include educational activities, provider meetings, and training sessions (Becker & Gillespie, 2021; Salmanizadeh et al., 2022). Telemedicine is a subfield of telehealth that has a specific focus. Initially has been coined by Thomas Bird in 1970, with a literal translation that denotes the concept of "healing at a distance" (Strehle & Shabde, 2006). Telemedicine typically refers to clinical care alone providing a range of services, from phone consultations with doctors to robotic surgery performed by healthcare providers using video conferencing equipment across borders (Becker & Gillespie, 2021). *"Telepractice is the delivery of services using telecommunication and Internet technology to remotely connect clinicians to clients, other health care providers, and/or educational professionals for screening, assessment, intervention, consultation, and/or education"* (American Speech-Language-Hearing Association, 2020).

Telepractice services, based on the timing and nature of communication, can be delivered through synchronous, asynchronous or hybrid communication (American Speech-Language-Hearing Association, 2020; Becker & Gillespie, 2021; Hao et al., 2021). Synchronous communication refers to participants being active at the same time from different places, involving immediate communication and real-time interaction between the care provider and the patient, like a face-to-face session. It typically takes place through video conferencing, phone calls, or live chat. Synchronous telepractice allows for direct conversations, instant feedback, and dynamic engagement. It is particularly useful for activities that require immediate interaction and response, such as assessments, therapy sessions, and discussions (American Speech-Language-Hearing Association, 2020).

Alternatively, asynchronous communication can be employed referring to participants' activation on different time and place, communicating at their own convenience. The care provider reviews patient data or material that is not in real-time, such as video stroboscopic or still images recorded by another qualified provider. Asynchronous methods can include email, messaging platforms, recorded videos, and discussion forums. This approach allows for flexibility in terms of when participants engage with the content and respond (American Speech-Language-Hearing Association, 2020; Hao et al., 2021).

A hybrid approach can also be utilized, combining synchronous and asynchronous elements (American Speech-Language-Hearing Association, 2020). This approach leverages real-time interactions, when necessary, while also incorporating asynchronous components for flexibility and resource sharing. For example, a therapy session might be conducted through video conferencing, but the therapist and client also exchange messages and resources between sessions using a messaging platform.

The corona pandemic urged overcoming the physical separation between the clinician and the patient, allowing them to connect through video conferencing or other digital platforms, eliminating the need for in-person visits telepractice to be used rapidly and broadly in all facets of healthcare (Ward et al., 2022a). With telepractice as a support modality, care delivery for dysphagia is typical (Ward et al., 2022a). Likewise, research findings report that telepractice achieves the same therapeutic outcomes as in-person therapy, improving feeding function in children with disabilities when receiving feeding therapy (Malandraki et al., 2014, 2021; Tamura et al., 2023). It is essential to look at the big picture and assess the efficacy of providing care over telepractice as a sustainable service option (Thomas et al., 2022) integrated into ordinary dysphagia care.

1.3. Aim of This Chapter

The aim of this chapter is to thoroughly pinpoint modern diagnostic and intervention methods performed by trained specialists to ensure accurate diagnosis and aid in the development of an individualized rehabilitation program in the era of telepractice. Critical considerations for the current and future usage of telepractice in pediatric dysphagia services, are mainly presented in this chapter.

It is therefore clear that the management of feeding and swallowing problems is a major issue that every communication specialist should prioritize, as it is essential for both survival and social engagement. Consequently, the resolution of any feeding and swallowing problems to smoothly manage the daily problems of those with mild, moderate, or severe swallowing issues, should come first. Telepractice can be an innovative and sustainable solution to enhance pediatric dysphagia services.

2. HOW TELEPRACTICE CAN CONTRIBUTE TO PEDIATRIC DYSPHAGIA?

Due to the risk of poor nutrition, development, and wellness, precise and prompt assessment, diagnosis, and management of feeding difficulties in infants and children is crucial (Berlin et al., 2011). To help readers better understand the practical implications of telepractice contributing to pediatric dysphagia issues, and how it could benefit them, next we provide more concrete examples of how telemedicine and telehealth can be used in real-world settings. While the text does mention several different applications of telepractice, it would be helpful to include more specific examples of how these services can be used in practice.

Best practices as well limitations for providing care over telepractice on dysphagia for children include issues regarding assessment, continuous monitoring, collaboration, education and training, therapeutic sessions, accessibility, and technical considerations.

2.1. Telepractice in Assessment of Pediatric Dysphagia

Telepractice can be used for initial assessments of children with dysphagia. SLPs may utilize video consultations to observe the child's swallowing function, review medical history, and gather information from parents or caregivers (Malandraki et al., 2014, 2021; Ward et al., 2022a).

The first study investigating telepractice for evaluating dysphagia in children, assessed 19 children with cerebral palsy, aged 6.9 to 17.5 years were using the Dysphagia Disorder Survey (DDS) during three mealtimes (Kantarcigil et al., 2016). Three clinicians conducted face-to-face evaluations, while a remote clinician completed about one-third of the evaluations in person. The study found a high level of understanding between face-to-face and remote assessments, with agreement percentages ranging from 78% to 100%. When separate raters conducted the assessments, agreement percentages ranged from 69% to 89%. The level of dysphagia severity showed excellent interrater agreement, with a 100% agreement rate and a Kappa value of 1. Interrater agreement was substantial, with an 85% agreement rate and a

Figure 2. Telepractice assessment in pediatric dysphagia

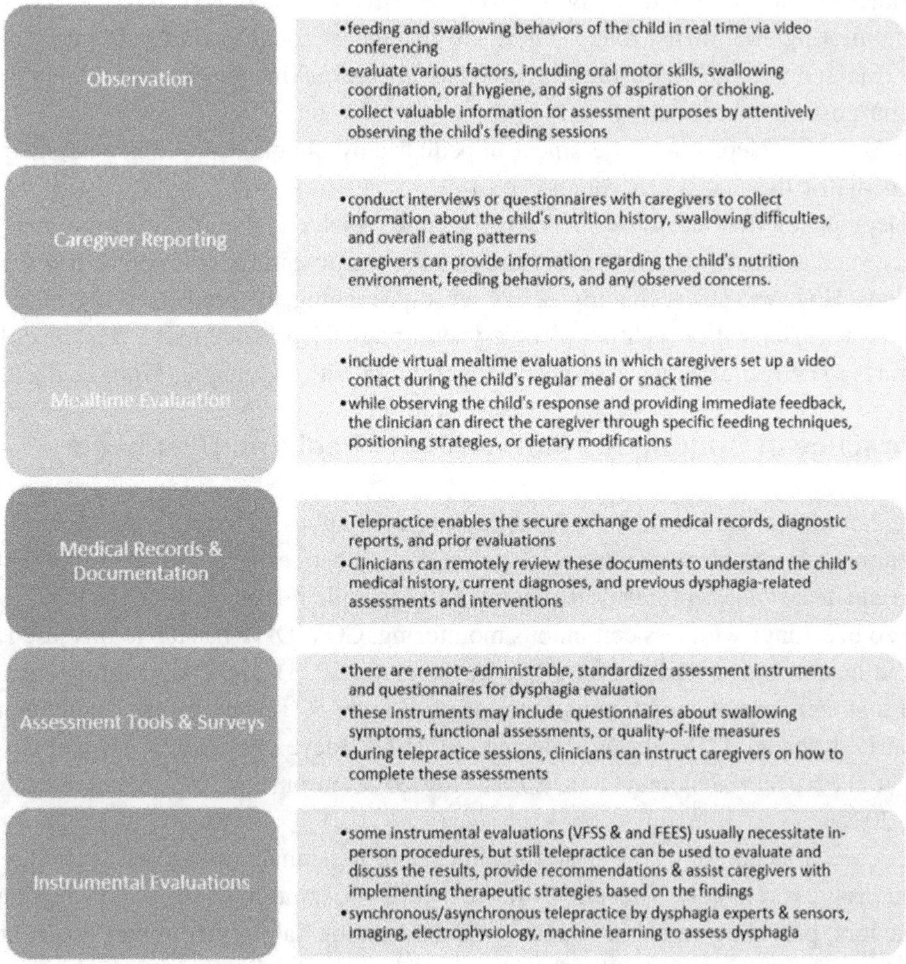

Kappa value of 0.76. Asynchronous clinical assessments of swallowing via standardized instruments provide satisfactory levels of concordance with in-person evaluations, serving as a viable option for children with limited access to specialized swallowing healthcare services.

In another study, reliability, clinician and parent satisfaction of synchronous telepractice bottle-feeding assessments were examined (M. Raatz, Ward, Marshall, & Burns, 2021). A remote telepractice SLP and an in-person SLP at the family home assessed 30 children aged 1 month-2 years. Developmental level, state, color, breathing, oral motor skills, newborn oral reflexes, tongue tie, non-nutritive suck, bottle-feeding, feeding abilities, and suggestions were assessed. Most evaluation components met agreement criteria, although palate integrity, non-nutritive suck assessment, and tongue tie screen were tough. Parent and clinician satisfaction was excellent, with SLPs saying they would give telepractice to 93% of families again.

Further, although swallowing science has advanced, there is still a lack of consensus on managing dysphagia due to limited understanding of underlying processes. Accurate tools and individualized analysis are needed to enhance assessment and treatment efficacy (Malandraki, 2023). Technology advances are reported with two new technologies that were developed by the author's team: SimulScan, which examines swallow and brain activity during an MRI sequence, and i-Phagia, a wearable EMG sensor for monitoring swallowing rehab. These advancements could lead to more individualized dysphagia care (Malandraki, 2023). Further research can also reveal insights of such tools for telepractice assessment purposes.

Next, in Figure 2. Telepractice assessment in pediatric dysphagia, we outline telepractice modal in assessment pediatric dysphagia procedures.

While telepractice offers numerous benefits for child dysphagia therapy, it's important to note that some aspects, such as hands-on assessments and certain instrumental assessments, may still require in-person sessions. However, new technologies like sensors, imaging, electrophysiology, machine learning can be utilized together with synchronous or asynchronous telepractice may offer novel flexible and accessible ways to deliver effective assessment for children with dysphagia (Ward et al., 2022b).

2.2. Telepractice in Continuous Monitoring of Pediatric Dysphagia

Telepractice can play a significant role in facilitating continuous monitoring of pediatric dysphagia, allowing healthcare professionals to track progress, detect changes, and provide timely interventions. Telepractice can make it harder for private practice SLPs to build relationships with clients, but it may be easier to do so in settings with less continuous monitoring. COVID-19 has led to increased telepractice monitoring in hospitals and rehab centers (De Taeye et al., 2023). Next, we summarize activities for telepractice that can promote continuous monitoring (Figure 3. Telepractice for continuous monitoring in pediatric dysphagia) (Becker & Gillespie, 2021; De Taeye et al., 2023; Dodrill & Gosa, 2015; Kantarcigil et al., 2016; Malandraki et al., 2021; Moroco & Aaronson, 2022; M. K. Raatz et al., 2020; Ward et al., 2022b):

Telepractice is a technology that allows healthcare professionals to monitor a child's swallowing function and progress remotely. This allows for real-time observation of the child's feeding and swallowing behaviors, providing valuable insights into their eating habits, oral motor skills, and potential difficulties. Caregivers can record video diaries of mealtime or feeding sessions, which can be shared with healthcare professionals for review (Ward et al., 2022b). Telepractice platforms also offer tools for caregivers to track and report symptoms related to dysphagia, such as coughing, choking, or difficulty swallowing (Raatz et al., 2020). Emerging technologies like wearable sensors or smart instruments can provide real-time data on swallowing movements and patterns (Malandraki, 2023; Malandraki et al., 2014, 2021; Ward et al., 2022a). SLPs can provide educational resources and guidelines for monitoring specific aspects of dysphagia at home, empowering caregivers to be proactive in identifying changes. Telepractice enables multidisciplinary teams to collaborate and share insights on the child's progress, ensuring comprehensive monitoring and care. It also allows easy storage and access to historical data, enabling healthcare professionals to make data-driven decisions (Raatz et al., 2019; Raatz et al., 2020; Ward et al., 2022b).

By incorporating these approaches, telepractice can establish a continuous feedback loop between healthcare professionals and caregivers, enabling proactive monitoring and enhancing the overall management of pediatric dysphagia.

Figure 3. Telepractice for continuous monitoring in pediatric dysphagia

2.3. Collaboration in Telepractice for Pediatric Dysphagia

Telepractice offers the opportunity for collaboration between SLPs, parents, caregivers, and other members of the child's healthcare team. With clear communication and sharing of information, a comprehensive treatment plan can be developed and implemented. Telepractice improves dysphagia care by facilitating virtual meetings for healthcare experts, encouraging family involvement, offering instructional workshops and real-time consultations, and allowing for remote monitoring and care transitions. It also promotes sharing of findings and resources among researchers and educators, ultimately leading to better understanding and management of dysphagia (Becker & Gillespie, 2021; Berlin et al., 2011; Malandraki et al., 2021; Ward et al., 2022b).

2.4. Telepractice for Education and Training in Child Dysphagia

Telepractice is an effective method for educating caregivers, parents, and colleagues about child dysphagia (Ward et al., 2022b). Virtual workshops, seminars, and webinars can be hosted by healthcare providers to cover topics such as dysphagia, oral motor exercises, safe feeding, and diet (American

Speech-Language-Hearing Association, 2020). Caregiver SLPs can also provide feeding and swallowing method demonstrations (Aggarwal et al., 2021). Personalized training programs can be tailored to the individual needs and difficulties of each child. SLPs can provide real-time feedback on feeding interactions, organize virtual mealtimes, and conduct feeding therapy sessions. Telepractice SLPs can support caregivers as they apply training methodologies for parent coaching, troubleshoot issues, and provide approval for feeding video recordings (Malandraki et al., 2014). Online materials, videos, and visual aids can be utilized to help caregivers understand child dysphagia and intervention. Telepractice enables group learning, continuous education, and cultural and language sensitivity. This method provides caregivers with the flexibility and convenience to receive education and training for supporting children with dysphagia on a daily basis (American Speech-Language-Hearing Association, 2020).

2.5. Telepractice in Therapy for Child Dysphagia

The first published study utilizing telepractice in intervention was a pilot study that examined teleconferencing to address the requirements of children with complex feeding disorders, regardless of distance (Clawson et al., 2008). The study involved 15 participants over a 26-month period from September 2002 to October 2004. The intervention improved long-term outcomes, treatment quality, family satisfaction, provider satisfaction, and clinical results. The study also analyzed the intervention's impact on variables such as family expenditures, provider contentment, and clinical outcomes. Likewise, another rehabilitation pediatric dysphagia study, highlights the need for evidence-based programs built with proper competence and consideration for patient and family needs, clinician qualifications, technological requirements, and technical assistance (Malandraki et al., 2014). Further, in a study examining teleconsultation for treating a child with eating issues, different approaches were used to increase the child's willingness to eat less favored foods, and the intervention was well-received by all parties involved. There was also strong agreement and adherence to the treatment plan (Bloomfield et al., 2019).

Telepractice aids in treating dysphagia in children by allowing speech-language pathologists (SLPs) to use video conferencing to teach oral motor control, sensory exploration, and swallowing exercises in real-time (Clawson et al., 2008; Malandraki et al., 2014; Thomas et al., 2022). Visual modeling can help SLPs demonstrate proper swallowing and oral exercises during therapy sessions and provide instant feedback. SLPs can also explain and demonstrate activities on video for their home exercise programs and advise parents and caregivers on pace, utensil use, and placement to improve a child's swallowing during meals (Marshall et al., 2023). Telepractice also allows SLPs to work with dietitians to advise dysphagia-afflicted youngsters on food changes. Furthermore, in therapy, SLPs help parents become effective partners in their child's rehabilitation efforts (American Speech-Language-Hearing Association, 2020). Telepractice platforms allow SLPs to track progress and make data-driven therapy plan adjustments. Telepractice also helps children and caregivers prepare for feeding and swallowing routines or intervention adjustments. Additionally, telepractice can apply motivational and behavioral tactics to treat food aversions and eating and swallowing anxieties. Ultimately, telepractice allows SLPs to work with other childcare experts to provide a holistic therapy plan.

To conclude, telepractice allows SLPs to remotely provide therapy, guidance, and support for children with dysphagia. SLPs can hold regular therapy sessions, create customized programs, instruct and cue parents and caregivers, and collaborate with other professionals to enhance swallowing function and quality of life (Marshall et al., 2023).

2.6. Telepractice Accessibility

Telepractice offers many accessibility benefits for child dysphagia assessment, therapy, and management. It allows children and families in rural or underdeveloped areas to receive specialized treatments without traveling (Mohan et al., 2017). Telepractice provides professional access, minimizes wait times, and assures rapid response (Ward et al., 2022b). It also makes scheduling therapy sessions around the child's routine and family obligations easier. Additionally, telepractice encourages family involvement, improving home care continuity. It also reduces travel costs, making therapy more affordable for families (American Speech-Language-Hearing Association, 2020). Finally, it improves language and cultural awareness, helping children and families understand and participate in their treatment (Raatz et al., 2020). Children are more engaged when they feel comfortable at home, and telepractice systems enable transdisciplinary data sharing among childcare experts. Telepractice also makes transitioning from hospital to home or between healthcare facilities easier, allowing SLPs to educate families on how to support the child's needs, ensuring that children receive the care they need.

2.7. Technical Considerations

Effective child dysphagia telepractice requires careful consideration of technology. Platform selection, internet connection, devices, accessibility features, privacy and security, testing, camera positioning, lighting, and engagement tools all contribute to a smooth and helpful experience (Becker & Gillespie, 2021; Raatz et al., 2019; Raatz et al., 2020; Ward et al., 2022b). In detail, a secure, HIPAA-compliant platform is essential for video conferencing, screen sharing, and data storage. A fast internet connection is crucial for smooth communication. Both the child and clinician should have compatible cameras and microphones. Screen reader compatibility and closed captioning are also important. Encryption and secure logins are necessary to protect sensitive health data. Pre-session checks and troubleshooting enable good communication, while clear camera location is necessary to capture oral and swallowing actions accurately (American Speech-Language-Hearing Association, 2020). Sufficient illumination is needed for video visibility. Interactive games, virtual prizes, and multimedia resources help engage children throughout therapy. Telepractice platform navigation requires parent/caregiver training. Consent, secrecy, and backup communication mechanisms are necessary in case of technical issues. Record sessions for future reference and maintain technology comfort through ongoing training.

3. TELEPRACTICE PROS AND CONS

Telepractice provides numerous advantages for pediatric patients with dysphagia, encompassing factors such as enhanced accessibility, heightened convenience, more flexibility, greater parental engagement, improved continuity of care, facilitated data sharing, promoted multi-disciplinary collaboration, streamlined transition of care, and potential cost savings.

Positive cost savings have also been reported regarding with pediatric telepractice feeding services (Burns et al., 2020; M. Raatz, Ward, Marshall, Burns, et al., 2021; Ward et al., 2022b). The cost of pediatric dysphagia therapy can vary depending on factors such as location, professional skill level, services offered, duration and frequency of sessions. Telepractice therapy includes therapist fees, technology expenses, travel savings, and flexible scheduling. In-person therapy costs vary based on therapist qualifications, local market rates, and travel expenses. The selection should be based on the child's specific needs, family preferences, and available resources while considering the quality of care, accessibility, and convenience.

The utilization of this telepractice enables children residing in geographically isolated or underserved regions to avail themselves of specialized dysphagia treatment, thereby mitigating the necessity for extensive travel and fostering a familiar setting. Telepractice also facilitates more convenient scheduling, thereby accommodating the child's established schedule and family obligations.

The promotion of parent/caregiver involvement is advocated, resulting in enhanced consistency of care within the home environment. Telepractice provides a means of maintaining uninterrupted therapeutic interventions in the face of adverse weather conditions or public health emergencies. The sharing of data is enabled by telepractice platforms, so facilitating the collaboration of professionals engaged in the provision of care for children.

Nevertheless, telepractice is not without its issues, including technical obstacles, restrictions in hands-on assessment, restricted physical manipulation, and potential difficulties in engaging children. Both therapists and families require access to suitable gadgets equipped with functional cameras and microphones. Privacy concerns are a notable issue, given that establishing a private and secure atmosphere for therapy sessions can present greater difficulties inside a home setting. Therapists encounter reduced control over the child's environment and potential distractions in telepractice sessions. The variability of reimbursement rules and regulations pertaining to telepractice services across different locations can influence the accessibility of healthcare services. Furthermore, it is imperative that both therapists and caregivers possess a level of proficiency and familiarity with the technological aspects of telepractice, potentially necessitating training in order to effectively utilize the telepractice platform. An obstacle for clinicians, as specified in this study is the *"limited training on telepractice for themselves and/or the client parents. The scope of training goes beyond technology to the abilities of offering intervention via telecommunication and training parents as service facilitators"* (Hao et al., 2021).

It's important to note that telepractice can complement traditional in-person interventions, offering an additional option for pediatric dysphagia care. Careful consideration of its pros and cons, along with the child's specific needs, can help determine if telepractice is an appropriate and effective approach for a particular case.

4. FUTURE PERSPECTIVES

The use of telepractice in pediatric dysphagia shows promise for enhancing accessibility, patient participation, and efficiency of assessment, therapy, and management. Novel tools like wearable sensors and intelligent utensils enable more precise remote estimates of swallowing function as technology evolves. Virtual reality can allow toddlers to practice swallowing exercises in immersive surroundings to enhance coordination. AI-Assisted Assessment demonstrates the possibility of analysing video footage and providing objective measures of swallowing patterns using artificial intelligence algorithms. Telepractice can provide data for researchers to acquire deeper insights into dysphagia, leading to more specifically focused therapies. Hybrid models with in-person and telepractice sessions can provide tailored hands-on assessments. Telepractice increases accessibility on a global scale, allowing for worldwide partnerships and remote monitoring of swallowing function. Gamification strategies can be introduced to keep children interested and motivated during therapy. Telepractice can enhance standardization and guidelines for dysphagia assessments and therapy, as well as the number of comprehensive online training and teaching platforms available to doctors and caregivers. Telepractice can be integrated with multidisciplinary teams, allowing professionals to contribute simultaneously and in real-time. Ethical and legal frameworks that govern telepractice will undoubtedly change over time. In conclusion, telepractice shows promise in advancing our understanding of dysphagia and can play a transformative role in improving the lives of children with swallowing difficulties.

5. CONCLUSION

In conclusion, telepractice has emerged as a valuable and versatile tool in addressing pediatric dysphagia, offering a range of benefits and considerations for both therapists and families. Its ability to transcend geographical boundaries, enhance accessibility to specialized care, and foster collaboration among multidisciplinary teams has transformed the landscape of pediatric dysphagia management. By providing remote assessments, therapy sessions, education, and training, telepractice has demonstrated its potential to empower families, engage children, and ensure consistent and timely interventions.

The convenience and flexibility that telepractice affords, allowing therapy sessions to seamlessly integrate into the child's daily routine, offer a significant advantage. However, challenges such as technical limitations, the inability to conduct certain hands-on assessments remotely, and the need for careful privacy considerations underscore the importance of thoughtful implementation and ongoing evaluation.

As telepractice in pediatric dysphagia continues to evolve, it should not be viewed as a replacement for traditional in-person interventions, but rather as a complementary approach. Effective outcomes rely on a balanced approach that harnesses the strengths of telepractice while acknowledging its limitations. By embracing telepractice as a dynamic tool within a comprehensive care framework, clinicians, caregivers, and children can collectively navigate the path to improved swallowing function, enhanced quality of life, and optimal developmental outcomes.

REFERENCES

Achenbach, S. J. (2020). Telemedicine: Benefits, challenges, and its great potential. *Health L. & Pol'y Brief, 14*, 1.

Aggarwal, K., Patel, R., & Ravi, R. (2021). Uptake of telepractice among speech-language therapists following COVID-19 pandemic in India. *Speech, Language and Hearing (London, England), 24*(4), 228–234. doi:10.1080/2050571X.2020.1812034

American Psychiatric Association. (2015). *Feeding and eating disorders: DSM-5® selections*. American Psychiatric Pub.

American Speech-Language-Hearing Association. (2020). *Telepractice*. ASHA. https://www.asha.org/practice-portal/professional-issues/telepractice/#collapse_1

Arvedson, J. C. (1998). MANAGEMENT OF PEDIATRIC DYSPHAGIA. *Otolaryngologic Clinics of North America, 31*(3), 453–476. doi:10.1016/S0030-6665(05)70064-5 PMID:9628944

Arvedson, J. C. (2008). Assessment of pediatric dysphagia and feeding disorders: Clinical and instrumental approaches. *Developmental Disabilities Research Reviews*, *14*(2), 118–127. doi:10.1002/ddrr.17 PMID:18646015

ASHA. (n.d.). *Feeding and Swallowing Disorders in Children*. American Speech-Language-Hearing Association; American Speech-Language-Hearing Association. https://www.asha.org/public/speech/swallowing/feeding-and-swallowing-disorders-in-children/

Becker, D. R., & Gillespie, A. I. (2021). In the Zoom Where It Happened: Telepractice and the Voice Clinic in 2020. *Seminars in Speech and Language*, *42*(01), 064–072. doi:10.1055/s-0040-1722750

Benfer, K. A., Weir, K. A., Bell, K. L., Ware, R. S., Davies, P. S. W., & Boyd, R. N. (2014). Oropharyngeal dysphagia in preschool children with cerebral palsy: Oral phase impairments. *Research in Developmental Disabilities*, *35*(12), 3469–3481. doi:10.1016/j.ridd.2014.08.029 PMID:25213472

Benfer, K. A., Weir, K. A., Bell, K. L., Ware, R. S., Davies, P. S. W., & Boyd, R. N. (2017). Oropharyngeal Dysphagia and Cerebral Palsy. *Pediatrics*, *140*(6), e20170731. doi:10.1542/peds.2017-0731 PMID:29167377

Berlin, K. S., Davies, W. H., Silverman, A. H., & Rudolph, C. D. (2011). Assessing Family-based Feeding Strategies, Strengths, and Mealtime Structure with the Feeding Strategies Questionnaire. *Journal of Pediatric Psychology*, *36*(5), 586–595. doi:10.1093/jpepsy/jsp107 PMID:19995867

Bhattacharyya, N. (2015). The prevalence of pediatric voice and swallowing problems in the United States: Pediatric Voice and Swallowing. *The Laryngoscope*, *125*(3), 746–750. doi:10.1002/lary.24931 PMID:25220824

Bloomfield, B. S., Fischer, A. J., Clark, R. R., & Dove, M. B. (2019). Treatment of Food Selectivity in a Child with Avoidant/Restrictive Food Intake Disorder Through Parent Teleconsultation. *Behavior Analysis in Practice*, *12*(1), 33–43. doi:10.100740617-018-0251-y PMID:30918768

Borowitz, K. C., & Borowitz, S. M. (2018). Feeding Problems in Infants and Children. *Pediatric Clinics of North America*, *65*(1), 59–72. doi:10.1016/j.pcl.2017.08.021 PMID:29173720

Burns, C. L., Wishart, L. R., Kularatna, S., & Ward, E. C. (2020). Knowing the costs of change: An introduction to health economic analyses and considerations for their use in implementation research. *Speech, Language and Hearing (London, England)*, *23*(1), 30–36. doi:10.1080/2050571X.2019.1693750

Calis, E. A., Veugelers, R., Sheppard, J. J., Tibboel, D., Evenhuis, H. M., & Penning, C. (2008). Dysphagia in children with severe generalized cerebral palsy and intellectual disability. *Developmental Medicine and Child Neurology*, *50*(8), 625–630. doi:10.1111/j.1469-8749.2008.03047.x PMID:18754902

Caron, C. J. J. M., Pluijmers, B. I., Joosten, K. F. M., Mathijssen, I. M. J., Van Der Schroeff, M. P., Dunaway, D. J., Wolvius, E. B., & Koudstaal, M. J. (2015). Feeding difficulties in craniofacial microsomia: A systematic review. *International Journal of Oral and Maxillofacial Surgery*, *44*(6), 732–737. doi:10.1016/j.ijom.2015.02.014 PMID:25771070

Clawson, B., Selden, M., Lacks, M., Deaton, A. V., Hall, B., & Bach, R. (2008). Complex pediatric feeding disorders: Using teleconferencing technology to improve access to a treatment program. [+. Gale Academic OneFile.]. *Pediatric Nursing*, *34*(3), 213. PMID:18649810

Davis, F. A. (1993). *Taber's cyclopedic medical dictionary*.

De Taeye, R., Van Lierde, K., & Alighieri, C. (2023). Telepractice in the diagnosis and treatment of pediatric speech-language disorders: The opinions and experiences of speech-language pathologists. *International Journal of Pediatric Otorhinolaryngology*, *169*, 111560. doi:10.1016/j.ijporl.2023.111560 PMID:37116275

De Vries, I. A. C., Breugem, C. C., Van Der Heul, A. M. B., Eijkemans, M. J. C., Kon, M., & Van Der Molen, A. B. M. (2013). Prevalence of feeding disorders in children with cleft palate only: A retrospective study. *Clinical Oral Investigations*. doi:10.100700784-013-1117-x PMID:24122307

Dharmaraj, R., Elmaoued, R., Alkhouri, R., Vohra, P., & Castillo, R. O. (2023). Evaluation and Management of Pediatric Feeding Disorder. *Gastrointestinal Disorders (Basel, Switzerland)*, *5*(1), 75–86. doi:10.3390/gidisord5010008

Dodrill, P., & Gosa, M. M. (2015). Pediatric Dysphagia: Physiology, Assessment, and Management. *Annals of Nutrition & Metabolism*, *66*(Suppl. 5), 24–31. doi:10.1159/000381372 PMID:26226994

Duncan, S., McAuley, D. F., Walshe, M., McGaughey, J., Anand, R., Fallis, R., & Blackwood, B. (2020). Interventions for oropharyngeal dysphagia in acute and critical care: A systematic review and meta-analysis. *Intensive Care Medicine*, *46*(7), 1326–1338. doi:10.100700134-020-06126-y PMID:32514597

Ekberg, O., Hamdy, S., Woisard, V., Wuttge-Hannig, A., & Ortega, P. (2002). Social and psychological burden of dysphagia: Its impact on diagnosis and treatment. *Dysphagia*, *17*(2), 139–146. doi:10.100700455-001-0113-5 PMID:11956839

Erkin, G., Culha, C., Ozel, S., & Kirbiyik, E. G. (2010). Feeding and gastrointestinal problems in children with cerebral palsy. *International Journal of Rehabilitation Research. Internationale Zeitschrift fur Rehabilitationsforschung. Revue Internationale de Recherches de Readaptation*, *33*(3), 218–224. doi:10.1097/MRR.0b013e3283375e10 PMID:20216224

Farri, A., Accornero, A., & Burdese, C. (2007). Social importance of dysphagia: Its impact on diagnosis and therapy. *Acta Otorhinolaryngologica Italica*, *27*(2), 83. PMID:17608136

Groher, M. E., & Crary, M. A. (2020). *Dysphagia-E-Book: Clinical management in adults and children*. Elsevier Health Sciences.

Hao, Y., Zhang, S., Conner, A., & Lee, N. Y. (2021). The Evolution of Telepractice Use during the COVID-19 Pandemic: Perspectives of Pediatric Speech-Language Pathologists. *International Journal of Environmental Research and Public Health*, *18*(22), 12197. doi:10.3390/ijerph182212197 PMID:34831952

Harrington, B. M., & Maybee, J. L. (2022). Pediatric FEES: What It Takes to Achieve Optimal Outcomes. *Perspectives of the ASHA Special Interest Groups*, *7*(6), 1972–1983. doi:10.1044/2022_PERSP-22-00106

Horton, J., Atwood, C., Gnagi, S., Teufel, R., & Clemmens, C. (2018). Temporal Trends of Pediatric Dysphagia in Hospitalized Patients. *Dysphagia, 33*(5), 655–661. doi:10.100700455-018-9884-9 PMID:29464395

Kakodkar, K., & Schroeder, J. W. Jr. (2013). Pediatric dysphagia. *Pediatric Clinics of North America, 60*(4), 969–977. doi:10.1016/j.pcl.2013.04.010 PMID:23905831

Kantarcigil, C., Sheppard, J. J., Gordon, A. M., Friel, K. M., & Malandraki, G. A. (2016). A telehealth approach to conducting clinical swallowing evaluations in children with cerebral palsy. *Research in Developmental Disabilities, 55*, 207–217. doi:10.1016/j.ridd.2016.04.008 PMID:27132060

Kostanjsek, N. (2011). Use of The International Classification of Functioning, Disability and Health (ICF) as a conceptual framework and common language for disability statistics and health information systems. *BMC Public Health, 11 Suppl 4*(Suppl 4). doi:10.1186/1471-2458-11-S4-S3

Kovacic, K., Rein, L. E., Szabo, A., Kommareddy, S., Bhagavatula, P., & Goday, P. S. (2021). Pediatric Feeding Disorder: A Nationwide Prevalence Study. *The Journal of Pediatrics, 228*, 126–131.e3. doi:10.1016/j.jpeds.2020.07.047 PMID:32702429

Kumin, L., Von Hagel, K. C., & Bahr, D. C. (2001). An effective oral motor intervention protocol for infants and toddlers with low muscle tone. *Infant-Toddler Intervention, 11*(3/4), 181–200.

Lawlor, C. M., & Choi, S. (2020). Diagnosis and Management of Pediatric Dysphagia: A Review. *JAMA Otolaryngology-Head & Neck Surgery, 146*(2), 183–191. doi:10.1001/jamaoto.2019.3622 PMID:31774493

Lefton-Greif, M. A. (2008). Pediatric Dysphagia. *Physical Medicine and Rehabilitation Clinics of North America, 19*(4), 837–851. doi:10.1016/j.pmr.2008.05.007 PMID:18940644

Lefton-Greif, M. A., & Arvedson, J. C. (2007). Pediatric feeding and swallowing disorders: State of health, population trends, and application of the international classification of functioning, disability, and health. *Seminars in Speech and Language, 28*(3), 161–165. doi:10.1055-2007-984722 PMID:17647128

Logemann, J. A. (1995). Dysphagia: Evaluation and treatment. [IALP]. *Folia Phoniatrica et Logopaedica, 47*(3), 140–164. doi:10.1159/000266348 PMID:7640720

Malandraki, G. A. (2023). *Advances for Dysphagia in the Digital Age: Integrative Imaging and Wearable Technologies. Folia Phoniatrica et Logopaedica: Official Organ of the International Association of Logopedics and Phoniatrics*. IALP.

Malandraki, G. A., Arkenberg, R. H., Mitchell, S. S., & Malandraki, J. B. (2021). Telehealth for Dysphagia Across the Life Span: Using Contemporary Evidence and Expertise to Guide Clinical Practice During and After COVID-19. *American Journal of Speech-Language Pathology, 30*(2), 532–550. doi:10.1044/2020_AJSLP-20-00252 PMID:33555933

Malandraki, G. A., Roth, M., & Sheppard, J. J. (2014). Telepractice for Pediatric Dysphagia: A Case Study. *International Journal of Telerehabilitation*, 3–16. doi:10.5195/ijt.2014.6135 PMID:25945217

Marshall, J., Raatz, M., Ward, E. C., Penman, A., Beak, K., Moore, M., & Hill, A. E. (2023). Development and Pilot Testing of Telesimulation for Pediatric Feeding: A Feasibility Study. *Dysphagia, 38*(5), 1308–1322. doi:10.100700455-023-10556-3 PMID:36692653

McCarty, E. B., & Chao, T. N. (2021). Dysphagia and Swallowing Disorders. *The Medical Clinics of North America, 105*(5), 939–954. doi:10.1016/j.mcna.2021.05.013 PMID:34391544

AB-SSD Task Force-Pediatric Group:Miller, C. K., Reynolds, J., Kelchner, L. N., Scarborough, D., Langmore, S., & Gosa, M. (2023). Tutorial on Clinical Practice for Use of the Fiberoptic Endoscopic Evaluation of Swallowing Procedure With Pediatric Populations: Part 2. *American Journal of Speech-Language Pathology, 32*(1), 55–82. doi:10.1044/2022_AJSLP-22-00057 PMID:36538506

Miller, C. K., Schroeder, J. W. Jr, & Langmore, S. (2020). Fiberoptic Endoscopic Evaluation of Swallowing Across the Age Spectrum. *American Journal of Speech-Language Pathology, 29*(2S), 967–978. doi:10.1044/2019_AJSLP-19-00072 PMID:32650653

Miller, C. K., & Willging, J. P. (2020). Fiberoptic Endoscopic Evaluation of Swallowing in Infants and Children: Protocol, Safety, and Clinical Efficacy: 25 Years of Experience. *The Annals of Otology, Rhinology, and Laryngology, 129*(5), 469–481. doi:10.1177/0003489419893720 PMID:31845586

Mohan, H. S., Anjum, A., & Rao, P. K. S. (2017). A Survey of Telepractice in Speech-Language Pathology and Audiology in India. *International Journal of Telerehabilitation, 9*(2), 69–80. doi:10.5195/ijt.2017.6233 PMID:29238451

Moroco, A. E., & Aaronson, N. L. (2022). Pediatric dysphagia. *Pediatric Clinics of North America, 69*(2), 349–361. doi:10.1016/j.pcl.2021.12.005 PMID:35337544

Motion, S., Northstone, K., Emond, A., & Team, T. A. S. (2001). Persistent early feeding difficulties and subsequent growth and developmental outcomes. *Ambulatory Child Health, 7*(3–4), 231–237. doi:10.1046/j.1467-0658.2001.00139.x

Mourão, L. F., Friel, K. M., Sheppard, J. J., Kuo, H. C., Luchesi, K. F., Gordon, A. M., & Malandraki, G. A. (2017). The Role of the Corpus Callosum in Pediatric Dysphagia: Preliminary Findings from a Diffusion Tensor Imaging Study in Children with Unilateral Spastic Cerebral Palsy. *Dysphagia, 32*(5), 703–713. doi:10.100700455-017-9816-0 PMID:28597327

Newman, L. A., Keckley, C., Petersen, M. C., & Hamner, A. (2001). Swallowing Function and Medical Diagnoses in Infants Suspected of Dysphagia. *Pediatrics, 108*(6), e106–e106. doi:10.1542/peds.108.6.e106 PMID:11731633

Ongkasuwan, J., & Chiou, E. H. (2018). *Pediatric dysphagia: Challenges and controversies*. Springer. doi:10.1007/978-3-319-97025-7

Paik, N. J., & Kim, W. S. (2021). Recovery of Swallowing. *Clinical Pathways in Stroke Rehabilitation: Evidence-Based Clinical Practice Recommendations*, 85–95. doi:10.1007/978-3-030-58505-1_6

Park, M. I. (2021). [Approach of Dysphagia]. *The Korean Journal of Gastroenterology = Taehan Sohwagi Hakhoe Chi, 77*(2), 57–63. doi:10.4166/kjg.2021.017

Perlman, A. L., & Schulze-Delrieu, K. (1996). Deglutition and its Disorders: Anatomy, Physiology, Clinical Diagnosis and Management by, published by (1996). In *Singular Publishing Group Inc.* https://www.amazon.com/Deglutition-its-Disorders-Physiology-Schulze-Delrieu/dp/B00EKYZNZY

Perren, A., Zürcher, P., & Schefold, J. C. (2019). Clinical approaches to assess post-extubation dysphagia (PED) in the critically ill. *Dysphagia, 34*(4), 475–486. doi:10.100700455-019-09977-w PMID:30684017

Prasse, J. E., & Kikano, G. E. (2009). An overview of pediatric dysphagia. *Clinical Pediatrics, 48*(3), 247–251. doi:10.1177/0009922808327323 PMID:19023104

Raatz, M., Ward, E. C., Marshall, J., & Burns, C. L. (2019). Developing the system architecture for conducting synchronous paediatric feeding assessments via telepractice. *Journal of Telemedicine and Telecare, 25*(9), 552–558. doi:10.1177/1357633X19872091 PMID:31631759

Raatz, M., Ward, E. C., Marshall, J., & Burns, C. L. (2021). Evaluating the Use of Telepractice for Bottle-Feeding Assessments. *Children (Basel, Switzerland), 8*(11), 989. doi:10.3390/children8110989 PMID:34828701

Raatz, M., Ward, E. C., Marshall, J., Burns, C. L., Afoakwah, C., & Byrnes, J. (2021). A time and cost analysis of speech pathology paediatric feeding services delivered in-person versus via telepractice. *Journal of Telemedicine and Telecare*. doi:10.1177/1357633X211012883

Raatz, M. K., Ward, E. C., & Marshall, J. (2020). Telepractice for the Delivery of Pediatric Feeding Services: A Survey of Practice Investigating Clinician Perceptions and Current Service Models in Australia. *Dysphagia, 35*(2), 378–388. doi:10.100700455-019-10042-9 PMID:31363846

Raol, N., Schrepfer, T., & Hartnick, C. (2018). Aspiration and Dysphagia in the Neonatal Patient. *Clinics in Perinatology, 45*(4), 645–660. doi:10.1016/j.clp.2018.07.005 PMID:30396410

Reid, J., Kilpatrick, N., & Reilly, S. (2006). A prospective, longitudinal study of feeding skills in a cohort of babies with cleft conditions. *The Cleft Palate-Craniofacial Journal, 43*(6), 702–709. doi:10.1597/05-172 PMID:17105331

Reilly, S., Skuse, D., & Poblete, X. (1996). Prevalence of feeding problems and oral motor dysfunction in children with cerebral palsy: A community survey. *The Journal of Pediatrics, 129*(6), 877–882. doi:10.1016/S0022-3476(96)70032-X PMID:8969730

Robbins, J. A., Butler, S. G., Daniels, S. K., Gross, R. D., Langmore, S., Lazarus, C. L., Martin-Harris, B., McCabe, D., Musson, N., & Rosenbek, J. C. (2008). Swallowing and dysphagia rehabilitation: Translating principles of neural plasticity into clinically oriented evidence. *Journal of Speech, Language, and Hearing Research: JSLHR, 51*(1). Advance online publication. doi:10.1044/1092-4388(2008/021) PMID:18230851

Rosenbek, J. C., & Jones, H. N. (2007). *Dysphagia in movement disorders*.

Salmanizadeh, F., Ameri, A., & Bahaadinbeigy, K. (2022). Methods of Reimbursement for Telemedicine Services: A Scoping Review. *Medical Journal of the Islamic Republic of Iran*. doi:10.47176/mjiri.36.68 PMID:36128316

Seiverling, L., Towle, P., Hendy, H. M., & Pantelides, J. (2018). Prevalence of feeding problems in young children with and without autism spectrum disorder: A chart review study. *Journal of Early Intervention, 40*(4), 335–346. doi:10.1177/1053815118789396

Shaker, R., Easterling, C., Belafsky, P. C., & Postma, G. N. (2012). *Manual of diagnostic and therapeutic techniques for disorders of deglutition*. Springer Science & Business Media.

Sharp, W. G., Berry, R. C., McCracken, C., Nuhu, N. N., Marvel, E., Saulnier, C. A., Klin, A., Jones, W., & Jaquess, D. L. (2013). Feeding Problems and Nutrient Intake in Children with Autism Spectrum Disorders: A Meta-analysis and Comprehensive Review of the Literature. *Journal of Autism and Developmental Disorders*, *43*(9), 2159–2173. doi:10.100710803-013-1771-5 PMID:23371510

Speyer, R., Cordier, R., Kim, J., Cocks, N., Michou, E., & Wilkes-Gillan, S. (2019). Prevalence of drooling, swallowing, and feeding problems in cerebral palsy across the lifespan: A systematic review and meta-analyses. *Developmental Medicine and Child Neurology*, *61*(11), 1249–1258. doi:10.1111/dmcn.14316 PMID:31328797

Strehle, E. M., & Shabde, N. (2006). One hundred years of telemedicine: Does this new technology have a place in paediatrics? *Archives of Disease in Childhood*, *91*(12), 956–959. doi:10.1136/adc.2006.099622 PMID:17119071

Svystun, O., Johannsen, W., Persad, R., Turner, J. M., Majaesic, C., & El-Hakim, H. (2017). Dysphagia in healthy children: Characteristics and management of a consecutive cohort at a tertiary centre. *International Journal of Pediatric Otorhinolaryngology*, *99*, 54–59. doi:10.1016/j.ijporl.2017.05.024 PMID:28688566

Tamura, F., Kikutani, T., Machida, R., Isoda, T., Hobo, K., Yamada, H., Kodama, M., Genkai, S., Mizukami, M., Tanaka, Y., Sakuda, T., Furuya, H., & Takahashi, N. (2023). Usefulness of Telemedicine for Disabled Children Receiving Feeding Therapy. *Dysphagia*, *38*(1), 425–434. doi:10.100700455-022-10482-w PMID:35768661

Thomas, E. E., Taylor, M. L., Ward, E. C., Hwang, R., Cook, R., Ross, J.-A., Webb, C., Harris, M., Hartley, C., Carswell, P., Burns, C. L., & Caffery, L. J. (2022). Beyond forced telehealth adoption: A framework to sustain telehealth among allied health services. *Journal of Telemedicine and Telecare*, 1357633X2210744. doi:10.1177/1357633X221074499

Uher, R., & Rutter, M. (2012). Classification of feeding and eating disorders: Review of evidence and proposals for ICD-11. *World Psychiatry; Official Journal of the World Psychiatric Association (WPA)*, *11*(2), 80–92. doi:10.1016/j.wpsyc.2012.05.005 PMID:22654933

van den Engel-Hoek, L., de Groot, I. J., de Swart, B. J., & Erasmus, C. E. (2015). Feeding and swallowing disorders in pediatric neuromuscular diseases: An overview. *Journal of Neuromuscular Diseases*, *2*(4), 357–369. doi:10.3233/JND-150122 PMID:27858755

Ward, E. C., Raatz, M., Marshall, J., Wishart, L. R., & Burns, C. L. (2022a). Telepractice and Dysphagia Management: The Era of COVID-19 and Beyond. *Dysphagia*, *37*(6), 1386–1399. doi:10.100700455-022-10444-2 PMID:35428923

Ward, E. C., Raatz, M., Marshall, J., Wishart, L. R., & Burns, C. L. (2022b). Telepractice and Dysphagia Management: The Era of COVID-19 and Beyond. *Dysphagia*, *37*(6), 1386–1399. doi:10.100700455-022-10444-2 PMID:35428923

Wilkinson, J. M., Codipilly, D. C., & Wilfahrt, R. P. (2021). Dysphagia: Evaluation and Collaborative Management. *American Family Physician, 103*(2), 97–106. PMID:33448766

World Health Organization (WHO). (1993). *ICD-10: International statistical classification of diseases and related health problems: Tenth revision.* WHO. https://apps.who.int/iris/handle/10665/42980

Compilation of References

Mèredieu, F. (1974). *Le dessin d'enfant*. Éditions universitaires.

Aberson, B., Shure, M. B., & Goldstein, S. (2007). Social problem-solving intervention can help children with ADHD. *Journal of Attention Disorders*, *12*(5), 391–393. doi:10.1177/1087054707299409 PMID:17606767

Abrahamson, D., Nathan, M. J., Williams-Pierce, C., Walkington, C., Ottmar, E. R., Soto, H., & Alibali, M. W. (2020, August). The future of embodied design for mathematics teaching and learning. [). Frontiers Media SA.]. *Frontiers in Education*, *5*, 147. doi:10.3389/feduc.2020.00147

Abuya, B. A., Mutisya, M., Onsomu, E. O., Ngware, M., & Oketch, M. (2019). Family structure and child educational attainment in the slums of Nairobi, Kenya. *SAGE Open*, *9*(2), 2158244019855849. doi:10.1177/2158244019855849

Ackermann, K., Kirchner, M., Bernhard, A., Martinelli, A., Anomitri, C., Baker, R., Baumann, S., Dochnal, R., Fernandez-Rivas, A., Gonzalez-Madruga, K., Herpertz-Dahlmann, B., Hervas, A., Jansen, L., Kapornai, K., Kersten, L., Kohls, G., Limprecht, R., Lazaratou, H., McLaughlin, A., & Freitag, C. M. (2019). Relational Aggression in Adolescents with Conduct Disorder: Sex Differences and Behavioral Correlates. *Journal of Abnormal Child Psychology*, *47*(10), 1625–1637. doi:10.100710802-019-00541-6 PMID:30949882

Adams, K. A., Marchman, V. A., Loi, E. C., Ashland, M. D., Fernald, A., & Feldman, H. M. (2018). Caregiver talk and medical risk as predictors of language outcomes in full term and preterm toddlers. *Child Development*, *89*(5), 1674–1690. doi:10.1111/cdev.12818 PMID:28452393

Adlof, S. M., & Hogan, T. P. (2018). Understanding Dyslexia in the Context of Developmental Language Disorders. *Language, Speech, and Hearing Services in Schools*, *49*(4), 762–773. doi:10.1044/2018_LSHSS-DYSLC-18-0049 PMID:30458538

Adlof, S. M., Scoggins, J., Brazendale, A., Babb, S., & Petscher, Y. (2017). Identifying children at risk for language impairment or dyslexia with group-administered measures. *Journal of Speech, Language, and Hearing Research: JSLHR*, *60*(12), 3507–3522. doi:10.1044/2017_JSLHR-L-16-0473 PMID:29222567

Admin. (2023). Accuracy and Precision - Definition, Examples, Need for Measurement, Differences, Practice Questions and FAQs. *BYJUS*. https://byjus.com/physics/accuracy-precision-measurement/

Aftab, J. (2015). Teachers' Beliefs about Differentiated Instructions in Mixed Ability Classrooms: A Case of Time Limitation. *Journal of Education and Educational Development*, *2*(2), 94–114. doi:10.22555/joeed.v2i2.441

Ahmad, S. Z., Ludin, N. N. A. A. N., Ekhsan, H. M., Rosmani, A. F., & Ismail, M. H. (2012, December). Bijak Membaca—Applying Phonic Reading Technique and Multisensory Approach with interactive multimedia for dyslexia children. In *2012 IEEE Colloquium on Humanities, Science and Engineering (CHUSER)* (pp. 554-559). IEEE.

Ahtiainen, R., Pulkkinen, J., & Jahnukainen, M. (2021). The 21st century reforms (re) shaping the education policy of inclusive and special education in Finland. *Education Sciences*, *11*(11), 750. doi:10.3390/educsci11110750

Ainscow, M. (2005). Developing inclusive education systems: What are the levers for change? *Journal of Educational Change*, *6*(2), 109–124. doi:10.100710833-005-1298-4

Ainscow, M. (2020). Promoting inclusion and equity in education: Lessons from international experiences. *Nordic Journal of Studies in Educational Policy*, *6*(1), 7–16. doi:10.1080/20020317.2020.1729587

Ainscow, M., Slee, R., & Best, M. (2019). The Salamanca Statement: 25 years on. *International Journal of Inclusive Education*, *23*(7-8), 671–676. doi:10.1080/13603116.2019.1622800

Akhmetova, D. Z., Chelnokova, T. A., & Morozova, I. G. (2017). Theoretical and Methodological Basis of Inclusive Education in the Researches of Russian Scientists in the First Quarter of 20th Century. *International Education Studies*, *10*(2), 174–179. doi:10.5539/ies.v10n2p174

Alexander-Passe, N. (2006). How Dyslexic Teenagers Cope: An Investigation of Self-esteem, Coping and Depression. *Dyslexia (Chichester, England)*, *12*(4), 256–275. doi:10.1002/dys.318 PMID:17152342

Alexopoulos, N. (2019). Resolving school staffing problems in Greece: A strategic management approach. *Frontiers in Education*, *4*, 1–14. doi:10.3389/feduc.2019.00130

Alkahtani, M. A. (2016). Review of the Literature on Children with Special Educational Needs. *Journal of Education and Practice*, *7*(35), 70–83.

Al-Kandari, Y. Y., & Al-Sejari, M. M. (2021). Social isolation, social support and their relationship with smartphone addiction. *Information Communication and Society*, *24*(13), 1925–1943. doi:10.1080/1369118X.2020.1749698

Allen, L., Kelly, B., Children, Y. B. O., & Families. (2015). Transforming the Workforce for Children Birth Through Age 8. In *National Academies Press eBooks*. doi:10.17226/19401

Almansour, M. A., Alateeq, M. A., Alzahrani, M. K., Algeffari, M. A., & Alhomaidan, H. T. (2013). Depression and anxiety among parents and caregivers of autistic spectral disorder children. *Neuroscience Journal*, *18*(1), 58–63. https://nsj.org.sa/content/nsj/18/1/58.full.pdf PMID:23291799

American Psychiatric Association (Ed.). (2022). *Diagnostic and Statistical Manual of Mental Disorders* (Fifth Edition, Text Revision). American Psychiatric Publishing.

American Psychiatric Association. (2013). *Diagnostic and statistical manual of mental disorders* (5th ed.). American Psychiatric Association.

American Psychiatric Association. (2013). Neurodevelopmental Disorders. In Diagnostic and statistical manual of mental disorders (5th ed.).

Amin, M. S., & Harrison, R. L. (2009). Understanding Parents' Oral Health Behaviors for Their Young Children. *Qualitative Health Research*, *19*(1), 116–127. doi:10.1177/1049732308327243 PMID:18997150

Anagnostopoulou, M., & Kantartzi, E. (2008). The spelling errors of primary school students in written expression. In A. Trillianos & I. Karaminas (Eds.), *Hellenic Pedagogical & Educational Research*. Conference Proceedings (*Vol. b*, pp. 995-1004). Atrapos. [in Greek]

Anastopoulos, A. D., Guevremont, D. C., Shelton, T. L., & DuPaul, G. J. (1992). Parenting stress among families of children with attention deficit hyperactivity disorder. *Journal of Abnormal Child Psychology*, *20*(5), 503–520. doi:10.1007/BF00916812 PMID:1487593

Anderson, B. (2022). *Category Theory for Cognitive Science*. eScholarship. https://escholarship.org/uc/item/1wt4q967#main

Anderson, A. (2019). *Virtual reality, augmented reality and artificial intelligence in special education: A practical guide to supporting students with learning differences*. Routledge. doi:10.4324/9780429399503

Anderson, S. A. S., Hawes, D. J., & Snow, P. C. (2022). Oral language skills, callous and unemotional traits and high-risk patterns of youth offending. *European Child & Adolescent Psychiatry, 0123456789*. doi:10.100700787-022-01980-1 PMID:35403912

Andrade, E. M., Geha, L. M., Duran, P., Suwwan, R., Machado, F., & Do Rosario, M. C. (2016). Quality of life in caregivers of ADHD children and diabetes patients. *Frontiers in Psychiatry*, *7*, 127. doi:10.3389/fpsyt.2016.00127 PMID:27504099

Androusou, A., & Tsafos, V. (2018). Aspects of the professional identity of preschool teachers in Greece: Investigating the role of teacher education and professional experience. *Teacher Development*, *22*(4), 554–570. doi:10.1080/13664530.2018.1438309

Andzik, N. R., Chung, Y. C., Doneski-Nicol, J., & Dollarhide, C. T. (2019). AAC services in schools: A special educator's perspective. *International Journal of Developmental Disabilities*, *65*(2), 89–97. doi:10.1080/20473869.2017.1368909 PMID:34141328

Angenent, H. (1985). *Opvoeding en persoonlijkheids ontwikkeling*. Nijkerk: Uitgevery Intro.

Antoniazzi, D., Snow, P., & Dickson-Swift, V. (2010). Teacher identification of children at risk for language impairment in the first year of school. *International Journal of Speech-Language Pathology*, *12*(3), 244–252. doi:10.3109/17549500903104447 PMID:20433343

Antonopoulou, K., Koutrouba, K., & Babalis, T. (2011). Parental involvement in secondary education schools: The views of parents in Greece. *Educational Studies*, *37*(3), 333–344. doi:10.1080/03055698.2010.506332

Antony-Newman, M. (2019). Parental involvement of immigrant parents: A meta-synthesis. *Educational Review*, *71*(3), 362–381. doi:10.1080/00131911.2017.1423278

Anzieu, D. (1993). La fonction contenante de la peau, du moi et de la pensée: conteneur, contenant, contenir. In D. Anzieu (Ed.), *Les contenants de pensée* (pp. 15–40). Dunod.

Arango-Tobon, O. E., Pinilla-Monsalve, G. D., Grisales-Aguirre, A. M., Gómez-Tabare, A. S., & Carmona-Cardona, C. A. (2022). Consistency and validity of the inventory of callous- unemotional traits in a multi-centric community sample. *Heliyon*, *8*(6), e09789. doi:10.1016/j.heliyon.2022.e09789 PMID:35800728

Archambault, L., Leary, H., & Rice, K. (2022). Pillars of online pedagogy: A framework for teaching in online learning environments. *Educational Psychologist*, *57*(3), 178–191. doi:10.1080/00461520.2022.2051513

Archibald, L. M. (2017). SLP-educator classroom collaboration: A review to inform reason-based practice. *Autism & Developmental Language Impairments*, *2*, 2396941516680369. doi:10.1177/2396941516680369

Archibald, L. M. (2017). Working memory and language learning: A review. *Child Language Teaching and Therapy*, *33*(1), 5–17. doi:10.1177/0265659016654206

Arens, A. K., Jansen, M., Preckel, F., Schmidt, I., & Brunner, M. (2021). The structure of academic self-concept: A methodological review and empirical illustration of central models. *Review of Educational Research*, *91*(1), 34–72. doi:10.3102/0034654320972186

Armstrong, D., & Humphrey, N. (2009). Reactions to a Diagnosis of Dyslexia Among Students Entering Further Education: Development of the 'resistance-Accommodation' Model. *British Journal of Special Education, 36*(2), 95–102. doi:10.1111/j.1467-8578.2008.00408.x

Armstrong, M., Morris, C., Abraham, C., & Tarrant, M. (2017). Interventions utilising contact with people with disabilities to improve children's attitudes towards disability: A systematic review and meta-analysis. *Disability and Health Journal, 10*(1), 11–22. doi:10.1016/j.dhjo.2016.10.003 PMID:27780687

Arts, E., Orobio de Castro, B., Luteijn, E., Elsendoorn, B., & Vissers, C. T. W. M. (2022). Improving social emotional functioning in adolescents with Developmental Language Disorders: A mini review and recommendations. *Frontiers in Psychiatry, 13*(1), 966008. Advance online publication. doi:10.3389/fpsyt.2022.966008 PMID:36569624

Ash, A. C., Christopulos, T. T., & Redmond, S. M. (2020). "Tell me about your child": A grounded theory study of mothers understanding of language disorder. *American Journal of Speech-Language Pathology, 29*(2), 819–840. doi:10.1044/2020_AJSLP-19-00064 PMID:32348158

Astramovich, R. L., Lyons, C., & Hamilton, J. N. (2015). Play Therapy for ChildrenWith Intellectual Disabilities. *Journal of Child and Adolescent Counseling, 1*(1), 27–36. doi:10.1080/23727810.2015.1015904

Atkinson, C., Dunsmuir, S., Lang, J., & Wright, S. (2015). Developing a competency framework for the initial training of educational psychologists working with young people aged 16–25. *Educational Psychology in Practice, 31*(2), 159–173. doi:10.1080/02667363.2015.1004038

Aujoulat, I., Libion, F., Bois, H., Martin, F., & Deccache, A. (2002). Communication difficulties of healthcare professionals and family caregivers of HIV infected patients. *Patient Education and Counseling, 47*(3), 213–222. doi:10.1016/S0738-3991(01)00197-5 PMID:12088599

Auza, B. A., Murata, C., & Penaloza, C. (2023). Predictive validity of a parental questionnaire for identifying children with developmental language disorders. *Frontiers in Psychology, 14*, 14. doi:10.3389/fpsyg.2023.1110449

Avramidis, E. (2013). Self-concept, social position and social participation of pupils with SEN in mainstream primary schools. *Research Papers in Education, 28*(4), 421–442. doi:10.1080/02671522.2012.673006

Awadalla, E. N., Khattab, A. N., & El-ella, E. I. A. (2023). Language Profile In Conduct Disorder Children Aged Between 7 To 12 Years Old. *74*, 143–152.

Axline, V. M. (1969). *Play Therapy: The inner Dynamics of Childhood.* Houghton Miffli.

Azazy, S., Nour-Eldein, H., Mikhail, H., & Ismail, M. (2018). Quality of life and family function of parents of children with attention deficit hyperactivity disorder. *Eastern Mediterranean health journal=La revue de santé de la Méditerranée orientale=al-Majallah al-ṣiḥḥīyah li-sharq al-mutawassiṭ. 24*. 579-587.

Baddeley, A. (2020). Working memory. In *Memory* (pp. 71–111). Routledge. doi:10.4324/9780429449642-4

Banks, T. (2008). *Foreign Language Learning Difficulties and Teaching Strategies*. Online Submission.

Barber, B. K., & Buehler, C. (1996). Family cohesion and enmeshment: Different constructs, different effects. *Journal of Marriage and Family, 58*(2), 433–441. doi:10.2307/353507

Barbiero, C., Lonciari, I., Montico, M., Monasta, L., Penge, R., Vio, C., Tressoldi, P. M., Ferluga, V., Bigoni, A., Tullio, A., Carrozzi, M., & Ronfani, L. (2012). The Submerged Dyslexia Iceberg: How Many School Children Are Not Diagnosed? Results from an Italian Study. *PLoS One, 7*(10), 1–9. doi:10.1371/journal.pone.0048082 PMID:23118930

Barker, E. D., Tremblay, R. E., van Lier, P. A., Vitaro, F., Nagin, D. S., Assaad, J. M., & Séguin, J. R. (2011). The neurocognition of conduct disorder behaviors: Specificity to physical aggression and theft after controlling for ADHD symptoms. *Aggressive Behavior*, *37*(1), 63–72. doi:10.1002/ab.20373 PMID:21046606

Barkley, R. (2005). *Taking Charge of AD/HD: The complete, authoritative guide for parents* (Rev.ed.). Guilford.

Barkley, R. A., Fischer, M., Edelbrock, C., & Smallish, L. (1991). The adolescent outcome of hyperactive children diagnosed by research criteria-III: Mother–child interactions, family conflicts and maternal psychopathology. *Journal of Child Psychology and Psychiatry, and Allied Disciplines*, *32*(2), 233–255. doi:10.1111/j.1469-7610.1991.tb00304.x PMID:2033106

Barnett, R. M., Maruff, P., & Vance, A. (2009). Neurocognitive function in attention-deficit-hyperactivity disorder with and without comorbid disruptive behaviour disorders. *The Australian and New Zealand Journal of Psychiatry*, *43*(8), 722–730. doi:10.1080/00048670903001927 PMID:19629793

Barnhill, L. R. (1979). Healthy family systems. *The Family Coordinator*, *28*(1), 94–100. doi:10.2307/583274

Barry, T. D., Marcus, D. K., Barry, C. T., & Coccaro, E. F. (2013). The latent structure of oppositional defiant disorder in children andadults. *Journal of Psychiatric Research*, *47*(12), 1932–1939. doi:10.1016/j.jpsychires.2013.08.016 PMID:24075326

Barua, P. D., Vicnesh, J., Gururajan, R., Oh, S. L., Palmer, E., Azizan, M. M., Kadri, N. A., & Acharya, U. R. (2022). Artificial intelligence enabled personalised assistive tools to enhance education of children with neurodevelopmental disorders—A review. *International Journal of Environmental Research and Public Health*, *19*(3), 1192. doi:10.3390/ijerph19031192 PMID:35162220

Bashalkhanov, S., Pandey, M., & Rajora, O. P. (2009). A simple method for estimating genetic diversity in large populations from finite sample sizes. *BMC Genetics*, *10*(1), 84. doi:10.1186/1471-2156-10-84 PMID:20003542

Baudin, K., Mullersdorf, M., Sundstrom, A., & Gustafsson, C. (2020). The policies of provision of assistive and welfare technology - a literature review. *Societies (Basel, Switzerland)*, *10*(1), 22. doi:10.3390oc10010022

Baumeister, R. F., Campbell, J. D., Krueger, J. I., & Vohs, K. D. (2003). Does high self-esteem cause better performance, interpersonal success, happiness, or healthier lifestyles? *Psychological Science in the Public Interest*, *4*(1), 1–44. doi:10.1111/1529-1006.01431 PMID:26151640

Beck, A. T. (2002). Cognitive models of depression. In R. Leahy & T. Dowd (Eds.), *Clinical advances in cognitive psychotherapy: Theory and application* (pp. 29–61). Springer Publishing Company.

Beck, J. S. (2020). *Cognitive behavior therapy: Basics and beyond.* Guilford Publications.

Bekhet, A. K., Johnson, N. L., & Zauszniewski, J. A. (2012). Effects on resilience of caregivers of persons with autism spectrum disorder: The role of positive cognitions. *Journal of the American Psychiatric Nurses Association*, *18*(6), 337–344. doi:10.1177/1078390312467056 PMID:23139377

Belda-Medina, J. (2022). Promoting inclusiveness, creativity and critical thinking through digital storytelling among EFL teacher candidates. *International Journal of Inclusive Education*, *26*(2), 109–123. doi:10.1080/13603116.2021.2011440

Bell, H. (2018). Creative interventions for teaching empathy in the counseling classroom. *Journal of Creativity in Mental Health*, *13*(1), 106–120. doi:10.1080/15401383.2017.1328295

Bender, W. N. (2012). *Project-based learning: Differentiiated instruction for the 21st century.* Corwin.

Benson, P. L., Leffert, N., Scales, P., & Blyth, D. A. (1998). Beyond the "Village" Rhetoric: Creating Healthy Communities for Children and Adolescents. *Applied Developmental Science*, *2*(3), 138–159. doi:10.12071532480xads0203_3

Berendt, B., Littlejohn, A., & Blakemore, M. (2020). AI in education: Learner choice and fundamental rights. *Learning, Media and Technology*, *45*(3), 312–324. doi:10.1080/17439884.2020.1786399

Berghs, M., Atkin, K., Hatton, C., & Thomas, C. (2019). Do disabled people need a stronger social model: A social model of human rights? *Disability & Society*, *34*(7-8), 1034–1039. doi:10.1080/09687599.2019.1619239

Beveridge, S. (2013). *Children, families and schools: Developing partnerships for inclusive education.* Routledge. doi:10.4324/9780203464700

Biggs, E. E., Bumble, J. L., & Hacker, R. E. (2022). Professional networks of special educators and speech-language pathologists working with students who use augmentative and alternative communication. *Remedial and Special Education*, 07419325221128497.

Binos, P., Papastefanou, T., & Psillas, G. (2023). Socio-Economic Status and Language Development in Hearing Loss: A Critical Appraisal. *Audiology Research*, *13*(1), 151–159. doi:10.3390/audiolres13010015 PMID:36825953

Birbili, M., & Myrovali, A. (2020). Early childhood teachers' relationship with the official curriculum: The mediating role of professional and policy contexts. *Education Inquiry*, *11*(2), 110–125. doi:10.1080/20004508.2019.1687080

Bird, J., & Bishop, D. V. M. (1992). Perception and awareness of phonemes in phonologically impaired children. *European Journal of Disorders of Communication*, *27*(4), 289–311. doi:10.3109/13682829209012042 PMID:1308694

Bishop, D. V. (2006). What causes specific language impairment in children? *Current Directions in Psychological Science*, *15*(5), 217–221. doi:10.1111/j.1467-8721.2006.00439.x PMID:19009045

Bishop, D. V. (2010). Which neurodevelopmental disorders get researched and why? *PLoS One*, *5*(11), e15112. doi:10.1371/journal.pone.0015112 PMID:21152085

Bishop, D. V. (2014). Pragmatic language impairment: A correlate of SLI, a distinct subgroup, or part of the autistic continuum? In D. V. M. Bishop & L. Leonard (Eds.), *Speech and languageimpairments in children* (pp. 113–128). Psychology Press. doi:10.4324/9781315784878

Bishop, D. V. M., Snowling, M. J., Thompson, P. A., & Greenhalgh, T. (2017). Phase 2 of CATALISE: a multinational and multidisciplinary Delphi consensus study of problems with language development: Terminology. *Journal of Child Psychology and Psychiatry, and Allied Disciplines*, *58*(10), 1068–1080. doi:10.1111/jcpp.12721 PMID:28369935

Bishop, D. V. M., Snowling, M. J., Thompson, P. A., & Greenhalgh, T.Catalise Consortium. (2016). CATALISE: A multinational and multidisciplinary Delphi consensus study. Identifying language impairments in children. *PLoS One*, *11*(7), e0158753. doi:10.1371/journal.pone.0158753 PMID:27392128

Bishop, D. V., & McDonald, D. (2009). Identifying language impairment in children: Combining language test scores with parental reports. *International Journal of Language & Communication Disorders*, *44*(5), 600–615. doi:10.1080/13682820802259662 PMID:19387886

Blair, E. (2015). A reflexive exploration of two qualitative data coding techniques. *Journal of Methods and Measurement in the Social Sciences*, *6*(1), 14–29. doi:10.2458/v6i1.18772

Blair, R. J. (2003). Neurobiological basis of psychopathy. *The British Journal of Psychiatry*, *182*(1), 5–7. doi:10.1192/bjp.182.1.5 PMID:12509310

Boada, R., & Pennington, B. F. (2006). Deficient implicit phonological representations in children with dyslexia. *Journal of Experimental Child Psychology, 95*(3), 153–193. doi:10.1016/j.jecp.2006.04.003 PMID:16887140

Bodovski, K., & Youn, M.-J. (2010). Love, discipline and elementary school achievement: The role of family emotional climate. *Social Science Research, 39*(4), 585–595. doi:10.1016/j.ssresearch.2010.03.008

Boonk, L., Gijselaers, H. J., Ritzen, H., & Brand-Gruwel, S. (2018). A review of the relationship between parental involvement indicators and academic achievement. *Educational Research Review, 24*, 10–30. doi:10.1016/j.edurev.2018.02.001

Borbajo, M. N. M., Malbas, M. H., & Dacanay, L. R. (2023). Reforming Education: The Global Impact of Integrating Artificial Intelligence in the Classroom Environment. *American Journal of Language, Literacy and Learning in STEM Education (2993-2769), 1*(5), 16-27.

Boslaugh, S. (n.d.). *Statistics in a Nutshell, 2nd Edition.* O'Reilly Online Learning. https://www.oreilly.com/library/view/statistics-in-a/9781449361129/ch01.html

Bossaert, G., Colpin, H., Pijl, S. J., & Petry, K. (2013). Truly included? A literature study focusing on the social dimension of inclusion in education. *International Journal of Inclusive Education, 17*(1), 60–79. doi:10.1080/13603116.2011.580464

Bourke. (2005). *Journal of Child Psychology and Psychiatry*, 1200–1210.

Bowleg, L. (2008). When Black+ lesbian+ woman≠ Black lesbian woman: The methodological challenges of qualitative and quantitative intersectionality research. *Sex Roles, 59*(5-6), 312–325. doi:10.100711199-008-9400-z

Boyes, M. E., Leitão, S., Claessen, M., Badcock, N. A., & Nayton, M. (2020). Correlates of externalising and internalising problems in children with dyslexia: An analysis of data from clinical casefiles. *Australian Psychologist, 55*(1), 62–72. doi:10.1111/ap.12409

Boyes, M. E., Tebbutt, B., Preece, K. A., & Badcock, N. A. (2018). Relationships between reading ability and child mental health: Moderating effects of self-esteem. *Australian Psychologist, 53*(2), 125–133. doi:10.1111/ap.12281

Bradshaw, J., Koegel, L. K., & Koegel, R. L. (2017). Improving functional language and social motivation with parent-mediated intervention for toddlers with autism spectrum disorder. *Journal of Autism and Developmental Disorders, 47*(8), 2443–2458. doi:10.100710803-017-3155-8 PMID:28536956

Bratton, S. C., Ray, D., Rhine, T., & Jones, L. (2005). The Efficacy of Play Therapy with Children: A Meta-Analytic Review of Treatment Outcomes. *Professional Psychology, Research and Practice, 36*(4), 376–390. doi:10.1037/0735-7028.36.4.376

Braun, V., & Clarke, V. (2006). Using thematic analysis in psychology. *Qualitative Research in Psychology, 3*(2), 77–101. doi:10.1191/1478088706qp063oa

Braun, V., & Clarke, V. (2012). *Thematic analysis.* American Psychological Association. doi:10.1037/13620-004

Bray, M. (2021). Shadow education in Europe: Growing prevalence, underlying forces, and policy implications. *ECNU. Review of Education, 4*(3), 442–475.

Briley, D. A., Livengood, J., Derringer, J., Tucker-Drob, E. M., Fraley, R. C., & Roberts, B. W. (2019). Interpreting behavior genetic models: Seven developmental processes to understand. *Behavior Genetics, 49*(2), 196–210. doi:10.100710519-018-9939-6 PMID:30467668

Brooks, M. (2009). Drawing, visualisation and young children's exploration of "big ideas". *International Journal of Science Education, 31*(3), 319–341. doi:10.1080/09500690802595771

Broomhead, K. E. (2019). Acceptance or rejection? The social experiences of children with special educational needs and disabilities within a mainstream primary school. *Education 3-13, 47*(8), 877-888. doi:10.1080/03004279.2018.1535610

Brown, C. S. (2019). The importance and the challenges to ensuring an inclusive school climate. *Educational Psychologist, 54*(4), 322–330. doi:10.1080/00461520.2019.1655646

Brown, G. T. (2017). *Assessment of student achievement*. Routledge. doi:10.4324/9781315162058

Bruhn, S. (2022). Intersectional recognition: Immigrant motherhood in a gentrifying sanctuary city's schools. *Journal of Ethnic and Migration Studies*, 1–20.

Brunner, M., Keller, U., Dierendonck, C., Reichert, M., Ugen, S., Fischbach, A., & Martin, R. (2010). The structure of academic self-concepts revisited: The nested Marsh/Shavelson model. *Journal of Educational Psychology, 102*(4), 964–981. doi:10.1037/a0019644

Bryant, D. P., Bryant, B. R., & Smith, D. D. (2019). *Teaching students with special needs in inclusive classrooms*. Sage Publications.

Buono, S., & Jang, E. E. (2021). The effect of linguistic factors on assessment of English language learners' Mathematical ability: A differential item functioning analysis. *Educational Assessment, 26*(2), 125–144. doi:10.1080/10627197.2020.1858783

Burden, R. (2005). *Dyslexia and self-concept*. Whurr Publishers.

Burden, R. (2008). Is dyslexia necessarily associated with negative feelings of self-worth? A review and implications for future research. *Dyslexia (Chichester, England), 14*(3), 188–196. doi:10.1002/dys.371 PMID:18646275

Burden, R., & Burdett, J. (2005). Factors Associated with Successful Learning in Pupils with Dyslexia: A Motivational Analysis. *British Journal of Special Education, 32*(2), 100–104. doi:10.1111/j.0952-3383.2005.00378.x

Burnley, A., St Clair, M., Bedford, R., Wren, Y., & Dack, C. (2023). Understanding the prevalence and manifestation of anxiety and other socio-emotional and behavioral difficulties in children with DLD. *Journal of Neurodevelopmental Disorders, 15*(17).

Burr, C., & Leslie, D. (2023). Ethical assurance: A practical approach to the responsible design, development, and deployment of data-driven technologies. *AI and Ethics, 3*(1), 73–98. doi:10.100743681-022-00178-0

Burton, L. M., & Jarrett, R. L. (2000). In the Mix, Yet on the Margins: The Place of Families in Urban Neighborhood and Child Development Research. *Journal of Marriage and Family, 62*(4), 1114–1135. doi:10.1111/j.1741-3737.2000.01114.x

Burton, L. M., & Price-Spratlen, T. (1999). Through the eyes of children: An ethnographic perspective on neighborhoods and child development. In A. Masten (Ed.), *Minnesota symposium on child psychology: Cultural processes in child development* (Vol. 29, pp. 77–96). Erlbaum.

Burton, S. (2004). Self-esteem groups for secondary pupils with dyslexia. *Educational Psychology in Practice, 20*(1), 55–73. doi:10.1080/0266736042000180410

Buschgens, C., van Aken, M., Swinkels, S., Altin, M., Fliers, E., & Rommelese, N. (2008). Differential family and peer environmental factors are related to severity and comorbidity in children with ADHD. *Journal of Neural Transmission (Vienna, Austria), 115*(2), 177–186. doi:10.100700702-007-0838-x PMID:18200433

Camargo, S. P. H., Rispoli, M., Ganz, J., Hong, E. R., Davis, H., & Mason, R. (2014). A review of the quality of behaviorally-based intervention research to improve social interaction skills of children with ASD in inclusive settings. *Journal of Autism and Developmental Disorders, 44*(9), 2096–2116. doi:10.100710803-014-2060-7 PMID:24781498

Campbell, A. (2023, July 1). How can you measure test validity and reliability? *Turnitin*. https://www.turnitin.com/blog/how-to-measure-test-validity-reliability

Cappe, E., Bolduc, M., Rouge, M. C., Saiag, M. C., & Delome, R. (2017). Quality of life, psychological characteristics, and adjustment in parents of children with attention- deficit /hyperactivity disorder. *Quality of Life Research: An International Journal of Quality of Life Aspects of Treatment, Care and Rehabilitation*, *26*(5), 1283–1294. doi:10.100711136-016-1446-8 PMID:27798755

Cardon, G., Campbell, J., & Sharma, A. (2012). Plasticity in the developing auditory cortex: Evidence from children with sensorineural hearing loss and auditory neuropathy spectrum disorder. *Journal of the American Academy of Audiology, 23*(6), 396-411(16). doi:10.3766/jaaa.23.6.3

Carmichael, K. D., & Atchinson, D. H. (1997). Music in Play Therapy: Playing my feelings. *International Journal of Play Therapy*, *1*(6), 63–72. doi:10.1037/h0089414

Carter, R. (2023). *Helping yourself help others: A book for caregivers*. University of Arkansas Press. doi:10.2307/jj.2354066

Caserini, C., Ferro, M., Nobile, M., Scaini, S., & Michelini, G. (2023). Shared genetic influences between depression and conduct disorder in children and adolescents: A systematic review. *Journal of Affective Disorders, 322*(July 2022), 31–38. doi:10.1016/j.jad.2022.11.001

Casey, B. M., & Fell, H. (2018). Spatial reasoning: A critical problem-solving tool in children's mathematics strategy toolkit. *Visualizing mathematics: The role of spatial reasoning in mathematical thought*, 47-75.

Caskey, M., Stephens, B., Tucker, R., & Vohr, B. R. (2014). Adult talk in the NICU with preterm infants and developmental outcomes. *Pediatrics*, *133*(3), e578–e584. doi:10.1542/peds.2013-0104 PMID:24515512

Caspari-Sadeghi, S. (2023). Artificial Intelligence in Technology-Enhanced Assessment: A Survey of Machine Learning. *Journal of Educational Technology Systems*, *51*(3), 372–386. doi:10.1177/00472395221138791

Casserly, A. M. (2013). The socio-emotional needs of children with dyslexia in different educational settings in Ireland. *Journal of Research in Special Educational Needs*, *13*(1), 79–91. doi:10.1111/j.1471-3802.2011.01227.x

Catts, H. W., Adlof, S. M., Hogan, T. P., & Weismer, S. E. (2005). Are specific language impairment and dyslexia distinct disorders. *Journal of Speech, Language, and Hearing Research: JSLHR*, *48*(6), 1378–1396. doi:10.1044/1092-4388(2005/096) PMID:16478378

Catts, H., Adlof, S., & Ellis Weismer, S. (2006). Language Deficits in Poor Comprehenders: A Case for the Simple View of Reading. *Journal of Speech, Language, and Hearing Research: JSLHR*, *49*(2), 278–293. doi:10.1044/1092-4388(2006/023) PMID:16671844

Chambers, D. (2020). Assistive technology supporting inclusive education: Existing and emerging trends. *Assistive technology to support inclusive education*, 1-16.

Chan, B. S. M., Deng, J., Li, Y., Li, T., Shen, Y., Wang, Y., & Yi, L. (2020). The role of self-compassion in the relationship between post-traumatic growth and psychological distress in caregivers of children with autism. *Journal of Child and Family Studies*, *29*(6), 1692–1700. doi:10.100710826-019-01694-0

Chande, A. T., Nagar, S. D., Rishishwar, L., Mariño-Ramírez, L., Medina-Rivas, M. A., Valderrama-Aguirre, A., Jordan, I. K., & Gallo, J. (2021). The Impact of Ethnicity and Genetic Ancestry on Disease Prevalence and Risk in Colombia. *Frontiers in Genetics*, *12*, 690366. Advance online publication. doi:10.3389/fgene.2021.690366 PMID:34650589

Chang, C. C., Chen, Y. M., Liu, T. L., Hsiao, R. C., Chou, W. J., & Yen, C. F. (2020). Affiliate stigma and related factors in family caregivers of children with attention deficit/hyperactivity disorder. *International Journal of Environmental Research and Public Health, 17*(2), 576. doi:10.3390/ijerph17020576 PMID:31963190

Chang, J. P. C., & Gau, S. S. F. (2017). Mother-child relationship in youths with attention-deficit hyperactivity disorder and their siblings. *Journal of Abnormal Child Psychology, 45*(5), 871–882. doi:10.100710802-016-0218-9 PMID:27771825

Chapman, J. W. (1988). Cognitive-motivational characteristics and academic achievement of learningdisabled children: A longitudinal study. *Journal of Educational Psychology, 80*(3), 357–365. doi:10.1037/0022-0663.80.3.357

Chapter 2: The Nature of Mathematics. (n.d.). Project http://www.project2061.org/publications/sfaa/online/chap2.htm

Charman, T., Baron-Cohen, S., Swettenham, J., Baird, G., Drew, A., & Cox, A. (2003). Predicting Language Outcome in Infants with Autism and Pervasive Developmental Disorder. *International Journal of Language & Communication Disorders, 38*(3), 265–285. doi:10.1080/1368203100001004830 PMID:12851079

Charron, C., Fitzpatrick, E. M., & McSweeney, E. (2016). Language ENvironment Analysis (LENA) with children with hearing loss: A clinical pilot. *CJSLPA, 40*, 93–104.

Cheatham, G. A., & Lim-Mullins, S. (2018). Immigrant, bilingual parents of students with disabilities: Positive perceptions and supportive dialogue. *Intervention in School and Clinic, 54*(1), 40–46. doi:10.1177/1053451218762490

Chen, J. Y., & Instone, S. L. (2008). *Family resilience and functioning in child with DMD: Functioning and resilience in families with children with Duchenne muscular dystrophy.* VDM Verlag Dr. Muller Aktiengesellschaft.

Chen, J., Justice, L. M., Rhoad-Drogalis, A., Lin, T. J., & Sawyer, B. (2020). Social networks of children with developmental language disorders in inclusive preschool programs. *Child Development, 91*(2), 471–487. doi:10.1111/cdev.13183 PMID:30417944

Chen, S. Y., & Wang, J. H. (2021). Individual differences and personalized learning: A review and appraisal. *Universal Access in the Information Society, 20*(4), 833–849. doi:10.100710209-020-00753-4

Chen, X., & Ma, R. (2023). Adolescents' Self-Esteem: The Influence Factors and Solutions. J*ournal of Education. Humanities and Social Sciences, 8*, 1562–1566.

Ching'oma, C. D., Mkoka, D. A., Ambikile, J. S., & Iseselo, M. K. (2022). Experiences and challenges of parents caring for children with attention-deficit hyperactivity disorder: A qualitative study in Dar es salaam, Tanzania. *PLoS One, 17*(8), e0267773. doi:10.1371/journal.pone.0267773 PMID:35921363

Chou, W. J., Liu, T. L., Hsiao, R. C., Chen, Y. M., Chang, C. C., & Yen, C. F. (2020). Application and perceived effectiveness of complementary and alternative intervention strategies for attention-deficit/hyperactivity disorder: Relationships with affiliate stigma. *International Journal of Environmental Research and Public Health, 17*, 1505.

Chow, J. C., Morse, A., & Senter, R. (2022). Intentional collaboration with speech-language pathologists to support language outcomes of students with emotional and behavioral disorders. *Beyond Behavior, 31*(3), 140–150. doi:10.1177/10742956221108350

Christakis, D. A., Gilkerson, J., Richards, J. A., Zimmerman, F. J., Garrison, M. M., Xu, D., Gray, S., & Yapanel, U. (2009). Audible television and decreased adult words, infant vocalizations, and conversational turns. *Archives of Pediatrics & Adolescent Medicine, 163*(6), 554. doi:10.1001/archpediatrics.2009.61 PMID:19487612

Christopulos, T., & Kean, J. T. (2020). General education teachers' contribution to the identification of children with language disorders. *American Speech-Language Hearing Association, 5*, 770–777. doi:10.1044/2020_PERSP-19-00166

Ciucci, E. B. (2014). *The association between callous-unemotional traits and behavioral and academic adjustment in children: Further validation of the Inventory of Callous-Unemotional Traits.*

Clarke, P. B., Adams, J. K., Wilkerson, J. R., & Shaw, E. G. (2016). Wellness-based counseling for caregivers of persons with dementia. *Journal of Mental Health Counseling, 38*(3), 263–277. doi:10.17744/mehc.38.3.06

Clegg, J., Hollis, C., Mawhood, L., & Rutter, M. (2005). Developmental language disorders – a follow-up in later adult life. Cognitive, language and psychosocial outcomes. *Journal of Child Psychology and Psychiatry, and Allied Disciplines, 46*(2), 128–149. doi:10.1111/j.1469-7610.2004.00342.x PMID:15679523

Cobley, D. (2018). *Disability and international development: A guide for students and practitioners.* Routledge. doi:10.4324/9781315208558

Cochet, H., & Byrne, R. W. (2016). Communication in the second and third year of life: Relationships between nonverbal social skills and language. *Infant Behavior and Development, 44*, 189–198. doi:10.1016/j.infbeh.2016.07.003 PMID:27450099

Coelho, V. A., Bear, G. G., & Brás, P. (2020). A Multilevel Analysis of the Importance of School Climate for the Trajectories of Students' Self-concept and Self-esteem Throughout the Middle School Transition. *Journal of Youth and Adolescence, 49*(2), 1793–1804. doi:10.100710964-020-01245-7 PMID:32356038

Cole, M., & Cole, S. R. (2002). *The development of children, the beginning of life, pregnancy, childbirth and infancy.* Typothito/Dardanos.

Colins, O. F., Andershed, H., & Pardini, D. A. (2015). Psychopathic traits as predictors of future criminality, intimate partner aggression, and substance use in young adult men. *Law and Human Behavior, 39*(6), 547–558. doi:10.1037/lhb0000148 PMID:26301710

Collins, P. H., & Bilge, S. (2020). *Intersectionality.* John Wiley & Sons.

Collis, J., & Bloch, S. (2012). Survey of UK speech and language therapists' assessment and treatment practices for people with progressive dysarthria. *International Journal of Language & Communication Disorders, 47*(6), 725–737. doi:10.1111/j.1460-6984.2012.00183.x PMID:23121530

Content Analysis. (2023, March 30). Columbia University Mailman School of Public Health. https://www.publichealth.columbia.edu/research/population-health-methods/content-analysis

Conti-Ramsden, G., & Botting, N. (2008). Emotional health in adolescents with and without a history of specific language impairment (SLI). *Journal of Child Psychology and Psychiatry, and Allied Disciplines, 49*(5), 516–525. doi:10.1111/j.1469-7610.2007.01858.x PMID:18221347

Conti-Ramsden, G., Durkin, K., Simkin, Z., & Knox, E. (2009). Specific language impairment and school outcomes. Identifying and explaining variability at the end of compulsory education. *International Journal of Language & Communication Disorders, 44*(1), 15–35. doi:10.1080/13682820801921601 PMID:18608604

Conti-Ramsden, G., Durkin, K., Toseeb, U., Botting, N., & Pickles, A. (2018). Education and employment outcomes of young adults with a history of developmental language disorder. *International Journal of Language & Communication Disorders, 53*(2), 237–255. doi:10.1111/1460-6984.12338 PMID:29139196

Conti-Ramsden, G., Mok, P., Durkin, K., Pickles, A., Toseeb, U., & Botting, N. (2019). Do emotional difficulties and peer problems occur together from childhood to adolescence? The case of children with a history of developmental language disorder (DLD). *European Child & Adolescent Psychiatry, 28*(7), 993–1004. doi:10.100700787-018-1261-6 PMID:30519863

Corey, G. (2012). *Theory and practice of counseling and psychotherapy*. Cengage learning.

Correa, V. I., Bonilla, Z. E., & Reyes-MacPherson, M. E. (2010). Support Networks of Single Puerto Rican Mothers of Children with Disabilities. *Journal of Child and Family Studies*, *20*(1), 66–77. doi:10.100710826-010-9378-3

Cozolino, L. (2010). *The neuroscience of psychotherapy: Healing the social Brain* (2nd ed.). Norton.

Crenshaw, K. (1989). Demarginalizing the intersection of race and sex: A black feminist critique of antidiscrimination doctrine, feminist theory and antiracist politics. *u. Chi. Legal f.*, 139.

Cristia, A., Bulgarelli, F., & Bergelson, E. (2020). Accuracy of the language environment analysis system segmentation and metrics: A systematic review. *Journal of Speech, Language, and Hearing Research: JSLHR*, *63*(4), 1093–1105. doi:10.1044/2020_JSLHR-19-00017 PMID:32302262

Cristia, A., Lavechin, M., Scaff, C., Soderstrom, M., Rowland, C., Räsänen, O., Bunce, J., & Bergelson, E. (2021). A thorough evaluation of the Language Environment Analysis (LENA) system. *Behavior Research*, *53*(2), 467–486. doi:10.375813428-020-01393-5 PMID:32728916

Cristofori, I., Cohen-Zimerman, S., & Grafman, J. (2019). Executive functions. *Handbook of Clinical Neurology*, *163*, 197–219. doi:10.1016/B978-0-12-804281-6.00011-2 PMID:31590731

Cross, A. M., Joanisse, M. F., & Archibald, L. M. (2019). Mathematical abilities in children with developmental language disorder. *Language, Speech, and Hearing Services in Schools*, *50*(1), 150–163. doi:10.1044/2018_LSHSS-18-0041 PMID:30950775

Crossley, S., Liu, R., & McNamara, D. (2017, March). Predicting math performance using natural language processing tools. In *Proceedings of the Seventh International Learning Analytics & Knowledge Conference* (pp. 339-347). ACM. 10.1145/3027385.3027399

Croteau, C., McMahon-Morin, P., Morin, C., Jutras, B., Trudeau, N., & Le Dorze, G. (2015). Life habits of school-aged children with specific language impairment as perceived by their parents and by school professionals. *Journal of Communication Disorders*, *58*, 21–34. doi:10.1016/j.jcomdis.2015.07.005 PMID:26342290

Crothers, L. M., Hughes, T. L., Kolbert, J. B., & Schmitt, A. J. (2020). *Theory and cases in school-based consultation: A resource for school psychologists, school counselors, special educators, and other mental health professionals*. Routledge. doi:10.4324/9780429029974

Cruz, R. A., Manchanda, S., Firestone, A. R., & Rodl, J. E. (2020). An examination of teachers' culturally responsive teaching self-efficacy. *Teacher Education and Special Education*, *43*(3), 197–214. doi:10.1177/0888406419875194

Cuccio, V., & Graziano, M. (2022). A Two-Level Model of Embodied Mathematical Thinking. Body Schema, Body Image and Language. In *Metaphors and Analogies in Sciences and Humanities: Words and Worlds* (pp. 87–113). Springer International Publishing. doi:10.1007/978-3-030-90688-7_5

Cummings, E. M., & Cummings, J. S. (2002). Parenting and Attachment. In M. H. Bornstein (Ed.), Handbook of Parenting: Vol. 5. *Practical Issues in Parenting* (pp. 35–58). Erlbaum.

Cummings, L. (2023). Communication disorders: A complex population in healthcare. *Language and Health*, (June). doi:10.1016/j.laheal.2023.06.005

Cummins, C., Pellicano, E., & Crane, L. (2020). Autistic adults' views of their communication skills and needs. *International Journal of Language & Communication Disorders*, *55*(5), 678–689. doi:10.1111/1460-6984.12552 PMID:32618026

Cunningham, C. E. (2007). A family-centered approach to planning and measuring the outcome of interventions for children with attention-deficit/hyperactivity disorder. *Ambulatory Pediatrics*, *7*(1), 60–72. doi:10.1016/j.ambp.2006.05.003 PMID:17261485

Cunningham, C. E., & Boyle, M. H. (2002). Preschoolers at risk for attention-deficit hyperactivity disorder: Family, parenting, and behavioral correlates. *Journal of Abnormal Child Psychology*, *30*(6), 555–569. doi:10.1023/A:1020855429085 PMID:12481971

Cussen, A., Sciberras, E., Ukoumunne, O. C., & Efron, D. (2012). Relationship between symptoms of attention-deficit/hyperactivity disorder and family functioning: A community-based study. *European Journal of Pediatrics*, *171*(2), 271–280. doi:10.100700431-011-1524-4 PMID:21743986

Cvencek, D., Fryberg, S. A., Covarrubias, R., & Meltzoff, A. N. (2018). Self-Concepts, Self-Esteem, and Academic Achievement of Minority and Majority North American Elementary School Children. *Child Development*, *89*(4), 1099–1109. doi:10.1111/cdev.12802 PMID:28386954

Daniel, G. R., & McLeod, S. (2017). Children with speech sound disorders at school: Challenges for children, parents and teachers. *The Australian Journal of Teacher Education*, *42*(2), 81–101. doi:10.14221/ajte.2017v42n2.6

Danielsen, A. G., Samdal, O., Hetland, J., & Wold, B. (2009). School-related social support and students' perceived life satisfaction. *The Journal of Educational Research*, *102*(4), 303–318. doi:10.3200/JOER.102.4.303-320

Danino, M., & Shechtman, Z. (2012). Superiority of group counseling to individual coaching for parents of children with learning disabilities. *Psychotherapy Research*, *22*(5), 592–603. doi:10.1080/10503307.2012.692953 PMID:22694319

Darling-Hammond, L., Cook-Harvey, C. M., Flook, L., Gardner, M., & Melnick, H. (2018). *With the whole child in mind: Insights from the Comer School Development Program*. ASCD.

Dattilio, F. M., & Epstein, N. B. (2015). Cognitive-behavioral couple and family therapy. In *Handbook of family therapy* (pp. 89–119). Routledge. doi:10.4324/9780203123584-6

Davenport, S., & Zolnikov, T. R. (2022). Understanding mental health outcomes related to compassion fatigue in parents of children diagnosed with intellectual disability. *Journal of Intellectual Disabilities*, *26*(3), 624–636. doi:10.1177/17446295211013600 PMID:34027745

Davis, C. M. (1990). What is empathy, and can empathy be taught? *Physical Therapy*, *70*(11), 707–711. doi:10.1093/ptj/70.11.707 PMID:2236214

De Bruin, K. (2019). The impact of inclusive education reforms on students with disability: An international comparison. *International Journal of Inclusive Education*, *23*(7-8), 811–826. doi:10.1080/13603116.2019.1623327

De Clercq-Quaegebeur, M., Casalis, S., Vilette, B., Lemaitre, M. P., & Vallée, L. (2018). Arithmetic abilities in children with developmental dyslexia: Performance on French ZAREKI-R test. *Journal of Learning Disabilities*, *51*(3), 236–249. doi:10.1177/0022219417690355 PMID:28134569

De Klerk, E. D., & Palmer, J. M. (2022). Technology inclusion for students living with disabilities through collaborative online learning during and beyond COVID-19. *Perspectives in Education*, *40*(1), 80–95. doi:10.18820/2519593X/pie.v40.i1.5

De Lopez, K. J., Feiberg, J., Baena, S., Lyons, R., & Harding, S. (2021). So I told him to look for friends" Barriers and protecting factors that may facilitate inclusion for children with Language Disorder in every day social settings: Cross-cultural qualitative interviews with parents. *Research in Developmental Disabilities*, 115.

De Smedt, B., & Boets, B. (2010). Phonological processing and arithmetic fact retrieval: Evidence from developmental dyslexia. *Neuropsychologia*, *48*(14), 3973–3981. doi:10.1016/j.neuropsychologia.2010.10.018 PMID:20965205

De Vroey, A., Struyf, E., & Petry, K. (2016). Secondary schools included: A literature review. *International Journal of Inclusive Education*, *20*(2), 109–135. doi:10.1080/13603116.2015.1075609

Deater-Deckard, K., & Scarr, S. (1996). Parenting stress among dual-earner mothers and fathers: Are there gender differences? *Journal of Family Psychology*, *10*(1), 45–59. doi:10.1037/0893-3200.10.1.45

Deault, L. C. (2010). A systematic review of parenting in relation to the development of comorbidities and functional impairments in children with attention-deficit/hyperactivity disorder (ADHD). *Child Psychiatry and Human Development*, *41*(2), 168–192. doi:10.100710578-009-0159-4 PMID:19768532

DeBoer, G. (2000). Scientific literacy: Another look at its historical and contemporary meanings and its relationship to science education reform. *Journal of Research in Science Teaching*, *37*(6), 582–601. doi:10.1002/1098-2736(200008)37:6<582::AID-TEA5>3.0.CO;2-L

Decety, J. M., Michalska, K. J., & Kinzler, K. D. (2012). The contribution of emotion and cognition to moral sensitivity: A neurodevelopmental study. *Cerebral Cortex (New York, N.Y.)*, *22*(1), 209–220. doi:10.1093/cercor/bhr111 PMID:21616985

Decision 104671/CD4. (2021). Pilot Implementation of Curricula in Primary and Secondary Education. *Gazette of the Government of the Hellenic Republic* (4003/B/30-8-2021).

Decision 21072b/C2 (2003). Interdisciplinary Unified Framework of Curricula (D.E.P.P.S.) and Analytical Curricula (A.P.S.). *Gazette of the Government of the Hellenic Republic* (304/B/13-3-2003).

Dell'Anna, S., Pellegrini, M., & Ianes, D. (2021). Experiences and learning outcomes of students without special educational needs in inclusive settings: A systematic review. *International Journal of Inclusive Education*, *25*(8), 944–959. doi:10.1080/13603116.2019.1592248

Developmental Language Disorder. (2023, May 8). NIDCD. https://www.nidcd.nih.gov/health/developmental-language-disorder

Dey, M., Castro, R. P., Haug, S., & Schaub, M. P. (2019). Quality of life of parents of mentally-ill children: A systematic review and meta-analysis. *Epidemiology and Psychiatric Sciences*, *28*(5), 563–577. doi:10.1017/S2045796018000409 PMID:30078381

Diamanti, V., Goulandris, N., Stuart, M., & Campbell, R. (2014). Spelling of derivational and inflectional suffixes by Greek-speaking children with and without dyslexia. *Reading and Writing*, *27*(2), 337–358. doi:10.100711145-013-9447-2

Dillon, S., Armstrong, E., Goudy, L., Reynolds, H., & Scurry, S. (2021). Improving special education service delivery through interdisciplinary collaboration. *Teaching Exceptional Children*, *54*(1), 36–43. doi:10.1177/00400599211029671

Dixon, F. A., Yssel, N., McConnell, J. M., & Hardin, T. (2014). Differentiated Instruction, Professional Development, and Teacher Efficacy. *Journal for the Education of the Gifted*, *37*(2), 111–127. doi:10.1177/0162353214529042

Dockrell, J. E., George, R., Lindsay, G., & Roux, J. (1997). Professionals' understanding of specific language impairments: Implications for assessment and identification. *Educational Psychology in Practice*, *13*, 27–35.

Dockrell, J. E., & Howell, P. (2015). Identifying the challenges and opportunities to meet the needs of children with speech, language and communication difficulties. *British Journal of Special Education*, *42*(4), 411–428. doi:10.1111/1467-8578.12115

Dockrell, J. E., Howell, P., Leung, D., & Fugard, A. J. (2017). Children with speech language and communication needs in England: Challenges for Practice. [). Frontiers.]. *Frontiers in Education*, *2*, 35. doi:10.3389/feduc.2017.00035

Dockrell, J. E., & Lindsay, G. (2001). Children with specific speech and language difficulties—The teachers' perspective. *Oxford Review of Education*, *27*(3), 369–394.

Dockrell, J., Lindsay, G., Roulstone, S., & Law, J. (2014). Supporting children with speech, language and communication needs: An overview of the results of the Better Communication Research Program. *International Journal of Language & Communication Disorders*, *49*(5), 543–557. doi:10.1111/1460-6984.12089 PMID:24961589

Doungyota, T., Prasoetsuk, T., Kirdpitak, P., & Pinyoanuntapong, B. (2010). A study and development of resilience of psychiatric patient caregivers through individual counseling. *Journal of Behavioral Science*, *16*(2), 51.

Downes, D. M. (2007). *Designing evaluation tools for the differentiated instruction staff development initiative* [Doctoral dissertation, Retrieved from ProQuest Dissertations & Theses Full Text]

Drigas, A., & Karyotaki, M. (2019). Executive Functioning and Problem Solving: A Bidirectional Relation. *Int. J. Eng. Pedagog.*, *9*(3), 76–98. doi:10.3991/ijep.v9i3.10186

Drigas, A., & Mitsea, E. (2020). The 8 pillars of metacognition. [iJET]. *International Journal of Emerging Technologies in Learning*, *15*(21), 162–178. doi:10.3991/ijet.v15i21.14907

Du, X. (2021). *Technology and Special Education: Designing Effective Professional Development for Equitable and Inclusive Classrooms* [Doctoral dissertation, Teachers College, Columbia University].

Dubois, P., St-Pierre, M.-C., Desmarais, C., & Guay, F. (2020). Young Adults With Developmental Language Disorder: A Systematic Review of Education, Employment, and Independent Living Outcomes. *Journal of Speech, Language, and Hearing Research: JSLHR*, *63*(11), 3786–3800. doi:10.1044/2020_JSLHR-20-00127 PMID:33022192

Dubow, E. F., & Ullman, D. G. (1989). Assessing Social Support in Elementary School Children: The Survey of Children's Social Support. *Journal of Clinical Child Psychology*, *18*(1), 52–64. doi:10.120715374424jccp1801_7

Ducharme, S. M. (2016). *Childhood speech and language disorders: Supporting children and families on the path to communication*. Rowman & Littlefield.

Duncan, R. J., Anderson, K. L., King, Y. A., Finders, J. K., Schmitt, S. A., & Purpura, D. J. (2023). Predictors of Preschool Language Environments and Their Relations to Children's Vocabulary. *Infant and Child Development*, *32*(1), e2381. doi:10.1002/icd.2381

Dunn, R., Hattie, J., & Bowles, T. (2019). Exploring the experiences of teachers undertaking Educational Design Research (EDR) as a form of teacher professional learning. *Professional Development in Education*, *45*(1), 151–167. doi :10.1080/19415257.2018.1500389

Dunst, C. J., Trivette, C. M., & Deal, A. (1988). *Enabling and empowering families: Principles & guidelines for practice*. Brookline Books.

Đurišić, M., & Bunijevac, M. (2017). Parental involvement as an important factor for successful education. *Center for Educational Policy Studies Journal*, *7*(3), 137–153. doi:10.26529/cepsj.291

Eaude, T. (1999). *Learning Difficulties: dyslexia, bullying and other issues*. Letts Educational.

Eden, G. F., & Moats, L. (2002). The role of neuroscience in the remediation of students with dyslexia. *Nature Neuroscience*, *5*(S11), 1080–1084. doi:10.1038/nn946 PMID:12403991

Eden, S. (2020). Technology Makes Things Possible. In *The Oxford handbook of deaf studies in learning and cognition* (p. 407). Oxford University Press.

Efthymiou, E. (2023). Amplifying Voices, Empowering Perspectives: Exploring the Experiences of Children with Disabilities in Inclusive Education During the Pandemic. In Inclusive Phygital Learning Approaches and Strategies for Students with Special Needs (pp. 1-32). IGI Global.

Efthymiou, E. (2023b). Examining Teachers' Perspectives on Equitable Digital Education: A Case Study on Delivering High-Quality and Inclusive Learning Experiences in Special Education. In E. Efthymiou (Ed.), *Inclusive Phygital Learning Approaches and Strategies for Students with Special Needs* (pp. 97–130). IGI Global. doi:10.4018/978-1-6684-8504-0.ch005

Efthymiou, E. (Ed.). (2023a). *Inclusive Phygital Learning Approaches and Strategies for Students with Special Needs.* IGI Global. doi:10.4018/978-1-6684-8504-0

Elder, J. H., Kreider, C. M., Brasher, S. N., & Ansell, M. (2017). Clinical impact of early diagnosis of autism on the prognosis and parent–child relationships. *Psychology Research and Behavior Management*, *10*, 283–292. doi:10.2147/PRBM.S117499 PMID:28883746

Elias, C. M., Vargas, S. I., & Castillo, K. V. B. (2021). La Realidad Virtual en la experiencia educativa de pregrado. *Delectus*, *4*(1), 139–145. doi:10.36996/delectus.v4i1.72

Elliott, J. G., & Grigorenko, E. L. (2014). *The dyslexia debate*. Cambridge University Press. doi:10.1017/CBO9781139017824

Ellis, W. E., & Zarbatany, L. (2007). Explaining friendship formation and friendship stability. The role of children's and friends' aggression and victimization. *Merrill-Palmer Quarterly*, *53*(1), 79–104. https://www.jstor.org/stable/23096292. doi:10.1353/mpq.2007.0001

Elsahar, Y., Hu, S., Bouazza-Marouf, K., Kerr, D., & Mansor, A. (2019). Augmentative and alternative communication (AAC) advances: A review of configurations for individuals with a speech disability. *Sensors (Basel)*, *19*(8), 1911. doi:10.339019081911 PMID:31013673

Emam, M. M., & Saad Abu-Serei, U. (2014). Family Functioning Predictors of Self-Concept and Self-Esteem in Children at Risk for Learning Disabilities in Oman: Exclusion of Parent and Gender Contribution. *International Education Studies*, *7*(10), 89–99. doi:10.5539/ies.v7n10p89

Epstein, J. L. (2001). Introduction to the special section. New directions for school, family, and community partnerships in middle and high schools. *NASSP Bulletin*, *85*(627), 3–6. doi:10.1177/019263650108562701

Erbeli, F., Hart, S. A., & Taylor, J. (2019). Genetic and environmental influences on achievement outcomes based on family history of learning disabilities status. *Journal of Learning Disabilities*, *52*(2), 135–145. doi:10.1177/0022219418775116 PMID:29790411

Evans, S.W., Owens, J.S., & Bunford, N. (2013). Evidence-based psychosocial treatments for children and adolescents with attention deficit/hyperactivity disorder. *Journal of Clinical Child andvAdolescent Psychology.*

Fabiano, G. A. (2007). Father participation in behavioral parent training for ADHD: Review and recommendations for increasing inclusion and engagement. *Journal of Family Psychology*, *21*(4), 683–693. doi:10.1037/0893-3200.21.4.683 PMID:18179340

Factors that Influence Language Development. (2010, January 1). Encyclopedia on Early Childhood Development. https://www.child-encyclopedia.com/language-development-and-literacy/according-experts/factors-influence-language-development

Fairchild, G. P., Passamonti, L., Hurford, G., Hagan, C. C., von dem Hagen, E. A. H., van Goozen, S. H. M., Goodyer, I. M., & Calder, A. J. (2011). Brain structure abnormalities in early-onset and adolescent-onset conduct disorder. *The American Journal of Psychiatry, 168*(6), 624–633. doi:10.1176/appi.ajp.2010.10081184 PMID:21454920

Fairchild, G., Van Goozen, S. H. M., Calder, A. J., Stollery, S. J., & Goodyer, I. M. (2009). Deficits in facial expression recognition in male adolescents with earlyonset or adolescence-onset conduct disorder. *Journal of Child Psychology and Psychiatry, and Allied Disciplines, 50*(5), 627–636. doi:10.1111/j.1469-7610.2008.02020.x PMID:19432683

Fang, J., Wang, X., Yuan, K. H., & Wen, Z. (2020). Childhood psychological maltreatment and moral disengagement: A moderated mediation model of callous-unemotional traits and empathy. *Personality and Individual Differences, 157*(January), 109814. doi:10.1016/j.paid.2020.109814

Fanti, K. A., Kimonis, E. R., Hadjicharalambous, M. Z., & Steinberg, L. (2016). Do neurocognitive deficits in decision making differentiate conduct disorder subtypes? *European Child & Adolescent Psychiatry, 25*(9), 989–996. doi:10.100700787-016-0822-9 PMID:26832949

Farquharson, K., Therrien, M., Barton-Hulsey, A., & Brandt, A. F. (2022). How to recruit, support, and retain speech-language pathologists in public schools. *Journal of School Leadership, 32*(3), 225–245. doi:10.1177/1052684620966062

Fazio-Griffith, L. J., & Ballard, M. B. (2014). Cognitive behavioral play therapy techniques in school-based group counseling: Assisting students in the development of social skills. *Vistas online, 18*, 1-14.

Feldman, D. B., Einav, M., & Margalit, M. (2018). Does family cohesion predict children's effort? The mediating roles of sense of coherence, hope, and loneliness. *The Journal of Psychology, 152*(5), 276–289. doi:10.1080/00223980.2018.1447434 PMID:29652639

Fenson, L., Dale, P. S., Reznick, J. S., Bates, E., Thal, D. J., Pethick, S. J., Tomasello, M., Mervis, C. B., & Stiles, J. (1994). Variability in early communicative development. *Monographs of the Society for Research in Child Development, 59*(5), 1–185. doi:10.2307/1166093 PMID:7845413

Ferjan Ramirez, N., Lytle, S. R., Fish, M., & Kuhl, P. K. (2019). Parent coaching at 6 and 10 months improves language outcomes at 14 months: A randomized controlled trial. *Developmental Science, 22*(3), e12762. doi:10.1111/desc.12762 PMID:30318708

Ferjan Ramirez, N., Lytle, S. R., & Kuhl, P. K. (2020). Parent coaching increases conversational turns and advances infant language development. *Proceedings of the National Academy of Sciences of the United States of America, 117*(7), 3484–3491. doi:10.1073/pnas.1921653117 PMID:32015127

Ferjan Ramírez, N., Weiss, Y., Sheth, K. K., & Kuhl, P. K. (2023). Parentese in infancy predicts 5-year language complexity and conversational turns. *Journal of Child Language*, 1–26. doi:10.1017/S0305000923000077 PMID:36748287

Fernandez-Villardon, A., Alvarez, P., Ugalde, L., & Tellado, I. (2020). Fostering the Social Development of Children with Special Educational Needs or Disabilities (SEND) through Dialogue and Interaction: A Literature Review. *Social Sciences, 9*(6), 97. MDPI AG. doi:10.3390/socsci9060097

Figley, C. R. (2002). Compassion fatigue: Psychotherapists' chronic lack of self care. *Journal of Clinical Psychology, 58*(11), 1433–1441. doi:10.1002/jclp.10090 PMID:12412153

Finkelstein, S., Sharma, U., & Furlonger, B. (2021). The inclusive practices of classroom teachers: A scoping review and thematic analysis. *International Journal of Inclusive Education, 25*(6), 735–762. doi:10.1080/13603116.2019.1572232

Firmin, M. W., & Phillips, A. (2009). A qualitative study of families and children possessing diagnoses of ADHD. *Journal of Family Issues, 30*(9), 1155–1174. doi:10.1177/0192513X09333709

Fitzgerald, P. B., Williams, C. L., Corteling, N., Filia, S. L., Brewer, K., Adams, A., De Castella, A. R. A., Rolfe, T., Davey, P., & Kulkarni, J. (2001). Subject and observer-rated quality of life in schizophrenia. *Acta Psychiatrica Scandinavica, 103*(5), 387–392. doi:10.1034/j.1600-0447.2001.00254.x PMID:11380309

Fleetwood, D. (2023). Quantitative Research: What It Is, Tips & Examples. *QuestionPro*. https://www.questionpro.com/blog/quantitative-research/

Flickinger, T. E., Waselewski, M., Tabackman, A., Huynh, J., Hodges, J., Otero, K., Schorling, K., Ingersoll, K., Tiouririne, N. A. D., & Dillingham, R. (2022). Communication between patients, peers, and care providers through a mobile health intervention supporting medication-assisted treatment for opioid use disorder. *Patient Education and Counseling, 105*(7), 2110–2115. doi:10.1016/j.pec.2022.02.014 PMID:35260260

Florian, L., Black-Hawkins, K., & Rouse, M. (2016). *Achievement and inclusion in schools*. Routledge. doi:10.4324/9781315750279

Florian, L., & Spratt, J. (2013). Enacting inclusion: A framework for interrogating inclusive practice. *European Journal of Special Needs Education, 28*(2), 119–135. doi:10.1080/08856257.2013.778111

Folia, V., Uddén, J., Forkstam, C., Ingvar, M., Hagoort, P., & Petersson, K. M. (2008). Implicit learning and dyslexia. *Annals of the New York Academy of Sciences, 1145*(1), 132–150. doi:10.1196/annals.1416.012 PMID:19076394

Forrest, C. L., Gibson, J. L., Halligan, S. L., & St Clair, M. C. (2018). Longitudinal analysis of early language difficulty and peer problems on later emotional difficulties in adolescence: Evidence from the Millennium Cohort Study. *Autism & Developmental Language Impairments, 3*, 2396941518795392. doi:10.1177/2396941518795392

Forrest, C. L., Gibson, J. L., & St Clair, M. C. (2021). Social functioning as a mediator between developmental language disorder (Dld) and emotional problems in adolescents. *International Journal of Environmental Research and Public Health, 18*(3), 1–17. doi:10.3390/ijerph18031221 PMID:33572993

Forrest, C. L., Gibson, J. L., & St Clair, M. C. (2021). Social functioning as a mediator between Developmental Language Disorder (DLD) and emotional problems in adolescents. *International Journal of Environmental Research and Public Health, 18.*

Forrest, C. L., Lloyd-Esenkaya, V., Gibson, J. L., & St Clair, M. C. (2022). Social Cognition in Adolescents with Developmental Language Disorder (DLD): Evidence from the Social Attribution Task. *Journal of Autism and Developmental Disorders*. doi:10.100710803-022-05698-6 PMID:35971042

Forteza, D., Fuster, L., & Moreno-Tallón, F. (2018). Barriers to Learning and School Participation for Students with Dyslexia: Voices of Families. *Int. J. Educ. Soc. Justice, 8*, 113–130.

Foster, R. H., Kozachek, S., Stern, M., & Elsea, S. H. (2010). Caring for the Caregivers: An Investigation of Factors Related to Well-Being Among Parents Caring for a Child with Smith-Magenis Syndrome. *Journal of Genetic Counseling, 19*(2), 187–198. doi:10.100710897-009-9273-5 PMID:20151318

Fredrickson, B. L. (2004). The broaden–and–build theory of positive emotions. *Philosophical Transactions of the Royal Society of London. Series B, Biological Sciences, 359*(1449), 1367–1377. doi:10.1098/rstb.2004.1512 PMID:15347528

Freedman, B. H., Kalb, L. G., Zablotsky, B., & Stuart, E. A. (2012). Relationship status among parents of children with autism spectrum disorders: A population-based study. *Journal of Autism and Developmental Disorders, 42*(4), 539–548. doi:10.100710803-011-1269-y PMID:21590433

Freer, J. R. R. (2021). Students' attitudes toward disability: A systematic literature review (2012–2019). *International Journal of Inclusive Education*, 1–19. doi:10.1080/13603116.2020.186668

Freud, A. (1965). *Normality and Pathology in Childhood International.* Universities Press.

Freud, S. (2008). *The Ego and the Id* (N. Mylonas, Trans.). Nikas. (Original work published 1923)

Freud, S. (2014). *Five medical histories* (K. Liaptsi & A. Anagnostou, Trans.). Epikouros. (Original work published 1905)

Frith, U. (1999). Paradoxes in the Definition of Dyslexia. *Dyslexia (Chichester, England)*, *5*(4), 192–214. doi:10.1002/(SICI)1099-0909(199912)5:4<192::AID-DYS144>3.0.CO;2-N

Frith, U. (2002). Resolving the paradoxes of dyslexia. *Dyslexia and Literacy. Theory into Practice*, 69–83.

Frith, U. (2017). Beneath the surface of developmental dyslexia. In *Surface dyslexia* (pp. 301–330). Routledge. doi:10.4324/9781315108346-18

Fuchs, L. S., Fuchs, D., Seethaler, P. M., & Craddock, C. (2020). Improving language comprehension to enhance word-problem solving. *Reading & Writing Quarterly*, *36*(2), 142–156. doi:10.1080/10573569.2019.1666760 PMID:32542068

Gabriel, F., Marrone, R., Van Sebille, Y., Kovanovic, V., & de Laat, M. (2022). Digital education strategies around the world: Practices and policies. *Irish Educational Studies*, *41*(1), 85–106. doi:10.1080/03323315.2021.2022513

Galaburda, A. M. (1993). Neuro anatomic basis of developmental dyslexia. *Neurologic Clinics*, *11*(1), 161–173. doi:10.1016/S0733-8619(18)30175-0 PMID:8441368

Gallagher, A. L., Murphy, C. A., Conway, P., & Perry, A. (2019). Consequential differences in perspectives and practices concerning children with developmental language disorders: An integrative review. *International Journal of Language & Communication Disorders*, *54*(4), 529–552. doi:10.1111/1460-6984.12469 PMID:30945410

Gallagher, S., & Hannigan, A. (2014). Depression and chronic health conditions in parents of children with and without developmental disabilities: The growing up in Ireland cohort study. *Research in Developmental Disabilities*, *35*(2), 448–454. doi:10.1016/j.ridd.2013.11.029 PMID:24361813

Gallagher-Thompson, D., & Coon, D. W. (2007). Evidence-based psychological treatments for distress in family caregivers of older adults. *Psychology and Aging*, *22*(1), 37–51. doi:10.1037/0882-7974.22.1.37 PMID:17385981

Gallaway, C., & Richards, B. J. (Eds.). (1994). *Input and interaction in language acquisition.* Cambridge University Press., doi:10.1017/CBO9780511620690

Galuschka, K., Görgen, R., Kalmar, J., Haberstroh, S., Schmalz, X., & Schulte-Körne, G. (2020). Effectiveness of spelling treatment approaches for learners with dyslexia – A meta-analysis and systematic review. *Educational Psychologist*, *55*(1), 1–20. doi:10.1080/00461520.2019.1659794

Ganek, H., & Eriks-Brophy, A. (2017). Language ENvironment analysis (LENA) system investigation of day long recordings in children: A literature review. *Journal of Communication Disorders*, *72*, 77–85. doi:10.1016/j.jcomdis.2017.12.005 PMID:29402382

Ganek, H., Smyth, R., Nixon, S., & Eriks-Brophy, A. (2018). Using the Language Environment Analysis (LENA) System to Investigate Cultural Differences in Conversational Turn Count. *Journal of Speech, Language, and Hearing Research: JSLHR*, *61*(9), 2246–2258. doi:10.1044/2018_JSLHR-L-17-0370 PMID:30076420

Gargiulo, R. M., & Metcalf, D. (2022). *Teaching in today's inclusive classrooms: A universal design for learning approach.* Cengage Learning.

Garrote, A., Dessemontet, R. S., & Opitz, E. M. (2017). Facilitating the social participation of pupils with special educational needs in mainstream schools: A review of school-based interventions. *Educational Research Review*, *20*, 12–23. doi:10.1016/j.edurev.2016.11.001

Genova, A. (2015). Barriers to inclusive education in Greece, Spain and Lithuania: Results from emancipatory disability research. *Disability & Society*, *30*(7), 1042–1054. doi:10.1080/09687599.2015.1075867

Gerber, Z., & Anaki, D. (2021). The Role of Self-compassion, Concern for Others, and Basic Psychological Needs in the Reduction of Caregiving Burnout. *Mindfulness*, *12*(3), 741–750. doi:10.100712671-020-01540-1 PMID:33224308

Ghandour, H., Eldin, S., Sallam, Y., & Mahmoud, S. (2018). Associated comorbidities of specific language impairment. *Benha Medical Journal*, *35*(2), 115. doi:10.4103/bmfj.bmfj_155_17

Ghazarian, S. R., & Buehler, C. (2010). Interparental conflict and academic achievement: An examination of mediating and moderating factors. *Journal of Youth and Adolescence*, *39*(1), 23–35. doi:10.100710964-008-9360-1 PMID:20091214

Giannouli, V., Sarris, D., & Bannou, M. (2019). Differences between dyslexic students and controls matched for educational level in word intelligibility and text comprehension presented via synthetic and natural speech. *European Journal of Special Education Research, 4*(3), 200-225, (ISSN: 2501 - 2428). doi:10.5281/zenodo.3246839

Gibby-Leversuch, R., Hartwell, B. K., & Wright, S. (2021). Dyslexia, literacy difficulties and the self-perceptions of children and young people: A systematic review. *Current Psychology (New Brunswick, N.J.), 40*(11), 5595–5612. doi:10.100712144-019-00444-1

Gilbert, P. (2010). *Compassion focused therapy: Distinctive features*. Routledge. doi:10.4324/9780203851197

Gilkerson, J., Richards, J. A., Warren, S. F., Oller, D. K., Russo, R., & Vohr, B. R. (2018). Language experience in the second year of life and language outcomes in late childhood. *Pediatrics*, *142*(4), e20174276. doi:10.1542/peds.2017-4276 PMID:30201624

Gillam, S. L., Holbrook, S., & Kamhi, A. G. (2021). Developmental Language Disorder. The Handbook of Language and Speech Disorders, 171–191. Dld, doi:10.1002/9781119606987.ch9

Girard, L. C., Pingault, J. B., Doyle, O., Falissard, B., & Tremblay, R. E. (2016). Developmental Associations Between Conduct Problems and Expressive Language in Early Childhood: A Population-Based Study. *Journal of Abnormal Child Psychology*, *44*(6), 1033–1043. doi:10.100710802-015-0094-8 PMID:26496905

Gkaintartzi, A., Kiliari, A., & Tsokalidou, R. (2015). 'Invisible'bilingualism–'invisible'language ideologies: Greek teachers' attitudes towards immigrant pupils' heritage languages. *International Journal of Bilingual Education and Bilingualism*, *18*(1), 60–72. doi:10.1080/13670050.2013.877418

Glasby, J., Graham, L. J., White, S. L. J., & Tancredi, H. (2022). Do teachers know enough about the characteristics and educational impacts of Developmental Language Disorder (DLD) to successfully include students with DLD? *Teaching and Teacher Education*, *119*, 103868. doi:10.1016/j.tate.2022.103868

Glazzard, J. (2010). The impact of dyslexia on pupils' self-esteem. *Support for Learning*, *25*(2), 63–69. doi:10.1111/j.1467-9604.2010.01442.x

Gliaou, Christodoulou, N. (2002). Project method, the importance of the method, what is the final project, the project method in kindergarten. *Modern Kindergarten*, *25*, 14–19.

Glover, A., McCormack, J., & Smith-Tamaray, M. (2015). Collaboration between teachers and speech and language therapists: Services for primary schoolchildren with speech, language and communication needs. *Child Language Teaching and Therapy*, *31*(3), 363–382. doi:10.1177/0265659015603779

Goldfus, C. (2012). Knowledge foundations for beginning reading teachers in EFL. *Annals of Dyslexia*, *62*(3), 204–221. doi:10.100711881-012-0073-5 PMID:22815105

Göransson, K., & Nilholm, C. (2014). Conceptual diversities and empirical shortcomings–a critical analysis of research on inclusive education. *European Journal of Special Needs Education, 29*(3), 265–280. doi:10.1080/08856257.2014.933545

Goswami, U., Ziegler, J. C., & Richardson, U. (2005). The effects of spelling consistency on phonological awareness: A comparison of English and German. *Journal of Experimental Child Psychology, 92*(4), 345–365. doi:10.1016/j.jecp.2005.06.002 PMID:16087187

Gough Kenyon, S. M., Palikara, O., & Lucas, R. M. (2021). Consistency of Parental and Self-Reported Adolescent Wellbeing: Evidence From Developmental Language Disorder. *Frontiers in Psychology, 12*, 12. doi:10.3389/fpsyg.2021.629577 PMID:33776852

Graham, L. (Ed.). (2020). *Inclusive education for the 21st century: Theory, policy and practice.* Routledge. doi:10.4324/9781003116073

Greenberg, M. T., Speltz, M. L., & Deklyen, M. (1993). The role of attachment in the early development of disruptive behavior problems. *Development and Psychopathology, 5*(1-2), 191–213. doi:10.1017/S095457940000434X

Gregory, G. H., & Chapman, C. (2012). *Differentiated instructional strategies: One size doesn't fit all.* Corwin.

Gremillion, M. L., & Martel, M. M. (2014). Merely misunderstood? Receptive, expressive, and pragmatic language in young children with disruptive behavior disorders. *Journal of Clinical Child and Adolescent Psychology, 43*(5), 765–776. doi:10.1080/15374416.2013.822306 PMID:23924073

Griffin, C. P., & Murtagh, L. (2015). Increasing the sight vocabulary and reading fluency of children requiring reading support: The use of a precision teaching approach. *Educational Psychology in Practice, 31*(2), 186–209. doi:10.1080/02667363.2015.1022818

Griva, E., & Kofou, I. (2017). *Alternative assessment in Language learning: Challenges and Practices.* Kyriakidis.

Grunwald, B. B., & McAbee, H. (2013). *Guiding the family: Practical counseling techniques.* Routledge. doi:10.4324/9780203768143

Guba, E. G., & Lincoln, Y. S. (1989). *Fourth generation evaluation.* Sage.

Guerreiro, M. M., Hage, S. R. V., Guimarães, C. A., Abramides, D. V., Fernandes, W., Pacheco, P. S., Piovesana, A. M. S. G., Montenegro, M. A., & Cendes, F. (2002). Developmental language disorder associated with polymicrogyria. *Neurology, 59*(2), 245–250. doi:10.1212/WNL.59.2.245 PMID:12136065

Guralnick, M. J. (2017). Early intervention for children with intellectual disabilities: An update. *Journal of Applied Research in Intellectual Disabilities, 30*(2), 211–229. doi:10.1111/jar.12233 PMID:26764896

Gurevitz, M., Geva, R., Varon, M., & Leitner, Y. (2012). Early markers in infants and toddlers for development of ADHD. *Journal of Attention Disorders.* PMID:22751678

Güroğlu, B. (2022). The power of friendship: The developmental significance of friendships from a neuroscience perspective. *Child Development Perspectives, 16*(2), 110–117. doi:10.1111/cdep.12450

Gustafsson, P., Thernlund, G., Besjakov, J., Karrlsson, M. K., Ericsson, I., & Svedin, C. G., & (2008). ADHD symptoms in primary school children. *Acta Paediatrica (Oslo, Norway), 97*(2), 233–238. doi:10.1111/j.1651-2227.2007.00608.x PMID:18177440

Haakonsen Smith, C., Turbitt, E., Muschelli, J., Leonard, L., Lewis, K. L., Freedman, B., Muratori, M., & Biesecker, B. B. (2018). Feasibility of coping effectiveness training for caregivers of children with autism spectrum disorder: A genetic counseling intervention. *Journal of Genetic Counseling, 27*(1), 252–262. doi:10.100710897-017-0144-1 PMID:28879629

Hadjipanayis, A., Efstathiou, E., Altorjai, P., Stirs, T., Laliulis, A., Lonetzko, B., & Fonseca, H. (2019). Social Media and Children: What Is the Pediatrician's Role? *European Journal of Pediatrics*, *178*(10), 1605–1612. doi:10.100700431-019-03458-w PMID:31468108

Haft, S. L., Chen, T., LeBlanc, C., Tencza, F., & Hoeft, F. (2019). Impact of mentoring on socio-emotional and mental health outcomes of youth with learning disabilities and attention-deficit hyperactivity disorder. *Child and Adolescent Mental Health*, *24*(4), 318–328. doi:10.1111/camh.12331 PMID:31649490

Hallahan, D. P., Pullen, P. C., Kauffman, J. M., & Badar, J. (2020). Exceptional learners. In Oxford Research Encyclopedia of Education.

Hamilton, L. G., Hayiou-Thomas, M. E., Hulme, C., & Snowling, M. J. (2016). The home literacy environment as a predictor of the early literacy development of children at family-risk of dyslexia. *Scientific Studies of Reading*, *20*(5), 401–419. doi:10.1080/10888438.2016.1213266 PMID:28250707

Hampden-Thompson, G. (2013). Family policy, family structure, and children's educational achievement. *Social Science Research*, *42*(3), 804–817. doi:10.1016/j.ssresearch.2013.01.005 PMID:23521996

Han, A., Yuen, H. K., & Jenkins, J. (2021). Acceptance and commitment therapy for family caregivers: A systematic review and meta-analysis. *Journal of Health Psychology*, *26*(1), 82–102. doi:10.1177/1359105320941217 PMID:32659142

Hancock, A., Northcott, S., Hobson, H., & Clarke, M. (2023). Speech, language and communication needs and mental health: The experiences of speech and language therapists and mental health professionals. *International Journal of Language & Communication Disorders*, *58*(1), 52–66. doi:10.1111/1460-6984.12767 PMID:36117337

Harborne, A., Wolpert, M., & Clare, L. (2004). Making sense of ADHD: A battle for understanding parents' views of their children being diagnosed with ADHD. *Clinical Child Psychology and Psychiatry*, *9*(3), 327–339. doi:10.1177/1359104504043915

Harold, G. T., Leve, L. D., Barrett, D., Elam, K., Neiderhiser, J. M., Natsuaki, M. N., Shaw, D. S., Reiss, D., & Thapar, A. (2013). Biological and rearing mother influences on child ADHD symptoms: Revisiting the developmental interface between nature and nurture. *Journal of Child Psychology and Psychiatry, and Allied Disciplines*, *54*(10), 1038–1046. doi:10.1111/jcpp.12100 PMID:24007415

Harrar-Eskinazi, K. L., De Cara, B., Leloup, G., Nothelier, J., Caci, H., Ziegler, J. C., & Faure, S. (2022). Multimodal intervention in 8- to 13-year-old French dyslexic readers: Study protocol for a randomized multicenter controlled cross-over trial. *BMC Pediatrics*, *22*(1), 741. doi:10.118612887-022-03701-8 PMID:36578007

Harrar, V., Tammam, J., Pérez-Bellido, A., Pitt, A., Stein, J., & Spence, C. (2014). Multisensory integration and attention in developmental dyslexia. *Current Biology*, *24*(5), 531–535. doi:10.1016/j.cub.2014.01.029 PMID:24530067

Harrison, C., & Sofronoff, K. (2002). ADHD and parental psychological distress: Role of demographics, child behavioural characteristics and parental cognitions. *Journal of the American Academy of Child and Adolescent Psychiatry*, *41*(6), 703–711. doi:10.1097/00004583-200206000-00010 PMID:12049445

Hartas, D. (2004). Teacher and speech-language therapist collaboration: Being equal. and achieving a common goal? *Child Language Teaching and Therapy*, *20*(1), 33–54. doi:10.1191/0265659004ct262oa

Hartas, D. (2012). Children's social behavior, language, and literacy in early years. *Oxford Review of Education*, *38*(3), 357–376. doi:10.1080/03054985.2012.699748

Hart, B., & Risley, T. R. (1999). *The social world of children: Learning to talk*. Brookes Publishing Company.

Hassall, R., Rose, J., & McDonald, J. (2005). Parenting stress in mothers of children with an intellectual disability: The effects of parental cognitions in relation to child characteristics and family support. *Journal of Intellectual Disability Research, 49*(6), 405–418. doi:10.1111/j.1365-2788.2005.00673.x PMID:15882391

Hastings, R. P., & Taunt, H. M. (2002). Positive perceptions in families of children with developmental disabilities. *American Journal of Mental Retardation, 107*(2), 116–127. doi:10.1352/0895-8017(2002)107<0116:PPIFOC>2.0.CO;2 PMID:11853529

Hawes, Z., Moss, J., Caswell, B., Naqvi, S., & MacKinnon, S. (2017). Enhancing children's spatial and numerical skills through a dynamic spatial approach to early geometry instruction: Effects of a 32-week intervention. *Cognition and Instruction, 35*(3), 236–264. doi:10.1080/07370008.2017.1323902

Helland, T. (2022). Trends in Dyslexia Research during the Period 1950 to 2020 - Theories, Definitions, and Publications. *Brain Sciences, 12*(10), 1323. doi:10.3390/brainsci12101323 PMID:36291256

Helland, W. A., Lundervold, A. J., Heimann, M., & Posserud, M. B. (2014). Stable associations between behavioral problems and language impairments across childhood - The importance of pragmatic language problems. *Research in Developmental Disabilities, 35*(5), 943–951. doi:10.1016/j.ridd.2014.02.016 PMID:24642228

Hendricks, A., Adlof, S., Alonzo, C., Fox, A., & Hogan, T. (2019). Identifying children at risk for developmental language disorder using a brief, whole-classroom screen. *Journal of Speech, Language, and Hearing Research: JSLHR, 62*(4), 1–13. doi:10.1044/2018_JSLHR-L-18-0093 PMID:30986146

Hendrickson, B., Rosen, D., & Aune, R. K. (2010). An analysis of friendship networks, social connectedness, homesickness, and satisfaction levels of international students. *International Journal of Intercultural Relations, 15*, 1–15. doi:10.1016/j.ijintrel.2010.08.001

Henry, A. (2021). Motivational connections in language classrooms: A research agenda. *Language Teaching, 54*(2), 221–235. doi:10.1017/S0261444820000026

Henry, L. A., & Botting, N. (2017). Working memory and developmental language impairments. *Child Language Teaching and Therapy, 33*(1), 19–32. doi:10.1177/0265659016655378

Hens, K., Peeters, H., & Dierickx, K. (2016). Genetic testing and counseling in the case of an autism diagnosis: A caregivers perspective. *European Journal of Medical Genetics, 59*(9), 452–458. doi:10.1016/j.ejmg.2016.08.007 PMID:27544064

Herba, C. M. (2004). Annotation: Developmental psychopathology: The role of emotion regulation in the development of psychopathology. *Journal of Child Psychology and Psychiatry, and Allied Disciplines.*

Herbert, M. R., Ziegler, D. A., Makris, N., Bakardjiev, A., Hodgson, J., Adrien, K. T., Kennedy, D. N., Filipek, P. A., & Caviness, V. S. (2003). Larger brain and white matter volumes in children with developmental language disorder. *Developmental Science, 6*(4), 11–22. doi:10.1111/1467-7687.00291

Hertberg-Davis, H., & Brighton, C. M. (2006). Support and sabotage: Principals' influence on middle school teachers' responses to differentiation. *Journal of Secondary Gifted Education, 17*(12), 90–102. doi:10.4219/jsge-2006-685

Hiatt, K. D., Lorenz, A. R., & Newman, J. P. (2002). Assessment of emotion and language processing in psychopathic offenders: Results from a dichotic listening task. *Personality and Individual Differences, 32*(7), 1255–1268. doi:10.1016/S0191-8869(01)00116-7

Hickendorff, M. (2021). The demands of simple and complex arithmetic word problems on language and cognitive resources. *Frontiers in Psychology, 12*, 727761. doi:10.3389/fpsyg.2021.727761 PMID:34733206

Hill, K. (2017). Role of Speech–Language Pathologists in Assistive Technology Assessments. In *Assistive technology assessment handbook* (pp. 301–324). CRC Press.

History of the English Language and Literature. (n.d.). Gutenberg. https://www.gutenberg.org/files/21665/21665-h/21665-h.htm

Hoag, A. (2014). Mothers' perceptions of family communication patterns when having an ADHD child. In Family Relationships and Familial Responses to Health Issues (pp. 211-246). Emerald Group Publishing Limited.

Hobson, H., Kalsi, M., Cotton, L., Forster, M., & Toseeb, U. (2022). Supporting the mental health of children with speech, language and communication needs: The views and experiences of parents. *Autism & Developmental Language Impairments, 7*.

Hodson, D. (2014). Learning Science, Learning about Science, Doing Science: Different goals demand different learning methods. *International Journal of Science Education, 36*(15), 2534–2553. doi:10.1080/09500693.2014.899722

Hoff, E., Core, C., Place, S., Rumiche, R., Señor, M., & Parra, M. (2012). Dual language exposure and early bilingual development. *Journal of Child Language, 39*(1), 1–27. doi:10.1017/S0305000910000759 PMID:21418730

Höft, L., Bernholt, S., Blankenburg, J. S., & Winberg, M. (2019). Knowing more about things you care less about: Cross-sectional analysis of the opposing trend and interplay between conceptual understanding and interest in secondary school chemistry. *Journal of Research in Science Teaching, 56*(2), 184–210. doi:10.1002/tea.21475

Holanda, C. M. A., Andrade, F. L. J. P., Bezerra, M. A., Silva Nascimento, J. P., Fonseca Neves, R., Alves, S. B., & Silva Ribeiro, K. S. Q. (2015). Support networks and people with physical disabilities: Social inclusion and access to health services. *Ciencia & Saude Coletiva, 20*(1), 175–184. doi:10.1590/1413-81232014201.19012013 PMID:25650611

Hollo, A., Wehby, J. H., & Oliver, R. M. (2014). Unidentified language deficits in children with emotional and behavioral disorders: A meta-analysis. *Exceptional Children, 80*(2), 169–186. doi:10.1177/001440291408000203

Holmes, L. F. (2008). *Teachers' perceptions of a differentiated instruction professional development program*. The University of Alabama.

Hooda, M., Rana, C., Dahiya, O., Rizwan, A., & Hossain, M. S. (2022). Artificial intelligence for assessment and feedback to enhance student success in higher education. *Mathematical Problems in Engineering, 2022*, 2022. doi:10.1155/2022/5215722

Hornby, G. (2011). Inclusive education for children with special educational needs: A critique. *International Journal of Disability Development and Education, 58*(3), 321–329. doi:10.1080/1034912X.2011.598678

Hornstra, L., Denessen, E., Bakker, J., van den Bergh, L., & Voeten, M. (2010). Teacher attitudes toward dyslexia: Effects on teacher expectations and the academic achievement of students with dyslexia. *Journal of Learning Disabilities, 43*(6), 515–529. doi:10.1177/0022219409355479 PMID:20445201

Horsfield, P., Stolzenburg, S., Hahm, S., Tomczyk, S., Muehlan, H., Schmidt, S., & Schomerus, G. (2020). Self-labeling as having a mental or physical illness: The effects of stigma and implications for help-seeking. *Social Psychiatry and Psychiatric Epidemiology, 55*(7), 907–916. doi:10.100700127-019-01787-7 PMID:31641830

Horton, T. V., & Wallander, J. L. (2001). Hope and social support as resilience factors against psychological distress of mothers who care for children with chronic physical conditions. *Rehabilitation Psychology, 46*(4), 382–399. doi:10.1037/0090-5550.46.4.382

Ho, S.-W., Chien, W., & Wang, L.-Q. (2011). Parents' perceptions of care-giving to a child with attention deficit hyperactivity disorder: An exploratory study. *Contemporary Nurse, 40*(1), 41–56. doi:10.5172/conu.2011.40.1.41 PMID:22545905

Houston-Price, C., Mather, E., & Sakkalou, E. (2007). Discrepancy between parental reports of infants' receptive vocabulary and infants' behaviour in a preferential looking task. *Journal of Child Language, 34*(4), 701–724. doi:10.1017/S0305000907008124 PMID:18062356

Hou, T., Zhang, T., Cai, W., Song, X., Chen, A., Deng, G., & Ni, C. (2020). Social support and mental health among health care workers during Coronavirus Disease 2019 outbreak: A moderated mediation model. *PLoS One, 15*(5), e0233831. doi:10.1371/journal.pone.0233831 PMID:32470007

Howe, D. (2010). The safety of children and the parent-worker relationship in cases of child abuse and neglect. *Child Abuse Review, 19*(5), 330–341. doi:10.1002/car.1136

Hulme, C., & Snowling, M. J. (2016). Reading disorders and dyslexia. *Current Opinion in Pediatrics, 28*(6), 731–735. doi:10.1097/MOP.0000000000000411 PMID:27496059

Humphrey, N., & Mullins, P. M. (2002). Self-concept and self-esteem in developmental dyslexia. *Journal of Research in Special Educational Needs, 2*(2). http://www3.interscience.wiley.com/cgi-bin/fulltext/120188296/

Humphrey, N. (2002). Teacher and pupil ratings of self-esteem in developmental dyslexia. *British Journal of Special Education, 29*(1), 29–36. doi:10.1111/1467-8527.00234

Humphrey, N. (2003). Facilitating a positive sense of self in pupils with dyslexia: The role of teachers and peers. *Support for Learning, 18*(3), 130–136. doi:10.1111/1467-9604.00295

Hurt, E. A., Hoza, B., & Pelham, W. E. Jr. (2007). Parenting, family loneliness, and peer functioning in boys with attention-deficit/hyperactivity disorder. *Journal of Abnormal Child Psychology, 25*(4), 413–424. doi:10.100710802-007-9111-x PMID:17333361

Hymel, S., & Katz, J. (2019). Designing classrooms for diversity: Fostering social inclusion. *Educational Psychologist, 54*(4), 331–339. doi:10.1080/00461520.2019.1652098

Im-Bolter, N., & Cohen, N. J. (2007). Language Impairment and Psychiatric Comorbidities. *Pediatric Clinics of North America, 54*(3), 525–542. doi:10.1016/j.pcl.2007.02.008 PMID:17543908

In Defense of Patentability of Mathematical Formulas and Relationships. (2022, November 10). Patents & Intellectual Property Law. https://ipwatchdog.com/2022/11/10/defense-patentability-mathematical-formulas-relationships/id=152875/

Iosifidis, T. (2003). *Qualitative data analysis in the social sciences*. Kritiki.

Irwin, D. A., Arslan-Ari, I., & Morris, W. (2022). Teachers' value beliefs and usage of one- to-one devices for students with dyslexia: A descriptive study. *Education and Information Technologies*. doi:10.100710639-022-11450-5 PMID:36438651

Isaacs, D., & Swartz, L. (2022). "Stammering less so that I can be more of a man": Discourses of masculinities among young adult men in the Western Cape, South Africa, who stutter. *Psychology of Men & Masculinity, 23*(1), 74–85. doi:10.1037/men0000302

Jabbari, B., & Rouster, A. S. (2023). Family dynamics. In *StatPearls*. StatPearls Publishing. https://www.ncbi.nlm.nih.gov/books/NBK560487/

Jackson, D., & Mannix, J. (2004). Giving voice to the burden of blame: A feminist study of mothers' experiences of mother blaming. *International Journal of Nursing Practice, 10*(4), 150–158. doi:10.1111/j.1440-172X.2004.00474.x PMID:15265225

Jamal Al-deen, T., & Windle, J. (2017). 'I feel sometimes I am a bad mother': The affective dimension of immigrant mothers' involvement in their children's schooling. *Journal of Sociology (Melbourne, Vic.), 53*(1), 110–126. doi:10.1177/1440783316632604

Jayasree, K. (2016). A Holistic Approach to Learning: Remedial Intervention for Students with Learning Disabilities (Dyslexia). *International Journal of New Technology and Research, 2*(11), 60–61.

Jiang, M. (2023). The Impact and Potential of Educational Technology: A Comprehensive Review. *Research and Advances in Education, 2*(7), 32–49. doi:10.56397/RAE.2023.07.05

Jiménez-Fernández, G., Vaquero, J. M., Jiménez, L., & Defior, S. (2011). Dyslexic children show deficits in implicit sequence learning, but not in explicit sequence learning or contextual cueing. *Annals of Dyslexia, 61*(1), 85–110. doi:10.100711881-010-0048-3 PMID:21082295

Johnson, E. (2010). *Improving students' academic achievement through differentiated instruction* [Doctoral dissertation, Retrieved from ProQuest Dissertations & Theses Full Text].

Johnston, C., & Mash, E. J. (2001). Families of children with attention deficit/ hyperactivity disorder: Review and recommendations for future research. *Clinical Child and Family Psychology Review, 4*(3), 183–207. doi:10.1023/A:1017592030434 PMID:11783738

Johnston, C., Mash, E. J., Miller, N., & Ninowski, J. E. (2012). Parenting in Adults with Attention-Deficit/Hyperactivity Disorder (ADHD). *Clinical Psychology Review, 32*(4), 215–228. doi:10.1016/j.cpr.2012.01.007 PMID:22459785

Johnston, V. (2019). Dyslexia: What reading teachers need to know. *The Reading Teacher, 73*(3), 339–346. doi:10.1002/trtr.1830

Jørgensen, C. R., Dobson, G., & Perry, T. (2021). Migrant children with special educational needs in European schools–a review of current issues and approaches. *European Journal of Special Needs Education, 36*(3), 438–453. doi:10.1080/08856257.2020.1762988

Joshi, R. M., Binks, E., Graham, L., Dean, E., Smith, D., & Boulware-Gooden, R. (2009). Do textbooks used in university reading education courses conform to the instructional recommendations of the National Reading Panel? *Journal of Learning Disabilities, 42,* 458e463.

Jovanova, N. C., & Radojichikj, D. D. (2013). Parents of children with developmental disabilities: Stress and support. *Journal of Special Education and Rehabilitation, 14*(1-2), 7–19. doi:10.2478/v10215-011-0029-z

Jurchiş, R., & Dienes, Z. (2023). Implicit learning of regularities followed by realistic body movements in virtual reality. Psychonomic Bulletin & Review, 30(1), 269-279.

Juvonen, J., Lessard, L. M., Rastogi, R., Schacter, H. L., & Smith, D. S. (2019). Promoting social inclusion in educational settings: Challenges and opportunities. *Educational Psychologist, 54*(4), 250–270. doi:10.1080/00461520.2019.1655645

Kaczorowski, T. L., Hashey, A. I., & Di Cesare, D. M. (2019). An exploration of multimedia supports for diverse learners during core math instruction. *Journal of Special Education Technology, 34*(1), 41–54. doi:10.1177/0162643418781298

Kahn, R. E., Frick, P. J., Youngstrom, E., Findling, R. L., & Youngstrom, J. K. (2012). Diagnosis of Conduct Disorder. *Journal of Child Psychology and Psychiatry, and Allied Disciplines, 53*(3), 271–282. doi:10.1111/j.1469-7610.2011.02463.x PMID:21950481

Kalkanis, G., Gkikopoulou, O., Kapotis, E., Gousopoulos, D., Patrinopoulos, M., Tsakonas, P., Dimitriadis, P., Papatsimpa, L., Mitzithras, K., Kapogiannis, A., Sotiropoulos, D., Politis, S. (2013). *Physics with experiments for the 1st grade of Lower Secondary School. [I Fysiki me Peiramata A΄ Gymnasiou].* Institute of Computer Technology and Publishing "Diophantus".

Kalliontzi, E., Ralli, A. M., Palikara, O., & Roussos, P. (2022). Examining the relationship between oral language skills and executive functions: Evidence from Greek-speaking 4–5-year-old children with and without Developmental Language Disorder. *Research in Developmental Disabilities*, *124*(March), 104215. doi:10.1016/j.ridd.2022.104215 PMID:35298958

Kansas State Department of Education. (2018). *Kansas full-day kindergarten guide*. KSDE. https://files.eric.ed.gov/fulltext/ED598986.pdf

Karakasidou, E. Yotsidis, & Papadimitriou, A. (2020). Self-compassion: The technique to take care of myself. In A. Stalikas, V. Yotsidis & E. Karakasidou (Eds.) Conquering prosperity (pp. 197-215). Topos.

Kefallinou, A., Symeonidou, S., & Meijer, C. J. (2020). Understanding the value of inclusive education and its implementation: A review of the literature. *Prospects*, *49*(3-4), 135–152. doi:10.100711125-020-09500-2

Kelly, M. L., Yeigh, T., Hudson, S., Willis, R., & Lee, M. (2022). Secondary teachers' perceptions of the importance of pedagogical approaches to support students' behavioural, emotional and cognitive engagement. *Australian Educational Researcher*, 1–23.

Kelly, S. W., Griffiths, S., & Frith, U. (2002). Evidence for implicit sequence learning in dyslexia. *Dyslexia (Chichester, England)*, *8*(1), 43–52. doi:10.1002/dys.208 PMID:11990224

Kempes, M. M., Matthys, W., de Vries, H., & van Engeland, H. (2005). Reactive and proactive aggression in children: A review of theory, findings and the relevance for child and adolescent psychiatry. *European Child & Adolescent Psychiatry*, *14*(1), 11–19. doi:10.100700787-005-0432-4 PMID:15756511

Keown, L. J. (2012). Predictors of boys' ADHD symptoms from early to middle childhood: The role of father–child and mother–child interactions. *Journal of Abnormal Child Psychology*, *40*(4), 569–581. doi:10.100710802-011-9586-3 PMID:22038253

Kepic, M., Randolph, A., & Hermann-Turner, K. M. (2019). Care for caregivers: Understanding the need for caregiver support. *Adultspan Journal*, *18*(1), 40–51. doi:10.1002/adsp.12068

Kerch, C. J., Donovan, C. A., Ernest, J. M., Strichik, T., & Winchester, J. (2020). An exploration of language and social-emotional development of children with and without disabilities in a statewide pre-kindergarten program. *Education & Treatment of Children*, *43*(1), 7–19. doi:10.100743494-020-00002-6

Khatin-Zadeh, O. (2022). How does representational transformation enhance mathematical thinking? *Axiomathes*, *32*(S2, Suppl 2), 283–292. doi:10.100710516-021-09602-2

Khursheed, F., & Ansari, U. (2012). Effects of innovative teaching strategies on students' performance. *Global Journal of Human Social science. Linguistics and Education*, *12*(10), 46–54.

Kibria, N., & Becerra, W. S. (2021). Deserving immigrants and good advocate mothers: Immigrant mothers' negotiations of special education systems for children with disabilities. *Social Problems*, *68*(3), 591–607. doi:10.1093ocpropaa005

Kim, T. H., Lee, S. M., Yu, K., Lee, S., & Puig, A. (2005). Hope and the meaning of life as influences on Korean adolescents' resilience: Implications for counselors. *Asia Pacific Education Review*, *6*(2), 143–152. doi:10.1007/BF03026782

Kirwan, B., & Leather, C. (2011). Students' voices: A report of the student view of dyslexia study skills tuition. *Support for Learning*, *26*(1), 33–41. doi:10.1111/j.1467-9604.2010.01472.x

Klang, N., Olsson, I., Wilder, J., Lindqvist, G., Fohlin, N., & Nilholm, C. (2020). A Cooperative Learning Intervention to Promote Social Inclusion in Heterogeneous Classrooms, Secondary. *Educational Psychology*, *11*. doi:10.3389/fpstg.2020.586489

Kloomak, S., & Cosden, M. (1994). Self-concept in children with learning disabilities: The relationship between global self-concept, academic 'discounting', non-academic self-concept and perceived social support. *Learning Disability Quarterly*, *17*(2), 140–153. doi:10.2307/1511183

Knight, C. (2018). What is dyslexia? An exploration of the relationship between teachers' understandings of dyslexia and their training experiences. *Dyslexia (Chichester, England)*, *24*(3), 207–219. doi:10.1002/dys.1593 PMID:30019501

Koch, A., Kozhumam, A. S., Seeler, E., Docherty, S. L., & Brandon, D. (2021). Multiple roles of parental caregivers of children with complex life-threatening conditions: A qualitative descriptive analysis. *Journal of Pediatric Nursing*, *61*, 67–74. doi:10.1016/j.pedn.2021.03.017 PMID:33780717

Köller, O., & Baumert, J. (2006). Self-Esteem, Academic Self-Concept, and Achievement: How the Learning Environment Moderates the Dynamics of Self-Concept. *Journal of Personality and Social Psychology*, *90*(2), 334–349. doi:10.1037/0022-3514.90.2.334 PMID:16536654

Kong, A., Thorleifsson, G., Frigge, M. L., Vilhjalmsson, B. J., Young, A. I., Thorgeirsson, T. E., Benonisdottir, S., Oddsson, A., Halldorsson, B. V., Masson, G., Gudbjartsson, D. F., Helgason, A., Bjornsdottir, G., Thorsteinsdottir, U., & Stefansson, K. (2018). The nature of nurture: Effects of parental genotypes. *Science*, *359*(6374), 424–428. doi:10.1126cience.aan6877 PMID:29371463

Konrad, K., Kohls, G., Baumann, S., Bernhard, A., Martinelli, A., Ackermann, K., Smaragdi, A., Gonzalez-Madruga, K., Wells, A., Rogers, J. C., Pauli, R., Clanton, R., Baker, R., Kersten, L., Prätzlich, M., Oldenhof, H., Jansen, L., Kleeven, A., Bigorra, A., & Freitag, C. M. (2022). Sex differences in psychiatric comorbidity and clinical presentation in youths with conduct disorder. *Journal of Child Psychology and Psychiatry, and Allied Disciplines*, *63*(2), 218–228. doi:10.1111/jcpp.13428 PMID:34008879

Kormos, J. (2020). Specific learning difficulties in second language learning and teaching. *Language Teaching*, *53*(2), 129–143. doi:10.1017/S0261444819000442

Kormos, J., & Nijakowska, J. (2017). Inclusive practices in teaching students with dyslexia: Second language teachers' concerns, attitudes and self-efficacy beliefs on a massive open online learning course. *Teaching and Teacher Education*, *68*, 30–41. doi:10.1016/j.tate.2017.08.005

Koster, M., Nakken, H., Pijl, S. J., & Van Houten, E. (2009). Being part of the peer group: A literature study focusing on the social dimension of inclusion in education. *International Journal of Inclusive Education*, *13*(2), 117–140. doi:10.1080/13603110701284680

Kotob, M. M., & Abadi, M. A. (2019). The influence of differentiated instruction on academic achievement of students in mixed ability classrooms. *International Linguistics Research*, *2*(2), 8–28. doi:10.30560/ilr.v2n2p8

Kougias, K., & Efstathopoulos, J. (2020). The operational framework of the Greek educational system as an obstacle to the implementation of sustainable school. *Frontiers in Education*, *5*, 1–11. doi:10.3389/feduc.2020.00142

Koutrouba, K., Antonopoulou, E., Tsitsas, G., & Zenakou, E. (2009). An investigation of Greek teachers' views on parental involvement in education. *School Psychology International*, *30*(3), 311–328. doi:10.1177/0143034309106497

Koutsoklenis, A., & Papadimitriou, V. (2021). Special education provision in Greek mainstream classrooms: Teachers' characteristics and recruitment procedures in parallel support. *International Journal of Inclusive Education*, 1–16. doi:10.1080/13603116.2021.1942565

Krischler, M., Powell, J. J., & Pit-Ten Cate, I. M. (2019). What is meant by inclusion? On the effects of different definitions on attitudes toward inclusive education. *European Journal of Special Needs Education, 34*(5), 632–648. doi:10.1080/08856257.2019.1580837

Krishnan, S., Cler, G. J., Smith, H. J., Willis, H. E., Asaridou, S. S., Healy, M. P., Papp, D., & Watkins, K. E. (2022). Quantitative MRI reveals differences in striatal myelin in children with DLD. *eLife, 11*, 2020–2022. doi:10.7554/eLife.74242 PMID:36164824

Kuiack, A. K., & Archibald, L. M. D. (2019). Developmental Language Disorder: The Childhood Condition We Need to Start Talking About. *Frontiers for Young Minds, 7*, 94. doi:10.3389/frym.2019.00094

Kumar, R., Zusho, A., & Bondie, R. (2018). Weaving cultural relevance and achievement motivation into inclusive classroom cultures. *Educational Psychologist, 53*(2), 78–96. doi:10.1080/00461520.2018.1432361

Kütük, M. Ö., Tufan, A. E., Kılıçaslan, F., Güler, G., Çelik, F., Altıntaş, E., Gökçen, C., Karadağ, M., Yektaş, Ç., Mutluer, T., Kandemir, H., Büber, A., Topal, Z., Acikbas, U., Giray, A., & Kütük, Ö. (2021). High depression symptoms and burnout levels among parents of children with autism spectrum disorders: A multi-center, cross-sectional, case–control study. *Journal of Autism and Developmental Disorders, 51*(11), 1–14. doi:10.100710803-021-04874-4 PMID:33459915

Kuvac Kraljevic, J. (2023). Can prevalence data help us identify developmental language disorder? *The Lancet Regional Health. Western Pacific, 34*(February), 100714. doi:10.1016/j.lanwpc.2023.100714 PMID:37283974

Kwilas, A. R., Donahue, R. N., Tsang, K. Y., & Hodge, J. W. (2015). 乳鼠心肌提取 HHS Public Access. *Cancer Cell, 2*(1), 1–17. doi:10.1111/jora.12170.Gender

Kytö, M. (2016, May 1). *Analyses*. Cambridge Core. https://www.cambridge.org/core/books/abs/cambridge-handbook-of-english-historical-linguistics/analyses/C54DDEFBBE99C711DBAF4DB01EB573B3

Laasonen, M., Smolander, S., Lahti-Nuuttila, P., Leminen, M., Lajunen, H., Heinonen, K., Pesonen, A., Bailey, T. M., Pothos, E. M., Kujala, T., Leppänen, P. H. T., Bartlett, C. W., Geneid, A., Lauronen, L., Service, E., Kunnari, S., & Arkkila, E. (2018). Understanding developmental language disorder - the Helsinki longitudinal SLI study (HelSLI): A study protocol. *BMC Psychology, 6*(1), 24. doi:10.118640359-018-0222-7 PMID:29784061

Lachowicz-Tabaczek, K., & Śniecińska, J. (2011). Self-concept and self-esteem: How the content of the self-concept reveals sources and functions of self-esteem. *Polish Psychological Bulletin, 42*(1), 24–35. doi:10.2478/v10059-011-0005-y

Lafrance, A., Henderson, K. A., & Mayman, S. (2020). *Emotion-focused family therapy: A transdiagnostic model for caregiver-focused interventions*. American Psychological Association. doi:10.1037/0000166-000

Lajunen, H., Laasonen, M., Lahti-Nuuttila, P., Leminen, M., Smolander, S., Kunnari, S., Arkkila, E., & Lauronen, L. (2023). Is epileptiform activity related to developmental language disorder? Findings from the HelSLI study. *Clinical Neurophysiology Practice, 8*, 65–70. doi:10.1016/j.cnp.2023.03.004 PMID:37188277

Lal, R. S., & Kishore, M. T. (2020). Evidence-based Practices for Teaching Students with Learning Disabilities. In Oxford Research Encyclopedia of Education. doi:10.1093/acrefore/9780190264093.013.1222

Lambert, R., & Tan, P. (2017). Conceptualizations of students with and without disabilities as mathematical problem solvers in educational research: A critical review. *Education Sciences, 7*(2), 51. doi:10.3390/educsci7020051

Lamborn, S., Mounts, N., Steinberg, L., & Dornbusch, S. (1991). Patterns of competence and adjustment among adolescents from authoritative, authoritarian, indulgent and neglectful families. *Child Development, 62*(5), 1049–1065. doi:10.2307/1131151 PMID:1756655

Lammertink, I., Boersma, P., Wijnen, F., & Rispens, J. (2017). Statistical learning in specific language impairment: A meta-analysis. *Journal of Speech, Language, and Hearing Research: JSLHR*, *60*(12), 3474–3486. doi:10.1044/2017_JSLHR-L-16-0439 PMID:29149241

Landa, R. J. (2018). Efficacy of early interventions for infants and young children with, and at risk for, autism spectrum disorders. *International Review of Psychiatry (Abingdon, England)*, *30*(1), 25–39. doi:10.1080/09540261.2018.1432574 PMID:29537331

Landreth, G. (2002, 2012). Play therapy: The art of relationship. Brunner-Routledge.

Lange, G., Sheerin, D., Carr, A., Dooley, B., Barton, V., Marshall, D., Mulligan, A., Lawlor, M., Belton, M., & Doyle, M. (2005). Family factors associated with attention deficit hyperactivity disorder and emotional disorders in children. *Journal of Family Therapy*, *27*(1), 76–96. doi:10.1111/j.1467-6427.2005.00300.x

Lara-Díaz, M. F., Mateus-Moreno, A., & Beltrán-Rojas, J. C. (2021). Reading and Oral Language Skills in Children With Developmental Language Disorder: Influence of Socioeconomic, Educational, and Family Variables. *Frontiers in Psychology*, *12*, 718988. doi:10.3389/fpsyg.2021.718988 PMID:34690876

Larson, C., Mathée-Scott, J., Kaplan, D., & Weismer, S. E. (2023). Cognitive processes associated with working memory in children with developmental language disorder. *Journal of Experimental Child Psychology*, *234*, 105709. doi:10.1016/j.jecp.2023.105709 PMID:37285760

Lasky, P., Buckwalter, K. C., Whall, A., Lederman, R., Speer, J., McLane, A., King, J. M., White, M. A., Woods, N. F., & Rees, B. L. (1985). Developing an instrument for the assessment of family dynamics. *Western Journal of Nursing Research*, *7*(1), 40–57. doi:10.1177/0092055X8500700105 PMID:3850686

Law 3699 (2008). Special Education and Education of Persons with Disabilities or Special Educational Needs. [Eidiki Agwgi kai Ekpaidefsi atomwn me anapiria i me eidikes ekpaideftikes anagkes]. *Government Gazette 199*, Vol. A, 2-10-2008. (in Greek)

Law 4368 (2016). Measures to speed up government work and other provisions. [Metra gia tin epitaxynsi tou kyvernitikoy ergou kai alles diatakseis]. *Government Gazette 21,* Vol. A, 21-2-2016. (in Greek)

Law 4547 (2018). Reorganisation of primary and secondary education support structures and other provisions. [Anadiorganwsi twn domwn ypostiriksis tis prwtovathmias kai defterovathmias ekpaidefsis kai alles diatakseis]. *Government Gazette 102*, Vol. A, 12-6-2018. (in Greek)

Law 4823 (2021). School upgrading, teacher empowerment and other provisions. [Anavathmisi tou sxoleiou, endynamwsi twn ekpaideftikwn kai alles diatakseis]. *Government Gazette 136*, Vol. A, 3-8-2021. (in Greek)

Law, J., McBean, K., & Rush, R. (2011). Communication skills in a population of primary school-aged children raised in an area of pronounced social disadvantage. *International Journal of Language & Communication Disorders*, *46*(6), 657–664. doi:10.1111/j.1460-6984.2011.00036.x PMID:22026567

Law, J., Rush, R., Schoon, I., & Parsons, S. (2009). Modeling developmental language difficulties from school entry into adulthood: Literacy, mental health, and employment outcomes. *Journal of Speech, Language, and Hearing Research: JSLHR*, *52*(6), 1401–1416. doi:10.1044/1092-4388(2009/08-0142) PMID:19951922

Lawrence, D. (2006). *Enhancing self-esteem in the classroom.* SAGE Publications Ltd. doi:10.4135/9781446213513

Lazaratou, H., Kalogerakis, Z., Petroutsou, A., Bali, P. P., Konsta, A., Pirlympou, M., & Dikeos, D. (2018). Differences in verbal and performance IQ in conduct disorder: Research findings from a Greek sample. *Journal of Psychiatry and Behavioral Science*, *2*(2), 1–6. doi:10.33582/2637-8027/1010

Lee, C. C. (2001). Culturally responsive school counselors and programs: Addressing the needs of all students. *Professional School Counseling*, *4*(4), 257.

Lee, J. C., Nopoulos, P. C., & Tomblin, J. B. (2020). Procedural and declarative memory brain systems in developmental language disorder (DLD). *Brain and Language*, *205*(February), 104789. doi:10.1016/j.bandl.2020.104789 PMID:32240854

Lee, Y. J., Park, H. J., & Recchia, S. L. (2015). Embracing each other and growing together: Redefining the meaning of caregiving a child with disabilities. *Journal of Child and Family Studies*, *24*(12), 3662–3675. doi:10.100710826-015-0175-x

Leiss, D., Plath, J., & Schwippert, K. (2019). Language and mathematics-key factors influencing the comprehension process in reality-based tasks. *Mathematical Thinking and Learning*, *21*(2), 131–153. doi:10.1080/10986065.2019.1570835

LENA Research Foundation. (2015). *User Guide LENA Pro*. LENA. http://www.lenafoundation.org/

Leonard, L. B. (2014). Specific language impairment across languages. *Child Development Perspectives*, *8*(1), 1–5. doi:10.1111/cdep.12053 PMID:24765105

Leonard, L. B., & Bortolini, U. (1998). Grammatical morphology and the role of weak syllables in the speech of Italian-speaking children with specific language impairment. *Journal of Speech, Language, and Hearing Research: JSLHR*, *41*(6), 1363–1374. doi:10.1044/jslhr.4106.1363 PMID:9859891

Leonard, N. R., Jha, A. P., Casarjian, B., Goolsarran, M., Garcia, C., Cleland, C. M., Gwadz, M. V., & Massey, Z. (2013). Mindfulness training improves attentional task performance in incarcerated youth: A group randomized controlled intervention trial. *Frontiers in Psychology*, *4*, 792. doi:10.3389/fpsyg.2013.00792 PMID:24265621

Levin-Asher, B., Segal, O., & Kishon-Rabin, L. (2023). The validity of LENA technology for assessing the linguistic environment and interactions of infants learning Hebrew and Arabic. *Behavior Research Methods*, *55*(3), 1480–1495. doi:10.375813428-022-01874-9 PMID:35668342

Levy, A. J. (2011). Neurobiology and the Therapeutic Action of Psychoanalytic Play Therapy with Children. *Clinical Social Work Journal*, *39*(1), 50–60. doi:10.100710615-009-0229-x

Levy, D. (1939). Release therapy. *The American Journal of Orthopsychiatry*, *9*(4), 713–736. doi:10.1111/j.1939-0025.1939.tb05641.x

Leyenaar, J. K., Tolpadi, A., Parast, L., Esporas, M., Britto, M. T., Gidengil, C., Wilson, K. M., Bardach, N. S., Basco, W. T. Jr, Brittan, M. S., Williams, D. J., Wood, K. E., Yung, S., Dawley, E., Elliott, A., Manges, K. A., Plemmons, G., Rice, T., Wiener, B., & Mangione-Smith, R. (2022). Collaborative to increase lethal means counseling for caregivers of youth with suicidality. *Pediatrics*, *150*(6), e2021055271. doi:10.1542/peds.2021-055271 PMID:36321386

Libretexts. (2022). Propagation of Error. *Chemistry LibreTexts*. https://chem.libretexts.org/Bookshelves/Analytical_Chemistry/Supplemental_Modules_(Analytical_Chemistry)/Quantifying_Nature/Significant_Digits/Propagation_of_Error

Li, K. C., & Wong, B. T. M. (2021). A literature review of augmented reality, virtual reality, and mixed reality in language learning. *International Journal of Mobile Learning and Organisation*, *15*(2), 164–178. doi:10.1504/IJMLO.2021.114516

Lindner, K. T., Schwab, S., Emara, M., & Avramidis, E. (2023). Do teachers favor the inclusion of all students? A systematic review of primary schoolteachers' attitudes towards inclusive education. *European Journal of Special Needs Education*, 1–22. doi:10.1080/08856257.2023.2172894

Lindsay, G., & Dockrell, J. E. (2012). Longitudinal patterns of behavioral, emotional, and social difficulties and self-concepts in adolescents with a history of specific language impairment. *Language, Speech, and Hearing Services in Schools*, *43*(4), 445–460. doi:10.1044/0161-1461(2012/11-0069) PMID:22826367

Lindsay, G., Ricketts, J., Peacey, L., Dockrell, J., & Charman, T. (2016). Meeting the educational and social needs of children with language impairment or autism spectrum disorder: The parents' perspectives. *International Journal of Language & Communication Disorders*, *51*(5), 495–507. doi:10.1111/1460-6984.12226 PMID:26952185

Lindsay, S., & Edwards, A. (2012). A systematic review of disability awareness interventions for children and youth. *Disability and Rehabilitation*, *35*(8), 623–646. doi:10.3109/09638288.2012.702850 PMID:22831703

Lin, L. Y., Yu, W. H., Lin, W. P., Chen, C. C., & Tu, Y. F. (2022). Agreement Between Caregivers' Concerns of Children's Developmental Problems and Professional Identification in Taiwan. *Frontiers in Pediatrics*, *10*, 804427. doi:10.3389/fped.2022.804427 PMID:35295704

Lipkin, P. H., Macias, M. M., Norwood, K. W. Jr, Brei, T. J., Davidson, L. F., Davis, B. E., Ellerbeck, K. A., Houtrow, A. J., Hyman, S. L., Kuo, D. Z., Noritz, G. H., Yin, L., Murphy, N. A., Levy, S. E., Weitzman, C. C., Bauer, N. S., Childers, D. O. Jr, Levine, J. M., Peralta-Carcelen, A. M., ... Voigt, R. G. (2020). Promoting optimal development: Identifying infants and young children with developmental disorders through developmental surveillance and screening. *Pediatrics*, *145*(1), e20193449. doi:10.1542/peds.2019-3449 PMID:31843861

Lithari, E. (2019). Fractured academic identities: Dyslexia, secondary education, self-esteem and school experiences. *International Journal of Inclusive Education*, *23*(3), 280–296. doi:10.1080/13603116.2018.1433242

Little, W. (2014, November 6). *Chapter 2. Sociological Research*. Pressbooks. https://opentextbc.ca/introductiontosociology/chapter/chapter2-sociological-research/

Livingston, E. M., Siegel, L. S., & Ribary, U. (2018). Developmental dyslexia: Emotional impact and consequences. *Australian Journal of Learning Difficulties*, *23*(2), 107–135. doi:10.1080/19404158.2018.1479975

Lloyd-Esenkaya, V., Russell, A. J., & Clair, M. C. S. (2020). What are the peer interaction strengths and difficulties in children with developmental language disorder? A systematic review. *International Journal of Environmental Research and Public Health*, *17*(9), 3140. doi:10.3390/ijerph17093140 PMID:32365958

Lloyd, J., Muers, J., Patterson, T. G., & Marczak, M. (2019). Self-compassion, coping strategies, and caregiver burden in caregivers of people with dementia. *Clinical Gerontologist*, *42*(1), 47–59. doi:10.1080/07317115.2018.1461162 PMID:29723129

Locke, J., Ishijima, E. H., Kasari, C., & London, N. (2010). Loneliness, friendship quality and the social networks of adolescents with high- functioning autism in an inclusive school setting. *Journal of Research in Special Educational Needs*, *10*(2), 74–81. doi:10.1111/j.1471-3802.2010.01148.x

Long, M., Wood, C., Littleton, K., Passenger, T., & Sheehy, K. (2011). *The Psychology of Education* (2nd ed.). Routledge.

Lozano-Álvarez, M., Rodríguez-Cano, S., Delgado-Benito, V., & Mercado-Val, E. (2023). A Systematic Review of Literature on Emerging Technologies and Specific Learning Difficulties. *Education Sciences*, *13*(3), 298. doi:10.3390/educsci13030298

Lu, F., Guo, Y., Luo, W., Yu, Y., Zhao, Y., Ni, S., Chen, J., Cai, X., Shen, C., Wang, X., He, J., Yang, G., Gao, Q., He, Z., & Zhou, J. (2023). Disrupted functional networks within white-matter served as neural features in adolescent patients with conduct disorder. *Behavioural Brain Research*, *447*(January), 114422. doi:10.1016/j.bbr.2023.114422 PMID:37030546

Lumen Learning. (n.d.). *Language Development | Lifespan Development*. LL. https://courses.lumenlearning.com/wm-lifespandevelopment/chapter/language-development/

Luquet, G. H. (1927; reprint ed. 1967). Le dessin enfantin. Paris: Alcan.

Lynch, S. H., Shuster, G., & Lobo, M. L. (2018). The family caregiver experience–examining the positive and negative aspects of compassion satisfaction and compassion fatigue as caregiving outcomes. *Aging & Mental Health, 22*(11), 1424–1431. doi:10.1080/13607863.2017.1364344 PMID:28812375

Lyon, G. R., Shaywitz, S. E., & Shaywitz, B. A. (2003). A definition of dyslexia. *Annals of Dyslexia, 53*(1), 1–14. doi:10.100711881-003-0001-9 PMID:24234186

M.(2011). Long-term reading and spelling outcome in Italian adolescents with a history of specific language impairment. *Cortex, 47*(8), 955-973.

Maia, L., Simões, F., Rodrigues, P., Santos, B., Monteiro, F., Castanho, L., Magalhães, M., Mendes, P., Augusto, T., & Eusébio, A. (2017). Dyslexia how it survived (or not) to classification alterations all over the years Implications to assessment and intervention. *Cuadernos de Neuropsicología / Panamerican. Journal of Neuropsychology, 11*(3), 151–165. doi:10.7714/CNPS/11.3.209

Malatesha, J. (2009). Do textbooks used in university reading education courses conform to the instructional recommendations of the National Reading Panel? *Journal of Learning Disabilities, 42*(5), 458–463. doi:10.1177/0022219409338739 PMID:19531632

Malik, S., & Janjua, F. (2011). Learning styles and teaching strategies: Creating a balance. *Language in India, 11*, 268–278.

Mamas, C. (2012). Pedagogy, social status and inclusion in Cypriot schools. *International Journal of Inclusive Education, 16*(11), 1223–1239. doi:10.1080/13603116.2011.557446

Marchetti, R., Pinto, S., Spieser, L., Vaugoyeau, M., Cavalli, E., El Ahmadi, A., & Colé, P. (2023). Phoneme Representation and Articulatory Impairment: Insights from Adults with Comorbid Motor Coordination Disorder and Dyslexia. Brain Sciences, 13(2), 210.

Marini, A., Piccolo, B., Taverna, L., Berginc, M., & Ozbič, M. (2020). The complex relation between executive functions and language in preschoolers with developmental language disorders. *International Journal of Environmental Research and Public Health, 17*(5), 1–14. doi:10.3390/ijerph17051772 PMID:32182903

Markic, S., & Childs, P. E. (2016). Language and the teaching and learning of chemistry. *Chemistry Education Research and Practice, 17*(3), 434–438. doi:10.1039/C6RP90006B

Márquez-González, M., Romero-Moreno, R., & Losada, A. (2010). Caregiving issues in a therapeutic context: New insights from the acceptance and commitment therapy approach. In N. A. Pachana, K. Laidlaw, & B. Knight (Eds.), *Casebook of clinical geropsychology: International perspectives on practice* (pp. 33–53). Oxford University Press. doi:10.1093/med/9780199583553.003.0003

Marsh, H. W., & Craven, R. G. (2006). Reciprocal effects of self-concept and performance from a multidimensional perspective: Beyond seductive pleasure and unidimensional perspectives. *Perspectives on Psychological Science, 1*(2), 133–163. . 1745- 6916. 2006. 00010.x doi:10.1111/j

Marsh, A. F., Finger, E. C., Fowler, K. A., Adalio, C. J., Jurkowitz, I. T. N., Schechter, J. C., Pine, D. S., Decety, J., & Blair, R. J. R. (2013). Empathic responsiveness in amygdala and anterior cingulate cortex in youths with psychopathic traits. *Journal of Child Psychology and Psychiatry, and Allied Disciplines, 54*(8), 900–910. doi:10.1111/jcpp.12063 PMID:23488588

Marshall, J., Harding, S., & Roulstone, S. (2017). Language development, delay and intervention—The views of parents from communities that speech and language therapy managers in England consider to be under-served. *International Journal of Language & Communication Disorders, 52*(4), 489–500. doi:10.1111/1460-6984.12288 PMID:27995697

Marsh, H. W. (1990). A Multidimensional, Hierarchical Model of Self-Concept: Theoretical and Empirical Justification. *Educational Psychology Review*, *2*(2), 77–172. doi:10.1007/BF01322177

Marsh, H. W., & Hau, K. T. (2003). Big-fish-little-pond effect on academic self-concept. A cross-cultural (26-country) test of the negative effects of academically selective schools. *The American Psychologist*, *58*(5), 364–376. doi:10.1037/0003-066X.58.5.364 PMID:12971085

Marsh, H. W., & O'Mara, A. (2008). Reciprocal effects between academic self-concept, self-esteem, achievement, and attainment over seven adolescent years: Unidimensional and multidimensional perspectives of self-concept. *Personality and Social Psychology Bulletin*, *34*(4), 542–552. doi:10.1177/0146167207312313 PMID:18340036

Marsico, P., Graser, J. V., & van Hedel, H. J. (2021). Effectiveness of Facilitation, Arrangement of Task and Situation, (Non-) verbal Communication, and Counseling of Caregivers in Children with Neuromotor Disorders: A Systematic Review. *Advances in Neurodevelopmental Disorders*, *5*(4), 1–21. doi:10.100741252-021-00220-y

Martin-Key, N., Brown, T., & Fairchild, G. (2017). Empathic accuracy in male adolescents with conduct disorder and higher versus lower levels of callous-unemotional traits. *Journal of Abnormal Child Psychology*, *45*(7), 1385–1397. doi:10.100710802-016-0243-8 PMID:28032270

Mash, E. J., & Johnston, C. (1983). Parental perceptions of child behaviour problems, parenting self-esteem, and mothers' reported stress in younger and older hyperactive and normal children. *Journal of Consulting and Clinical Psychology*, *51*(1), 86–99. doi:10.1037/0022-006X.51.1.86 PMID:6826870

Mason, J. (2003). *Conducting qualitative research.* Hellenic Literature.

Masten, A. S. (2018). Resilience theory and research on children and families: Past, present, and promise. *Journal of Family Theory & Review*, *10*(1), 12–31. doi:10.1111/jftr.12255

Mastropieri, M. A., & Scruggs, T. E. (2014). *The inclusive classroom: Strategies for effective differentiated instruction* (5th ed.). Pearson.

Maurer, B. T., & Taylor, L. C. (2020). The Effect of Digital Media on Children in Their Formative Years. *Journal of the American Academy of Physician Associates*, *33*, 46–51. PMID:32345948

Mazurek, M. O., Shattuck, P. T., Wagner, M., & Cooper, B. P. (2012). Prevalence and correlates of screen-based media use among youths with autism spectrum disorders. *Journal of Autism and Developmental Disorders*, *42*(8), 1757–1767. doi:10.100710803-011-1413-8 PMID:22160370

Mazurek, M. O., & Wenstrup, C. (2013). Television, video game and social media use among children with ASD and typically developing siblings. *Journal of Autism and Developmental Disorders*, *43*(6), 1258–1271. doi:10.100710803-012-1659-9 PMID:23001767

McAleavy, T., Hall-Chen, A., Horrocks, S., & Riggall, A. (2018). Technology-Supported Professional Development for Teachers: Lessons from Developing Countries. Education Development Trust. Highbridge House. United Kingdom.

McAllister, S., Lincoln, M., Ferguson, A., & McAllister, L. (2011). A systematic program of research regarding the assessment of speech-language pathology competencies. *International Journal of Speech-Language Pathology*, *13*(6), 469–479. doi:10.3109/17549507.2011.580782 PMID:21846166

McCabe, P. C. (2005). Social and behavioral correlates of preschoolers with Specific Language Impairment. *Psychology in the Schools*, *42*(4), 373–387. doi:10.1002/pits.20064

McCoy, S., & Banks, J. (2012). Simply academic? Why children with special educational needs don't like school. *European Journal of Special Needs Education*, *27*(1), 81–97. doi:10.1080/08856257.2011.640487

McGarry, L. M., & Russo, F. A. (2011). Mirroring in Dance/Movement Therapy: Potential mechanisms behind empathyenhancement. *The Arts in Psychotherapy*, *38*(3), 178–184. doi:10.1016/j.aip.2011.04.005

McGillion, M., Pine, J. M., Herbert, J. S., & Matthews, D. (2017). A randomised controlled trial to test the effect of promoting caregiver contingent talk on language development in infants from diverse socioeconomic status backgrounds. *Journal of Child Psychology and Psychiatry, and Allied Disciplines*, *58*(10), 1122–1131. doi:10.1111/jcpp.12725 PMID:28429816

McGregor, K. K. (2020). How we fail children with developmental language disorder. *Language, Speech, and Hearing Services in Schools*, *51*(4), 981–992. doi:10.1044/2020_LSHSS-20-00003 PMID:32755505

McGregor, K. K., Goffman, L., Van Horne, A. O., Hogan, T. P., & Finestack, L. H. (2020). Developmental language disorder: Applications for advocacy, research, and clinical service. *Perspectives of the ASHA Special Interest Groups*, *5*(1), 38–46. doi:10.1044/2019_PERSP-19-00083

McIntyre, R., & Hennessy, E. (2012). 'He's just enthusiastic. Is that such a bad thing?' Experiences of parents of children with attention deficit hyperactivity disorder. *Emotional & Behavioural Difficulties*, *17*(1), 65–82. doi:10.1080/13632752.2012.652428

McKee, T. E., Harvey, E., Danforth, J. S., Ulaszek, W. R., & Friedman, J. L. (2004). The Relation Between Parental Coping Styles and Parent-Child Interactions Before and After Treatment for Children With ADHD and Oppositional Behavior. *Journal of Clinical Child and Adolescent Psychology*, *33*(1), 158–168. doi:10.1207/S15374424JCCP3301_15 PMID:15028550

McLaughlin, D. P., & Harrison, C. A. (2006). Parenting practices of mothers of children with ADHD: The role of maternal and child factors. *Child and Adolescent Mental Health*, *11*(2), 82–88. doi:10.1111/j.1475-3588.2005.00382.x PMID:32811096

MDAhellas. (2023). *Leukodystrophies*. MD Ahellas. https://mdahellas.gr/leukodystrophies/?lang=en

Measuring What Counts. (1993). *National Academies Press eBooks*., doi:10.17226/2235

Medina-García, M., Doña-Toledo, L., & Higueras-Rodríguez, L. (2020). Equal opportunities in an inclusive and sustainable education system: An explanatory model. *Sustainability (Basel)*, *12*(11), 4626. doi:10.3390u12114626

Menassa, B. M. (2009). 2018). Theoretical Orientation and Play Therapy: Examining Therapist Role, Session Structure, and Therapeutic Objectives. *Journal of Professional Counseling, Practice, Theory, & Research*, *37*(1), 13–26. doi:10.1080/15566382.2009.12033852

Merkaj, V., Kika, M., & Simaku, A. (2013). Symptoms of stress, depression and anxiety between parents of autistic children and parents of tipically developing children. *Academic Journal of Interdisciplinary Studies*, *2*(2), 345–352. doi:10.5901/ajis.2013.v2n2p345

Messiou, K. (2017). Research in the field of inclusive education: Time for a rethink? *International Journal of Inclusive Education*, *21*(2), 146–159. doi:10.1080/13603116.2016.1223184

Messiou, K., & Ainscow, M. (2020). Inclusive Inquiry: Student–teacher dialogue as a means of promoting inclusion in schools. *British Educational Research Journal*, *46*(3), 670–687. doi:10.1002/berj.3602

Metcalf, L. (2021). *Counseling toward solutions: A practical, solution-focused program for working with students, teachers, and parents*. Routledge. doi:10.4324/9781003122128

Meuser, S., Piskur, B., Hennissen, P., & Dolmans, D. (2023). Targeting the school environment to enable participation: A scoping review. *Scandinavian Journal of Occupational Therapy*, *30*(3), 298–310. doi:10.1080/11038128.2022.2124190 PMID:36170879

Michielsen, P. J. S., Habra, M. M. J., Endendijk, J. J., Bouter, D. C., Grootendorst-van Mil, N. H., Hoogendijk, W. J. G., & Roza, S. J. (2022). Callous-unemotional traits and anxiety in adolescents: A latent profile analysis to identify different types of antisocial behavior in a high-risk community sample. *Child and Adolescent Psychiatry and Mental Health*, *16*(1), 1–12. doi:10.118613034-022-00493-8 PMID:35854316

Miguel, F. S. (2021). Assistive technology integration for children with specific learning disabilities: A systematic literature review perspective from Mexico. *African Journal of Emerging Issues*, *3*(5), 40–49.

Ministerial Decision 134960/D3. Unified regulation on the operation of the School Educational Support Networks (S.D.E.Y.) and the Interdisciplinary Support Committees (E.D.Y.) of general and vocational education school units and definition of the specific duties of their members. Government Gazette 5009, Vol. B, 27-10-2021. (in Greek)

Ministerial Decision 27922/C6. Tasks of integration teachers. No 3. Determination of the specific duties and responsibilities (a) The teaching staff, who serve as teachers working in special education units (SEU) primary and secondary education (special schools, integration departments), and in primary and secondary special education programmes (parallel support) and (b) special education staff and special auxiliary staff serving in school establishments of special education, primary and secondary schools. Government Gazette 449, Vol. B, 3-4-2007. (in Greek)

Ministry of Education and Religious Affairs 46978/ CD4 (2023). Call for expressions of interest for the submission of applications for participation in the process of evaluation and inclusion of textbooks in the Register of Textbooks and the Digital Library of Textbooks, 25-04-2023. (in Greek)

Miodrag, N., & Hodapp, R. M. (2010). Chronic stress and health among parents of children with intellectual and developmental disabilities. *Current Opinion in Psychiatry*, *23*(5), 407–411. doi:10.1097/YCO.0b013e32833a8796 PMID:20592593

Mitchell, D., & Sutherland, D. (2020). *What really works in special and inclusive education: Using evidence-based teaching strategies*. Routledge. doi:10.4324/9780429401923

Moffitt, T. E.-l. –5. (2006). Life-course-persistent versus adolescence-limited antisocial behavior. In D. Cicchetti & D. J. Cohen (Eds.), Developmental psychopathology, Vol. 3: Risk, disorder, and adaptation (pp. 570–598). John Wiley & Sons.

Mohammadi, M. R., Salmanian, M., & Keshavarzi, Z. (2021). The global prevalence of conduct disorder: A systematic review and meta-analysis. *Iranian Journal of Psychiatry*, *16*(2), 205–225. doi:10.18502/ijps.v16i2.5822 PMID:34221047

Mok, P. L. H., Pickles, A., Durkin, K., & Conti-Ramsden, G. (2014). Longitudinal trajectories of peer relations in children with specific language impairment. *Journal of Child Psychology and Psychiatry, and Allied Disciplines*, *55*(5), 516–527. doi:10.1111/jcpp.12190 PMID:24410167

Molina, M.F., & Musich, F.M. (2016). Perception of parenting style by children with ADHD and its relation with inattention, hyperactivity/impulsivity and externalizing symptoms. *Ni*(5), 1656-1671.

Monn, E. R. (2015). *Social Communication Across Language Environments in Nonverbal Children with ASD from English and non-English Speaking Families.* [Doctoral dissertation, University of Minnesota]. ProQuest Dissertations and Theses Global.

Morocco World News. (n.d.). *French Influence on the English Language Under Norman Occupation*. MWN. https://www.moroccoworldnews.com/. https://www.moroccoworldnews.com/2022/07/350430/french-influence-on-the-english-language-under-norman-occupation

Morris, A. S., Silk, J. S., Steinberg, L., Myers, S. S., & Robinson, L. R. (2007). The role of the family context in the development of emotion regulation. *Social Development, 16*(2), 361–388. doi:10.1111/j.1467-9507.2007.00389.x PMID:19756175

Morton, J. (2004). *Understanding developmental disorders: A causal modelling approach.* Blackwell Publishing. doi:10.1002/9780470773307

Mountford, H. S., Braden, R. O., Newbury, D. F., & Morgan, A. T. (2022). The Genetic and Molecular Basis of Developmental Language Disorder: A Review. *Children (Basel, Switzerland), 9*(5), 586. doi:10.3390/children9050586 PMID:35626763

Mouzaki, A., & Protopapas, A. (2010) (Eds.). Orthography, learning and disorders. Gutenberg. [in Greek]

Mozeiko, J., Le, K., Coelho, C., Krueger, F., & Grafman, J. (2011). The relationship of story grammar and executive function following TBI. *Aphasiology, 25*(6–7), 826–835. doi:10.1080/02687038.2010.543983

Muarifah, A., Widyastuti, D. A., & Fajarwati, I. (2019). The effect of social support on single mothers' subjective well-being and its implication for counseling. *Jurnal Kajian Bimbingan dan Konseling, 4*(4), 143-149. doi:10.17977/um001v4i42019p143

Mugambi, M. M. (2017). Approaches to inclusive education and implications for curriculum theory and practice. *International Journal of Humanities Social Sciences and Education, 10*(4), 92–106.

Mulligan, A., Anney, R., Butler, L., O'Regan, M., Richardson, T., Tulewicz, E. M., Fitzgerald, M., & Gill, M. (2011). Home environment: Association with hyperactivity/impulsivity in children with ADHD and their non-ADHD siblings. *Child: Care, Health and Development, 39*(2), 202–212. doi:10.1111/j.1365-2214.2011.01345.x PMID:22168816

Mundy, P., Delgado, C., Block, J., Venezia, M., Hogan, A., & Seibert, J. (2003/2023). *A manual for the Abridged Early Social Communication Scales (ESCS).* Coral Gables, FL: University of Miami. http://www.ucdmc.ucdavis.edu/mind-institute/ourteam/faculty_staff/ escs.pdf

Muñoz, L. C., Frick, P. J., Kimonis, E. R., & Aucoin, K. J. (2008). Verbal ability and delinquency: Testing the moderating role of psychopathic traits. *Journal of Child Psychology and Psychiatry, and Allied Disciplines, 49*(4), 414–421. doi:10.1111/j.1469-7610.2007.01847.x PMID:18081757

Müürsepp, I., Aibast, H., Gapeyeva, H., & Pääsuke, M. (2014). Sensorimotor function in preschool-aged children with expressive language disorder. *Research in Developmental Disabilities, 35*(6), 1237–1243. doi:10.1016/j.ridd.2014.03.007 PMID:24685939

Nalavany, B. A., Logan, J. M., & Carawan, L. W. (2018). The relationship between emotional experience with dyslexia and work self-efficacy among adults with dyslexia. *Dyslexia (Chichester, England), 24*(1), 17–32. doi:10.1002/dys.1575 PMID:29230916

Navarro-Haro, M. V., Modrego-Alarcón, M., Hoffman, H. G., Lopez-Montoyo, A., Navarro-Gil, M., Montero-Marin, J., García-Palacios, A., Borao, L., & García-Campayo, J. (2019). Evaluation of a mindfulness-based intervention with and without virtual reality dialectical behavior therapy mindfulness skills training for the treatment of generalized anxiety disorder in primary care: A pilot study. [CrossRef]. *Frontiers in Psychology, 10*, 55. doi:10.3389/fpsyg.2019.00055 PMID:30745888

Neff, K. (2003). Self-compassion: An alternative conceptualization of a healthy attitude toward oneself. *Self and Identity, 2*(2), 85–101. doi:10.1080/15298860309032

Neiss, M. B., Stevenson, J., Sedikides, C., Kumashiro, M., Finkel, E. J., & Rusbult, C. E. (2005). Executive self, self-esteem, and negative affectivity: Relations at the phenotypic and genotypic level. *Journal of Personality and Social Psychology*, *89*(4), 593–606. doi:10.1037/0022-3514.89.4.593 PMID:16287421

Nevill, T., Savage, G. C., & Forsey, M. (2023). It'sa diagnosis for the rich: Disability, advocacy and the micro-practices of social reproduction. *British Journal of Sociology of Education*, *44*(2), 239–258. doi:10.1080/01425692.2022.2145931

Newcombe, F. R. I. E. D. A., & Marshall, J. C. (2017). Reading and writing by letter sounds. In *Surface dyslexia* (pp. 35–52). Routledge. doi:10.4324/9781315108346-4

Newman, J., Gozu, H., Guan, S., Lee, J. E., Li, X., & Sasaki, Y. (2015). Relationship between maternal parenting style and high school achievement and self-esteem in China, Turkey and U.S.A. *Journal of Comparative Family Studies*, *46*(2), 265–288. https://www.jstor.org/stable/43613115. doi:10.3138/jcfs.46.2.265

Nicolae, M. (2013). Teachers Beliefs as the Differentiated Instruction Starting Point: Research Basis. *Procedia: Social and Behavioral Sciences*, *128*, 426–431. doi:10.1016/j.sbspro.2014.03.182

Nicolson, R. I., & Fawcett, A. J. (1990). Automaticity: A new framework for dyslexia research? *Cognition*, *35*(2), 159–182. doi:10.1016/0010-0277(90)90013-A PMID:2354611

Nicolson, R. I., & Fawcett, A. J. (1994). Comparison of deficits in cognitive and motor skills among children with dyslexia. *Annals of Dyslexia*, *44*(1), 147–164. doi:10.1007/BF02648159 PMID:24234050

Niemec, C. P., & Ryan, R. M. (2009). Autonomy, competence and relatedness in the classroom. Applying self-determination theory to educational practice. *Theory and Research in Education*, *7*(2), 133–144. doi:10.1177/1477878509104318

Ni, H. C., & Gau, S. S. F. (2015). Co-occurrence of attention-deficit hyperactivity disorder symptoms with other psychopathology in young adults: Parenting style as a moderator. *Comprehensive Psychiatry*, *57*, 85–96. doi:10.1016/j.comppsych.2014.11.002 PMID:25465651

Nilholm, C. (2021). Research about inclusive education in 2020–How can we improve our theories in order to change practice? *European Journal of Special Needs Education*, *36*(3), 358–370. doi:10.1080/08856257.2020.1754547

Nilsen, E. S., & Bacso, S. A. (2017). Cognitive and behavioural predictors of adolescents' communicative perspective-taking and social relationships. *Journal of Adolescence*, *56*(1), 52–63. doi:10.1016/j.adolescence.2017.01.004 PMID:28157666

Nilsson, K., & Jensen de López, K. (2016).Theory of mind in children with Specific Language Impairment: A systematic review and meta-analysis. *Child Development, 87* (1), 143 153, doi:10.1111/cdev.12462

Nitin, R., Shaw, D. M., Rocha, D. B., Walters, C. E. Jr, Chabris, C. F., Camarata, S. M., Gordon, R. L., & Below, J. E. (2022). Association of Developmental Language Disorder with Comorbid Developmental Conditions Using Algorithmic Phenotyping. *JAMA Network Open*, *5*(12), E2248060. doi:10.1001/jamanetworkopen.2022.48060 PMID:36580336

Noble, K. G. (2021). Early childhood: The opportunity to untap human potential. *The scale-up effect in early childhood and public policy: Why interventions lose impact at scale and what we can do about it*, 25-40.

Norbury, C. F., Gooch, D., Wray, C., Baird, G., Charman, T., Simonoff, E., Vamvakas, G., & Pickles, A. (2016). The impact of nonverbal ability on prevalence and clinical presentation of language disorder: Evidence from a population study. *Journal of Child Psychology and Psychiatry, and Allied Disciplines*, *57*(11), 1247–1257. doi:10.1111/jcpp.12573 PMID:27184709

NORD-National Organization for Rare Disorders. (2023). *Leukoencephalopathy with Brain Stem and Spinal Cord Involvement and Lactate Elevation.* NORD. https://rarediseases.org/rare-diseases/leukoencephalopathy-brain-stem-spinal-cord-involvement-lactate-elevation/

Nordquist, R. (2020). Understanding the Use of Language Through Discourse Analysis. *ThoughtCo*. https://www.thoughtco.com/discourse-analysis-or-da-1690462

Nouzari, R., Najafi, S. S., & Momennasab, M. (2019). Post-traumatic growth among family caregivers of cancer patients and its association with social support and hope. *International Journal of Community Based Nursing and Midwifery*, *7*(4), 319–328. doi:10.30476/IJCBNM.2019.73959.0 PMID:31641681

Nteropoulou-Nterou, E., & Slee, R. (2019). A critical consideration of the changing conditions of schooling for students with disabilities in Greece and the fragility of international in local contexts. *International Journal of Inclusive Education, 23*(7-8), 891–907. doi:10.1080/13603116.2019.1623331

Nteropoulou-Nterou, E., Zoniou-Sideri, A., Lampropoulou, N., & Tsermidou, L. (2017). Views and Perceptions of Senior Early Childhood Education Students Regarding Inclusive Education and Disability. *Mediterranean Journal of Social & Behavioral Research, 1*(1), 12–21.

Nudel, R., Christensen, R. V., Kalnak, N., Schwinn, M., Banasik, K., Dinh, K. M., Consortium, D. G., Erikstrup, C., Pedersen, O. B., Burgdorf, K. S., Ullum, H., Ostrowski, S. R., Hansen, T. F., & Werge, T. (2023). Developmental language disorder – a comprehensive study of more than 46,000 individuals. *Psychiatry Research, 323*(October 2022), 115171. doi:10.1016/j.psychres.2023.115171

Nygreen, K. (2019). Neoliberal reform and family engagement in schools: An intersectional gender analysis. *Policy Futures in Education, 17*(2), 205–221. doi:10.1177/1478210318788416

Non profit organization for research into LBSL. (2023). *About LBSL.* A cure for Ellie. http://acureforellie.org/

O'Mara, A. J., Marsh, H. W., Craven, R. G., & Debus, R. L. (2006). Do Self-Concept Interventions Make a Difference? A Synergistic Blend of Construct Validation and Meta-Analysis. *Educational Psychologist, 41*(3), 181–206. doi:10.120715326985ep4103_4

Oden, K. A., Miner-Holden, J., & Balkin, R. S. (2009). Required counseling for mental health professional trainees: Its perceived effect on self-awareness and other potential benefits. *Journal of Mental Health (Abingdon, England), 18*(5), 441–448. doi:10.3109/09638230902968217

Ogletree, B. T., Brady, N., Bruce, S., Dean, E., Romski, M., Sylvester, L., & Westling, D. (2017). Mary's case: An illustration of interprofessional collaborative practice for a child with severe disabilities. *American Journal of Speech-Language Pathology, 26*(2), 217–226. doi:10.1044/2017_AJSLP-15-0065 PMID:28514476

Ohene-Djan, J., & Begum, R. (2008). Multisensory games for dyslexic children. In *2008 Eighth IEEE International Conference on Advanced Learning Technologies* (pp. 1040-1041). IEEE. 10.1109/ICALT.2008.98

Oliver, M., Schofield, G. M., & Kolt, G. S. (2007). Physical activity in preschoolers. *Sports Medicine (Auckland, N.Z.), 37*(12), 1045–1070. doi:10.2165/00007256-200737120-00004 PMID:18027993

Olivier, M. A., Gomes, A. M., & Greyling, A. J. (2009). Attention Deficit Hyperactivity Disorder (ADHD)—Dilemmas and Solutions. *Journal of Psychology in Africa, 19*(2), 237–241. doi:10.1080/14330237.2009.10820285

Oller, K. (2000). *The Emergence of the Speech Capacity*. Lawrence Erlbaum Associates. doi:10.4324/9781410602565

Ostafin, B. D., & Proulx, T. (2020). Meaning in life and resilience to stressors. *Anxiety, Stress, and Coping, 33*(6), 603–622. doi:10.1080/10615806.2020.1800655 PMID:32755239

Otaiba, A. S., Rouse, A. G., & Baker, K. (2018). Elementary grade intervention approaches to treat specific learning disabilities, including dyslexia. *Language, Speech, and Hearing Services in Schools, 49*(4), 829–842. doi:10.1044/2018_LSHSS-DYSLC-18-0022 PMID:30458544

Ottosson, S., Lorentzon, U. S., Kadesjo, B., Gillberg, C., & Miniscalco, C. (2022). Neurodevelopmental problems and quality of life in 6-year-olds with a history of developmental language disorder. *Acta Paediatrica (Oslo, Norway)*, *111*(1), 115–122. doi:10.1111/apa.16104 PMID:34516681

Pahlavanzadeh, S., Mousavi, S., & Maghsoudi, J. (2018). Exploring the needs of family caregivers of children with attention deficit hyperactivity disorder: A qualitative study. *Iranian Journal of Nursing and Midwifery Research*, *23*, 149–154. PMID:29628964

Palacio, G. C., Krikorian, A., Gómez-Romero, M. J., & Limonero, J. T. (2020). Resilience in caregivers: A systematic review. *The American Journal of Hospice & Palliative Care*, *37*(8), 648–658. doi:10.1177/1049909119893977 PMID:31830813

Palikara, O., Lindsay, G., Cullen, M. A., & Dockrell, J. (2007). Working together?:the practice of educational psychologists and speech and language therapists with children with specific speech and language difficulties. *Educational and Child Psychology*, *24*(4), 77–88. doi:10.53841/bpsecp.2007.24.4.77

Palikara, O., & Ralli, A. M. (2013). Specific language impairment in childhood and adolescence: Educational and clinical implications. *Psychology (Irvine, Calif.)*, *20*, 243–266.

Paradice, R. (2001). An Investigation into the Social Construction of Dyslexia. *Educational Psychology in Practice*, *17*(3), 213–225. doi:10.1080/02667360120072747

Pardini, D. A., & Fite, P. J. (2010). Symptoms of conduct disorder, oppositional defiant disorder, attention-deficit/hyperactivity disorder, and callous-unemotional traits as unique predictors of psychosocial maladjustment in boys: Advancing an evidence base for DSM-V. *Journal of the American Academy of Child and Adolescent Psychiatry*, *49*(11), 1134–1144. doi:10.1097/00004583-201011000-00007 PMID:20970701

Park, S., & Holloway, S. D. (2017). The effects of school-based parental involvement on academic achievement at the child and elementary school level: A longitudinal study. *The Journal of Educational Research*, *110*(1), 1–16. doi:10.1080/00220671.2015.1016600

Paseka, A., & Schwab, S. (2020). Parents' attitudes towards inclusive education and their perceptions of inclusive teaching practices and resources. *European Journal of Special Needs Education*, *35*(2), 254–272. doi:10.1080/08856257.2019.1665232

Patra, S., Arun, P., & Chavan, B. S. (2015). Impact of psychoeducation intervention module on parents of children with autism spectrum disorders: A preliminary study. *Journal of Neurosciences in Rural Practice*, *6*(04), 529–535. doi:10.4103/0976-3147.165422 PMID:26752898

Paul, R., Norbury, C. F., & Gosse, C. (2018). Models of child language disorders. In Language Disorders from Infancy Through Adolescence (5th ed.). doi:10.1016/B978-0-323-44234-3.00010-5

Paulus, M., Licata, M., Gniewosz, B., & Sodian, B. (2018). The impact of mother-child interaction quality and cognitive abilities on children's self-concept and self-esteem. *Cognitive Development*, *48*, 42–51. doi:10.1016/j.cogdev.2018.07.001

Pavlidis, G. Th., & Giannouli, V. (2003). Spelling errors accurately differentiate USA-English speakers from Greek dyslexics: Implications for causality and treatment. In R. M. Joshi, C. K. Leong, & L. J. Kaczmarek (Eds.), *Literacy acquisition: The role of phonology, morphology and orthography*. IOS Press.

Pavlidou, E. V., Louise Kelly, M., & Williams, J. M. (2010). Do children with developmental dyslexia have impairments in implicit learning? *Dyslexia (Chichester, England)*, *16*(2), 143–161. doi:10.1002/dys.400 PMID:20440744

Pavlidou, E. V., & Williams, J. M. (2014). Implicit learning and reading: Insights from typical children and children with developmental dyslexia using the artificial grammar learning (AGL) paradigm. *Research in Developmental Disabilities, 35*(7), 1457–1472. doi:10.1016/j.ridd.2014.03.040 PMID:24751907

Peasgood, T., Bhardwaj, A., Biggs, K., Brazier, J. E., Coghill, D., Cooper, C. L., & Sonuga-Barke, E. J. (2016). The impact of ADHD on the health and well-being of ADHD children and their siblings. *European Child & Adolescent Psychiatry, 25*(11), 1217–1231. doi:10.100700787-016-0841-6 PMID:27037707

Pegrum, M., Hockly, N., & Dudeney, G. (2022). *Digital literacies.* Routledge. doi:10.4324/9781003262541

Pelz, P. B. (n.d.-a). *Chapter 7 Scale Reliability and Validity | Research Methods for the Social Sciences.* LL. https://courses.lumenlearning.com/suny-hccc-research-methods/chapter/chapter-7-scale-reliability-and-validity/

Pelz, P. B. (n.d.-b). *Chapter 12 Interpretive Research | Research Methods for the Social Sciences.* LL. https://courses.lumenlearning.com/suny-hccc-research-methods/chapter/chapter-12-interpretive-research/

Peng, H., Ma, S., & Spector, J. M. (2019). Personalized adaptive learning: An emerging pedagogical approach enabled by a smart learning environment. *Smart Learning Environments, 6*(1), 1–14. doi:10.118640561-019-0089-y

Peng, P., Wang, C., & Namkung, J. (2018). Understanding the cognition related to mathematics difficulties: A meta-analysis on the cognitive deficit profiles and the bottleneck theory. *Review of Educational Research, 88*(3), 434–476. doi:10.3102/0034654317753350

Pennington, B. F., & Bishop, D. V. (2009). Relations among speech, language, and reading disorders. *Annual Review of Psychology, 60*(1), 283–306. doi:10.1146/annurev.psych.60.110707.163548 PMID:18652545

Peñuelas-Calvo, I., Palomar-Ciria, N., Porras-Segovia, A., Miguélez-Fernández, C., Baltasar-Tello, I., Perez-Colmenero, S., & Baca-García, E. (2021). Impact of ADHD symptoms on family functioning, family burden and parents' quality of life in a hospital area in Spain. *European Journal of Psychiatry, 35*(3), 166–172. doi:10.1016/j.ejpsy.2020.10.003

Peräkylä, A. (2004). Conversation analysis. *Qualitative research practice,* 165-179.

Petersen, I. T., & LeBeau, B. (2021). Language ability in the development of externalizing behavior problems in childhood. *Journal of Educational Psychology, 113*(1), 68–85. doi:10.1037/edu0000461

Peters, K., & Jackson, D. (2009). Mothers' experiences of parenting a child with attention deficit hyperactivity disorder. *Journal of Advanced Nursing, 65*(1), 62–71. doi:10.1111/j.1365-2648.2008.04853.x PMID:19120583

Peterson, R. L., & Pennington, B. F. (2012). Developmental dyslexia. *Lancet, 379*(9830), 1997–2007. doi:10.1016/S0140-6736(12)60198-6 PMID:22513218

Peterson, R. L., & Pennington, B. F. (2015). Developmental dyslexia. *Annual Review of Clinical Psychology, 11*(1), 283–307. doi:10.1146/annurev-clinpsy-032814-112842 PMID:25594880

Petry, K. (2018). The relationship between class attitudes towards peers with a disability and peer acceptance, friendships and peer interactions of students with a disability in regular secondary schools. *European Journal of Special Needs Education, 33*(2), 254–268. doi:10.1080/08856257.2018.1424782

Pfenninger, S. (2014). Taking L3 learning by the horns: Benefits of computer-mediated intervention for dyslexic school children. *Innovation in Language Learning and Teaching.*

Pham, A. V., & Riviere, A. (2015). Specific learning disorders and ADHD: Current issues in diagnosis across clinical and educational settings. *Current Psychiatry Reports, 17*(6), 1–7. doi:10.100711920-015-0584-y PMID:25894357

Piaget, J. (1950). Épistémologie génétique et méthodologie dialectique II. *Dialectica*, *4*(4), 287–295. doi:10.1111/j.1746-8361.1950.tb01029.x

Piaget, J. (1964). Cognitive development in children. *Journal of Research in Science Teaching*, *2*(2), 176–186. doi:10.1002/tea.3660020306

Piot, L., Havron, N., & Cristia, A. (2022). Socioeconomic status correlates with measures of Language Environment Analysis (LENA) system: A meta-analysis. *Journal of Child Language*, *49*(5), 1037–1051. doi:10.1017/S0305000921000441 PMID:34180383

Pitt, S., & Soni, A. (2017). Students' experiences of academic success with dyslexia: A call for alternative intervention. *Support for Learning*, *32*(4), 387–405. doi:10.1111/1467-9604.12182

Planas, N., Morgan, C., & Schütte, M. (2018). Mathematics education and language: Lessons and directions from two decades of research. *Developing research in mathematics education. Twenty years of communication, cooperation and collaboration in Europe*, 196-210.

Podolski, C. L., & Nigg, J. T. (2001). Parent stress and coping in relation to child ADHD severity and associated child disruptive behavior problems. *Journal of Clinical Child Psychology*, *30*(4), 503–513. doi:10.1207/S15374424JCCP3004_07 PMID:11708238

Pokrivčáková, S. (2015). *Teaching Foreign Languages to Learners with Special Educational Needs: e-textbook for foreign language teachers*. Constantine the Philosopher University., doi:10.17846/SEN.2015.7-28

Polanczyk, G., de Lima, M. S., Horta, B. L., Biederman, J., & Rohde, L. A. (2007). The worldwide prevalence of ADHD: A systematic review and metaregression analysis. *The American Journal of Psychiatry*, *164*(6), 942–948. doi:10.1176/ajp.2007.164.6.942 PMID:17541055

Polychroni, F., Koukoura, K., & Anagnostou, I. (2006). Academic self-concept, reading attitudes and approaches to learning of children with dyslexia: Do they differ from their peers? *European Journal of Special Needs Education*, *21*(4), 415–430. doi:10.1080/08856250600956311

Pomerantz, E. M., Moorman, E. A., & Litwack, S. D. (2007). The how, whom, and why of parents' involvement in children's academic lives: More Is not always better. *Review of Educational Research*, *77*(3), 373–410. doi:10.3102/003465430305567

Portnoy, J., Cui, N., Raine, A., Frazier, A., Rudo-Hutt, A. S., & Liu, J. (2020). Autonomic nervous system activity and callous-unemotional traits in physically maltreated youth. *Child Abuse and Neglect, 101*(November 2019), 104308. doi:10.1016/j.chiabu.2019.104308

Pretorius, J. W. M. (Ed.). (1998). *Sociopedagogics 2000*. Van Schaik Publishers.

Principles of Child Development and Learning and Implications That. (n.d.). NAEYC. https://www.naeyc.org/resources/position-statements/dap/principles

Protopapas, A., Fakou, A., Drakopoulou, S., Skaloumbakas, C., & Mouzaki, A. (2013). What do spelling errors tell us? Classification and analysis of errors made by Greek schoolchildren with and without dyslexia. *Reading and Writing*, *26*(5), 615–646. doi:10.100711145-012-9378-3

Puglisi, M. L., Hulme, C., Hamilton, L. G., & Snowling, M. J. (2017). The home literacy environment is a correlate, but perhaps not a cause, of variations in children's language and literacy development. *Scientific Studies of Reading*, *21*(6), 498–514. doi:10.1080/10888438.2017.1346660 PMID:29930486

Quinn, C., Clare, L., & Woods, R. T. (2012). What predicts whether caregivers of people with dementia find meaning in their role? *International Journal of Geriatric Psychiatry*, *27*(11), 1195–1202. doi:10.1002/gps.3773 PMID:22334416

Qvortrup, A., & Qvortrup, L. (2018). Inclusion: Dimensions of inclusion in education. *International Journal of Inclusive Education, 22*(7), 803–817. doi:10.1080/13603116.2017.1412506

Radecki, L., Sand-Loud, N., O'Connor, K. G., Sharp, S., & Olson, L. M. (2011, July 01). Trends in the use of standardized tools for developmental screening in early childhood: 2002–2009. *Pediatrics, 128*(1), 14–19. doi:10.1542/peds.2010-2180 PMID:21708798

Rahul, D. R., & Ponniah, J. (2021). Educational Insights into Dyslexia. *Rupkatha Journal on Interdisciplinary Studies in Humanities, 13*(4), 1–12. doi:10.21659/rupkatha.v13n4.35

Ralli, A. M., Chrysochoou, E., Roussos, P., Diakogiorgi, K., Dimitropoulou, P., & Filippatou, D. (2021). Executive Function, Working Memory, and Verbal Fluency in Relation to Non-Verbal Intelligence in Greek-Speaking School-Age Children with Developmental Language Disorder. *Brain Sciences, 11*(5), 604. doi:10.3390/brainsci11050604 PMID:34066872

Ralli, A. M., Kalliontzi, E., & Kazali, E. (2022). Teachers views of children with Developmental Language Disorder in Greek mainstream schools. *Frontiers in Education, 7*, 832240. doi:10.3389/feduc.2022.832240

Ralli, A. M., Kazali, E., Kanellou, M., Mouzaki, A., Antoniou, F., Diamanti, V., & Papaioannou, S. (2021). Oral Language and Story Retelling During Preschool and Primary School Years: Developmental Patterns and Interrelationships. *Journal of Psycholinguistic Research, 50*(5), 949–965. doi:10.100710936-021-09758-3 PMID:33515178

Ramus, F., Marshall, C. R., Rosen, S., & van der Lely, H. K. (2013). Phonological deficits in specific language impairment and developmental dyslexia: Towards a multidimensional model. *Brain, 136*(2), 630–645. doi:10.1093/brain/aws356 PMID:23413264

Raschle, N. M., Menks, W. M., Fehlbaum, L. V., Steppan, M., Smaragdi, A., Gonzalez-Madruga, K., Rogers, J., Clanton, R., Kohls, G., Martinelli, A., Bernhard, A., Konrad, K., Herpertz-Dahlmann, B., Freitag, C. M., Fairchild, G., De Brito, S. A., & Stadler, C. (2018). Callous-unemotional traits and brain structure: Sex-specific effects in anterior insula of typically-developing youths. *NeuroImage: Clinical, 17*(November 2017), 856–864. doi:10.1016/j.nicl.2017.12.015

Rathore, G., Star, L., Larsen, P., & Rizzo, W. (2017). Novel mutation of DARS2 gene leads to a rare and aggressive presentation of leukoencephalopathy with brainstem and spinal cord involvement and lactate elevation (LBSL). *Neurology, 88*(16 Supplement) P4.174 https://n.neurology.org/content/88/16_Supplement/P4.174/tab-article-info

Raufelder, D., Kittler, F., Braun, S. R., Lätsch, A., Wilkinson, R. P., & Hoferichter, F. (2013). The interplay of perceived stress, self-determination and school engagement in adolescence. *School Psychology International, 35*(4), 405–420. doi:10.1177/0143034313498953

Reaves, S., Martinez-Torteya, C., & Kosson, D. S. (2022). Understanding the relation between family engagement in education and preschoolers' socioemotional and behavioral functioning in a primarily Latinx sample. *Urban Education, 57*(4), 630–661. doi:10.1177/0042085920974073

Regression with Two Independent Variables. (n.d.). USF. http://faculty.cas.usf.edu/mbrannick/regression/Reg2IV.html

Reid Chassiakos, Y., Radesky, J., Christakis, D., Moreno, M. A., Cross, C., Hill, D., Ameenuddin, N., Hutchinson, J., Levine, A., Boyd, R., Mendelson, R., & Swanson, W. S. (2016). Children and Adolescents and Digital Media. *Pediatrics, 138*(5), e20162593. doi:10.1542/peds.2016-2593 PMID:27940795

Reilly, S., Bishop, D. V., & Tomblin, B. (2014). Terminological debate over language impairment in children: Forward movement and sticking points. *International Journal of Language & Communication Disorders, 49*(4), 452–462. doi:10.1111/1460-6984.12111 PMID:25142092

Rentzsch, K., Wenzler, M. P., & Schütz, A. (2016). The structure of multidimensional self-esteem across age and gender. *Personality and Individual Differences*, *88*, 139–147. doi:10.1016/j.paid.2015.09.012

Richards, D., Caldwell, P. H. Y., & Go, H. (2015). Impact of Social Media on the Health of Children and Young People. *Journal of Paediatrics and Child Health*, *51*(12), 1152–1157. doi:10.1111/jpc.13023 PMID:26607861

Richards, J. A., Xu, D., Gilkerson, J., Yapanel, U., Gray, S., & Paul, T. (2017). Automated assessment of child vocalization development using LENA. *Journal of Speech, Language, and Hearing Research: JSLHR*, *60*(7), 2047–2063. doi:10.1044/2017_JSLHR-L-16-0157 PMID:28609511

Richards, S. B., Brady, M. P., & Taylor, R. L. (2014). *Cognitive and intellectual disabilities: Historical perspectives, current practices, and future directions*. Routledge. doi:10.4324/9780203508251

Ricketts, J. (2011). Research Review: Reading comprehension in developmental disorders of language and communication. *Journal of Child Psychology and Psychiatry, and Allied Disciplines*, *52*(11), 1111–1123. doi:10.1111/j.1469-7610.2011.02438.x PMID:21762147

Riddick, B. (1995). Dyslexia: Dispelling the myths. *Disability & Society*, *10*(4), 457–473. doi:10.1080/09687599550023453

Riddick, B. (1996). *Living With Dyslexia: The social and emotional consequences of specific learning difficulties/ disabilities* (1st ed.). Routledge. doi:10.4324/9780203432600

Riddick, B. (2001). Dyslexia and Inclusion: Time for a Social Model of Disability Perspective? *International Studies in Sociology of Education*, *11*(3), 223–236. doi:10.1080/09620210100200078

Riddick, B., Sterling, C., Farmer, M., & Morgan, S. (1999). Self-Esteem and Anxiety in the Educational Histories of Adult Dyslexic Students. *Dyslexia (Chichester, England)*, *5*(4), 227–248. doi:10.1002/(SICI)1099-0909(199912)5:4<227::AID-DYS146>3.0.CO;2-6

Rief, S. F. (2005). *How to reach and teach children with ADD/ADHD: Practical Techniques, strategies and interventions* (2nd ed.). Jossey-Bass.

Rinaldi, S., Caselli, M. C., Cofelice, V., D'Amico, S., De Cagno, A. G., Della Corte, G., Di Martino, M. V., Di Costanzo, B., Levorato, M. C., Penge, R., Rossetto, T., Sansavini, A., Vecchi, S., & Zoccolotti, P. (2021). Efficacy of the treatment of developmental language disorder: A systematic review. *Brain Sciences*, *11*(3), 407. doi:10.3390/brainsci11030407 PMID:33806938

Ringer, N. (2019). Young people's perceptions of and coping with their ADHD symptoms: A qualitative study. *Cogent Psychology*, *6*(1), 1608032. doi:10.1080/23311908.2019.1608032

Robb, C. E., De Jager, C. A., Ahmadi-Abhari, S., Giannakopoulou, P., Udeh-Momoh, C., McKeand, J., Price, G., Car, J., Majeed, A., Ward, H., & Middleton, L. (2020). Associations of social isolation with anxiety and depression during the early COVID-19 pandemic: A survey of older adults in London, UK. *Frontiers in Psychiatry*, *11*, 591120. doi:10.3389/fpsyt.2020.591120 PMID:33132942

Roberts, D. A., & Bybee, R. W. (2014). Scientific Literacy, Science Literacy, and Science Education. In N. G. Lederman & S. K. Abell (Eds.), *Handbook of Research on Science Education* (pp. 545–558). Routledge.

Robinson, B. A., Azores-Gococo, N., Brennan, P. A., & Lilienfeld, S. O. (2016). The Roles of Maternal Psychopathic Traits, Maternal Antisocial Personality Traits, and Parenting in the Development of Child Psychopathic Traits. *Parenting, Science and Practice*, *16*(1), 36–55. doi:10.1080/15295192.2016.1116894

Robledo-Ramón, P., García-Sánchez, J.-N., Robledo-Ramón, P., & García-Sánchez, J.-N. (2012). The family environment of students with learning disabilities and ADHD. In *Learning Disabilities*. IntechOpen. doi:10.5772/32507

Roebers, C. M. (2017). Executive function and metacognition: Towards a unifying framework of cognitive self-regulation. *Developmental Review*, *45*, 31–51. doi:10.1016/j.dr.2017.04.001

Roello, M., Ferretti, M. L., Colonnello, V., & Levi, G. (2015). When words lead to solutions: Executive function deficits in preschool children with specific language impairment. *Research in Developmental Disabilities*, *37*, 216–222. doi:10.1016/j.ridd.2014.11.017 PMID:25528081

Rogers, C. R. (1942). *Counseling and psychotherapy*. Houghton Mifflin.

Rohmer, O., Doignon-Camus, N., Audusseau, J., Trautmann, S., Chaillou, A. C., & Popa-Roch, M. (2022). Removing the academic framing in student evaluations improves achievement in children with dyslexia: The mediating role of self-judgement of competence. *Dyslexia (Chichester, England)*, *28*(3), 309–324. doi:10.1002/dys.1713 PMID:35623893

Roitsch, J., & Watson, S. M. (2019). An overview of dyslexia: Definition, characteristics, assessment, identification, and intervention. *Science Journal of Education*, *7*(4), 81–86. doi:10.11648/j.sjedu.20190704.11

Romeo, R. R., Leonard, J. A., Robinson, S. T., West, M. R., Mackey, A. P., Rowe, M. L., ... Gabrieli, J. D. E. (2020). Beyond the 30-Million-Word Gap: Children's conversational exposure is associated with language-related brain function. *Psychological Science*, *31*(5), 586–598. doi:10.1177/0956797617742725 PMID:29442613

Romeo, R. R., Segaran, J., Leonard, J. A., Robinson, S. T., West, M. R., Mackey, A. P., Yendiki, A., Rowe, M. L., & Gabrieli, J. D. E. (2018). Language Exposure Relates to Structural Neural Connectivity in Childhood. *The Journal of Neuroscience : The Official Journal of the Society for Neuroscience*, *38*(36), 7870–7877. doi:10.1523/JNEUROSCI.0484-18.2018 PMID:30104336

Romski, M. A., Sevcik, R. A., King, M., DeLeo, G., Branum-Martin, L., & Bornman, J. (2023). Using a self-guided app to provide communication strategies for caregivers of young children with developmental disorders: A pilot investigation. *Journal of Policy and Practice in Intellectual Disabilities*, *20*(1), 73–88. doi:10.1111/jppi.12436

Roodenrys, S., & Dunn, N. (2007). Unimpaired implicit learning in children with developmental dyslexia. *Dyslexia (Chichester, England)*, *14*(1), 1–15. doi:10.1002/dys.340 PMID:17624907

Rose, D., Bartoli, A. J., & Heaton, P. (2018). Learning a Musical Instrument can benefit a Child with Special Educational Needs. Psychomusicology: Music, Mind, and Brain. *American Psychological Association, 28*(2), 71-81. doi:10.1037/pmu0000209

Rosenberg, M., Schooler, C., Schoenbach, C., & Rosenberg, F. (1995). Global Self-Esteem and Specific Self-Esteem: Different Concepts, Different Outcomes. *American Sociological Review*, *60*(1), 141–156. doi:10.2307/2096350

Rossetti, Z., Burke, M. M., Hughes, O., Schraml-Block, K., Rivera, J. I., Rios, K., & Lee, J. D. (2021). Parent perceptions of the advocacy expectation in special education. *Exceptional Children*, *87*(4), 438–457. doi:10.1177/0014402921994095

Ross, H. (2021). 'I'm Dyslexic but What Does That Even Mean?': Young People's Experiences of Dyslexia Support Interventions in Mainstream Classrooms. *Scandinavian Journal of Disability Research*, *23*(1), 284–294. doi:10.16993jdr.782

Rott, L., & Marohn, A. (2018). Choice2explore – a teaching concept for inclusive science education in primary schools. In: O. Finlayson, E. McLoughlin, S. Erduran, & P. Childs, (Eds.), Proceedings of the 12th *ESERA 2017 Conference, Research, practice and collaboration in science education* (pp. 2194-2202). Dublin: Dublin City University.

Roulstone, S. (2015). Exploring the relationship between client perspectives, clinical expertise and research evidence. *International Journal of Speech-Language Pathology*, *17*(3), 211–221. doi:10.3109/17549507.2015.1016112 PMID:25850604

Roulstone, S. E., Marshall, J. E., Powell, G. G., Goldbart, J., Wren, Y. E., Coad, J., & Coad, R. A. (2015). *Evidence based intervention for preschool children with primary speech and language impairments: Child Talk – An exploratory mixed-methods study*. NHS National Institute for Health Research.

Rowe, M. L. (2012). A longitudinal investigation of the role of quantity and quality of child-directed speech in vocabulary development. *Child Development, 83*(5), 1762–1774. doi:10.1111/j.1467-8624.2012.01805.x PMID:22716950

Rudolph, J. M. (2017). Case history risk factors for specific language impairment: A systematic review and meta-analysis. *American Journal of Speech-Language Pathology, 26*(3), 991–1010. doi:10.1044/2016_AJSLP-15-0181 PMID:28672377

Rüsseler, J., Gerth, I., & Münte, T. F. (2006). Implicit learning is intact in adult developmental dyslexic readers: Evidence from the serial reaction time task and artificial grammar learning. *Journal of Clinical and Experimental Neuropsychology, 28*(5), 808–827. doi:10.1080/13803390591001007 PMID:16723326

Rydell, A.-M., & Brocki, K. C. (2019). Cognitive and emotional profiles of CU traits and disruptive behavior in adolescence: A prospective study. *Journal of Abnormal Child Psychology, 47*(6), 1039–1051. doi:10.100710802-018-0496-5 PMID:30523475

Sahu, A., Bhargava, R., Sagar, R., & Mehta, M. (2018). Perception of families of children with specific learning disorder: An exploratory study. *Indian Journal of Psychological Medicine, 40*(5), 406–413. doi:10.4103/IJPSYM.IJPSYM_148_18 PMID:30275614

Salmon, K., O'Kearney, R., Reese, E., & Fortune, C.-A. (2016). The role of language skill in child psychopathology: Implications for intervention in the early years. *Clinical Child and Family Psychology Review, 19*(4), 352–367. doi:10.100710567-016-0214-1 PMID:27678011

Samsari, E. P., Nikolaou, G., & Palaiologou, N. (2022). Multicultural diversity and special needs education: Small steps towards a successful inclusive environment in Greece. In *International Issues in SEND and Inclusion* (pp. 95–106). Routledge. doi:10.4324/9781003177135-12

SAMSHA. (2016). *DSM-5 Changes: Implications for Child Serious Emotional Disturbance (unpublished internal documentation)*. APA. www.ncbi.nlm.nih.gov/books/NBK519712/table/ch3.t8/

Sanderson, K. A. (2023). "Be Prepared to Fight Like Hell": Parent Advice for IEP Meetings. *Exceptionality,* 1-18.

Sands, D. J., & Kozleski, E. B. (1994). Quality of life differences between adults with and without disabilities. *Education and Training in Mental Retardation and Developmental Disabilities, 29*, 90–101.

Santín, D., & Sicilia, G. (2016). Does family structure affect children's academic outcomes? Evidence for Spain. *The Social Science Journal, 53*(4), 555–572. doi:10.1016/j.soscij.2016.04.001

Sarbarzeh, P. A., Karimi, S., Jalilian, M., & Mosafer, H. (2020). Depression, anxiety, stress and social isolation in hepatitis patients. *SciMedicine Journal, 2*(4), 225–233. doi:10.28991/SciMedJ-2020-0204-5

Satrazemi, M., Mpakagianni, A., Sarris, D., Vergou, M., & Zakopoulou, V. (2017). Tite: establishing an integrated diagnostic profile of Autism Spectrum Disorder (ASD) through the use of essence framework. The case study of a 3-year-old infant. European Journal of Special Education Research, 2(5), 11-52, (ISSN: 2501 - 2428) doi:10.5281/zenodo.573377

Saunders, M. C., Anckarsäter, H., Lundström, S., Hellner, C., Lichtenstein, P., & Fontaine, N. M. G. (2019). The Associations between Callous-unemotional Traits and Symptoms of Conduct Problems, Hyperactivity and Emotional Problems: A Study of Adolescent Twins Screened for Neurodevelopmental Problems. *Journal of Abnormal Child Psychology, 47*(3), 447–457. doi:10.100710802-018-0439-1 PMID:29728890

Schalock, R. L., & Luckasson, R. (2021). Intellectual disability, developmental disabilities, and the field of intellectual and developmental disabilities. In L. M. Glidden, L. Abbeduto, L. L. McIntyre, & M. J. Tassé (Eds.), *APA handbook of intellectual and developmental disabilities: Foundations* (pp. 31–45). American Psychological Association. doi:10.1037/0000194-002

Schalock, R. L., Luckasson, R., & Tassé, M. J. (2021). An overview of intellectual disability: Definition, diagnosis, classification, and systems of supports. *American Journal on Intellectual and Developmental Disabilities*, *126*(6), 439–442. doi:10.1352/1944-7558-126.6.439 PMID:34700345

Scherrer, V., & Preckel, F. (2019). Development of Motivational Variables and Self-Esteem During the School Career: A Meta-Analysis of Longitudinal Studies. *Review of Educational Research*, *89*(2), 211–258. doi:10.3102/0034654318819127

Schietecatte, I., Roeyers, H., & Warreyn, P. (2012). Exploring the nature of joint attention impairments in young children with autism spectrum disorder: Associated social and cognitive skills. *Journal of Autism and Developmental Disorders*, *42*(1), 1–12. doi:10.100710803-011-1209-x PMID:21360019

Schlebusch, L., Chambers, N., Rosenstein, D., Erasmus, P., & de Vries, P. J. (2022, November 09). WHO CST Team, & de Vries, P. J. (2022). Supporting caregivers of children with developmental disabilities: Findings from a brief caregiver well-being programme in South Africa. *Autism*. doi:10.1177/13623613221133182 PMID:36352758

Schneeweiß, N., & Gropengießer, H. (2019). Organising Levels of Organisation for Biology Education: A Systematic Review of Literature. *Education Sciences*, *9*(3), 207. doi:10.3390/educsci9030207

Schneider, W. (2008). The Development of Metacognitive Knowledge in Children and Adolescents: Major Trends and Implications for Education. *Mind, Brain and Education : the Official Journal of the International Mind, Brain, and Education Society*, *2*(3), 114–121. doi:10.1111/j.1751-228X.2008.00041.x

Schuelka, M. J. (2018). Social dimensions of inclusion in education of 4th and 7th grade pupils in inclusive and regular classes: Outcomes from Austria. *Research in Developmental Disabilities*, *43*, 72–79. doi:10.1016/j.ridd.2015.06.005

Schulte-Körne, G. (2016). Mental Health Problems in a School Setting in Children and Adolescents. *Deutsches Ärzteblatt International*, *113*(11), 183–190. doi:10.3238/arztebl.2016.0183 PMID:27118666

Schumacher, J., Hoffman, P., Schmaeil, C., Schulte-Korne, G., & Nothen, M. (2007). Genetics of dyslexia: The evolving landscape. *Journal of Medical Genetics*, *44*(5), 289–297. doi:10.1136/jmg.2006.046516 PMID:17307837

Schutte, N. S., & Malouff, J. M. (2019). The impact of signature character strengths interventions: A meta-analysis. *Journal of Happiness Studies*, *20*(4), 1179–1196. doi:10.100710902-018-9990-2

Schwab, S., Gebhardt, M., Krammer, M., & Gasteiger-Klicpera, B. (2015). Linking self-rated social inclusion to social behaviour. An empirical study of students with and without special education needs in secondary schools. *European Journal of Special Needs Education*, *30*(1), 1–14. doi:10.1080/08856257.2014.933550

Sebastian, C. L., Fontaine, N. M. G., Bird, G., Blakemore, S.-J., De Brito, S. A., McCrory, E. J. P., & Viding, E. (2012). Neural processing associated with cognitive and affective theory of mind in adolescents and adults. *Social Cognitive and Affective Neuroscience*, *7*(1), 53–63. doi:10.1093can/nsr023 PMID:21467048

Seifert, K. (2019, September 1). *Ch. 16 Standardized and other formal assessments*. Pressbooks. https://granite.pressbooks.pub/teachingdiverselearners/chapter/standardized-and-other-formal-assessments-2/

Seipp, C. M., & Johnston, C. (2005). Mother-son interaction in families of boys with attention deficit/hyperactivity disorder with and without oppositional behavior. *Journal of Abnormal Child Psychology*, *33*(1), 87–98. doi:10.100710802-005-0936-x PMID:15759593

Selenius, H., & Strand, S. (2015). Superficiality in forensic psychiatric patients is related to superior phonological, semantic and syntactic skills. *Nordic Journal of Psychiatry*, *69*(5), 392–396. doi:10.3109/08039488.2014.994031 PMID:25592288

Semantic Features Analysis Definition, Examples, Applications. (2022, June 16). Spiceworks. https://www.spiceworks.com/tech/artificial-intelligence/articles/what-is-semantic-analysis/

Serpell, Z. N., & Mashburn, A. J. (2012). Family–school connectedness and children's early social development. *Social Development*, *21*(1), 21–46. doi:10.1111/j.1467-9507.2011.00623.x

Shahaeian, A., Wang, C., Tucker-Drob, E., Geiger, V., Bus, A. G., & Harrison, L. J. (2018). Early shared reading, socioeconomic status, and children's cognitive and school competencies: Six years of longitudinal evidence. *Scientific Studies of Reading*, *22*(6), 485–502. doi:10.1080/10888438.2018.1482901 PMID:34108838

Shavelson, R. J., & Bolus, R. (1982). Self concept: The interplay of theory and methods. *Journal of Educational Psychology*, *74*(1), 3–17. doi:10.1037/0022-0663.74.1.3

Shavelson, R. J., Hubner, J. J., & Stanton, G. C. (1976). Self-Concept: Validation of Construct Interpretations. *Review of Educational Research*, *46*(3), 407–441. doi:10.3102/00346543046003407

Shaywitz, S. (2003). *Overcoming dyslexia: A new and complete science-based program for reading problems at any level*. Alfred A. Knopf.

Shelton, T. L., Barkley, R. A., Crosswait, C., Moorehouse, M., Fletcher, K., Barrett, S., Jenkins, L., & Metevia, L. (1998). Psychiatric and psychological morbidity as a function of adaptive disability in preschool children with aggressive and hyperactive impulsive inattentive behaviour. *Journal of Abnormal Child Psychology*, *26*(6), 475–494. doi:10.1023/A:1022603902905 PMID:9915654

Sheng, L., Yu, J., Su, P. L., Wang, D., Lu, T. H., Shen, L., Hao, Y., & Lam, B. P. W. (2023). Developmental language disorder in Chinese children: A systematic review of research from 1997 to 2022. *Brain and Language*, *241*(June 2022), 105268. doi:10.1016/j.bandl.2023.105268

Shimojima, K., Higashiguchi, T., Kishimoto, K., Miyatake, S., Miyake, N., Takanashi, J. I., Matsumoto, N., & Yamamoto, T. (2017). A novel *DARS2* mutation in a Japanese patient with leukoencephalopathy with brainstem and spinal cord involvement but no lactate elevation. *Human Genome Variation*, *4*(1), 17051. doi:10.1038/hgv.2017.51 PMID:29138691

Shneiderman, B. (2020). Bridging the gap between ethics and practice: Guidelines for reliable, safe, and trustworthy human-centered AI systems. [TiiS]. *ACM Transactions on Interactive Intelligent Systems*, *10*(4), 1–31. doi:10.1145/3419764

Sidlauskaite, J., González-Madruga, K., Smaragdi, A., Riccelli, R., Puzzo, I., Batchelor, M., Cornwell, H., Clark, L., Sonuga-Barke, E. J. S., & Fairchild, G. (2018). Sex differences in risk-based decision making in adolescents with conduct disorder. *European Child & Adolescent Psychiatry*, *27*(9), 1133–1142. doi:10.100700787-017-1024-9 PMID:28688012

Sigman, M., Ruskin, E., Arbeile, S., Corona, R., Dissanayake, C., Espinosa, M., Kim, N., López, A., & Zierhut, C. (1999). Continuity and change in the social competence of children with autism, Down syndrome, and developmental delays. *Monographs of the Society for Research in Child Development*, *64*(1), 1–114. doi:10.1111/1540-5834.00002 PMID:10412222

Silliman, E. R., & Berninger, V. W. (2011). Cross-disciplinary dialogue about the nature of oral and written language problems in the context of developmental, academic, and phenotypic profiles. *Topics in Language Disorders*, *31*(1), 6–23. doi:10.1097/TLD.0b013e31820a0b5b

Smythe, T., Zuurmond, M., Tann, C. J., Gladstone, M., & Kuper, H. (2021). Early intervention for children with developmental disabilities in low and middle-income countries–the case for action. *International Health, 13*(3), 222–231. doi:10.1093/inthealth/ihaa044 PMID:32780826

Snowling, M. J. (2013). Early identification and interventions for dyslexia: A contemporary view. *Journal of Research in Special Educational Needs, 13*(1), 7–14. doi:10.1111/j.1471-3802.2012.01262.x PMID:26290655

Snowling, M. J., Hayiou-Thomas, M. E., Nash, H. M., & Hulme, C. (2020). Dyslexia and Developmental Language Disorder: Comorbid disorders with distinct effects on reading comprehension. *Journal of Child Psychology and Psychiatry, and Allied Disciplines, 61*(6), 672–680. doi:10.1111/jcpp.13140 PMID:31631348

Sofologi, M., Kougioumtzis, G. A., & Koundourou, C. (2023). *Perspectives of Cognitive, Psychosocial, and Learning Difficulties From Childhood to Adulthood: Practical Counseling Strategies*. doi:10.4018/978-1-6684-8203-2

So, K. K. F., & To, C. K. S. (2022). Systematic Review and Meta-Analysis of Screening Tools for Language Disorder. *Frontiers in Pediatrics, 10*, 801220. doi:10.3389/fped.2022.801220 PMID:35281230

Sollie, H. (2014). Struggling with and for A Grounded Theory of Parents Managing Life with Hard-to-Treat ADHD Teenagers. *The Grounded Theory Review, 13*(1), 3–15.

Sommers-Flanagan, J., & Sommers-Flanagan, R. (2018). *Counseling and psychotherapy theories in context and practice: Skills, strategies, and techniques*. John Wiley & Sons.

Song, J., Mailick, M. R., & Greenberg, J. S. (2018). Health of parents of individuals with developmental disorders or mental health problems: Impacts of stigma. *Social Science & Medicine, 217*, 152–158. doi:10.1016/j.socscimed.2018.09.044 PMID:30333078

Sonna, L. (2005). *The everything parent's guide to children with ADD/ADHD*. Avon: F+W Publications.

Sonuga-Barke, E. J., Cortese, S., Fairchild, G., & Stringaris, A. (2016). Annual research review: Transdiagnostic neuroscience of child and adolescent mental disorders — differentiating decision making in attention-deficit/ hyperactivity disorder, conduct disorder, depression, and anxiety. *Journal of Child Psychology and Psychiatry, and Allied Disciplines, 57*(3), 321–349. doi:10.1111/jcpp.12496 PMID:26705858

Soriano-Ferrer, M., & Echegaray-Bengoa, J. (2014). A Scale of Knowledge and Beliefs about Developmental Dyslexia: Scale Development and Validation. *Procedia: Social and Behavioral Sciences, 132*, 203–208. doi:10.1016/j.sbspro.2014.04.299

Sosa, A. V. (2016). Association of the type of toy used during play with the quantity and quality of parent-infant communication. *JAMA Pediatrics, 170*(2), 132–137. doi:10.1001/jamapediatrics.2015.3753 PMID:26720437

Sousa, D. A., & Tomlinson, C. A. (2011). *Differentiation and the brain: How neuroscience supports the learner-friendly classroom*. Solution Tree Press.

Spadidakis, I. (2009). *Difficulties of writing production of school-age children. Diagnosis - Assessment - Treatment* (8th ed.). Hellenic Letters. [in Greek]

Speech and language: risk factors and disorders. (n.d.). Child Language Research Center. http://www.ouluclrc.fi/research/projects/speech-and-language-risk-factors-and-disorders/

St Clair, M. C., Pickles, A., Durkin, K., & Conti-Ramsden, G. A. (2011). Longitudinal study of behavioral, emotional and social difficulties in individuals with a history of specific language impairment (SLI). *Journal of Communication Disorders, 44*(2), 186–199. doi:10.1016/j.jcomdis.2010.09.004 PMID:20970811

Stagnitti, K., O'Connor, C., & Sheppard, L. (2012). Impact of the Learn to Play program on play, social competence and language for children aged 5-8 years who attend a specialist school. *Australian Occupational Therapy Journal, 59*(4), 302–311. doi:10.1111/j.1440-1630.2012.01018.x PMID:22934903

Stamatis, P., & Nikolaou, E. (2020). *Communication and mental health promotion in early childhood education.* Nova Publishers. doi:10.52305/QXVD5566

Stamm, B. H. (2005). *The ProQOL Manual: The Professional Quality of Life Scale: Compassion satisfaction, burnout & compassion fatigue/secondary trauma scales.* Sidran Press.

Stam, T., French, B., Lucassen, N., van Steensel, R., Godor, B., & Keizer, R. (2023). Not your cup of coffee? An ethnographic study on interparental dynamics during parental involvement activities in Dutch primary schools. *Ethnography and Education, 18*(2), 159–182. doi:10.1080/17457823.2022.2158748

Stein, J. (2018). What is developmental dyslexia? *Brain Sciences, 8*(2), 26. doi:10.3390/brainsci8020026 PMID:29401712

Stepanova, G. A., Tashcheva, A. I., Stepanova, O. P., Menshikov, P. V., Kassymova, G. K., Arpentieva, M. R., & Tokar, O. V. (2018). The problem of management and implementation of innovative models of network interaction in inclusive education of persons with disabilities. *International journal of education and information technologies.*

Stephany, U., & Aksu-Koç, A. (Eds.). (2021). Development of Modality in First Language Acquisition: A Cross-Linguistic Perspective (Studies on Language Acquisition 54). Berlin & Boston: De Gruyter Mouton.

Stephany, U., & Voeikova, M. (Eds.). (2009). Development of Nominal Inflection in First Language Acquisition: A Cross-Linguistic Perspective (Studies on Language Acquisition 30). Berlin & New York: Mouton de Gruyter.

Stevens, A., & Iowe, J. (1993). *Histology.* Paschalidis.

Stevens, D., Charman, T., & Blair, R. (2001). Recognition of emotion in facial expressions and vocal tones in children with psychopathic tendencies. *The Journal of Genetic Psychology, 162*(2), 201–211. doi:10.1080/00221320109597961 PMID:11432605

Stewart, A. L., Field, T. A., & Echterling, L. G. (2016). Neuroscience and the Magic of Play Therapy. *International Journal of Play Therapy, 25*(1), 4–13. doi:10.1037/pla0000016

Stone, B. G., Mills, K. A., & Saggers, B. (2019). Online multiplayer games for the social interactions of children with autism spectrum disorder: A resource for inclusive education. *International Journal of Inclusive Education, 23*(2), 209–228. doi:10.1080/13603116.2018.1426051

Stransky, M. L., Oshita, J. Y., & Morris, M. A. (2020). Prevalence of Behavioral Health Problems among Adults with and without Communication Disabilities. *Journal of the American Board of Family Medicine, 33*(6), 934–941. doi:10.3122/jabfm.2020.06.200216 PMID:33219072

Streisand, R., Mackey, E. R., Elliot, B. M., Mednick, L., Slaughter, I. M., Turek, J., & Austin, A. (2008). Parental anxiety and depression associated with caring for a child newly diagnosed with type 1 diabetes: Opportunities for education and counseling. *Patient Education and Counseling, 73*(2), 333–338. doi:10.1016/j.pec.2008.06.014 PMID:18692342

Strömberg, A. (2013). The situation of caregivers in heart failure and their role in improving patient outcomes. *Current Heart Failure Reports, 10*(3), 270–275. doi:10.100711897-013-0146-8 PMID:23857163

Styles, S. J., & Plunkett, K. (2008). What is 'word understanding' for the parent of a one-year-old? Matching the difficulty of a lexical comprehension task to parental CDI report. *Journal of Child Language, 36*(4), 895–908. doi:10.1017/S0305000908009264 PMID:19079845

Sucheta (2020). Gender differences on self-esteem in children with specific learning disability. *International Journal of Advances in Engineering and Management (IJAEM), 2*(7), 593-599.

Sue, D., Sue, D., & Sue, S. (1994). *Understanding abnormal behavior* (4th ed.). Houghton Miffin.

Sullivan, A. B., & Miller, D. (2015). Who is taking care of the caregiver? *Journal of Patient Experience, 2*(1), 7–12. https://journals.sagepub.com/doi/pdf/10.1177/237437431500200103. doi:10.1177/237437431500200103 PMID:28725810

Sultana, N., Wong, L. L. N., & Purdy, S. C. (2020). Natural language input: Maternal education, socioeconomic deprivation, and language outcomes in typically developing children. *Language, Speech, and Hearing Services in Schools, 51*(4), 1049–1070. doi:10.1044/2020_LSHSS-19-00095 PMID:32755504

Surendran, A. (2023). Qualitative Data – Definition, Types, Analysis and Examples. *QuestionPro*. https://www.questionpro.com/blog/qualitative-data/

Suzuki, M., Yamada, A., Watanabe, N., Akechi, T., Katsuki, F., Nishiyama, T., ... Furukawa, T. A. (2014). A failure to confirm the effectiveness of a brief group psychoeducational program for mothers of children with high-functioning pervasive developmental disorders: A randomized controlled pilot trial. *Neuropsychiatric Disease and Treatment, 10*, 1141–1153. doi:10.2147/NDT.S60058 PMID:25061301

Szukiel, B., Górska, M., & Kruk, U. (2017). Differential Diagnosis of Specific Language Impairment-Sli. *Pol. J. Appl. Sci, 3*, 5–10.

Tait, K. (2020). Preparing Educators to Collaborate with Professionals Who Work With Learners With Complex Conditions. In Oxford Research Encyclopedia of Education. doi:10.1093/acrefore/9780190264093.013.1204

Tamboer, P., Vorst, H. C. M., & Oort, F. J. (2016). Five describing factors of dyslexia. *Journal of Learning Disabilities, 49*(5), 466–483. doi:10.1177/0022219414558123 PMID:25398549

Tannock, R. (1998). Attention deficit hyperactivity disorder: Advantages in cognitive, neurobiological, and genetic research. *Journal of Child Psychology and Psychiatry, and Allied Disciplines, 39*(1), 65–99. doi:10.1111/1469-7610.00304 PMID:9534087

Tantaros, S. (2004). Family and child and adolescent development: Theoretical approaches and considerations. In S. Tantaros (Ed.), *Human development and family* (pp. 15–34). [in Greek]

Tasiou, K., & Nikolaou, E. N. (2022). Resilience in Families with children with special needs. In P. I. Stamatis & E. N. Nikolaou (Eds.), *Counselling and communication in education* (pp. 271–295). Diadrasis.

Tasiou, K., & Nikolaou, E. N. (2023). The psychological resilience of families of children with attention deficit hyperactivity disorder. In D. B. Katsarou, C. Koundourou, & G. P. Reppa (Eds.), *New trends and approaches in child and adult psychopathology and mental health* (pp. 99–121). Gutenberg.

Taunt, H. M., & Hastings, R. P. (2002). Positive impact of children with developmental disabilities on their families: A preliminary study. *Education and Training in Mental Retardation and Developmental Disabilities*, 410–420. https://www.jstor.org/stable/23880074

Taxitari, L., Floros, G., Kambanaros, M., & Grohmann, K. K. G. (2017). Early language development in a bilectal context: The Cypriot adaptation of the MacArthur-Bates CDI. In E. Babatsouli, D. Ingram, & N. Müller (Eds.), *Cross-linguistic encounters in language acquisition: Typical and atypical development* (pp. 145–171). Multilingual Matters. doi:10.21832/9781783099092-010

Taylor, E. (2009). Developing Adhd. *Journal of Child Psychology and Psychiatry, and Allied Disciplines, 50*(1-2), 126–132. doi:10.1111/j.1469-7610.2008.01999.x PMID:19076263

Tedeschi, R. G., & Calhoun, L. G. (2004). Posttraumatic growth: Conceptual foundations and empirical evidence. *Psychological Inquiry*, *15*(1), 1–18. doi:10.120715327965pli1501_01

Tekola, B., Kinfe, M., Girma, F., Hanlon, C., & Hoekstra, R. A. (2020). Perceptions and experiences of stigma among parents of children with developmental disorders in Ethiopia: A qualitative study. *Social Science & Medicine*, *256*, 113034. doi:10.1016/j.socscimed.2020.113034 PMID:32446155

Terras, M., Thompson, L. C., & Minnis, H. (2009). Dyslexia and psycho-social functioning: An exploratory study of the role of self-esteem and understanding. *Dyslexia (Chichester, England)*, *15*(4), 304–327. doi:10.1002/dys.386 PMID:19384920

Thapliyal, M., Ahuja, N. J., Shankar, A., Cheng, X., & Kumar, M. (2022). A differentiated learning environment in domain model for learning disabled learners. Journal of Computing in Higher Education, 34(1), 60-82.

Themane, M., & Thobejane, H. R. (2019). Teachers as change agents in making teaching inclusive in some selected rural schools of Limpopo Province, South Africa: Implications for teacher education. *International Journal of Inclusive Education*, *23*(4), 369–383. doi:10.1080/13603116.2018.1434690

Theodoratou, M. M., Tafiadis, D., Mpekos, V., Euaggelatou, M., Kiritsi, B., Plitsi, A., & Pistola, D. (2006). Coping strategies of Greek students. *Annals of General Psychiatry*, *5*(S1, Suppl 1), S222. doi:10.1186/1744-859X-5-S1-S222

Theodoratou, M., Farmakopoulou, I., Kougioumtzis, G., Kaltsouda, A., Siouti, Z., Gkintoni, E., Sofologi, M., Flora, K., & Tsitsas, G. (2023a). Emotion-focused coping, social support and active coping among university students: Gender differences. *J Psychol Clin Psychiatry*, *14*(1), 5–9. doi:10.15406/jpcpy.2023.14.00720

Theodoratou, M., Kougioumtzis, G., Kaltsouda, A., Katsarou, D., Siouti, Z., Sofologi, M., Tsitsas, G., & Flora, K. (2023). Neuropsychological Aspects and Interventions for Internet Addiction in Adolescents with Asperger's Syndrome - Narrative Review. *Neurology & Neuroscience*, *4*(3), 1–10.

Thoits, P. A. (2011). Mechanisms linking social ties and support to physical and mental health. *Journal of Health and Social Behavior*, *52*(2), 145–161. doi:10.1177/0022146510395592 PMID:21673143

Thomas, S., Schulz, J., & Ryder, N. (2019). Assessment and diagnosis of Developmental Language Disorder: The experiences of speech and language therapists. *Autism & Developmental Language Impairments*, *4*, 4. doi:10.1177/2396941519842812

Thompson, J. (2020). *Measuring Student Success Skills: A Review of the Literature on Complex Communication. 21st Century Success Skills*. National Center for the Improvement of Educational Assessment.

Thompson, R. A. (2015). *Counseling techniques: Improving relationships with others, ourselves, our families, and our environment*. Routledge. doi:10.4324/9781315886114

Thordardottir, E., Ellis Weismer, S., & Evans, J. L. (2015). Continuity in lexical and morphosyntactic development from 2;6 to 21. *Journal of Speech, Language, and Hearing Research: JSLHR*, *58*(3), 587–602. doi:10.1017/S0305000900009302

Thordardottir, E., & Topbaş, S. (2021). How aware is the public of the existence, characteristics and causes of language impairment in childhood and where have they heard about it? A European survey. *Journal of Communication Disorders*, *89*, 106057. doi:10.1016/j.jcomdis.2020.106057 PMID:33279754

Tilahun, D., Hanlon, C., Fekadu, A., Tekola, B., Baheretibeb, Y., & Hoekstra, R. A. (2016). Stigma, explanatory models and unmet needs of caregivers of children with developmental disorders in a low-income African country: A cross-sectional facility-based survey. *BMC Health Services Research*, *16*(1), 1–12. doi:10.118612913-016-1383-9 PMID:27117326

Timimi, S., & Taylor, E. (2004). ADHD is best understood as a cultural construct. *The British Journal of Psychiatry*, *184*(1), 8–9. doi:10.1192/bjp.184.1.8 PMID:14702221

Timler, G. R. (2018, April). Let's Talk: Review of Conversation Intervention Approaches for School-Aged Children and Adolescents with Autism Spectrum Disorder. []. Thieme Medical Publishers.]. *Seminars in Speech and Language*, *39*(02), 158–165. doi:10.1055-0038-1628367 PMID:29558770

Tindall, J. A. (1989). *Peer counseling: An in-depth look at training peer helpers*. Muncie Accelerated Development Inc.

Toffalini, E., Chen, X., Pastore, M., Carretti, B., Fraccadori, F., & Szűcs, D. (2021). Dyslexia treatment studies: A systematic review and suggestions on testing treatment efficacy with small effects and small samples. *Behavior Research Methods*, *53*(5), 1954–1972. doi:10.375813428-021-01549-x PMID:33694077

Toliao, P. S. (2017). *Underprepared, First-Year College Student Experiences with Academic Integration* [Doctoral dissertation, Northcentral University].

Tomaševski, K. (2001). *Human rights obligations: making education available, accessible, acceptable and adaptable. (Right to Education Primers No. 3)*. Sida.

Tomblin, J. B., Records, N. L., Buckwalter, P., Zhang, X., Smith, E., & O'Brien, M. (1997). Prevalence of specific language impairment in kindergarten children. *Journal of Speech, Language, and Hearing Research: JSLHR*, *40*(6), 1245–1260. doi:10.1044/jslhr.4006.1245 PMID:9430746

Tomblin, J. B., Zhang, X., Buckwalter, P., & O'Brien, M. (2003). The stability of primary language disorder: Four years after kindergarten diagnosis. *Journal of Speech, Language, and Hearing Research: JSLHR*, *46*(6), 1283–1296. doi:10.1044/1092-4388(2003/100) PMID:14700355

Tomlinson, C. (2017). *How to differentiate instruction in academically diverse class- rooms*. ASCD.

Tomlinson, C. A. (1995). Deciding to differentiate instruction in middle school: One school's journey. *Gifted Child Quarterly*, *39*(2), 77–87. doi:10.1177/001698629503900204

Tomlinson, C. A. (1999). Mapping a route toward differentiated instruction. *Educational Leadership*, *57*, 12–17.

Tomlinson, C. A. (2001). *How to differentiate instruction in mixed-ability classrooms*. Ascd.

Tomlinson, C. A. (2003). *Differentiation into practice. A resource guide for differentiating curriculum, grades K-5*. Association for Supervision and Curriculum Development.

Tomlinson, C. A. (2014). *The differentiated classroom: Responding to the needs of all learners* (2nd ed.). Association for Supervision and Curriculum Development.

Tomlinson, C. A., & Imbeau, M. (2010). *Leading and managing a differentiated classroom*. ASCD.

Tomlinson, C. A., & McTighe, J. (2006). *Integrating differentiated instruction & understanding by design: Connecting content and kids*. Association for Supervision and Curriculum Development.

Tomlinson, C. A., & Moon, T. R. (2013). *Assessment and student success in a differentiated classroom*. Association for Supervision and Curriculum Development.

Tomopoulos, S., Dreyer, B. P., Berkule, S., Fierman, A. H., Brockmeyer, C., & Mendelsohn, A. L. (2010). Infant media exposure and toddler development. *Archives of Pediatrics & Adolescent Medicine*, *164*(12), 1105–1111. doi:10.1001/archpediatrics.2010.235 PMID:21135338

Torff, B. (2011). Teacher beliefs shape learning for all students. *Phi Delta Kappan*, *93*(3), 21–23. doi:10.1177/003172171109300305

Torres, F., Fuentes-López, E., Fuente, A., & Sevilla, F. (2020). Identification of the factors associated with the severity of the speech production problems in children with comorbid speech sound disorder and developmental language disorder. *Journal of Communication Disorders, 88*(June 2019). doi:10.1016/j.jcomdis.2020.106054

Torsheim, T., & Wold, B. (2001). School-related stress, support, and subjective health complaints among early adolescents: A multilevel approach. *Journal of Adolescence*, *24*(6), 701–713. doi:10.1006/jado.2001.0440 PMID:11790051

Toulia, A., Alves, S., Avramidis, E., Sanches-Ferreira, M., & Silveira-Maia, M. (2022). Qualitative evaluation of an intervention programme fostering students' social participation implemented by Greek and Portuguese elementary school teachers. *International Journal of Educational Research Open*, *3*, 100205. Advance online publication. doi:10.1016/j.ijedro.2022.100205

Touretzky, D., Gardner-McCune, C., Martin, F., & Seehorn, D. (2019, July). Envisioning AI for K-12: What should every child know about AI? *Proceedings of the AAAI Conference on Artificial Intelligence*, *33*(01), 9795–9799. doi:10.1609/aaai.v33i01.33019795

Traianou, A. (2023a). Evaluation and its politics: trade unions and education reform in Greece. *Education Inquiry*, 1-20.

Traianou, A. (2023b). The intricacies of conditionality: Education policy review in Greece 2015–2018. *Journal of Education Policy*, *38*(2), 342–362. doi:10.1080/02680939.2021.1986641

Trecha, S., & Tsibidaki, A. (2021). Spelling mistakes and performance on an intelligence assessment test. In V. Chiou, L. Geunis, O. Holz, N. O. Ertürk & F. Shelton (Eds), Voices from the classroom: A celebration of learning (pp. 385-397). Waxmann Verlag.

Trecha, S., & Tsibidaki, A. (2022). Correlation of spelling errors with intelligence and family dynamics of primary school students. In S. G. Soulis & M. Liakopoulou (Eds.), *Education in the 21st century: Contemporary challenges and concerns*. Proceedings of the International Scientific Conference (Vol. 2, pp. 54-67). Gutenberg. [in Greek]

Treiman, R. (2017). Learning to spell: Phonology and beyond. *Cognitive Neuropsychology*, *34*(3–4), 3–4. doi:10.1080/02643294.2017.1337630 PMID:28628367

Triga-Mertika, E. (2010). *Learning difficulties. General and specific learning difficulties - Dyslexia*. Gregory. [in Greek]

Tripp, G., Schaughnecy, E. A., Langlands, R., & Mouat, K. (2007). Family interactions in children with and without ADHD. *Journal of Child and Family Studies*, *16*(3), 385–400. doi:10.100710826-006-9093-2

Tryfon, M., Anastasia, A., & Eleni, R. (2021). Parental perspectives on inclusive education for children with intellectual disabilities in Greece. *International Journal of Developmental Disabilities*, *67*(6), 397–405. doi:10.1080/20473869.2019.1675429 PMID:34925772

Tseng, Y. T., & Hsu, H. (2022, October). jen. (2023). Not only motor skill performance but also haptic function is impaired in children with developmental language disorder. *Research in Developmental Disabilities*, *134*, 104412. doi:10.1016/j.ridd.2022.104412 PMID:36638673

Tsibidaki, A. (2021). Resilience, meaning in life and self-efficacy in families with or without a member with special educational needs and disability during the COVID-19 pandemic. *Psychology: the Journal of the Hellenic Psychological Society*, *26*(3), 3. doi:10.12681/psy_hps.29161

Tsou, Y. T., Wiefferink, C. H., Broekhof, E., & Rieffe, C. (2023). Short report: Longitudinal study on emotion understanding in children with and without developmental language disorder. *Research in Developmental Disabilities, 137*(January 2022), 104493. doi:10.1016/j.ridd.2023.104493

Tunali, B., & Power, T. G. (1993). Creating Satisfaction: A Psychological Perspective on Stress and Coping in Families of Handicapped Children. *Journal of Child Psychology and Psychiatry, and Allied Disciplines*, *34*(6), 945–957. doi:10.1111/j.1469-7610.1993.tb01100.x PMID:8408377

Turnbull, A. P., Turnbull, R., Erwin, E. J., & Soodak, L. C. (2005). *Families, professionals, exceptionality: Positive outcomes through partnership and trust* (5th ed.). Prentice Hall.

Ullman, M. T., Earle, F. S., Walenski, M., & Janacsek, K. (2020). The neurocognition of developmental disorders of language. *Annual Review of Psychology*, *71*(1), 389–417. doi:10.1146/annurev-psych-122216-011555 PMID:31337273

UNESCO. (1994). *The Salamanca Statement and Framework for Action on Special Needs Education.* World Conference on Special Needs Education: Access and Quality, Salamanca, Spain.

UNESCO. (2020). *Global education monitoring report, 2020: Inclusion and education: all means all.* UN. https://unesdoc.unesco.org/ark:/48223/pf0000373718

Upadhyaya, R. G., & Havalappanavar, N. B. (2008). Coping in parents of the mentally challenged. *Journal of the Indian Academy of Applied Psychology*, *34*(2), 221–225.

Uppstad, P. H., & Tønnessen, F. E. (2007). The notion of 'phonology' in dyslexia research: Cognitivism—and beyond. *Dyslexia (Chichester, England)*, *13*(3), 154–174. doi:10.1002/dys.332 PMID:17624910

Uziel, G., Ghezzi, D., & Zeviani, M. (2011). Infantile Mitochondrial Encephalopathy. Seminars in Fetal & Neonatal Medicine. *Elsevier, 16*(4), 205- 215. https://doi.org/ doi:10.1016/j.siny.2011.04.003

Vail, P. L. (2001). *Treating the whole person: emotion, denial, disguises, language, and connectedness. Dyslexia: theory and good practice*. Whurr Publishing.

Valle, J. W., & Connor, D. J. (2019). *Rethinking disability: A disability studies approach to inclusive practices*. Routledge. doi:10.4324/9781315111209

Vallerand, R. J., Fortier, M. S., & Guay, F. (1997). Self-determination and persistence in real life setting: Toward a motivational model of high school drop out. *Journal of Personality and Social Psychology*, *72*(5), 1161–1176. doi:10.1037/0022-3514.72.5.1161 PMID:9150590

Van Daal, J., Verhoeven, L., & van Balkom, H. (2007). Behavior problems in children with language impairment. [PubMed: 17995490]. *Journal of Child Psychology and Psychiatry, and Allied Disciplines*, *48*(11), 1139–1147. doi:10.1111/j.1469-7610.2007.01790.x PMID:17995490

Van den Bedem, N. P., Dockrell, J. E., van Alphen, P. M., Kalicharan, S. V., & Rieffe, C. (2018). Victimization, bullying, and emotional competence: Longitudinal associations in (Pre)adolescents with and without developmental language disorder. *Journal of Speech, Language, and Hearing Research: JSLHR*, *61*(8), 2028–2044. doi:10.1044/2018_JSLHR-L-17-0429 PMID:29998317

Van Mieghem, A., Verschueren, K., Petry, K., & Struyf, E. (2020). An analysis of research on inclusive education: A systematic search and meta review. *International Journal of Inclusive Education*, *24*(6), 675–689. doi:10.1080/13603116.2018.1482012

VanDam, M., & Yoshinaga-Itano, C. (2019). Use of the LENA Autism Screen with Children who are Deaf or Hard of Hearing. *Medicina*, *55*(8), 495. doi:10.3390/medicina55080495 PMID:31426435

Vansteenkiste, M., Simons, J., Lens, W., Sheldon, K. M., & Deci, E. L. (2004). Motivating learning, performance, and persistence: The synergistic role of intrinsic goals and autonomy support. *Journal of Personality and Social Psychology*, *87*, 246–260. doi:10.1037/0022-3514.87.2.246 PMID:15301630

Varsamidou, D., & Spadidakis, G. (2007). Relationship between written language production and comprehension. In M. Vlassopoulou, A., Giannetopoulou, M. Diamanti, L., Kirpotin, E., Levantis, E., Leftheri & G. Sakellariou (Eds.), Language difficulties and written language in the context of school learning (pp.377- 389). Grigoris. [in Greek]

Vasconcelos, M., Viding, E., Sebastian, C. L., Faria, S., Almeida, P. R., Gonçalves, Ó. F., Gonçalves, R. A., Sampaio, A., & Seara-Cardoso, A. (2021). Callous-Unemotional Traits Moderate Anticipated Guilt and Wrongness Judgments to Everyday Moral Transgressions in Adolescents. *Frontiers in Psychiatry*, *12*(March), 1–11. doi:10.3389/fpsyt.2021.625328 PMID:33762977

Vasileiadis, I., Koutras, S., & Stagiopoulos, P. (2021). Changing the attitudes of high school students towards intellectual disabilities: The contribution of a social coexistence programme. *Journal of Research in Special Educational Needs*, *21*(1), 49–62. doi:10.1111/1471-3802.12498

Verenikina, I. (2003). Vygotsky' s Socio-Cultural Theory and the Zone of Proximal Development. In H. M. Hasan, I. M. Verenikina, & E. L. Gould (Eds.), *Expanding the Horizon. Information Systems and Activity Theory* (pp. 4–14). University of Wollongong Press.

Vernes, S. C., Newbury, D. F., Abrahams, B. S., Winchester, L., Nicod, J., Groszer, M., Alarcón, M., Oliver, P. L., Davies, K. E., Geschwind, D. H., Monaco, A. P., & Fisher, S. E. (2008). A Functional Genetic Link between Distinct Developmental Language Disorders. *The New England Journal of Medicine*, *359*(22), 2337–2345. doi:10.1056/NEJMoa0802828 PMID:18987363

Vernon-Feagans, L., Bratsch-Hines, M., Reyonlds, E., & Willoughby, M. (2020). How early maternal language input varies by race and education and predicts later child language. *Child Development*, *91*(4), 1098–1115. doi:10.1111/cdev.13281 PMID:31317532

Vervoort, T., Logan, D. E., Goubert, L., De Clercq, B., & Hublet, A. (2014). Severity of pediatric pain in relation to school-related functioning and teacher support: An epidemiological study among school-aged children and adolescents. *Pain*, *155*(6), 1118–1127. doi:10.1016/j.pain.2014.02.021 PMID:24631587

Vetoniemi, J., & Kärnä, E. (2021). Being included–experiences of social participation of pupils with special education needs in mainstream schools. *International Journal of Inclusive Education*, *25*(10), 1190–1204. doi:10.1080/13603116.2019.1603329

Vicari, S., Finzi, A., Menghini, D., Marotta, L., Baldi, S., & Petrosini, L. (2005). Do children with developmental dyslexia have an implicit learning deficit? *Journal of Neurology, Neurosurgery, and Psychiatry*, *76*(10), 1392–1397. doi:10.1136/jnnp.2004.061093 PMID:16170083

Vickery, K. S., Reynolds, V. A., & Cochran, S. W. (1987). Multisensory teaching approach for reading, spelling, and handwriting, Orton-Gillingham based curriculum, in a public school setting. *Annals of Dyslexia*, *37*(1), 189–200. doi:10.1007/BF02648066 PMID:24234994

Vietze, P., & Lax, L. E. (2020). Early intervention ABA for toddlers with ASD: Effect of age and amount. *Current Psychology (New Brunswick, N.J.)*, *39*(4), 1234–1244. doi:10.100712144-018-9812-z

Vincent, L., & Chiwandire, D. (2019). Funding and inclusion in higher education institutions for students with disabilities. *African Journal of Disability*, *8*(1), 1–12. PMID:30899686

Vitiello, V., & Williford, A. P. (2016). Relations between social skills and language and literacy outcomes among disruptive preschoolers: Task engagement as a mediator. *Early Childhood Research Quarterly*, *36*, 136–144. doi:10.1016/j.ecresq.2015.12.011

Vivanti, G., Fanning, P. A. J., Hocking, D. R., Sievers, S., & Dissanayake, C. (2017). Social Attention, Joint Attention and Sustained Attention in Autism Spectrum Disorder and Williams Syndrome: Convergences and Divergences. *Journal of Autism and Developmental Disorders*, *47*(6), 1866–1877. doi:10.100710803-017-3106-4 PMID:28349363

Vlachos, F., Avramidis, E., Dedousis, G., Chalmpe, M., Stalla, I., & Giannakopoulos, M. (2013). Prevalence and Gender Ratio of Dyslexia in Greek Adolescents and its Association with Parental History and Brain Injury. *American Journal of Educational Research*, *1*(1), 22–25. doi:10.12691/education-1-1-5

Vlachou, A., & Fyssa, A. (2016). 'Inclusion in practice': Programme practices in mainstream preschool classrooms and associations with context and teacher characteristics. *International Journal of Disability Development and Education*, *63*(5), 529–544. doi:10.1080/1034912X.2016.1145629

Vlachou, A., & Papananou, I. (2018). Experiences and perspectives of Greek higher education students with disabilities. *Educational Research*, *60*(2), 206–221. doi:10.1080/00131881.2018.1453752

Von Cheong, E., Sinnott, C., Dahly, D., & Kearney, P. M. (2017). Adverse childhood experiences (ACEs) and later-life depression: Perceived social support as a potential protective factor. *BMJ Open*, *7*(9), e013228. doi:10.1136/bmjopen-2016-013228 PMID:28864684

Vula, E., Avdyli, R., Berisha, V., Saqipi, B., & Elezi, S. (2017). The impact of metacognitive strategies and self-regulating processes of solving math word problems. *International Electronic Journal of Elementary Education*, *10*(1), 49–59. doi:10.26822/iejee.2017131886

Vygotsky, L. S. (1978). *Mind in Society: The development of higher psychological processes*. Harvard University Press.

Vygotsky, L. S. (2012). *Thought and language*. MIT press.

Wadlington, E. M., & Wadlington, P. L. (2005). What educators really believe about dyslexia. *Reading Improvement*, *42*(1), 16–33.

Wadman, R., Botting, N., Durkin, K., & Conti-Ramsden, G. (2011). Changes in emotional health symptoms in adolescents with specific language impairment. *International Journal of Language & Communication Disorders*, *46*(6), 641–656. doi:10.1111/j.1460-6984.2011.00033.x PMID:22026566

Wagner, R. K., Zirps, F. A., Edwards, A. A., Wood, S. G., Joyner, R. E., Becker, B. J., Liu, G., & Beal, B. (2020). The prevalence of dyslexia: A new approach to its estimation. *Journal of Learning Disabilities*, *53*(5), 354–365. doi:10.1177/0022219420920377 PMID:32452713

Wakschlag, L. S. (2005). Disruptive behavior disorders: Developmental pathways to conduct disorder. In D. Cicchetti & D. J. Cohen (Eds.), *Developmental psychopathology*. Developmental psychopathology.

Waller, R., Wagner, N. J., Barstead, M. G., Subar, A., Petersen, J. L., Hyde, J. S., & Hyde, L. W. (2020). A meta-analysis of the associations between callous-unemotional traits and empathy, prosociality, and guilt. *Clinical Psychology Review, 75*(April 2019), 101809. doi:10.1016/j.cpr.2019.101809

Wang, Y., Xiong, M., & Olya, H. (2020, January). Toward an understanding of responsible artificial intelligence practices. In *Proceedings of the 53rd Hawaii international conference on system sciences* (pp. 4962-4971). International Conference on System Sciences (HICSS). 10.24251/HICSS.2020.610

Wang, P., Michaels, C. A., & Day, M. S. (2011). Stresses and coping strategies of Chinese families with children with autism and other developmental disabilities. *Journal of Autism and Developmental Disorders*, *41*(6), 783–795. doi:10.100710803-010-1099-3 PMID:20859670

Wang, Y., Hartman, M., Aziz, N. A., Arora, S., Shi, L., & Tunison, E. (2017). A Systematic Review of the Use of LENA Technology. *American Annals of the Deaf, 162*(3), 295–311. doi:10.1353/aad.2017.0028 PMID:28824021

Wang, Y., Williams, R., Dilley, L., & Houston, D. (2020). A meta-analysis of the predictability of LENA automated measures for child language development. *Developmental Review, 57*, 100921. Advance online publication. doi:10.1016/j.dr.2020.100921 PMID:32632339

Washburn, E. K., Joshi, R. M., & Binks-Cantrell, E. S. (2011). Teacher knowledge of basic language concepts and dyslexia. *Dyslexia, 17,* 165e183.

Watson, R. M., & Pennington, L. (2015). Assessment and management of the communication difficulties of children with cerebral palsy: A UK survey of SLT practice. *International Journal of Language & Communication Disorders, 50*(2), 241–259. doi:10.1111/1460-6984.12138 PMID:25652139

WattA. (2014, August 14). *14. Quality Planning*. Pressbooks. https://opentextbc.ca/projectmanagement/chapter/chapter-14-quality-planning-project-management/

Wehmeyer, M. L. (2019). *Strengths-based approaches to educating all learners with disabilities: Beyond special education*. Teachers College Press.

Weisleder, A., & Fernald, A. (2013). Talking to children matters: Early language experience strengthens processing and builds vocabulary. *Psychological Science, 24*(11), 2143–2152. doi:10.1177/0956797613488145 PMID:24022649

Wendt, G. W., Bartoli, A. J., & Arteche, A. (2017). Dimensions of youth psychopathy differentially predict concurrent pro- and antisocial behavior. *Revista Brasileira de Psiquiatria (Sao Paulo, Brazil), 39*(3), 267–270. doi:10.1590/1516-4446-2016-2143 PMID:28813114

Westwood, P. (2018). *Inclusive and adaptive teaching: Meeting the challenge of diversity in the classroom*. Routledge. doi:10.4324/9781351061261

Wetherby, A. M., & Prutting, C. A. (1984). Profiles of communicative and cognitive-social abilities in autistic children. *Journal of Speech and Hearing Research, 27*(3), 364–377. doi:10.1044/jshr.2703.364 PMID:6482406

Wetherby, A. M., Watt, N., Morgan, L., & Shumway, S. (2007). Social communication profiles of children with autism spectrum disorders late in the second year of life. *Journal of Autism and Developmental Disorders, 37*(5), 960–975. doi:10.100710803-006-0237-4 PMID:17066310

Whitehouse, A. J., Robinson, M., & Zubrick, S. R. (2011). Late talking and the risk for psychosocial problems during childhood and adolescence. [PubMed: 21727106]. *Pediatrics, 128*(2), e324–e332. doi:10.1542/peds.2010-2782 PMID:21727106

White, M., & Elander, G. (1992). Translation of an instrument. *Scandinavian Journal of Caring Sciences, 6*(3), 161–164. doi:10.1111/j.1471-6712.1992.tb00145.x PMID:1439377

Wiggins, G. P., & McTighe, J. (2005). *Understanding by design*. Association or Supervision and Curriculum Development.

Wiig, E. (2004). Assessing Students for Successful Inclusion. In *Count Me In - Developing Inclusive International Schools*. Overseas Schools Advisory Council, Department of State, Washington, D.C. https://2009-2017.state.gov/m/a/os/45070.htm

Wilcox, M. J., Gray, S., & Reiser, M. (2020). Preschoolers with developmental speech and/or language impairment: Efficacy of the Teaching Early Literacy and Language (TELL) curriculum. *Early Childhood Research Quarterly, 51*, 124–143. doi:10.1016/j.ecresq.2019.10.005

Willcutt, E. G., Doyle, A. E., Nigg, J. T., Faraone, S. V., & Pennington, B. F. (2005). Validity of the executive function theory of attention-deficit/hyperactivity disorder: A meta-analytic review. *Biological Psychiatry*, *57*(11), 1336–1346. doi:10.1016/j.biopsych.2005.02.006 PMID:15950006

Willinger, U., Brunner, E., Diendorfer-Radner, G., Sams, J., Sirsch, U., & Eisenwort, B. (2003). Behaviour in Children with Language Development Disorders. *Canadian Journal of Psychiatry*, *48*(9), 607–614. doi:10.1177/070674370304800907 PMID:14631881

Willoughby, M. T.-K. (2014). Measuring callous unemotional behaviors in early childhood: Factor structure and the prediction of stable aggression in middle childhood. *Journal of Psychopathology and Be.*

Wilson, L., McNeill, B., & Gillon, G. T. (2017). Inter-professional education of prospective speech–language therapists and primary school teachers through shared professional practice placements. *International Journal of Language & Communication Disorders*, *52*(4), 426–439. doi:10.1111/1460-6984.12281 PMID:27624388

Winnicott, D. W. (1971). *Playing and Reality*. Penguin Books.

Winnicott, D. W. (1975). *Through pediatrics to psycho-analysis: Collected papers*. Brunner/Mazel.

Wong, K., Thomas, C., & Boben, M. (2020). Providence talks: A citywide partnership to address early childhood language development. *Studies in Educational Evaluation*, *64*, 100818. doi:10.1016/j.stueduc.2019.100818

Woodward, D., Wilens, T. E., Yule, A. M., DiSalvo, M., Taubin, D., Berger, A., Stone, M., Wozniak, J., Burke, C., & Biederman, J. (2023). Examining the clinical correlates of conduct disorder in youth with bipolar disorder. *Journal of Affective Disorders*, *329*(February), 300–306. doi:10.1016/j.jad.2023.02.119 PMID:36863464

Writing@CSU. (n.d.). https://writing.colostate.edu/guides/guide.cfm?guideid=65

Wu, J., Chen, L., Li, X., Yue, S., Huang, X., Liu, J., Hou, X., & Lai, T. (2022). Trends in the prevalence of conduct disorder from 1990 to 2019: Findings from the Global Burden of Disease Study 2019. *Psychiatry Research, 317*(May 2021), 114907. doi:10.1016/j.psychres.2022.114907

Wymbs, B. T., & Pelham, W. E. (2010). Child effects on communication between parents of youth with and without ADHD. *Journal of Abnormal Psychology*, *119*, 366–375. doi:10.1037/a0019034 PMID:20455609

Xanthi, S. (2017). Qualitative analysis of 4th - 6th grade students' errors in dictation and free writing spelling tasks. [in Greek]. *Research in Education*, *6*(1), 1–17.

Xu, S., Zhang, H., & Wang, J. (2020). Caregiver burden and depression among Chinese family caregivers: The role of self-compassion. *Mindfulness*, *11*(7), 1647–1654. doi:10.100712671-020-01378-7

Yang, L., Li, C., Li, X., Zhai, M., An, Q., Zhang, Y., Zhao, J., & Weng, X. (2022). Prevalence of developmental dyslexia in primary school children: A systematic review and metaanalysis. *Brain Sciences*, *12*(2), 240. doi:10.3390/brainsci12020240 PMID:35204003

Yew, S. G. K., & O'Kearney, R. (2013). Emotional and behavioural outcomes later In childhood and adolescence for children with specific language impairments: Meta-analyses of controlled prospective studies. *Journal of Child Psychology and Psychiatry, and Allied Disciplines*, *54*(5), 516–524. doi:10.1111/jcpp.12009 PMID:23082773

Yokota, R., Okuhara, T., Okada, H., Goto, E., Sakakibara, K., & Kiuchi, T. (2022). Association between stigma and anxiety, depression, and psychological distress among Japanese women undergoing infertility treatment. *Health Care*, *10*(7), 1300. doi:10.3390/healthcare10071300 PMID:35885826

Zachos, G. H., & Zachos, D. H. (1998). *Dyslexia. Treatment-Rehabilitation. Program implementation instructions.* Center for Psychological Studies.

Zarić, J., Hasselhorn, M., & Nagler, T. (2021). Orthographic knowledge predicts reading and spelling skills over and above general intelligence and phonological awareness. *European Journal of Psychology of Education*, *36*(1), 21–43. doi:10.100710212-020-00464-7

Zdravkova, K. (2022). The potential of artificial intelligence for assistive technology in education. In Handbook on Intelligent Techniques in the Educational Process: Vol 1 Recent Advances and Case Studies (pp. 61-85). Cham: Springer International Publishing. doi:10.1007/978-3-031-04662-9_4

Zelazo, P. D. (1996). Impulse control in aggressive children. *Aggressive Behavior*, 1098–2337.

Zeleke, S. (2004). Self-concepts of students with learning disabilities and their normally achieving peers: A review. *European Journal of Special Needs Education*, *19*(2), 145–170. doi:10.1080/08856250410001678469

Zhang, J., & Lee, D. T. (2017). Meaning in stroke family caregiving: A literature review. *Geriatric Nursing*, *38*(1), 48–56. doi:10.1016/j.gerinurse.2016.07.005 PMID:27671537

Zhang, L. F. (2010). Do age and gender make a difference in the relationship between intellectual styles and abilities? *European Journal of Psychology of Education*, *25*(1), 87–103. doi:10.100710212-009-0006-9

Zhang, R., Bashford-Largo, J., Lukoff, J., Elowsky, J., Carollo, E., Schwartz, A., Dobbertin, M., Bajaj, S., Blair, K. S., Leibenluft, E., & Blair, R. J. R. (2021). Callous-Unemotional Traits Moderate the Relationship Between Irritability and Threatening Responding. *Frontiers in Psychiatry*, *12*(November), 1–12. doi:10.3389/fpsyt.2021.617052 PMID:34867494

Zhang, S., Fan, H. J., & Zhang, Y. (2021). The 100 Top-Cited Studies on Dyslexia Research: A Bibliometric Analysis. *Frontiers in Psychiatry*, *12*, 714627. doi:10.3389/fpsyt.2021.714627 PMID:34366943

Zheng, B., Warschauer, M., Lin, C. H., & Chang, C. (2016). Learning in one-to-one laptop environments: A meta-analysis and research synthesis. *Review of Educational Research*, *86*(4), 1052–1084. doi:10.3102/0034654316628645

Zhou, Y., Yin, H., Wang, M., & Wang, J. (2019). The effect of family-focused psychoeducational therapy for autism spectrum disorder children's parents on parenting self-efficacy and emotion. *Archives of Psychiatric Nursing*, *33*(1), 17–22. doi:10.1016/j.apnu.2018.08.002 PMID:30663619

Zhu, M., Cai, D., & Leung, A. W. (2017). Number line estimation predicts mathematical skills: Difference in grades 2 and 4. *Frontiers in Psychology*, *8*, 1576. doi:10.3389/fpsyg.2017.01576 PMID:28955282

Ziegenfusz, S., Paynter, J., Flückiger, B., & Westerveld, M. F. (2022). A systematic review of the academic achievement of primary and secondary school-aged students with developmental language disorder. *Autism & Developmental Language Impairments*, *7*, 23969415221099397. doi:10.1177/23969415221099397 PMID:36382072

Zimmerman, F. J., Gilkerson, J., Richards, J. A., Christakis, D. A., Xu, D., Gray, S., & Yapanel, U. (2009). Teaching by listening: The importance of adult-child conversations to language development. *Pediatrics*, *124*(1), 342–349. doi:10.1542/peds.2008-2267 PMID:19564318

About the Contributors

Dimitra Katsarou is an Assistant Professor of Developmental Psychopathology and Language Disorders at the Department of Preschool Education Sciences and Educational Design of the University of the Aegean. She has more than 30 scholarly publications in influential peer-reviewed journals and more than 100 conference presentations, she has authored a monograph, four co- editing books, and three editing books in Greek language, as well as participated in several chapters in other scientific publications. She is academically responsible for education, training and education programs of Greek and international organizations and participates as a key researcher in Greek and international research programs, such as Erasmus Plus, Alliance edu, Cost.eu, Erasmus Sport. In parallel with the University of the Aegean, she has worked as adjunct faculty at University of Nicosia, University of Derby, University of Thessaly, Aristotle University of Thessaloniki, Hellenic Open University, Neapolis University of Paphos and Frederick University. Her research interests focus on the special education of children with intellectual disabilities, neurolinguistics, cognitive processes, autism, developmental psychopathology, speech and language development, genetic syndromes and intergenerational activities.

***

Maria Alexandri was born in Athens in 1997. She studied Psychology at the University of Athens. She completed an internship at a neurodevelopmental care centre for children in Piraeus. She holds two certifications from the University of Athens in infant, child, and adolescent psychopathology, as well as special treatment: "interdisciplinary convergence practices". She is currently in her second year of a Master's degree in Clinical and Cognitive Neuropsychology at the University of Strasbourg. She works as a psychologist, specializing in children, adolescents, and families in Athens. She delivered a speech during Brain Awareness Week 2023. Her passion lies in assisting individuals with any disabilities to achieve their full potential.

Anastasia Barbouni was born in Athens. She studied Medicine at the University of Athens, Greece. She is Paediatrician and is specialised in Paediatric Intensive Care Unit. She holds a Master of Public Health (MPH) from the National School of Public Health and Doctorate (PhD) from the University of Athens in the field of Epidemiology . Her research interests covers the epidemiology of the developmental diseases of the first years of life, paediatrics issues, nutrition and the development of prevention and intervention programs and efforts for the control of smoking habit in Greece. She has published in Greek and international journals and has co-authored books and educational material within Greek and European programs . Since 2016 she has been elected Professor of Public Health at the Department of

Public Health of the National School of Public Health, Athens, Greece. She was member of National Nutrition Commitee, National vaccination Commitee and representative of Greece to the Council of Europe (CDSP -Public Health Committee)

Christos Charmpatsis is a PhD Candidate, Pedagogical Department of Early Childhood Education, University of Ioannina.

Pineio Christodoulou is a graduate of the Pedagogical Department of Kindergarten Teachers of the School of Humanities and Social Sciences of the University of Patras, Greece. She holds a master's and doctoral degree in Special Education. She was a scholarship holder of National Scholarships Foundation (IKY) at undergraduate, postgraduate and doctoral level. She has taught in primary, secondary and tertiary education. She has taught in the postgraduate program of Special Education at the University of Nicosia in Cyprus. She participated as a delegate, but also as a speaker at Greek and international scientific conferences. Publishes articles in reputable Greek and international scientific journals. She is the co-author of a book. She has been a reviewer of articles in Greek and international scientific journals, as well as conference presentations. She has attended many specialization seminars in Special Education. She is a certified instructor in adult education (National Organization for Certification of Qualifications & Professional Guidance-EOPPEP).

Foteini Christopoulou is a graduate of the Department of Philology of the University of Patras, Greece. She holds a master's degree in Special Education and is a PhD candidate in Special Education at the Department of Preschool Education at the University of Ioannina, Greece. She has participated as a speaker in Greek scientific conferences. She publishes articles in reputable international scientific journals. She was a reviewer of articles in an international scientific journal. She has attended specialization seminars in Special Education.

Antonios I. Christou is an Assistant Professor in Child Neurocognitive Development at the University of Thessaly, Volos, Greece and Coordinator of the Section of Neuropsychology at the Hellenic Psychological Society. He holds a Ph.D. in Psychology (2016) and an M.A. in Inclusion and Special Educational Needs (2011) from the University of Birmingham, UK. His primary research interests are on the investigation of neurocognitive mechanisms of emotion processing, emotion regulation and sensitivity in early childhood.

Efthymia Efthymiou is a professional in the field of special education, currently serving as an Assistant Professor at Zayed University in the United Arab Emirates (UAE). With a strong background in special education, her research focuses on inclusive teaching practices, classroom discourse, and creating educational environments that support the inclusion of all students, including those with special needs. Her work centers on understanding the perspectives of various stakeholders, such as teachers and children with special needs, to develop more inclusive educational systems. She explores the role of both physical and psychological environments in shaping attitudes, positioning, and inclusion. Her research aims to identify and overcome barriers to inclusive education, with particular emphasis on leveraging technology-based teaching practices to address digital exclusion and promote inclusive teaching methods. In addition to her research efforts, Dr. Efthymiou actively contributes to the advancement of inclusive education through her workshops and seminars conducted for teachers and principals in federal schools within the UAE.

Vasiliki Folia earned her graduate degree from the Department of Psychology at Aristotle University of Thessaloniki and holds a master's degree in Cognitive Neuroscience from Radboud University in The Netherlands. Her PhD, completed at Karolinska Institutet in Sweden, focused on Implicit Learning of Linguistic Syntax in the Department of Clinical Cognitive Neuroscience. Following her doctoral studies, Dr. Folia held various positions at the Amsterdam University of Applied Sciences (AUAS), starting as an Assistant from 2009 to 2012, then advancing to become an Associate Professor from 2013 to 2018. During this time, she also served as a Research Chair from 2016 to 2018. She joined the Department of Psychology in Aristotle University in 2021. Her primary research interests lie in the field of neuropsychology of language, both in healthy and clinical populations. Specifically, her work revolves around investigating neural mechanisms, serial language processing, and cognitive functions that contribute to syntactic and linguistic ability. To achieve these objectives, she employs a combination of neuropsychological, neurophysiological, and neuroimaging methods.

Theodore Karakasidis is a Professor at the Physics Department, University of Thessaly, University of Thessaly in Greece. His research interests include Computational Materials Modeling, CFD, Nanotechnology, Nano fluidics, Nanomaterials, biomaterials as well as data analytics, machine learning, econophysics. He has conducted research in many different aspects materials modeling using atomistic and coarse grained d methods and is actively working in the field of multiscale materials in the field of grain boundaries and surfaces, crack propagation modeling, as well in several aspects of nano-fluidics. Recently he is working in the modeling of water purification and desalination procedures using magnetic nanoparticles. He is also working in the field of dynamical systems modeling using advanced time series analysis methods and data analytics methods for system identification and event detection from multisensory measurement, especially in spatiotemporal phenomena like fluid motion, weather data, traffic analysis and prediction etc. He has published more than 150 articles in scientific journals and conference proceedings and participated in the organization of Scientific Conferences and Symposia in Greece and Abroad. He is actively involved either as a Principal Investigator or Senior researcher in research projects- funded by the European Union or national sources.

Eirini Karakasidou is a Psychologist, who holds a Master's degree (MSc) with a specialization in Sports Psychology and a PhD in Clinical Psychology from the Panteion University of Social and Political Sciences. Alongside her academic studies, she has completed 4 years of training in Existential Psychotherapy and 2 years of training in Behavioural Therapy for Anxiety Disorders. Her research interests are in the field of Counselling Psychology, Positive Psychology, Psychometrics, and Psychotherapy and she has participated as a principal investigator and coordinator in several European-funded projects. She has authored articles in peer-reviewed journals, and book chapters and has a number of presentations and experiential workshops at Greek and international conferences, NGOs, schools, businesses, and hospitals. She works privately as a psychologist and psychotherapist in individual and group settings, teaches in various educational institutions in Greece and abroad, and is a lecturer in seminars for special and general audiences.

Vasia Karra is a teacher in secondary education researching linguistics, new technologies in education, DI differentiated instruction in education.

Eleni Kazali is an Assistant Professor in Cognitive Experimental Psychology.

Georgios A. Kougioumtzis shares his love and scientific involvement in the fields of Counseling, Sciences of Education and Teaching Methodology and CTI. He is a postdoctoral researcher at the Department of Philosophy, Education, and Psychology of the University of Athens and holds a Ph.D. (Pedagogy, Didactics, and Counseling - Teacher Mentoring) of the same department. He studied Classics (National and Kapodistrian University of Athens) and Social Theology (National and Kapodistrian University of Athens) and also has a Master's Degree (M.Ed.) in Educational Sciences (focusing on Adult Education - Hellenic Open University). He has specialized in the fields of Learning Difficulties [SNE - Dyslexia (Department of Special Education, University of Thessaly)], of Information Technology (Piraeus University of Applied Sciences) and Counseling (University of the Aegean). He has taught "Counseling Psychology" at the Hellenic Open University, ASPAITE and in Programs of Mental and Community Health at the University of the Aegean. He has worked as a Counseling Specialist / Expert and Evaluator in many of the programs of the Ministry of Education. He is married and father of three daughters.

Afroditi Malisiova is an EFL teacher and a Ph.D. candidate at the Department of Psychology at the Aristotle University of Thessaloniki. She has studied English Language and Literature at the Aristotle University of Thessaloniki and holds a Master's degree in Teaching English as a Foreign Language (TEFL) from the Hellenic Open University and a Master of Science in Educational Psychology from the University of Neapolis, Pafos. She has been working as an English language teacher in Greek primary and secondary schools in the private and state sector since 2005. Her research interests lie in the fields of teaching English as a foreign language, cognitive psychology, special education, intercultural education, and pedagogies.

Fani Nasika is a graduate of Philology (Linguistics stream) of the National and Kapodistrian University of Athens (Greece) and of Speech and Language Therapy of the Higher Technological Educational Institute of Western Greece. She holds an MA in Language Disorders from the University of Essex (UK) and a PhD in Clinical Language Sciences from the University of Reading (UK). She has taught at the Department of Philology and the Department of Speech and Language Therapy at the University of Patras (Greece), at the MA in Sciences of Language and Culture at the Aristotle University of Thessaloniki (Greece) and she has been a Scientific Collaborator at the Hellenic Open University, for the MEd Education Science: Special Education for People with Oral and Written Language Difficulties. She has also worked as an Associate Lecturer with Canterbury Christ Church University and she has collaborated with the University of Essex via Aegean Omiros College (Greece). Her research interests involve developmental and acquired language disorders as well as special educational needs.

Eleni Nikolaou is an Assistant Professor (tenured) at the department of Sciences of Preschool Education and Educational Design, University of the Aegean. She has been teaching at the University of the Aegean, as an adjunct lecturer, since 2002 and as an elected lecturer since 2014. In addition to her teaching duties at the undergraduate level, she also teaches in the Postgraduate Programs of "Environmental Education", as well as in the "Models of Educational Planning and Development" of T.E.P.A.E.S of the University of the Aegean. She has worked for almost fifteen consecutive years in a counseling and mental health service for children, adolescents and their families in Rhodes, Greece. During her career she has given a lot of lectures in schools regarding mental health issues and she has been participated in professional development training courses for teachers. She holds a Ph.D. from the Department of Preschool Education and Educational Design, University of the Aegean (2005). She completed her postgraduate studies at City University, London (M.Sc. in Counseling Psychology, 1999). She holds a Bachelor's Degree in Psychology from the University of Crete (1996). Her articles have been published in reputable scientific peer reviewed journals and Conferences, both nationally (in Greek) and internationally (in English language).

Olympia Palikara is a Professor of Educational Psychology and co-director of postgraduate research programmes in the University of Warwick, UK. Olympia is currently Convener of the Psychology in Education Standing Committee of the European Federation of Psychologists' Association (EFPA) and co-chair of the Division of Educational and Child Psychology (DECP) of the British Psychological Society. Her research interests concern the educational and psychosocial outcomes of children with developmental disorders, including those with Developmental Language Disorder, Williams Syndrome, Down Syndrome and Autism Spectrum Disorders. She is also particularly interested in the effect of educational transitions, including from primary to secondary education and secondary education to post-compulsory education on children's mental health and wellbeing. Previous studies have been funded by Baily Thomas Charitable Fund, British Academy and Williams Syndrome Foundation. Olympia has written over 50 peer-reviewed articles and two co-edited books.

Anna Papadimitriou is Psychologist and CBT Psychotherapist who specializes in working with adults, children, and teenagers. Simultaneously, she holds a position within the educational staff and serves as a supervisor for undergraduate and postgraduate degree theses in the Department of Psychology at Metropolitan College, in collaboration with the University of East London. Additionally, she is an accomplished seminar trainer (e.g. training for intercultural mediators). She holds a master's degree in Positive Psychology and Business Psychology, and she has completed extensive training in Cognitive Behavioral Therapy, Acceptance and Commitment Therapy, as well as Counseling and Psychotherapy for LGBTQI individuals. Actively engaged in research projects, Ms. Papadimitriou has also contributed to the writing of articles, book chapters, and conference presentations.

Panagiotis Papalexopoulos has a BSc in Physics, Physics Department, University of Patras,1988. MA in Instruction and Evaluation, Philospophy-Psychology-Pedagy Department, University of Athens, 1998. PhD in Dyslexia and Physics, Philospophy-Psychology-Pedagy Department, University of Athens, 2004. Post doc in Learning Disabilities and Science Education, Special Education Department, University of Thessaly, 2018. Post doc in Differentiated Pedagogy and Science Education, Physics Department, University of Thessaly, in progress. Lecturer, University of Thessaly, 2010. Lecturer, University of Nicosia, since 2021. Teacher of Science in Secondary Education, General Education, 1991-2020. Teacher of Science in Secondary Education, Special Education, since 2020.

. M. Nazmuz Sakib was born in Bangladesh on the 16th of April in 2001. He achieved his Primary School Certificate (PSC) from Cotton Research Station School, Sreepur, Gazipur and after several months of studying Class 6 in Alhaz Dhanai Bepari Memorial High School, Sreepur, Gazipur, he relocated to

Jashore. He accomplished his Junior School Certificate (JSC) from Jagodishpur Mirzapur Ismail Secondary School, Jagodishour, Chaowgacha, Jashore and his Secondary School Certificate (SSC) from A. K. High School And College, Dhania, Dhaka-1236. He obtained his Higher Secondary Certificate (HSC) from Chowgacha Government College, Chowgacha, Jashore. He received a BSc in Business Studies, earning a CGPA of 4 out of 4 (1st class 1st) with 97.06% marks from School of Business and Trade, an online business school situated in Switzerland. He completed an MBA in Human Resources from International MBA Institute, an online business institute in Switzerland. He studied Bachelor of Laws (Hon's) or LLB(Hon's) at Dhaka International University, Dhaka, Bangladesh and obtained 1st class. He has accomplished CPD verified advanced diploma and diploma programs i.e. Advanced Diploma in Tissue Engineering, Advanced Diploma in Genetic Engineering - Theory and Application, Diploma in Fashion Design, Diploma in Nutrition, Therapeutics and Health, Diploma in Biology, Diploma in Pharmacy Technician, Software Test Engineer Diploma (Advanced), Advanced Diploma in Soil Science and Technology, Diploma in Energy Economics, Energy Systems and Environmental Impact, Advanced Diploma in Political Ideologies, Diploma in Community Psychology, Diploma in Training of Trainers, Advance Diploma in Principles of Industrial Engineering, Advanced Diploma in Production & Operation Management, Advanced Diploma in Modelling and Analytics for Supply Chain Management, Business Administration Diploma (Foundation), Diploma in Effective Human Resource Administration, Diploma in Audio System Engineering, Diploma in ISO Standards - Integrated Management System (IMS), Diploma in Lean Manufacturing - Productive Management with Fundamental Tools, Advanced Diploma in Tourism and Hospitality Management, Diploma in Web Design, Diploma in Human Resources, and Diploma in Basic English Grammar, Diploma in River Engineering and has obtained certifications such as TESOL from Arizona State University, TEFL from Teacher Record, Scrum Master Professional Certificate (SMPC®), EF SET Certificate (C2 Level), Google IT Support Professional Certificate, Google Data Analytics Professional Certificate, Google Project Management Professional Certificate, Google Business Intelligence Professional Certificate, Google Digital Marketing & E-commerce Professional Certificate and IBM New Collar: Customer Engagement Specialist credential etc. As a multidisciplinary researcher, he has published several articles in the Asian Pacific Journal of Environment and Cancer, Simulacra, Journal of Innovation Information Technology and Application (JINITA), Waste Technology, and The IUP Journal of Electrical and Electronics Engineering. Several of his articles are published by Cambridge Open Engage, a publication of Cambridge University Press. Some of the titles of his published research works include "The Impact of Oil and Gas Development on the Landscape and Surface in Nigeria," "Assessing the Impact of Arctic Melting in the Predominantly Multilateral World System," "LiDAR Technology - An Overview," "Exploring the Intersection of Software Engineering and Mobile Technology from 2010 to 2021: A Review of Recent Research", This paper presents a comprehensive review of recent research on the intersection of software engineering and mobile technology. The review method involves a systematic literature search and analysis of relevant research articles. The study identifies key trends and challenges in the field, including the need for better testing and debugging tools, and the emergence of new technologies such as mobile cloud computing. Innovative solutions are proposed to address these challenges. The research focuses on topics such as mobile application development, mobile databases, and mobile security. The paper provides a concise summary of the major findings and proposed solutions. The study concludes that the field of software engineering and mobile technology is rapidly evolving, and further research is needed to effectively address the challenges and keep pace with the dynamic nature of the field; "Comparing the sociology of culture in Bangladesh and India: Similarities and differences in Bangladeshi and Indian cultures", The sociology of culture is an important field that examines how societies create, maintain, and transform their cultural practices and beliefs. In the context of Bangladesh and India, this field is particularly relevant due to their rich and diverse cultural heritage. This paper explores the sociology of culture in these countries, focusing on cultural similarities and differences. Through a literature review of research from anthropology, sociology, history, and related fields, we will examine the historical background of cultural development in both countries, considering the impact of colonialism, nationalism, globalization, language, ethnicity, and religion. We will then present a comparative analysis of cultural practices, beliefs, and values, drawing on empirical data and case studies. This paper aims to contribute to our understanding of the sociology of culture in Bangladesh and India by shedding light on their diverse cultural heritage and exploring the ways in which cultural practices and values are shaped by historical, social, and political factors. By comparing the cultural similarities and differences between these nations, we hope to deepen our understanding of how culture is influenced by the broader social and political context; "Electrochemical Waste Water Treatment.". Published chapters i.e. "Chapter 3: Artificial Intelligence Model for Analyzing the Buying Patterns of Customers" and "Chapter 11: Restaurant Sales Prediction Using Machine Learning" of the book titled "Handbook of Research on AI and Machine Learning Applications in Customer Support and Analytics", "Chapter 15: The Role of Innovation in Driving the Bioeconomy: The Challenges and Opportunities (pages 288-311)" of the book, "Handbook of Research on Bioeconomy and Economic Ecosystems"; The bioeconomy presents a promising opportunity for sustainable economic growth, but it also poses several challenges that require innovative solutions. This chapter provides an overview of the bioeconomy and its key components, including biotechnology, agriculture, and forestry. It then explores some of the challenges associated with the bio economy, such as the need to balance economic growth with environmental sustainability, the potential risks of genetically modified organisms, and the need to ensure that the benefits are shared equitably across society. Finally, it discusses the potential for new bio-based products and services, the creation of new jobs and economic opportunities, and the potential to contribute to global sustainability goals.. He developed a sociological concept "Sakibphobia" which has impact on several fields including Psychology, Sociology, Health Science etc. 82 scientists, researchers, students and others contributed in the research titled, "S M Nazmuz Sakibs Toxic Comparative Theory, Sakibphobia with Structural Functionalism, Symbolic Interactionism, and Conflict Perspective, A Sociological Analysis" which is published in the International Journal of Nursing Care and Research, a publication of CME Live publishes. Sakibphobia is a relatively new concept that describes the fear or hatred of individuals towards those who they perceive as more successful or accomplished than themselves. In this research article, we conduct a comparative analysis of Sakibphobia with three major sociological perspectives: Structural Functionalism, Symbolic Interactionism, and Conflict Perspective. Our study utilizes a literature review approach to analyze the theoretical frameworks, assumptions, and implications of these perspectives on Sakibphobia. The result of our analysis suggests that while each perspective provides unique insights and explanations, none of them can fully capture the complexity and dynamics of Sakibphobia. However, a synthesis of these perspectives can help to develop a more comprehensive understanding of Sakibphobia and its implications for individuals and society."

Dimitrios Sarris is an Associate Professor, Department of Early Childhood Education, School of Education, University of Ioannina, Greece.

Zoi Siouti is a Clinical and Counseling Psychologist for children, adolescents and adults, specializing in Cognitive Behavioral Therapy (CBT), Eye Movement Desensitization and Reprocessing (EMDR) and Acceptance and Commitment Therapy (ACT). She has studied Psychology at the University of Crete and holds five postgraduate degrees. Mrs Siouti has conducted research and participated in Psychology Conferences as well as she has worked as a Psychologist in Public and Private institutions. At the moment Mrs Siouti works as an external scientific associate – Psychologist at the Department of Clinical and Translational Research in Endocrinology of the Medical School (University of Athens) and maintains a private practice in Attica.

Maria Sofologi is an Adjunct Ass. Professor at the Department of Early Childhood and Education at the University of Ioannina in Greece. She delivers the courses "Cognitive Psychology", and "Developmental Psychology". She is also a postdoctoral researcher at the University of Ioannina in Greece. She holds a Ph.D. in Cognitive Psychology from the Aristotle University of Thessaloniki. She also holds a Master of Science degree in Cognitive Psychology from the Aristotle University of Thessaloniki. During her master's degree years she trained and practiced different assessment cognitive tools to evaluate all cognitive functions like memory, attention, language, executive functions both in adults and children. She is the key speaker in many European and Hellenic conferences concerning cognitive psychology, educational psychology, special education in children and adults, as well. Her academic work includes a series of many scientific publications, books, and book chapters concerning Cognitive Psychology, Special Education, Educational Psychology, and Cognitive impairments in children and adults as well.

Anastassios Stalikas is a Psychology professor at Panteion University of Social and Political Sciences, an adjunct professor at McGill University, and a visiting professor and research associate at several universities, such as the National and Kapodistriako University of Athens, the University of Thessaly,the University of Cyprus and the Sigmund Freud University in Vienna. He is the current President of the Hellenic Society of Positive Psychology, a business consultant, trainer, coach, clinical psychologist, and psychotherapist. His research interests spring from the fields of Clinical and Counselling Psychology and his research initiatives aim in understanding the manner in which people "flourish" psychologically by implementing their character strengths, experiencing positive emotions, finding meaning in their lives, and developing their psychological resilience. He is the author of 10 scientific books, more than 60 chapters in scientific books, and 200 articles in scientific journals and conference presentations at the international scientific community.

Kyriaki Tasiou is a special education teacher and works for the last 14 years at a primary school in Kos. She holds a Master's degree on the topic: ''Gender and New Educational and Working Environments in the Information Society" of the Department of Sciences of Preschool Education and Educational Design-University of the Aegean and Master's degree with the title: "Education Sciences: Special Education and Education of People with Speech and Writing Difficulties'' of the Inter-University MSc of the EAP with the University of Thessaly. She has been trained in Greek Sign Language. She has been trained in Assessment & Diagnostic Tests for individuals with Autism Spectrum Disorder (ADOS,ADI-R) & in Early Detection of Autism Spectrum Disorders with the "PAIS" test. She has participated in several chapters in other scientific publications in Greek language. Her research interests lie in the fields of special education, students with special education needs and families raising a child with special education needs or other difficulties. She is a PhD candidate at the University of the Aegean. She is married and a mother of one daughter.

Loukia Taxitari is a Lecturer in Research Methods in the Department of Psychology at Neapolis University. In 2009, she received a PhD in experimental psychology and, in 2004, an M.Phil. in General Linguistics from the University of Oxford, UK. She specializes in language acquisition and development, and various methods to investigate it. She has worked as a post-doctoral researcher in Cyprus (University of Cyprus and Cyprus University of Technology), Germany (University of Potsdam) and Italy (CNR, Pisa), employing different techniques to the study of language in various populations. She has adapted the MacArthur-Bates CDI to Cypriot Greek and she has been working on the development of novel methodologies for the study of language, such as tablet apps. She has taught extensively in public and private universities in Cyprus as a part-time lecturer and she has published several articles and chapters in specialized books whilst also presenting at international conferences. She is also a reviewer for peer-reviewed journals and the annual CogSci conference. She is passionate about the communication of science to the public and has been involved in various types of activities promoting science and its understanding, such as the Mediterranean Science Festival, as well as the Famelab (where she won the 2nd local prize) and S-Factor competitions.

Maria Theodoratou-Bekou is a Clinical Psychologist with a Ph.D. in Clinical Psychology from the National and Kapodistrian University of Athens, Greece. Her academic journey began with a Bachelor's degree in Philosophy, Pedagogy and Psychology from the University of Athens, followed by another Bachelor's degree in Psychology in France. She then successfully completed her Master's degree in Clinical Psychology and Psychopathology at the University of Aix-Marseille I, Provence, France. With a wealth of experience spanning over 25 years, she has been teaching Psychology as an Adjunct Lecturer at the Hellenic Open University, Greece and the Neapolis University of Pafos, Cyprus since 2017. Her insights extend to her work as a psychologist in the private sector. Balancing her professional commitments, she is married and the mother of two students.

Theodosia Thoma is a graduate of the Department of Philosophy, Pedagogy, and Psychology (Psychology stream) of the National and Kapodistrian University of Athens (Greece). She holds a MEd in Special Educational Needs, an MSc in Educational Research, and a PhD in Education from the University of Exeter (UK). She has worked as a Scientific Collaborator at the Hellenic Open University, for the MEd Education Science: Special Education for People with Oral and Written Language Difficulties and she has also collaborated with Canterbury Christ Church University via Aegean Omiros College (Greece). She works as a Special Educational Needs teacher (Philologist) in secondary education. Her research interests include dyslexia, specific learning difficulties, special educational needs, and inclusive educational practices.

Stergoulla Trecha is a PhD holder in the Department of Primary Education at the University of the Aegean (Greece). She works as an English language teacher in primary education. Her research interests include teaching of students with learning difficulties and family dynamics in families raising children who have learning difficulties in spelling. Her published work includes articles in Greece and abroad, as well as various participations in Greek and international conferences.

Georgios Tsakirakis emerges as the visionary author of this chapter, combining his expertise as an esteemed mathematician with his unwavering passion for education. Throughout his academic journey, Georgios has demonstrated relentless dedication and exceptional prowess in the realm of Mathematics. With resounding success in his undergraduate and graduate studies at renowned universities, he has honed his mastery of abstract reasoning and profound problem-solving abilities. Drawing from a wealth of experience gained through diverse academic engagements at universities worldwide, Georgios has developed a profound understanding of the intricacies of the subject. Currently, as a dedicated educator at Zayed University in the United Arab Emirates, Georgios shares his vast knowledge and unwavering passion for Mathematics with students, shaping the minds of future mathematicians. However, his aspirations extend far beyond personal accolades. Driven by an innate passion for teaching, Georgios ventured into the realm of self-efficacy research, propelled by an unwavering commitment to advancing mathematics education. Recognizing the paramount importance of self-efficacy in shaping the effectiveness of mathematics instructors and its profound impact on student outcomes, Georgios embarked on a quest to explore innovative strategies that nurture the confidence and belief in their own abilities among mathematics instructors. His research is driven by a profound understanding of the transformative power of self-efficacy and its ability to empower educators and inspire students. Georgios Tsakirakis stands not only as a consummate mathematician but also as a tireless advocate for equitable Mathematics instruction. With an unwavering belief in the transcendent power of education, he embraces the noble mission of empowering students and fostering a sense of inclusivity within the realm of Mathematics. Through his research, teaching and advocacy, Georgios seeks to break down barriers, promote equity and inspire a new generation of mathematicians to explore the boundless possibilities within the captivating realm of Mathematics.

Assimina Tsibidaki is an Associate Professor of Special Education in the Department of Primary Education at the University of the Aegean (Greece). Her research interests focus on the following areas: Students with special educational needs and disabilities (SEND), families raising a child with SEND, home-school collaboration, social support networks, technology and inclusive education, disability in children's literature and cinema. Her published work includes two books, editing and articles in Greece and abroad, as well as various participations in Greek and international conferences.

Ilias Vasileiadis is a school psychologist with research interests in the inclusion of students with and without disabilities. He has teaching and research experience at universities in Greece.

Denis Vavougios holds a BSc in Physics, Physics Department, University of Patras (1982) & PhD in Theoretical Physics of the Physics Department Faculty of Sciences University of Patras, (1989). Professor of Physics and Science Education at the Physics Department of University of Thessaly. Research Interests: Theoretical Physics, Science Education (Experimental Science Teaching, Science Concepts in Early Childhood Education and Teaching Science, ICT in Science Education).

Ourania Veneti was born in Thessaloniky/Greece. Ourania Veneti is a graduate of the Department of Preschool Education of the Aristotle University of Thessaloniki, Greece. She holds a master's degree in Special Education from the University of Nicosia, Cyprus. She has participated as a speaker at Greek scientific conferences. For many years, she has been participating in voluntary groups that are active in the field of Special Education. She has attended specialization seminars in Psychology and Special

Education. She works in an Interdisciplinary Center for Special Treatments (Skepsi kai Praxi) as a special educator. At the same time, she is currently completing her second master's degree, entitled "Educational Sciences through Innovative Technologies and Biomedical Approaches" at the University of Western Attica, while she is in her second year of education on contemporary interpersonal psychodynamic therapy, at the Psychotherapeutic Institute Centre for Southern Suburbs (ICPA).

Index

P

Q

S

T

www.ingramcontent.com/pod-product-compliance
Lightning Source LLC
LaVergne TN
LVHW080121011026
849160LV00013B/1148